CATHOLIC CITIZENS
IN THE THIRD REICH
Psycho-Social Principles
and Moral Reasoning

DONALD J. DIETRICH

Transaction Books
New Brunswick (U.S.A.) and Oxford (U.K.)

Copyright © 1988 by Transaction, Inc.
New Brunswick, New Jersey 08903

Library of Congress Catalog Number: 86-19344
ISBN: 0-88738-131-6
Printed in the United States of America

Library of Congress Cataloging in Publication Data

Dietrich, Donald J., 1941-
    Catholic citizens in the Third Reich.

    Bibliography: p.
    Includes index.
        1. Catholics—Germany—History—20th century.
    2. Catholic Church—Germany—History—20th century.
    3. Germany—Church history—1933-1945.   4. Church
    and state—Germany—1933-1945.   I. Title.
    BX1536.D54   1986   282'.43   86-19344
    ISBN 0-88738-131-6

To Coralie, Kathy, Steve, and Martin

Contents

Preface

Over fifty years after its inception, the Third Reich remains not only the central historical experience of modern Germany, a referent for past and present, but also an enigma. Varied schools of historical interpretation have developed, attempting to explain the phenomenon of the emergence of Nazi totalitarianism in twentieth-century European civilization.[1] Despite the mass of works devoted to the Third Reich, a definitive analysis has not been forthcoming and the emergence as well as the durability of Nazism is difficult to comprehend or accept. The enigma, then, could well remain shrouded in mystery, although investigations will not and should not cease.

Reflecting on the Third Reich as a historical phenomenon reveals that conscience and spiritual values failed to control conduct, and that the foundation of that decency on which our civilized community rests proved most fragile indeed. In light of this seeming collapse of our accepted value structure from 1933 to 1945, attention has increasingly in the post-World War II era been riveted on the Holocaust. For Christians, the Holocaust has necessitated a confrontation[2] with certain fundamental aspects of the Christian tradition and teaching, and has elicited a variety of questions: Can one still be a Christian after Auschwitz? How is anti-Judaism endemic to the very nature of Christianity? Will a new Christian theology be any greater guarantee against anti-Semitism than the old? What is the relationship of religion to society? How can moral values control patterns of behavior? Because of the nature of their institutional church, Catholic responses have been scrutinized most rigorously.

Some areas of human experience are so vast in implication and so complex in emotion that distance from the event seems necessary for a balanced perspective. Rolf Hochuth's controversial play *The Deputy* encouraged a scholarly analysis of the role of Catholics and their Church in the maintenance of Nazi Germany. The works of Günter Lewy and Gordon Zahn laid bare the reactions of clerical leaders to Nazism and highlighted their less than valorous responses.[3] To help further explain the decisions and behavior of Catholic leaders, the *Kommission für Zeitgeschichte* of the Catholic Academy in Bavaria, under the inspired leadership of Konrad Repgen, has issued well-edited volumes of pertinent documents.[4] The sheer bulk of material published to explicate the role of the Catholic Church in the Third Reich and to reveal the reactions of German Catholics to Nazism has raised complex questions in such diverse areas as history, political science, theology, ethics, and sociology.[5] But virtually no attempt has been made to focus on the psychological dynamics acting on Catholics as they dealt with the moral conundrums posed by the Third Reich.

What social-psychological dynamics lay behind the religious reactions of German Catholics (hierarchy, theologians, publicists, and laymen) to political and, in the final analysis, moral issues during the late Weimar and Nazi eras? Like other Germans, Catholics were trapped in a cruel dilemma. To conform to the Nazi system could easily lead to a loss of moral credibility; to oppose could result in the full force of the state being used against the Church and her members. Both accommodation and resistance highlighted the story of German Catholicism. Unavailable from preceding historical narratives, however, is a coherent psychological analysis of the behavior of Catholics toward totalitarianism, anti-Semitism, and the systematic execution of Nazi-defined undesirables, as well as the reasons for the Catholic resistance that did develop. Using rigorously tested psychological principles, the values of Catholics can, however, be analyzed in relation to their patterns of behavior. Ultimately the goal is to clarify the apparent value versus behavior inconsistency apparent among German Catholics as well as to provide a strategy to analyze similar issues that focus on belief versus behavior dilemmas, problems that remain as current as today's newspaper. However one assesses the role that Catholic teaching, the Church, or Pius XII played in the drama of Nazi Germany, none can claim dissociation from the event. In the face of Hitler and the "Final Solution," neutrality becomes apathy, noninvolvement becomes guilt.

Like every scholarly work, this book is the result of an extensive support network without which the project could never have been completed. The University Personnel Development Committee at the University of Wisconsin-Stevens Point has made available several grants that have helped support the collection of data. The American Philosophical society has provided a grant that made possible a trip to the *Institut für Zeitgeschichte* (Munich) and the Berlin Document Center. A Rockefeller Foundation Humanities Stipend provided time for writing the monograph, free from the day-to-day interruptions of university life. Lorraine Swanson and Linda Kieliszewski in the Faculty Typing Office have patiently typed several drafts of this book. The interlibrary loan staff, especially Kathleen Halsey, has shown great ingenuity in finding obscure materials and providing me with them in record time. In particular, Irving Louis Horowitz,

Hannah Arendt distinguished professor of sociology at Rutgers University, and Otto P. Pflanze, professor of history at Indiana University, have encouraged me in this project and offered their support through the years. Naturally, I must thank my wife Coralie, professor of psychology at the University of Wisconsin-Stevens Point. She has provided not only the traditional support that I have come to rely on, but has also been instrumental in my attempt to fuse the psychological methodologies and historical data into a tool useful in explicating the complexities that have arisen in understanding the role of Catholics in the rise and duration of Nazi Germany. Like most scholars, I acknowledge the errors of this work as my own.

Notes

1. Theodore S. Hamerow, "Review Essay: Guilt, Redemption, and Writing German History," *American Historical Review* 88 (1983):53-72; Konrad Jarausch, "Illiberalism and Beyond: German History in Search of a Paradigm," *Journal of Modern History* 55 (1983):268-284 (A variety of interpretations are offered in this essay. For a particularly trenchant analysis of the *Sonderweg* thesis and its critics in Hans-Ulrich Wehler, *Das deutsche Kaiserreich, 1871-1918* Göttingen: Vanderhoeck und Ruprecht, 1973); Otto Pflanze, "Bismarcks Herrschaftstechnik als Problem der gegenwartigen Historiographie," *Historische Zeitschrift* 234 (1982):562-599; David Blackbourn and Geoff Eley, *Mythen deutscher Geschichtschreibung! Die gescheiterte bürgerliche Revolution* (Frankfurt am Main: Ullstein, 1980).
2. A variety of conferences have been held on the Holocaust, and their proceedings have helped illuminate some issues, while raising new questions. See, for example, Franklin H. Littell and Hubert G. Locke (eds.), *The German Church Struggle and the Holocaust* (Detroit: Wayne State University Press, 1974); Eva Fleischner (ed.), *Auschwitz: Beginning of a New Era? Reflections on the Holocaust* (New York: Ktav Publishing Co., 1977); Henry Friedlander and Sybil Milton, (eds.), The Holocaust: Ideology, Bureaucracy, and Genocide (Millwood, NY: Kraus International Publications, 1980); Joel Dimsdale (ed.) *Survivors, Essays on the Nazi Holocaust* (Washington: Hemisphere Publishing Corp., 1980).
3. Rolf Hochhuth, *The Deputy* (New York: Grove Press, 1964); Guenter Lewy, *The Catholic Church and Nazi Germany* (New York: McGraw Hill, 1964); Gordon C. Zahn, *German Catholics and Hitler's Wars: A Study in Social Control* (New York: E.P. Dutton, 1969); for a recent treatment of *The Deputy* controversy, see Donald J. Dietrich, "Historical Judgments and Eternal Verities," *Society* 20 (1983):31-35.
4. For an analysis of several of these volumes and a well-organized review of the *Kirchenkampf* literature up until the early 1970s, see Owen Chadwick, "The Present Stage of the '*Kirchenkampf*' Enquiry," *Journal of Ecclesiastical History* 24 (1973):33-50.
5. The literature on the Church's confrontation with Nazism is enormous, but several analyses are outstanding. See Ernst Christian Helmreich, *The German Churches under Hitler: Background, Struggle, and Epilogue* (Detroit: Wayne

State University Press, 1979); John Conway, *The Nazi Persecution of the Churches, 1933-1945* (New York: Basic Books, Inc., 1968); Heinz Boberach (ed.), *Berichte des Sd und der Gestapo über Kirchen und Kirchenvolk in Deutschland 1934-1944* (Mainz: Matthias-Grünewald-Verlag, 1971); Hermann Greive, *Theologie und Ideologie. Katholizismus und Judentum in Deutschland and Österreich 1918-1935* (Heidelberg: Lambert Schneider Verlag, 1969).

Introduction

Sigmund Freud's work on Leonardo, the first psychoanalytic life-study, and Moses, a variety of short articles in *Psychoanalytic Review* during the 1920s and 1930s, and Erik Erikson's work launched psychohistory as a discipline. When William Langer[1] urged historians onto "the next assignment" (i.e., the application of psychology to history), he reinforced the intense, enduring controversy swirling around psychobiography. The resultant output of psychohistorians has been prodigious.[2] Scholarly analyses and polemics on the use of psychology by the historian have focused on a series of methodological difficulties as well as on the opportunities at hand for understanding behavior.[3] Especially during the last two decades, a substantial number of historical figures have been subject to what psychoanalytically oriented Fawn Brodie has referred to as the "surgical operation" of psychohistory.[4] The quality of effort ranges from the elegant and sensitive works of such scholars as Erik Erikson, Rudolph Binion, Peter Loewenberg, and Kenneth Keniston to the eccentric disquisitions of Lloyd de Mause and his disciples.[5]

The initially dominant, and still popular, theme in psychohistorical methodology has been the strict application of psychoanalysis to history. Ironically, however, during the last fifty years, the psychoanalytic model itself has grown increasingly unpopular among psychologists. The potential for applying principles extricated from developmental psychology, political socialization theories, and, in particular, cognitive theories indicates that psychohistory is emerging as a multifaceted discipline and that the use of psychology by historians is seen as a fruitful approach to the analysis of complex issues.[6] Within social psychology such models as cognitive dissonance, attribution theories, social exchange theories, and social behaviorism[7] can prove particularly useful to the historian analyzing interpersonal behavior in typical, contemporary settings.

Up to now, however, such principles have rarely been applied to historical phenomena, although such a cross-disciplinary analysis could be beneficial to both history and psychology. Some scholars have argued that culture and historical experiences shape the specific psychological patterns that characterize a specific people. One implication of this view would be

1

that our understanding of psychological functioning must necessarily be limited to a particular culture and historical period. Psychological models would be considered ahistorical and applicable only to contemporary society, but human beings have certain basic commonalities, e.g., active nervous systems, self-concepts, and motives, which certainly may vary. The development, learning, and growth of people, moreover, takes place in terms of a limited number of such principles as conditioning, modeling, identification, and learning through the resolution of cognitive discrepancies.[8]

The last decade has seen social psychologists themselves engaged in a lively debate about the nature and future direction of their discipline and its relationship to history.[9] This debate has led to at least one conclusion—that social psychology could benefit from devoting more attention to the study of historical events, since there is a dialectical relationship between the developing individual and a changing society both in the past and present. A socio-historical perspective could provide social psychologists with an opportunity to analyze the development of the individual and society based on lived experiences and directive actions. Such a perspective would also address the methodological criticism that social psychology limits itself to the study of mundane and artificial phenomena and thus generates models of human behavior that lack experiential realism. On the one hand, then, historical phenomena appear able to offer the social psychologist a situation analagous to the controlled laboratory setting of the experimentalist. On the other, coherent and rigorous psychological models can offer the historian a tool with which to help uncover the mysterious "why" of historical human behavior.

Social exchange theories, for example, are very general, as they ought to be if they are to cover a great variety of situations. To understand what happens in a particular group, the exact details that the propositions do not reveal must be explicated. Why specific people behave as they do cannot be understood without knowing precisely what they want from their interactions and the influences that guide and limit the social, economic, or political exchanges they make. These factors include the nature of the activities in which they engage; whether the role differentiation in the group is assigned from outside or reached internally through interactions; and the beliefs, values, and status investments the members bring from outside the group. Such factors are the "givens" of the situation, which determine the concrete ways in which the general propositions operate under varying circumstances.[10]

As opposed to the historian, the psychologist may not have to know how actions come about; he needs to know only what the norms, values, and beliefs are, and these are frequently embodied in the religions practiced in the society. By providing a unified and unifying value system, religion seems to contribute to the integration of society and to the functioning of social institutions. Religion is seen by some as the most general mechanism for integrating meaning and motivation in action systems. As such, it contributes to social stability and to the adaptation to the whole social system. There are good and bad aspects to this adaptation phenomenon, depending on the strength of religious commitment. In the analysis of religious behavior and values, for example, studies have indicated that conventional churchgoers demonstrate a high degree of racial prejudice. Those whose religious practice can be characterized as committed seem to be less prejudiced. The psychological issue is not exclusively why people hold specific good or bad values, but given that they do hold them, what they do about them. The focus, then, is on *what* values are held and *how* these norms interact to explain specific patterns of behavior. To understand, however, how societies, groups, and individuals have developed norms, values, and beliefs requires scrutiny of the past histories of the peoples concerned. In essence, using psychological principles, the historian can add a new dimension in explaining the maintenance of certain patterns of behavior in given past societies. Analyzing the historical exchanges that occur in the separate parts of complex social systems helps clarify the psychological patterns of behavior. The overall degree of interdependence in a large society can be measured by summing up the exchanges occurring among its parts, just as psychologists measure the cohesiveness of groups by adding up the interactions and interpersonal attractions between different pairs of members.[11] Psychological principles, then, have the potential of revealing the devastating interaction that occurred in the Third Reich as part of the "normal" life of German Catholics. Traditionally, psychologists have viewed their discipline as an asocial and ahistorical focus on the individual, i.e., as a person-centered subject area. Built into psychology, however, is the polarity between man *and* society. From the moment of birth the individual organism is a social organism, which means embeddedness in patterned family relationships that are part of an array of such relationships rooted in a social, political, economic, and cultural history. Even a psychological model whose primary focus may be the individual cannot understand its subject matter in isolation from the social and historical context. Hence, history and psychology seem to be related as disciplines, since scholars in both try to understand why persons in society act as they do.

Although few developments in European history have received as much attention as Nazi Germany, there still remain questions whose answers could shed light on the nature of the nation-state as a totalitarian polity and could help social scientists reflect on the lethal potential of any twentieth-century society, especially one that has reached a high industrial level. With remarkable success social scientists over the past forty years have diagnosed nearly every facet of the Third Reich.[12] Using psychoanalytical models, such historians as Rudolph Binion and R.G. Waite have provided an empathetic understanding of the private world of Adolf Hitler and have aided readers in perceiving how Hitler's internal, subjective world became externalized and politically significant. They have not, however, effectively explained the behavior of specific groups in Nazi Germany. Avoiding psychoanalytical concepts, then, appears to offer some hope of describing the relationship between Hitler and other Germans by the same principles that govern other known forms of social and group behavior. These theories can provide a useful way of linking the events of the external world with the behavior of individuals in groups.[13] The "Final Solution," in particular, has become a pressing issue for virtually anyone attempting to understand the historical development of modern European societies.[14] Hitler was a challenge to the moral and political traditions as well as to the assumptions about man's nature, accepted as part of western tradition. The challenge is still being met. To explain the Third Reich, the relationship between Nazi ideas and their bloody results is still being pondered.[15]

Genocide among nation-states occurs not merely with the successful liquidation of a group. In the view of Irving Louis Horowitz,[16] for example, genocide is a fundamental mechanism for the unification of national policy, and examples have appeared with unfortunate frequency since the French Revolution. The nation-state as the basis for genocide poses very serious questions about state power, collectivism, bureaucracy, human rights, and individualism. Nazi Germany, however, offers the unusual concrete case of an advanced technological society virtually eliminating a targeted group. The psychological, social, and political factors that made this possible should offer a reflective model for a continuing analysis of the state and the preservation of individual rights. The phenomenon of Nazi Germany with its Holocaust and the Catholic contribution through omission and commission has emphasized the need for the continuing careful reflection on all aspects of contemporary life to insure that individual and group rights are not being transposed into obligations fulfilled through the power of such a state as Nazi Germany.

In National Socialism, an ideology stressing the dehumanization of racial, religious, national, and ethnic groups received its most systematic formulation as a theory of society and as a blueprint for political renewal and military expansion. Rejecting traditional Western moral and religious concepts about the nature of man and his inalienable dignity as a human personality, Hitler and others proclaimed the virtue of violence and of blood; worship of the German "race" replaced concern for the individual and the other "weak" values of Christian humanism. Endowed with the supreme mission to lead and dominate other races, the Aryan race, according to the Nazi ideologues, had the right to subjugate other peoples, to use them purely as means, as expendable slave labor, or indeed to slaughter them. In a grandiose design for world hegemony, Nazi ideology organized other peoples in a hierarchy that delineated their right to survival, or the conditions of their incorporation into the living space of the Greater German Reich, or of subjugation as auxiliary affiliated groups. Ultimately, anti-Semitism in Germany was to serve as a unifying factor among radical Nazis and as the motor driving the "Final Solution."[17]

In analyzing Nazi Germany and the Catholic response, attention should be focused on the emergence of specific German value and behavior patterns, including those of the Catholic community since the foundation years of the Second Reich when a heightened nationalism was fused with Christian and racial anti-Semitism. The economic and social dislocations that accompanied Germany's rapid industrialization in the second half of the nineteenth century, some have suggested, stimulated an intensified anti-Semitism both among the rural farmers and within the nationalistic bourgeois class. Others have stressed the particular socio-political structure that Bismarck and the Junkers imposed on Germany in 1871, leaving power in their hands and exploiting the craving of the bourgeois for state protection. Still others have uncovered the chief cause of heightened nationalism in the three wars successfully fought by Prussia to unite Germany. These wars fused nationalism, militarism, and authoritarianism in the minds of most Germans as the conjunction of forces leading to the long-sought unification. Some have uncovered the chief cause of anti-Semitism in the basic ideological change that occurred when intellectuals abandoned rationalistic, humanistic principles and the Christian outlook in favor of radical attitudes sustained partially by a vulgar social Darwinism, popular on the left, and racial or eugenic theories in general.[18] The roots of the Catholic reaction to the Third Reich can be traced in part to their German unification experiences. During the 1860s and more pressingly after 1871, German Catholics had to confront an apparently hostile Protestant authoritarian state governed by Wilhelm I and Bismarck behind the facade of a liberal parliament openly opposed to Catholicism as a political and religious force. In real life, a person deals with a complex environment and behavior rooted in a complex history. Human behavior is learned within a society that has historically developed. Man is distinguished by his extraordinary ability to learn and to base his actions on his knowledge. Catholics, then, confronted Hitler with patterns of behavior and values developed through their historical experiences in Germany.

Notes

1. Sigmund Freud, "Leonardo da Vinci and a Memory of His Childhood," in Sigmund Freud, *The Standard Edition of the Complete Psychological Works,*

trans. and ed. James Strachey et al., 24 vols. (London: International Psychoanalytic Press, 1953-1975), 11:59-137; Freud, "The Moses of Michelangelo," in *Standard Works*, 13:211-238; Erik Erikson's *Childhood and Society* (New York: Norton, 1950) is a collection of essays spanning his early career; William Langer, "The Next Assignment," *American Historical Review* 63 (1958):283-304. For a recent review of the psychohistorical literature, see Donald J. Dietrich, "Psychohistory: Clio on the Couch—or Off?" *Historical Methods* 15 (1982):83-90.

2. Rather than including the innumerable works that reflect psychohistorical insights, a number of bibliographical surveys can serve as an initial guide into the literature. Faye Sinofsky et al., "A Bibliography of Psychohistory," *History of Childhood Quarterly* 2 (1975):517-562; Dirk Blasius, "Psychohistorie und Sozialgeschichte," *Archiv für Sozialgeschichte* 17 (1977):383-403; William J. Gilmore, "Critical Bibliography," *Psychohistory Review* 5 (1976):4-33; 6 (1977):88-96; 6 (1977-78):106-111; 6 (1978):60-65; 7 (1978):40-47. Gilmore's reviews of the literature emphasize the methodologies being used by psychohistorians. Two journals with contributions of uneven scholarly value, *History of Childhood Quarterly* (currently *Journal of Psychohistory)* and *Psychohistory Review,* contain articles and reviews, which offer materials on the current state of the discipline.

3. Terry H. Anderson, "Becoming Sane with Psychohistory," *Historian* 41 (1978):1-20; Robert J. Brugger (ed.), *Our Selves/Our Past: Psychological Approaches to American History* (Baltimore: Johns Hopkins University Press, 1981). Brugger's collection of studies relates history and applied psychology and highlights some of the conceptual difficulties which have resulted from the fusion of these two disciplines.

4. Fawn M. Brodie, "Who Defends the Abolitionist?" in Martin Duberman (ed.), *The Anti-Slavery Vanguard: New Essays on the Abolitionist (*Princeton: Princeton University Press, 1965), p. 66; her application of psychoanalytical techniques may be found in Fawn Brodie, *Thomas Jefferson: An Intimate History* (New York: Norton, 1974).

5. Erik Erikson, *Young Man Luther* (New York: Norton, 1958); Rudolph Binion, *Frau Lou: Nietzsche's Wayward Disciple* (Princeton: Princeton University Press, 1968): Peter Loewenberg, "The Psychohistorical Origins of the Nazi Youth Cohort," *American Historical Review* 76 (1971):1457-1502; Kenneth Keniston, "Psychological Development and Historical Change," in Robert J. Lifton (ed.), *Explorations in Psychohistory* (New York: Simon and Schuster, 1974), pp. 149-164; the "Special Carter Issue" of *Journal of Psychohistory* 5 (1977), edited by Lloyd de Mause.

6. Harvey Asher, "Non-Psychoanalytic Approaches to National Socialism," *Psychohistory Review* 7 (1979):13-21; George Forgie, *Patricide in a House Divided: A Psychological Interpretation of Lincoln and His Age* (New York: Random House, 1979); Uri Wernick, "Cognitive Dissonance Theory, Religious Reality and Extreme Interactionism," *Psychohistory Review* 7 (1979):207-232; Charles M. Radding, "The Evolution of Medieval Mentalities: A Cognitive-Structural Approach," *American Historical Review* 83 (1978):577-597; Donald J. Dietrich, "The Holocaust as Public Policy: The Third Reich," *Human Relations* 34 (1981):445-462; Richard L. Schoenwald, "The Psychological Study of History," in George G. Iggers and Harold T. Parker, (eds.), *International Handbook of Historical Studies: Contemporary Research and Theory* (Westport, CT: Greenwood Press, 1979), pp. 77-85.

7. Leon Festinger, *A Theory of Cognitive Dissonance* (Stanford: Stanford University Press, 1957); G.C. Homans, *Social Behavior: Its Elementary Forms* (New York: Harcourt, Brace, and World, 1961); J.W. Thibaut and H.H. Kelley, *The Social Psychology of Groups* (New York: Wiley, 1959); F. Heider, *The Psychology of Interpersonal Relations* (New York: International Universities Press, 1958); H.H. Kelley, "The Process of Causal Attribution," *American Psychologist* 28 (1973):107-128.
8. Ervin Staub, *Positive Social Behavior and Morality* (New York: Academic Press, 1978), 1:430.
9. Klaus F. Riegel, *Psychology of Development and History* (New York: Plenum Press, 1976); Kenneth Gergen, "Social Psychology as History," *Journal of Personality and Social Psychology* 26 (1973):309-320.
10. Homans, *Social Behavior*; Thibault and Kelley; Peter M. Blau, "Interaction IV: Social Exchange," in David L. Sills (ed.), *International Encyclopedia of the Social Sciences* (New York: MacMillan, 1968), 7:452-458.
11. Homans, p. 48; Peter M. Blau, *The Dynamics of Bureaucracy* (Chicago: University of Chicago Press, 1955), pp. 99-116; Peter M. Blau, *Exchange and Power in Social Life* (New York: J. Wiley, 1964); Michael Argyle and Benjamine Beit–Hollahmi, *The Social Psychology of Religion* (London: Routledge and Kegan Paul, 1975), p. 203; R.N. Bellah, *Beyond Belief* (New York: Free Press, 1970), p. 12; C. Bagley, "Relation of Religion and Racial Prejudice in Europe," *Journal for the Scientific Study of Religion* 9 (1970):219; G.W. Allport, "The Religious Context of Prejudice," *Journal for the Scientific Study of Religion* 5 (1966):447-457; G.W. Allport and J.M. Ross, "Personal Religious Orientation and Prejudice," *Journal of Personality and Social Psychology* 5 (1967):432-443; N. Dickson Reppucci, "Psychology and Public Policy," in Robert Kidd and Michael Saks (eds.), *Advances in Applied Social Psychology* (Hillsdale, NJ: L. Erlbaum, 1980), 1:163-166; S.B. Sarason, "The Nature of Problem Solving in Social Action," *American Psychologist* 33 (1978):370-380; S.B. Sarason, *Psychology Misdirected* (New York: Collier MacMillan, 1981), pp. 175-176; J. Saunders and N. Reppucci, "The Social Identity of Behavior Modification," in M. Hersen et al. (eds.), *Progress in Behavior Modification,* vol. 6 (New York: Basic Books, 1978); W. Bevan, "On Getting in Bed with a Lion," *American Psychologist* 35 (1980):787.
12. Since 1953 the *Bibliographie Zur Zeitgeschichte,* under the editorship of Thilo Vogelsang, published as a supplement to the *Vierteljahrshefte für Zeitgeschichte,* has been the standard source on the growing literature on National Socialism. A variety of current and provocative analyses are available; see, Martin Broszat, *The Hitler State: The Foundation and Development of the Internal Structure of the Third Reich* (New York: Longman, 1981); Fred Weinstein, *The Dynamics of Nazism: Leadership, Ideology, and the Holocaust* (New York: Academic Press, 1980); Richard Hamilton, *Who Voted for Hitler?* (Princeton: Princeton University Press, 1982); Otis Mitchell, *Hitler Over Germany: The Establishment of the Nazi Dictatorship (1918-1934)* (Philadelphia: Institute for the Study of Human Issues, 1983).
13. J.R.P. French, Jr. and Bertram Raneu, "The Bases of Social Power," in D. Cartwright and F. Zander (eds.), *Group Dynamics: Research and Theory,* 2nd ed., New York: Harper and Row, 1960), p. 613.
14. Fritz Stern, *The Failure of Illiberalism: Essays on the Political Culture of Modern Germany* (New York: Knopf, 1972); p. xi; Lucy S. Davidowicz, *The Holo-*

caust and the Historians (Cambridge: Harvard University Press, 1981), p. 31; recent works on intellectual patterns predisposing Germans on both the Right and Left of the political spectrum to accept Nazism are Geoffrey Field, *Evangelist of Race: The Germanic Vision of Houston Stewart Chamberlain* (New York: Columbia University Press, 1981); Alfred Kelley, *The Descent of Darwin: The Popularization of Darwinism in Germany, 1860-1917* (Chapel Hill: University of North Carolina Press, 1981).

15. Secretariat of State of His Holiness, *Actes et Documentes du Saint Siege relatifs a'la Seconde Guerre Mondiale,* ed. Pierre Blet, Robert Graham, Angelo Martini, and Burkhart Schneider (Vatican City: Libreria Editrice Vaticana, 1965-1975), 9 vols.; John S. Conway, "The Present State of Research and Writing on the Church Struggle," in Littel and Lock, pp. 31-39; Michael R. Marrus and Robert O. Paxton, *Vichy France and the Jews* (New York: Schocken Books, 1983).

16. Irving Louis Horowitz, *Genocide: State Power and Mass Murder* (New Brunswick, NJ: Transaction Books, 1976), p. 189.

17. E. Jäckel, *Weltanschauung: A Blueprint for Power* (Middletown, CT: Wesleyan University Press, 1972); Karl Schleunes, *The Twisted Road to Auschwitz: Nazi Policy Toward German Jews, 1933-1939* (Urbana, IL: University of Illinois Press, 1970); Leo Kuper, *Genocide: Its Political Use in the Twentieth Century* (New Haven: Yale University Press, 1981); Norman Rich, *Hitler's War Aims: Ideology, The Nazi State, and the Course of Expansion,* vol. I (New York: Norton, 1973); Gerhard Weinberg, *The Foreign Policy of Hitler's Germany: Starting World War II, 1937-1939* (Chicago: University of Chicago Press, 1980).

18. Uriel Tal, *Christians and Jews in Germany: Religion, Politics, and Ideology in the Second Reich, 1870-1914* (Ithaca: Cornell University Press, 1975); H. Huss and A. Schroeder (eds.), *Antisemitismus Zur Pathologie der Bürgerlichen Gesellschaft* (Frankfurt: Europäische Verlagsanstalt, 1966); H.S. Chamberlain, *Worte Christi* (Munich: Oldenbourg, 1903); G.C. Mosse, *The Crisis of German Ideology: Intellectual Origins of the Third Reich* (New York: Grosset, 1964); Otto Pflanze, *Bismarck and the Development of Germany: The Period of Unification, 1815-1871* (Princeton: Princeton University Press, 1963); Kelley, *Darwin's Descent*; Richard Rubenstein in his *The Cunning of History: The Holocaust and the American Future* (New York: Harper and Row, 1978) has suggested that the Final Solution in fact was a logical derivative of the rational, Christian *Weltanschauung* of European civilization, thereby differing from that entire school of thought that stresses the irrational and romantic roots of anti-Semitism, e.g., Mosse, *Crisis* and Fritz Stern, *The Politics of Cultural Despair* (Berkeley: University of California Press, 1961).

1

Catholics Confront Authoritarianism: The Prelude

The issue of Catholic integration into the authoritarian German states was exacerbated by the unification of 1871 after which Protestant Prussia completely dominated the pluralistic empire, 30 percent of which was Catholic and 1 percent Jewish. Adding to the tensions were the final emancipation of the Jews on July 3, 1869, the dominance of the anti-Catholic National Liberals in the new empire, and the great depression hovering over much of the 1870s. Both the remarkable economic growth prior to 1873 and the sharp decline in prosperity that developed thereafter produced a dislocation in German society which gave added impetus to attacks on liberal policies.[1]

In the nineteenth century Germany was experiencing the strains of its transition from a rural, agrarian to an urban-centered, industrializing society. This modernization phenomenon was characterized by a concentration of the population in cities, mass consumption, the increasing participation of citizens in economic and political affairs, an extensive, but not universal, breakdown of communal and hereditary social groupings leading to more mobility, the spread of secular orientations, mass communication, the construction of large-scale socioeconomic institutions, and rapidly developing nationalism. In its *extreme* form, such a pluralistic society historically in the Western experience has been characterized by a superimposition of inequalities. The same sections are dominated or subordinated, favored or discriminated against, in the political structure, in the economy, in opportunities for education, in human rights, in access to amenities. And issues of conflict tend also to be superimposed along the same lines of cleavage and inequality. Such structural conditions are likely to be conducive to political conflict and, if the stresses are sufficiently intense, to genocide.[2]

9

Catholic Opposition Against Classical Liberalism

Latent as well as blatant suspicion and enmity between Catholicism and Protestantism in Germany had been intense and in the nineteenth century had been highlighted, for example, by the "Cologne Troubles" (1837-41), which earlier had galvanized the Catholic community into political action. During the Austro-Prussian War (1866) the *Norddeutsche Allgemeine Zeitung* referred to the Catholic Hapsburgs as "the mortal enemy of the Evangelical Church," a sentiment reinforced by the *Kreuzzeitung's* assertion that "a religious war was brewing, perhaps as bloody as the Thirty Years War 200 years ago."[3] Still, it was not the lack of religious guarantees or even Protestantism per se, but rather the absence of a responsible ministry and the dangerously centralized character of the constitution that impelled, for example, Ludwig Windthorst, a leader of the post-1871 Center party, to join the Progressives and Poles voting against the adoption of the constitution in 1867. Not surprisingly, then, by the time of the unification, Catholics felt an acute need for a political party to safeguard their religious rights. Simultaneously, the swelling tide of liberal, nationalist euphoria that accompanied the founding of the empire created a political climate hostile to all political minorities and made national politicization seem even more imperative.[4]

Due to the accelerated modernization in Germany as well as to the specific historical conditions present in the Prussian-dominated state, Catholics felt threatened in the Second Reich. There were a number of general socioeconomic factors that are generally held responsible for the alienization and dehumanization so apparent in modern times. Bureaucratization, technology, automation, urbanization, and high social mobility all have led people to relate to one another in anonymous, impersonal ways and have induced dehumanizing behavior. When the environment appears complex and yields a scarcely tolerated ambiguity, individuals seem to become available for mobilization by political movements because of anxieties arising from uncertainty and alienation. In Germany this activist response has supported political movements in which individuals have sought to replace, sometimes only partially, an unwanted reality with a collective and acceptable one. Karl Jentsch summed up the Catholic feeling of inferiority when he said: "Every day the Catholic had to read in his *Käseblättchen* as well as in the great newspapers that he was the enemy of the Fatherland, a little papist, a dumbhead, and that his own clergy were the scum of humanity."[5] Either Catholics could oppose the newly centralized German state and so remain outside the general stream of development and system of political rewards or could identify with the state even though it was embedded in a predominantly Protestant, industrial, authoritarian socio-political culture.

In choosing political integration through the Center party, Catholics opted for inclusion in the authoritarian and successful Second Reich. For Bismarck, however, the Center was by definition subversive, and Windthorst's repeated assertion that it was not a confessional but a *political* party, in which Protestants were welcome, certainly was not comforting. Too powerful to be left autonomous, and once clear that the Center was bent on an independent status, Bismarck struck at what was for him the root of its power, the Catholic Church. Bismarck's attack led to a Catholic defense mounted on anti-Semitism, a response fraught with psychological and political ramifications. In this case, anti-Semitism and antiliberalism were synonymous and provided an acceptable Catholic vehicle initially for an assault on Bismarckian authoritarianism without in turn being labeled totally disloyal to the monarchy. The choice of anti-Semitism, deeply embedded in the Christian and European tradition, was not surprising since a similarity of belief can act as a major determinant in the acceptance of others or their rejection.[6] During the 1870s Catholics sought a common political ground with the conservative Protestant elite by attacking a common enemy—the Jew. Initially, they opposed Bismarck and his liberal allies; only after 1879 did they achieve a detente with Bismarck and the potential for political activity in the Reichstag.

The issues during the 1870s were not, of course, purely ideological. The "iron chancellor" manipulated the *Reichstag* and *Bundesrat* through constant threats of resignation, dissolution, and new elections. There were growing threats after 1877 to discipline the *Reichstag* and limit its authority. Retrospectively, the *Kulturkampf* could be seen as an antiparlimentary diversionary policy on a grand scale, perhaps even a conscious Bismarckian plot. The Liberals' alliance with the government in the *Kulturkampf,* of course, like their support for Bismarck's foreign policy, reduced their ability to mount a sustained drive for political reform. At the time, however, responding to the perceived political threat, Catholics developed a complex defensive posture toward Bismarck, liberals, socialists, democracy, and secularism. Ultimately, as the *Kulturkampf* waned, a Catholic identity was forged within the authoritarian state, which allowed the Center to join nearly any coalition government. The struggle forced Catholics to define their values and goals, carve out issues, take positions, and, in general, to establish a political and cultural identity. Anti-Semitism facilitated this process.[7] The role of religion has traditionally been to unify the community of believers around a concensus of values, while at the same time making in-group and out-group distinctions that can contribute to social divisions. Evidence exists, for example, that about 25 percent of the anti-Semitism found among Christians has been due to the Church's teaching about Jews.[8]

Given the hostility focused on Catholics in the Second Reich, not surprisingly they carefully compared themselves to other groups as they sought political and religious safeguards. Out of this defensiveness there emerged strong pressure toward uniformity with, and conformity to, those whose beliefs resembled their own, i.e., those Protestant Junkers who were not supporters of Bismarck until the late 1870s. In the final analysis, like-minded persons can validate one another's belief structure, and during the *Kulturkampf* this dynamic reinforced as well as intensified Catholic patterns of faith and prejudice. Having political and religious viewpoints in many cases similar to the Protestant Junker elite, Catholics under pressure to integrate themselves into the body politic turned against those who violated their perceived moral and personal principles, the Jews. Since the Catholics desired to be integrated into the Protestant political community, their assault logically could be made against those Jews who conveniently had chosen liberal politics to safeguard their own recently acquired emancipation. Jews, liberals, and businessmen were opposed by Catholics, who as a group could be classified sociologically as lower middle class and rural agrarian.[9] Catholics did not seem to be sharing in the *Gründerjahre* benefits.

In times of stress and change, divisions can become politicized with opposing groups demanding the right to the resolution of issues through the political processes. As Catholics attacked "Jewish" governmental policies, liberals branded their Catholic opponents as beyond the political or social pale. Anti-Semites tend to be highly dogmatic as well as nationalistic. Hence, the political debate became quite rabid and was based on widespread support. There are indications that conventional churchgoers (i.e., the majority for whom religion is not the master motive in life) tend to be intolerant and prejudiced toward deviant minorities. Such an anti-Semite typically ascribed all manner of evil to his Jewish enemies, foreign or domestic, while attributing good to himself. Such prejudice expresses deep passions and historically has reflected the basic needs and inner conflicts of such individuals as those lower middle class and rural agrarian Catholics struggling for political identity and against economic anxiety.[10] In these early days of the Second Reich, Germany offers a classic case of anti-Semitism as a politicization mechanism.

Catholic Anti-Semitism in the Second Empire

Catholics had already assimilated traditional anti-Semitic patterns of thought. In 1848, the Catholic theologian, Sebastian Brunner, and Bishop

Konrad Martin of Paderborn, for example, had isolated the dangers of "talmudic anti-Christianity" whose principle articles were the obdurate refusal of the Jews to acknowledge the truths of salvation, proclaimed by the Church, as well as Jewish economic power, political guile, and moral corruption, which could ultimately subvert Christian life, if unchecked. This threatening danger to the political state and its Christian culture naturally increased, Catholics felt, when the Jews were granted equal rights and their historical disabilities were removed. As early as 1873 the *Historisch-politische Blätter,* a leading Catholic paper, spoke of a plan according to which the emancipation of the Jews would lead to the ultimate subjugation of Christians. Political unification and the great depression of 1873 served to mobilize Catholics. Hostility or fear normally is generalized from a frustration not to *any* object or group, but to previously disliked individuals or groups.[11]

During the *Kulturkampf,* Catholics accused the Jews of being liberals and enemies of the Church, grain speculators, lords of the exchange, and terrorists. These epithets had already been used by Bishop Wilhelm Emanuel von Ketteler in 1862 when he attacked what he called the destructive and corrupting influence of capitalism, industrialism, and the Jews on the national economy, the family, and the public morality of Christian society. The traditional values of discipline, modesty, family integrity, and ecclesiastical authority, he asserted, were being undermined by the laissez-faire financial power of the Jews. Ketteler declared that in 1872 liberal Jewish dominance had reached a point where even "German character" was being warped. *Der Katholik* (1873) reinforced this point by stressing that undoubtedly it was the influence of Judaism, which was causing the progressive de-Christianization and the weakening of public morality in society as well as undermining the strength of German national life. The assault on liberalism and the Jews is not surprising, perhaps, because religious values come from the top down. At least until recently, Catholics have tended to respect authority and tradition. The Catholic anti-Semitic movement, historically nurtured since the early Church, has been characterized by a contempt for Jews on the one hand and a fear of their power on the other. This viewpoint is apparent in the interpretation given by Georg Ratzinger, member of the Bavarian Parliament, and Ludwig Erler, Bishop of Mainz, to the religious thrust of the *Kulturkampf* and to the economic and social crisis of that period, which they attributed to rapid industrial expansion, reckless speculation, and the financial crash. From the moment the Jews appeared on the stage of history, maintained these theologians, they betrayed monotheism and as cunning nomads roamed among cultures, subverting the Christian cultures in which they lived. An economic ethos of work and not simply profit and investments, a discipline of obedience based on love, faith, and humility, a sense of responsibility to one's work and family as well as qualities of probity, devotion, and fidelity were all repugnant to the Jewish character. Anti-Semitism was reinforced from the Vatican as well. In 1872, Pius IX attacked Jewish journalism; in 1873 he assaulted Jewish avarice and participation in the *Kulturkampf*.[12]

Anti-Semitic agitation continued throughout the 1870s. In 1874 the Catholic theologian and popular writer Alban Stolz stated that Catholics had been educated by the punitive May Laws, the initial *Kulturkampf* legislation. In particular they aggressively sought to counteract the influence of liberalism and Judaism on the Christian German citizen. In this period, the polemical works of Canon August Rohling, professor of Catholic theology and, subsequently, professor of Semitic languages at the German University of Prague, enjoyed a great popularity. He analyzed the *Talmud* and *Schulchan Aruch,* the authoritative code of Jewish laws and customs compiled by the sixteenth century Talmudic scholar, Joseph Caro. These commentaries described the "inhuman" character of rabbinic Judaism and the corrupting influence of the Jews on German culture and the economy. Rohling treated the *Talmud* as a Jewish breviary in which Christians were vilified as servants of Baal, and Jews were permitted usury as well as the practice of sodomy with Christians and the violation of non-Jewish women. The *Talmud* supposedly referred to Christians as swine and dogs, using animal imagery to dehumanize Christians, and was a program for world domination by the chosen people. Rohling's work, moreover, analyzed "ritual murder," whereby the spilling of Christian blood was viewed as a sacrifice to God.[13]

By 1875 leading Catholic newspapers had also begun to echo the Protestant-Conservative *Kreuzzeitung's* attacks. The major Catholic daily *Germania* denounced the prevailing *Judenwirtschaft* and demanded a boycott of Jewish firms. Jewish financiers, for example, were condemned for subscribing to the French war loan in 1870 while they were simultaneously reluctant to finance the North German Confederation. The Jews, in short, were unpatriotic—an accusation usually aimed at Catholics! The temptation to equate the liberals with the Jews was too great for *Germania:* "The *Kulturkampf* is in fact and in many of its manifestations exclusively a consequence of Jewish activities. On account of the *Kulturkampf,* we are pleased that the Jewish problem has for some time now been highlighted clearly and decisively."[14] Or again: "The true *Kulturkampf,* directed not against the religion of the Jews, not against the Jewry as such, but against Jewish spirit which threatens Christianity and the German character and against the Jewish money domination which is the death of our national prosperity, has become an urgent necessity and fortunately has already become widely popular."[15]

This Catholic assault on the "Jewish problem" can be explained in part by focusing on the function of prejudice in intergroup relationships. Frequently incidents that evoke aggressive behavior in persons have gained this potency through learning experiences. Such significant aggression elicitors as personal insults or status threats instigate responses. Attribution of blame to a group can become an expedient mechanism, useful for self-assuaging purposes. Aggressors frequently perceive themselves as persons of goodwill who are forced into punitive actions by villainous opponents. Hence, the Jewish victims in the Second Reich could be condemned for bringing suffering on themselves either by their character defects or by their provocative behavior. For Catholics, self-vindication could be achieved by selecting a chain of wrongs or instances of real or imagined aggression by their opponents and interpreting these as the cause of incitement. Likewise, seeing victims suffer punitive physical or verbal treatment for which they were held partially responsible historically has reinforced others to devalue the Jew. In case the perpetrator doubts the efficacy of his action, discomfort can be reduced through the simple expedient of designating the victim as a bad person rather than by challenging bad practices that are an accepted part of the social order. Catholic anti-Semitism developed both extensively and intensively through psychological reinforcement.[16]

In 1876, the second edition of Bishop Martin's book was published by the Catholic theologian Joseph Rebbert, one of the editors of the periodical *Leo,* as part of his polemical booklet against the Jews. Rebbert emphasized themes that by this time had become part of the normal anti-Semitic arsenal. The Jewish question was not the property of ultramontanist groups, but belonged to all parties. Significantly, he asserted that assimilated or reformed Jews were merely *Juden mit Schweinefleisch.* Also he stressed that historically *all* Christians had been plundered and degraded into slavery by the Jews. Rebbert continued by insisting that although Jews had lived among Germans for centuries, race distinctions had always remained. In fact, Jews could be referred to as a "ferment of cosmopolitanism and of national decomposition." Finally, as long as Liberals were ascendant, he insisted, the regeneration of Germany through the Christian spirit was unthinkable. As a solution to the "Jewish question," he proposed the elimination of the National Liberal party and its Jewish allies.[17]

Beginning with the second half of the 1870s more socioeconomic Catholic theorists were drawn into the process of consolidating anti-Jewish feeling. Taking part in this process were the Dominican theologian Albert M. Weiss, the historian and jurist Simon Eichner, and Constantin Frantz. In this assault, traditional arguments focusing on "Jewish moral corruption" were used. Such "racial" characteristics as Jewish avarice and such esthetic traits as garlic odors were specified as the product of blood and could not be changed by external circumstances. Emphasizing such qualities and social practices, Catholic commentators were effectively dividing the population into in-group and out-group members and so were producing a human estrangement that could be conducive to dehumanization. The leaders of this anti-Jewish revival gave a more or less coherent account of what they termed to be the historical image and character of the Jews. In the early days of Christianity, they explained, and as Christianity was extended throughout the pagan world, the Jews were regarded (as in the period of the *Kulturkampf*) as shameless intrigants, swindlers, venal, unscrupulous exploiters who lived like parasites and who seduced and slandered all Christians. The persecution of the Catholics by the Prussian authorities was linked to that of the Christians in the Roman Empire as the insidious work of the crafty Jews.[18]

Hostile attitudes along such lines of ethnic, political, or class cleavage have originated in a variety of ways: from a history of group conflict, from the threatening demands of a subordinated group for greater privileges, or from frequent contact between people adhering to different ideational systems. All of these conditions existed in the Germany of the 1870s. Given the historical existence of intergroup hostilities, an actual or fancied attack by members of a specific group provided the sufficient justification for organized aggression. Like other hostile acts, anti-Semitism also developed through the modeling and social reinforcement of anti-Judaism that had been operant since early Christian times. In the final analysis, identification through aggression could serve to reduce anxiety not by assimilating the external threat but by appropriating a variety of forceful tactics and responses that could assure better control over the social environment. As late as 1879, *Germania* was still attacking the Jewish *Geldherrschaft,* which focused on monetary enrichment without productive work and on furthering moral corruption through newspapers and popular literature. Jewish power was even perceived as supporting such radical and revolutionary movements as socialism or Marxism—a convenient shift in light of Bismarck's future intentions.[19]

Both conservative Protestants and Catholics found that they could identify the Jewish ethnic or religious minority as the source of deprivation, hence as a justifiable target of attack. From a psychological perspective, if people already dislike an outgroup for varied reasons, they tend to be susceptible to rumors and beliefs that associate their present discontents with the group. The anti-Semitism of the 1870s is a classic example of this dynamic. The more visible or "different" the outgroup is, the more readily can discontented people learn external or mental cues that associate such groups with their discontent. The more vulnerable an outgroup appears to be, the more readily can blame be attributed to it and aggression directed against it. After 1870, with increasing frequency the notion spread that this alien force (Judaism) was part of a vast international conspiracy "set on ruining and then dominating the rest of mankind." After 1879 the fuel for the German anti-Semitism engine became nationalism and anticapitalism. The "Jewish Question" was reduced to a minority problem.[20]

In the anti-Jewish, antiliberal campaign, Catholic anti-Prussianism and Protestant-Conservative ultra-Prussianism found their common ground. This community of interests propelled the two major antiliberal forces toward further political cooperation. An alliance was constructed through which Bismarck ultimately found his great opportunity to escape the liberal forces within the Reichstag, which were threatening the delicate political structure that he had established. Even while attacked by this Conservative-Catholic coalition, Bismarck sensed his opportunity for a political shift that would topple the liberals as governmental partners and isolate the socialist Left.[21]

During the *Kulturkampf* the mood of the Center was to beat the Bismarckian liberal coalition with an anti-Semitic stick. This anti-Jewish perspective did not totally disappear once Bismarck reversed his political alliances. After 1880 anti-Semitic articles in the Catholic press appeared both in major and provincial papers. For example, the *Kölnische Volkszeitung,* one of the party's two leading organs, commented that the Rhenish Center party had paid far too little attention to the *Kulturkampf.* The party should have declared its attitude toward the anti-Semitic movement at its public meetings. Although this attitude should have been a decisive rejection of demagogic and inflammatory anti-Semitism, the party should have energetically acted against existing Jewish excesses, particularly in commercial life, but only on a legal basis. Use the law, they felt, to press the anti-Semitic issue. Anti-Semitism had served its initial purpose in helping Catholics integrate themselves into the body politic. In an 1880 letter to Wilhelm Marr, a leading Protestant anti-Semite, Vicar Arnold Bongartz, editor of the *Christlich-sozialen Blätter,* stated that the Catholic press, in particular that served by the Catholic clergy and intellectuals, had battled *Judentum* most energetically. Because of their intimate connection with the *Volk,* he continued, Catholics had developed a perceptive understanding of the Jews. From the 1880s onward, the Center officially refused to embrace anti-Semitism. Various reasons may be suggested for this policy. Having been the victim of discriminatory legislation, Catholics were on weak ground proposing such laws to others. Catholic leaders were in general more cosmopolitan than their Bavarian or Galician followers. Windthorst, for example, insisted that Catholics should oppose anti-Semitism even when it was not in their interest to do so. Still, a popular or vulgar anti-Semitism, overt at the local level and covert on the national stage, continued creeping into Catholic responses to political and socioeconomic issues right up to the Nazi era.[22]

Catholic rediscovery of Christian tolerance, at least publicly, was directly related to the position of Catholicism in the Reich. After 1879, the year of the protective tariff and Bismarck's coalition shift, the Catholic Center, at last a respectable party, gained a strategic position in the Reichstag and began acting less defensively. The only major party not tied predominately to a single social group, it could join the Right or Left in coalitions without fearing the loss of its popular base. Bismarck's liquidation of the *Kulturkampf* opened the door for conditional Catholic parliamentary support. The National Liberal era was then over, and with it disappeared some of the socioeconomic and political inducements that anti-Semitism could offer Catholicism. The concept of "minority" as applied to Catholic and Jewish groups is also apt to conceal essential distinctions. Following the *Kulturkampf,* Catholics, for example, slowly gained access to the governmental machinery, while Jews did not. Industrial expansion in Catholic regions gave rise to a Catholic trade union movement and established Catholic influence in a sphere of power where the Jewish weakness was glaring. Germany's close diplomatic relations to predominantly Catholic states (the Hapsburg Empire and Italy) also strengthened the German Catholic group. Seemingly, Catholics could afford to be tolerant.

After the *Kulturkampf,* anti-Semitism was no longer, at least in official circles of the Center, a crucial component in the campaign to integrate Catholics into the mainstream of German life.[23] In general, until 1933, across Germany rabid anti-Semites fared poorly in districts with a Catholic majority. The explanation for this disparity may lie in the Catholics' strong group identity, for which the *Kulturkampf* was a powerful reinforcement. This religious identity became political identity. For all their persecution by the state and their bewilderment at rapid socioeconomic change, German Catholics did not feel severed from the German or Catholic communities nor abandoned by their natural leaders. Catholics stayed with their leaders and, thanks to Windthorst, with few exceptions the leadership avoided officially sanctioned anti-Semitic politics. The Catholic *Mittelstand* was not available for the Christian Social party (Stöcker) in the 1880s nor a similar Catholic group. One has only to remember Karl Lueger of Vienna, admired by Hitler, who mobilized political Catholicism in Austria, to realize it might have been otherwise.[24] Yet anti-Semitism ran strongly beneath the surface in German-Catholic strongholds and the underlying strains of modernization had not been eliminated.

The development of aggressive behavior is directly related to the social contexts, the targets, the role occupied by the performer, and any other cues that reliably illuminate the potential consequences for aggressive action, without relying on the performer alone. Man is neither driven by inner forces nor buffeted helplessly by environmental influences. Rather, psychological functioning is derived from the continuous reciprocal interaction between behavior and its controlling conditions. The environment is only a potentiality, not a fixed property, which inevitably impinges upon individuals and to which their behavior eventually adapts. Hostile behavior, real or alleged, elicits unfriendly responses[25]—hence the emergence of varied degrees of anti-Semitism in the Second Reich among all the socioeconomic classes.

Through anti-Semitism the Center initially was able to identify itself with powerful conservative groups who were anticapitalist and antiliberal. When Bismarck decided to jettison the National Liberals, the Center was in an ideal position to be integrated into subsequent governmental coalitions. After 1880 anti-Semitism was still used by some Catholics as they assaulted modernism and reminded the dominant majority that they were "loyal" Germans, but it did not have to be used overtly and officially as a device to assure the integration of Catholics into mainstream politics. Socialism, represented by the Social Democratic party purportedly supported by the Jews, could now be assaulted as a system hostile to Catholicism and to the ruling elites of authoritarian Germany. Perhaps some Catholics had initially adopted anti-Semitism to become the attackers rather than the attacked and could now abandon this vulgar bias. Likewise, anti-Semitism may well have provided the language and vehicle for the symbolic, as opposed to physical, aggression which the Center needed to battle Catholicism's politico-economic enemies during the *Kulturkampf.* After 1879 some Catholics could jettison overt anti-Semitism; it had served its tactical function. Others saw the Jew as a continuing problem and covertly insinuated anti-Semitism into their politics.

Antipathy to the Social Democratic party was accompanied by a widespread distrust of the city, the symbol of wealth, political power, administrative caprice, and immorality. These attitudes had been equally apparent in the anti-Semitic response of Catholics to the *Kulturkampf.* The Center from 1870 until 1914 created a demonology, composed of anti-Semitism and later attached to antisocialism, to appeal to its supporters' apprehensions. The economic backwardness among Catholics[26] and their anti-urban bias helped align the party to the Right. Generally, prejudiced Catholics became respectable, verbal anti-Semites, not demagogues. In 1907 Hans Rost, for example, insisted that Christianity certainly forbade the hatred of races, but did not "prohibit defense against the harmful influences caused by the peculiarities of a certain race."[27]

While it has usually been argued that anti-Semitism among Catholics and in the Center Party had reached its zenith in the 1870s,[28] this prejudice remained meaningful among various segments of Catholic local communities during the entire period of the Second Reich. Biased Catholics were anti-Semitic because of their socioeconomic position. They were overrepresented in the poorer countryside and small towns as well as in agriculture and small business. Under external attack, such Catholics as Martin Spahn could make Jews a scapegoat for the turn to the Left in Germany and Hans Rost could describe a number of universities as *verjudet*. The Catholic variant of "respectable" bourgeois anti-Semitism could focus on "bewitching Jewish department stores," "pushy Jewry," and resentment among the peasantry against the Jewish money lender and cattle dealer.[29]

In one respect, Catholic anti-Semitism readily formed part of a broader antiliberal and antibureaucratic appeal. Within their threatened "tower," Catholic leaders found covert anti-Semitism an important tool for Center party politics throughout the period of the Second Reich. Although liberalism may well have declined nationally after 1879, liberal governmental groups remained powerful on the local level, frequently gerrymandering districts at the expense of Catholics. Politicians used anti-Semitic appeals against liberals. Catholic leaders warned peasants to stay out of the clutches of the Jew.[30] On local levels reports on meetings of the *Volksverein für das katholische Deutschland,* usually addressed by the town or village priest, almost automatically included condemnation of officials, liberals, Freemasons, and Jews. At one meeting a speaker commented on local proposals, supported by the Left liberals, to extend an educational provision: "The Democrats want everyone who attends school to be brought to the stage that they can later secure themselves against any need, and no longer fall into the hands of the Jew. Against this it must be said that already highly educated peasants have fallen victim to the usurious Jew."[31]

In essence, then, during the Second Reich anti-Semitism was generated by the Catholics' own experience of backwardness, repression, discrimination, and neglect. The rural and small-town base of German political Catholicism insured against the emergence of an urban, Catholic, extremist anti-Semitism. Among Catholic peasantry and the petty bourgeois was constituted a set of reactions that expressed a sense of exploitation and neglect—economic, social, and institutional. Center leaders could subtly harness this populistic anti-Semitism, without risking embarrassment. Such policies with such popular anti-Semitic overtones as department store taxation were officially adopted by the party and stripped of those offensive terms in which they continued to be discussed in small towns and villages. Anti-Semitic labels were missing, but everyone understood the "real" issues.[32]

Christian and Racial Anti-Semitism

Like so many other Central Europeans, a significant number of Catholics used anti-Semitism as a lens through which to analyze the issues erupting in the modernizing Germany of their era. The anti-Semitic movement had become more than an attempt to reverse emancipation; it was for many an important component of a comprehensive *Weltanschauung.* To some, the Jewish question was the key to understanding the political, economic, and cultural problems of the era. To others it was a convenient vehicle to facilitate integration. Catholic intolerance during the *Kulturkampf* may be seen as an event that at least reinforced a latent anti-Semitism while simultaneously aiding Catholics in their struggle for integration into a potentially hostile authoritarian Reich. Parliamentary liberalism was not accepted in the 1870s nor would it be approved thereafter enthusiastically by a significant number of Catholics. Anti-Semitism served the Center as a functional mechanism for political mobilization to the Right. After 1880 it seemed directed by some against the liberal Jews, but by many against their surrogates and puppets, the Social Democrats, or against any problem that seemed insoluble or rooted in an "anti-German" conspiracy. Although many Catholics were not blatantly anti-Semitic, they could hardly be jaundiced toward the Nazis in light of their own *Kulturkampf* defense and subsequent experiences.

Catholics and Conservatives were not alone in their support of anti-Semitism. By the 1880s even the conservative wing of the National Liberal party was reluctant to appoint Jewish candidates. Jews now began leaning increasingly toward the Progressives and Socialists. This spontaneous concentration of Jews in leftist politics gave rise to an imposed seclusion from the main scene of activity, thus completing Jewish social segregation.[33] In the domain of public administration, including appointments in the universities and promotions in the army, the law guaranteeing civil rights irrespective of religious confession remained a dead letter, notably so in Prussia. This set the tone for the country as a whole. Even baptized Jews had difficulty in being accepted and promoted in the army or public administration. Once the anti-Semitic movement engulfed society, the liberalizing tendencies of the 1870s, if ever they really existed, were reversed. The exclusion of Jews from public positions, perhaps even more than their social and political segregation, demonstrated their exceptional and precarious situation, recalling once again the condition of the pariah.[34]

Basically, Christian anti-Semitism was not as virulent as racial anti-Semitism. The former stigmatized Jewish perfidy, but it permitted the Jew to exist as the living witness to the truth of Christianity. The Jew, it was thought, was ordained to act out his predestined, perfidious role as villain in the drama of salvation, at the end of which he would be justified. But he was always free according to Christian theorists to abrogate his covenant with Jehovah and accept the benevolent efforts of the Church to redeem him. According to racial theory, on the contrary, even baptism could not penetrate the tainted Jewish seed; the deep stain could only be removed by destroying the source of infection and its bearer, the physical Jew. The Jew must not only be excoriated, but eliminated. Insofar as it had succumbed to Jewish influences, Christianity also seemed culpable since the *agape,* like the Jewish *logos,* had alienated man from nature and weakened him in his struggle for existence. In the final analysis, as the Nazis insisted, the values of the Jews and Christians were opposite sides of the same coin.

In the days of the Second Reich vulgar racial theories as such were not embraced by the majority of the German people, although Gustav Freytag's popular novel *Soll und Haben* must have struck a resonant chord when the "good Jew" Bernhard led the reader to conclude that Judaism alone was not capable of giving its adherents morality and culture.[35] Literary examples of anti-Semitism could be multiplied and the tabloid press reveled in unending racial incidents. People bought this sensationalism and did not appear offended. The prejudicial stereotype gained popular currency in the Second Reich and Weimar Republic. A respondent to the 1934 Abel contest,[36] Kurt Winkler (b.1908), mentioned in his biography that in his youth it was considered shameful for a young Christian girl even to dance with a Jew and that no academic could risk being surprised in the company of a Jewess. Winkler suggests that part of this reaction, at least in his Munich peer group and apparently in Hitler's perception as well, had originated among *völkisch* Germans born in Austria who feared any mixture with the different races of the empire.[37] Most Germans did not make anti-Semitism the central premise for their activity, although the images and stereotypes did enjoy a common currency and seemed a part of their general cultural baggage. The *völkisch* ideology, reinforced by anti-Semitism, for example, was given respectability by such intellectuals as Lagarde, Langbehn, H.S. Chamberlain, and the antiintellectualist Rembrandt movement before transmission to such leading Nazis as Alfred Rosenberg and to the leaders of the Deutsch-Christian movement.[38]

For the racial anti-Semites on the intellectual fringe, blood became an absolute value because it eliminated the distinction between the symbol and that which was symbolized. They hoped to create a total identity connecting the individual sphere and public domain, the society and state. These thinkers felt that man's life must be saved from the anemic ideals of Christianity and restored to its root and anchor in blood. By placing spirit above matter, conscience above intuition, and speculative thought above the experience of blood, Christianity had polluted the noblest instincts in man and severed him from his natural roots. In the minds of these racists, true anti-Semitism would finally cleanse civilization of Christian corruption as well. It would seem, then, that traditional Christianity and racial anti-Semitism, although starting at opposite poles and with no discernible principle of reconciliation, were powered by a common impulse directed either to the conversion or to the extermination of the Jews. Racial anti-Semites adapted and used basic Christian ideas and terminology. According to some racial anti-Semites, the Jews were the essence of evil and must therefore be exterminated not only spiritually (as Christianity had attempted) but also in the flesh.[39]

Given the long history of anti-Semitism,[40] Christianity materially aided in reinforcing the patterns of prejudice, hatred, and calumny, which justified violence to cure the ills of society. The anti-Christian elements of racial anti-Semitism were so camouflaged that the traditional concepts of Christianity were not completely rejected; only their meanings were transformed by using a pseudoscientific jargon which the racists applied to the historical realities of that day, ignoring the salutary correction of Christian discipline and belief. Racial anti-Semitism and the subsequent Nazi movement were not simply the result of mass hysteria or the work of single propagandists. Despite their antagonism toward traditional Christianity, the racial anti-Semites learned much from Christianity and succeeded in producing a systematic and logical ideology that reached its culmination in the Third Reich.[41] In the Second Reich anti-Semitism pervaded society but can be distinguished according to its degree of virulence.

Patterns of populistic prejudice were delineated and supported by Catholics in the Second Reich and certainly no strenuous effort was made by them to integrate the Jewish minority into status positions. After all, Catholics themselves felt they were in a besieged fortress.[42] A number of general values either emerged or were reinforced as a result of Catholic experiences in the Second Reich. Jews, liberals, and socialists all were lumped together as evildoers. Catholics tended to support the value structure of the authoritarian state in opposition to a liberal political system that emphasized civil rights for all in a system of political pluralism. Catholics were politicized in the authoritarian state and accepted their identity as Catholic German citizens in the Bismarckian Second Reich. For Catholics, nationalism and anti-Semitism were commingled in the 1870s, and the Second Reich became the political home of Catholics prospering in the mainstream of their nation, although still suffering discrimination and suspected by some of a lack of patriotism.

The leaders of the Catholic Church during World War I, Weimar, and then Nazi Germany had matured during the period of oppression labeled the *Kulturkampf.* Bismarck's assault and the subsequent discrimination against Catholics in governmental and university positions left a long-lasting impression that Roman Catholics were second-class citizens in Imperial Germany. In defense, Catholics attempted to prove themselves loyal—even 200 percent German—during the war. Catholics by 1918 had assimilated a pattern of values highlighting nationalism, anti-Semitism as a "normal" German bias, and opposition to liberalism as well as to the vices associated with an urban-industrial civilization that was opposed to the traditional rural milieu where values were rooted in the past. Thus, many had serious reservations about the Weimar Republic itself. The Center party ultimately maintained its constituency against the Nazis, partly because of its successful, even if less strident, demagogy. Catholic anti-Semitism already offered supporters of the Center a muted and respectable form of the vulgar Nazi racism. The Center, however, also helped establish a nationalist-authoritarian political milieu in which some Nazis could appear respectable, and the party could be supported if such rabid racists as Streicher and Rosenberg could be relegated to obscurity. As a result, the Center could prosper politically until 1933, but could not offer any strenuous moral or political resistance after the Nazis seized power,[43] in light of their contribution to the heightened nationalistic anti-Semitism during the Weimar era.

To understand the reasons for the pervasive anti-Semitism and the rise of Nazism, scholars have analyzed the fundamental precepts of Western civilization and Christian morality. No better expression of the scholarly conundrum exists than that provided by Dwight MacDonald in 1945. "What had previously been done only by individual psychopathic killers has now been done by the rulers and servants of a great modern state. This is something new."[44] In Nazi Germany, human extermination represented a logical national, racial, and social policy needed for the evolution of Hitler's Reich. This Final Solution has been a major historical and religious issue in the twentieth century—a veritable crisis focusing on human behavior and values. Roman Catholic Germans participated in this event, but were also simultaneously the heirs of the Church's claim to being the moral arbiter through the centuries and the mediatrix of God's word to man. The Church, of course, is a human institution subject to the environmental-personal dynamics typical of all human interactions of men in states and societies. German Catholics, then, carried the burden of their history as well as the challenges of their faith as they began the tortuous path that led into the Third Reich and its frightening implications for the twentieth-century human condition. The Catholic Church formed one of the only counterweights to Nazi totalitarianism, opposing it with their own claims on the individual. But religion frequently finds itself peculiarly tailored to the nationalistic, class, and ethnic cleavages and outlooks that sustain the prevailing social order. A striking instance is the extent to which German Catholics capitulated to the political and cultural demands of Nazi pressure and in the final analysis were indifferent toward Nazi racism. Had the pope or the German bishops spoken out *publicly* against the deportation of Jews, for example, some evidence suggests that the German government might have modified its policy,[45] although there are grave doubts as well that such a change would have occurred. Catholics did not speak and their behavior has been questioned since 1945.

As a community, the Church theoretically plays a vital role in the formation of its members' ethical responses to the secular environment. The Church influences character in three ways: as shaper of moral identity, as bearer of moral tradition, and as the community of moral deliberation. Where moral identity is concerned, it is clear that the Church's actions (liturgy, preaching) function as socializing factors. This moral mission of the Church has been consistently challenged by the pressures generated through the secular society of the twentieth century. Increasingly in modern times religious values, however, seem to have little demonstrable relationship to what people actually do in work and politics. Secularization has led to the result that adherence to any single set of beliefs, values, and norms is increasingly difficult in any society at an advanced level of differentiation. The effects of pluralism and the mass media have combined to reduce beliefs to opinions and matters of ultimate commitment to matters of personal preference. Secularization has not driven religion from modern society, but rather has fostered a type of religion that has no major functions for the *entire* society.[46] In light of this twentieth-century development, for the Church to fulfill its religious mission in a modern secularized society would be surprising indeed. But if prelates and theologians do not examine the ultimate values surrounding the human condition and critique sociopolitical developments, which institution has the power and prestige to replace organized religion, at least theoretically involved both in social interaction and in a position to judge the secular milieu? From a psychological perspective, such a dual role may not even be possible. The examination of the Church's activity in Nazi Germany focuses on the problems that religion faces in modern society and highlights the operative psychosocial dynamics that widen the gap between St. Augustine's heavenly city and man's metropolis.

In his book *Social Behaviorism,* Arthur Staats has offered a psychological paradigm for the study of man. A paradigm has a philosophy of science as well as a philosophy for gaining knowledge. Of central importance in the paradigm is its ability to direct the observations of those who accept the paradigm and to organize what might otherwise be disparate investigatory activity. In Staats' social behaviorism, learning and behavior theory are central. In general, Staats maintains that people can and do learn fantastically complex sequences, arrays, and combinations of responses under complex stimulus-eliciting conditions. Such a theory of learning behavior must be concerned with the length of the individual's learning history[47] and that would include the culture in which the person lives.

Since the social environment itself is a determinant of the individual's behavior, when he affects his milieu he in turn helps determine what his own and his descendants' future behavior will be. Persons interacting with their social environments develop attitudes, respond to positive and negative reinforcements, and utilize discriminatory capabilities. In essence, they acquire a system of preferences, which causes them to select particular activities, pursue specific objects, and determine which events are potentially rewarding. Staats has pointed out that social practices or systems that result in stronger positive reinforcers will control supportive behaviors more strongly than a competitive practice or system that results in little positive reinforcement or much negative reinforcement. Naturally, different institutions or value systems in society may be in competition and higher rewards would attract more adherents.[48]

The formation of values, the activities of individuals, and the interactions between individuals and their social milieu can be delineated through the social behavioristic paradigm. Catholics politicized after 1871 matured in an anti-Semitic, antiliberal, authoritarian, and nationalistic sociopolitical environment. They were rewarded for patriotism, and their religion was politically suspect. Hence, their learning experiences, attitudinal reinforcers, and their discriminatory abilities finely honed in the political struggles of Wilhelmine Germany had basically placed them by 1918 in the mainstream of German historical development with their fellow citizens. They had won a hard-fought battle, but now had to deal with the National Socialist party led by Hitler who hoped to redefine German society in accordance with his *Weltanschauung*.

Notes

1. Felix Gilbert, "Bismarckian Society's Image of the Jew" (New York: Leo Baeck Institute, 1978); Christoph Weber, *Aufklärung und Orthodoxie am Mittelrhein 1820-1850* (Paderborn: Schöningh, 1973); Jonathan Sperber, "Roman Catholic Religious Identity in Rhineland-Westphalia, 1800-1870: Quantitative Examples and Some Political Implications," *Social History 7* (1982):306, 311; for an analysis of the post-1850 formation of Catholic associations, characterized by a strict religious and moral atmosphere as well as by a basically conservative sociopolitical outlook, see Jonathan Sperber, "The Transformation of Catholic Associations in the Northern Rhineland and Westphalia, 1830-1870" *Journal of Social History 14* (1981):253-263; Ismar Schorsch, *Jewish Reactions to Ger-*

man Anti-Semitism, 1870-1914 (New York: Columbia University Press, 1972), p. 27. The Reichstag declared for Jews the rights of full citizenship and the holding of public office wholly independent of religious affiliation. The *Allgemeine Zeitung des Judentums,* 1869, 717, stated: "The sorrowful days, thank God, have passed for German Israelites." The *Nationalzeitung,* Berlin, February 25, 1872 stated: "The German does not intend to tolerate within his own nation any spiritual kinship with Rome; he rejects the ascendance of priests and all attempts to blunt the people's intelligence; he stands for enlightenment . . . an honest conscience and work. . . . Our German states and our German Reich are a truly moral community of a much higher order than that represented by the ecclesiastical societies, either those misguided by the ultramontanes or the selfstyled Evangelical Orthodox." Joseph N. Moody (ed.), *Church and Society: Catholic Social and Political Thought and Movements, 1789-1950* (New York: Arts, Inc., 1953), p. 453; the Center party leader, Ludwig Windthorst, on May 14, 1872, delineated the issue between Catholics and Liberals. "Gentlemen, I am quite aware of the fact that your notion of liberty is totally different from that held in North America. Your understanding of liberty consists of according the state all sorts of rights, then making every effort to take hold of state power, and, finally, crushing by this state power those who hold different views." Engelbert Pulke, "Geschichte der politischen Parteien in Kreis Recklinghausen bis zum Ende des Kulturkampfes 1848-1859," *Vestische Zeitschrift* 41 (1934):3-163.

2. S.M. Eisenstadt, *Traditions, Change, and Modernity* (New York: Wiley, 1973); Richard J. Evans and W.R. Lee (eds.), *The German Family: Essays on the Social History of the Family in Nineteenth and Twentieth Century Germany* (London: Croom Helm, 1981); Kuper, 58.

3. Ronald Ross, *The Beleaguered Tower: The Dilemma of Political Catholicism in Wilhelmine Germany* (Notre Dame, IN: University of Notre Dame Press, 1976), p. 11; the *Kreuzzeitung* was a conservative Junker newspaper.

4. Margaret Anderson, *Windthorst: A Political Biography* (Oxford: Clarendon Press, 1981), pp. 113, 134.

5. Ibid., p. 151; Albert Bandura, *Aggression: A Social Learning Analysis* (Englewood Cliffs, NJ: Prentice Hall, 1973), p. 213; V. Bernard et al. "Dehumanization: A Composite Psychological Defense in Relation to Modern War," in M. Schwebel (ed.), *Behavioral Science and Human Survival* (Palo Alto, CA: Science and Behavior Books, 1965), pp. 64-82; Ted Robert Gurr, *Why Men Rebel* (Princeton: Princeton University Press, 1970), pp. 199-200; William Kornhauser, *The Politics of Mass Society* (New York: Routledge and Kegan Paul, 1959), p. 112.

6. Howard J. Ehrlich, *The Social Psychology of Prejudice: A Systematic Theoretical Review and Propositional Inventory of the American Social Psychological Study of Prejudice* (New York: John Wiley & Sons, 1973), p. 82; Jacob Katz, *From Prejudice to Destruction: Anti-Semitism, 1700-1933* (Cambridge: Harvard University Press, 1980); for essays on earlier forms of anti-Semitism, see David Winston, "Pagan and Early Anti-Semitism" and Garvin I. Langmuir, "Medieval Anti-Semitism," in Friedlander and Milton, pp. 15-36; Ernst Heinen, "Anti-Semitische Strömungen in politschen Katholizismus während des Kulturkampfes," in Ernst Heinen and Julius Schoeps (eds.), *Geschichte in der Gegenwart* (Paderborn: Schöningh, 1972); Anderson *Windthorst,* p. 145; M. Rokeach, *The Open and Closed Mind* (New York: Basic Books, 1960); H.

Bornkamm, "Die Staatsidee in Kulturkampf," *Historische Zeitschrift* 170 (1950):41ff.

7. James J. Sheehan, *German Liberalism in the Nineteenth Century* (Chicago: University of Chicago Press, 1978), p. 136; Douglas W. Hatfield, "*Kulturkampf:* The Relationship of Church and State and the Failure of German Political Reform," *Journal of Church and State* 23 (1981):465-484; Anderson, 197; Gordon R. Mork, "Bismarck and the Capitulation of German Liberalism," *Journal of Modern History* 43 (1971), 59-75, Michael Stürmer, *Regierung und Reichstag im Bismarcksstaat, 1871-1880: Cäsarismus oder Parlementarismus* (Düsseldorf: Droste, 1974), pp. 46-87; Seymour Martin Lipset, *The First Nation* (New York: Basic Books, 1963), p. 16; Hans Rost, *Die Parität und die deutschen Katholiken* (Cologne: J.P. Bachem, 1914), pp. 32-33; for a sound study of the Catholic Center party, see David Blackbourn, *Class, Religion and Local Politics in Wilhelmine Germany: The Centre Party in Württemberg before 1914* (New Haven: Yale University Press, 1980); for a study of anti-Semitism and political parties, see P.G.J. Pulzer, *The Rise of Political Anti-Semitism in Germany and Austria* (New York: John Wiley and Sons, 1964), and Paula Hyman, "The History of European Jewry: Recent Trends in the Literature," *Journal of Modern History* 54 (1982):303-319.

8. Argyle, pp. 115ff.; R.M. Williams, "Religion, Value Orientation, and Intergroup Conflict,"*Journal of Social Issues* 12 (1956):12-20; C.Y. Glock and R. Stark, *Christian Beliefs and Anti-Semitism* (New York: Harper and Row, 1966).

9. L. Festinger, "A Theory of Social Comparison Processes" *Human Relations* 7 (1954):117-140; Louise H. Kidder and V. Mary Stewart, *The Psychology of Inter-Group Relations: Conflict and Consciousness* (New York: McGraw Hill, 1975), p. 23; Bandura, *Aggression*, p. 211; K. Keniston, "Student Activism, Moral Development, and Morality," *American Journal of Ortho-Psychiatry* 40 (1970), 577-592; Ehrlich, p. 55; for 'Catholic backwardness,' see J. Rost, *Die wirtschaftliche und kulturelle Lage der deutschen Katholiken* (Cologne: J.P. Bachem, 1911); C. Bauer, *Deutscher Katholizismus. Entwicklungslinien und Profile* (Frankfurt: Josef Knecht, 1964).

10. I.L. Horowitz and M. Liebowitz, "Social Deviance and Political Marginality: Toward a Redefinition of the Relation Between Sociology and Politics," *Social Problems* 15 (1968):280-296; D.J. Levinson, "Authoritarian Personality and Foreign Policy," *Journal of Conflict Resolution* 1 (1957):37-47; P.E. Johnson, *The Psychology of Religion* (New York: Abingdon Press, 1959). For a succinct study of the anti-Semitism pervasive in the Second Reich, see Gilbert.

11. Leonard Berkowitz, *Aggression: A Social Psychological Analysis* (New York: McGraw Hill, 1962), chap. 6; Bandura, *Aggression*, pp. 135-136; D. Weatherly, "Anti-Semitism and the Expression of Fantasy Aggression," *Journal of Abnormal and Social Psychology* 62 (1961):454-457; E.E. Jones and R.E. Nisbett, *The Actor and the Observer: Divergent Perceptions of the Causes of Behavior* (New York: Appleton-Century-Croft, 1967), pp. 79-80; "Die Jüdische Frage," in *Historisch-politische Blätter für das katholische Deutschland* 2 (1838), p. 393; J.A. Köfler, *Katholische Kirche und Judenthum* (Munich: F. Enke, 1928), p. 42; Konrad Martin, "Blicke ins talmudische Judenthum," *Theologische Vierteljahresschrift* (1848).

12. Wilhelm Freiherr von Ketteler, *Freiheit, Autorität und Kirche. Erörterungen über die grossen Probleme der Gegenwart* (Mainz: Matthias-Grünewald, 1862), p. 125; Tal, pp. 93-103; *Der Katholik* in Stefan Uhr, *Antisemitismus religiöse*

Motive in sozialen Vorurteil, aus der Frühgeschichte des Antisemitismus in Deutschland, 1870-1914 (Munich: Oldenbourg, 1974), p. 133; Argyle, pp. 91-94; the Rokeach study (see footnote 6) on the open and closed mind suggests that at least U.S. Catholics emerge as more dogmatic than other religious groups; Georg Ratzinger, *Die Volkswirtschaft in ihren sittlichen Grundlagen, ethisch-soziale Studien über Cultur und Civilisation* (Freiburg: Herder, 1881), pp. 287ff., 377ff.; Ludwig Erler, *Historischkritische Übersicht der nationalökonomischen und sozialpolitischen Literatur* (Mainz: Matthias-Grünewald, 1879-1885), 43:361; Amine Hoose, *Katholische Presse und die Judenfrage: Inhaltsanalyse katholischer Periodika am Ende des 19. Jahrhunderts* (Berlin:Brückenverlag, 1875), p. 43.

13. August Rohling, *Der Talmudjude Zur Beherzingung für Juden und Christen aller Stände*, 4th ed. (Münster: Adolph Russell's Verlag, 1873), pp. 8, 9, 35; George L. Mosse, *Toward the Final Solution: A History of European Racism* (New York: Howard Fertig, 1978), p. 138.

14. Quoted in Paul W. Massing, *Rehearsal for Destruction: A Study of Political Anti-Semitism in Imperial Germany* (New York: Harper, 1949), pp. 14-15.

15. Quoted in Fritz Stern, *Gold and Iron. Bismarck, Bleichröder and the Building of the German Empire* (New York: Knopf, 1977), pp. 502-503.

16. Bandura, *Aggression*, pp. 116, 214; M.J. Lerner, "Observer's Evaluation of a Victim: Justice, Guilt, and Veridical Perception," *Journal of Personality and Social Psychology* 20 (1971):127-135.

17. Joseph Rebbert, *Blicke in's Talmudische Judenthum. Nach den Forschungen von Dr. Konrad Martin, Bischof von Padenborn, dem Christlichen Volke enthüllt* (Paderborn: J.W. Schröder, 1876), pp. 8, 13-14, 81, 88-89; Tal, pp. 90-91, the Jewish *Gemeindebund* and the Prussian Prosecution preferred charges against Rebbert and his publishers and won.

18. Fritz Schmidt-Clausing, "Judengegnerische Strömungen in deutschen Katholizismus des 19. Jahrhunderts, eine religionspolitsche Untersuchung," unpub. diss., University of Jena, 1942, p. 83; Tal, pp. 92-93; Bandura, *Aggression*, pp. 213-214.

19. Bandura, *Aggression*, pp. 36, 89; H.W. Stevenson, "Studies of Racial Awareness in Young Children," in W.W. Hartup and N.L. Smothergill (eds.), *The Young Child: Review of Research* (Washington, D.C.: National Association for the Education of Young Children, 1967), pp. 206-213; Bornkamm, pp. 41ff.; Hajo Holborn, "Der deutsche Idealismus in sozialgeschichtlicher Bedeutung," *Historische Zeitschrift* 174 (1952): 366ff.; Reinhard Rürup, "Emanzipation und Krise. Zur Geschichte der 'Judenfrage' in Deutschland von 1890," in Werner Mosse (ed.), *Juden in Wilhelminischen Deutschland, 1890-1914* (Tübingen: J.C.B. Mohr, 1976), p. 50.

20. Pulzer, pp. 274-276; Hans Rost, "Der Zerfall des deutschen Judentums," *Hochland*, 11 (1913-1914):545-558; Matthias Erzberger, *Christliche oder sozialdemokratische Gewerkschaften* (Stuttgart: Deutscheverlagsanstalt, 1898), pp. 29-30.

21. Ross, p. 11.

22. Anderson, pp. 251, 257, 259; Pulzer, pp. 274-276; Massing, p. 216; Werner Jochmann, "Struktur und Funktion des deutschen Antisemitismus," in Werner Mosse, *Juden in Wilhelminischen*, p. 398; David Blackbourn, "Roman Catholics, the Centre Party and Anti-Semitism in Imperial Germany," in Paul Kennedy and Anthoyn Nicholls (eds.), *National and Racialist Movements in Britain and Germany Before 1914* (London: MacMillan Press, 1981).

23. See Blackbourn, "Roman Catholics"; Carl H.E. Zangerl, "Courting the Catholic Vote: The Center party in Baden, 1903-1913," *Central European History* 10 (1977):239-240, 220-221; for the anti-Catholic bias in court circles, see Field, p. 259, and Ross, *Beleagured Tower.*

24. Rudolf Lill, "Die deutschen Katholiken und die Juden in der Zeit von 1850 bis zur Machtübergreifung," in Karl Heinrich Rengstorf and Siegfried Kortzfleisch (eds.), *Kirche und Synagogue. Handbuch zur Geschichte von Christen und Juden,* 2 vols. (Stuttgart: Ernst Klett Verlag, 1970), 2:370-420; Ellen Lovell Evans, *The Center Party, 1870-1933: A Study in Political Catholicism* (Carbondale, IL: University of Southern Illinois Press, 1981); John W. Boyer, *Political Radicalism in Late Imperial Vienna: Origins of the Christian Social Movement, 1848-1897* (Chicago: University of Chicago Press, 1981).

25. Bandura, *Aggression*, pp. 40, 43; H.L. Rausch, "Interaction Sequences," *Journal of Personality and Social Psychology* 2 (1965):487-499.

26. Ross, pp. 12-13; Anderson, p. 224; T. Nellessen-Schumacher, *Sozialprofil der deutschen Katholiken: Eine konfessionsstatistischen Analyse* (Mainz: Matthias-Grünewald, 1978); Hans Rost, *Gedanken und Wahrheiten zur Judenfrage* (Trier: Paulinus, 1907); Sperber, "Transformation of Catholic Associations," pp. 257-258.

27. Sperber, "Roman Catholic Religious Identity," p. 315.

28. See Massing and Pulzer. Both of these writers accept the continued existence of Catholic anti-Semitism in later years, but this is denied by R.S. Levy, *The Downfall of the Anti-Semitic Political Parties in Imperial Germany* (New Haven: Yale University Press, 1975).

29. Ross, pp. 26-28; Rost, *Wirtschaftliche und kulturelle Lage*, p. 202; Heinen p. 282, n.99a; H. Cardauns, *Adolf Gröber* (M. Gladbach: H. Ludwig, 1921), p. 152; B. Gottron, *Erlebtes und Erlauschtes aus dem Mainzer Metzgergewerbe im 19. Jahrhundert* (Mainz: Matthias-Grünewald, 1928), p. 33.

30. L. Gall, "Die Problematik des badischen Kulturkampfes," *Zeitschrift für die Geschichte Oberrheins* 113 (1965):151-196; Rürup, *Emanzipation*, pp. 37-73; K. Möckl, *Die Prinzregentenzeit. Gesellschaft und Politik während der Ära des Prinzregenten Luitpold in Bayern* (Munich: Oldenbourg, 1972), pp. 36-39.

31. *Waldse'er Wochenblatt*, May 13, 1897.

32. Blackbourn in Kennedy, pp. 120-123.

33. Edward von Hartmann, *Das Judenthum in Gegenwart und Zukunft*, 2nd ed. (Leipzig: W. Friedrich, 1885); Jacob Toury, *Die politischen Orientierungen der Juden in Deutschland* (Tübingen: J. Möhr, 1966), pp. 110-123.

34. Katz, p. 272; Stern, *Gold and Iron*, pp. 501-507, 516-519.

35. Gustav Freytag, *Soll und Haben* (Berlin: Wegweiser, 1855), p. 432.

36. The Abel Collection consists of 581 autobiographical statements from early members of the NSDAP. The vitae were collected by means of an essay contest run in June 1934 by Theodore Abel, a Columbia sociology professor. The original number of essays was reduced by 100 cases in 1951 when the FBI confiscated the documents for unstated reasons and has written this author that they have no knowledge of such an action. For an analysis of the Abel collection, see Peter Merkl, *Political Violence under the Swastika* (Princeton: Princeton University Press, 1975). The collection is currently housed at Stanford University.

37. Respondent No. 258, Abel Collection, Stanford: Hoover Institution. For Hitler's Vienna experiences and the development of his "intellectual racism,"

see Bradley F. Smith, *Adolf Hitler: His Family, Childhood, and Youth* (Stanford: Stanford University Press, 1967), pp. 147-151.

38. Stern, *Politics of Cultural Despair;* Field, *Chamberlain,* Tal, p. 302.

39. Tal, pp. 303-304; Saul Friedländer, *L'Antisemitisme Nazi: Histoire d'une psychose collective* (Paris: Editions du Sevil, 1971), pp. 13ff., 53ff.; Katz, *Anti-Semitism.*

40. Mosse, *Toward a Final Solution;* Rosemary Ruether, *Faith and Fratricide: Theological Roots of Anti-Semitism* (New York: Seabury Press, 1974); Leon Poliakov, *The Aryan Myth: A History of Racist and Nationalist Ideas in Europe* (New York: Basic Books, 1974).

41. Tal, p. 305.

42. See Ross, *Beleagured Tower.*

43. Günter Plum, *Gesellschaftstruktur und politsches Bewusstsein in einer Katholischen Region, 1928-1933* (Stuttgart: Deutsche-Verlags Anstalt, 1977), pp. 152-165; Blackbourn in Kennedy, pp. 123-124; for a study of Streicher and populist anti-Semitism, see Dennis Showalter, *"Little Man, What Now?" Der Stürmer in the Weimar Republic* (Hamden, CT: Anchor Books, 1982).

44. Dwight MacDonald, *Memoirs of a Revolutionist: Essays in Political Criticism* (New York: Farrar, Strauss, and Cudahy, 1957), pp. 33-44.

45. On the capitulation of German Catholic leaders, see Lewy and Zahn; Henry V. Dicks, "Personality Traits and National Socialist Ideology: A War-Time Study of German Prisoners of War," *Human Relations* 3 (1950):141; Kuper, p. 136; Allport, "The Religious Context of Prejudice," 450-451; Helen Fein, *Accounting for Genocide: National Responses and Jewish Victimization during the Holocaust* (New York: Free Press, 1979), p. 67.

46. Jeremy Miller, O.P., "Ethics Within an Ecclesial Context," *Angelicum* 57 (1980):32-44; Richard K. Fenn, "Toward a New Sociology of Religion," *Journal for the Scientific Study of Religion* 11 (1972):21, 31; Peter Berger and Thomas Luckmann, *The Social Construction of Reality* (New York: Doubleday, 1967), p. 125.

47. Arthur W. Staats, *Social Behaviorism* (Homewood, IL: Dorsey Press, 1975), pp. 45, 63.

48. Arthur Staats, *Child Learning, Intelligence, and Personality* (Kalamazoo: Behaviordelia, 1977); Arthur Staats (ed.), *Human Learning* (New York: Holt, Rinehart, and Winston, 1964), p. 336.

2

The Rise of Nazism and the Institutional Church, 1919-1933

A person's learned behavior patterns and the rewarding reinforcements are intimately connected. There are events that a person finds rewarding and punishing, satisfying and dissatisfying, and these events have an important effect upon a person's behavior, even that which is relevant to ethical and political considerations. From experiences, a person builds a language repertoire that largely embodies the knowledge he has. This language repertoire provides the basis for personal and social decisions for all kinds of behavior. Human cognitive characteristics are derived, then, from the repertoire of behavior the individual has learned and repeated. In fact, previously learned complex repertoires are the reason the person can learn so readily and even vicariously. In the Second Reich, Catholics experienced discrimination because Bismarck and others perceived potential disloyalty and because they were overrepresented in poorly paid occupations. In the historical environment of the Second Reich, anti-Semitism and nationalism were reinforced and rewarded. Not surprisingly, for economic and political reasons Catholics adopted both the terminology and the societally accepted viewpoints as they attempted and succeeded in joining the mainstream of German development. As a nation, Germany had achieved unprecedented prosperity and possessed political as well as military force, which made the country a world power of the first magnitude. It was predicted that World War I would be brief, but gloriously successful. From his balcony, the kaiser proclaimed to cheering crowds that he knew no parties, but only Germans, and a *Burgfrieden* followed.[1]

By 1914 Catholics were unequivocally loyal members of the *Volk*. Their nationalistic as well as *völkisch* language and behavior were rewarded. Catholics assimilated nationalistic vocabulary and constructed their behavioral patterns accordingly. These rewarded patterns allowed Catholics to apply their cognitive and behavioral repertoires to the new conditions prevalent in Germany after 1918. But to understand the reaction of the Catholics to the Nazis, a brief summary of the extensive social and po-litico-cultural support for Hitler must be presented. To evaluate the poten-tial force that the Catholic Church could wield in Germany, a sketch of the Church as an institution must be drawn.

Germans and the 1918 Defeat

The effect of the unprecedented wartime struggle was heightened by the wave of early enthusiasm and patriotic displays of solidarity, which papered over the socio-political fissures of prewar society. By 1917, if not earlier, it had become abundantly clear, however, that after the war it would no longer be possible to send the workers back to their menial jobs, the agri-cultural laborers to their feudal estates, or the women back to the kitchen, without major readjustments or open battle or both. In 1917, the parlia-mentary majority in the Reichstag resolutely expressed its disagreement with the kaiser and his chancellor, while the shadow of the Bolshevik revo-lution fell over Germany. Political grievances and social injustices resur-faced despite the *Burgfrieden* proclaimed by the kaiser in 1914. At the same time greatly exaggerated expectations of glory and territory as well as feel-ings of loyalty and patriotism were commingled with fears of internal reform or revolution. The patriots and their associations realized they had a lot more to lose than just the war. This was one reason for their strong hostility toward anyone who opposed or failed to support the war effort to the bitter end.[2]

Many of the Abel respondents have eloquently described the impact of World War I on their lives and on German society. "The experience at the front gave me a great deal for my whole life," wrote a schoolteacher (b. 1884). "I took it for granted that I had to fulfill my duty as a man, con-vinced then and for all time of the justice of our sacred cause. We had been attacked and had fought for our most sacred goods."[3] Faulhaber, the future Munich cardinal, for example, also served with the army in World War I, and this experience reinforced a deep affection for his military uniform. Such sentimentalism mingled with patriotism appears almost romantic as he spoke of his devotion to the "Fatherland" in his sermons.[4] The Abel documents also attest to the bitterness felt over the lost war which resulted in the imposition of liberal democracy. One typical response was the fol-lowing:

> Unfortunately the struggle came to a different end than our soldiers' hearts had dreamt of. Ruthless elements had long prepared to undermine this iron front, to rob it of its faith in the fatherland, and to make it tired of the war.

> They sold out their own fatherland with their treason. Thus, we returned humiliated but undefeated. . . . Until the last minute, we had hoped that our military leader, von Hindenburg, whom we trusted and loved, would succeed after all, but this turned out to be an illusion.[5]

This respondent saw Jews and Freemasons as the problem. With his purple prose, a retired officer (b. 1878) embodied the cultural shock experienced by many as they returned from the front.

> Returning home we no longer found an honest German people, but a mob stirred up by its lowest instincts. Whatever virtues were once found among the Germans seemed to have sunk once and for all into the muddy flood. . . . Promiscuity, shamelessness, and corruption ruled supreme. German women seemed to have forgotten their German ways. German men seemed to have forgotten their sense of honor and honesty. Jewish writers and the Jewish press could 'go to town' with impunity dragging everything into the dirt. They stopped not even before our most sacred feelings and dared to mock our crucified Lord in public exhibitions. While criminals and Jewish 'big-time operators' were wallowing in feasts and traitors were floating in champagne, the poorest of the poor hungered and suffered the most dire need.[6]

In 1916-17 the Germans had also suffered through the infamous "turnip winter," after which hunger and privation became common experiences. The official food ration for the summer of 1917 was 1,000 calories a day, although the health ministry estimated that 2,280 calories was a subsistence minimum. From 1914 to 1918, 750,000 people died of starvation in Germany. Not even the armistice of November ll, 1918 brought relief to the weary and hungry Germans. The ordeal of the previous three years was intensified into famine in the winter of 1918-19. The blockade was continued until the Germans turned over their merchant fleet to the Allies. In his closely reasoned analysis of the cohort that matured into adulthood during World War I, Peter Loewenberg has concluded that this youthful generation ultimately sought a restitution of a lost childhood characterized by warmth, closeness, security, power, and love and so supported the rise of Hitler.[7] From all indications, then, the German experience in World War I was traumatic—visions of victory turned into defeat, prosperity transformed into starvation, the traditional socio-political order exiled and humiliated in defeat.

Confronted by the World War I defeat in 1918, a revolution resulting in a scarcely tolerated republic, and a serious depression followed by a disastrous inflation and then another depression, the Jew as scapegoat again gained prominence.[8] The decisive turning point in recent German history was 1918. The monarchy collapsed; the war, surprisingly for many, was lost; the liberal-democratic-socialist parties, seemingly dominated by Jewish notables, replaced the now defunct aristocracy. The superficial changes came rapidly, but the established opposition in the army, bureaucracy, judiciary, and war veterans remained to cripple the new republic. The political uneasiness was intensified by the 1919 depression; the political assassinations of Mathias Erzberger, one of the "November Criminals," and Walther Rathenau, the foreign minister; and the inflation of 1923, which threatened middle-class wealth. The depression of 1929 proved to be the final straw. Germans needed someone or some political party to explain the issues and seek solutions.[9]

Hitler's ultimate success rested on the fact that he and his fellow Nazis could simplistically state the problems for Germans, although he could not always offer realistic solutions. The Nazi party before 1924 was concentrated in the urban centers of South Germany, but was spreading rapidly to smaller towns in that area and into other areas of Germany as well. It was a young, overwhelmingly masculine movement that drew a disproportionately large percentage of its membership from the lower middle class and from the *Mittelstand*. Yet it was not wholly a class movement, for it had representatives from all strata of German society; nor was it wholly a generational revolt, although both of these characteristics must be included in any description of Nazism. Through an instinctive grasp of the many diverse social and economic tensions present in postwar Germany, Hitler was able to forge a movement that transcended traditional party affiliations, class lines, and age barriers, and to unite persons from diverse social backgrounds into an effective and fanatical protest movement. While the party failed to achieve its objectives in 1923, the foundation was laid for the refounded party which legally assumed power in 1933.[10] Although the NSDAP was broadly based, the Nazis failed to attract the Catholic peasantry into the movement during the initial years and to an extent even until 1945. Perhaps most important was the hold Catholicism retained over most South German peasants, coupled with their adherence to the Bavarian Peoples' party during the Weimar era and their dislike of outside interference thereafter.[11] The Center party itself retained a constant proportion of the electorate until the dissolution of the party in 1933, in part because Center leaders responded to the religious needs and local grievances of their Catholic clients.

On one level, Nazism was a religious rebellion against a Christianity whose own history had provided the raw material for the hatred and prejudice in German society. In his *Mein Kampf,* Hitler described a Germany suffering from a spiritual and physical disease, the toleration of which had criminal implications. The German body politic stank with rottenness, cowardice, and half-heartedness, he asserted. Germans had forsaken their national ideals and had come to worship money just as did the leaders of international finance capital, the Jews. Marxists and Jews were attempting to undermine all national loyalty and health. Jews were responsible for prostitution as well as the spread of syphilis, of which he wrote: "The sin against blood and race is the original sin of this world and the end of that humanity that gives itself over to it." For Hitler, "all of these signs of decay were in the last analysis the result of the lack of a definite, generally acknowledged, world view." Germany was suffering from a lack of leadership in its hour of trial. Why, he asked? Germany had fallen into a general condition of moral and physical weakness because, as Hitler insisted, it had failed to recognize "the race problem and its significance for the historical development of nations."[12]

Anti-Semitism was vital to rabid National Socialists and the cornerstone of Hitler's own messianic, biological racism, even though not all Nazis were anti-Semites. Hitler's ideology interpreted history as a Manichaean struggle between *good* Aryanism and *evil* Judaism. Hitler was to save Germany and the world from the Jews, biologically motivated to destroy the "true" historical process because of their inability to wage the Darwinian struggle fairly.[13] By 1933, Hitler's ideology consisted primarily of two related systems of ideas acquired and developed in chronological sequence. The doctrine of race had been formed first and had been clearly delineated by 1923; the partly derivative doctrine of space came to be defined, in the formulation to which Hitler subsequently adhered, in the years immediately following. Hitler's doctrine of race was a vulgarized version of the Social Darwinism that found increasing acceptance in Germany and elsewhere, both in learned circles and, especially in the years between 1900 and 1914, among the masses.[14] The elimination of categories of persons was to be judged solely by standards of utility, not morality.

Scholars have differed on the impact of anti-Semitism. For Lucy Dawidowicz anti-Semitism was crucial to Hitler's rise to power. Golo Mann sees it as one ingredient in a poisonous soup of hatred, while Sebastian Haffner asserts that Hitler's virulent hatred alienated "normal" anti-Semites.[15] Regional, sexual, and generational studies agree that anti-Semitism was rarely the vitally attractive element in Hitler's electoral campaigns. Still, anti-Semitism is an identifiable component among the varied groups studied. It is not that Germans were enthralled by or receptive to anti-Semitism a' la Hitler, but that they were not so repelled by it that they rejected the other planks in the party's platform.[16]

In part, what caused the rise of Nazism was the perceived discontinuity between the empire and the republic in virtually all ideological and political dimensions.[17] Traditional political ties had dissolved. Because the Catholic Church formed an unbroken bridge between the old and new order, its leaders had a unique opportunity to show forceful leadership during these perilous years of the Republic. In some political areas, however, the "apolitical" Church tried only to identify itself with the old order despite its close connection to the Center party, a stable component of the "Weimar coalition." In general, then, such nationalist parties as the National-sozialistischen Deutsche Arbeiterpartei were able to build on the anomie in post-1918 German society. Hitler appealed to those persons who were adrift after the collapse of the Empire and experienced Weimar Germany as a socio-political maelstrom, caused in some indefinable fashion by the Jews.

Between 1918 and 1933, Germans experienced a series of economic, social, and political anxiety-producing events. Not surprisingly after 1929 and the sustained disaster of the depression they could be influenced by fear-arousing politicians. The more vulnerable Germans perceived themselves to be, the higher their level of emotional arousal as they received threatening information or experienced disconcerting events. During the years of 1929-33 the Nazis enjoyed ever increasing electoral success. Also, the Nazi terminology, although frequently sounding radical, had already enjoyed extended acceptance among most Germans, including Catholics. To attack Jews, the Republic, and liberalism or to extol nationalism did not sound foreign to Germans in general. Throughout the 1920s a link was being forged between an ever increasing number of Germans and the *führer*. Both the leader and the led appeared to share a set of beliefs and values created by exposure to common experiences, crises, as well as behavioral responses, thus allowing many Germans later to obey a regime whose total array of ideas they may not necessarily have fully shared and whose concrete actions they may actually have abhorred.[18]

Certainly it cannot be overlooked that many believed that the National Socialists did not necessarily mean precisely what they said; that Hitler's more extreme ideas should not be taken seriously; that once in power, the movement would find itself forced into a more reasonable course by the impact of responsibility and reality. Many of those who deluded themselves argued after World War II that Hitler had deluded them, but in reality they had misled themselves. In many instances this self-delusion was constructed on the hope that Hitler *did* mean what he said about destroying the Social Democratic party and the trade unions, regardless of the methods used and the purposes for which this might be done. There was also the hope of the older generation of German leaders that the dynamism of National Socialism could be harnessed to their more limited goals. But above all, there was the opposition of millions to the Weimar Republic, its ideals and its practice, and the whole tradition of liberalism and humanism to which they were related. Hitler could, many felt, lead Germany back to strength; he could overcome the psychological depression of past defeat and the economic depression of Germany's contemporary situation.[19]

To many, the nineteenth-century emancipation of the Jews found its culmination in the rise of the much vilified Weimar liberalism and the attendant sundering of relations between Jews and Germans. Far from being an insignificant event in German history, the emancipation can be seen as an important symptom of the disintegration of liberal bourgeois society. The "Jewish question" became part of the social and political conflicts of modern Germany. Observing right-wing attacks on Jews and the "Jewish press," anti-Semitism can be seen as a function of anti-Weimar politics. Anti-Semitism appeared not alone, but in attacks on Weimar policies. Foremost in the agitation on the Right was antagonism to the Republic; the Jewish question, while there, was subordinate to these other concerns. Anti-Semitism may be seen, then, as a source of terminology and images with which to flagellate the Republic. Many *völkisch* Germans believed the differences separating Germans and Jews precluded genuine assimilation, but they were not aggressively anti-Semitic. Moderate volkists spoke of a separation between Germans and Jews, but never specified what actual forms this exclusion should have. The differences separating German nationalists from the fanatical *völkisch* minority were, however, more than mere nuance. Too often in retrospect, the dimensions of the Jewish issue in the last years of the Republic have been overestimated. Still, among the majority of Germans who did not succumb to systematic racism, there prevailed little sympathy for the Jews who were unjustly vilified, and, seemingly, little awareness that any danger threatening the Jews concomitantly imperiled German democracy and the Catholic Church.[20]

The Catholic Church in Germany

In this fluid political situation, the potentially powerful Church could not fully succeed in resolving at least such issues as those of parity and education, which retarded the integration of Catholics fully into mainstream German society. Lack of success reflects the fact that democratic Germany was doomed by its internal fragmentation and overall stagnation. Institutionally, the Church was a religious power in its own right. Its firm organization since the early nineteenth century, the slow but steady elimination of the *Staatskirchentum* as it had developed in the eighteenth century, the negotiated agreements which followed acrimonious church-state conflicts, the steady expansion of monastic orders, lay organizations, and an articulate press were not only factors in the development of Catholicism, but also signified the position the Church had achieved in nineteenth-century Germany. On the eve of World War I, Germany had two cardinals (later to be three) and was organized into five archbishoprics

(Bamberg, Freiburg, Gnesen-Posen, Cologne, and Munich-Freising), twenty bishoprics, three apostolic vicarates, and two apostolic prefectures. According to the 1910 census, Catholics numbered 23,821,453; according to the 1915 census, they were served by 18,417 secular clergy. In addition, there were 1,072 regular clergy chiefly concerned with school duties, 891 institutional clergy, and 1,287 holding no church office. There were 335 male monastic establishments, with 1,860 priests, 579 other clergy and scholastics, 3,651 lay brothers, and 274 novices. Female monastic establishments numbered 6,246, with 64,249 members and 4,784 novices.[21] After the war, the number of clergy grew. By 1920 there were 366 monastic establishments for men with 7,030 members and 616 novices; in 1932 there were 640, with 13,206 members and 1,910 novices. Meanwhile the number of secular clergy had increased from 19,369 in 1920 to 21,358 in 1932. The total number of Catholics in Germany, the figures adjusted to the postwar German territory but including the Saar, according to the census of 1910, was 20,594,816 and in 1933, 21,765,614.[22]

There are no figures available on church attendance, but at least by European standards and official comments, German Catholics regularly attended services. Statistics on the sacramental life of the Church help to indicate the relationship of individuals to the Church. In 1915, out of 71,093 civil marriages where both bride and groom were Catholic, 66,670 were later solemnized by the Church; out of 32,072 mixed civil marriages, 11,072 were later solemnized by the Church. Baptismal figures were higher. There were 530,616 live births to Catholic families in 1915 and 531,400 baptisms, which presumably indicates some carryover from the previous year. Of 62,749 children born to parents of mixed marriages, only 29,831 received Catholic baptism, a figure which, like the one on mixed marriages, disturbed Church authorities. Of 55,369 illegitimate children born to Catholic mothers, 54,220 were baptized. Of the 418,744 Catholics who died, 399,459 received Church burials. There were 224,758,673 communicants, but only 13,893,147 fulfilled their Easter obligation. This last figure suggests that a significant number of Catholics were "conventional" Church members, not possessing a particularly strong commitment to their religion.[23] This fact would prove significant as the Church reacted to Nazism. Being Catholic in name alone would not suffice as the persecution of the Church began.

Church membership and the conventional fulfillment of duties, however, is an unsatisfactory measure of the institution's actual power, because it fails to reveal the depth of commitment in individual Catholics. Religious behavior, of course, cannot be isolated from the total social environment. The statistics do tell us the potential that a mobilized Catholicism could have had, but also suggest that the bishops would have had a difficult time effectively guiding such a mass of people in opposition to a legitimate government. In a scenario alluded to after 1933, Church spokesmen feared that they might find themselves without followers if the bishops tried to actualize religious values in the political world. Although the religious basis for the normative order has become less necessary, religion has continued to have functions for certain social strata and for private individuals, but these functions have become expressive rather than utilitarian. Recent research has indicated, and there is no reason to believe that the 1920s and 1930s offer a radically different socio-political environment, that religious values for most people appear to have a minimal *demonstrable* relationship to what people actually do in work and politics. In essence, the modern world has produced an increasing number of individuals who, when convenient, look upon the world and their own lives without the benefit of religious interpretations.[24] It seems, then, that religious values generally are not the sole norms for political behavior. The Center party certainly benefited from its religious affiliation, but other planks in its platform likewise attracted voters. The Church had potential power, but its full strength could probably never be mobilized against a popular regime, especially in Germany where Church leaders were reluctant to oppose the national government. The *Kulturkampf* experience could not be forgotten.

Economically growing stronger, the Church acquired property and received gifts and inheritances. It also received direct subsidies—often the continuation of ancient grants and payments resulting from the secularization of land and titles. In some states the Church could levy taxes on its members. These were set by the diocesan and state officials and were usually collected by the state for the Church. In many instances the states indirectly assumed a large part of the cost of Catholic education by supporting a confessional school system and by paying teachers of religion in schools that were not divided confessionally. Indeed, the Catholic Church in imperial Germany and thereafter was satisfactorily situated financially, and it drew heavily on state support. In other ways as well the Catholic Church had achieved organizational success. It possessed a strong and well-administered ecclesial organization, amply staffed, with a tightly woven network of organizations related to the daily life of its members. Politically, it was supported by the seasoned Center party and by the widely diffused confessional and private school system that fulfilled the Church's basic educational needs. The old fear that Catholicism was a minority religion in danger of being overwhelmed by a Protestant majority no longer haunted the Church, although the spectre could not be completely dissolved. Basically, then, the Church had institutionally a standing throughout Germany such as it had not known since the days before the Reformation.[25]

Within these parameters the Church would react to the 1918 defeat and to political democracy in Weimar by renewing its pledge to support national values.

Several factors shaped the response of the Church to the Republic. Territorial adjustments demanded at Versailles ultimately had the effect of making the German Catholic Church as national as the Protestant churches, despite the former's connection to the papacy and worldwide Catholicism. Prior to 1918 some spoke of a Catholic ghetto, and there was a constant clamor that Catholics did not receive their share of lucrative state appointments. Politically, the Center party had usually been swimming against the tide, but now became part of the governing political coalition. Still, Catholic students at universities were disproportionately small compared to Protestants and Jews. Answering this Catholic criticism, it was pointed out that the Catholic population was largely rural and was not as interested in higher education as were the more urban Protestants and Jews. Economically also, Catholics generally were not as well off as other segments of the population. But the historic socioeconomic position of Catholics could not be immediately reversed. For example, in 1907 Catholics comprised 35.8 percent of the population, but only paid 15 percent of the income tax. To change this situation would take time. This economic situation remained largely unchanged during the 1920s.[26]

The shedding of non-German groups did something to bolster the confidence and assertiveness of postwar German Catholicism now reinforced by the new liberties guaranteed in the national and state constitutions. The Center party participated in every coalition government during the Weimar era, contributing four chancellors to the system. The persistent feeling that Catholics were being discriminated against began to evaporate. Public manifestations of Catholic religious strength became more numerous. Annual Catholic assemblies developed into mass gatherings. The festive outdoor mass held at Dortmund in 1927 for example, was reputedly attended by 80,000 people. Corpus Christi Day processions became more elaborate and were held in many predominately Protestant cities where previously they had not been customary, a clear sign of integration into mainstream Germany. One Corpus Christi Day procession even moved down *Unter den Linden* in Berlin, with the chancellor and other governing officials carrying candles.[27]

No data on church attendance is available, but the figures on participation in the sacraments indicate there was little change between earlier decades and the 1920s. Figures indicate that the external loyalty of the laity to the Church remained approximately at the same level despite the increasing secularization of the time. A long list of Catholic organizations, founded in the 1920s as well as pre-1918, is given in the 1930-31 *Ka-*

tholisches Handbuch and illustrates the obvious vitality of the institutional Church. In addition to the daily press, Catholics by 1932 were served by 420 periodicals and other publications. Among these, 29 had editions of over 100,000.[28]

The quality as well as the quantity of Catholic literature indicates the vigorous religious life. Periodicals changed format, new writers emerged, and Catholics played an increasingly significant role in the cultural life of Germany. The big Catholic dailies added Sunday supplements in which they discussed the problems of the times. The names of these supplements reflect the new spirit that prevailed. The *Germania* had "The New Shore," the *Kölnische Volkszeitung* had "In Step With the Times," and the *Essener Volkszeitung* had "From the Intellectual Life of the Present." In 1920 Friedrich Muckermann, S.J., undertook the editorship of the literary periodical *Der Gral,* developing it into one of the liveliest cultural magazines of the era. He founded a correspondence bureau and soon was delivering copy to some 400 daily Catholic papers in Germany. He also established a separate news bureau for church papers. He and his brother founded a *Film Rundschau* that reviewed films from the Catholic viewpoint, and soon exercised a considerable influence on the German film industry. It was not surprising that this influential journalist would be one of the first to experience the Nazi *Gleichschaltung.* He fled to exile in Holland, where he ultimately gave the Gestapo the hard chore of trying to stop the papers he was smuggling across the border.[29]

Because of the strength and integration of the associational components, characteristic of the institutional Church, Catholic voting patterns remained intact throughout the Weimar era as the demographics indicate despite the post-1928 "rural" strategy of the Nazis. The most decisive political move of the Nazis was into the countryside from 1928 to 1932 because that is where the majority of Germans lived. In general, the Nazis here could take advantage of manipulating a population whose party loyalties were loose, at least in the Protestant areas. The largest segment of new Nazi voting support came from Protestant villages with the next largest from Protestant middle-sized communities. The decision to go into the countryside seems to have been crucial for the 1930 and then 1932 Nazi successes. Several reasons can account for Nazi gains in these areas. Many local leaders had died in the war and so middle and small community leadership was superannuated. Many of these liberal leaders were not veterans and so were labeled with the failure of republican policies, especially its bankrupt farm policies. Nazi leaders were young, aggressive, organized, and innovative. In the rural Catholic countryside, however, the hierarchy and pastors, exuding conservative nationalism, were able to maintain their hold on the electorate. In middle-sized Catholic towns, the populace also maintained its loyalty to the Center party. This is not to suggest that the

Nazis could make no inroads, but rather that Catholics in rural areas and towns were less vulnerable than their Protestant counterparts. In general, the Nazis could get 25-35 percent of even the Catholics to support them, certainly a fair number, but even more significantly for their future success, 62 percent of the Protestant electorate.[30]

In large cities religion did not seem to be a political factor. The political struggle was more likely a class struggle and possibly helps explain the church's antimodernist vehemence, useful in identifying itself with the older imperial Germany. Using statistics alone, Richard Hamilton has maintained that a rigorous and verifiable analysis cannot be made. But conceivably, the urban lower middle class voted Right with the workers voting Left in mixed districts. The lower middle class probably perceived the Nazis as nationalists capable of achieving German cultural goals. Big business theoretically opposed Nazism, but felt that government responsibility would "tame" the party. Apparently many upper-and middle-class individuals saw in the Nazis their best option since their favorite nationalist parties had all but disappeared by 1930. Rightists in general and the Nazis most enthusiastically trumpeted the communist danger and helped generate an intense anxiety that actually aided their own relatively weak parties to disintegrate. In no city was there a definitive Nazi strength centered exclusively in the lower middle class. Three groups led to success: (1) Nazi party activists in number and ability appear to have outdone all their competitors in carrying their party's lessons to the public; (2) the press, much of it friendly to virtually any conservative party, attacked the German Communist party and so helped establish Nazism as acceptable for a role in a conservative nationalist coalition; (3) many elite notables vouched for and made the party acceptable. Where all three agents worked in the party's favor, Nazism succeeded.[31]

The rise of National Socialism, then, stemmed in large measure from the inflexibility of the existing party system and its inability to respond satisfactorily to the structural transformations that German society had undergone since the beginning of the twentieth century and in particular after 1918. Increasingly it appeared to many that only the NSDAP was capable of creating a genuine *Staatsvolk* out of the agglomeration of private interests that the bourgeois parties had come to represent. Although much in vogue during the 1920s, the German word *Volk* cannot be defined, but is a "highly charged" word in modern Germany history. Volkists turned into political questions of the greatest magnitude issues that normally are resolved in the private arena: sex, ethics, religion. They chased goals that could not have any positive effects: *Volk* unity, racial purity, *Lebensraum*. They methodically rejected as sterile the problems that politics can resolve, i.e., issues revolving around institutional and legal frameworks.[32]

Catholics as German Citizens

Political predilections are embedded in interpersonal networks, i.e., are based on a people's historio-political socialization. Versailles and Weimar had upset the traditional order. Thus, many voters were searching for security and were open to new options from the beginning. A structural political indeterminancy existed in Germany as well as a desire to return to the past, which eventually allowed Catholics to accept the legally installed Nazi government, once established on what appeared to be a traditionalist foundation. The Treaty of Versailles had reduced the army and shifted future recruits to other career opportunities. Strong feelings of resentment, not necessarily mere anxiety, existed. The history of Weimar Germany was an intense and continuous struggle of parties and classes, depending on the locality, more a conflict of idealogues than of the citizens who seemed to be trying to avoid conflict and the damage being done to them by the political system. Political leaders fought with intransigence and ultimately broke down the normal political processes. In the long run, most Germans could accept the Nazi program of nationalism and order by assuming, if they wished, that the anti-Semitic or stormtrooper activities emanated from the radical wing of the party and not Hitler, since, it was felt by conservative leaders, he could be controlled. The bishops and theologians unknowingly through their nationalistic anti-Semitism paved the way for the acceptance of Nazism, but as leaders they were in a very real sense only responding to their followers. Prejudice enhances self-esteem; religion provides a tailored security. Both satisfy the same psychological needs and can reinforce one another.[33]

Karl Dietrich Bracher has offered a verifiable description of the fall of the Weimar Republic. He emphasizes the patterned and sequential character of the breakdown process through the phases of loss of power, power vacuum, and the takeover of power. It was not the technical characteristics of the problems in the fledgling Republic, but the political context in which they were to be resolved, the constraints upon the regime, and the alternatives offered by the disloyal Nazi opposition, which in the final analysis triggered the breakdown. Constitutionally, Article 48 facilitated the abdication of responsibility by the democratic parties, created the artificial government of presidential cabinets and emergency legislation, and encouraged tendencies toward antidemocratic, authoritarian, and bureaucratic rule consistent with the pre-1918 tradition. In Germany, this ramshackle solution proved too unstable to withstand a dynamic and disloyal opposition led by the charismatic Hitler and dedicated to rallying broad support for a legal 1933 revolution.[34]

Unsolvable problems, an opposition ready to exploit them to challenge the regime, the decay of democratic authenticity among loyal parties, the loss of effectiveness when confronted by violence, all led to a loss of legitimacy. In this atmosphere of tension, a widespread feeling evolved that something had to be done. The dissatisfaction with democracy, economic panic, and anxiety led to a heightened politicization shared in the final years of the Republic by even the so-called apolitical. The less politically committed segments of the population seemed to accept the cooperation of the disloyal opposition, apparently hoping that such a move would result in a stable government and an end to the politically inspired violence that they had been suffering as bystanders. Paradoxically, the Nazi party, which had caused the disorder, was seen by 1933 as the final chance for order.[35]

In the Second Empire, Catholics developed a system of nationalistic and in some cases latent anti-Semitic preferences that led them to act in specific ways that would be rewarding. After 1918, their active participation in the political life of the Republic convinced them that their days as second-class citizens were over. Such problems as the state support of confessional schools had not been resolved, but the right time and the right coalition would provide the opportunity. Staats has suggested that the group itself constitutes a learning environment for a person. Hence, the characteristics of socio-political groupings and the culture itself as it is reflected in patterns of behavior can also help illuminate the characteristics of the individuals who compose the group.[36] Many Catholics apparently supported the Center until the end of Weimar Germany, apparently seeing in the Republic the political arena in which they could unburden themselves of their social, economic, and political liabilities. Some Church leaders[37] viewed the Republic as a merely tolerated form of government. In their eyes democratic institutions were tolerated only because they were superior to communism.

Whether Catholics identified with a democratic constitution or longed for the Empire, they were highly charged nationalists, favored at least a latent anti-Semitism, and did not seem to object by 1933 to an authoritarian government if the Church's institutional life could be safeguarded. Like so many others, Catholics were convinced that religious loyalties could be maintained separately from political loyalties. In fact, Hitler probably generated more intense fervor for his cause than any of the bishops could for theirs. Given the political socialization process after 1870 and the eventful years fraught with anxiety after 1918, not surprisingly the bulk of the Catholic laity, many of whom were "Sunday morning" Christians, and their clergy accepted Hitler assuming he probably could be tamed and his force channeled for the good of the *Volk*.

Focusing merely on the institutional life and vitality of the Church offers a deceptive image of the true strength of Catholicism. From 1870 to 1933, the basic tenets and values of Catholicism as a religion had never been assaulted politically. As the depression deepened after 1929, however, the Nazis with their *Weltanschauung,* alien to religion, began to gain in political strength. By 1933 the Nazis were prepared to challenge the Church as a religion and were sure of a broad-based political support for their nationalist and racist ideas.

Notes

1. Staats, *Social Behaviorism*, pp. 145, 154-159, 511; Michael Balfour, *The Kaiser and His Times* (Boston: Norton, 1972), p. 355; Gerhard Masur, *Imperial Berlin* (New York: Basic Books, 1970). For a recent analysis of the discontinuity syndrome driving Germans from 1918 to 1933, see Mitchell, *Hitler Over Germany.*
2. Merkl, *Political Violence*, pp. 154-155; Werner Conze, *Die Zeit Wilhelms II und die Weimarer Republik* (Tübingen: Wunderlich, 1964); for an analysis of the 1914 spirit as the antidote to the anomie, which had resulted from the sweep of powerful forces from the recent past—urban, capitalistic, and technological forces tearing up primeval bonds and forcing people into a crisis of social relationships, see Roland N. Stromberg, *Redemption by War: The Intellectuals and 1914* (Lawrence, KS: University of Kansas Press, 1982).
3. Merkl, p. 154, respondent 210.
4. Mary Alice Gallin, "The Cardinal and the State: Faulhaber and the Third Reich," *Journal of Church and State* 12 (1970):388; Ludwig Volk, S.J., "Kardinal Faulhabers Stellung zur Weimarer Republik und zum NS-Staat," *Stimmen der Zeit* 177 (1966):193.
5. Merkl, p. 169, respondent 263.
6. Ibid., p. 173, respondent 173.
7. Karl Dietrich Erdmann, "Die Zeit der Weltkriege," in Bruno Gebhardt (ed.), *Handbuch der deutschen Geschichte* (Stuttgart: Union Deutsche Verlagsgesellschaft, 1963), 4:49, 77, 88; James A. Huston, "The Allied Blockage of Germany, 1918-1919," *Journal of Central European Affairs* 10 (1950): 161; Peter Loewenberg, "The Psychohistorical Origins of the Nazi Youth Cohort," *American Historical Review* 76 (1971):1473, 1502.
8. Norman Cohn, *Warrant for Genocide* (New York: Harper, 1967); Hellmut Andics, *Der Ewige Jude. Ursachen und Geschichte des Anti-Semitismus* (Vienna: Molder, 1965). For a seminal, but controversial, study of anti-Semitism and authoritarianism, see Theodor Adorno et al., *The Authoritarian Personality* (New York: Harper, 1950).
9. Mitchell, pp. 259ff.; David Abraham, *The Collapse of the Weimar Republic: Political Economy and Crisis* (Princeton: Princeton University Press, 1981). Abraham's book has aroused controversy focusing on his scholarly interpretations and because of his research techniques. For a comprehensive scholarly treatment of German big business and industry, see Henry Ashby Turner, *German Big Business and the Rise of Hitler* (New York: Oxford University Press, 1985). Harold J. Gordon, *Hitler and the Beerhall Putsch* (Princeton: Princeton University Press, 1972) stresses that the Nazi party was only a portion of a broader movement.

10. Paul Madden, "Some Social Characteristics of Early Nazi Party Members, 1919-1923," *Central European History* 15 (1982):51-52; Barbara Miller Lane, "Nazi Ideology: Some Unfinished Business," *Central European History* 7 (1974):3-30. The membership of Hitler's party has been described as a movement composed of small-town inhabitants rebelling against urbanization and modernity; see Reinhard Bendix, "Social Stratification and Political Power," *American Political Science Review* 6 (1952):357. Some have seen it as a green revolt of irate farmers; see C.P. Loomis and J.A. Beegle, "The Spread of German Nazism in Rural Areas," *American Sociological Review* 11 (1946):724-34. As a regional movement, see Dietrich Orlow, *The History of the Nazi Party: 1919-1933* (Pittsburgh: University of Pittsburgh Press, 1969), pp. 56, 86, 104. And as a class movement, see Heinrich August Winkler, *Mittelstand, Demokratie und Nationalsozialismus* (Cologne: Kiepenheuer und Witsch, 1972). A recent thesis identifies the Nazis as primarily the disaffected youth of the Weimar Republic and Nazism as a generational revolt; see Loewenberg, "Psychohistorical Origins"; Allen B. Spitzer, "The Historical Problem of Generations," *American Historical Review* 78 (1973):1353-85.

11. Johnpeter Horst Grill, "The Nazi Party's Rural Propaganda Before 1928," *Central European History* 15 (1982):149-185; Madden, p. 47. For studies that attribute the rural electoral swing after 1928 to a combination of factors which usually include the farmers' deteriorating economic prospects, the farmers' alienation from the "Weimar System," and the NSDAP's anti-urban propaganda which appealed to a variety of deep-seated resentments, see Rudolf Heberle, *From Democracy to Nazism: A Regional Case Study on Political Parties in Germany* (Baton Rouge: Louisiana State University Press, 1945).

12. Adolf Hitler, *Mein Kampf* (Munich: Eher, 1935), pp. 250, 255, 272, 292, 310.

13. Showalter, p. viii; Graham S. Gibbard et al., *Analysis of Groups* (San Francisco: Jossey-Bass, 1974), p. 334; messianic fantasies appear at times when anxiety and depression, the psychological equivalent of the anthropologist's "spiritual deprivation," cannot be dealt with in a familiar and viable manner. Messianism is most in evidence when "political," active, problem-solving behavior is not effective in coping with problems confronting a specific group; see also James Rhodes, *The Hitler Movement: A Modern Millenarian Revolution* (Stanford: Hoover Institution Press, 1980).

14. Günter Schubert, *Anfänge Nationalsozialistischer Aussenpolitik* (Cologne: Verlag Wissenschaft und Politik, 1963); Pulzer, *The Rise of Political Anti-Semitism;* Ernst Deuerlein, "Hitlers Eintritt in die Politik und die Reichswehr," *Vierteljahrshefte für Zeitgeschichte* 7 (1959):177-227; Reginald Phelps, "Hitler als Parteiredner im Jahre 1920," *Vierteljahrshefte für Zeitgeschichte* 11 (1963):274-330. For treatments, although controversial, of this interrelation of Hitler and the German people from a psychoanalytical, psychohistorical perspective, see Robert G.L. Waite, *The Psychopathic God: Adolf Hitler* (New York: Basic Books, 1977) and Rudolph Binion, *Hitler Among the Germans* (New York: Elsevier, 1976).

15. Lucy Dawidowicz, *The War Against the Jews, 1933-1945* (New York: Holt, Rinehart and Winston, 1975), pp. 163ff; Golo Mann, *Der Anti-Semitismus* (Munich: Ner-Tamidverlag, 1960), pp. 32-33; Sebastian Haffner, *The Meaning of Hitler* (New York: Appleton-Century-Croft, 1979), pp. 91ff.

16. Examples include Geoffrey Pridham, *Hitler's Rise to Power: The Nazi Movement in Bavaria, 1923-1933* (New York: Harper, 1973), pp. 237ff; Jeremy

Noakes, *The Nazi Party in Lower Saxony, 1921-1933* (London: Oxford University Press, 1971), pp. 209-210; H.W. Koch, *The Hitler Youth: Origins and Development 1922-45* (London: MacDonald and Jane's, 1975), pp. 116ff; Schleunes, pp. 55ff; Showalter, p. ix; Blackbourn, "Roman Catholics, the Centre Party and Anti-Semitism in Imperial Germany," pp. 120-124; Michael Billig, *Fascists: A Social Psychological View of the Nationalist Front* (London: Academic Press, 1978), pp. 8, 46. Studies that indicate that people joined the NSDAP for heterogeneous reasons would include: Claudia Koonz, "Nazi Women before 1933: Rebels Against Emancipation," *Social Science Quarterly* 56 (1976):553-563, and Merkl, *Political Violence*. In general, forcefully simplified explanations of Nazism are probably wrong.

17. Fred Weinstein, *The Dynamics of Nazism*. Weinstein's main arguments are roughly these: the Germans' grounds for accepting Hitler varied individually, and his appeal was heterogeneous socially. After 1929 all Germans faced a disruptive, potentially chaotic situation and his following increased. His supporters ignored his ideological stress on the Jewish menace. When his personal goal led logically, although in a convoluted fashion, to the death camps, concerned Germans followed their varied commitments to his leadership, including his ideology. For a critical review of Weinstein's approach, see Rudolph Binion's review in the *Journal of Modern History* 54 (1982):409-411.

18. Irving Janis, Vigilance and Decision Making in Personal Crises," in George Coelho et al., *Coping and Adaptation* (New York: Basic Books, 1974), pp. 165, 169; R. Lazarus, *Psychological Stress and the Coping Process* (New York: McGraw-Hill, 1966); Shaul Esh, "Words and Their Meanings: Twenty-Five Examples of Nazi Idiom," *Yad Vashem Studies* (1963):134-135. For a trenchant analysis of the current psychohistorical literature on establishing a pathology for both individuals and a group, see Asher, pp. 13-14; attempts to isolate the individual or small groups as pathological are flawed and Asher argues against the "National Character" approach as well.

19. William S. Allen, *The Nazi Seizure of Power: The Experience of a Single German Town, 1930-1935* (Chicago: University of Chicago Press, 1965); Karl Dietrich Bracher et al., *Die nationalsozialistische Machtergreifung,* 2nd ed. (Cologne: Westdeutschen Verlag, 1962), pp. 22-77.

20. Werner Mosse (ed.), *Deutsches Judentum in Krieg und Revolution, 1916-1923. Ein Sammelband* (Tübingen: Mohr, 1971); Werner Mosse (ed.), *Entscheidungsjahr 1932. Zur Judenfrage in der Endphase der Weimarer Republik. Ein Sammelband* (Tübingen: Mohr, 1965).

21. *Kirchliches Handbuch. Amtliches statistisches Jahrbuch der katholischen Kirche Deutschlands* (Freiburg: Herder, 1914 +), hereafter cited *KH.*

22. *KH,* (1922-1923), p. 405; (1927-28), p. 420; (1935-36), p. 367.

23. Ernst Helmreich, *The German Churches Under Hitler;* Allport, "The Religious Context of Prejudice," pp. 447-457.

24. Argyle, p. 2; Fenn, p. 16; Robin Gill, *The Social Context of Theology: A Methodological Enquiry* (London: Mowbrays, 1975), pp. 85-86; Peter Berger, *The Social Reality of Religion* (London: Faber, 1969).

25. Helmreich, pp. 59-60; Adolf Fellmeth, *Das kirchliche Finanzwesen in Deutschland* (Karlsruhe: G. Braun, 1910); Friedrich Thiele, et al., *Das Kirchensteuerrecht* (Herne, Westfalen: Neue Wirtschaftsbriefe, 1947).

26. Wilhelm Spael, *Das katholische Deutschland im 20. Jahrhundert. Seine Pionier und Krisenzeiten 1890-1945* (Würzburg: Echterverlag, 1967), pp. 264-265; Fritz

von der Heydt, *Die Parität bei der Anstellung der Beamten* (Berlin: Saemann, 1931), pp. 3, 29; *KH,* (1927-28), pp. 283-292; (1930-31), pp. 288-298.

27. Helmreich, pp. 98-101; Gerhard Anschütz, *Die verfassung des deutschen Reichs vom 11. August 1919. Ein Kommentar für Wissenschaft und Praxis,* 3rd ed. (Berlin: G. Stilke, 1930), pp. 503, 539.

28. *KH,* (1919-1920), pp. 246-267; (1925-26), pp. 458-459; (1930-31), pp. 108-239; (1935-36), pp. 364-365; *Die Religion in Geschichte der Gegenwart. Handwörterbuch für Theologie und Religionswissenschaft,* 3rd ed. (Tübingen: Mohr, 1957-62), 5:556-68.

29. Spael, pp. 282-287; Friedrich Muckermann, *Der deutsche Weg. Aus den Widerstandsbewegung der deutschen Katholiken von 1930-1945* (Zürich: NZN Verlag, 1946), pp. 28-29.

30. Hamilton, *Who Voted for Hitler?,* pp. 361-74.

31. Ibid., pp. 421-422.

32. Larry Eugene Jones, "'The Dying Middle': Weimar Germany and the Fragmentation of Bourgeois Politics," *Central European History* 5 (1972):23-54; Louis Edwin Pease, "After the Holocaust: West Germany and Material Reparation to the Jews—From the Allied Occupation to the Luxemburg Agreements," Ph.D. diss., Florida State University, 1976, p. 1089; Hartmut Scheible, *Joseph Roth: Mit einem Essay über Gustave Flaubert* (Stuttgart: Kohlhammen, 1971).

33. Hamilton, pp. 426, 444, 459-461; Allport, "Religious Context of Prejudice," 451; see the Abel collection at Stanford University, especially respondents 258, 466, 281, 232, 520.

34. Juan Linz, "Introduction," in Juan Linz and Alfred Stepan (eds.), *The Breakdown of Democratic Regimes* (Baltimore: Johns Hopkins University Press, 1978), pp. 55-70; M. Rainer Lepsius, "From Fragmented Party Democracy to Government by Emergency Decree and National Socialist Takeover: Germany," in Linz, *Breakdown,* pp. 34-79; Karl Dietrich Bracher, "Auflösung einer Demokratie: Das Ende der Weimarer Republik als Forschungsproblem," in Arkadij Gurland (ed.), *Faktoren der Machtbildung* (Berlin: Duncker und Humblot, 1952), pp. 39-98.

35. Linz, *Breakdown,* pp. 75, 79.

36. Staats, *Social Behaviorism,* p. 100.

37. See chap. 3.

3

Catholics in Weimar Germany

The episcopate in Germany was a well-organized and coherent leadership force, forged in the fires of the *Kulturkampf* and periodically reinforced in its dedication by the modern secularistic assaults on the Church. In general, the German bishops historically have refused to compromise with secular rulers only when a specific issue focused on established dogma. Opposition to a regime or disobedience to the government, however, was generally alien to them. They could be classified as apolitical in day-to-day activities, leaving such responsibilities to the Center party. But they had definitely assimilated the nationalistic values that provided the sinew for the Second Reich's body politic. A brief survey of the episcopal efforts at organization is necessary to understand how this official organ of the German Church came into existence.

To unite German Catholics and to better interact more effectively with the state from a position of strength, the bishops from the northern and southern Church provinces began meeting in plenary sessions at the shrine of St. Boniface in 1867. The defeat of Austria in 1866 had already shattered the dream of Catholic-Protestant parity in a *Grossdeutschland*. The post-1870 *Kleindeutsch* solution meant that German Catholics north of the Alps would be in a permanent minority. Faced with the prospect of incorporation into a state which, whether liberal and secularist or conservative and absolutist, would endanger Catholicism, the bishops closed ranks. For seven years they continued to meet at Fulda, but in 1873 Bismarck's *Kulturkampf* caused them to separate into two conferences. It was felt that such a tactical maneuver would allow the northern and southern Church provinces greater flexibility and freedom in dealing with the diverse challenges created by the *Kulturkampf.* It had also been discovered over the seven years that the antagonisms between the Bavarian bishops (traditionally separatist and anti-Prussian) and the northern bishops had resulted in too many disagreements and left the Church too vulnerable to Bismarck's attacks. The northern and eastern church provinces of Cologne, Paderborn, the Upper Rhenish province, and Breslau continued to meet at Fulda and retained the title of Fulda Bishops' Conference; the southern provinces of Bavaria and Würzburg, referred to as the Freising Bishops' Conference, met under the leadership of the archbishop of Munich at Freising.[1]

The German Episcopate

Over the years, faint attempts were made to coordinate the activities of both conferences; but it was not until Adolf Bertram, cardinal of Breslau, became chairman of the Fulda Conference that a partial accord was reached. The establishment of the Weimar Republic had created a new situation for the Church, and it was felt that closer cooperation between the two conferences would now be desirable. At the suggestion of the papal nuncio, Msgr. Eugenio Pacelli, Bertram and Michael Faulhaber, the Munich cardinal and chairman of the Freising Conference, respectively, agreed to attend each other's annual meetings. They also agreed to exchange information on the issues and problems confronting their episcopal associations and to report the decisions made, resulting from the respective conferences.[2] Increased collaboration became necessary throughout the period of the Weimar Republic. With the appearance of National Socialism as a major influence in German politics, the bishops began to view the custom of meeting separately in a different light. The attacks of the Nazis against the Church, the appearance of Alfred Rosenberg's *Myth of the Twentieth Century,* and the significant increase of Catholics leaving the Church to join the party alarmed the bishops. Hitler's appointment as chancellor in 1933 made the problem even more acute. After the March elections, the passage of the Enabling Act, and Hitler's promises to support the Church, the German hierarchy was once again convinced of the need to unite their forces as they prepared for a new *Kulturkampf.* Consequently, under the leadership of Bertram, the Fulda Conference began meeting in May 1933 along with the members of the Freising Conference. It became the official organization representing the Church in Germany. From 1933 to 1944, the Fulda Conference continued to meet. In 1945 it was renamed the German Bishops' Conference and has continued meeting to the present. But it was the historical experiences of the bishops that guided them in accepting Hitler's Reich in 1933 and in attempting cooperation as far as possible thereafter.

With the exception of Bishop Konrad Preysing of Eichstatt (later Berlin), who had studied secular law and seems to have had an astute sense of the totalitarian aspirations of Nazism, the other bishops had come to office as theologians or administrators, but possessed only limited understanding of political matters. Their average age was slightly above sixty. Their outlooks on politics had been shaped by life in Imperial Germany before World War I. Many were still convinced monarchists; all had a basically conservative outlook and were distrustful of liberalism and democracy. Nationalism above all focused on the hated Treaty of Versailles, influenced the thought of more and more Catholics. Once won to the "Fatherland ideal," Catholics became fanatic. Political pluralism was, in general, assaulted, and democracy was ideologically dismissed. In 1922 Faulhaber, for example, asserted that the revolution, i.e., Marxism, was high treason and was marked by the sign of Cain. A latent anti-Semitism was also present and was manifested in conjunction with nationalism. The views of the Nazis and many Catholics on political questions were also quite similar, at least on first reading. Hence, the Catholic hierarchy found itself opposing the Nazis primarily on cultural grounds. Such opposition focused on the Nazi assertion that race, not religion, was the source of moral norms. The hierarchy did not oppose anti-Semitism as such, except when it led to violence. The pastoral opposition to National Socialism, the Bavarian bishops insisted, remained generically the same as that against nineteenth-century liberals and against contemporary socialists.[3]

While Church leaders were uncomfortable with Hitler's movement, neither they nor the conservative Center leadership had shown any strong affinity for the Weimar Republic. The conservative leaders in the Center as well as many individual Catholic bishops at first condemned the revolution of 1918, even though the Erzberger wing of the party had been readily coopted into the Weimar coalition. Reflecting the attitudes of so many of his episcopal brethren, Faulhaber provides evidence in his letters and sermons of ultra-conservative and pro-monarchist sentiments.[4] His thinking was permeated by his deep attachment to Bavaria and its kings; his refusal to accept fully the Weimar Republic stemmed from his personal, staunchly authoritarian frame of reference. The "state" had a mystical and religious significance for him and his views are outlined in works that do not indicate even a partial understanding of the democratic process theoretically dominant in Weimar Germany. His view reflects a determined adherence to the antidemocratic, antiliberal view of the state so popular in the Church that had experienced the strains of the *Kulturkampf.* Along with his episcopal colleagues he favored state protection of the Church and looked forward with hope to the day when the Church and state would not only coexist peacefully, but would constitute one single authority each reinforcing the actions of the other. To such a man, the liberal secularization of the state was blasphemy and the promises of Hitler to base the Nazi program on strong religious foundations could certainly be supported.[5] Faulhaber's dislike of the democratic new order in Germany was nourished by three sources: (1) his love for the monarchy, (2) his dislike of leftist politics, (3) his appreciation of the monarchial structure of the Church government. The Munich cardinal always insisted that he had not condemned the Republic as a political system nor did he support the forceful overthrow of the Weimar constitution, but rather had merely declared the revolution as well as the varied portions of the constitution, which were against the commandments of God, sinful. Verbally, then, he opposed the Weimar government, while simultaneously supporting the state. Such a distinction was not always clear to those who heard him. Faulhaber also opposed the Center's tactic of cooperation with the SPD, because such a maneuver obscured the basic corporatist and solidarist Christian principles that Faulhaber and his episcopal colleagues supported.[6]

The archbishop of Munich was a prelate of great zeal who remained utterly faithful to the Church. What has been written of his forceful denunciations of the actions of the Nazi regime in persecuting the Church, destroying her schools, muzzling her press, and disbanding her organizations, remains a testimonial to his personal courage, but not to his early political acumen. Opening a national gathering of Catholics in Munich on August 27, 1922, Cardinal Faulhaber characterized the November revolution as "perjury and high treason." Pragmatically, the chairman of the Center party deputation in the National Assembly in his first speech on February 13, 1919, had declared that the party could not approve of the revolutionary upheaval that had overthrown the monarchy, though he added that the party now, "after all that has happened, takes its stand on the grounds of the accomplished facts."[7] In time, the Center became one of the mainstays of the Republic, consistently polling 12 to 13 percent of the vote. The bishops, of course, adjusted their tactics to the situation, but not their principles.

Most of the bishops were convinced monarchists who either opposed the Weimar Republic or accepted it with reservations simply because they had no choice. Unaccustomed to the free play of ideas within a democratic order and fearful for the existence of Catholic schools and associations, they wanted the government to prevent criticism of the Church. In 1931, for example, Bertram, who received his seminary education during the *Kulturkampf,* appealed to the Prussian government to control the agitation by the Free Thinkers in favor of the separation of Church and state and against Church schools. Even Bishop Preysing, a younger man, who became a strong opponent of the Nazi regime, compared the effort to build a stable government on the Weimar constitution to an attempt to build a pyramid from peas.[8]

In the 1920s, the political trend among Catholic bishops without exception was to the Right. In Bavaria particularly, but not solely, the forces of conservatism had encouraged the spread of nationalistic and anti-democratic ideas, which in the 1920s meant the rejection of the Treaty of Versailles and the demand for the reversal of the verdicts of 1918, both internal and external. The promise of an organic state, free from the divisions of a politically pluralistic society, appealed to many Catholic thinkers, while others openly expressed their dislike of the whole tide of events since the French Revolution, which had introduced the dangerous heresies of liberalism, individualism, and democracy. Count Galen, later bishop of Münster, for example, openly attacked the liberal constitution as being "godless." Fear of communism and the rejection of everything that smacked of Marxist heresies became a standard feature on the pronouncements of Catholic speakers on political developments in Germany. Dropping their loyalty to the Center, some Catholics supported the growing claims of nationalist propaganda by a determination to show that they could be as patriotic and nationalistic as anyone else. Whereas in the time of the *Kulturkampf* the percentage of Catholics voting for the Center party had exceeded 80 percent, the figure during the 1920s stood at about 60 percent.[9] A few Catholics supported the left-wing parties; others, resentful of the Versailles peace settlement, were attracted by the aggressively nationalistic politics of the nationalists and the new Nazi party. The former, a sizable minority, resented the way parish priests and clerical school teachers pressured the people to support Catholic political groups that were generally nationalist. An ultranationalist Catholic movement began to emerge with the inception of the Weimar Republic. Such groups were peculiarly susceptible to the appeal of authoritarianism in the Nazi program. Hitler welcomed these supporters, and the bishops saw a loss of Catholic political power.

As early as 1920 a small and obscure group of Catholics in Berlin had founded a *Katholikenbund für nationale Politik* (Catholic League for Patriotic Politics), which aimed at achieving a synthesis between right-wing radicalism and Catholicism. In 1924 the Munich branch participated in publishing the periodical *Der Rütlischwur,* a section of which was entitled "Der Völkisch Katholik." This *Bund* called for a fight against the three forces of evil which it considered the enemies of Germany as well as the Church: Marxists, Jews, and Freemasons. Such a struggle could be fought successfully only by an alliance of Catholics and the *völkisch* Right. A regular contributor to the *Rütlischwur* was the priest, Josef Roth, Heinrich Himmler's cousin and later an official in Hitler's Ministry for Ecclesiastical Affairs. Roth specialized in anti-Semitic tirades and published his opinions in a pamphlet distributed by the Franz Eher firm of Munich, the Nazi's official publishing house.[10]

In the early 1920s the Hitler movement was small in numbers, and the

Catholic membership almost miniscule. Because Bavaria was the center of "Catholic" Germany and because it was the place where the Nazis had originated, the other bishops often consulted the Munich prelate and deferred to his views. Faulhaber seems to have played a role midway between the immovable Preysing and the weak and yielding Konrad Gröber (the brown bishop); for that reason it was his view that often prevailed in the bishops' conferences. During the early 1920s, the German hierarchy issued few pronouncements on the program of the infant Nazi movement. Cardinal Faulhaber, speaking of Hitler and his movement before a meeting of Catholic students and academicians in the Löwenbräu Beer Cellar in Munich on February 15, 1924, felt that the great tragedy was that the "originally pure spring of Catholic nationalism had been poisoned by later contemporaries and by the *Kulturkampf.*" The Bavarian episcopate agreed on September 9, 1924 not to celebrate the birthday of the Weimar constitution—an unusual stance in light of the later celebrations of Hitler's birthday. Striking a theme consistent during the Third Reich, Faulhaber in 1925 noted that Hitler knew better than others in his movement that the strengthening of nationalism could never be based on a hatred of Rome or on the so-called *Wotanskult.* This theme of separating Hitler from the radicals in his movement recurred consistently until 1945. Interestingly, Faulhaber equated obedience to the state and cooperation for the enhancement of the community (*Volksgemeinschaft*) with the fourth commandment. He emphasized that he was German by birth and Catholic by baptism. Both characteristics must be nurtured and developed with age. During the Weimar years the Nazi party made sizable gains, and many more Catholics made common cause with it, including such priests as Karl König in Berlin, Philipp Haeuser in Augsburg, and Wilhelm Senn in Flehingen. These men were attracted by the party's anticommunism, its fight against liberalism, parliamentarism, pacifism, and other "un-German" ideologies, as well as by its militant program of liberation from the Versailles Treaty.[11]

Faulhaber addressed the problem that seemed to cause the most difficulty for the Catholic clergy at the time. How was the priest to escape from the crossfire when national questions were debated? From the Left he was accused of having too much love for his fatherland. From the Right, he was mistrusted because he owed allegiance to both Berlin and Rome and was concerned with his earthly and heavenly fatherland.[12] Faced with this issue, priests were advised to emphasize their allegiance to patriotic groups whenever possible, only qualifying their views when necessary. Very shrewdly and early, Hitler had disavowed any interest in religious warfare and had relegated sniping against the Church and "political Catholicism" to the editors of the *Völkischer Beobachter. Mein Kampf* said little about religion or Christianity, probably from an instinctual awareness of the political risks involved in antagonizing Bavaria's Catholic majority. In fact, Article 24 of the program of the Nazi Party, adopted on February 20, 1920, had demanded "liberty for all religious denominations in the state, so far as they are not a danger to it and do not militate against the morality and the moral sense of the Germanic race. The party, as such, stands for positive Christianity, but does not bind itself in the matter of creed to any particular confession."[13] What was "positive Christianity?" This calculated ambiguity served Hitler well in his struggle for power.

Hitler's opposition to the Church was actually both ideological and political. He saw in the Church an organization whose power he resented and coveted. To his mind the unity, continuity, and authority of the Church were due, not to any spiritual force, but to its well-organized control over its followers, a control which the Nazi party would do well to emulate. Throughout the 1920s Hitler refused to campaign against the Catholic Church, fully realizing that by professing support for the Church's position in the state and by emphasizing the nationalist aspects of his program, Catholics could be persuaded to assist his rise to power. The Nazi principles dealing with religion did not draw any episcopal criticism until the Nazi party, benefiting from the economic collapse of 1929, had made impressive headway in the elections of September of 1930, returning a Nazi contingent to the Reichstag nine times the size of that of 1928 and controlling 18.5 percent. The rise in strength was smallest in the Catholic constituencies, but the small gains of the Nazis caused concern. Also, in 1930, Rosenberg's *Myth of the Twentieth Century* interpreted the party's "positive Christianity" in an ominous way, calling for the elimination of the "Jewish" Old Testament, for the purging of the New Testament from "obviously distorted and superstitious reports," and for the creation of a German Church anchored not in abstract dogma and denomination, but in the forces of blood, race, and soil. Despite a reserved attitude toward the democratic regime, the German hierarchy in the years immediately prior to the Nazi takeover frequently condemned such party doctrines as that of blood and race as the basis of morality. Unfortunately, the bishops excluded from their criticism of Nazism the following points: a recognition that Hitler intended to replace democracy with dictatorship, a perception of the possible consequences of the Nazi *Lebensraum* policy in foreign affairs, and a condemnation of racial anti-Semitism. Instead, they emphasized the Nazi threat to religious liberty, and they attacked only the aspects of the Nazi racist policy that exulted Germans above other peoples and which endeavored to promote a racist heathendom or a German national church. In 1923, Cardinal Faulhaber, for example, declared that every human life was precious, including that of a Jew—an insidious remark. Many public statements of the bishops likewise characterized the Nazi idea of the primacy of power rather than justice as contrary to Christian teaching. Yet the German hierarchy favored the Nazi destruction of the Communist party while simultaneously deploring the acts of terrorism against Germans.[14] Such politico-theological refinements did not totally clarify the Church's position vis-a-vis Nazism.

Keenly aware of the disturbances evoked by such issues as the 1929 Young Plan, Bertram and others began to recognize that the viable but radical alternatives to the much-maligned Republic could prove disastrous. Recognizing the seriousness of Nazi disturbances, Cardinal Bertram, as spokesman for the entire hierarchy, urged Catholics in 1929 to help counteract political unrest by exercising their right to vote now in support of the Republic. He said that the Republic had a "right of existence." Voting against it would only result in disorder and disturb the peace. He acknowledged that the Weimar Republic had now become worthy of preservation and must be supported. Any endeavor leading toward its downfall should be condemned.[15] The Republic was now seen as the lesser of evils, hardly a judgment designed to encourage enthusiastic support. The Church's policy on membership in the NSDAP also did not offer a clear direction.

Early in 1930, the vicar general of the Diocese of Mainz, Dr. Mayer, responding to a query, had informed the Nazi party's district office in Offenbach that Catholics could not be permitted membership in the NSDAP. The vicar general confirmed the position taken in a sermon by Father Weber in Kirchenhausen. Father Weber had told his parishioners (1) that Catholics were forbidden to belong to the Nazi party, (2) that members of the Nazi party would not be allowed to attend funerals or other Church functions in group formations, and (3) that a Catholic acknowledging adherence to the Nazi program could not be admitted to the sacraments. Father Weber had complied with the injunctions distributed by the diocesan chancery. Such instructions, Mayer stated, had been necessitated by the incompatibility of Catholic doctrines with Article 24 of the Nazi program. The guarantee of religious freedom in the Nazi program, Dr. Mayer pointed out, was qualified by conditions that seemed aimed at denying religious liberty to the Catholic faith. The Christian moral law was valid for all times and for all races, and "it therefore is a great error to demand that the Christian creed be made to conform to the ethical and moral sense of the Germanic race." The concept of "positive Christianity," under which the Nazi leaders demanded a German God and a German Christianity in effect involved the establishment of a German national church. The religious policies of National Socialism, he concluded, contradicted Catholic Christianity.[16] The Nazi press attacked Mayer, but he was defended by his bishop, Ludwig Hugo. In response to Mayer's action, the episcopate was not united. Bishop Buchberger remarked that the position was untenable and, perhaps even worse, inopportune. Mayer had been, he felt, tactically stupid.[17] But the bishops also expressed the hope that the many Catholics who had joined the Nazi party out of dissatisfaction with the prevailing difficult political and economic conditions would heed the warnings of their pastors.

When the Gauleiter (regional party leader) of Hesse sought permission for the laying of wreaths on November 9 at the graves of soldiers fallen in World War I and buried in Catholic cemeteries, his request was denied on the ground that a political party whose *Weltanschauung* conflicted with the doctrine of the Church could not be allowed to hold such ceremonies on Catholic soil. Confusing the signals being sent by the Church, Bishop Schreiber of Berlin during the same month indicated that Catholics of Berlin were not forbidden membership in the Nazi party. Clearly the German episcopate had not worked out a common stand on specific questions posed by the increasingly popular Nazi party.[18]

At the end of 1930, Bertram had cited as a grave error the one-sided glorification of the Nordic race and the contempt for divine revelation increasingly taught in all corners of Germany. He warned the faithful against the ambiguous "positive Christianity," which he felt meant nothing since everyone interpreted it differently. The Church could never recognize the fanatic nationalism that led to mutual hatred and to the worship of race, although he commended normal nationalism. "We are no longer dealing with political questions," Bertram continued, "but with a religious delusion which has to be fought with all possible vigor."[19] This episcopal warning was timely since some Catholics had countered the liberal democratic collapse of the Weimar experiment by seeking justification for the radical organization of society under the regime of National Socialism. Some Catholics felt they could accept, for example, those parts of National Socialism that appeared to be vaguely corporatist.[20]

In his New Year's message for 1931, Bertram reiterated his warning against false prophets and agitators, declaring that extreme nationalism, by glorifying the race, could lead only to a despisal of the revelation and commandments of God. "Away therefore with the vain imaginings of a national religious society, which is to be torn away from the Rock of Peter, and only guided by the racial theories of an Aryan—heathen teaching about salvation. This is no more than the foolish imaginings of false prophets."[21] And again:

> There is a nationalism that justifies itself, and its characteristics are love of the mother tongue, devotion to one's own people and the customs of the country, and recognition to God for all hereditary advantages. All this is justified so

long as truth and charity are not offended. It is justified only so long as one keeps an eye open to the value of other races and nations and recognizes God as the Creator of the soul, as the distributor of all the gifts of nature and sees in the progress of races and nations the evolution of the handiwork of God.[22]

The Breslau prelate distinguished between a "reasonable nationalism," which had the power to unite and conciliate, and a "fanatical nationalism," which was "the source of reciprocal misunderstanding and hatred among peoples and is outside the supernatural tie that should bind all men 'as sons of the Church, as brothers in Christ, as heirs of Christian civilization.'"[23] Even though the cardinal failed to indicate National Socialism by name, this omission should not be construed as proof that the Church did not recognize the dangers inherent in the teachings of the party. The Church was fully aware that there were many aspects of National Socialism that were opposed to Catholicism, but it was the usual practice in messages of this type, regretably perhaps, to omit mentioning specific movements by name. Because of the background it was clear that the Nazis were meant even though not specifically designated.[24] The distinction, however, between a reasonable and a fanatical nationalism may have been lost on those Catholics faced with the disastrous post-1929 depression.

In 1930 and 1931, when the issue was raised about Catholic membership in the NSDAP, Faulhaber also agreed with his fellow bishops that such membership was impossible to countenance. The Bavarian bishops condemned the doctrines of the party and forbade at least priests to work in any way with the movement. They condemned the movement on the five grounds that: (1) it put race before religion; (2) it rejected Old Testament revelation, even the Ten Commandments; (3) it denied the primacy of the pope because he represented an authority outside Germany; (4) it cherished the plan of an undogmatic national German church; and (5) in Article 24 it set up the "moral feeling of the German race" as the criterion of Christian morality. Hence Nazism had denied the universality of the Catholic Church and moral principles. Faulhaber did not, however, think that it was necessary to forbid specifically the wearing of the Nazi uniform in church. No one in Bavaria, therefore, was ever excommunicated for wearing the uniform in church or for belonging to the NSDAP—although such an interpretation had its episcopal supporters.[25] By 1931 the bishops realized that, because of the changing social and intellectual influences of the 1920s, their authority was considerably weaker than it had been in 1921 when they condemned socialism; they hesitated to assume the responsibility for excommunicating so many of the "faithful" and so proceeded cautiously. General condemnations were frequent; explicit applications were formulated with an eye to expediency.

The Freising Bishops' Conference hoped to prevent such embarrassing occurrences as the May 18, 1930 incident in which the SA in Regensburg had been allowed to bring flags and banners into the cathedral, and the December 14, 1930 instance in which Catholic priest Dr. Haeuser had given the principal address at the Nazi Christmas party in Augsburg. Significantly, the bishops denied any intention of passing judgment on the specific political aims of the Nazi movement, but as guardians of the faith, they felt called upon to warn against National Socialism "as long and insofar as it adheres to a religious and cultural program which is irreconcilable with Catholic teaching." The question of admitting National Socialists to the sacraments should be decided on an individual basis depending on whether the Catholics in question were mere fellow travelers or active members of the party having full knowledge of its anti-Catholic intentions. The bishops continued: "Should National Socialism, against our hope, adopt the methods of Bolshevism, we then, of course, could no longer assume the existence of good faith."[26] On March 5, 1931 the Cologne bishops stated that they could no longer delay warning the Nazis, "especially since our policy of waiting and watching the development of the National Socialist movement has already been misinterpreted." The bishops of the Paderborn province on March 10, 1931 ruled that membership in the Nazi party was not permitted. They stated: "National Socialism is not only a political party, it also represents a total world outlook. As such it involves an attitude toward religion and it poses demands in the area of religion."[27]

Some hesitation was felt by the bishops over being drawn further into partisan politics, an arena they always sought to avoid. The increasing number of Catholics aligned with right-wing parties, however, pressured the bishops to relinquish their unequivocal support of the Center and to adopt a more neutral attitude. Typical of this sentiment was the letter by 100 Catholics addressed to Archbishop Klein of Paderborn on July 20, 1931, complaining about the difficult position of those not belonging to the Center. A copy of this letter was only formally submitted to the Fulda Bishops' Conference.[28]

The bishops met at Fulda in August of 1931 to take up the challenge of the growing Nazi movement. Varied rules had been established since 1921 to ensure that Catholics did not join parties or groups hostile to the faith. Now the bishops confronted a draft that would specifically include the Nazis. The draft asserted that the principles developed in 1921 were now to be applied to the Nazi party, "which pretends to be no more than a political party with justified national goals, but which in fact stands in clearest conflict with the fundamental truths of Christianity and with the organization of the Catholic Church of Christ's founding."[29] The draft was eventually adopted by the Fulda Conference and later by the Freising

Conference as well. The NSDAP was equated with the Socialists, Communists, and other freethinkers, in essence just another hostile party. A set of directions to the clergy covering doubtful cases was formulated. The bishops worked to devise appropriate pastoral guidelines based on canon law and applicable to Catholics who joined the party out of fear, pressure, invincible ignorance, or an erroneous conscience. Many apparently also felt that the party was not beyond salvation since recently some Nazis had demonstratively resigned from the NSDAP on the grounds that it was not sufficiently bold in its opposition to Catholicism. The argument implied that some Nazis saw no obstacle to Nazi-Catholic reconciliation.

The bishops were somewhat united and temporarily adopted a shaky resolution that stressed that the Church's insidious enemies must be handled from a position of faith and not partisan politics. In practice, the bishops were far from united on how to deal with the Nazi issue. Hitler's propagandists were quick to note that even those bishops' declarations most critical of National Socialism had paid their respect to the nationalistic aspirations of the party, and they put these utterances to good use. National Socialism, one of them wrote, welcomes "the gratifying fact that the German bishops warmly acknowledge the importance of the national cause and that they approve and even support with religious arguments national aims which represent a main part of the National Socialist program of liberation."[30]

The bishops themselves had indeed thought it necessary to accompany their warnings against National Socialism with affirmations of their intense feeling of national solidarity. The bishops of the Paderborn province, for example, had written: "We love the fatherland, the country of our cradle, the country of our language, the country of our forefathers, the country of our graves." Some argued against the war-guilt issue; others praised the "new life" surging through Germany. Instead of weakening the nationalistic extreme Right, the constant stress on devotion to the fatherland reinforced nationalism among the faithful without really convincing those who questioned the Church's devotion to the national cause. The same tragic fate characterized post-1933 Catholic-Nazi relations.[31]

Echoing their bishops, the stress of many Catholic publicists on dynamically defeating National Socialism and then praising nationalism led logically to a certain ambivalence among the faithful in evaluating the Nazi movement. Publicists pointed out the anti-Christian elements in the Nazi program and declared these incompatible with Catholic teaching. But then they supported the healthy core of Nazism—its reassertion of the values of religion and love of fatherland, its standing as a strong bulwark against atheistic Bolshevism. Many expressed regret that National Socialism had become a *Weltanschauung* instead of simply remaining a patriotic movement "which every friend of the fatherland in principle could have supported." Nazism was not totally evil. In January 1932 even the highly esteemed Jesuit Friedrich Muckermann, later one of the most outspoken anti-Nazis, declared it a serious duty so to influence National Socialism that it developed its positive nucleus so that it could become a true reform movement. Father Mühler best expressed the quandary in which the bishops found themselves when he stated that the Nazi program was certainly better from a cultural standpoint than was that of the SPD, a coalition partner of the Center in Weimar Germany. But compared to the SPD the rowdy tactics of the Nazis left much to be desired. And Father Nötges, in his important quasi-official study of the Nazi problem, reminded his readers that the condemnation of the NSDAP by the episcopate was conditional because of the expectation "that National Socialism, notwithstanding everything, might succeed someday in eliminating from its program and its activities all that which conflicted in principle and in practice with Catholicism."[32] There is no suggestion that the principles of Catholicism and Nazism were basically irreconcilable.

One reason for this state of affairs was certainly the Catholic affinity for the nationalistic aims and the anticommunism of the Nazi movement; another was the lack of strong democratic conviction on the part of the leaders and intelligentsia of German Catholicism. There were those in the clergy who were openly hostile to the revolutionary origin of the Weimar Republic and who, like the future bishop of Münster, Count Galen, sharply criticized the acknowledgment of popular sovereignty made by a constitution that had omitted God. Many harbored resentments against a regime that had extended legal recognition to all religious denominations. Faulhaber had condemned the Weimar constitution, which gave truth and error the same rights. He had opposed the Nazi Putsch but only on the grounds that it was a "wild demonstration" and was motivated in part by excessive, as distinct from "normal," anti-Semitism. Even more widespread among so many Germans was the attitude of indifference to the Weimar democratic institutions. This attitude had its roots in the continued popularity of the authoritarian and organic ideas propagated by nineteenth-century Catholic romantics in opposition to the Enlightenment and to its progeny the "atheistic liberalism" that fed the Weimar Republic. Likewise, concern for the maintenance of political liberty was further weakened by preoccupation with the protection of the rights of the institutional Church and religion, not with the system of moral values, which they felt would be maintained. This restricted political consciousness, another of the unfortunate effects of the *Kulturkampf,* but not peculiar solely to German Catholics, meant that many of the faithful regarded the continuation of state subsidies to the Church and the protection of confessional schools as more important than the defense of democracy and the liberties at its base. In essence, democracy was tolerated only because the republic guaranteed specific and desired rights and privileges to the Church. Hence, the institutional Church could equally and perhaps even enthusiastically tolerate Nazism if the extremists were controlled and the Church's rights and privileges were supported. In judging the bishops at this point, historical hindsight offers a clear view of their attitudes and activities as well as of the seeds of the future disaster. But in the view of the bishops, from 1930 to 1933 their course was merely a continuation of the traditional *Kirchenpolitik,* only now under acute circumstances. In essence, then, the Catholic hierarchy themselves were nationalistic and resented Versailles. The bishops were convinced monarchists. Pre-1933, they did not condemn possible dictatorship (at least not strenuously), potential war, or anti-Semitism unless radical and vulgar. Basically they lacked interest in politics as long as the Church religiously was unimpeded. From 1930 onward, Catholics were increasingly influenced by the Nazi propaganda, which claimed to be rescuing the Church from communism, and many were carried away by the 'spirit of national renewal,' which Hitler and his party appeared to embody. Nevertheless, the official attitude of the Catholic Church on January 30, 1933 was one of reserve, at best passive acceptance. Some Catholic clergy and laity had given open support to the Nazi movement. The Catholic doctrinal position remained unaltered, but the political tactics and strategy were malleable.[33]

Responding to the argument that both Nazis and Catholics were battling Bolshevism, Bishop Buchberger in June 1932 had indicated that Catholics should not become Nazis to fight communists. His statement to the *Katholikentag* in Waldsassen suggests that some bishops were more politically astute than commentators have thought. He maintained that if the NSDAP insisted that it really was the savior of Christianity from Bolshevism, then Catholics should recall that the gospel said that one cannot drive out the devil with Beelzebub. Christianity should rely on Christian precepts, not on nationalism, socialism, or both in combination. The dictatorship of communism could not be eliminated by the dictatorship of the führer.[34]

Many Catholics felt that they could serve their faith best by choosing the Nazi party, however, since it was more vigorously opposed to communism than were the varied Catholic parties. But the Bavarian episcopate tried to reinforce an anti-Nazism as well as anticommunism among their clergy. In 1932 the bishops in a letter to their clergy insisted that help during the depression could not be found in communism *or* socialism. Nor could it be found in a chauvinistic nationalism. Class-hate and race-hate were unchristian and unholy.[35] Even so, the practical ramifications of these episcopal denunciations were never spelled out. Condemnation without a specific strategy was useless or at best confusing.

If the bishops opposed the NSDAP, they could not hide behind the fortifications of papal encyclicals as they could if they attacked socialism-communism, but would have to confront the full force of the Nazi program. Their opposition was made more untenable by the fact that a fair number of Germans after 1930 felt that they could be loyal Catholics and support Nazi aims. By 1932 the Baden Catholic leader Ernst Fohr, for example, certainly rejected the Nazi program and was not sure whether the NSDAP and Center could cooperate. But he sensed changes in the Nazi leadership and thought that giving the NSDAP responsibility might diffuse the revolutionary elements in the party. Likewise, from 1932 to 1933 Upper Bavarian Catholics still tended to avoid party membership, but did not see anything wrong with voting for Nazis in elections.[36] In its claim to the whole of a man's life, the inherent evil of Hitler's predicted totalitarian state was beyond the comprehension of the bishops and to the end they were caught in a web of groundless distinctions between the party and the state. Defending the rights of the Church, the bishops failed to support the rights of the political community. Had they followed Faulhaber's episcopal motto *Vox Dei, Vox Temporis* (The voice of God is the voice of his times), they might have urged political pluralism and halted the Nazi tide. But then they would have had to choose selectively what the dominant current of the era was, a complex task since many of the theologians and politicized laity supported rightest movements and a few even praised the Nazis from an early date.

Catholic Intellectuals and German Nationalism

In his analysis of anti-Semitism, Uriel Tal has emphasized the sharp division between the persistent influence of Christian anti-Semitism and the much more violent and radical racism of the secularists. Yet he points out how subtly the arguments could be combined, particularly by a sinister blending of Christian vocabulary with the more far-reaching concepts of racial segregation and discrimination.[37] When varied Catholics attacked anti-Semitism they used scriptural and ecclesiastical rather than ethical and humanitarian weapons. For their part the Nazis did not launch ideological campaigns against the Church, but rather assaulted political Catholicism, a vulnerable target even among Catholics, and after 1933 used administrative intimidation. Since Nazism was a mass movement, its leaders chose not to challenge Church doctrine, but to inculcate the masses with an intoxicating brew of racist, *völkisch,* and nationalistic propaganda. As Church officials, the bishops aided and abetted the development of the nationalist theme. These men, generally conservative monarchists in sentiment, elderly and from rural smalltown backgrounds, sought to avoid offending the growing number of devout Catholics who had increasingly shifted to the Right.[38] Taking their cue from the frequently ambivalent statements of their bishops, the theologians and average Catholics offered variations on the themes of nationalism and anti-Semitism, which were in the final analysis only different sides of the same coin.

Theology is written by persons living in society. The susceptibility of the German religious elite to the allurements of a nationalistically oriented authoritarianism is undeniable and ultimately helped open the way for the post-1933 accommodation, since Hitler did not publicly attack the Churches. There is evidence to indicate that individuals supporting religious dogmatism (e.g., conventional, church-going Catholics as well as most theologians) seem to care less for equality, freedom, and broadmindedness in religion, with some carryover effect to politics, than those low on the dogmatic scale. High dogmatics apparently value salvation, social recognition, and obedience. Also, dogmatism can be correlated to an intolerance of ambiguity. Such dogmatic individuals would not be expected to attempt to use the Church to control secular leaders in order to keep the political system open for all potential solutions to the issues of the era, or struggle for the ecclesial support of liberty against authoritarianism, even in its Nazi form.[39] To Herman Rauschning shortly after assuming power, Hitler privately said:

> Neither of the denominations—Catholic or Protestant, they are both the same—has any future left. At least not for the Germans. Fascism may perhaps make its peace with the Church in God's name. I will do it too. Why not? But that won't stop me from stamping out Christianity in Germany, root and branch. One is either Christian or German. You can't be both.[40]

The orientation taken by episcopal leadership was supported by the theologians and Catholic publicists. Within the Church the interaction between leaders and flock can be viewed as an exchange process. This framework stresses the critical importance of analyzing the transactions that took place between the bishops and their co-clergy as well as with German Catholics in general. Such an approach departs from the assumption that the influence was one way with the leaders directing the activities of the followers. A transactional analysis of leader-follower relations emphasizes the significance of the follower's influence on the leaders as well as the leaders' attempts to direct the group. To maintain authority, a leader must fulfill the expectations of group members, address potential or real challenges to authority, and provide the followers with sufficient rewards to maintain the relationship. In essence, then, the bishops' reactions to Nazism must be seen contextually as they responded to the Catholic intelligentsia and laity with their understanding of anti-Semitism and authoritarianism. Theology likewise does not live in a vacuum; theologians make claims about the society or culture within which they operate and then incorporate these claims into their works. Precisely because the theologian is concerned to communicate with his contemporaries, he is obliged to respond to the plausibility structures of his society. Theology, then, is a function of the dominant culture to which it belongs.[41]

The political effects, when Catholics had earlier not fully received the rewards of society, had significant consequences. The marginality and vulnerability of the Catholic middle classes and rural faithful suggest a potential susceptibility to radical movements. Fascist, right-wing, and anti-Semitic movements apparently have their social bases, at least in some respects, among the peasants and in the lower middle class of retailers, craftsmen, and petty officials. Standing in opposition both to big labor and big business, these social classes are assumed to become radicalized out of a perception of relative or absolute deprivation.[42] German Protestant peasants and *Kleinburger* deserted the liberal and conservative parties en masse, giving their votes by 1932 overwhelmingly to the Nazi party. Approximately 5.5 million Catholics continued to cast their ballots for the Catholic political parties, while about 6.5 million gave their votes to all other parties combined. A populistic anti-Semitism, based on resentment of Jewish wealth, was to be found in Catholic ranks especially among the southern agrarian wing. This anti-Semitism might link up with anti-socialism or a general repudiation of modern culture, but it was by no means identical with rabid antirepublicanism or sympathetic to Nazism. The Catholic Center could offer an antiliberal, anti-Semitic outlook and so retard the drift of Catholics to more radical parties, although simultaneously such views could predispose Catholics to accept the so-called moderate Nazism so frequently mentioned in the sources.[43] Earlier, Hans Rost had asserted that Christianity forbids the hatred of other races when he wrote, "Christianity does not prohibit defense against the harmful influences caused by the peculiarities of a certain race." Anton Otto Neher, a Catholic economist, attacked Jewish businessmen for allegedly unscrupulous practices, but then extolled the Weimar *Volksstaat* for ending the political oppression of Catholics and making possible the social improvement of the Catholic proletariat. In his work Neher indicates that any *Volkstaat* would have his allegiance.[44] Unlike its Austrian counterpart, German Catholicism, however, never produced a prominent anti-Semite of the Karl Lueger variety. But the undercurrents and latent support or acceptance were there and frequently in the academic arena as well.

Between 1918 and 1933 a significant number of Catholic scholars and publicists concentrated their efforts on developing a *Reichstheologie*. At least intellectually, the political theologians supporting this system of ideas helped usher in the Third Reich. Erich Przywara, for example, stressed a hierarchical conception of being and even as late as 1964 still maintained that "*Reich und Kreuz*" were basic Christian concepts. The term *Reich* and the concept of a strict hierarchical order were antithetical to the pluralistic value structure necessary for the support of the fledgling Republic and, although without realizing the consequences, clearly a religiously rooted anti-Weimar fabric was being woven.[45] In 1926, Przywara wrote an article on Christianity and Judaism that also helps illuminate a fundamental theme prominent in the Catholicism of the era. He stated that he wanted to analyze the Jewish religion, *the* contemporary question to be faced by Christians. He pointed to the rabid anti-Semitism of his day, but then maintained that Judaism should be overcome by a Christianity characterized by the consistent, unconditional surrender through faith to the supernatural God revealed in the New Testament. Other attempts to deal with the Jewish problem would only result in driving Judaism into peripheral areas of concentration. Jewish capitalism, for example, resulted because the money market was restricted originally to Jews. Also, he emphasized that Judaism would remain a tragic actor on the stage of world history as long as it was not fulfilled in Christianity.[46] Essentially he was promoting religious, although certainly not physical, extermination.

During the Weimar Republic, organized German Catholicism came into repeated conflicts with the growing Nazi movement, but anti-Semitism was not necessarily one of the primary bones of contention. On the contrary, such Catholic publicists as the Franciscan father, Erhard Schlund, agreed in 1923 with the Nazis on the importance of fighting the Jews' "hegemony in finance, the destructive influence of the Jews in religion, morality, literature and art, and political and social life." The nationalist movement, the same author observed, had a healthy core, "the endeavor to maintain the purity of the German blood and German race." Around this good core there lay merely the bad shell of extremism, which he proceeded to diagnose in subsequent years. The implication would seem to be that a reformed Nazism could be acceptable.[47]

Agreeing with an article in the 1923 *Bayerische Kurier,* Schlund wrote that Nazism was anti-Semitic, antisocialist, and opposed to the Freemasons. Nazism was not a positive Christianity, but rather only attacked the enemies of Christianity. Thus, the "Christian" ideas of Nazism essentially were negative, not positive. Schlund's remarks highlight the problem of dealing with the National Socialist ideology since it reinforced several Catholic viewpoints as well. The ability of a Catholic to make a sound moral decision was weakened by the leadership mechanism in the Church. As Pius XII would do later, Schlund insisted that National Socialism was a German phenomenon, and so the German bishops should make appropriate responses; but he failed to recognize that as loyal Germans the bishops would have difficulty in attacking a popular nationalist party, even though *Osservatore Romano* (1930) had stated that belonging to the Nazi party was incompatible with the Catholic conscience, just as belonging to socialist movements of any hue was unacceptable for Catholics. On February 12, 1931, the Bavarian episcopate offered, as Schlund remarked, typical guidance that failed to help Catholics. The bishops attacked the cultural goals of Nazism, but said that the strictly political goals were beyond their purview. As previously seen, the bishops opposed Paragraph 24 of the Nazi program and the entire idea of race as the basis of religion. How was this condemnation implemented? Columns of Nazis could not appear in Church, but single Nazis, if they did not disturb the services, could.[48]

In 1931, Schlund maintained that any Christian who had real love for his fatherland must view Nazism as a political misfortune. Nazism had not developed into a simple "fatherland movement" as other parties had. National Socialism had developed a new and, according to Hitler, unchangeable *Weltanschauung* that would continue to oppose traditional religion. Since the Church had already attacked the Social Democratic-Marxist world view and opposed the communist as well as liberal political programs, it could not tolerate the all-pervading Nazi viewpoint. The state, Schlund insisted, was to be oriented toward religion and not religion to the state. In opposition to the romanticism so basic for such *völkisch* movements as Nazism, Schlund reminded his readers that revelation and the Church's pronouncements were binding and must be accepted by a reasoning faith, not by feeling.[49]

Also responding in 1931 to the increasing Nazi prominence was the highly respected Jesuit, Gustav Gundlach. His plea for a moderate anti-Semitism was a fairly typical and perfectly respectable view in the Church. Writing in a reference work edited by Buchberger, Gundlach argued that a political anti-Semitism fighting the Jews' "exaggerated and harmful influence" was permitted as long as it utilized morally admissible means.[50] Even with such anti-Semitic views, however, Gundlach could support the Republic, but not all the values usually associated with pluralistic democracy, a system stressing toleration and pragmatism. He had voted, he told a good friend, for Wilhelm Marx against Paul von Hindenburg, the "Mythos von Tannenberg," in 1925. Seeking the traditional Aristotelian "mean," Gundlach by 1929-31 saw dangers inherent in both Bolshevism and National Socialism, and criticized a syndrome of intellectual biases that could endanger the Weimar Republic. He was, for example, particularly disturbed by such Catholic tendencies as the antiintellectual emotionalism so popular in many circles, which condemned rational approaches to political issues. In the *Staatslexikon der Görresgesellschaft,* even Gundlach pointed out that the Marxist support of class conflict, usually anathema to Catholics, might actually be necessary under some conditions for the realization of specific social goals. This did not mean that he was pro-Bolshevik, since most of his works pointed to the dangerous parallels existing between communism and Nazism.[51] It did mean that he could accept "healthy" elements normally declared anathema by contemporary commentators. The emphasis on reasoning faith for both Schlund and Gundlach was one way to attack the obviously emotive Nazism. Even as opponents of Nazism, however, both men could still retain an anti-Semitic outlook.

The Nazis emphasized the totality of their movement, and their *Weltanschauung* was one of the primary attractions for many. Gundlach insisted that the Catholic *Weltanschauung* was rooted in a 2,000 year history, initiated through Christ's salvific act. Catholic doctrine guided mankind to God, the completion of the earthly pilgrimage. Since this religious view might suggest to some that they should ignore Weimar politics, Gundlach insisted that theoretical orientations were designed to help focus on the present milieu and be relevant. In other words, theory must be rooted in reality. God can be found in His created world, and so religion should offer a view corresponding to the harmonic totality of life. Historical events are an outgrowth of the unity of God's will with human action. In this context, the theocentric Christian view must oppose the purely anthropocentric racism on strictly rational grounds. The Church is Christ living among men and should affect the historical development of mankind. Naturally, this religious axiom was acceptable to nearly everyone within the Church.[52] The problem, of course, was how to apply such an axiom to specific conditions.

Gundlach felt that democracy as a Christian political theory had its roots in the natural law theory of late scholastic, but not Thomistic, philosophy. He supported the view of Suarez, which appreciated the individual man with his metaphysical and natural autonomy, because man was a member of a real society and a citizen of a political state. He remarked that natural law theory promoted the inalienable rights of the individual opposed to feudalism, absolutism, and even to any unenlightened authorities ruling the Church and religious orders. Catholicism emphasized the supernatural origins of Catholic democracy, i.e., the equality of all of redeemed men before God. Hence, Catholicism could not be viewed necessarily as an antidemocratic *Weltanschauung*. Membership in the authoritative Church actually provided the individual a valid system of values with which to view the political world.[53] Gundlach's sole stress on the "saved," however, could be perceived as anti-Semitic; his theory does not seem to take into account Jewish members of his political society, although he saw Catholicism as a support for the democratic order. Gundlach saw in the Catholic religion, united through its connection to the objective hierarchy and dogma, a good protection from the assaults of radical individuals or the masses. Catholicism could introduce a vital dynamic into the democratic state which he felt could be an organic entity. With its objective natural law and revelation, Catholicism could offer a sound foundation for democracy.[54]

In defending corporate thought as developed by his friend Heinrich Pesch, Gundlach was attacking liberalism. This is probably not too surprising since Gundlach had intellectually assimilated Pesch's sociopolitical principles. Solidarism was the only Catholic theory of society that proved able to formulate Catholic basic philosophy in a general socio-philosophical system, and then to apply it in a concrete manner to the industrialized social order. The system postulates the essentially social character of man as a person at the center of its religious anthropology. Such an approach opposed those who wanted to take property ownership as the guiding principle, i.e., the socialists. Catholic social solidarity can only be realized in a natural (i.e., a fair) ordering of the relations between the individual and the common good. Social order is hierarchical, ascending from the person to the family to the nation and state. Thus, the socioeconomic principle of solidarity can only be realized through an objective, fair order supporting the vocational needs of the industrial society. Under the influence of Weimar, Catholics even reevaluated socialism by dividing the movement into a pre- and post-1918 continuum. By 1919 solidarists had developed a new positive Catholic approach to the ideal of socialism now reinterpreted as "a superior, more perfect community of life and fortune than was ever achieved before, which takes its vital strength from the unselfish loyalty and devotion of one man for another."[55]

For confronting classical liberalism, communism, and national socialism, Pesch had delineated the general framework within which Gundlach worked. Pesch wrote:

> Christianity makes no distinctions between races, nations or classes with regard to human solidarity. For it, there is no class of pariahs who have no rights . . . ; there is no privileged class of capitalistic overlords who combine egoistic striving for wealth with simultaneous expansion of power and progressive domination of man over man; there is no International which proclaims the permanence of class hatred. . . . The state is more than a mass of individual beings. It is a moral-organic unity, a community of people governed by public well-being as its objective. Citizens are morally obligated to assist this objective. They should serve the public welfare with their labor, positively by their economic achievements, negatively by respecting the rights of others and the public well being in their striving for income.[56]

Gundlach accepted this form of corporate democracy which demanded organic linkage for its member components. For him, the political community is organically united, but he fails to specify, except for his essay in the *Lexikon,* what is to be done about those who do not "fit" into the sociopolitical patterns. He also ignores the implication of the organic theory, i.e., the individual exists for the community and not the reverse.

Supporting organic corporatism, Gundlach portrayed liberalism as a mechanistic world-view stressing individualism and emphasizing freedom *from* rather than freedom *for.* The state is more than the sum of individuals; it reflects an organically interconnected social life. Only by accident had secular liberalism succeeded in paving the way to some of the goals sought by the solidarists, namely freedom. Basically, the pluralistic arbitrariness of liberalism frustrated the desired organic development of the state.[57] This assault on liberalism was rooted in such Catholic experiences in the nineteenth century as the *Kulturkampf.* Gundlach encouraged Catholics to work within the Weimar milieu, but openly assaulted such political values as pluralism. Stressing organicism, moreover, made it difficult to support the tolerant pluralism so necessary to the foundation of democratic possibilities. Others veered further to the radical Right and saw intricate connections among Jews, liberals, and capitalists. They assaulted this conspiracy, even though one stream in the Catholic tradition developed since the *Kulturkampf* had stressed that the freedom of Catholics, Protestants, and Jews were all bound together no matter what their political coloration. But representing a large rural population, Catholic leaders connected liberalism and its Jewish representatives. The position of the official Church, which condemned racial anti-Semitism in 1928, tolerated social anti-Semitism of the Gundlach variety. Even in referring to the *Judenfrage,* the implication would eventually have to emerge that there had to be an answer to the question.[58] The terminology itself, then, implied a problem.

The charge of excessive Jewish influence in German public life was factually false and morally indefensible. In the press of the Left, for example, which was attacked as totally *verjudet,* less than 20 of the 400 editors were Jews. Statistics do not matter. Reasoned argument was, of course, notably absent from the anti-Semitic agitation, especially in that emanating from the extreme camp. A number of Catholic clergy identified with this extremist wing. In the eyes of Curate Roth, an early supporter of the Hitler movement, the Jews were a morally inferior race who should be eliminated from public life.

> If in the course of proceeding against the Jews as a race some good and harmless Jews, with whom immorality because of inheritance is latent, will have to suffer together with the guilty ones, this is not a violation of the

Christian love of one's neighbor as long as the Church recognizes also the moral justification of war, for example, where many more 'innocents' than 'guilty' have to suffer.[59]

Roth was allowed to wield his poisonous pen without ever being formally disciplined by the Church.

Similar views were propounded by Dr. Haeuser, whose book appeared in 1923 with the *Imprimatur* of the diocese of Regensburg. Haeuser called the Jews Germany's cross, a people disowned by God and under their own curse. They carried much of the blame for Germany having lost the war, and they had taken a dominant role in the revolution of 1918. The time had come to put them in their place, though Haeuser stressed that the Jews should be allowed to live as guests in Germany. Father Senn called even German Catholicism *verjudet* and termed the Hitler movement, despite certain exaggerations, "the last big opportunity to throw off the Jewish yoke." In the same vein, J.A. Köfler (1929) wanted to free Germany from the Judaised Jesuit Order.[60]

Other cliches appeared that also indicate the depth of anti-Semitism. Ziesche, for example, labeled Judaism a "rational" religion in opposition to Christianity with its reliance on mystery. Guardini wrote that a *Volk* is that segment of mankind currently existing with an essence, natural and living because of its unbroken roots into the past. Even Georg Schreiber, who certainly was not anti-Semitic, was impressed by the fact that political order and greatness as well as cultural potency stemmed from the *Volkstum*. And Alois Dempf asserted that the *Volk* was the living unity of blood (*Blut*) and fate (*Schicksal*) greater than the state. Theodor Haecker translated Hilaire Belloc's *The Jews* and highly recommended it in an article appearing in *Hochland,* a Jesuit periodical; and E. Przywara, S.J., praised Haecker's translation because it again opened the possibility of rational discussion of the *Judenfrage.*[61]

Karl Eschweiler, Michael Schmaus, and Joseph Lortz, all noted Catholic intellectuals, discussed the Church as a community alongside other communities rooted in nature and insisted that the German *Volk* could be traced back to *germanischer Quellen.* Naturally, given many peoples there was no worthless race. But just as the values of individuals can be different, so also the values of races can vary. Even this defense of Judaism carried an implied bias. J. Bernhart, for example, stressed that Jewish uniqueness was to be respected as was any other. The meaning is clear—Jews cannot be Germans. Karl Adam went even further in potentially uniting the Catholic Church and Nazism when he stressed that grace presupposes nature. Grace completes nature, i.e., the living and national *Volk.*[62] Of course, in this work Adam was justifying the support given to the Nazis after January

1933, but his work logically capped Catholic political analyses during the Weimar era.

The general aspect of the crisis in post-1918 Germany can be derived from the precipitous decline of liberalism, where it had been a class outlook instead of a national tradition expressing itself in national institutions. As a class creed, liberalism no longer had content or a program to meet the serious problems besetting German society. It was doomed to be swept away by a postwar integral nationalism that seemed able to confront and answer the demands for a new economic and social order. Within this political context, Hitler appeared to many differing German groups as a leader who could fulfill their wishes; he owed his success to the fact that he appealed to most segments of the population or, at least, did not alienate significant groups, even with his anti-Semitism.

Populist Nationalism and Anti-Semitism

Catholic anti-Semitism manifested itself in the popular culture as well as in theological discourses and episcopal pronouncements. The people of Deggendorf in Bavaria, for example, had long commemorated the miraculous emergence of "a lovely little child" from a consecrated wafer that allegedly had been "stolen and tortured" by the Jews of the town on September 30, 1337. On the same day, the chroniclers reported, the pious citizens of Deggendorf, acting "out of legitimate zeal pleasing to God," killed off all the Jews. "God grant," the inscription under a picture depicting the massacre and exhibited in one of the town's churches said, "that our fatherland be forever free from this hellish scum." In a play composed by a Benedictine and performed every year during the week-long celebrations, the Jews were called such names as "brood of Judas," "hordes of the devil," "poison mixers," etc. The historical accuracy of this tale of blasphemy and miraculous recovery had never been certified, but in view of the 100,000 guests that every year attended the commemoration exercises and the "wholesome" religious atmosphere created by them, the Church authorities saw little reason to be sticklers for historical truth. The effects of this perpetuation of the worst medieval anti-Jewish prejudices upon contemporary attitudes toward the Jews are not difficult to guess.[63]

Much of the Weimar anti-Semitism had its roots in the discontinuous sociopolitical continuum. As the occupants of the economic positions that seemed to threaten the non-Jewish middle class, Jews were the objects of considerable ill feeling. Because they had a different religious and cultural tradition, often bore distinguishable physical characteristics, and had been recently and only partially integrated into German society, they were natural "outsiders." Those Germans who needed membership in a special group excluded Jews. There are a number of indications that anti-Semitism was a popular bias among educated Catholics as well as the laity who might well not follow the thought-provoking articles in the Catholic press. Anti-Semitism in elements of the Catholic press was not abnormal. In general, the conservative and anti-Semitic Austrian journal *Schönere Zukunft* regularly carried articles that attributed social, economic, and political misfortunes or opposition to the Jewish community. Articles that were pro-*völkisch* and anti-Semitic were "normal."[64] Populistic anti-Semitism was also alive in the streets. In the beerhalls a popular folk-song in Munich rendered by the Platzl Folksingers gives ample testimony that anti-Semitism was acceptable to a broad spectrum of the populace:

> *Cohen and Sarah*
> *Are driving their car;*
> *Up front it stinks of garlic*
> *And at the back of gasoline.*[65]

Weiss Ferdl, a popular singer, proclaimed a very attractive message and confirmed the popular view of Jews as "outsiders." Occasionally, the folksinger even received requests from the audience that he provide some amusing lyrics on Jews.[66]

Catholics proved very susceptible to anti-Semitism in part because of their sensitivity to the "outsider" epithet. Bismarck had branded members of the Center *Reichsfeinde* (enemies of the Reich), lumping them together with Poles and Socialists. The most common term used in German Catholic historiography to characterize their own situation was "ghetto." Rallying and organizing the broad masses of the laity, *Verbandskatholizismus* (associations to create a cultural and social *Weltanschauung)* made use of liberal freedoms to create an anti-Semitic movement on a basis that was simultaneously populist and hierarchical—the masses of the excluded minority led by their natural leaders. The ghetto church remained, then, a church of the people. During the Weimar era the Catholic population was still concentrated in rural areas and underrepresented especially in the larger cities. Catholics worked in disproportionate numbers in farming and traditional handicrafts. They were underrepresented in banking, commerce, technical industry, and professional pursuits. In the Rhineland they worked in coal and steel industries, but these were owned by Protestants. Catholic craftsmen and retailers were economically marginal, employing little help and relying disproportionately on family members. Catholic miners and steelworkers adhered to their labor unions, had job and class interests in common with their socialist or communist colleagues, and suspected the reactionary nature of Hitler's movement. Catholic peasants appear to have specialized less than Protestant peasants, practicing a more traditionally mixed agriculture and so were less economically vulnerable than were other social groups.[67] The Catholic economic position and rural concentration apparently helped insulate them to a degree from direct Nazi incursions, but they probably were not repelled by Nazi anti-Semitism as such. A populistic anti-Semitism, based on the resentment of Jewish wealth, was to be found in some Catholic ranks, but was not a vital issue in the southern agrarian wing. The anti-Semitism might link up with anti-socialism or a general repudiation of modern culture, but it was not necessarily identical with political revolution or sympathy with the Nazis.[68] In fact, between 1928 and 1932, when the nationalist party lost 40 percent of its vote and the bourgeois parties 80 percent of theirs—presumably to the Nazis—the Catholic Center party, which drew about one-half of the votes of German Catholics, maintained throughout a proportion of the vote equal to about 15 percent of the total. This would seem to suggest a general stability among Catholics, including the youth, who supported the Center.[69] The antirepublican bias was there undermining Catholic resistance to Nazism and did introduce some Catholics into the NSDAP as the Abel materials so aptly document. The attitude toward Catholicism within the party is equally important for understanding Catholic responses to their situation in Weimar, since once again they were being labeled unpatriotic.

Some respondents saw Jews, socialists, and Catholics as the governing clique in Weimar Germany and said the flag (gold, red, black) reflected the true political situation. Respondent 44, a Protestant from a Rhenish village, became involved in *völkisch* groups. He joined the Nazis in 1928 "because all the other parties had ideologies invented by Jews and were subordinate to the 'supranational powers,'" meaning the Catholic Church, Bolshevism, and international finance. The ethnocentrics in the sample vent their spleen naturally on the Jews and liberals, but also on ultramontanism.[70] Clearly, then, many in the party distrusted Catholics and suspected a lack of patriotism, which might help to explain why the Catholic clergy was so patriotic and generally *völkisch* during the 1920s. On a less sophisticated level, a similar reaction can be observed among Catholics in the party who reflected the same proportion that existed in Germany as a whole. Catholics in the NSDAP tend to be anti-Semitic, superpatriots, and "solidarists" as if reacting against the attacks so frequently leveled against them. This dimension of practical solidarism is similar in spirit to the traditional Catholic social philosophy of Heinrich Pesch. The Jesuits saw this social theory as a means to heal society and bind the wounds. On a more popular level, all the social yearning for comradeship, for fraternal acceptance, and for community engendered by the social tensions of Imperial Germany and then the Republic, seemed to culminate in the call for the *Volksgemeinschaft*. The Nazi slogan *Gemeinnutz geht vor Eigennutz* (The common good is more important than self-interest) had an appeal to the right wing and could even appeal to Catholics convinced of the efficacy of practical or theoretical solidarism.[71] German youth, including Catholics, had been politicized in World War I and were also anxious to find a national political identity, which for many became possible in the NSDAP. The absence of the fathers and the changing role of the mothers, together with the visible collapse of many prewar social norms, may explain the new attitude of youth. To meet the welter of new ideas, Catholics in the NSDAP seemed to react by continuing their traditional support for antipluralists and authoritarians.[72]

Before 1933 the Church responded, of course, to local Catholics who joined the Nazis. Respondent 342 offers an intimate view of the allegiance issue and the dynamics that drove him into the party.

> I began to show my fighting spirit toward the outside. Having thrown aside the Marxist idea long ago, I thought and thought. I wanted in the future an equal right to a living. I did not like the "interest parties" but professed to be above parties. In 1928-1929 I read and heard about Adolf Hitler and his words went right to my marrow. Since the Catholic clergy always warned us against him, I thought at first that my conscience would not permit me to follow him. But the worsening economic situation once more threatened to ruin my laboriously built-up livelihood and I began to worry about the future of my four sons.

The Church pressured him not to join. When he finally joined, the Church withheld the sacraments from him notwithstanding an appeal to his bishop. He continues: "My spiritual struggle with the clergy tore wounds that are still bleeding today."[73]

A young man (born 1907) from Mühlheim on the Ruhr recounted how he had rung the Church bells when the German army had been victorious early in World War I. He remembered the defeat and revolution, in particular "the shame of seeing the red revolutionaries tear off officers' insignia before our eyes at school." He continues: "The Center party fought us hardest. The clergy refused our dead comrades a regular funeral and we were not allowed to enter the church in uniform although we National Socialists stand on Christian principles."[74] The young man was under stress and so was the institutional Church. The concern of both the bishops and theologians to remain in the mainstream of nationalism is clear. Even their nationalist statements did not seem to offer enough reinforcement to keep this young man in the fold. He was, however, an extremist. There is some personal documentary evidence indicating that a few were informed by the clergy that they could not belong to the Center and still be nationalists. Others saw the Center as soft on nationalism.

Respondent 466, for example, stated that he felt that the Center party was not nationalist enough and did not support a valid Christian *Weltanschauung*. The *Hakenkreuz* was seen by Respondent 281 to be the old germanic sign of the victory of good over evil. He also felt that one could only be German by possessing German blood. He naturally disagreed with Marxism, which preached the equality between Germans and French, Blacks and Jews. The NSDAP stood for the *Volk* and would fight against the class of estate owners. He added that all of the treason had begun with Erzberger. Respondent 492 asserted that the Jew was the *Unglück des Vaterlandes*. One Catholic Nazi (Respondent 232) contended that National Socialism embodied real Christianity. Perhaps Respondent 204 expressed the strands of hatred that the NSDAP could weave so effectively into the fabric of revolution. He stated: "I began to study the Jewish question after the murder of Rathenau in the early summer of 1922. I devoured written works and increasingly understood the connections between international Marxism and the Jewish problem, learned the underlying causes for the political, moral, and cultural collapse of my fatherland."[75] This respondent reflected the observation of at least some Catholic leaders. Such rightest Catholic politicians as Martin Spahn (1875-1945) attacked the Weimar constitution since it was, he insisted, created by the Berlin Jew Hugo Preuss using Western models. Such rightist comments could easily build bridges to Nazism by 1933. These politicians were supported directly by such theologians as the pastor A. Hecker in his book *Vor Judas Weltherrschaft?*, an attack against the Jews in the press and the economy and, of course, against their protectors, the liberals and socialists.[76]

These sentiments of Catholics who became Nazis must have unnerved the clergy, trying to guide their Church through the shoals of post-World War I Germany. Equally as upsetting were the statistics on Church commitment. Statistics on increasing mixed marriages and on Catholics converting suggest that Catholicism in general lacked respectability among the elite or managerial class. Generally, growing numbers of Catholics were making their individual union with the nation, ignoring the religious split and disregarding the teachings of Church and school. Catholic reactions to the Republic, however, were not uniform. For example, Catholic women did not share the revulsion of Protestants toward the Weimar settlement. There were benefits that had been obtained from democracy, which had brought women the vote, an active role in the economy, an opportunity to formulate public policy, and an escape from the cultural ghetto.[77] Even after the depression the journal *Frauenland* urged its readers to support the state and to take an active part in the elections of 1930.[78] In the Weimar Republic, Catholic gains in nationalistic respectability were bought at a price. As limited as they were, they provoked a hostile reaction, which centered around the Protestant League, Protestant Civil Servant Associations, and the Nationalist and German People's parties. Protestant officials found in Catholic gains yet another reason or pretext to drift away from the Republic.[79] Catholics were in a no-win situation. If they were not identified with the nation, then they were trapped in their "ghetto" and excluded from the mainstream. If they did integrate into the nation, then the opposing political elite groups lent less support to the Republic to show their anti-Catholicism.

On January 8, 1919, the bishops of the Cologne province warned the faithful of the leftist socialism and communism hostile to the Church. It must be recalled, of course, that the extensive Spartacus Revolution was mounting an offensive against the relatively moderate government. On February 13, 1919, Gröber urged the Center to support the republic for expediency; a democratic republic was the only political form available to rescue society from chaos—hardly committed support. Even the respected theologian Karl Muth could maintain his support of democratic theory, but not of the specific republic of the 1920s. The support for the political system developed of necessity but had no deep roots. A sizable segment of Catholics can probably be classified as *Vernunftrepublikaner,* and only the social integration provided Catholics through their Church may have kept them from voting for the Nazis.[80]

Thus, for the bishops to retain an influence among their followers, nationalism and anti-Semitism had to be highlighted, an easy task in view of the past reactions of Catholics to the political pressures associated with their integration into the Second Reich. The bishops tried to offer a nationalist position that would permit "normal" anti-Semitism, while constructing a defense against the radical Right. The theologians followed suit. The chief problem confronted by the laity is that the nuances were not all that clear and the bishops were not completely united. At a 1922 rally as seen already, Faulhaber condemned the November Revolution as perjury and high treason, and blamed Germany's distress on the Weimar Constitution. But the episcopacy took pains to indicate that it opposed the most extreme right-wing organizations as well. The Fulda Bishops Conference, composed of the Prussian bishops, warned Catholics in 1924 against membership in the paramilitary organizations and forbade participation by the clergy in these associations. The hierarchy likewise stood firm against other attempts of right-wing Catholics to assimilate themselves into the culture of German nationalism, refusing, for example, to lift the ban on dueling among university students. Indicative of the problem, Catholics increasingly spoke of adhering to the Catholic *Weltanschauung* (world view) rather than Catholic *Lehre* (doctrine), even their terminology reflecting their assimilation of national values. The reaction of the Catholic laity to Nazism suggests that village Catholics, for example, not only separated religion from politics, but could offer an enticing array of reasons in support for or opposition to the NSDAP. Rinderle has indicated that Nazism had a very heterogeneous appeal, but on practical, not ideological grounds. Some of the inhabitants of the village Rinderle studied supported the Nazis because they promised jobs and to raise prices for the farmers. The Nazis attacked the Weimar coalition for its string of economic blunders. Young persons were attracted by slogans of "community" and "commonweal before private gain." Also, apparently many thought the NSDAP would merely form another coalition and do something, viewing the Nazi party as just another political *tendenz*. In answering the question of how these villagers of Kirchheim came to know Nazism and its program, Rinderle suggests that most of these Catholic villagers received news of the NSDAP from the local Catholic *Anzeiger* that was answering Nazi charges. Thus, for the Nazis any publicity was good publicity. Pastors in the pulpit were the main opponents of the Nazis, and later *Sicherheitsdienst* reports indicate that this resistance also continued during the war years. In this particular Catholic village in the election of September 14, 1930, the Nazi vote jumped from 1 percent (1928) to 28 percent, although the Center still retained a good share. The pastor was ill and so this might explain the Nazi jump, but the attractions of the NSDAP could explain the vote shift of Catholics to Hitler's party. Catholics apparently left non-Center parties to vote NSDAP.[81] Catholics committed to the Center continued their support; the others drifted to the political Right.

The German bishops during these years spoke up against the Nazi glorification of race and blood, but they had practically nothing to say specifically about the widespread anti-Semitic propaganda, which could be construed as vulgar nationalism, and acts of violence. In 1932, Cardinal Schulte, in reply to a letter from a Jewish organization seeking help, expressed only his sympathy in the face of numerous acts of vandalism, especially the desecration of Jewish graves, which had occurred in Cologne.[82] A Church that justified moderate anti-Semitism and tried to answer the "Jewish question," merely objecting to extreme and immoral acts, was ill-prepared to provide an effective antidote to the Nazis' gospel of hate, especially as the depression worsened and the "Jew Republic" seemed impotent to end the suffering. Psychological research indicates that there is some evidence that a positive or negative experience with another person affects subsequent behavior toward that person. Also, peoples' behavior toward others can create their attitudes toward them. Describing people in negative terms enhances aggression against them. Finally, internalized moral codes do not necessarily lead to moral conduct, because "reprehensible" behavior can be made personally or socially acceptable by construing it in terms of high moral principle.[83] Anti-Semitism could be accepted by Christians proclaiming brotherly love. Catholic historical experiences could support such a seemingly contradictory reaction.

While countless anti-Semitic references can be uncovered in the pronouncements of bishops and theologians as well as in the materials generated from the laity, there were Catholics who opposed anti-Semitism, although even they often qualified their position. But their reaction itself tells us how virulent this stream of hatred was in the Republic. Already at the first Reichsparteitag (1920) the theologian Georg Schreiber attacked radical anti-Semitism. The leading Center newspapers *Germania* (Berlin) and the *Kölnische Volkszeitung* sought by the late 1920s to awaken sympathy for the insulted Jewish community. Here again, however, the newspapers succeeded in reinforcing an insider-outsider dichotomy that in the long run would prove disastrous. The *Bavarian Volkspartei* repudiated racial anti-Semitism, but also opposed the atheistic elements of international Judaism with its East European origins. International Judaism had been influential in assaulting the German economy during the war and had helped destroy the political structure of Germany at the end of the war.[84] Tolerance of this nature did not serve the Republic, since one could easily attach the German Jewish community to this international conspiracy.

A variety of theologians, however, did unequivocally attack Nazi anti-Semitism and would continue their critique into the Nazi era: Heinrich Kaupel, Friedrich Muckermann, S.J., W. Schmidt, Jakob Nötges, Hans Rost, and Anton Scharnagl.[85] Fritz Gerlich and Ingbert Naab in the weekly *Der gerade Weg* continued the fight against the Nazi party and ideology.[86] But these opponents did not answer the practical needs of the laity in this economic depression, nor could they mobilize the force that the Nazis did on behalf of national goals. They were "voices crying in the desert," but do remind us that there was "another" Church that saw the dangers in the NSDAP program even before 1933 and would not compromise, although Rost's periodic references, for example, to the *Judenfrage* or to Jewish business influences ultimately helped lend credence to the Nazi charges.

Catholics as Assimilated Germans

Some of the roots of the Church's failure to protest or act against the later National Socialist policy of extermination can be uncovered in the highly ambivalent attitude of the Church itself toward the Jews from the early days of Christianity up to the Third Reich.[87] Fearing political isolation, the Center and the clergy, both hierarchy and theologians, eventually supported Hitler's government as legitimate, although frequently opposing the

Nazi ideology. The trauma of having been branded *Reichsfeinde* continued its pernicious effects.[88] In a very real sense the German Catholics had established their scenario before World War I and were its captives in the Weimar era. The middle-class politicians of the post-Windthorstian Center had engaged in an "orgy of overassimilation" politically while maintaining the intellectual and social ghettoization of Catholicism out of habit, out of need for a retreat, and out of a desire to continue the *Kulturkampf*-era unity.[89] They sought full integration into the national *Volk* and simultaneously protection of a cultural *Weltanschauung* that opened them to charges of internationalism and ghettoism. The water was muddied and the issues not clearly drawn as the Church faced the opening stages of Hitler's chancellorship. Leaders in the Church and Center entered the fray, thinking in terms of tactics rather than principles.

The German Catholic bishops and theologians never taught their flocks to believe that National Socialism had to be repudiated for conscience's sake, even though the values of the political and cultural program were clear. The majority continued to hold to the idea that their national and theological loyalties could be reconciled. The excesses of the Nazis were regarded as incidental, or at worst inimical, to the true form of German patriotism, which the Church strove to uphold. Popular feeling against the Republic as well as the theological ambivalence with respect to the cutting issues were perhaps too much to overcome. The Catholic position can perhaps best be seen in the themes developed at two general meetings. The 69th general meeting of German Catholics at Münster, September 4-8, 1930, reflected on one theme suggesting the direction of Catholicism in this crucial year. The progressive de-Christianization of the era was analyzed in a very antimodern polemic within an anti-Semitic framework, and then in 1931 at a meeting of the same group in Nürnberg the theologian Georg Schreiber developed the theme that too much effort was being expended focusing on the *state;* concentration should be on the *nation.* In other works Schreiber had already repudiated National Socialism and its brand of virulent anti-Semitism, but had acknowledged the significance of the concepts of race and nation for any analysis of Weimar Germany.[90]

Catholics, then, appeared to advocate love, peace, and brotherhood as well as nationalistic racism—two contradictory, but not mutually exclusive, sets of values. Ideological development or accommodation does not follow the orderly process of abandoning one set of beliefs and replacing it with another. Rather, each set of beliefs develops within its own cognitive context—within a framework of what is realistically achievable as against a context of what is historically just—and each assumes its place alongside the other. Which set of beliefs predominates at any given moment or prevails over time depends very much on the options and opportunities available to the individual.[91] Both brotherly love and anti-Semitism had enjoyed a healthy, vigorous growth since the patristic Church. There was no reason to assume from 1870 until World War II that both patterns could not continue to flourish beside one another. Neither had ever been followed to its logical conclusion and so Nazism could not be seen in 1933 as an ultimate evil. In any attempt to attribute reasons for specific behavior, fundamental problems arise. There is a pervasive tendency for actors to attribute their actions to situational requirements, whereas observers tend to attribute the same actions to the stable personalities of the actors. In essence, however, a situation that evokes a response common to many persons can likely be seen as causing a behavior. When a person acts in a similar fashion on many different occasions, the act can be seen to reflect a personal disposition. Out of needs to impose structure on the environment, moreover, the actor as well as observer often make premature judgments on the nature of the entities observed. The values of nationalism, anti-Semitism, and antiliberalism were pervasive and shaped the reactions of the Catholic episcopate, clergy, and populace in the 1918-33 period. These values were also deeply rooted in the nineteenth century.[92]

Given the post-1918 psychological anomie, it was simpler to put one's faith in one man who would take care of everything than to assume a share of the responsibility for the agonizing choices to be made in daily political life. Those who agreed that one man was to lead and decide, while they would obey and follow, could not thereby escape the responsibility for his decisions; they simply accepted that responsibility in advance without realizing what they had done. A further factor of great significance was the general acceptance of racial ideology among the citizens of Germany. Although probably not ready to agree to all its horrible implications, vast numbers were prepared to accept its premises. It is significant that in a country where academic persons were high in prestige, the pseudoscience of racism had made very rapid inroads in the university community. Also, it is clear from all accounts of National Socialist gatherings that anti-Semitism was a popular part of Hitler's appeal to his audiences. If so many followed, it was in part that they were enthusiastic about the direction he wanted to take.[93]

By 1933 German Catholics resembled the National Liberals of 1866-70 who were willing to subordinate their liberalism to their national ideals. Catholics likewise found that they could accept the national revival while they delayed obtaining other sociopolitical goals. On the surface it would seem that the delay would be short as Concordat negotiations commenced, but as Naab so perceptively asked: How can unbelievers be trusted in any negotiations? Catholic leaders had repeatedly condemned pluralism in society and had seen advantages in a strong man as a substitute for constant parliamentary changes. Moreover, the anti-Semitism in Catholicism came from sources other than the Nazis, but should not on that account be undervalued. The bottom line of the Catholic response to the problems inherent in the Weimar Republic was to "baptize" elements of Hitler's *Weltanschauung* and form Catholics susceptible to the Nazi national and cultural program, even if not to the full-blown racism of the party. Hitler carefully camouflaged his intent both before and after 1933. He and his minions were supposedly not battling the Church, but rather political Catholicism. Because of the Bismarckian political system that supported the Empire and because of the chaotic milieu in which the Republic was introduced, Germans in general and Catholics in this case were unable to make coherent and insightful political judgments. On political issues the Nazi and Catholic leadership read from the same text, and so the opposition of Catholics focused on the cultural aspects of their respective *Weltanschauungen.* Catholics saw compromise possible with Hitler, even if not with some of his radical followers. Hitler reinforced this tendency, but in reality his opposition to religion was unconditional.[94] When the Catholic leaders began negotiating with Hitler in 1933 for a secure niche in his national program, they had already lost the ideological battle because their followers were committed to the traditional German value structure, and to maintain their leadership, they also had to conform.

It would be reasonable to conclude that the Nazis were skillful at developing and using a variety of issues that succeeded at gaining increasing popular support for the party. Nationalism, sometimes but not necessarily, coupled with anti-Semitism by the Nazi party hierarchy was generally well-received by the rank-and-file Nazis and accepted by a significant portion of the German populace, Catholics included. Even indifference toward anti-Semitic themes would encourage the Nazi leaders to continue their course after 1933, thus creating a vicious circle that could ultimately evolve into a behavioral rule as norm. Nationalistic anti-Semitism was not the result of one twisted mind, but was a prominent social attitude in Germany which was not combated effectively by Catholics before 1933 and Hitler's *Gleichschaltung.*

When a cultural norm is dominant, relatively uniform motives, values, or behavior may characterize the members of the culture. Psychologically, the more stereotypes a person assigns to a target group, the more these will be evaluative, intense, salient, and important, and so the greater their directing consistency. In a culture with a majority and a minority, a high level of prejudice is likely to exist. The ongoing denigration and dehumanization of the Jews can be regarded as a dominant aspect in the Weimar environment. Cultures may vary in the extent to which they emphasize the common humanity of all persons or devalue outsiders, even members of subcultures. Persons within a culture learn the behavior patterns that are accepted. In Germany, nationalism and various forms of anti-Semitism were reinforced and provided vehicles for sociopolitical integration or segregation. Racism and nationalism were dominant motifs in the Germany of the 1920s. Thus, Weimar Germans shaped their own environment and vice-versa. Their behavior determined one another's responses and the kind of interaction that resulted.[95]

In countless pastoral pronouncements before 1933, the bishops had condemned the erroneous doctrines of the National Socialist movement, had warned of its dangers, and forbidden active endorsement of the goals of the NSDAP and even mere membership in the party. But Catholic authorities were also united in a deeply rooted antiliberalism, rejected democracy and modern society, leaned toward authoritarian government, and supported an organic concept of public order. A fair selection of Catholic publicists seemed to agree with their bishops.[96] The Church's natural law orientation placed the politico-sociological foundation outside the concrete state as well as the existing society and in the Church. From this vantage point Catholics were to make decisions on their political conduct *within* the state with an emphasis on religion, the Church, and schools as the building blocks of good political order.[97] Because of this natural law orientation, given its modern form by Leo XIII, Catholics tended to think in terms of ecclesiastical-cultural and not political goals. Normative force was seen as rooted in natural law principles, separated from historical forms and systems, which are viewed as "mere reality." Such a declaration of neutrality regarding political forms, first precisely argued by Leo XIII, demanded total dedication only to that which was directly demanded by the principles of natural law.[98]

The earlier *Kulturkampf* situation and the ahistorical natural law doctrine of the state were attached to a deeply rooted antiliberalism which has characterized Catholic thought since the nineteenth-century reaction against the Enlightenment and the individualistic political systems which it spawned.[99] By 1933 in wide Catholic circles an ideological bias and detachment from reality had caused many to accept the popular National Socialist movement as a means for battling liberalism and for promoting a Christian order that would realize natural law. Full acceptance would grow as Hitler stressed his religious and nonthreatening goals after January 30, 1933.

Franklin Littell has asserted that in theological terms, Nazism was the true—if illegitimate—offspring of a false relationship between the Christian Church and the ethnic bloc or nation (*Volk*). When such ethnic history was infused with "spirituality," and a political program was mounted on disciplined cadres to lead a people to past values, a frontal challenge to the true Church—on pilgrimage and supranational—was thrown down. In light of its post-1870 formation, it was not surprising that the Catholic Church failed to meet the challenge of the 1933 Nazi "legal revolution."[100] Its accommodating behavior in the Third Reich politically, however, is not as surprising as its complete betrayal of presumably accepted Christian values. Catholics had accepted or were indifferent to the crucial axioms of the Nazi *Weltanschauung*—Nationalism and anti-Semitism.

There is a determining relationship between man's conception of the world and the way he behaves. This *Weltanschauung* involves the individual's conception of the universe, others' activities in the world, and the relationship between individuals in this world. Such a world view also includes philosophical and religious beliefs and the necessary prescriptive demands of social interaction modes, i.e., acceptable behavioral responses. This *Weltanschauung* helps determine complex social interactions. Staats suggests that what frequently is labeled the "world view" can also be seen as a constellation of behavior—especially language behaviors—of great complexity. The individual usually acquires in the course of his learning history very complex systems of behaviors cemented by language, which can be applied to the situations faced and to the actions taken in response to the social, economic, cultural, and political environment. Through his learning experiences, the individual acquires very complex forms of thought (language), which may be imbued with emotional value and are associated with specific behaviors. Such language and emotional systems can affect the way the individual behaves toward others in a variety of situations. This type of system can also help determine an individual's decisions with respect to such activities as the support of a political system or voting for a politician. Human cognitive characteristics are derived from repertoires of behaviors that the individual has learned. Previously learned complex patterns are the reason the individual can learn readily as well as reason, think, and plan. Language repertoires involve personality patterns, and so there will probably be variations in the responses among persons who may well have lived through the same experiences. Nevertheless, certain commonalities will most likely be present and cause responses to the socio-economic and political stimuli to differ only by degree. Language is both intrapersonal and interpersonal. Hence, a person's own patterns of behavioral response can be reinforced as he deals with others.[101]

The anti-Semitic responses of Catholics to a hostile world had an extensive history in modern Germany. Designated as second-class citizens, Catholics after 1871 frequently reacted to attacks in a supernationalistic fashion. Although the Center had an enthusiastic, pro-republican faction, the leadership, especially after 1929, veered sharply to the Right. Moreover, during the Weimar years Catholics increasingly voiced adherence to a Catholic *Weltanschauung*. Even their terminology reflected the acceptance of national norms. Branded *Reichsfeinde* by Bismarck, Catholics wanted acceptance as Germans. Minority consciousness or a desire to be in the mainstream of the nation did not interfere with the Center's political cooperation with democratic parties during the normal years of the Weimar era, but as the depression precipitated political crises, the Center reacted to the initiatives of others and ceased positive activity. Clerical leaders, bishops, and theologians exhibited anti-Semitic, *völkisch* patterns of thought. Their intellectual ruminations reflect their adherence to the *Volk* as the conceptual norm organizing their political behavior and politico-theological philosophy. In this German context, *völkisch* can be seen as a racist populism, a brew in which is mixed anti-Semitism, intolerant nationalism, and, for some, the rejection of modernity. Catholics may not have gulped the brew, but they were sipping as Hitler became chancellor.

Notes

1. The *Kulturkampf* was firmly located within a field of socioeconomic contradictions, which pitted the liberals against a growing constellation of conservative interests that found its natural articulation in a newly politicized Catholicism, which would become increasingly influential until 1933. Thus a narrow, i.e., merely political interpretation of the *Kulturkampf* era is no longer tenable. See Gert Zang (ed.), *Provinzialisierung einer Region. Regionale Unterentwicklung und liberale Politik in der Stadt und im Kreis Konstanz im 19. Jahrhundert Untersuchungen zur Entstehung der bürgerlichen Gesellschaft in der Provinz* (Frankfurt: Syndikat, 1978); Gerhart Binder, *Irrtum und Widerstand. Die deutschen Katholiken in der Auseinandersetzung mit dem Nationalsozialismus* (Munich: Verlag Pfeiffer, 1968), p. 216; Ludwig Volk, *Der Bayerische Episkopat und der Nationalsozialismus, 1930-1934*, 2nd ed. (Mainz: Matthias Grünewald, 1966), p. 1.
2. Ludwig Volk, "Adolf Kardinal Bertram (1859-1945)," in Rudolf Morsey (ed.), *Zeitgeschichte in Lebensbildern* (Mainz: Matthias Grünewald, 1973), pp. 275-276; Volk, *Episkopat*, pp. 1-2. For an excellent recent study of Bertram, using the Bertram papers from the Archdiocesan archives in Wroclaw (Breslau), Poland, see Richard Rolfs, "The Role of Adolf Cardinal Bertram, Chairman of the Fulda Bishops Conference, in the Church's Struggle in the Third Reich: 1933-1938," Ph.D. diss., University of California, Santa Barbara, 1976.
3. K. Speckner, *Die Wächter der Kirche* (Munich: K. Kösel and F. Pustet, 1934), p. 23; Volk, "Stellung," p. 177. For Faulhaber's speech at the Katholikentag in 1922, see Binder, p. 219. For examples of Catholic nationalism that made the Concordat with Hitler possible, see *Rhein-Mainische Volkszeitung*, 1930-1933; Hans Müller, *Katholische Kirche und Nationalsozialismus. Dokumente, 1930-35* (Munich: Nymphenburger Verlagshandlung, 1963), pp. 5-12. For an example of pastoral advice focusing on the rising Nazi threat, see

"Nationalsozialismus and Seelsorge, Pastorale Anweisungen für den Klerus bestimmt" (1931), in Müller, *Katholische Kirche*, pp. 21-23.

4. Erzberger, for example, was hated because he swung the Center from opposition to advocacy of international conciliation in foreign policy and democratic development in domestic policy. See Klaus Epstein, *Matthias Erzberger and the Dilemma of German Democracy* (Princeton: Princeton University Press, 1959); Volk, *Episkopat*, pp. 5-7, see especially Faulhaber's sermon on November 5, 1921 in honor of the former king and queen of Bavaria.

5. By 1939, however, even Faulhaber was willing to accept Hitler's apparent desire for the separation of Church and state. See Pierre Blet et al., *Lettres de Pie XII aux eveques allemands 1939-1944* (Vatican City: Libreria Editrice Vaticana, 1966), p. 395ff.

6. Volk, "Stellung," pp. 178-180.

7. Mary Alice Gallin, "The Cardinal and the State: Faulhaber and the Third Reich," *Journal of Church and State* 12 (1970):385. The Faulhaber papers and Munich diocesan archives have been used by Ludwig Volk in his work *Bayerische Episkopat* (1965); useful for understanding Faulhaber and his colleagues are the *Amtsblatt für die Erzdiocese München und Freising*, 1931 ff. for the pastoral letters and sermons; *Münchener Katholische Kirchenzeitung*, July 31, 1932, p. 332; Karl Bachem, *Vorgeschichte, Geschichte und Politik der Deutschen Zentrumspartei* (Cologne: J.P. Bachem, 1931), 7:362.

8. Walter Adolph, *Hirtenamt und Hitler-Diktatur*, 2nd ed. (Berlin: Morus Verlag, 1965), pp. 17, 31-32; Ethel Mary Tinnemann, "Attitudes of the German Catholic Hierarchy Toward the Nazi Regime: A Study in German Psycho-Political Culture," *Western Political Quarterly* 22 (1969):334.

9. For Catholics, the French Revolution epitomized a variety of evils, e.g., subjectivism and democracy, to nineteenth-century scholastic theologians and seems to have carried over into the twentieth as well. See Joseph Fitzer, "J.S. Drey and the Search for a Catholic Philosophy of Religion," *Journal of Religion* 63 (1983):244-246; Lewy, pp. 271-274; Karl Dietrich Bracher, *Die Auflösung der Weimarer Republik*, 3rd ed. (Villingen: Ring Verlag, 1960), p. 91.

10. *Der Rütlischwur* 1 (1924), p. 4; in Weimar Germany, the word *Volk* is nearly synonymous with racism and nationalism; J. Roth, *Katholizismus und Judenfrage* (Munich: Eher Verlag, 1923).

11. Michael Faulhaber, *Deutsches Ehrgefühl und katholisches Gewissen* (Munich: Pfiffer Verlag, 1925), pp. 13, 38-39; Binder, p. 220.

12. Faulhaber, *Ehrgefühl*, pp. 40-41.

13. Walther Hofer (ed.), *Der Nationalsozialismus: Dokumente 1933-1945* (Frankfurt: Fischer-Bücherei, 1957), pp. 28-31.

14. John Conway, *The Nazi Persecution of the Churches*, pp. 3-4; Bracher, *Auflösung*, pp. 648-656; Alfred Rosenberg, *Der Mythus des 20. Jahrhunderts* (Munich: Hoheneichenverlag, 1934), p. 603; Müller, *Kirche*, p. 7; Tinnemann, p. 334; Johann Neuhäusler, *Kreuz und Hakenkreuz; Der Kampf des Nationalsozialismus gegen die katholische Kirche und der kirchliche Widerstand* (Munich: Katholische Kirche Bayerns, 1946), 2 parts; the works of both Müller and Neuhäusler are not fully reliable or correct and so must be read with care; crucial texts should be confirmed from other sources such as those of the Bavarian Commission; Faulhaber, *Ehrgefühl*, pp. 13, 19.

15. David Ried, "The Official Attitude of the Roman Catholic Hierarchy in Ger-

many toward National Socialism, 1933-1945," Ph.D. diss., State University of Iowa, 1957, pp. 26-27; N.C.W.C., *News Bulletin*, November 4, 1929.

16. Alfons Wild, *Nationalsozialismus und Religion: Kann Ein Katholik Nationalsozialist sein* (Augsburg: Haas und Grabherr, 1930), pp. 10-11.

17. Buchberger to Faulhaber, December 9, 1930 (Nachlass Faulhaber).

18. Jakob Nötges, S.J., *Nationalsozialismus und Katholizismus* (Cologne: J.P. Bachem, 1931), pp. 107-108; *Ecclesiastica: Archiv für zeitgenössische Kirchengeschichte* 11 (1931):138. See Paul Schnitzer, "Die katholische Kirche und der Nationalsozialismus bis 1933" (unpub. *Staatsexamenarbeit*, University of Frankfurt, 1960) for a discussion of Bertram's letter of December 2, 1930 and the response of the German bishops.

19. Adolf Bertram, *Die Stellung der katholischen Kirche zu Radikalismus und Nationalismus: Ein offenes Wort in erster Stunde am Jahresschlusse 1930* (Breslau: G.P. Aderholz, 1930), pp. 7-8.

20. James Donohoe, *Hitler's Conservative Opponents in Bavaria, 1930-1945: A Study of Catholic, Monarchist, and Separatist Anti-Nazi Activities* (Leiden: E.J. Brill, 1961), pp 29-30. Some Catholics were initially favorably impressed by the NSDAP; see Alois Natterer, *Der Bayerische Klerus in der Zeit dreier Revolutionen: 1918, 1933, 1945*, 3rd ed. (Munich: Verlag der Kath. Kirche Bayerns, 1946), pp. 240ff. The most famous Catholic apologia for National Socialism was written by an Austrian bishop, resident in Rome, cf. Alois Hudal, *Die Grundlagen des Nationalsozialismus: Eine ideengeschichte Untersuchung* (Leipzig: Johannes Günther Verlag, 1937).

21. Bertram in Müller, *Katholische Kirche*, p. 17; Rolfs pp. 28ff.

22. N.C.W.C., *News Bulletin*, March 30, 1931.

23. Ibid.

24. Bernhard Stasiewski, *Akten Deutscher Bischöfe über die Lage der Kirche 1933-1945* (Mainz: Matthias Grünewald, 1968), 1:viii. Official documents do not usually show the process of opinion formation which is why the work of the Bavarian Commission is so useful.

25. Volk, *Episkopat*, p. 35; pastoral letter of the Bavarian bishops, *Amtsblatt*, no. 4, February 10, 1931.

26. Lewy, p. 10; *Ecclesiastica* 11 (1931):117ff; Adolph, *Hirtenamt*, pp. 21, 25, 33, 36, 43; Tinnemann, pp. 335-336.

27. Wilhelm Corsten (ed.), *Kölner Aktenstücke zur Lage der Katholischen Kirche in Deutschland 1933-1945* (Cologne: J.P. Bachem, 1949), p. 1; Müller, *Kirche*, p. 30.

28. Diocesan Archive Aachen, folder "Fuldaer Konferenz 1931."

29. Ibid.; Stasiewski, *Akten*, docs. 11, 12, 13, 14, 15, pp. 814-843; Müller, *Kirche*, pp. 49-58; Armin Roth, *Nationalsozialismus und Katholische Kirche* (Munich: Ludendorff Volkswarte-Verlag, 1931).

30. Johannes Stark, *Nationalsozialismus und Katholische Kirche I* (Munich: Eher, 1931), p. 50; Johannes Stark, *Nationalsozialismus und Katholische Kirche II. Teil: Antwort auf Kundgebungen der deutschen Bischöfe* (Munich: Eher, 1931), p. 4.

31. Lewy, p. 15; Müller, *Kirche*, pp. 31, 36; Corsten, p. 2.

32. Erhard Schlund, O.F.M., "Religion, Christentum, Kirche und Nationalsozialismus," *Gelbe Hefte* 9 (1931): 115; Friedrich Muckermann, S.J., "Die positive Überwindung des Nationalsozialismus," *Der Gral* 26 (1932): 269; Nötges, p. 210.

33. Graf Clemens von Galen, *Die Pest des Laizismus* (Münster: Aschendorff, 1932), pp. 40-56; Heinrich Lutz, *Demokratie im Zwielicht: Der Weg der deutschen Katholiken aus dem Kaiserreich in die Republik, 1914-1925* (Munich: Kösel-Verlag, 1963), p. 82; Binder, pp. 219-222; Ernst Wolfgang Böckenförde, "Der deutsche Katholizismus im Jahre 1933: Eine kritische Betrachtung," *Hochland* 53 (1961): 233; Tinnemann, pp. 333-336. For an analysis of the reasons why liberal democracy never took root in pre-1945 Germany, see Rolf Dahrendorf, *Society and Democracy in Germany* (Garden City, NY: Doubleday, 1967); Conway, *Persecution*, p. 9

34. Volk, *Episkopat*, p. 45.

35. *Ibid.*, p. 43; *Amtsblatt München*, 1932, pp. 166ff; Ernst Deuerlein, *Der Deutsche Katholizismus 1933* (Osnabrück: A. Fromm, 1963), p. 78.

36. Volk, *Episkopat*, p. 37; Conway, *Persecution*, 331; Johnpeter Horst Grill, *The Nazi Movement in Baden, 1920-1945* (Chapel Hill: University of North Carolina Press, 1983, p. 239; Michael Kater, *The Nazi Party: A Social Profile of Members and Leaders, 1919-1945* (Cambridge: Harvard University Press, 1983), p. 59.

37. Uriel Tal, *Religious and Anti-Religious Roots of Modern Anti-Semitism* (New York: Leo Baeck Institute, Inc., 1971). The Christian and theological roots of anti-Semitism have been traced in a variety of works; see Ruether, *Faith and Fratricide: The Theological Roots of Anti-Semitism*; Charlotte Klein, *Anti-Judaism in Christian Theology* (Philadelphia: Fortress Press, 1978); Jeremy Cohen, *The Friars and the Jews: The Evolution of Medieval Anti-Judaism* (Ithaca: Cornell University Press, 1983). For a controversial and opinionated analysis of Christianity as the source of the Holocaust, see Rubenstein, *The Cunning of History: The Holocaust and the American Future*.

38. Conway, *Persecution*, pp. 203-205; James Hunt, "Between the Ghetto and the Nation: Catholics in the Weimar Republic," in Michael Dobkowski and Isidor Wallimann (eds.), *Towards the Holocaust: The Social and Economic Collapse of the Weimar Republic*, (Westport, CT: Greenwood Press, 1983), pp. 213-226.

39. Dahrendorf, pp. 13ff; Elizabeth Simpson, "Preference and Politics: Values in Political Psychology and Political Learning," in Stanley Allen Renshon (ed.), *Handbook of Political Socialization: Theory and Research* (New York: Free Press, 1977): 379-380; M. Rokeach, "Long Range Experimental Modification of Values, Attitudes, and Behavior," *American Psychologist* 26 (1971):453-459; Y. Rim, "Values and Attitudes," *Personality: An International Journal* 1 (1970):243-250; R. Christie and R.K. Merton, "Procedures for the Sociological Study of the Value Climate of Medical Schools," *Journal of Medical Education* 18 (1958):125-153; S. Budner, "Intolerance of Ambiguity as a Personality Variable," *Journal of Personality* 30 (1962):29-50; Gill, p. 7; Berger, *The Social Reality of Religion*, pp. 182-183.

40. G. van Norden, *Kirche in der Krise* (Düsseldorf: Pressenerband der Evangelischen Kirche im Rheinland, 1963), p. 181.

41. E. P. Hollander, *Leadership Dynamics: A Practical Guide to Effective Relationships* (New York: Free Press, 1978); Robert Gill, "From Sociology to Theology," in David Martin (ed.), *Sociology and Theology: Alliance and Conflict* (New York: St. Martin's Press, 1980), p. 105; Gregory Baum, "The Sociology of Roman Catholic Theology," in Martin, p. 128.

42. The classic treatment of this theory is Seymour Martin Lipset, *Political Man*, (Baltimore: Johns Hopkins University Press, 1981), chap. 5. Among recent

scholars, see Richard Levy, *The Downfall of the Anti-Semitic Liberal Parties in Imperial Germany* (New Haven: Yale University Press, 1975) and Timothy Tilten, *Nazism, Neo-Nazism and the Peasantry* (Bloomington: Indiana University Press, 1975).

43. Hans Rost, for example, identified Jewishness with socialism and the corrupting influences of modern society, but was simultaneously a zealous opponent of the Nazis; Rost, *Gedanken und Wahrheiten zur Judenfrage*; Hans Rost, *Katholiken Familienkultur* (Augsburg: Haas und Grabherr, 1926); Hans Rost, *Erinnerungen aus dem Leben eines beinahe glücklichen Menschen* (Westheim, 1962).

44. Rost, *Gedanken*, p. 89; Anton Neher, *Die wirtschaftliche und soziale Lage der Katholiken im westlichen Deutschland* (Rottweil: Druck und Verlag des Emmanuel, 1927), pp. 22-31, 100-113.

45. Klaus Breuning, *Die Vision des Reiches. Deutscher Katholizismus zwischen Demokratie und Diktatur 1919-1934* (Munich: Max Hueber Verlag, 1969), pp. 298-299; Erich Przywara, S.J., *Analogia Entis, Metaphysik* (Munich: Kösel u. Pustet, 1932), p. 126; Erich Przywara, *Logos, Abendland, Reich, Commercium* (Düsseldorf: Patmos Verlag, 1964), p. 106.

46. Erich Przywara, S.J., "Judentum und Christentum," *Stimmen der Zeit* 110 (1926):83, 98-99.

47. Erhard Schlund, O.F.M., *Katholizismus und Vaterland* (Munich: F.A. Pfeiffer, 1923), pp. 32-33.

48. *Bayerische Kurier*, May 21, 1923; Erhard Schlung, "Religion, Christentum, Kirche und Nationalsozialismus," *Gelbe Heft* 8 (1931):124-141.

49. Schlund, "Religion," pp. 115-121.

50. Gustav Gundlach, S.J., "Antisemitismus," *Lexikon für Theologie und Kirche*, 2nd rev. ed. (Freiburg: Herder, 1930), 1:504. After the downfall of Nazism, the new edition of this work has replaced Gundlach's piece with an article that condemns Nazism.

51. For a comprehensive analysis Gundlach's sociopolitical philosophy, see Johannes Schwarte, *Gustav Gundlach, S.J. (1882-1963). Massgeblicher Repräsentant der katholischen Soziallehre während der Pontifikate Pius XI und Pius XII* (Munich: Schöningh, 1975), pp. 27-31, 43ff; K. Sontheimer, *Antidemokratisches Denken in der Weimarer Republik. Die politischen Ideen des deutschen Nationalismus zwischen 1918-1933* (Munich: Nymphenburger Verlagshandlung, 1968); Breuning, *Vision des Reiches*; K. Breuning, *Der Weg in die Diktatur 1918 bis 1933. Zehn Beiträge* (Munich: Nymphenburger Verlagshandlung, 1962); Gustav Gundlach, "Klasse," in *Staatslexikon der Görres Gesellschaft*, 5th ed. (Freiburg: Herder, 1929), 3:394-399.

52. Gustav Gundlach, *Zur Soziologie der Katholischen Ideenwelt und des Jesuitenordens* (Freiburg: Herder, 1927), pp. 38-39, 48, 50.

53. Ibid., pp. 72-73.

54. Ibid., p. 74.

55. Edgar Alexander, "Church and Society in Germany," in Moody, pp. 519-526.

56. Alexander in Moody, pp. 545-546.

57. Gustav Gundlach, S.J., "Fragen um die berufsständische Ordnung," *Stimmen der Zeit* 125 (1933):218, 220, 225.

58. Rudolf Lill, "Die deutschen Katholiken und die Juden in der Zeit von 1850 bis zur Machtübernahme Hitlers," in Rengstorf und von Kortzfleisch (eds.), 2:380, 386, 392, 394-395; Karl Thieme, "Deutsche Katholiken," in Mosse, *Entscheidungsjahr*, pp. 272, 279.

59. Harry Pross (ed.), *Die Zerstörung der deutschen Politik* (Frankfurt: Fischer Bücherei, 1959), p. 242; Roth, *Katholizismus und Judenfrage*, p. 5; Lill in Rengstorf, p. 403; H. Heiber, *Walter Frank und sein Reichsinstitut für die Geschichte des neuen Deutschland* (Stuttgart: Deutsche Verlags Anstalt, 1966), pp. 374ff, 623.

60. Philipp Häuser, *Jud und Christ oder Wem gehört die Weltherrschaft?* (Regensburg: G.J. Manz, 1923), pp. 12, 15, 17, 19, 21, 36ff; Philipp Häuser, *Pazifismus und Christentum* (Augsburg: Aschendorff, 1925); Philipp Häuser, *Wir deutsche Katholiken und die moderne revolutionäre Bewegung* (Regensburg: G.J. Manz, 1921). A good response to Häuser's 1921 book is C. Walterbach's *Katholiken und Revolution: Eine Verteidigung gegenüber den Angriffen auf die Führer der deutschen Katholiken* (Berlin: E. Schmidt, 1922); Thieme in Mosse, *Entscheidungsjahr*, p. 283; Wilhelm Maria Senn, *Katholizismus und Nationalsozialismus* (Münster: Abwehr-Verlag, 1931), p. 80.

61. For a thorough study of the relationship between Catholic theology and anti-Semitism, see Greive, pp. 43, 107; K. Zeische, *Das Königtum Christi in Europe* (Regensburg: G.J. Manz, 1926), p. 3; G. Schreiber, *Auslandsdeutschtum und Katholizismus* (Münster: Aschendorff, 1927), p. 18; A. Dempf, "Individualistische und universalistische Staatsauffassung," in G.J. Ebers (ed.), *Katholische Staatslehre und Volksdeutsche Politik* (Freiburg: Herder, 1929), p. 6; Theodor Haecker, "Zur europäischen Judenfrage," *Hochland* 24 (1926/27):607ff.

62. K. Eschweiler, "Die Kirche im neuen Reich," *Deutsches Volkstum* 15 (1933):454; M. Schmaus, *Begegnungen zwischen katholischem Christentum und nationalsozialistischer Weltanschauung* (Münster: Verlag der Aschendorffschen Verlagsbuchhandlung, 1934), p. 23; J. Lortz, *Katholischer Zugang zum Nationalsozialismus*, 2nd ed. (Münster: Verlag der Aschendorffschen Verlagsbuchhandlung, 1934), p. 12; J. Peitzmeier, "Vom Sinn der Rasse," *Theologie und Glaube* 26 (1934):413; J. Bernhart, "Um das Alte Testament," *Hochland* 32 (1934/35):101; K. Adam, "Deutsches Volkstum und katholisches Christentum," *Theologische Quartalschrift* 114 (1933):40ff.

63. Lewy, p. 273. In 1960, Franz Rödel, a retired Catholic priest and organizer of the *Katholisch-Judaeologischen Institut* (Jetzendorf/Ilm), unsuccessfully appealed to the Bavarian Bishops Conference to abolish the commemoration exercises at Deggendorf and to remove the offensive artifacts. He exposed the historical inaccuracies, but achieved no results until *Der Spiegel* publicized the story. Church authorities have now changed the ceremony into an annual call for forgiveness for the wrongs done to the Jews.

64. Robert Sackett, *Popular Entertainment, Class and Politics in Munich, 1900-1923* (Cambridge, MA: Harvard University Press, 1982), p. 6. A good example of "normal" Catholic anti-Semitism may be found in Richard V. Schankol, "Studentenrecht und Judenfrage," *Schönere Zukunft* (December 27, 1931): 303-304; Joseph Eberle, *Zum Kampf um Hitler. Ein Reformprogram für Staats-, Wirtschafts-und Kulturpolitik zur Überwindung des Radikalismus* (Vienna: Verlag Schönere Zukunft, 1931); Deuerlein, *Der deutsch Katholizismus 1933*, p. 47.

65. Sackett, p. 56.

66. Ibid., p. 145.

67. Hunt in Dobkowski; Rost, *Die Parität und die deutschen Katholiken*, pp. 32-33; *Statistik des deutschen Reiches*, Neue Folge, vol. 203, pp. 54-75 (census

returns from 1907); Rost, *Wirtschaftliche und Kulturelle Lage*; Traute Nellessen-Schumacher, *Sozialstruktur und Ausbildung der deutschen Katholiken* (Weinheim: Beltz, 1969); Nellessen-Schumacher, *Sozialprofil der deutschen Katholiken*; Günter Golde, *Catholics and Protestants: Agricultural Modernization in Two German Villages* (New York: Academic Press, 1975); Helmut Hahn, *Der Einfluss der Konfessionen auf die Bevölkerungs-und Sozialgeographie des Hunsrück* (Bonn: Geographischen Instituts der Universität, 1950).

68. For an anti-Semitic opponent of the Nazis, see Rost, *Katholische Familienkultur*. For an anti-Semitic supporter of the Weimar Republic, who contended that the government had ended Catholic oppression and made possible the social improvement of the Catholic proletariat, see Neher, pp. 22, 31, 100-113.

69. Seymour Martin Lipset, *Political Man* (Garden City, NY: Doubleday, 1963), pp. 138-139, 145. Along these general lines Lawrence Walker has offered a succinct, but penetrating, criticism of Peter Loewenberg's article, "Psychohistorical Origins"; see Lawrence Walker, "The Nazi 'Youth Cohort': The Missing Variable," *Psychohistory Review* 9 (1980):71-83; Rainer Hambrecht, *Der Aufstieg der NSDAP in Mittel und Oberfranken 1925-1933* (Nürnberg: Stadtarchiv, Korn u. Berg, 1976), pp. 284-292. In general, Protestants seemed to have had a greater affinity for National Socialism; see Loren K. Waldman, "Models of Mass Movements: The Case of the Nazis," Ph.D. diss., University of Chicago, 1978, p. 78.

70. Merkl, *Political Violence*, pp. 55, 90, 341, 364; roughly 28 percent of the anti-Semitic Abel respondents were Catholic; 33 percent of Germany was Catholic. Sarah Ann Gordon, "German Opposition to Nazi Anti-Semitic Measures between 1933 and 1945, with Particular Reference to the Rhine-Ruhr Area," Ph.D. diss., SUNY-Buffalo, 1979, p. 420; Theodore Abel, *The Nazi Movement: Why Hitler Came to Power* (New York: Atherton Press, 1965), p. 164; 60 percent of the autobiographies make no mention of anti-Semitism and 4 percent actually disapproved of anti-Semitism.

71. Merkl, *Political Violence*, pp. 96-97, 687.

72. Ibid., pp. 235, 491.

73. Ibid., p. 89.

74. Ibid., pp. 259-260.

75. Abel Collection, Hoover Library, Stanford, Respondents 281, 492, 232, 204; even some members of the Center had a blind rage toward Erzberger's leftist orientation and had even questioned the sincerity of his Catholicism; see K. Epstein, pp. 371-394.

76. M. Spahn, "Das deutsche Zentrum und die Wahlen," *Das Neue Reich* (May 9, 1920): 512; A. Hecker, *Vor Judas Weltherrschaft?* (Achern: Unitas, 1921), pp. 26, 31ff.

77. Hunt in Dobkowski; Helmreich, pp. 98-99. A succinct summary of Catholic reservations centering on the republic can be found in Plum, pp. 152-165.

78. *Frauenland*, 1930, p. 226.

79. Dr. Geerbig, *Die Parität an den öffentlichen höhere Schulen der Rheinprovinz im Schuljahr 1928* (Birkenfeld: Volk u. Wissen, 1928); Fritz von der Heydt, *Die Parität bei der Anstellung der Beamten* (Berlin: Säemann-Verlag, 1931).

80. Ernst Deuerlein, "Zur Vergegenwärtigung der Lage des deutschen Katholizismus 1933," *Stimmen der Zeit* 168 (1961):11, 13; K. Muth, "Res Pub-

lica 1926. Gedanken zur politischen Krise der Gegenwart," *Hochland* 24 (1926/27): 1ff; Corsten, p. 1; Waldman, pp. 75, 77. Waldman maintains that religion can have an effect on voting behavior, but it is only one variable.

81. Lewy, pp. 8-15; Walter J. Rinderle, "Struggle for Tradition: One German Village in a Radical Era, 1929-1936," Ph.D. diss., Notre Dame University, 1977, pp. 80-88. A good solid analysis of the role of the SD in the Third Reich as well as a sound edited collection of materials on SD activities and the churches may be found in Boberach, *Berichte.*

82. Lill in Rengstorf, p. 406; Faulhaber, *Deutsches Ehrgefühl*, p. 19; "Der Erzbischof von Köln für den inneren Frieden," *Münchener Katholische Kirchenzeitung* (April 10, 1932), p. 170.

83. Staub, 1:154, 318-319; K. Kelley and D. Bryne, "Attraction and Altruism: With a Little Help from my Friends," *Journal of Research in Personality* 10 (1976):59-68; A. Bandura et al., "Disinhibition of Aggression through Diffusion of Responsibility and Dehumanization of Victims," *Journal of Research in Personality* 9 (1975):253-269; Bandura, *Aggression: A Social Learning Analysis.*

84. Rudolf Morsey, *Die deutsche Zentrumspartei* (Düsseldorf: Droste, 1966).

85. H. Kaupel, *Die antisemitische Bekämpfung des Alten Testaments, vom Standpunkt katholischer Bibelbetrachtung beleuchtet* (Münster: Aschendorff, 1933); Muckermann, *Der deutsche Weg*; W. Schmidt, *Die Stellung der Religion zu Rasse und Volk* (Augsburg: Haas und Grabherr, 1932); Nötges, *Nationalsozialismus und Katholizismus*; H. Rost, *Christus, nicht Hitler* (Augsburg: Haas und Grabherr, 1932); Anton Scharnagl, *Die völkische Weltanschauung und wir Katholiken* (Munich: Graphische Kunstanstalt, 1932).

86. Lill in Rengstorf, p. 410.

87. David Winston, "Pagan and Early Christian Anti-Semitism," in Friedlander and Milton, pp. 15-26; Gavin Langmuir, "Medieval Anti-Semitism," in Friedlander and Milton, pp. 27-36; Eugen Weber, "Modern Anti-Semitism," in Friedlander and Milton, pp. 37-52.

88. See the forthcoming doctoral dissertation by Herr Vogel, "Katholische Bischöfe, Weimar und nationale Opposition," written under the direction of Konrad Repgen at Bonn.

89. James Hunt, "Review: Margaret Lavinia Anderson, *Windthorst: A Political Biography*," *Review of Politics* 44 (1982):465.

90. John S. Conway, "The Churches," in Friedlander and Milton, p. 202; Thieme in Mosse, *Entscheidungsjahr*, pp. 284-285.

91. Herbert C. Kelman, "Attitudes are Alive and Well and Gainfully Employed in the Sphere of Action," *American Psychologist* 29 (1974):310-324.

92. See chap. I, H.H. Kelley, "Attribution Theory in Social Psychology," in D. Levine (ed.), *Nebraska Symposium on Motivation, 1967* (Lincoln: University of Nebraska Press, 1967); E.E. Jones and K.E. Davis, "From Acts to Dispositions," in L. Berkowitz (ed.), *Advances in Experimental Social Psychology* (New York: Academic Press, 1965); Jones and Nisbett, *The Actor and the Observer: Divergent Perceptions of the Causes of Behavior.*

93. George L. Mosse, *The Crisis of German Ideology*; Hermann Glaser, *Spiesser-Ideologie, von der Zerstörung des deutschen Geistes im 19. und 20. Jahrhundert* (Freiburg: Rombach, 1964).

94. Müller, *Katholische Kirche*, pp. 10-12.

95. Ehrlich, pp. 55, 59; Staub, 2:275.
96. Ernst-Wolfgang Böckenförde, "German Catholicism in 1933," *Cross Currents* 11 (1961):291-293; Schmaus, *Begegnungen*; Josef Pieper, *Das Arbeitsrecht des neuen Reiches und die Enzyklika Quadragesimo anno* (Münster: Verlag der Aschendorffschen Verlagsbuchhandlung, 1934); Jakob Hommes, "Katholisches Staats-und Kulturdenken u.d. Nationalsozialismus," *Deutsches Volk* (1933):285ff.
97. In 1933 such Jesuits as Max Pribilla and Ivo Zeiger called for recognition of the political facts and for cooperation with the state; see Max Pribilla, S.J., "Nationale Revolution," *Stimmen der Zeit* 125 (1933):156ff and Ivo Zeiger, S.J. "Das Reichskonkordat," *Stimmen der Zeit* 125 (1933):126.
98. Böckenförde, "German Catholicism," pp. 298-299.
99. Franz Schnabel, *Deutsche Geschichte im neunzehnten Jahrhundert*, vol. 4, *Die Religiösen Kräfte* (Freiburg: Herder, 1951), pp. 44-46, 164-202; Böckenförde, "German Catholicism," p. 300.
100. Franklin H. Littell, "*Kirchenkampf* and Holocaust: The German Church Struggle and Nazi Anti-Semitism in Retrospect," *Journal of Church and State* 13 (1971):210.
101. R. Redfield, "The Primitive World View," *Proceedings of the American Philosophical Society*, 96 (1952):30-36; Staats, *Social Behaviorism*, pp. 158-160; A.W. Staats, *Learning, Language, and Cognition* (New York: Holt, Rinehart, and Winston, 1968); A.W. Staats, *Child Learning*; A.W. Staats, "Linguistic-Mentalistic Theory versus an Explanatory S-R Learning Theory of Language Development," in D.I. Slobin (ed.), *The Ontogenesis of Grammar* (New York: Academic Press, 1971).

4

The Church Confronts the Reich

Totalitarianism is a relatively new form of government, a dictatorship in which technologically advanced instruments of political power are wielded without apparent restraint by the centralized leadership of an elite to effect a total social revolution, including the conditioning of man through arbitrary ideological assumptions, proclaimed by the leadership to a population, at least theoretically united. Both the Church and the Nazis were attempting to gain or maintain the adherence of Catholics to a specific normative pattern. A norm is a rule or standard that governs conduct in social situations and is a description of society's values in a specific area of behavior. It is a societal expectation, a standard to which persons are expected to conform whether they actually do so or not. It is a cultural specification that guides conduct in society and is the essential instrument of social control.[1] Since until relatively recent times totalitarian systems have been rare, the Church leadership understandably was ignorant of what Hitler would actually do once in power. Only from hindsight is his activity not surprising.

National Socialism appealed to the desire to belong. It concentrated on the alienated, the confused, the frightened—on people who, whatever their objective circumstances, perceived themselves as actual or potential losers. In this context the Jew could serve many as the ideological symbol of and for the lower middle classes, the real reason for everything that had gone wrong in Germany since the Enlightenment, the Industrial Revolution, and the Versailles Treaty. He was the principal negative image, the antitype juxtaposed to the new world the Nazis proposed to create. Mobilizing the German masses against the Jew or for the *Volk* were means of achieving the consensus National Socialism required not merely to take and exercise power, but to carry out its revolutionary visions of a Germany and a world reborn.[2]

In *Mein Kampf,* Hitler had written that every power that does not grow out of a firm intellectual base will remain wavering and insecure. It lacks the stability that can only rest on a fanatical *Weltanschauung*. Hitler's *Weltanschauung* consisted basically of a radical anti-Semitism and an imperialism of living space. Hitler himself had started out with the conventional *völkisch* and anti-Weimar notions held by the man on the street and even by the elite, which may explain why his ideas resonated so well in the maelstrom of Weimar politics. As the Nazi movement matured, he gave his ideas of race and space less conventional traits by radicalizing anti-Semitism for his fanatic followers and lower middle class, and finally by launching his war in the East directed to expansion. The long process by which he fitted together into a system these ideological bits and pieces acquired haphazardly so that finally every one of them was put into place where it belonged in the general picture of the world,[3] was truly an unusual phenomenon which revealed an intricate mind. Early in his career he had already insisted that a *Weltanschauung* must be the basis of the *völkisch* community. In *Mein Kampf* Hitler stated:

> Every philosophy of life, even if it is a thousand times correct and of the highest benefit to humanity, will remain without significance for the practical shaping of a people's life as long as its principles have not become the banner of the fighting movement which for its part in turn will be a party as long as its activity has not found completion in the victory of its ideas and its party dogmas have not become the new state principle of a people's community.[4]

In supporting nationalism since 1871, Catholics were already predisposed to accept a substantial portion of Hitler's *Weltanschauung*. The genesis of this normative system and then its implementation can be viewed as a slow development from the ordinary to the extraordinary. Perhaps this fact is what made it so difficult for the Church to realize fully the extent of the threat that had to be faced. Hitler's ideology seems to reflect the aspirations of a large group in Weimar Germany and was solidly rooted in the socio-historical context.[5]

The sociopolitical activities of this era can be seen as an exchange process between Hitler and his supporters. Specifically, such a transactional analysis of leader-follower relations[6] is useful for understanding the power of Hitler in the Third Reich. This approach emphasizes the significance of the follower's influence on the leader as well as the leader's attempts to direct the group. To maintain authority a leader must fulfill the expectations of the group members, address potential or real challenges to authority, and provide his followers with sufficient rewards to maintain the interaction. The relation between the ideology of the Nazi party embodied in its leadership and the perceptions and motivations of the German populace can be conceptualized as a mutual process of interaction. Catholics maintained a stable voting bloc opposed to the NSDAP, although not necessarily immune to some of Hitler's blandishments. In general, the conclusion seems warranted that participation in the Church for Catholics, except for marginal members, acted as a buffer against the Nazis even in the election of 1933 when overall Catholic resistance to the Nazi appeal appears to have been lowest in all the elections of the 1930s. The electoral statistics made it even more imperative for the Nazis to reach agreement and/or destroy the Church. Conversely, it was important to keep Catholics in the Church and practicing the faith, even if only by force of habit, to maintain the institutional integrity of Catholicism. While nationalism was a significant source of Nazi votes, both the Church and the NSDAP sounded this theme from 1919 to 1933, thereby signaling future grounds for reconciliation, uneasy though it might be.[7]

The Concordat of 1933

The opposition of the bishops to the NSDAP had been echoed in the pastoral letters of several conferences during 1930-32. By the summer of 1932 the condemnation had been endorsed by the entire German hierarchy, when the Fulda Episcopal Conference went on record against Catholic membership in the party.[8] The Church concentrated on the inculcation of values, thus contributing either to political consensus or to conflict. Not surprisingly, when the NSDAP gained control of Germany in January 1933, it was on very poor terms with the Catholic Church, despite the fact that the clerical leaders could support individual planks of the Nazi platform. Fascist and Catholic propaganda were effective to the extent that their key elements corresponded to the fundamental beliefs of their audiences. Both stressed the importance of the "national community" and so had a common basis for agreement. Such a potential existed since historically a person could be considered a good Catholic while supporting authoritarian forms of government and anti-Semitic movements, thereby offering at least a psychological empathy between some Church leaders and the Nazi ideology. In 1933, who was to say that Hitler was not a "normal" leader? There were indications that Church leaders were already trying to come to terms. The Center leader, Ludwig Kaas, tried to join Hitler's cabinet. The papal nuncio, Orsenigo, was reported to be jubilant since he saw in Hitler's accession to power the possibility of a Vatican-Mussolini type of agreement. Pacelli refrained from sending even private letters to Germany, but members of the curia told German visitors that the Vatican was anxious for German Catholicism to come to terms with Hitler as a bulwark against communism. On the surface, at least, as the last "free" election approached, the bishops warned the Catholic faithful to choose candidates whose character and proven fidelity would guarantee their attitude for the defense of the confessional school, for the Catholic religion, and for the Catholic Church. The voters were also told to "beware of agitators and of parties which are not worthy of the confidence of the Catholic community." Although seemingly a clear statement to modern readers, the bishops had again not stated a definitive position. A group of Catholic Nazis in Koblenz, for example, thanked Bishop Bornewasser for not having supported the Center party and for urging the election of Catholic National Socialists, for only those men were truly dedicated to the defense of the Church. Of course, many persons join a social movement in a tentative fashion, with only superficial acquaintance with its ideology and aims. Faulhaber on February 10 merely discussed the rights and duties of the state toward its citizens and vice-versa. Opposition was evaporating into meaningless generalities. In the final analysis, collective behavior cannot be understood except in relation to the organization of a society. Groups of individuals who are subjected to common historical conditioning experiences will acquire common systems of preferences that can help organize their political behavior.[9] The ultimate question is: Were Catholics politically naive or merely politicized to accept Hitler as a legitimate agent for negotiating purposes or both?

A variety of specific psychological mechanisms can be identified that probably enabled individual Catholics to banish or sharply reduce the motivational conflicts they experienced in making a decision or, when exposed to pressures, in reexamining decisions already made. They are:

1. Cognitive restructuring that can help the individual avoid or minimize the cognitive dissonance occasioned by new information and facts that are relevant to the decision being made, or that challenge the presuppositions of decisions already made.
2. The tactic of devaluating a value or a position held by the self or significant others when that value loses out in the competition with other norms or, for example, political decisions.
3. The tactic of *reducing or abandoning one's identification with significant others* who suffer utilitarian loss as a result of political, social, economic, or cultural changes.[10]

Several authors[11] have indicated that the Catholic hierarchy was not crystal clear in its opposition to Nazism in 1933, and that, in fact, the contrary was the case. Although up to the time of the Nazi takeover of power Catholics were enjoined to have nothing to do with Nazism, a sudden and disastrous change took place. Basically, the Center party leaders led their party into self-immolation and the hierarchy welcomed the concordat. Clearly the Church was hoping for a working solution and reevaluated its former position against Nazism in light of the cold political reality of 1933. Papen, Pius XI, Pacelli, Buttmann, and Gröber sought to formulate a Concordat. By compromising themselves in this way, the Catholic hierarchy was never able to lead the Church in wholehearted opposition to the Nazis, even after their hostile intentions were all too plainly revealed,[12] although the Concordat could offer a basis for limited protest.

In March 1933, a *rapprochement* between the party and the Church became discernible. Nazi and Catholic propaganda were successful because their key elements corresponded to the fundamental beliefs of their audiences. Both stressed the importance of the "national community" and so had a common basis for discussion. The comprehension of similarities between the Nazis and Catholic leaders is perhaps a more complex intellectual task than the comprehension of differences would be, and this may well be partially the reason why the exact roles and goals of the negotiators has been debated for years.[13]

On March 23 Hitler sought his Enabling Act and promised that his government would respect all agreements concluded between the Church and the state. The entire German hierarchy met at Fulda on March 28 and agreed upon a conciliatory attitude to the Nazi movement. The ban on National Socialism was formally raised, and membership in the Nazi party and Catholic Church were no longer held to be incompatible. Reciprocally, Hitler publicly disavowed any anti-Christian intentions or objectives. Following the Enabling Act and the March 23 speech of Hitler, the bishops suggested reconciliation with the government was possible, hoping that Catholics could continue their tradition of loyalty to the legitimate authority. Pacelli's reaction, according to his secretary, Robert Leiber, S.J., was: "Why must the German bishops come to terms with the government so quickly? If it must be done, couldn't they wait a month or so?"[14] Clearly the Church was hoping for a working solution. Papen, Pius XI, Pacelli, Buttmann, and Gröber negotiated the Concordat. To help pave the way to agreement, Hitler assured Bertram that Rosenberg's *Myth* was a private work and that schools and associations would remain under Catholic control.[15] Hitler had no problems with Catholic associations as long as they entertained no partisan notions.

On April 7, 1933, before his first trip to Rome, Papen told a representative of the Berlin Foreign Office that the removal of the clergy from party politics would be "one of the principal demands on our side." He said on April 27 that the limitation of this exclusion to parish clergy only was "completely inadequate" in Hitler's view. Early in the Concordat discussions, the interests of the Vatican in the conclusion of a treaty with the Reich came into collision with the Center's need to retain as much assistance from the Church as could be mustered. Hitler, of course, sought the

Concordat to persuade the curia that it could obtain most of its goals in Germany, with the exception of an explicit pledge from the Nazi regime that the legal existence of all Catholic associations would be guaranteed, if the Vatican would prohibit priestly participation in German politics. On May 17 Papen termed the total exclusion of the clergy from party politics a *conditio sine qua non,* adding on May 26 that this would be "the crucial point" on which the success of the Concordat negotiations depended. On June 16 the German ambassador to the Holy See, Diego von Bergen, was instructed to find out whether Pacelli was prepared to grant this demand, since there would be no point in Papen's coming to Rome for final negotiations if the Holy See were intransigent on this matter. In his final answer to Bergen's inquiry, Pacelli, ever the careful diplomat, avoided any commitment on this point.[16]

The Fulda bishops, now for the first time including the Bavarian episcopate, issued its annual letter (June 3, 1933). It was both conciliatory and admonitory toward the government. It supported nationalism, but warned of excessive nationalism. It accepted that fact that strong authority is sometimes necessary, but cautioned against the unnecessary curtailment of human liberty. It attacked the proposal for a sterilization law and criticized racial persecution. But then it continued: "The fact that we German bishops make the above enumerated demands does not imply that they conceal a mental reservation to the State." A final prayer was added that "the prudence and energy of Germany's leader will succeed in extinguishing all those sparks and glowing coals which, here and there, certain people would like to fan into a terrible conflagration against the Catholic Church."[17] Such was the position of the German hierarchy regarding the new Nazi Reich as the negotiations for the Concordat reached their critical stages.

Having read *Mein Kampf* and consistently attacked the anti-Christian character of Nazism, Pacelli preferred to adopt a wait-and-see attitude. This was particularly easy to do since Hitler had promised to respect the previous Concordats with Bavaria (1924), Prussia (1929), and Baden (1932), which protected eighteen of the approximately twenty million Catholics in Germany. But Hitler was anxious for an agreement, and against extremists in the party Papen had urged generosity. The Reich insisted on the exclusion of the Catholic clergy from party politics. This was not a particularly difficult point for the Church to concede, not only because it appeared that true parliamentary government had already been abolished in Germany, but also because the Holy See was not obsessed with the survival of the Center party. The Church was in a vulnerable position. Hence Pius XI and his cardinal secretary had to pursue a realistic strategy. In essence, the Vatican was certainly far more interested in the guarantees for nonpolitical activities it might obtain for the Catholic faithful living in a state rapidly becoming totalitarian.[18]

But German Catholics were by no means as hesitant as the cardinal secretary. On the whole the German bishops were pressured to respond to the proffered hand of friendship extended by Hitler and to rescind their opposition toward joining the movement. They were besieged to surrender their reservations. Bornewasser stated Catholics were prepared to serve the regime with all their powers of body and soul. But the bishops were in a very difficult position. Publicly, Gröber on April 27, 1933 had already said that Catholics could not oppose the new state; they must positively affirm it and cooperate with it unflinchingly. But privately Gröber had doubts about Nazi intentions as early as March when he noted the migration of youth to National Socialism and saw that he was unable to intercede successfully to aid converted Jews in Karlsruhe. Abbot Ildefons Herwegen of Maria Laach at the end of May 1933 in Cologne said that the *Volk* and *Staat* had again become one through Adolf Hitler. The führer, he continued, had total faith in the German people, wanted to serve them, and so had garnished the support of millions. In June, J. Nattermann, general secretary for the *Deutsche Gesellentag* proclaimed in Munich that once again the German nation had seized its shield against unbelievers and pagans. Again the German people had responded to their mission.[19] Such public responses from so many varied quarters suggested that many Catholics were now prepared to adapt to the times.

The depoliticizing of the clergy could be viewed as *protection* for the Church against future attempts to enlist the clergy in the Nazi party. Leiber pointed this out to Pacelli on June 29. On June 22 Cardinal Bertram had already written Pacelli that in his diocese the state possessed, on the basis of centuries of old law and custom, the right to nominate a third of the pastors of parishes in an area having some two million Catholics. He warned that the new government was likely to make membership in the Nazi party a condition for any priest who wished to be nominated to a pastorate. Catholic clergy did not join the Nazi Party prior to Hitler's seizure of power because of the clear warnings of their bishops against Nazi errors. In the brief period of euphoria that prevailed among some of the clergy following the signing of the Concordat, they were prevented from joining the Nazi party by Article 32 of the treaty. When, in 1935, the Nazis began to claim that in the Third Reich state and party were identical, so that the prohibition of party membership in Article 32 could not possibly apply to the Nazi party, there was little temptation for Catholic clergy to join a party which by that time had clearly embarked on a deliberate policy of Church persecution.[20] The Concordat, then, can be viewed as a treaty made with a hostile state to preserve the institutional Church, not simply as an acknowledgement indicating support for the government.

Those in charge of negotiations recognized the dangers to the Church. Nazi violence resulted in injury to some Catholic journeymen and the death of a Bavarian priest. The Vatican threatened to break off negotiations, and on July 2 *Osservatore Romano* declared that the conclusion of a Concordat would in no way imply the approval of National Socialist teachings. Various motives for the terror campaign have been cited. It may have been organized to sabotage the negotiations or at least to destroy Catholic organizations in Germany before the Concordat provisions protecting them became effective. Or it may even be that Hitler had come to doubt the value of the Concordat and was simply playing for time in order to reset his course. The fear of the second possibility explains why on July 1, within an hour of receiving the telephoned news of the terror campaign against Catholic organizations in Germany, Archbishop Gröber could urge Pacelli to press on with the Concordat as quickly as possible; Gröber had second thoughts the next day, however, when the news from Germany got worse. The same reasoning lay behind the recommendation of the German bishops at the end of August that the Concordat be ratified as soon as possible despite the continuing harassment of Catholic organizations. There were two reasons for this seemingly paradoxical advice: any delay in ratification would strengthen Nazi party opposition to the Concordat in Germany, where Hitler's supporters were claiming that he had made too many concessions to the Church; and only by ratification, it was argued, would the bishops be able to protest effectively against Church persecution. The latter argument, it must be added, was also used by the German government to pressure the Vatican into ratifying the Concordat.[21]

In sending the agreed text of the Concordat to Hitler on July 2, Papen complained that the reports about numerous arrests and mistreatment of clergy, the seizing of diocesan funds, etc., have created an atmosphere that makes the conclusion of this Concordat very difficult. The Concordat was concluded in three stages: July 8, initialing of the agreed text; July 20, formal signing; September 19, exchange of ratifications. Actually, negotiations were conducted only under great pressure from the Berlin government; Pacelli said shortly afterward that a pistol had been pointed at his head and that he really had no alternative. In his view he had been offered a choice between concessions, greater than any previous German government had agreed to, and the threat of the virtual elimination of the Catholic Church in Germany. Not only that, he had been given only a week to make a decision. He knew that the Nazis would violate the agreement, but at least the Holy See would have a treaty on which to base its protests, a stronghold behind which Catholics might be shielded. In any case, the cardinal secretary of state insisted that the Germans would probably refrain from violating all the articles of the Concordat simultaneously. The Reich government had already applied pressure by occupying the headquarters of specific Catholic associations and by threatening a propaganda campaign orchestrated by Goebbels against the alleged immorality in Catholic monasteries. In the second week of June (1933), stormtroopers, SS, and Hitler Youth assaulted delegates to the national congress of the *Gesellenverein* (the Catholic young journeyman's association) that was being held in Munich, and by menacing the assembly ultimately forced cancellation of the congress.[22] The Nazis alternated threats with promises. Apparently papal negotiators tried to maintain some limited involvement of the Catholic clergy in the Center, but finally yielded to win the Concordat. On July 5, two weeks before signing the Concordat, the Center party dissolved itself. In all likelihood the Center would have come apart at the seams regardless of the course of negotiations between the Curia and Hitler. Leaders of the Center felt themselves weak and isolated.

The Concordat was provisionally signed July 8, 1933 and von Papen at the Holy See's insistence issued a communique that halted repressive measures effected against Catholic associations recognized in the new agreement. Papen declared that future oppressive measures would incur the full rigor of the law. For the Church's part, it accepted without protest the dissolution of the Center and Bavarian People's party, accomplished a few days earlier. On July 9, the day after the Concordat was initialed, Hitler announced triumphantly to an SA meeting in Dortmund that it was "now for all time forbidden for priests to be active in a political party." In the cabinet meeting of July 14 at which the Concordat was discussed, Hitler claimed that the dissolution of the Center could be called permanent only with the conclusion of the Concordat after the Vatican had ordered the permanent withdrawal of the priests from party politics. Hitler and his associates manifested a complete lack of sincerity by enacting at this same cabinet meeting a law forbidding the formation of any new parties, thus achieving by virtue of the special emergency powers vested in his government the very thing for which Hitler claimed it was necessary to sign an international treaty with the Holy See.[23] In this decisive meeting of the cabinet on July 14, Hitler rejected any debate about the particulars of the Concordat, pointing out that an atmosphere of confidence would be created in Germany, which would facilitate the work of political reconstruction. No doubt the fact that his government would secure its first international agreement and would take on an air of international respectability loomed large in his thoughts as well. He told the opponents of the Concordat at this conference that a few months before he would not have considered the Church's signing such an agreement possible, that it was "an indescribable success." Besides, he remarked, whatever defects the agreement might have for Germany could be changed later when the international situation had been altered.[24]

On July 20, 1933 the Reich Concordat was signed to regulate the relations between the Church and the state "in a permanent manner and on a basis acceptable to both parties." It purported to give the Church an official guarantee of its rights, including freedom for its organizations, and the right to maintain Catholic schools and to preserve its general influence upon the education of the German youth. In return, the entire clergy was forbidden membership in a political party or activity on behalf of any party. The Concordat also provided that Catholic religious instruction should emphasize the patriotic duties of the Christian citizen and an attitude of loyalty toward the fatherland. By the summer of 1933, therefore, the single-party state was now a reality. The NSDAP's absolute monopoly as a political party meant that legal political activity was only possible within the NSDAP, and Hitler's position of absolute leadership in the party was also transferred to the government and the state. The National Socialist single-party state meant, at the same time, the führer state. It was a logical step, therefore, when the Reich's minister of the interior, Frick, informed civil servants on July 20 that the Hitler salute was to be used generally as the German greeting now that the party system was finished and the entire government of the German Reich was under the control of Reich Chancellor Adolf Hitler.[25]

Nazi centralization in Germany destroyed the value of the separate Concordats with the various German states, thus making a Reich Concordat necessary if the Church were to have a strong legal position in education, youth organizations, and similar matters. The Vatican was deeply suspicious of Hitler's motives; at the same time it did not dare to reject his advances. Since Germany accepted the major demands of the Holy See, opposition to the Concordat might have led to an open struggle between Church and state in Germany; this the Vatican did not want to provoke as it sought to contain Nazism. Although the signing of the Concordat brought about the immediate removal of such difficulties of recent origin as the occupation of certain Catholic association headquarters by local Nazi authorities, other points of conflict were quickly evident. On July 25 the government published a sterilization law that was in sharp opposition to the teachings of the Church. In August the propaganda attacks against the Catholic associations were suddenly renewed, and vehement, although not coordinated, attacks began against the Catholic schools and press. The German hierarchy sought an immediate ratification of the Concordat, with the hope that such a step might truly protect the Church's position. Also, the German government informed the Holy See that only after the ratification could it proceed with all the weight of its authority against those who were opposed to the Concordat.[26]

With this in mind, the Holy See accepted the idea of a September ratification, but it reminded the German government that while the Concordat excluded priests from party politics, it also guaranteed the Church the right to teach and to defend publicly Catholic principles. Until 1945 the question of whether Catholic doctrinal principles had a political bearing would be subject to almost continual debate between the bishops and Nazi cadre. The Holy See called attention to improper restrictions and pressures enforced against Catholic associations and press, and demanded public assurances regarding the Reich's willingness to begin negotiations dealing with all points of conflict on the Concordat's interpretation and application. For its part, the government protested its good faith and simultaneously with the ratification of the Concordat on September 10 gave the assurances the Holy See had requested.[27]

Hitler's initial intention had been to use a Concordat to dissolve the Center party, but the clergy themselves deserted the party, which by early July had dissolved itself. The argument then shifted to new grounds. Papen convinced Hitler that the Concordat would signify the Vatican's agreement to the permanent dissolution of the Center. Hitler was now convinced that the conclusion of the Concordat would greatly raise the international prestige of the new Nazi state. He now stressed the prestige arguments by July 14. Throughout these negotiations, Pacelli had serious misgivings about Hitler's willingness to observe the pledges he had given. Hitler, however, claimed that the Concordat had three great advantages: it refuted the charge that National Socialism was anti-Christian, it extended Vatican recognition to his regime, and it withdrew the clergy permanently from party politics.[28] Because of these assertions the Vatican has received a great deal of criticism.[29] Clearly the Vatican had some interest in the Concordat. It takes two to conclude a Concordat, however, and clearly the Holy See had its motives as well.

Hitler's emergency powers removed not only the Reichstag's ability to prevent a Concordat, because by giving Hitler the power to suspend the constitution at will, such powers removed as well the guarantees of freedom of religion written into the Weimar constitution. Given the consolidation of Hitler's power in the Reich, it was incumbent on the pope and his advisers to examine with care any offer of a Concordat, especially since they had been seeking such a document throughout the Weimar era, but had been obstructed by the SPD in the Reichstag.[30] One must also attend here to the general thrust of German constitutional theory.[31] This theory assumes an authoritarian state in which individuals and institutions have only those rights that the state confers and recognizes. To engage in Concordat negotiations, then, was not a hastily made decision.

The Concordat guaranteed rights sought throughout the Weimar years, e.g., generous guarantees for schools and other organizations. Confronted with this offer, refusal was never more than a theoretical possibility for the Holy See. The consequences of a refusal were clearly discerned at the time by Archbishop Gröber, one of the German bishops who was most optimistic about the possibilities of cooperation with the Nazi state. Should the Concordat be rejected, he wrote to Pacelli on July 1, "everything we have will soon be smashed. Catholics could say: 'the Holy See could have helped us and did not.' The government would publish the text of the Concordat and blame the Holy See for blocking the accomplishment of such a good work."[32] The Church could only have delayed by contending that Hitler's word was not to be trusted, almost an impossibility at such an early date.

The Vatican, guided in large measure by Kaas, refused to concede the "depoliticizing" of the clergy until it was clear that the Catholic parties were already doomed.[33] As the Center party collapsed, however, the Vatican felt it needed protection for the Church against future attempts to enlist the clergy in the one remaining party, especially at a time when all except the Nazi party were disappearing in Germany into a movement greeted by all as one of "national renewal." Any attempt by the Vatican to support or "rescue" the Center party would have been denounced by Germans in general as unwarranted outside interference in domestic political affairs. Far from desiring the precipitate collapse of the Catholic parties or bargaining them away in return for the Concordat, the swiftness of the dissolution was an acute embarrassment to the Vatican. When he learned from press reports on July 5 of the Center's dissolution, Pacelli expressed deep regret that the party had not been able to hold out at least until the Concordat had been signed: "The mere fact of its existence was still an advantage for us in the negotiating."[34]

The Concordat was an attempt by Church leaders, many possessing greater realism about what the future held for the Church in Hitler's Germany than they have yet been credited with, to build a defense against the attacks that they feared were coming. Evidence of the hierarchy's realism in reacting to Nazism is widespread during this period. To Ivone Kirkpatrick's suggestion that Hitler would settle down in time and behave himself, Pacelli "replied with emphasis that he saw no ground for such easy optimism." He said the German government was certain to violate the Concordat, but that the Germans would probably not violate all the articles at the same time. Meeting in plenary conference in Fulda at the end of May 1933, the German bishops noted that they were "seriously concerned that all the Catholic youth organizations will die out within a few years." They warned against the desire of the Nazis to exclude the clergy from the public forum completely and confine the Church to the sacristy, pointing out the grave effect this would have for the Church's pastoral work. Further doubts appeared among a variety of bishops during the summer. Bishop Preysing of Eichstätt doubted (July 3, 1933), in view of the lawless state of Germany and the Nazi claim that whatever was advantageous to the state was legal, whether any Concordat would be possible. The release of imprisoned clergy would be an empty gesture that would change nothing in principle. On July 20 he feared that the suspension of Church persecution not as a *condition* for further Concordat negotiations but as a *reward* for initialing the treaty was an ominous sign; he called this "peace negotiations and the conclusion of peace before the cease-fire." On July 27 Preysing feared that despite the "depoliticizing" of the clergy the state would encourage the clergy to be active in the Nazi party on the pretense that it was no longer a political party but identical with the state. Cardinal Bertram wrote Faulhaber on August 10 that he could not accept the suggestion of Bishop Berning of Osnabrück that a *Te Deum* of thanksgiving for the Concordat be sung in all the German churches. "It is not yet time to join in the general bell ringing and jubilation. That is not lack of gratitude on my part or a wet blanket reaction but simply grave concern."[35]

Father Leiber sent an especially significant report to Pacelli on his (Leiber's) trip through Germany in August 1933. He stated that Gröber could be considered an optimist, Bornewasser a pessimist along with Faulhaber. Further, he reminded Pacelli that it should not be forgotten that most people could not say publicly or even in correspondence what they really thought. All correspondence was subject to surveillance. Critics of the Vatican policy claim, however, that the defense erected in the Concordat was worthless since Hitler broke his promises from the start. This claim ignores both the limited nature of the defense and the fact that those who erected it were aware of this limitation. Even the often culpably optimistic Gröber claimed merely that the Concordat "would establish order at least for the time being." This modest expectation was fulfilled. On July 8, the day the Concordat was initialed in Rome, Hitler ordered varied acts of harassment to cease.[36]

An indication of the realism with which the Church's leadership responded is evident in the muted Vatican reaction to the treaty. Even the expressions of gratitude by the German bishops for the Concordat were couched in language certainly suggesting no great confidence that its provisions would be heeded. Bertram coupled his thanks with the urgent wish that the provisions of the Concordat would be carried out by Hitler in such a way that the Church could cooperate in "the promotion of faith in God, morality and loyal obedience to the leading authorities," which would rebound with blessing to the welfare of people and fatherland. The public declarations of the bishops to which Bertram referred at the outset of his statement were those of March 28 and June 3, 1933. The former was a qualified and conditional retraction of previous warnings against Nazism because of Hitler's unexpectedly strong assurances of respect for the churches and Christianity in his Reichstag declaration of March 23 which had been crucial in the Center's assent to the Enabling Act. The bishops' far stronger statement of June 3 was a skillful attempt to emphasize the positive elements in National Socialism (patriotism, emphasis on obedience to the constituted authority, the common welfare vs. selfish individualism), but it interpreted these in a way designed to give maximum offense to the Nazis and added a long list of demands and warnings that they could never accept. The June statement was understood at the time to constitute "a clear *no* to National Socialist intentions"; this is clear from contemporary documents. Hochhuth and Lewy failed to understand such statements in their historical context and so their critiques are not exactly accurate, at least according to current interpretations. But a case can certainly be made that the Church did not offer guidance clear enough for the average lay Catholic.[37]

Faulhaber's fulsome letter to Hitler, for example, ran the gamut from seemingly unqualified jubilation to hardly disguised skepticism, and is in keeping with the personality of this colorful and volatile prelate. He made a number of points. The Concordat had strengthened Germany's reputation in the world, not Hitler's nor that of the Nazi party or state. After stating that the Concordat *could* contribute to the moral strength of the people, Faulhaber expressed the hope that its provisions "will not remain on paper," but would be put into practice. The prelate's letter highlights the political attitude of German Catholicism: "What the old parliaments and parties did not accomplish in sixty years, your far-seeing statesmanship realized in six months of world-historical significance." The bishops seemed to be acting in an almost apolitical fashion; instead they could only think in terms of ecclesiastical-cultural goals, perhaps because of a combination of the *Kulturkampf* and natural law mentality. Their political acumen was lacking not only on this point but in the subsequently expressed hope that the lower ranks of the first, second, and third level would not remain all too far behind the statesmanlike greatness of the führer. Indeed the only person to rejoice over the Concordat was Hitler, who in a July 14 cabinet meeting refused to discuss the details of the agreement, saying that "one should see only the great success" that it embodied. The price paid for this success was not small. From the start the long list of Church rights solemnly pledged in the Concordat was in reality a foreign element in Hitler's totalitarian system. Typical was the complaint of a Nazi party newspaper on the fourth anniversary of the Concordat that it had been designed "to make every National Socialist educational policy impossible." Had the Concordat done nothing more than hamper and delay Hitler in his campaign against the Church, as in the case of the Catholic youth organizations, it would still have been preferable, from the Church's point of view, to a refusal of the proffered Concordat. The latter scenario would have left Hitler free to persecute the Church with virtually no restrictions. Goebbel's propaganda machine would have claimed that the persecution was fitting retribution for the stubbornness of Church leaders in spurning the more than generous terms which Hitler had offered. But the Concordat had a long-term effect very damaging for Hitler. The Holy See now had the right to criticize all aspects of Hitler's religious policy without risking the reply that these were purely domestic matters and thereby ignoring Vatican advice and protests. Especially valuable from the Church's point of view were the generous guarantees proposed for both Catholic schools and organizations. The desire for precisely such guarantees, especially for schools, had been a principal motive for the Church's efforts to obtain a Reich Concordat during the Weimar period.[38]

Criticism of the Church's leaders for signing the Concordat is somewhat misplaced, since it ignores the fact that in the situation actually prevailing in the summer of 1933, rejection of Hitler's Concordat with its generous terms, judged in the light of the Vatican's previous efforts to obtain such a treaty, was at no time a real possibility. Criticism could be directed at Church policy after the Concordat had been accepted by both sides. Too much reliance was probably placed on diplomatic protests; too little was done to acquaint rank and file Catholics in Germany with the existence and content of these protests and to mobilize them in support of Church rights. On one hand, the fundamental cause of this failure was theological: the view of the Church as consisting of a more or less passive laity, an obedient body of pastoral clergy, and a hierarchy that directed and led both laity and clergy, making all decisions in lonely and splendid isolation. On the other hand, psychologically, both the pope and the bishops had pursued a Concordat for so long that consistency with past actions was a force that could not easily be turned aside. It is, moreover, always easy to repudiate the actions of others from historical hindsight.

Theoretically, a totalitarian political party seeks to gain a monopoly of control or at least dominance over other pluralistic components of the state. But the actual party based on mass mobilization and declared ideological commitments frequently seems to lose that dynamism and increasingly begins to share its power with a variety of selected interest groups. The totalitarian and arrested totalitarian tendencies, therefore, may be depleted into various forms of conservative quasi-pluralistic or pluralistic authoritarian regimes. But by eliminating "democratic pluralism" during the Third Reich, the Nazi party did manage to absorb the aspirations and criticisms of the distinct socioeconomic segments of society without endangering the Nazi goals of *Lebensraum* and eugenic purification. Party pluralism, it has been argued, weakened monolithic control, but in the final analysis actually seems to have strengthened the Nazi control of German society by fragmenting social and economic interests.[39] By working within the system, the Catholic Church may well have been trying to position itself to become part of a future authoritarian Germany or perhaps there was hope that Hitler could be tamed and his party coopted into the conservative Right. Unfortunately, the curia and German bishops were either naive or failed to respond with the courage of their convictions and to provide the leadership necessary to counter Hitler's *Gleichschaltung* (coordination) policy.

A credible source can more easily change opinion than can an isolated person resisting the system. The bishops were the credible source of interpretation of an accepted and viable *Weltanschauung,* but had already capitulated to the nationalist thrust in German politics, which they now followed to one of its possible conclusions. To distinguish for their followers the good from the bad in the Nazi *credo* was becoming increasingly difficult as Hitler tightened his hold. Having visibly supported nationalism since 1871, the Catholic hierarchy tried to maintain consistency after 1933, not realizing apparently that to Hitler nationalism meant racism. Their misjudgment meant that traditional Church values did not help minimize the effect of the Nazis. A person must feel that a truism has been threatened before he can assimilate supportive material as an aid to increasing his resistance. In signing the Concordat, the Church signaled that a normalization between state and Church had apparently been reached.[40]

The Concordat should have offered a useful illustration of the lack of values underlying Hitler's political goals. The long series of Vatican protests over violations of the Concordat, including the searing public indictment of Nazi faithlessness in *Mit Brennender Sorge* (1937),[41] constituted a demonstration of Hitler's duplicity the like of which has not been attempted by any other power prior to World War II. Such an illumination of the essence of Nazi totalitarianism would have been impossible without the Concordat. Unfortunately, foreign governments chose to overlook this massive demonstration of Hitler's character. At the time, the bishops had to urge dealing with Hitler's government. They would not have had their whole flock behind them had they outlined an uncompromising stand against National Socialism. The bishops had clearly not undergone an inner conversion, but had taken careful note that the political situation had changed.

Unfortunately people tend to be most influenced by well-known leaders of opinion in their community. The Concordat was by no means an approval by the Vatican, and presumably by the bishops, of the National Socialist political state, but Catholics would find it difficult to accept such a treaty as the opening volley in a prolonged conflict between the Church and the Reich. Pacelli himself made the institution's position abundantly clear on January 31, 1934: "It is not for the Catholic Church to reject any form of government or reshaping of the organization of the state. She lives in correct and proper relation to States with a variety of governments and of different internal structures. She has made Concordats with monarchies and republics, with democracies and totalitarian states. Her Concordats are acts dealing with religion and Church matters and are not simply acts of political significance."[42]

The distinction between embracing the system and preparing a defense for the Church was probably lost for most Catholics. The bishops' joint pastoral letter of June, characterized by d'Harcourt as "professions of loyalty, seasoned with drops of vinegar," could not have been otherwise. Reacting to the German political developments, the bishops could not refrain from making a statement, but they knew that most Catholics would not have followed them and certainly would not have opposed their legitimate government. The speed of the bishops' reconciliation, however, is bewildering until the rapidity of the Center's dissolution process is recalled. Although the Concordat may have helped the Church in its long-run protests and its defense, it also tied the hands of the bishops. The Concordat checked them from coming out too openly against the overall dominance of the totalitarian state. Too much protest could endanger the rights that had been left untouched.[43] The Concordat offered a vehicle for protest, but not necessarily for resistance. In the post-Concordat era, the Church as an institution placed itself in a position of evaluating the policies of the government and seemed intent on providing leadership in the political struggle orchestrated by Hitler. The real issues, however, were not immediately apparent because Hitler's state only gradually emerged as the threat that some, of course, had already predicted it would be.

Indications of future problems rapidly emerged. No sooner was the Concordat signed than the altercations between the German government and Holy See began. The dispute concerned the government's refusal to appoint to the civil service Catholic officials of Jewish descent. The Vatican, ignoring racial criteria, wanted such appointments to be nondiscriminatory. The government refused; it considered the matter an internal problem, outside the jurisdiction of the Vatican. It was not possible to give these people equal status, Eugen Klee, the German charge d'affaires at the Vatican, explained to the cardinal secretary of state, because "the Jewish question was not a religious but a race problem." Both sides eventually found fault with the Concordat. The battle line drawn around the Church's organizations proved to be much less clearly demarcated than it ought to have been, leaving many lay organizations dangerously exposed. On the Nazi side, even that porous barrier proved noisome to the ever-expanding state.[44]

Catholic responses to National Socialism throughout the Third Reich era were motivated essentially by the pastoral concerns of Church leaders and their responsibility to maintain public worship and the efficacy of the sacraments. Their actions should also be judged in pastoral terms, not only by applying extraneous political standards.[45] The correspondence between Preysing with his episcopal colleagues and the Holy See supports the contention that Vatican officials approached Hitler hoping not so much to gain short-term tactical advantages as to guarantee the long-term spiritual integrity of the Catholic Church.[46] The great unresolved question is not whether the hierarchy's pastoral concerns should be judged by "extraneous" political standards but whether, in an age of totalitarian political religions, the pastoral concerns themselves were adequate, or were they too limited? Should Church leaders have focused more intensely on human rights and the legitimacy of a racist regime? Also, in an authoritarian or totalitarian context, opposition must be voiced in circuitous ways, which might elude outsiders or later generations, when leaders try to influence despots and communicate with their followers. Thus, the episcopal pronouncements must be studied *in tota* and very carefully.

The episcopate, of course, was again to some extent merely mirroring the sentiments of other German Catholics, while trying to control the euphoria erupting after the successful conclusion of the Concordat. The signing of the Concordat was welcomed since most people would rather accept an explanation as a way to avoid anxiety than to question a controversial issue. But several priests' comments on the Concordat are extant and suggest the confusion that existed among the lower echelon clergy and presumably among the lay Catholics as well. Curate Fürstl of Gauting (Munich Achdiocese) apparently had great confidence in it, for when called to account for his actions in publicly leading a uniformed Catholic youth group on an outing, he snapped at his accusers, "The Concordat will ruin you yet." Pastor Bruckmaier of Wolfakirchen (Passau Diocese) was more pessimistic. In his Thanksgiving Festival sermon (October 10, 1933) he stated that the Church and priests were being persecuted. "There is a Concordat to be sure, but it exists only on paper." He was convinced that worse things were going to happen than at the time of Bismarck's *Kulturkampf.*[47]

The Reconciliation Phase

The success of the Nazis in attracting the intelligensia into its ranks or in neutralizing the hostility of some despite the inconsistencies in the party platform is not easily explained. That so many members from this group could join or accept a political movement that was openly dedicated to the overthrow of the Weimar government as well as accepted religious values— and concurrently gave the party an air of respectability it otherwise would not have gained—is indicative of the political trauma of interwar Germany, culminating in 1933. Opportunists emerged and published articles and booklets outlining the numerous affinities thought to exist between National Socialism and Catholicism. In reality the themes developed were merely extensions of earlier works, only now their assertions appeared more orthodox in light of the apparent *modus vivendi* reached between the hierarchy and Hitler, symbolized in the Concordat. Church leaders had serious reservations with respect to the regime, but their signals lacked clarity, especially when directed to political Catholic publicists. Writing on the "new nationalism (Nazism) as a religious metaphysical movement," Gerhart in 1932 struck virtually all the themes to which Catholics as well as other Germans were sensitive. He asserted, for example, that the ideals of the French Revolution offered Judaism a chance to corrupt Christian peoples everywhere. He noted the fact that the Catholic world view would actually be weaker in a Nazi state because the state itself would support an exclusivistic *Weltanschauung*. The National Socialists would define what was national and endanger the historical particularism of Germany. Ultimately, Gerhart affirmed the concept of an authoritarian democracy to make possible the connection between *Autorität und Volkswillen.* An authoritarian democracy would overcome the *Volksstaat-Obrigkeitstaat* antithesis and in place of a liberal atomistic society would organize a political entity featuring organic connections. Not surprisingly many Germans were susceptible to Hitler's political platform, given the general desire for a stable, authoritarian government modeled on that of the Second Reich. Gerhart favored planks in Hitler's platform, albeit not the entire program. The heteronomous control of the ideological content of Catholic thought by a universal Church and specifically by the pope was one of the most serious obstacles to the creation of a truly totalitarian system by nondemocratic rulers claiming to implement Catholic corporatist doctrine in their states (e.g., the Dollfuss' Austria, Franco's Spain, Salazar's Portugal).[48] This controlled ideology could potentially block a *Weltanschauung* hostile to the Church. Hitler had cause to see in Catholicism a serious competitor.

A number of well-known Catholic scholars and theologians, however, found a theoretical justification for the reconciliation of church and state.

Joseph Lortz, a prominent church historian, saw basic similarities between the Nazi and the Catholic *Weltanschauungen*. Both were opposed to Bolshevism, liberalism, relativism, atheism, and public immorality, and had in common the espousal of corporatist principles, the return to the Teutonic sources of the German people, and the importance of faith as something grand and heroic. The German Catholics, according to Lortz, were morally obligated in conscience to support National Socialism wholeheartedly, since it represented not merely the legal authority, but, to an overwhelming degree, Germany itself. Not all theologians, of course, saw Nazism as the antidote to Bolshevism: Gundlach almost immediately saw the dangers of National Socialism, which he felt paralleled Bolshevism. The assaults by both ideologies on personal values and the stress on fixed norms for the individual and society were almost identical. Both world views were too simplistic.[49]

Still, a significant number sought reconciliation because they perceived threatening political divisions. In the autumn of 1933 there appeared a pamphlet by Otto Helmut, "Our People in Danger: The Decline in the Birthrate and its Meaning for the Future of Germany" (published by I.F. Lehmann, Munich). In an appendix to this work, Dr. Gütt, an official of the Ministry of the Interior, accused the Catholic Church and Judaism of an anti-German attitude:

> All "internationalism," whether Jewish or clerical, considers the ideal condition of any country to be a peace-loving intermingling of racial strains which knows nothing of Race or Fatherland or national honor, a community which worships the golden calf by a life devoted to pleasure and personal property. . . . They care nothing for the physical or spiritual welfare of the people or for the happiness of future generations; they care solely for an international domination of which the foundations were laid centuries ago. With their outlook thus oriented, these groups despise all racial or national political views or theories which may lead, through internal purity and stability, to the higher development and improvement of any given race.[50]

To cope with such discrepancies between opposing views and patterns of behavior, the cognitively confused person has recourse to several strategies. He can exaggerate the value of what was chosen. In the Germans' case, the citizen could glorify the value of submitting to the führer over the value of independent action. One could also devalue the rejected alternative, for example, by assessing the Weimar Republic as completely bankrupt. Still another way of reducing dissonance would be to find others who agree with the person in dissonance.[51] Attitudes believed long dead came to life once more under the stresses that produced the Weimar Republic. In Bavaria, Catholic youth movements in 1919 were discussing a pamphlet *Judas, der*

Weltfeind, by the same author who later wrote for *Der Stürmer* under the name of "Heimdal." Institutional Christianity failed to take even a neutral position against the increasingly rabid offensive mounted against the Jewish minority in Germany during the Weimar years. And theological subtleties were likely to have limited effect on the casual churchgoer who knew what he saw, or what he sang, or, with growing frequency, what he heard from the pulpit.[52]

Michael Schmaus, professor of dogmatic theology at Münster, reminded his readers that the German bishops would not have revoked the ban on membership in the Nazi party if they had thought that Catholic and National Socialist ideas were in conflict. Whereas Catholic and Liberal thinking could never be reconciled, Catholicism and National Socialism could and should march hand in hand. The new stress on authority in the state represented the counterpart in the natural sphere to the Church's authority in the supernatural realm. Catholics had in the past viewed the fate of the people, anchored in blood and soil, as a manifestation of divine providence, and for that reason they would also have to share "the just concern for maintaining the purity of the blood, the basis for the spiritual structure of the people.[53] Both of these books by Lortz and Schmaus appeared in the series *Reich und Kirche* that was published with ecclesiastical permission and had a variety of aims attractive to the government.

> *Reich und Kirche* is a series that has the purpose of building the Third Reich by uniting the forces of the National Socialist state and Catholic Christianity. The series is motivated by the conviction that no basic conflict exists between the natural renaissance of our people to be witnessed today and the supernatural life of the Church. In fact, the restoration of the political order calls for its completion through the resources of religion. To awaken and deepen the understanding for this undertaking is perhaps the biggest spiritual task of contemporary German Catholicism, and its best contribution to the success of that great work of German renewal to which the Führer has summoned us. . . . Being entirely German and entirely Catholic, the series will examine and promote the relations and encounter between Catholicism and National Socialism and it will point the way toward the kind of fruitful cooperation that is outlined in the *Reichskonkordat.*[54]

The theologian Max Pribilla analyzed National Socialism in 1933-34 in light of the post-January 30, 1933 developments, and came to some surprising conclusions that contradicted the accepted pre-1933 Catholic viewpoint. National Socialism, he felt, emphasized a conception of the state and not a *Weltanschauung.* Like the bishops, Pribilla offered what was probably more an appeal than a claim when he said:

> Either one desires to impose one and the same *Weltanschauung* upon the

whole German people—then it must be so constructed as to contain within it nothing contradicting the religious convictions of Catholics and Protestants; or one must contemplate the admission of different variants of the National Socialist *Weltanschauung* with differing content or differing interpretations according as the edition is intended for Catholics, Protestants, Deists, etc. . . . Careful note must be taken of the fact that the Government by its solemn declaration of 23 March 1933 has bound itself not to interfere with the rights of the two Christian denominations; it has thereby granted Catholics and Protestants the right to defend themselves against open or covert attacks on their religious creed.[55]

Up until this point the Nazis were more concerned with their political struggle than with a strictly ideological *Weltanschauung*. Hence Hitler appeared flexible, and many felt he cold be dealt with.

World-renowned theologian Karl Adam of Tübingen argued that not only were National Socialism and Catholicism not in conflict with one another, but belonged together as nature and grace. Hitler was the people's chancellor. Adam continued: "Now he stands before us, he whom the voices of our poets and sages have summoned, the liberator of the German genius. He has removed the blindfolds from our eyes and, through all political, economic, social, and confessional covers, has enabled us to see and love again the one essential thing: our unity of blood, our German self, the *Homo Germanus.*" Professor Theodor Brauer from Cologne stressed that the appreciation of national essence must also include the approval of racial purity. Catholics had to participate in the new Germany, even if at first they were given a cold shoulder. Theologian Karl Eschweiler of Braunsberg pointed out that the Nazi *Weltanschauung* and Catholic truths were not opposites and that the ideas which the bishops had condemned in earlier years did not constitute the official program of the current party leadership.[56]

A number of new periodicals, as well, dedicated themselves to the task of reconciliation. The weekly *Zeit und Volk,* published by the Catholic firm Kösel und Pustet, made its first appearance on July 20, 1933. Noting the depoliticizing of German Catholicism, the editor Alex Emmerich (later writing under the name Edgar Alexander) called upon Catholics to find new ways of particpating in building Germany's future and to accept the new state out of inner conviction. The monthly *Deutsches Volk* was similarly devoted to promoting the unity of will between Catholicism and National Socialism. Writing in its columns, Dr. Jakob Hommes pointed out that Catholics should find it easy to embrace the world of ideas of National Socialism, since Catholicism too was essentially conservative, opposed to individualism, liberalism, and materialism.[57]

There can be little doubt that these calls for ideological *Gleichschaltung* did much to facilitate the acceptance of National Socialism by German

Catholics. The fact that such prominent intellectuals as Adam, Lortz, and Schmaus aligned themselves with the new regime and movement was seen by many Catholics as proof that National Socialism, despite some superficial errors, could not really be so bad. Furthermore, practically all these books and periodicals appeared with the approval of Church authorities and thus carried the stamp of orthodoxy. Theology is supposed to be an encounter of the Church and world in which the meaning of the gospel illuminates man's world. The theologian is to make sense of the gospel in the light of contemporary experience and is to analyze contemporary experience in the light of the gospel injunction.[58] Following cues from their bishops, the German theologians seemed to be fulfilling their professional responsibilities. Initially, Catholic theologians in Germany seemed more concerned with reconciling religious principles with the new political order than with opposing heathen Nazi principles or transforming Nazism so that it conformed to Catholic values. But then again, Catholics were not the only Germans to accept Nazism as a legitimate ideology.

Respected theologians also expressed an anti-Semitism that they felt would facilitate the reconciliation. Karl Adam, for example, defended the preservation of the German people's pure blood as a justified act of self-defense, for blood was the physiological basis of all thinking and feeling, and "the myth of the German, his culture and his history are decisively shaped by blood." The repulsion of the Jewish influence in the press, literature, science, and art now undertaken by the state was a necessary measure, he continued, though the Christian conscience must insist that these legal ordinances be implemented in a spirit of justice and love. Anti-Semitism had a decisive voice in the relaionship of the Catholic population to National Socialism. Based on the common hostility to Jews, which generally was connected to an antiliberal and antisocialist resentment, a tenuous reconciliation was being developed between Catholicism and National Socialism. At least in its early phase (pre-1935) this was of greater importance than the cultural-political differences in their *Weltanschauungen*. To many, even after the war, and Michael Schmaus is a good example, the persecution of the Jews was not so much a breakdown of the human value system as much as an implementation of the punishing justice and love of God. Writing on Bolshevism in 1933, Algermissen connects it to the cold, decomposing liberal Judaism. Even Muckermann in 1933 saw how the *Blut und Boden* ideology could be connected to proper religious and theological views. And Max Müller announced that the new government was no "abstract state," but rather an organic one, because it was constructed on a historical Christian basis on one side and on the living *Volkstum* on the other. Such responses were necessary since some Nazis had accused Catholicism of being Judaised.[59]

In a sense the theologians were only reiterating the comments of Cardinal Bertram concerning the boycott of Jewish businesses (April 1, 1933). The dean of the Berlin Cathedral, Bernard Lichtenberg, had asked Bertram to mobilize the episcopate to intervene. Bertram cited several reasons for not intervening. One was that "this boycott is a matter of economics, of measures directed against an interest group which has no very close bond with the Church." He mentioned in passing, of course, that the press, *which is overwhelmingly in Jewish hands,* had remained consistently silent about the persecution of Catholics in various countries. Bertram was himself reflecting a prejudice shared by Pius XI and the Jesuits at least until the consequences of their ideas became clear. With respect to the Jews, the anti-Semitic attitude of the papacy as well as that of the Jesuits was contained in *Civilata Cattolica.* Such anti-Semitism in Jesuit publications was normal until Pope Pius XI condemned anti-Semitism as irreconcilable with Christianity. Any ambiguity in the position of the Jesuits regarding anti-Semitism disappeared before the outbreak of World War II. Other Catholics, however, sometimes saw both Nazism and Judaism as enemies because both identified race with religion. In this way, the Jewish question continued to be asked and answers sought. Before Hitler's reconciliation, the Church warned the faithful *on the basis of* the Nazi values, but after his famed speech of late March the Church affirmed National Socialism in spite of some of the perverted views. The problem then became one of dealing with Hitler's legitimized political regime, although not with the racist ideology accepted in popular culture which seemed to reflect a minimum acceptable denominator of some of its consumers' attitudes. Specifically, it is reasonable to suggest that those who purchased or read *Der Stürmer,* for example, during the Weimar years were not so disgusted by its message that Julius Streicher, anti-Semitism, and National Socialism became by extension equally repulsive.[60] One had to accept the good with the bad, they seemed to think.

Early Catholic Resistance to the Nazi State

An added complication emerged as a result of the dissatisfaction among pastors with the Nazis who interfered in village affairs. Such popular and local resistance would seem to suggest that these Church leaders may well have chosen a battleground where they had a chance of achieving success. This resistance to the regime can be documented until the end of the war and is apparent immediately in post-Concordat Bavaria. The Church's administrative structure was not slow to react to the dangers posed by Nazism. Based on local pastors possessing considerable prestige, the Church had esteemed leaders. Since only Hitler equaled the bishops in status, even the German prelates perhaps could have offered more resistance to the Nazi officials, at least in the early stages of the Third Reich. The SD reports indicate, for example, that Catholic pastors courageously kept membership down in local Nazi organizations. Even the removal of pastors apparently did not help the Nazis, since the Catholics of the parish were loyal to their Church and priest. Forcible removal seemed only to alienate parishoners.[61] In particular, the Nazis found it difficult to stop oral communication without attacking the entire institutional structure. German villages, which contained over 50 percent of the German population, proved to be particularly insular and, given a strong-willed and healthy pastor, resisted encroachment from outside authorities. These resisting pastors were at times as much a "cross" to their bishops as to the Nazis since they confronted their bishops with the tangible issues of defending the Church or compromising with the regime. In essence, theological and patriotic abstractions would not suffice to reconcile village pastors and their local Nazi neighbors. Quite early in the Third Reich, Heinrich Himmler, head of the political police in Bavaria, was confronted with this perennial problem of a resistant clergy.

A Bavarian political police report of 1933 offers an incisive view of the Catholic Church in Bavaria. The first section, entitled "Ecclesiastical Authorities," concerned the attempts of the Archdiocese of Munich-Freising to retaliate against Nazi newspapers, to which, along with a select number of pro-Nazi newspapers, the Bavarian government had granted the business of publishing official notices. The case of one pastor is treated there, Pastor Waldhauser of Zorneding, who threatened to withdraw publication of Church notices from the *Grafinger Anzeiger* because it recommended the book of Nazi party philosopher Alfred Rosenberg. The second section of the report, entitled "Clergy," detailed the offenses of nineteen priests who had in one way or another expressed opposition to National Socialism or to its leaders. The priests' offenses range at one end of the scale from refusing to return the "Heil Hitler" greeting, to reprimaning students for accosting them with it, to graver offenses such as reasoned attacks against Nazi policies explicated in sermons, or serious but less temperate outbursts against Hitler or his followers vented at a local inn. On October 10, 1933, Pastor Karl Graf of Dorfen (already arrested once) criticized the Nazi party by praising Hitler's official stand toward the Catholic Church and contrasting that with the actions of his subordinate leaders. Moreover, he preached that *Führertum* and authority came not from themselves, but from God alone, and in the eyes of God no one part of the *Volk* was better or had more rights than any other.[62]

The Church had hoped to maintain its strength by reinforcing its "non-political" associations. Here is where the Nazi regime repeatedly violated the Concordat. One function of integration and conscientization accounts for the importance assigned in totalitarian parties to such associations as the youth organization seen as the recruiting ground for future leaders and as a means to counteract the socializing influences of family and Church. The in-cadration of the masses not ready to join the party and participate in its many activities was to be achieved by the many functional organizations to which people have to belong to gain other ends. In the case of Nazi Germany, given the large number of organizations and their high rate of penetration into their constituencies, this required either the destruction or the infiltration and *Gleichschaltung* of those organizations.[63]

Had the Church no rights? In the eyes of the SD, the Church had the right to enjoy an unhindered care of souls. In education, for example, it had the exclusive rights to teach religion. The state was concerned with the totality of education in other spheres, namely those of physical education, occupational training, and strengthening the *Volk* community. Catholic leaders insisted that religion went beyond the Church doors and should pervade the whole life. In Cologne the Jesuit Fritz Vorspel stated the position very well in 1934: "The filling up of free time is more important even than the confessional schools. Because it knows what a great effect leisure time has on youth, the Church holds firmly to its youth outside of school and home."[64] He and others felt that the youth movement, and this could be generalized to other associations as well, was extremely effective in developing Christian character. Catholic associations and the Church itself as a national organization posed an obstacle to the dissemination among Catholics of neo-heathen doctrines.

In October 1933, Pastor Droll of Kalle near Dortmund summarized the basic Catholic position since the *Kulturkampf:* "Catholicism must be brought into politics. . . . It won't do that Catholicism and the effect of the clergy stop at the Church door; all politics and public life must be thoroughly leavened by Catholicism . . ." In 1934, a priest, pointing to Hitler's Austrian origins, emphasized that the Church was already national before Hitler had issued his orders. In 1933 the Hitler government was composed of a minority of Nazis; the "national" camouflage was effective. The mistaken support of Nazi nationalism by the Catholic leaders, then, may be seen as a traditional Catholic response to accusations of disloyalty. Most frequent in these years were priestly denunciations only of Nazi racism and neo-heathen practices. In some instances bishops transferred priests who were too outspoken in their criticisms, apparently fearing that local situations might get out of hand. It seems apparent that villagers followed local leaders rather than outsiders. Even when taking action against a priest, the SD was urged to limit itself to parishes with at least two priests, so that the following Sunday mass could be said as usual.[65]

Rinderle's study of a typically Catholic village indicates that occasionally a few voters had earlier blamed the Socialists for defeat and revolution in 1918, but no one thought of them as "November criminals." Nor did anti-Semitism win local favor, since Jews in nearby villages acted like other farmers. Nazi promises for a controlled economy fell on deaf ears, because many inhabitants believed this would result in more outside interference. Hence the villagers in Kirchheim probably were not too keen on dealing with the Nazis. In this village, resistance was possible because of the village's insignificance, its suspicion of all outsiders, its fierce dedication to self-government, and its intense loyalty to the Catholic pastor. But despite the pastor's anti-Nazism, his flock adopted a "live and let live" attitude toward many Nazi policies. By giving to the *Winterhilfe* campaign, joining the German Girls' League, and eating the *Eintopf,* ordinary citizens indicated that they were resigned to live with the NSDAP as best they could and concentrate on the economic improvements taking place.[66] The Nazis wisely did not precipitate any crises. Not just in 1933, but until 1945, the National Socialist ideological revolution had relatively little influence on Kirchheim's social, economic, and political structures. Similar to other Bavarian villages, Kirchheim remained quiet and normal and maintained remarkable continuity and stability during the entire Nazi era. Kirchheim's experience of Nazism was so mild that the village could have been located in another country. As far as Kirchheim and other small villages (about 5,000) are concerned, in Germany the twentieth century was not a "Nazi century," the Nazi years were not a separate era; the *Gleichschaltung* was not applied uniformly. In large cities under the leadership of Nazi fanatics, however, the experience was usually the opposite. It must be remembered, however, that villages like Kirchheim represented almost half of the German people.[67] Hence Church leaders had some good possibilities to politicize roughly half of the population, reinforce a natural resistance to outsiders, namely the Nazis, and reassert their moral leadership. The bishops failed to take advantage of this local situation so that they could mount an offensive on the national level. As a result, resistance to the regime persisted in an uncoordinated fashion in the villages of the Third Reich—a missed opportunity. Some Catholic laity, of course, did attempt a public reconciliation with the regime.

Members of the Sodality and Elizabeth Society, along with the vast majority of Catholic women, felt relieved rather than constrained by the signing of the Concordat. To most Catholics the Concordat signaled agreement between their Church and the National Socialist state, which therewith ended potential conflicts in their lives. The reaction of some organized segments of the Catholic populace to the new unity between the Church and the state found concrete expression in the election of

November 1933. Although this election was highly staged and organized, and can hardly be termed free, the turnaround in the Catholic vote was truly amazing. After having withheld their votes from the National Socialists in the previous March election, they reversed themselves in November, voting overwhelmingly Nazi, sometimes outdoing the Protestants. This new mood of unity was reinforced late in 1933 when the Catholic hierarchy urged their faithful to integrate themselves into the new state and work positively with it.[68] But some associations, including Catholic women's groups, for example, were not coopted by the regime.

Catholic women's newspapers contained virtually no copy on themes relating to the *Volk,* nor did they register a real concern for the fate of the *Volksdeutsch*—ethnic Germans living as minorities in other countries—over whom Hitler would later work himself and Germany into a fevered pitch.[69] They were reinforced in their viewpoints by the Catholic bishops who had railed against Nazi racism and a false *Volkstum.* Catholic women also did not subscribe to the Protestant idea that the rise of Nazism corresponded to a spiritual reawakening of the German people, but they were aware that Nazism stood for a new departure and in the difficult economic circumstances that faced the country, they wished the Nazis success as much as other Germans.[70] Writing in *Die Christliche Frau,* Gerta Krabbel gave poignant expression to this emotion: "We stand now before a new beginning. We have the feeling that everything bad since 1914 is over and we are going to move ahead. We hold our breath and our hearts pound as we think what the coming months and years will bring for Germany, Europe, and the world."[71] Although one misses the collective sigh of relief that came forth from others when the Nazis came to power, Catholic women seemed prepared to cooperate as much as possible with the new regime. These articles, however, probably do reflect rather than shape the ideas of the readers of these papers, since, in general, people prefer not to read anything antagonistic to their *Weltanschauung* if they know its purport in advance.[72] Among Catholics a limited acceptance of the Nazis seemed coupled with a healthy suspicion and critical analysis of Nazi activity.

Catholic Values in a Totalitarian System

In 1933 both the pope and the German bishops were concerned about the preservation of the Church as a viable institution. A basic pattern of thought governed their behavior during the Third Reich. The Church, they were convinced, could fulfill its mission only as a visible community, as a society constituted and ordered in this world. It was the duty of the Vatican and the bishops to insure the possibility of institutional survival through dignified relations with the extant worldly authorities: no pope—no bishops—no priests—no sacraments was the line of thought.[73] How to insure institutional survival and the vitality of traditional Catholic values in an alien totalitarian state was the cutting problem. There were few historical precedents they could rely on for guidance in opposing Hitler, but many that encouraged them to seek a reconciliation.

The relationship between religious and political values is profound; it involves beliefs, convictions, emotions, images of social life, norms and values—all of which are closely intertwined with cultural and political behavior patterns. Not moral axioms but moral reasoning is the clue to the relationship between morals and political beliefs. As with politics, one has a better understanding of what a person believes if one knows the compromises he makes than if one has a map of his beliefs.[74] Regularly practicing Catholics during the Weimar Republic along with their clergy tended to vote for the Right and not enthusiastically for the Left unless individual socialists in specific districts could be trusted within the nationalistic value system. In post-1918 Germany, Catholicism played a key historical role in the organization and consolidation of a system of images, perceptions, and sentiments that led to the exclusion of the Left from the universe of legitimate political options and to the inclusion of the Nazis after they became legitimized political authorities. Since the significance of sacred beliefs and the social influence of the Church deriving its authority from God decreases as the level of religious integration recedes, allowing for the impact of nonreligious factors and a greater receptivity to influences other than religion, Church leaders had to affirm again and again their national as well as Catholic credentials in Nazi Germany. Such a delicate balancing act was necessary to insure that the Catholic priests' belief system as well as the episcopal authority continued to have an impact on the 35 percent of the population who were nominally Catholic, and to allow dedicated Catholics to represent their faith. Statistically the number of priests in orders, for example, rose from 1933 until 1945. The secular priests, however, statistically fell beginning in 1939, probably as a result of the war.[75] Understandably, the bishops were concerned to nurture the committed faithful and so had to maintain the institution.

Catholic theology has always admitted the existence of conflict situations, and it has faced them with a set of exception-making categories (e.g., rule of double effect, material-formal cooperation, etc.). But only relatively recently has it begun to see the source of some conflicts in man's temporal situation. In the past, at least some of these conflicts were approached exclusively through the distinction between the objective-subjective. Thus, in the face of human weakness, some conduct was seen as objectively wrong, but subjectively guiltless. Without denying the usefulness of this distinction, but aware of the dangers in this approach, Fuchs notes that "there is a constant danger of using genuinely 'sin-conditioned' situations as a facile excuse for indulging in compromise."[76] When society is stripped of respect for a transcendent God, secular authority unchecked can become absolute, and can lead directly to the assumption of omnipotent power over life and death on the part of the state. Coupled with this political fact, the entry of the philosophical ideologies of racism and nationalism into Western culture produced after 1933 a tragedy unthought of before that time and necessitating after 1945 a rethinking of the relationship between morals and politics.[77]

If there is any single overriding lesson to be learned from this era, it would seem to be that the religious community must never become so enmeshed in its support for a given sociopolitical order that it loses its potential to be a source of dissent and disobedience. The Church must recognize that it has a stake in maintaining a separation of Church and state as that separation is defined from an historical and contingent perspective, since this can protect the Church as well as the state. The traditional readiness to grant "the presumption of justice" to "lawful authority" no longer suits the needs of a world where the secular rulers increasingly respect no guides but the maximization of power and expediency in determining their policies and programs.[78] In political matters, no doubt, goodwill is required, but simply willing the good cannot overcome the structural framework within which people pursue evil. Indeed, a structural constraint may be precisely the kind of institutional tool that buttresses the statistical impossibility of achieving moral good. As a result of the Christian-Nazi experience, contemporary Christians have become increasingly aware of how structural constraints engender activities that are morally noxious, at least by the normal canons of reprehensibility.[79] Psychologically, Catholic reactions to the Nazis had been consistent over time for the preceding twelve years. Leaders had condemned the vulgar racism, but praised the heartfelt nationalism. One key variable for understanding the Nazi phenomenon, however, is not to be found solely in the long-established national tradition, but in external, post-World War I events that made previous ways of responding to the political environment for virtually all Germans difficult, inappropriate, or useless. The political perceptions of the populace and of Hitler and his Nazis were congruent with one another, at least on the level of nationalistic support of the *Volk*. Post-1933 statements from the bishops seemed to reinforce the same theme. Their nationalistic reaction to Weimar was consistent and in general shaped their post-1933 response to the regime. Virtually all the bishops attributed nationalistic motives to the Nazis; only a few countered, at least in public, this good quality with the evil deeds wrought by the regime. After 1933, in the absence of other officially recognized sources of nationalism, the

NSDAP was viewed as the sole bearer of the national destiny by an array of Germans. The bishops and others were hard pressed to refute this opinion.[80] Increasingly, they supported the state while simultaneously condemning specific Nazi acts. Under the best of circumstances the laity would be hard pressed to make the distinction between state and government even if they felt that Church leaders had a right to enmesh themselves in politics.

Notes

1. Juan J. Linz, "Totalitarian and Authoritarian Regimes," in Fred Greenstein and Nelson Polsby (eds.), *Macropolitical Theory* (Reading, MA: Addison-Wesley, 1975), 3:188; Staats, *Social Behaviorism,* p. 516; R. Bierstedt, *The Social Order: An Introduction to Sociology* (New York: McGraw-Hill, 1957), p. 175.

2. See, particularly, Wolfgang Sauer, "National Socialism: Totalitarianism or Fascism?" *American Historical Review* 73 (1967):404-424; Kater, pp. 19-31.

3. Jäckel, *Weltanschauung: A Blueprint for Power,* trans. Herbert Arnold, (Middletown, CT, 1972), pp. 19, 119-120; see Binion, *Hitler Among the Germans,* and Waite, *Psychopathic God,* for studies of Hitler's goals from the psychoanalytic perspective; H.R. Trevor-Roper, "Hitler's Kriegsziele," *Vierteljahrshefte für Zeitgeschichte* 8 (1960):121ff.; Adolf Hitler, *Mein Kampf* (Boston: Houghton, Mifflin, 1939), p. 47. Hitler's planning as opposed to spontaneity have been much debated. In *Hitler's Strategie: Politik und Kriegsführung 1940-41* (Frankfurt: Bernard U. Graefe Verlag für Wehrwesen, 1965), Andreas Hillgruber reveals Hitler as a master of sources and a synthesizer of ideas. As opposed to Martin Broszat and Hans Mommsen, among others, who stress Hitler's opportunism, his improvisation, his Machiavellian character, Hillgruber suggests instead a well-thought-out, rational, and historically derived "program" in stages, which the führer developed after the debacle of 1918; see Broszat, *The Hitler State*; Hans Mommsen, *Beamtentum im Dritten Reich* (Stuttgart: Deutsche Verlags-Anstalt, 1966); Kater, pp. 32-71.

4. Hitler, *Mein Kampf* (Boston: Houghton Mifflin, 1943), p. 380.

5. Edward Sampson, "Cognitive Psychology as Ideology," *American Psychologist* 36 (1981):731.

6. See, Hollander, *Leadership Dynamics: A Practical Guide to Effective Relationships.*

7. Waldman, "Models of Mass Movements: The Case of the Nazis," pp. 86, 91-92, 237.

8. William Harrigan, "Nazi Germany and the Holy See, 1933-1936: The Historical Background of *Mit Brennender Sorge*," *The Catholic Historical Review* 47 (1961):166; Michele Maccarrone, *Il Nazionalsocialismo e la Santa Sede* (Rome: Editrice Studium, 1947), pp. 1-2; Wilhelm Corsten (ed.), *Kölner Aktenstücke*, pp. 3-4.

9. Renshon, p. 136; Russell O. Allen and Bernard Spilka, "Committed and Consensual Religion: A Specification of Religion-Prejudice Relationships," *Journal for the Scientific Study of Religion* 6 (1967):191-206; Lewy, pp. 27-29; Rudolf Morsey, "Hitlers Verhandlungen mit der Zentrumsführung Am 31 January

1933," *Vierteljahrshefte für Zeitgeschichte* 9 (1961):182-194; Robert Leiber, S.J., "Pius XII +," *Stimmen der Zeit* 163 (1958-59):95-96; DA Trier, 59/26 (February 20, 1933-signature illegible); *AB Munich*, February 21, 1933, pp. 57-64. Lewy has inculcated the Hochhuth myth, sticking to the recorded utterances of the bishops and accepting them at their face value. He uses them selectively, eliminating statements of opposition and taking silence as assent; for a study of collective behavior see Stanley Milgram and Hans Toch, "Collective Behavior: Crowds and Social Movement," in Gardner Lindzey and Elliot Aronson (eds.), *The Handbook of Social Psychology*, 2nd ed. (Reading, MA: Addison-Wesley, 1969), 4:593; John P. Hewitt, *Self and Society: A Symbolic Interactionist Social Psychology* (Boston: Allyn and Bacon, 1976), p. 180; Staats, *Social Behaviorism*, p. 523.

10. Alexander George, "Adaptation to Stress in Political Decision Making: The Individual, Small Group, and Organizational Contexts," in Coelho, pp. 183-184; O.R. Holsti, "Cognitive Dynamics and Images of the Enemy: Dulles and Russia," in D.J. Finlay et al. (eds.), *Enemies in Politics* (Chicago: University of Chicago Press, 1967):25-96.

11. Müller, *Katholische Kirche;* Böckenförde, "Der deutsche Katholizismus im Jahr 1933," pp. 215-239; Karl Amery, *Capitulation: The Lesson of German Catholicism*, trans. Edward Quinn (New York: Herder & Herder, 1967); Sontheimer, *Antidemokratisches ken in der Weimarer Republik.* Böckenförde was not quite just to the German bishops. But this was the real beginning of the revision of the early favorable picture; see John Brown Mason, *Hitler's First Foes: A Study of Religion and Politics* (Minneapolis: Burgess Publishing Co., 1936); Nathaniel Micklem, *National Socialism and the Roman Catholic Church, BEing an Account of the Conflict Between the National Socialist Government of Germany and the Roman Catholic Church 1933-1938* (London: Oxford University Press, 1939); and Neuhäusler, *Kreuz und Hakenkreuz.* For the reply to Böckenförde by Buchheim, see Hans Buchheim, "Der deutsche Katholizismus im Jahr 1933: Eine Auseinandersetzung mit Ernst-Wolfgang Böckenförde," *Hochland* 53 (1961):497-515; for Böckenförde's response, see Ernst-Wolfgang Böckenförde, "Der deutsche Katholizismus in Jahre 1933: Stellungnahme zu einer Diskussion," pp. 217-245. Böckenförde seems to be isolating some episcopal statements fro their contexts or at any rate not giving *enough* contexts; for thorough and succinct analysis of the early relationship between Catholics and Nazis, see Beate Ruhm von Oppen, "Catholics and Nazis in 1933," *iener Library Bulletin* 16 (1962):8. Documents from the Vatican and materials edited by the Catholic Academy in Bavaria have provided material that is necessary for an impartial analysis. Naturally, once in power, the Nazis had the initiative and the Church was placed in a position in which a response to Hitler's initiative may well have been the only defense; see Friedrich Zipfel, *Kirchenkampf in Deutschland, 1933-1945. Religionsverfolgung und Selbstbehauptung der Kirchen in der nationalsozialistischen Zeit* (Berlin: De Gruyter, 1965).

12. Amery, pp. xv, 49-50, 96; Conway, *Persecution*, pp. xxii-xxiii.

13. Billig, p. 62; Ehrlich, p. 149; W.E. Lambert and O. Klineberg, *Children's Views of Foreign Peoples*, (New York, 1967).

14. Harrigan, *Nazi Germany and the Holy See*, pp. 167-168; Corsten, pp. 4-5; Norman Baynes (ed.), *The Speeches of Adolf Hitler, April '22—August '39* (London: Oxford University Press, 1942), 1:102-107; Robert Leiber, S.J.,

"Reichskonkordat und Ende der Zentrumspartei," *Stimmen der Zeit* 167 (1960):217.

15. The most important collections of documents reflecting the arduous negotiations leading to the Concordat as well as the issues behind the diplomacy are: Alfons Kupper (ed.), *Staatliche Akten über die Reichskonkordat* (Mainz: Matthias-Grünewald-Verlag, 1969); Ludwig Volk, *Das Reichskonkordat vom 20 Juli 1933: Von den Ansätzen in der Weimarer Republik bis zur Ratifizierung am 10 September 1933* (Mainz: Matthias-Grünewald-Verlag, 1972); Germany, *Auswärtiges Amt, Documents on German Foreign Policy, 1918-1945*, Series C, I, 347-348, 361; hereafter DGFP.

16. Kupper, pp. 10, 30, 59, 72, 90, 118; John Jay Hughes, "The Pope's 'Pact With Hitler': Betrayal or Self-Defense?" *Journal of Church and State* 17 (1975):64-65; Konrad Repgen, "Zur vatikanischen Strategie beim Reichskonkordat," *Vierteljahrsheft für Zeitgeschichte* 38 (1983):506-535.

17. *Osservatore Romano*, June 21, 1933.

18. *DGFP*, C, I, 266-268 and nos. 54, 362, 278, 333, 347, 351, Franzevon Papen, *Der Wahrheit eine Gasse* (Munich: P. List, 1952), pp. 315-316; Hansjacob Stehle, "Motive des Reichskonkordats," *Aussenpolitik* 7 (1956):561-562; Bracher, *Nationalsozialistische Machtergreifung*, p. 53. For a good coherent study of the dissolution of the Center party and the role of the Vatican, see Rudolf Morsey, "Die Deutsche Zentrumspartei," in Erich Matthias and Rudolf Morsey (eds.), *Das Ende der Parteien: 1933* (Düsseldorf: Droste, 1960), pp. 281-452; Jean-Guy Vaillancourt, *Papal Power: A Study of Vatican Control over Lay Catholic Elites* (Berkeley: University of California Press, 1980), pp. 189-193.

19. Binder, pp. 119-120; Grill, *Nazi Movement*, p. 336.

20. Ludwig Volk (ed.), *Kirchliche Akten über die Reichskonkordatsverhandlungen 1933* (Mainz: Matthias-Grünewald-Verlag, 1969), pp. 89, 172ff.; Hughes, "Pope's Pact," p. 73.

21. Stehle, "Motive," p. 562; Ernst Deuerlein, *Da Reichskonkordat* (Düsseldorf: Patmos, 1956), p. 116; Volk, *Kirchliche Akten*, pp. 92ff., 107, 237; Kupper, p. 368.

22. Kupper, pp. 130-131; *DGFP*, C, I, Nos. 319, 341, 347, 611, 624; no 3268-PS, International Military Tribunal, *Trial of the Major War Criminals* (Nuremberg, 1947-49) 32:112-113; Francois Charles-Roux, *Huit Ans au Vatican, 1932-1940* (Paris: Flammarion, 1947), p. 95; Papen, p. 316; Lawrence Walker "'Young Priests' as Opponents: Factors Associated with Clerical Opposition to the Nazis in Bavaria, 1933," *Catholic Historical Review* 65 (1979):402.

23. *Völkischer Beobachter*, July 9-10, 1933; Volk, *Reichskonkordat*, pp. 171-172; Kupper, p. 237.

24. Otto Meissner, *Staatssekretär unter Ebert-Hindenburg-Hitler* (Hamburg: Hoffmann and Campe, 1950), p. 308.

25. The official text of the Concordat is printed in *Acta Apostolica Sedis*, 25:389-413; conflict over details in the last stages of the negotiations can be found in *DGFP*, C, I, nos. 333, 347, 348, 349, 351, 362, 371; Broszat, *The Hitler State*, p. 91.

26. Harrigan, "Nazi Germany," pp. 173-174.

27. *DGFP*, C, I, nos. 418, 419, 422, 425, 789.

28. Kupper, pp. 134, 138, 236-237; Volk, *Reichskonkordat*, pp. 171-173; Volk, *Kirchliche Akten*, p. 62; Thomas E. Hackey (ed.), *Anglo-Vatican Relations,*

1919-1939: Annual Reports of the British Ministers to the Holy See (Boston: Beacon Press, 1972), pp. 250-253.

29. Lewy, chap. 3; less vitriolic but requiring revision in light of recent publications is Conway, *Nazi Persecution*, pp. 24-30.
30. Hughes, p. 70.
31. See, for example, Joseph W. Bendersky, *Carl Schmitt: Theorist for the Reich* (Princeton: Princeton University Press, 1983).
32. Volk, *Kirchliche Akten*, p. 93.
33. Konrad Repgen, "Das Ende des Zentrumspartei und die Entstehung des Reichskonkordats," *Militärseelsorge* 12 (1970):83-122; Conway, *Nazi Persecution*, p. 25, offers an alternative interpretation, stressing that Kaas abandoned the Center.
34. Volk, *Kirchliche Akten*, pp. 72ff., 89, 162; Volk, *Reichskonkordat*, 185ff.; Leiber, "Reichskonkordat," 220.
35. Volk, *Kirchliche Akten*, pp. 72, 111, 177, 193, 220; Hughes, "Pope's Pact," 74.
36. Volk, *Reichskonkordat*, pp. 198, 245; Volk, *Kirchliche Akten*, pp. 59, 93; Kupper, *Staatliche Akten*, pp. 219ff.
37. Hughes, "Pope's Pact," p. 76; Kupper, *Staatliche Akten*, pp. 290ff.; Stasiewski, *Akten deutscher Bischöfe*, 1:30ff., 239-248.
38. Ludwig Volk, *Der bayerische Episkopat und der Nationalsozialismus 1930-1934* (Mainz: Matthias-Grünewald-Verlag, 1965), pp. 2-6; A. Kupper, "Zur Geschichte des Reichskonkordats," *Stimmen der Zeit* 163 (1958-59): 367; Kupper, *Staatliche Akten*, p. 236; Volk, *Reichskonkordat*, p. 213ff., 217.
39. Linz, 355-356; Grill, *Nazi Movement*, p. 530.
40. Arthur D. Cohen, *Attitude Change and Social Influence* (New York: Basic Books, 1964), pp. 31, 84, 125-127.
41. For the encyclical and the protests against the Nazi activities that contravened the Concordat, see Dieter Albrecht, *Der Notenwechsel zwischen dem Hl. Stuhl und der deutschen Reichsregierung, I: von der Ratifizierung des Reichskonkordats bis zur Enzyklika "Mit Brennender Sorge"* (Mainz: Matthias-Grünewald-Verlag, 1965).
42. Victor Conzemius, "German Catholics and the Nazi Regime in 1933," *Irish Ecclesiastical Record* 103 (1967):329-332; Albrecht, pp. 69-70; Elihu Katz, "The Two-Step Flow of Communication: An Up-to-Date Report on an Hypothesis," *Public Opinion Quarterly* 21 (1957): 61-78.
43. Conzemius, pp. 333-334; for a good study of resistance on the local level, see Rinderle, "Struggle for Tradition."
44. George O. Kent, "Pope Pius XII and Germany: Some Aspects of German-Vatican Relations, 1933-1943," *American Historical Review* 70 (1964):61; Walker, "Young Priests," 404.
45. A good analysis of the connundrum faced by the bishops can be found in Walter Adolph, *Kardinal Preysing und zwei Diktaturen: Sein Widerstand gegen die totalitäre Macht* (Berlin: Morus Verlag, 1971); see also Walter Adolph, *Hirtenamt und Hitler—Diktatur*, 2nd ed. (Berlin: Morus Verlag, 1965).
46. William Harrigan, "Hochhuth as Historian," *Continuum* (1964):166-182; Rolf Hochhuth, Deborah Lipstadt, Fred Katz, and Donald Dietrich, "The Papacy and the Holocaust: A Symposium," *Society* 20 (1983):4-35.
47. Jim C. Nunnally and Howard Bobren, "Attitude Change with False Information," *Public Opinion Quarterly* 23 (1959):260-266; *National Archives* Microfilm F120, roll 3310, frames E58048 and E580151.

48. Lewy, p. 107; Walter Gerhart, *Um des Reiches Zukunft, Nationale Wiedergeburt oder politische Reaktion?* (Freiburg: Herder, 1932), pp. 151, 171, 180, 207; Linz, p. 197.

49. Konrad Algermissen, *Die Gottlosenbewegung der Gegenwart und Ihre Überwindung* (Hannover: Verlag Joseph Giesel, 1933); Joseph Lortz, *Katholischer Zugang zum Nationalsozialismus kirchengeschichtlich gesehen* (Münster: Aschendorff, 1933), pp. 9-15, 26. Some research indicates that Catholics, at least in the United States, are likely to be more authoritarian and dogmatic than are Protestants and Jews; see Arthur Cryns, "Dogmatism of Catholic Clergy and Ex-Clergy: A Study of Ministerial Role Perseverance and Open-Mindedness," *Journal for the Scientific Study of Religion* 9 (1970): 239; Schwarte, pp. 43-44.

50. Walter Mariaux, S.J., *The Persecution of the Catholic Church in the Third Reich* (London: Burns & Oates, 1940), pp. 416-417.

51. Leon Berkowitz, *A Survey of Social Psychology* (Hinsdale, IL: Dryden Press, 1975), pp. 72-73, 149; Edward E. Sampson, *Social Psychology and Contemporary Society* (New York: Wiley, 1971), p. 110.

52. Scholarly analyses of Christian anti-Semitism may be found in Wm. Eckert and E.L. Ehrlich (eds.), *Judenhass-Schuld der Christen?!* (Essen: H. Driewer, 1964) and Grieve, *Theologie und Ideologie.*

53. Schmaus, *Begegnungen*, pp. 7, 23, 29, 42.

54. Bookjacket of Lortz, *Katholischer Zugang.*

55. Pribilla in Micklem.

56. Karl Adam, "Deutsches Volkstum und katholisches Christentum," *Theologische Quartalschrift* 114 (1933):42, 59; Theodor Brauer, *Der Katholik im neuen Reich: Seine Aufgaben und sein Anteil* (Munich: Kösel u. Pustet, 1933), pp. 32, 77; Karl Eschweiler, "Die kirche im neuen Reich," *Deutsches Volkstum* 15 (1933):454; Rosenberg in *Mitteilungen zur Weltanschaulichen Lage* 2 (1936):11.

57. Alex Emmerich, "Katholizismus ohne Politik," *Zeit und Volk* 1 (1933):5; Edgar Alexander, *Der Mythus Hitler* (Zurich: Europa-Verlag, 1937); Hommes, "Katholisches Staats," 285-288. In his *Lebens-und Bildungsphilosophie als völkische und katholische Aufgabe* (Freiburg: Herder, 1934), p. 135, Jakob Hommes characterized the new nationalist movement as "the return to natural law and God."

58. Lewy, p. 109; C. Ernst, "Theological Methodology," in Karl Rahner et al. (eds.), *Sacramentum Mundi: An Encyclopedia of Theology* (London: Burns & Oates, 1970), 6:218.

59. Gustav Lehmacher, S.J., "Rassenwerte," *Stimmen der Zeit* 126 (1933):81; Greive, pp. 225-226; Friedrich Muckermann, *Vom Rätsel der Zeit* (Munich: Kösel U. Pustet, 1933), p. 120; Max Müller, "Neudeutsche Jugend und neuer Staat," *Leuchtturm* 27 (1933-34):136ff.; A. Wiedemann, "Stimme aus der katholischen Jugend," *Deutsches Volkstum* 15 (1933):568.

60. Peter Matheson (ed.), *The Third Reich and the Christian Churches* (Grand Rapids, MI: William B. Eerdmans Publishing Co., 1981), p. 11; Vincent A. Lapomarda, "The Jesuits and the Holocaust," *Journal of Church and State* 23 (1981):241; see Richard A. Webster, *The Cross and the Fasces* (Stanford: Stanford University Press, 1960), p. 126; Pinchas E. Lapide, *Three Popes and the Jews* (New York: Hawthorne Books, Inc., 1967), pp. 80-82, 96, 106-109; Bartolemeo Sorge, "Civilata Cattolica," *The Jesuits* (1975-76): 147-55; Celia S.

Heller, *On the Edge of Destruction* (New York: Macmillan, 1970), p. 110; Helmreich, pp. 354, 520. The Jesuit Order itself had at least one superior general and one cardinal of Jewish background; Greive, pp. 205-206; Showalter, p. xi.

61. *National Archives*, roll 193, frames 2732373-84, 2732836, 2732915-19, 2732362; roll 410, frame 2933807; roll 193, frame 2732635. Studies of the resistance can also be found in Donald Wall, "The Reports of the *Sicherheitsdienst* on the Church and Religious Affairs in Germany, 1939-1944," *Church History* 40 (1971):437-456, and Boberach, *Berichte.*

62. *National Archives*, German Foreign Ministry, T-120, roll 3310, frames E580143-55.

63. Hans-Christian Brandenburg, *HJ-Die Geschichte der HJ* (Cologne: Verlag Wissenschaft und Politik, 1968); Arno Klonne, *Hitlerjugend. Die Jugend und die Organisation im Dritten Reich* (Hanover: O. Goedel, 1955).

64. *National Archives*, roll 193, frames 2732676, 2732930-33.

65. Buchheim, "Deutsche Katholizismus," 497ff; Lawrence D. Walker, *Hitler Youth and Catholic Youth, 1933-1936: A Study in Totalitarian Conquest* (Washington, D.C.: Catholic University of America Press, 1970), pp. 76-78, 85; Walker, "Young Priests," pp. 87-89, discusses SD procedures against clergy opposing the regime.

66. Rinderle, pp. 79-80, 111-112, 129; Friedrich Glum, *Der Nationalsozialismus, Werden U. Vergehen* (Munich: Beck, 1962), pp. 300-302.

67. Glum, pp. 241-244; Edward N. Peterson, *The Limits of Hitler's Power* (Princeton: Princeton University Press, 1969), p. 405.

68. A. Ihorst, "Zur Situation der katholischen Kirche und Ihren Caritative Tätigheit in der ersten Jahren des Dritten Reiches" (Diplomarbeit, University of Freiburg i. Br., 1971), pp. 1-5; Klaus Scholder, *Die Kirchen und das Dritte Reich* Bd. 1, *Vorgeschichte und Zeit der Illusionen, 1919-1934* (Frankfurt: Ullstein, 1977), p. 646.

69. See the three Catholic womens' papers: *Frauenland, Die Christliche Frau, Frau und Mutter.*

70. *Frau und Mutter*, 24: June 6, 1933, p. 41.

71. *Die Christliche Frau*, 21: September 9, 1933, p. 226.

72. Festinger, *Cognitive Dissonance*, p. 30. On many occasions, however, people do read both sides even if their minds are made up; see Guido H. Stempel III, "Selectivity in Readership of Political News," *Public Opinion Quarterly* 25 (1961):400-404.

73. Hansjakob Stehle, *Eastern Politics of the Vatican, 1917-1979*, tr. Sandra Smith (Athens, OH: Ohio University Press, 1981), p. 8.

74. Robert Lane, "Patterns of Political Belief," in Jeanne Knutson (ed.), *Handbook of Political Psychology* (San Francisco: Jossey-Bass, Inc., 1973), p. 113.

75. Franz Groner (ed.), *Kirchliches Handbuch: Amtliches statistisches Jahrbuch der katholischen Kirche Deutschlands* (Cologne: Bachem, 1957-1961), 25:524. For a comparative perspective on the role religion plays on the current French political scene, see Guy Michelat and Michael Simon, "Religion, Class, and Politics," *Comparative Politics* 10 (1977):159-186. For the most recent work on early Christian anti-Semitism, see John Gager, *The Origins of Anti-Semitism: Attitudes Toward Judaism in Pagan and Christian Antiquity* (New York: Oxford University Press, 1983). Gager concludes that anti-Semitism in antiquity was rare and that Paul—usually cited for his repudiation of Judaism—was, in fact, totally outside the mainstream of Christian anti-Judaism.

76. Richard McCormick, S.J., "Notes on Moral Theology: 1980," *Theological Studies* 42 (1981):83.

77. Desmond Fisher, *Pope Pius XII and the Jews: An Answer to Hochhuth's Play, Der Stellvertreter [the Deputy]* (Glen Rock, NY: Paulist Press, 1963); Irving Greenberg, "Cloud of Smoke, Pillar of Fire: Judaism, Christianity, and Modernity after the Holocaust," in Eva Fleischner (ed.), *Auschwitz: Beginning of a New Era?* (New York: Ktav Publishing Company, 1977):7-56.

78. Gordon C. Zahn, "Catholic Resistance? A Yes and A No," in Littell and Locke, *German Church Struggle*, pp. 234-235. For a penetrating socio-political analysis of the relationship between the emergence of the national state and genocide, see Irving Louis Horowitz, *Taking Lives: Genocide and State Power* (New Brunswick, NJ: Transaction Books, 1980).

79. David Martin, "The Sociological Mode and the Theological Vocabulary," in Martin (ed.), *Sociology and Theology*, pp. 50-51.

80. Muzafer Sherif, *Social Psychology* (New York: Harper, 1969). On attribution theory see H.H. Kelley, "Attribution Theory in Social Psychology," in D. Levine (ed.), *Nebraska Symposium on Motivation 1967* (Lincoln: University of Nebraska Press, 1967), p. 197.

5

Hierarchy on a Tightrope: Episcopal Tactics in the Third Reich

Once the Nazis began expanding their electoral support during the Weimar era, they drew votes from so many occupational groups that it has been easier to discover those that did not vote Nazi, specifically the skilled and unskilled workers as well as the Catholic bloc, than to determine those that did.[1] After January 30, 1933, the effects of group pressure probably accounted for the willingness of even more Germans to adhere to the Nazi party creed. Non-Nazi Germans increasingly received positive reinforcement from others for the Nazi attitudes held, the decisions made, and the actions performed. In all likelihood, of course, some Germans certainly followed the Nazi banner not out of any great sense of idealism or spiritual fervor, but simply because they did not want to offend unnecessarily the NSDAP as it tightened its hold on Germany.[2] Hitler's own goal was to develop values and attitudes, which would result in popular expressions of support initially for moderate political policies that would eventually lead to his ultimate radicalization of German society through his racial revolution. His goal was to eliminate dissent. To be effective, his propaganda had to relate the persuader, the presentation of the issues, and the audience as reacting individuals. The final goal of Nazi propaganda was to maintain the desired opinion change.[3]

Hitler as persuader had a high credibility rating since he was legally chancellor and embodied such specific values, which resonated with his audience, as the *Dolchstoss* legend, the need for a strong *Volk* and *Vaterland,* and a rabid dislike of Weimar democracy. Hitler's extremist views may also have been beneficial to the acceptance of his program, since there is evidence that the more extreme the opinion change that the persuader seeks, the more actual change he is likely to get. The image of the charismatic, omniscient führer, which was fostered by propaganda and reinforced by the economic and political rewards given Germans, helped

132

counter any personal characteristics that might negatively have influenced the acceptance of his arguments. The depression and the anxiety subsequently introduced favored his talents for developing popular empathy during this period of political, economic, and social uncertainty. Hitler's presentation of the Nazi program was brilliant. As he gained more control of the information channels in Germany, he could more effectively present his side of the issue for an immediate, even though sometimes only temporary, opinion change. Enough temporary opinion changes eventually helped develop either permanent attitude changes or an indifference leading to a "live and let live" frame of mind. There does seem to be a positive relationship between the intensity of anxiety and the degree of attitude change, especially if the recommendations for action are explicit and possible. Hitler's strategy to secure attitude change and adherence to his program and person was to state very explicitly the actions that he wanted taken to remedy the calamitous conditions existing in Germany after the lost war and the onset of economic depression.[4]

Hitler possessed an intuition for propaganda appropriate to his audience and their milieu; his anxiety-ridden audience was primed for manipulation and for the acceptance of almost any credible solution to the post-1929 economic catastrophe that had left the Weimar governments impotent. In general, individuals will selectively search for evidence consonant with their goals. Hitler's task was to help his audience recognize the correct path to follow. As the political "drummer," his successful persuasion techniques took cognizance of the socioeconomic and political bases of attitude formation. He seemed quite sensitive to the fact that an individual whose self-esteem has been threatened is easily influenced. Enlisting millions in public demonstrations of support for a regime that did renew patriotism and that did begin dissolving the anxieties rooted in the alien Weimar Republic helped increase the probability of attitude change along a broad spectrum of the German citizenry. Individuals' attitudes can also also influenced by the groups to which they belong. Generally, persons are rewarded for conforming to group standards. Hitler's *Gleichschaltung* aimed at eliminating all non-Nazi organized groups.[5] Agreement with Hitler's political goals, which were acceptable to most Germans anyway, made adherence to the moderate dimensions of his *Weltanschauung* painless. Most assumed the radicals in his movement could be tamed.

People attached to a group are least influenced by materials that conflict with group norms. Eliminating or at least restricting the activities of associations not attached to the party was a top priority. Integrating Germans into NSDAP organizations would offer a spectacle of mass support for the regime and discourage dissonant viewpoints. A boy, for example, could be politically indifferent in the *Hitlerjugend,* but he could not very well be hostile to a regime that seemed, at least in part, beneficial. The greater the identification with even part of the value system of the Nazis, the more the resistance that could be developed to all counternorm communications. Group pressure can also be weakened with the consistent opposition of even one component of the social system. Hence, one of the primary Nazi goals was to eliminate any dissident opinion. Securing an opinion change was the first step; Hitler desired the change to persist. Repeating his themes helped prolong their influence. His *Gleichschaltung* policy and mass rallies indicate that he and his advisers were cognizant of the fact that attitude change is more persistent over time if the receiver actively participates in, rather than passively receives, the communication. In general, people look to the environment for the information that they need in forming their attitudes. Useful information can be acquired from friends, the media, and many other sources.

There is a link between attitudes and behavior. Attitudes themselves depend on a variety of factors. The expectation of the outcome involved in adopting an attitude seems to be a salient factor. A positive and desired result supports the adoption of a specific attitude. Behavior also depends on beliefs about what other people think should be done. In essence, how people will act in a given situation depends on attitudes and social pressure.[6] How are new values selected? The intrusion of outside forces and the breakdown in the adequacy of existing institutions are two common explanations. Social environment is a major contributor. Values, therefore, can be transformed because of external changes in degree and the kind of information available as the result of a new intrusive social and political ideology.[7] The bishops could only maintain Catholic values by combating both Nazism and the historical patterns that supported Hitler's *Weltanschauung.* Historically, their support of nationalism condemned them to do neither. Their early public support of the "new spirit" in the land signaled their flock that Nazism might not be an unmitigated disaster. This attitude and Hitler's restrictions on Catholic propaganda efforts, combined with his apparent successes in domestic and foreign policy, seriously curtailed the ability of the episcopate to oppose radical Nazi policies during this entire period.

Particularly difficult to control through normal Church channels were statements made by leading members of the laity. Baron von Schorleman, an early Catholic Nazi, for example, disagreed with the 1932 policy of the bishops when he said:

> The Catholic Church through its clergy, thinks fit to attack the Hitler movement violently. We German Catholics get a sense of liberation when we find a Catholic priest resolutely supporting the German cause. All the powers of the

Church, all the attempts at intimidation will fail to stop us. Neither the Church nor any of its dignitaries has the right to silence a German Catholic when it is a matter of boldly confessing his faith in Christian Germanism.[8]

Issues raised by the Nazis could be answered by Church officials. Generally, however, conflicts in modern societies are more likely to be discussed in terms of priorities for public policy than in terms of the basic values of the society itself, especially when such values are part of the legitimating consensus.

Such an anachronistic authoritarian state as the Second Reich—by slowing the mature development of liberalism, democratic socialism, left-wing Catholicism, and responsible conservatism—provided a desirable prototype for Nazism and perhaps made it impossible to offer effective resistance to the onslaught of the Third Reich.[9] Possibilities for the control of the laity or for political attacks by bishops also were limited when the political neutrality of the Church in the Third Reich was accepted by the Concordat after it was clear that the Catholic parties were defunct.[10] Given this situation, if any criticism can be leveled against the Church, it would have to be its excessive reliance on diplomatic protests and the failure to acquaint Catholics with those protests to mobilize their support for the rights guaranteed by the Concordat. The reasons for this failure can be found in the nature of German Catholicism as a whole, the attitude of the faithful toward the hierarchy and clergy, and the peculiar relationships within the hierarchy itself. The Catholic bishops judged political forms from preconceived and, to an extent, ahistorical ideals, encouraging flight from the concrete problems and challenges presented by the Nazis. Hitler and the bishops frequently used the same political terminology, encouraging Catholics to assume that Hitler might well be introducing a national era rooted in the past.[11] By 1933 the pattern had been set of giving recognition to Hitler and his regime as the legitimate secular authority possessing full claim upon the loyalty and obedience of the individual German Catholic, not only as a civil duty but specifically as a moral obligation. If the Nazi radicals were not going to challenge the institutional structures of the Church, there seemed no substantial reason for any Church struggle. The Catholic hierarchy used its influence in 1933 to support the regime and so gain the unprecedented advantages of the Reich Concordat.[12] In order to continue administering the sacraments and performing other spiritual functions, Church leaders placed a high premium on institutional survival. The bishops said: "Under no circumstances would we seek to deprive the state of the virtues of the Church, and we may not do so; for only the power of the *Volk* combined with the power of God inexhaustibly streaming forth from the spiritual life can rescue and restore us."[13]

After 1933, many Catholics adapted to the new regime. The well known Catholic legal scholar, Carl Schmitt, almost immediately adjusted to the fact that National Socialism in 1933 had become the dominant force in German politics. Schmitt had always considered obedience to the legally constituted authority a fundamental political precept and, just as he had transferred his allegiance in 1919, he now felt bound to obey the newly constituted authority. He was not alone. After 1933 literally hundreds of thousands of Germans flocked to join the party; they were motivated by opportunism, fear, or in many cases enthusiasm.[14] Gröber insisted that the misgivings against the regime, voiced by some Catholics, did not involve the state, but were directed against those in the NSDAP who sought to block "the peaceful integration of Catholics into the new type of government." Bishop Berning's book linked Catholic thinking and national consciousness. The age of individualism, he declared, had surrendered to a new era that justifiably sought a return to the ties of blood.[15] Dr. Anton Stonner, an expert on religious instruction, maintained that the totalitarian character of the new state did not have to lead to difficulties in the relations between Church and state. The Church was also totalitarian, although her claims were on a different plane. The importance attributed by the Nazis to the values of *Volk* should be supported, for Christian revelation made the identification with one's own people a duty.[16] *Volk* connotes a people organized along national lines and somehow organically fused together using such varied cements as race, religion, and culture. In Germany, *Volk* was seen as the ultimate political reality, although not necessarily supported by the primacy of race.[17] In 1935, Bertram reminded his Breslau clergy that many National Socialist ideas already existed in Catholic teaching. The Church had always admitted the significance of race, soil, and blood, which were valuable divine gifts and received special consecration through Christianity.[18] Selectively assimilating Nazi ideas proved to be a very dangerous step on the part of the hierarchy and further confused German Catholics, although, in the light of past German Catholic experiences, such accommodation should not be surprising.

In Nazi Germany both the laity and clergy could generally be characterized by their passivity, because they usually obeyed the decisions of their leaders with little opposition. Many of the German bishops, most of whom had matured within the *Kulturkampf* experience, considered Nazism as another potential *Kulturkampf*. Resistance during the Bismarckian era had been costly, and so they eschewed that option. On the basis of the protection granted under previous *Länder* Concordats, they hoped for similar results in 1933. The Church had acknowledged the legitimacy of Hitler's government. The normal manner of dealing with a government in these circumstances was by way of petitions and appeals based on the terms of the agreement. From 1933 to 1938 the bishops supported, although not uniformly or always enthusiastically, Cardinal Bertram's policy of petitions and appeals.[19] Even though such an approach was not dynamic and seemed to be a least-common-denominator type of policy, it was hoped that it would provide security for schools, youth groups, and the press. The Church, moreover, expected to regulate its own nonpolitical affairs. Unfortunately, Hitler's and the bishops' definition of political activity differed. As a political movement, National Socialism required the elimination of all religious and cultural representatives not compatible with its *Weltanschauung*.[20]

Initial Episcopal Confusion

News that the Concordat had been ratified was greeted with welcome relief in many Catholic circles and obscured the few pockets of local resistance to the Nazi *Gleichschaltung*. Several dioceses scheduled special thanksgiving services to honor the achievement. In Berlin, Caesare Orsenigo, the papal nuncio, presided at a solemn high pontifical mass attended by Catholic members of the SA and SS. Overhead, the papal colors mingled with the swastika, while the faithful jammed into St. Hedwig's Cathedral and overflowed into the Kaiser Franz Josef Platz to participate in the celebration. The preacher struck the chord for the German episcopate for the duration of the Reich by eulogizing Hitler, but not necessarily others (i.e., the "radicals"), in the movement. Father Marianus Vetter emphasized that the Concordat was a symbol of peace and friendship between the Church and state. Hitler, he intoned, "was a man marked by his devotion to God and sincerely concerned for the well-being of the German people." Other bishops ordered the *Te Deum* to be sung in the parishes of their dioceses.[21] On October 9, 1933, Archbishop Gröber, a "sponsoring member" of the SS by this time, pledged his support of the Reich.[22]

Others as well supported the new order. Bishop Berning harmonized Catholic doctrine with the philosophy of "positive Christianity" as proposed in the National Socialist program. In a pamphlet entitled *Katholische Kirche und deutsches Volkstum* he sought to build a bridge between the Church and Third Reich. He saw, for example, in the "New Order" the basis for reestablishing the traditional Catholic idea of the *Sacrum Imperium;* throne and altar were to be united to form the basis of an earthly kingdom in which man, under the leadership of the secular and spiritual authorities, worked out his eternal salvation. Berning envisioned the beginning of the Third Reich and the subsequent agreement with the Vatican as the reincarnation of this medieval paradigm. The German *Volk* were the bearers of this ideal "in opposition to the formerly liberalistic culture."[23] Msgr. Franz Hartz applauded the führer for saving Germany from "the poison of liberalism . . . and the pest of communism."[24] On the more popular level, General Secretary Johannes Nattermann of the Kolping House Society not only claimed that the NSDAP and Kolping had the same goal, German unity, but that he would personally be very happy "if the staunch and loyal sons of Kolping would turn into equally loyal SA and SS men."[25]

The euphoria concealed a hostility between Church and state that time and the intensified totalitarianism would only exacerbate. Basically, inner-oriented man is a latent threat to the totalitarian system in which the conflict is between collective goals and private ones. Although in modern states religion has had to "evacuate" one area after another in the public sphere, it has generally been maintained as a public expression of the personal values of the individual.[26] Basically, therefore, the Nazis hoped that their policy of restriction would evolve into the elimination of the Church's influence. On September 19, just nine days after the ratification of the Concordat, Heydrich issued a set of secret instructions to the Bavarian Political Police. He advised his agents that ratification of the Concordat did not mean that the Nazis intended to relax their activities against the Church's organizations. The instructions continued, therefore, to insist that all organizations were to be limited to purely religious functions, and all public meetings, parades, and so on, were forbidden. Furthermore, any Catholic group suspected of engaging in "political activity" was to be immediately suppressed.[27] Increasingly mistrustful, Bavarian bishops turned to Rome for help. In early September Bertram had raised the question that would be crucial during the ensuing years. Would the ratification of the Concordat, Bertram asked Pacelli, leave the Vatican in a position to protect the rights of the Church, when such protection required that the spirit of agreement be based on a "friendly understanding" among the highest authorities?[28] As chairman of the Fulda Bishops' Conference, Bertram was unprepared to deal with the political realities of the Reich. He disliked politics, he suffered from a debilitating shyness, and his preference for pastoral duties outweighed his other talents. Once Pius XI ratified Article 32 of the Concordat, in essence he absolved the bishops from any political responsibility. By the time the bishops became fully aware that Hitler's campaign was directed not only against liberalism, Bolshevism, and the Jews, but also against the Church, the bishops were committed to a course of loyal obedience, difficult to reverse both psychologically and practically. Ultimately, they adopted a policy of reserve toward current political problems and events and refused intervention in matters not specifically ecclesiastical in nature. The tragic results were that they remained silent when issues arose in which moral questions were involved, even though the rights guaranteed by the Concordat were not threatened. Along with their fellow Germans the bishops had a political outlook molded by their national loyalty. They came to believe Hitler's promises to create a new order in which the evils of liberalism, atheism, and the spectre of communism would be eliminated. Generally, the bishops protested their loyalty to the führer, while simultaneously charging other party and government leaders with violating the Concordat. Robert d'Harcourt characterized this action by the bishops as an attempt to "reconcile the irreconcilable, to flatter the hangman and console the victim."[29]

The failure of the Church in August of 1933 to insist on a definite list of protected organizations before signing the Concordat was a serious tactical blunder and illustrates the naivete of Gröber, the political inexperience of such men as Berning, the inability of the Vatican to control or guide the German hierarchy, and the emphasis on pastoral over political duties of Bertram, the Fulda chairman.[30] In the interests of securing a *modus vivendi,* the bishops had unwittingly sealed the fate of Catholic organizations.[31] The Nazis felt free to attack any Catholic organization. Objections by the bishops or the Vatican could usually be ignored, or it was maintained that until a list appeared there was no violation of the Concordat. Episcopal unity also was already cracking. At the national conference of bishops in 1933 von Preysing urged his colleagues not to acknowledge the new order whose world view was incompatible with Christianity. Instead he beseeched them to issue a clear statement of the dogmatic and ethical errors in National Socialism which would open the eyes of Catholics to the dangers and give "them a measuring stick for truth and falsity in the movement." To fail to do this would leave the Catholic position regarding their organizations unintelligible and contradictory. After 1935 Preysing did not press ineffective protests until the war and devoted himself to personal works of mercy, including financial help to those Jews desiring to emigrate.[32]

Although the Concordat was ratified, the issue concerning an approved list of protected organizations continued to drag on. From October 23-28, 1933, Rudolf Buttmann, head of the department of *Kulturpolitik* in the Ministry of the Interior, met in Rome with Pacelli, Kaas, and Gröber, but accomplished virtually nothing.[33] Meanwhile, a situation arose that allowed the bishops to test their strength vis-a-vis Hitler to force him to honor the treaty obligations. In the process, however, they highlighted their own divisions and indicated that they possessed a fatal flaw similar to that of their old enemies, the Liberals, since the Catholic hierarchy also supported nationalism even when it meant political capitulation. On October 14, 1933, Hitler withdrew Germany from the League of Nations. Cleverly, he announced that a plebiscite would be held in combination with the

Reichstag elections on November 12, in which the people would be asked to approve the chancellor's decisions. In a letter to Bertram, Gröber suggested that the bishops publish a joint statement in support of the plebiscite. Such an action, Gröber pointed out, would be considered a patriotic act of the first magnitude. He warned that the omission of a declaration could lead to consequences which could "hardly be calculated."[34] Gröber believed that if the bishops came out in support of the plebiscite, Hitler would reciprocate by calling off the anti-Catholic campaign and by making generous concessions in the matter of Catholic organizations.

Upon receipt of Gröber's suggestions, Bertram forwarded the Freiburg prelate's advice to the other German bishops but significantly added that he was personally opposed to any public statement "which touches on a purely political matter." He feared that a precedent might be established "for all other, and probably still more difficult, situations that might arise in the new Reich." He agreed, however, to abide by the decision of the majority. Bertram also included a rough draft of a statement, in case the bishops decided to publish one, and requested a response by November 5, 1933. The draft stated that the bishops relinquished the decision about "the purely political aspects of the situation" to the conscientious judgment of the voters. But, insofar as the future of the people and the fatherland were concerned, it was the moral obligation of every Christian to support the efforts of the legitimate authorities.[35]

After Cardinal Faulhaber received a copy of Gröber's letter to Bertram, as chairman of the Freising Conference, he submitted his version of a public statement to the Bavarian bishops for comment and approval. More specific than Bertram's draft, Faulhaber's proposal was far less flattering to the regime than Gröber would have wished. It called for the loyal support of the faithful in the plebiscite issue but stressed that this call did not mean episcopal approval of the Nazi hostility against the Church. The statement clearly implied that the Church supported the government on condition that the Reich adhered to its Concordat obligations in the matter of schools, the press, youth organizations, and so on. The point was not lost on the Nazi leaders in Bavaria, who suppressed publication of the statement prior to the elections.[36] Meanwhile, Gröber and Berning composed their own version of a statement and submitted it to Bertram as a possible text. But before Bertram could comment, Gröber had already published a statement in his diocese on November 8, 1933. Unlike Bertram, Gröber did not distinguish between the plebiscite and the Reichstag election. Nor did he charge the Nazis with Concordat violations as Faulhaber had done.[37] Gröber's call to close ranks in the interests of unity, peace, and national honor was an unmistakable appeal for Catholic support of the Nazi slate of candidates as well as the plebiscite.

Episcopal reaction to the three proposals varied. Some thought Bertram's draft too vague or too insufficiently forthright. Ow-Felldorf of Passau thought it was an approval of all that the Third Reich had already inflicted on the Church "and was yet to come." The bishops of Speyer, Würzburg, and Eichstätt agreed with the Breslau proposal, while others like Kumpfmüller of Augsburg did not want any statement published.[38] To complicate matters, several bishops preferred Faulhaber's statement, while others thought there should be a compromise based on the Munich-Breslau statements. This entire episode reveals the unjustified optimism of several bishops as well as points to the lack of unity and leadership within the hierarchy. The situation continued to deteriorate.

In a letter dated November 5, Bertram revealed his frustration and impatience. Not only was it impossible to compose a statement that would satisfy everyone, he wrote, but there were some who did not want any statement whatever. Under the circumstances, he concluded, each bishop should do what he thought best. Bertram also enclosed a revised version of the original statement and declared that he intended to publish it in his diocese. He closed his letter on the sarcastic note that he did not think that it would meet with the approval of many bishops.[39] Bertram's reaction left the Fulda Conference without any official statement. The bishops of Berlin, Osnabrück, and Paderborn adopted Gröber's statement, whereas the bishop of Speyer elected to combine sections of Bertram's with portions of Faulhaber's statements. In Bavaria, however, Faulhaber sought to reach some agreement among the Bavarian bishops. By means of telephone calls and telegrams, he managed to secure a consensus from the Freising Conference. Although more mild, the new version retained its criticisms of the Nazi hostility toward the Church.[40]

Although there is no way to assess the impact of the episcopal action (or inaction) on the election itself, the fact is that the Nazis won an overwhelming victory. It is true that there were no rival parties to challenge the Nazi hegemony. Still, there is a temptation to speculate on the consequences for the regime had the bishops insisted that Catholics vote in favor of the plebiscite but refuse to cast votes for the slate of Nazi candidates. The Church was still a force to be reckoned with, especially in the Rhineland and Bavaria. Since the election was a Nazi tactic to publicize the popularity of the party and the unity of the people in support of the führer, a negative vote would have helped defeat this strategy. Not only would the Nazi image have been tarnished abroad as well as at home, but, more importantly, the Church would have been on record as opposed to injustice, violence, and the flagrant abuse of human rights. The bishops, however, were totally unprepared, and in many cases unwilling, to view the situation in this light. No doubt the popularity of the Hitler movement among many German Catholics caused them to hesitate. They had been conditioned to support the national cause, and their sympathy with some of the Nazi objectives reconciled them again to the regime and led to a further evaporation of their political influence.[41] Guarantees for Catholic organizations did not materialize, but Hitler's appetite for power was whetted.

The Bishops as Patriots

During the spring and early summer of 1934, Berning, Gröber, and Bares continued negotiations with the government on the implementation of Article 31, governing Catholic associations. The bishops had become conciliatory, insisting on the independence of Catholic associations while restricting their activities considerably. They discussed with Frick, Buttmann, and von Shirach, for example, the need to provide Catholic members of the Hitler Youth with religious services and instructions. Contrary to the previous year, the episcopal delegation was now well-informed and reasonably united, but too conciliatory in Pacelli's view.[42] It was agreed that youth organizations could exist only if they confined their activities to the religious and moral education of their members. Such restrictions would do much to dampen their popularity. During the course of the negotiations, Berning and Gröber met with Hitler. Thanking the chancellor for the audience, Berning pointed out "that the bishops have placed themselves squarely behind the new state and have instructed the people to do likewise. But they were very concerned whether the Concordat would be implemented in all of its provisions." Berning supported his arguments with a list of complaints against party leaders who continued to violate the Concordat. Hitler agreed that the state and the party should not engage in religious propaganda. However, he told the bishops that in return the Church should refrain from any criticism of the government and stay out of politics. At Berning's request, the chancellor promised to issue instructions to state and party organs, forbidding all neopagan propaganda.[43] Berning and Gröber left Hitler, feeling confident that they had successfully accomplished their mission, but instead of receiving support they faced vigorous criticism. Greater divisions now existed within the episcopacy, and Bertram was disturbed with thir concessions.[44] Pacelli insisted that the Holy See wanted some points clarified. Namely, Pius refused to accept Buttmann's point that Article 31 was inoperative until the negotiations were completed. Likewise, he insisted that the Vatican was not about to negotiate with party Leaders, but only with the Reich government.[45]

Following the "Night of the Long Knives,"[46] which they did not condemn, the bishops had become increasingly disenchanted with the regime.
The problem now became one of supporting traditional nationalistic values and criticizing Nazism. In essence the bishops had to remain "good
Germans" as well as opponents of Nazism. They generally failed to make
this distinction clear to their congregations. Their disenchantment increased when Alfred Rosenberg was appointed Hitler's deputy in charge of
the supervision and ideological training of the NSDAP and so of those
Catholics, now members of the party. The news of this appointment came
as an unpleasant shock to the bishops, who had been waging a daily battle
against Rosenberg's neopagan doctrines published in the *Mythus*. In April
1933, Hitler had assured Bishop Berning that he considered Rosenberg's
book a private publication and completely disavowed its contents. When
Cardinal Schulte (Cologne) met with the Chancellor on February 7, 1934,
Hitler brushed aside Schulte's complaints with the difficult-to-believe statement that he supported Rosenberg the party theoretician but not Rosenberg the author of *Mythus*.[47] While the bishops continued publicly to
criticize Rosenberg's anti-Christian philosophy, they were reluctant to
identify the book with what were to them, at least, the praiseworthy National Socialist views on blood, race, and soil. Perhaps they had secretly
hoped that Hitler would publicly renounce Rosenberg. Perhaps they also
feared that a more intense persecution would expose clergy and laity to
even greater hardships. In any event, for a long time the bishops insisted
that they were criticizing the neopagan ideas of some party leaders and not
the state and its legitimate government. The Fulda Conference of June
1934 highlighted the gravity of the issue. Primarily the work of Cardinal
Faulhaber, the Fulda letter protested against the spread of anti-Christian
propaganda and the harassment of Catholic organizations. The letter insisted on the bishops' right to speak out against such errors, but was careful to
state that what the bishops criticized was only that portion of the
Weltanschauung that undermined religion based on divine revelation as
taught by the Church.[48] Unwilling to tolerate this criticism, which should
have led the bishops to think they could potentially mobilize resistance, the
Nazi regime refused to permit the publication of the pastoral missive; the
Gestapo confiscated printed copies. Despite Bertram's appeals, the government upheld the prohibition.

Berning and his colleagues met with Buttmann September 14-20, 1934.
The request to permit Catholic organizations to engage in certain recrea-
tional activities was turned down by the Reich representative. The attempt
to prevent the dissolution of the occupational organizations and incorporate them into Catholic action also was refused. When Berning requested
that Hitler publicly acknowledge the rights of Catholic associations as

promised in the June deliberations, Buttmann responded that the delay and the new proposals required more time to reflect on the issues. The meetings were, for all practical purposes, of no benefit to the Church and held out little hope for future negotiations.[49] Still, neither side was ready to terminate the discussions. The bishops hoped to achieve some settlement that would provide them with minimal guarantees. For their part, the Reich leaders had another reason for wanting to resume negotiations in November.

One of the provisions of the Versailles Treaty called for the Saar Territory to hold a plebiscite fifteen years after the treaty had been implemented. As January 13, 1935, approached, Hitler became anxious to secure the support of the predominantly Catholic population in the Saar. The recent Nazi brutalities in the Röhm purge had caused many Saar Catholics to become disenchanted with the regime. Since the Nazis feared a loss of support in the plebiscite, they offered an olive branch to the bishops by suggesting new negotiations. The Gestapo ordered that attacks against Catholic organizations be halted as well. Prior to the Saar plebiscite (1935), Schulte, supported by Galen and the other German bishops, called for prayer. The Bavarian episcopate used the phrase "dictated peace of Versailles" and introduced a preamble that mentioned that the Cologne province had originated this call.

> On Sunday, January 13, a plebiscite will be held in the Saar Territory on the question whether this German land and its people shall remain under the separation from the German Reich forced upon them by the dictated peace of Versailles. This decision, to be made in a few days in the Saar and fraught with fateful consequences for the future of our fatherland, no true German can face with indifference. As German Catholics we are duty bound to stand up for the greatness, welfare, and peace of our fatherland.[50]

The reasons for the German bishops' stand lay primarily in their strong personal patriotism. Historically the Saar was German territory; they saw no reason to give it up, even temporarily, just because Germany was ruled by National Socialists, probably also temporarily. The episcopate also had consistently assailed the "dictated peace of Versailles" and had supported those calling for its revision.[51] The German bishops had not been deceived by the Nazi orders to halt the harassment of Church associations. In a letter to Pacelli, Bertram pessimistically noted that there was only a temporary truce. Once the elections were over, he predicted, the Nazis would resume their campaign. Bertram's prophecy proved to be true. Not only did the Nazis resume their anti-Catholic campaign, but they intensified it by launching a bold program of defamation of the clergy and bishops. By the end of January, meanwhile, any hope of reaching a settlement in the matter of the organizations had disappeared; the Foreign Office informed Pacelli that they would adhere to the outcome of the June 29, 1934, agreement between the German bishops and the government.[52] The Nazis succeeded in gaining the support of German Catholics in the Saar plebiscite at the expense of the bishops, who had in any case been eager to support the return of the Saar to the Reich. Hitler's government reached new heights of popularity, and the bishops could do nothing but follow a patriotic course, dooming their opposition to failure.

Catholic Publications Suppressed

Despite the efforts by the bishops and the Vatican, Catholic organizations, the cultural network of the Church, had nearly all disappeared by 1936. The bishops had failed to obtain a *modus vivendi* with the regime by their basic support of the nationalistic aims of the government. Presumably, most Catholics found it difficult to reconcile the bishops' condemnation of the government one day and their support the next. In retrospect, the Church's efforts to come to terms with the Reich leaders were doomed from the start. The Nazis clearly did not want the Church as an equal partner. A totalitarian system by definition seeks to exclude any institution that might encourage allegiance to a cause other than its own. The Catholic Church as seen in the Gestapo reports,[53] for example, presented a threat to the unanimity that a totalitarian regime pursues.[54] It was, therefore, only a question of time before the Church had to be brought to its knees. Although the Concordat had been signed to protect German Catholics, it actually became a means for National Socialism to consolidate power by "legally" neutralizing the potential for episcopal opposition. Likewise, instead of strengthening the Catholics' will to resist, the treaty appeared to many of the faithful as an approval of the regime. Quick to take advantage of the prestige won by the pact, the Nazis exploited the advantage at the expense of the German hierarchy. Disunity, desire for compromise, and a nationalistic value pattern made it impossible for the bishops with any consistency to oppose the Nazi elimination of Catholic organizations. The episcopal efforts to protect Catholic organizations were an example of political naivete, excessive optimism, a lack of leadership and unity, and an overriding concern to do nothing that would interfere with the administration of the sacraments. The bishops and Vatican had hoped to arrive at coexistence and so adhered to their self-imposed restrictions. Tragically this tactic did not free, but rather imprisoned, them. Control of organizations was crucial for the state. Equally, if not more significant, was the elimination of the thriving Catholic press and so of dissident opinions.

In 1932 the Catholic dailies had reached a circulation of over three million—about one-eighth of the total daily newspaper circulation in Germany. Catholic journals numbered over 9.5 million. Even after Hitler's rise to power, Catholic journal publications continued to increase their circulation to 11.5 million. By October 1935, however, the Catholic dailies ceased to exist. A few years later (1938), the government completely suppressed all Catholic weeklies and had turned its attention against other forms of Catholic publications. With the exception of twenty-seven theological journals and the official diocesan gazettes, Catholic publications were suppressed. Even the latter, which had traditionally served as a private but official means of communication between the bishops and their clergy, were watched carefully by the Gestapo and sometimes confiscated. A supplement to the *Diocesan Gazette* of the Munich-Freising diocese, for example, published an article in October 1935 entitled "The Religious Situation in Germany," translated from *L'Osservatore Romano*. The Gestapo confiscated the issue and forbade all future translations from the Vatican newspaper to appear in the diocesan paper. When the *Diocesan Gazette* in Freiburg dared to print a report on the events in Oldenbourg, where unsuccessful attempts were made to remove crucifixes from schoolrooms, the issue was confiscated and the paper subjected to the censorship of the Gestapo. The German hierarchy sought to retain some measure of control over the Catholic publications through a series of compromises. The failure by the bishops to achieve a workable agreement with the regime had resulted in charges that the bishops willingly cooperated with the regime. Defenders of the bishops' refusal to suspend publication as a form of protest have maintained that the bishops did exercise responsibility to the end, but could not prevent the final outcome because of Nazi terror, deception, and force. They avoided only a total capitulation before Nazism.[55] Throughout this period, Bertram and the Fulda Bishops' Conference basically resorted only to "petition politics"—their chief tactic in dealing with the leaders of the Reich.

As representatives of "political Catholicism," the Catholic dailies were immediately included among the publications destined to become the victims of the *Gleichschaltung*. Papers were suspended for a few days, several weeks, or permanently, following Hitler's ordinance of February 4, 1933, which proscribed all publications "whose contents are likely to endanger public security or order."[56] Again, however, the bishops compromised at the Fulda Conference on June 3, 1933. They advocated a free press and carefully pointed out that the Catholic press "has always and everywhere proven itself as a force that upholds the state . . . and calls on its readers to submit willingly to lawful authorities." Such professions of loyalty not only revealed episcopal uncertainty toward the new regime but, more importantly, indicated the bishops' unwillingness or inability to penetrate the facade of the patriotic and noble intentions of the National Socialists. Moreover, the Concordat contained no references to the rights and privileges of the press. Apparently neither the Vatican nor the German bishops were interested in protecting that part of the Catholic press that had been closely connected with political parties. In a letter to Bertram (July 18, 1933) Bornewasser of Trier reflected the general episcopal sentiment on this issue, when he stated that since the Catholic parties had dissolved themselves of their own accord, there was no further need for the Catholic press to continue assuming a political stance. Bornewasser recommended that Catholic newspapers should concentrate in the future on religious and cultural issues. In a similar vein, Hauck of Bamberg told Bertram that the Catholic press should focus on purely Catholic news and refrain completely from party politics. The German bishops generally supported these views. In the Freising and Fulda conferences of August 1933, the bishops maintained the right of the Church to enjoy full freedom of the press "in the proclamation and defense of Catholic teaching and principles." The Vatican concurred.[57]

The bishops were not concerned with the political press. A fair number of German bishops and clergy supported the nationalistic and anticommunist statements of National Socialism. Along with a lack of enthusiasm for democracy, many bishops harbored resentment against the Weimar spirit of toleration, which, according to Faulhaber, granted the same rights to truth as to error.[58] Clearly, the bishops were more interested in protecting the rights of the Church than in defending political liberty. A simple retreat from party politics, however, would not satisfy the Nazi leaders. While the Fulda Bishops' Conference discussed ways to preserve an apolitical press, the Nazis plotted to destroy it. On October 4, 1933, the government published its *Schriftleitergesetz*, scheduled to become effective January 1, 1934. The law stipulated that journalism was a "public vocation." Hence, all editors had to meet a number of qualifications, including Aryan descent and the ability to influence public opinion. Goebbels was to determine what constituted political news. Responding to the bishops' desire to have a voice in laws concerning editors, on September 27, 1933, Buttmann argued that since the Concordat failed to mention the press, the subject should not be negotiated between Reich and Church.[59] The law meant that political leaders or events could not be analyzed within a Catholic context.

Catholic dailies were virtually eliminated when on April 24, 1934, Max Amann, president of the *Reichspressekammer,* issued an`order prohibiting the publication of any article even with religious content. He also decreed that no newspaper could be supported or promoted by any confessional group. Publishers were ordered to develop a positive and cooperative attitude toward the ideology and practices of the Nazi state. The bishops were unwilling to assume greater responsibility in the conflict and historically had really never cooperated anyway with the Catholic press associations earlier connected to Catholic parties.[60] Hoping to preserve weeklies and journals as well as periodicals, Bertram appointed Bares and Walter Adolph to meet with representatives of the propaganda ministry and negotiate a settlement.[61]

In a meeting with Max Amann, Bares pointed out that the weekly papers and political journals had always refrained from publishing politically oriented articles. The bishop argued that they served to provide "instructions, ordinances, pastoral letters . . . and other enactments for the spiritual welfare of the faithful," in accordance with the provisions of Article 4 of the Concordat. Exemption from the new law seemed reasonable. The two sides reached a compromise. Diocesan weeklies were to remain exempted from registration with the *Reichspressekammer* but agreed to join the *Fachschaft der katholischen-kirchlichen Presse,* created as a compromise and part of the Nazi press association.[62] Joining the *Fachschaft* meant automatic membership in the *Reichskulturkammer,* the parent organization. Bertram and his fellow bishops surrendered the legal freedom to criticize in exchange for religious guarantees—not a good bargain when negotiating with totalitarians.

Initially, the disappearance of Catholic daily newspapers helped increase the circulation of diocesan weeklies and periodical journals. The price of success came high. Bishops instructed the editors to avoid all criticism of governmental policies except for religious questions involving Rosenberg and the neopagan movement. The bishops rightly considered Rosenberg's espousal of a religion based on loyalty to race, blood, and soil as anti-Christian but did not question racist *Blut und Boden* political ideals. Under the terms of the Concordat, they considered it their right and duty to publish statements "regarding the spiritual welfare of the faithful." Since Rosenberg's writings expressed the essence of the Nazi *Weltanschauung,* Goebbels, Amann, and other Nazi leaders, certainly with Hitler's approval, sought to curtail these criticisms.[63] The battle between Nazi ideology and the Church was now joined in discussion of the only public issue still remaining, i.e., in the dispute concerning precisely what was religious, as opposed to political, Catholicism.

The Fulda Bishops' Conference of June 1934 noted with surprise and anxiety that "contrary to earlier declarations of the führer, the National Socialist movement itself now wanted to constitute a *Weltanschauung.*" The joint pastoral letter, nevertheless, did not attack the Nazi party and its teachings but directed its criticism at the proponents and concepts of neopaganism. Religion, they felt, could not be based on blood and race or other dogmas of human creation, but only on divine revelation taught by the Church and her visible head, the pope. Through this tactic the Church could continue supporting the new regime while opposing the "erroneous" views of such followers of Hitler as Rosenberg. The tactic failed; the pastoral letter was forbidden to be read, and unsold copies were confiscated by the Gestapo. In vain did Bertram plead that the episcopate had had no intention of attacking state or movement. Rosenberg's *Mythus* was subjected to scathing criticisms in a concerted fashion in 1934, but even then Galen in a preface recommended his own sponsored book to the clergy as one written "in a spirit of love for the German fatherland, for the Holy Church and for the truth."[64]

The struggle to prevent the Nazi regime from seizing control of the Catholic press reached a climax in February 1936. Amann informed Adolph that all existing publications, regardless of format, were required to register and comply with the provisions of the *Schriftleitergesetz* no later than April 1, 1936. Amann complained that a number of diocesan weeklies were printing political articles, and he demanded that the *Fachschaft* should enforce the nonpolitical character of these publications, not only in the text but even in the advertisements. There followed a set of guidelines that restricted Catholic papers to purely religious topics—questions dealing with dogma and ethics, lives of the saints, and meditation themes. Amann warned that any publication that did not adhere to these guidelines would forfeit its independent status and become subject to control by the *Reichspressekammer.* Both Adolph and Preysing protested that the new decree created an entirely new situation for the Catholic press—one that required consultation and clarification. On February 28, Bertram registered a protest with Goebbels in which he appealed to the Church's rights as provided in Articles 1 and 15 of the Concordat, whereby the Reich had agreed to recognize the Church's right to order and administer its own affairs. Bertram argued that one of the modern means for accomplishing this was the printed word. Therefore, he concluded, the German bishops had the right to bring their messages of faith and discipline to the attention of the faithful. He strenuously disagreed with Goebbel's decree because it withdrew exemptions already granted to official ecclesiastical periodicals.[65]

Goebbels refused to back down. On March 18, Preysing threatened to inform the faithful unless Goebbels postponed the enforcement of the decree. In a milder tone Bertram requested Goebbels to postpone the decree and abide by the agreement permitting the diocesan weeklies to remain independent of the *Reichspressekammer.* Goebbels failed to comply and the bishops were faced with a crucial question: should they forego the continued publication of the weeklies or comply with the new order? To discontinue publication of the weeklies, Bertram maintained, would deprive the faithful of an important source of pastoral advice. Submission to the order, however, would mean that these publications could be classified as "political" and so be subjected to Nazi control. Either alternative could lead to the elimination of Catholic weeklies. The bishops continued defending the Church as best they could without risking a rupture in their working relations with the regime. They still did not attribute to Hitler and his government their problems but blamed those radicals who allegedly misunderstood the Nazi party's teaching of positive Christianity. A joint pastoral letter issued in January 1936, for example, emphasized that if the Church forbade the faithful to read certain books, periodicals, and newspapers, it did so without wanting to encroach upon the prerogatives of state or party.[66] Virtually underscoring the potential power of the bishops, Goebbels informed Bertram that he would postpone enforcement of the decree until the forthcoming Reichstag elections.[67] Goebbels probably changed his mind because of Preysing's threat rather than Bertram's mild response. Elections were set for March 29, and Hitler was seeking a strong, positive response for his Rhineland gamble.

On March 7, 1936, the Nazis had marched into the Rhineland, and Hitler needed full domestic support for his blatant violation of the Locarno Pact. On March 7 Cardinal Schulte dispatched the following telegram to the commander-in-chief of the German Wehrmacht, Baron von Blomberg:

> In this memorable hour, which celebrates the entry into the German Rhineland of the German *Wehrmacht,* again as the guardians of peace and order, I greet these competent armed men of our people and with deeply affected soul remember the lofty examples of ready sacrifice in love of the Fatherland, the earnest discipline and upright fear of God which our army has given at all times to the world.[68]

In 1949 the "real" meaning of this telegram was offered. The Cologne Archdiocese stated that the telegram was meant to welcome the army as the one organization that could check the Nazi terror in the Rhineland.[69] Never was Hitler more popular than after the Rhineland occupation and never was this popularity more shaped by religious fervor and intensity than in the short phase between 1936 and 1939. After 1936, Hitler began to thrive on his own image. Three interacting factors now moved the Reich: propagandistic manipulations, Hitler's own actions, and the public creation of collective fantasies.[70]

To add to the confusion on March 22, 1936, the bishops addressed the issue of the imminent elections:

> We know the coming elections will place many of you in a painful dilemma since your affirmative answer might be interpreted as approval of the anti-

Church and anti-Christian measures and statements which in past years have filled us with sorrow and affliction. In order to pave the way for a firm '*Ja*,' we bishops in the name of all German Catholics, whose guiding principle is the Catholic faith, declare: We give our vote to the Fatherland, but this does not signify approval of things we cannot, in conscience, justify.[71]

Goebbels did not wish to risk Catholic support by having the bishops speak out against the regime. In the end 98.8 percent voiced their approval of the regime. The active nationalistic support of the bishops and the clergy in this election helped convince German Catholics that the relationship between the regime and the Church was a healthy one. Thus, it would become increasingly difficult for the Church to marshal support among the faithful in the future. After Hitler had occupied the Rhineland (March 1936) and called a plebiscite to justify his decision, even Bishop Preysing of Berlin, who earlier had voiced serious reservations, now told his flock that they could vote for the honor and freedom of the fatherland and do so with the intention of promoting "the vital necessities of the German people, the peace of the world, internal peace."[72]

Within the month, in typical fashion the government launched a new assault against the press. Amann charged the diocesan weeklies with engaging in "political Catholicism" and publishing statements detrimental to the state and party. In response, Bertram engaged in "petition politics," writing numerous letters to Goebbels, Amann, and Hans Kerrl, Minister of Ecclesiastical Affairs. Adolph was replaced by Anton Willi, an SS leader. Preysing protested Adolph's dismissal, but the propaganda minister replied that the change was necessary because of the "conflict of duties necessarily encountered by a cleric in an official position of this nature."[73] The bishops now found themselves facing the same situation that had confronted the dailies in 1934. Petition politics had only gained time. Willi now ordered each diocese to designate one paper as the official *Bistumsblatt*. Roughly two-thirds of the weeklies would go out of existence. The remaining papers would be subject to the government and so would probably be run by editors chosen by Goebbels. In August, Willi issued new directives. Not only was there to be only one official diocesan paper, but all other forms of publication were subject to censorship by the Association of the German Press, an organization under the control of the government.[74]

When the bishops assembled at Fulda in August 1936, Preysing informed them of the recent developments and urged a firm stand. It was decided not to recognize the binding character of the *Schriftleitergesetz* in the matter of the diocesan weeklies and to forbid the clerical editors of these papers to register under the law. Bertram informed Goebbels of this decision in September and requested him to allow the bishops to control these publications. Like so many others, this appeal went unanswered for months. The government proceeded to impose even more stringent measures on the press. On September 9, 1936, at the annual party rally in Nuremberg, Hitler lashed out against the Bolshevik danger, while the same theme was struck, also that day, by Pius XI at the Vatican before a group of Spanish refugees. "The coincidence that these two great speeches were delivered on the same day and the congruence of their main ideas," remarked the chancery of Trier in a pamphlet, "appear to us as convincing demonstration of what the hour demands; to wit, a sympathetic cooperation of State and Church in Germany for the combined fight against the common enemy."[75] The tone suggests an attempt to convince Hitler that the Church could be a natural ally, if the stringent measures of the *Gleichschaltung* could only be eased.

On October 1, 1936, Kerrl forbade publication of pastoral letters in the diocesan weeklies "or in any other form," except in the official diocesan gazettes issued to the clergy. Kerrl accused the bishops of criticizing the state and party and said the situation was intolerable. Responding, Bertram insisted that no pastoral letter had ever criticized the state, the movement, or the führer. The memo ended in a pigeonhole on a bureaucrat's desk and had no effect. As the entire situation deteriorated, the bishops decided to hold a special session at Fulda on January 12-14, 1937. With respect to the press, Preysing reported that the government's efforts to throttle the diocesan weeklies had created a serious situation. To preserve their rights, he urged the bishops to take a stronger stand. The bishops decided to continue in noncompliance with the *Schriftleitergesetz*. Furthermore, if the government tried to force the editors to comply, they would close down all Catholic periodicals and inform the faithful of the reasons. The bishops were mistaken if they thought their threat to discontinue 400 weeklies and periodicals would cause Goebbels to rescind the order. Even if they were only bluffing, the failure of their tactic would further weaken their position. On March 30, 1937, Bertram informed the bishops of Goebbels' refusal to reconsider. Rather than eliminate Catholic publications, Bertram counseled retreat and compliance. The bishops, he suggested, should wait and see whether the authorities would "pose intolerable demands for the journals or their editors" in concrete cases.[76] The elimination of the press made protest very difficult and helps explain why journalistic contributions increasingly came to have a theological orientation. There was still hope, however, that Hitler could realign policy. In November 1936, Faulhaber, for example, had a memorable meeting with the führer at Obersalzberg. By this point the regime had failed to live up to the Concordat, shut down the Catholic press, and virtually extinguished Catholic organizations. Faulhaber's report to the bishops, nevertheless, emphasized Hitler's statesmanlike behavior, stating: "The Führer lives in the faith of God." Apparently the Cardinal was convinced that it was the SS, and not Hitler, which was responsible for the sad condition of things. There are other instances of the Bishop's praise of Hitler. On New Year's Eve in 1938, months after *Mit Brennender Sorge,* he shocked those listening to him when he declared: "It is the privilege of our time to have at the top of the Reich the example of a simple, sober life free of both alcohol and nicotine."[77]

Diocesan weeklies that did not cooperate with the government were closed. In a report to the Fulda Bishops' Conference of March 2, 1940, Preysing noted that from January 1, 1934, to October 19, 1939, Catholic weeklies decreased from 435 to 124, that is, by 71 percent. Of these, seventy-four were suppressed for not complying with the law and sixty-one for other reasons; 176 gave up because of a lack of newsprint. The final suppression of the diocesan weeklies came with the outbreak of the war. In September 1939 Willi reminded the editors and publishers of the Catholic press that everything published was to increase the power and readiness of the German people to make sacrifices to the highest possible degree. By June 1941 the end had arrived when the government refused the further allocation of newsprint. The only publications relatively unhindered until the end of the Reich were the official diocesan gazettes issued to the clergy. Even these, however, faced prior censorship. Occasionally they were forbidden to publish certain articles, and those that did found those issues confiscated by the Gestapo.[78]

Despite the increasing governmental violations of Church rights, the bishops continued to stress that Catholics owed obedience to the state since "every human authority is a reflection of divine rule and is a participation in the eternal authority of God." The state, they felt, had the obligation of giving each individual his due, "be it property, honor or freedom and should not limit human freedom more than the total well being demands since justice is the foundation of the state." The 1933 letter concluded that what was said did not imply any hidden reservations with regard to the new state. "Only the power of the *Volk* combined with the power of God . . . can save us." Later letters specifically maintained that if a state law conflicted with divine law, "man must obey God rather than man"; but the bishops, including von Galen, still preached loyalty to the legitimate authority. In a sermon delivered in September 1934, von Galen repeated the "stab in the back" legend and claimed that Catholics had no desire to return to the Weimar days. The 1935 letter that obligated Catholics to follow their consciences closed with the warning: "Catholics make no revolt and perform no violent resistance. Instead they should neither listen to nor pass on wild rumors which were spread against authority. Their best answer to complaints was to strive for unity with Rome and to be patient and pray."[79]

In all likelihood the bishops, given their support of political obedience, could not have prevented the Nazis from shackling the press. The Concordat had no specific guarantees and probably would not have been honored anyway. Bertram consistently stopped short of calling for concerted action or open resistance. For the German bishops, obedience to lawful authority was a moral obligation. The Concordat remained in force, reinforcing the hierarchy's legitimatization of Hitler's regime. Unwilling to promote active resistance, the bishops pursued a steady, though generally unsuccessful, campaign of defensive opposition against the equally and eminently successful "war of attrition" conducted by the Nazis. The struggle to preserve the Catholic press offers a good example of the futility of "petition politics." The initiative lay with the Nazis. The bishops could not fight back, seek redress in the courts, or bring vital information to the public. Their tactics were limited to formal protests, a policy of remonstrances, and petitions. Essentially, all that could be done was to keep the lines of communication open with the Nazi hierarchy and to state their case in lengthy memos. Their task was a futile and hopeless labor. The Nazis determined the areas of the contest and the timing; the bishops responded as best they could. Couched in language that appealed to patriotic sentiments, episcopal letters, sermons, and official correspondence served merely to intensify the listeners' identification and commitment to state and nation. The combination of patriotism and protest was not effective. Even as late as 1940, however, Cardinal Bertram refused to change this tactic, with the result that there developed within the episcopacy a strong current of opposition. Although the division never surfaced, it was an admission of the failure of his policy. Had this tactic been challenged earlier, perhaps the whole tragic history of the Church in the Third Reich might have been quite different. Such a challenge would have been difficult to mount, however, since the bishops gradually lost their traditional organizational and publishing vehicles with which to reach the laity as well as the unquestioning support of their flocks. The bishops' continuous compromises and the power of the modern totalitarian state robbed the hierarchy of its traditional influence.

Diverse Responses Among the Bishops

Although the bishops by 1936 no longer could hope for improvement in the Nazi regime, they occupied a difficult position because they now lacked organizations through which they might operate against the Nazi power. The bishops had no regular means for reaching Catholics except through sermons; the Catholic papers could print no articles critical of the state, and pastoral letters could appear only in an abridged form or not at all.

After 1937, moreover, the bishops seriously questioned their right to speak out, in view of the fact that the blows of the government fell on lay Catholics, not on the bishops. By 1937 the campaign to confine the Church to the sacristy appeared to be well on its way to success. Goebbels controlled the public media. The Hitler Youth Movement had captured the loyalty of many young people. Rosenberg's neopagan doctrines threatened to undermine traditional teachings. The Church's influence in education had been reduced. By 1937 in Bavaria, for example, only 4.4 percent of the elementary school students were enrolled in denominational schools.[80]

Even though the Concordat provided an outward semblance of autonomy, Bertram and his fellow bishops were aware of the growing loss of support from the faithful. In the SS of 1938 the entire membership can be divided as follows: 51 percent affiliated with the Evangelical Church, 26 percent with the Catholic Church, 23 percent *Gottgläubig*. The elite membership was divided as follows: 23.5 percent Protestant, 8.4 percent Catholic, 68.1 percent *Gottgläubig*. Given that the Catholic population of Germany was about 33 percent, Catholics were somewhat underrepresented in the total membership and greatly underrepresented in the elite, probably because of the pronounced religious antagonism of the latter. Still, this Catholic membership in the most ideologically oriented of all Nazi organizations must have given the bishops food for thought.[81] There is evidence that even the increased salience resulting from religious group membership fails to influence significantly perceptions of political matters not seen as relevant to religious group identification. Equally signficant, an intolerance of ambiguity is found not only in prejudiced persons, but also in religious individuals,[82] who are seeking universal norms. The bishops could probably not have generated support for Catholic anti-Nazism. The dissonance that Catholics would have experienced would have been too great and might have forced Catholics to choose between the state and the Church, hardly a welcome prospect. The response of the bishops to the Nazi regime can be characterized as an attempt to establish distinctions between state and party as well as between Hitler and his "radical" colleagues, so that Catholics could support both the state and Hitler. Such abstract distinctions were difficult to establish and even more difficult to translate into positive action.

Church leaders, moreover, also began to show signs of pessimism and weariness with the whole protracted struggle. In December 1936, reflecting episcopal discouragement, Bertram wrote Pacelli that to expect a basic change in the attitude of the National Socialist party and the government dependent on it was probably impossible for the time being. On the evidence of the residual loyalty of many Catholics to the Church, on the admittedly inconclusive reports that a majority of priests and laity opposed the Nazi government, and on the evidence that the Catholic press could still occasionally express at least religious opinions at variance with the official viewpoint, the bishops might have turned the Catholics actively against the state during the early years of Nazi power. A united episcopal plea to Catholics who looked to their bishops for political as well as spiritual leadership might have forced the government to modify its policies. To achieve this, the bishops would have had to stand by the principles and policies enunciated prior to 1933 and to realize that they could not save their institutions and people by a policy of expediency.[83] Each compromise merely reinforced the Church's capitulation to the regime and signaled the laity to support the Church as an institution by not mounting an organized resistance.

The joint pastoral letter of January 3, 1937, for example, more tightly bound the ties between the Church and Reich. The bishops warned that Russian Bolshevism had started its march on Europe. The letter maintained that the führer and chancellor of the Reich, Adolf Hitler, had sighted the advance of Bolshevism from afar and that his thoughts and aspirations aimed at averting the horrible danger from the German people and the entire continent. The German bishops considered it their duty to support the head of the German Reich by all those means the Church had at her disposal and to mobilize all the spiritual and moral forces of the Church in order to strengthen confidence in the führer. The Church's role in supporting the struggle of the Third Reich against Bolshevism, the bishops went on, could be far more forceful and effective if the constant attacks against Christianity would cease and if the Church were to enjoy those freedoms guaranteed her by divine law and by the Concordat. But Catholics continued following the führer despite their increasing lack of confidence in his reliability. "Even where we repulse inroads upon the rights of the Church, we want to respect the rights of the state in its proper jurisdiction and to see also the good and great elements in the work of the führer."[84] Obviously unimpeded, the Nazis continued their struggle with the Church, and the bishops insisted on the rights obtained through the Concordat as Pius XI now made his most forceful and public attack on the Nazi ideology and the emergent "Hitler State."

Pacelli, Faulhaber, Preysing, Bertram, and von Galen by 1937 saw the need for a more resolute stance against the Reich government. Their discussions eventually took the form of *Mit Brennender Sorge*. Basically, the bishops and pope agreed on the essentials of the persecution and left the drafting of the encyclical to Pacelli and Faulhaber.[85] It was decided that the encyclical concentrate on the ideological errors of Nazism but abstain from mentioning the party in order to avoid charges that the Church was mixing in politics, thereby violating the Concordat. *Mit Brennender Sorge* was smuggled into Germany and read from the pulpits on Palm Sunday March 23, 1937. The pope noted that the Concordat was being violated and the conscience of the faithful oppressed. Pius urged the faithful to uphold their faith and defend the rights given by the Concordat. Human laws that are contrary to natural law, he insisted, could not be made obligatory in conscience. He defended parental rights in education and called for the faithful to resist the idolatrous cult of race and *Volk*. The pope ended the letter with an admonition to priests and the religious in Germany to continue to serve truth and unmask and refute error, whatever its form or disguise.[86]

Hitler was furious; the Catholic clergy had defied his authority. Those distributing the encyclical were arrested. Twelve publishing houses were closed; the encyclical was not to be printed.[87] One of the worst consequences for the Church was the renewal of the currency and morality trials,[88] which had been begun in 1935 to discredit the clergy in the eyes of the public, but had been canceled shortly before the summer Olympics of 1936. By May 1937, Hitler was reported to be contemplating even stronger measures against the Church, including a reconsideration of the Concordat and a unilateral abrogation of some of its more important articles. Responding to this fissure between the Church and the Nazi state, Cardinal Mundelein of Chicago on May 18 undertook to defend the German clergy against the charges of immorality being leveled against them. Mundelein declared: "Perhaps you will ask how it is that a nation of 60 million intelligent people will submit in fear and servitude to an alien, an Austrian paperhanger, and a poor one at that, and a few associates like Goebbels and Göring, who dictate every move of the people's lives."[89] Such a question was insulting to the German government and to the majority of the Germans of that day. Shortly thereafter, however, the pope spoke to pilgrims from Chicago and praised Mundelein. In May 1937 (two months after *Mit Brennender Sorge*), the Austrian ambassador to Berlin sent a report to his foreign minister in Vienna on the religious situation in Germany:

> The attack on the Church is a systematic one. It has long-term goals and is unlikely to assume sharper outward forms than at present. It is a war of attrition which begins with the soul of the child and aims slowly and by degrees to do away with Catholic schools, and to drive the faithful away from the churches, religious houses, and other church institutions, so that these become, over decades, redundant.

The ambassador went on by noting that the attack was counterproductive and that the Church was actually more united in some respects than it had been in 1933. He cited the notable increase in church attendance and other purely religious activities.[90] But apparently no official resistance against the regime could be discerned.

The 1937 Fulda Conference split. Bertram's faction eschewed all notions of direct confrontation or the mobilization of public opinion against the government. Galen, Preysing, and Faulhaber preferred public protests against the religious and political ideology of Hitler's dictatorship. Bertram feared that opposition would lead to a *Kulturkampf* and deprive the faithful of their priests and bishops and so of the sacraments. Confusion, uncertainty, and bitterness characterized discussion among the hierarchy. Repression of newspapers, the virtual elimination of Catholic schools,[91] and the morality trials had built sufficient pressure to lead to a split in the episcopal ranks. In a memo, Preysing supported a new aggressive policy and made several salient points.[92] There should be, he asserted, no negotiations with the enemy while the regime was not prepared to accept an armistice; the Concordat had become a farce and every appeal to it that did not simultaneously unmask the insidious tactics of the party appeared ridiculous. He urged that the delicate diplomatic language be eliminated from the episcopal correspondence with the government and that the clergy be informed of the important letters to the government. Finally, he suggested that by means of short pastoral letters the faithful be enlightened about the real struggle facing the Church, its motives, and the events.[93]

Preysing's action shocked and angered Bertram. Negotiation on the school issue had already indicated that Pacelli favored Preysing's hard-line position rather than Bertram's, and the cardinal secretary of state did not feel that the bishops' conciliatory negotiations would be successful. Pacelli's specific instructions to Bertram that he was to remain within the provisions of the Concordat indicated that the Vatican saw Bertram as too accommodating. Responding to Preysing, Bertram insisted that before there could be an armistice on the part of the regime the Church must declare one by abandoning the tone of the encyclical and disassociating itself from such intemperate outbursts as that of Cardinal Mundelein. Bertram did not feel that blunt language was advisable since the bishops really could not defend themselves, and he concluded that he was appalled by the aggravating tone of the encyclical and so also disapproved of pastoral letters that embodied such hostile attitudes.[94] Despite these disagreements, an attempt to heal the breach between the Church and the state was made in 1938. The bishops would not exhibit dissension in public and so had to adopt a position that would be least offensive to them all.

Petition Politics

By the fall of 1938 the attacks against the Church had become more pronounced and the goals of the Nazis clearer. In fact, Hitler's complete dictatorship may be dated from the elimination of such conservatives as Neurath and Blomberg from his government in 1938. The reaction of the bishops reflects the change: "[the Nazis] are trying to restrict us on every side, to bleed our Catholic life to death; still more, they aim at the complete overthrow of the Catholic Church on German soil, and even at the entire elimination of Christianity of whatever sort, and the introduction in its place of a form of belief which is utterly alien to the true faith in God and belief in a future life."[95] The 1938 settlement of the *Sudetenland* dispute, however, was greeted by another burst of episcopal enthusiasm. A distinctly nationalistic tone overshadowed Cardinal Bertram's greeting to the 30,000 Sudeten Germans who had formerly been part of his Breslau diocese. He frankly avowed that an unqualified submission to secular authority as a civil and moral duty of citizenship was normative:

> How could the Catholic Church, which is a *Volk* church in the most exalted sense, silently ignore a development so rich in meaning for all in the bosom of the *Volk?* . . . . Gratitude to God for the preservation of international peace is joined in your community with the second blessed sensation of joy that you are once again united with the rest of Germany. All of us share your joy in the depths of our heart and pray to God that the new arrangement will bear richest blessings for the spiritual and temporal welfare of all communities. . . . There is no need to urge you to give respect and obedience to the new authorities of the German state. You all know the words of the apostle: let every man be subject to the powers placed over him.[96]

The occupation of the Sudetenland (1938) elicited several other statements of support. Archbishop Hauck of Bamberg, whose archdiocese was enriched by many new members, gave thanks for the safeguarding of peace that brought in its wake the peaceful *Anschluss* of the Sudeten German *Volksgenossen.* The diocesan Sunday paper of Munich declared that while thanking God Catholics "did not forget to thank the man who has preserved the peace for us and yet at the same time has achieved the freedom of our German brothers in Bohemia. Together with the German cardinals, the entire Catholic community in the Greater German Reich thanks the führer for the act of peace."[97]

Generally, Pacelli and the curia had followed the historically traditional policy of permitting local bishops as much leeway as possible, since they were most knowledgable on local conditions. The Vatican's decision to condemn the religious policies of Nazi Germany probably stemmed more from Pius XI than from Pacelli, whose basic objection to totalitarianism was the unsettling effect it could have on international relations. Pacelli's own attitude toward the German government may be seen in his response to the German Foreign Office in April 1937:

The Holy See, which has friendly, correct, or at least tolerable relations with the states of one or another constitutional form and orientation, will never interfere in the question of what concrete form of government a certain people chooses to regard as best suited to its nature and requirements. With respect to Germany also, it has remained true to this principle and intends to so continue.[98]

The differences between the acerbic Pius XI and the diplomatic Pacelli may be seen clearly in their approaches to racism in 1938. In the summer of 1938, Pius XI called the American Jesuit John LaFarge, leader in the fight against racism in America, to Rome and requested him to write an encyclical against racism, anti-Semitism, and totalitarianism. Along with Gustav Gundlach, S.J., LaFarge wrote the encyclical, but Pius died before it could be published. As Pius XII, Pacelli did not publish his predecessor's letter, but did author another, which he issued in October 1939 and in which he called for the peaceful resolution of international conflicts as well as expressed sympathy for all mankind, especially for those persecuted and oppressed. So innocuous was the encyclical that the Gestapo allowed it to be read. Further blunting the effect of the encyclical was the fact that Pius XII through Orsenigo offered his personal congratulations to the führer for his personal escape from the Munich assassination attempt (November 8, 1939).[99] The irony of all this patriotic behavior is that, whereas the Nazis were not likely to be at all impressed by this display of nationalistic enthusiasm, the bishops' congregations were more likely to be caught up in the surge of patriotic commitment than by the spirit of protest the sermons were intended to instill and express. For example, in defending a priest named Kraus, a veteran accused of opposing the state, Bishop Rachl stated: "No one loves his Fatherland as truly as the Catholic priest" and continued, "everything for Germany, and Germany for Christ."[100] Such a patriotism-protest approach could hardly send clear signals to the faithful. Pius XI clearly condemned racism and anti-semitism, whereas his successor's letter avoided any direct application of abstract principles.[101] Pius XII preferred to remain aloof from what he may have regarded as the rash impulsiveness of his predecessor. From this perspective it is not at all improbable that Pacelli by 1938 may have superficially favored Bertram's *Eingabenpolitik* (petition politics). Consequently, despite the papal encyclical and Preysing's protests, the majority of the bishops continued supporting Bertram's leadership and so his policies. The spirit of "petition politics" can be seen even in the "birthday greeting" policy of the bishops.

Since 1935 Bertram had customarily sent birthday greetings to Hitler on behalf of the Fulda Bishops' Conference. Even in the years of bitter persecution by the Nazis, the Fulda chairman carried out this practice. These birthday greetings reflected Bertram's *Eingabenpolitik*. They usually began with a birthday wish for the führer and a promise to continue to support the state and party in order to strengthen German unity. Couched in diplomatic language was an appeal to Hitler to preserve the Church's spiritual mission, which did not oppose the responsibilities of those civic leaders "who continually respect the obligations of the Church." Bertram seemed to hope that such an indirect appeal to the führer might soften his attitude and reduce the tensions between Church and state. Like most of the bishops, Bertram was either unwilling or unable to recognize that the responsibility for the repressive actions of the Nazis lay in the hands of Hitler himself. They never accused Hitler of being responsible for the persecution, and their protests preserved the polite fiction that the fault lay with lesser officials and subordinates. Although it may have been a wise tactic, unfortunately it also furnished the faithful with the opportunity to make false distinctions between Hitler's intentions and the acts and speeches of the Gestapo and Goebbels. Although Rosenberg's *Mythus,* for example, was never officially adopted as the party line, it was "recommended" for use by all teachers and pupils.[102] Thus, the regime saw nothing inconsistent in calling the bishops' attack on the book an act of disloyalty.

Preysing wanted to denounce Nazi tactics. In a pastoral letter (Fall 1937), Preysing accused the government of suppressing the Church's freedom under the subterfuge that the suppression of the press, the confiscation of papal encyclicals, and the attacks against the clergy were intended to purge the Church of "politics."[103] He accused the regime of assaulting the consciences of the German people. "In this spirit an attempt is being made to force the German people, by every means possible, to regard the world of revelation and the supernatural not only as superfluous, but even as a pernicious fabrication of 'cracked-brain papists.'" He called upon the faithful to prepare to defend the faith and pointed to the large number of the faithful who continued to attend Church services.[104] *Angriff,* the daily paper published by Goebbels, criticized Preysing's letter as an attempt to undermine the legitimate authority of the State.[105] Bertram remained silent, but had justified his policy in a letter of October 21, 1937. The cardinal argued that his protests were based on "clarity of presentation, sound reasons, and a candid response toward anti-Christian attitudes."[106] Preysing had objected to the compromising tone of these letters and had also regarded these protests as counterproductive unless the public were made aware of the nature and the course of events in the conflict. Government actions bore out this point. Protest letters were carefully and deliberately misquoted. Passages were selected that best suited Nazi justifications for attacking the Church. These were then published in the Nazi press. Instead of bringing these errors to the attention of the public by means of sermons and pastoral letters, the bishops registered their complaints with the very office that had created the deception in the first place. In Preysing's opinion, Bertram's failure to take the offensive made the Nazis' task easier, since it created great confusion in the minds of the faithful. The general episcopal attitude can also be seen in a conference Faulhaber had with Pius XII.

At the meeting of March 6, 1939, with the newly elected Pius XII, Faulhaber presented his views in writing to the pope. The bishop's document was basically a plea for peace between the Church and the state in Germany, and the issues listed as obstacles were basically procedural and legalistic matters rather than substantive questions. They included, among others, the point that the swastika was viewed by Hitler not as a sign of opposition to the cross but rather as a national emblem, and the conviction that Hitler wanted the separation of church and state. Perhaps, the bishop suggested, friendly birthday greetings on Hitler's fiftieth birthday would help. Faulhaber also noted that the Theological faculty at the Munich University had been closed by the Bavarian minister of education over a dispute about the appointment of a professor of canon law, but that it would be reopened (it was not). He pointed out that the party leaders had no desire for peace with the Church, but that the German bishops should act as if they did not see this and do all they could to bring about a peace. Pius, on the other hand, thought that they should approach the situation with eyes open, so that, although they would make every effort for peace, they would not refuse to fight if the state insisted on provoking them. Not surprisingly, as time went on, Pius came to sympathize with the opposition tactics of Preysing more than with those of Faulhaber.[107]

Further capitulation to the Nazi state could be seen in the April 20, 1939, celebration. Hitler's fiftieth birthday festivities were centered around the recent overwhelming success of the führer's daring foreign policy. In 1939 Faulhaber had continued to favor an attempt to improve relations with the state by signaling this intent through a birthday greeting to Hitler.[108] The basic thrust of this approach would persist into the next year. The church bells rang in the great day. Cardinal Bertram had left it to the discretion of each bishop whether he wanted to have a peal of bells, and all of them apparently ordered it. On April 20, Bertram, in the name of the episcopate, sent a telegram of congratulations to Hitler. Special votive masses in honor of the Archangel St. Michael, the patron saint of Germany, were celebrated in all the churches "to implore God's blessing on führer and people." The bishop of Mainz called for prayer for "the führer and chancellor, the inspirer, enlarger, and protector of the Reich." In all the dioceses the churches displayed the swastika. On April 20, Nuncio Orsenigo personally delivered the congratulations of Pius XII and, as dean of the diplomatic corps, those of the other ambassadors in Berlin as well. Such Catholic papers as the

Klerusblatt, the organ of the Bavarian Association of Diocesan Priests, celebrated the momentous changes in the history of Germany achieved by Hitler: "The frontiers imposed upon us by the 'hate-peace' of Versailles are broken, the *Lebensraum* of the German people has been widened, multitudes of unemployed again have work. God's holy providence has provided that in a decisive hour he [Hitler] be entrusted with the leadership of the German people."[109]

Bertram's birthday message to Hitler (April 1940) also illustrates what in Preysing's mind was wrong with the Fulda chairman's approach. Bertram's letter of April 10, 1940, of course, must be taken in the context of the successful war that Hitler seemed to be waging.

> The love of the *Volk* and the Fatherland offers us the opportunity on this festive occasion to make an urgent request to you, honored leader, to preserve a deep understanding for our dutiful and unremitting concern to preserve the Christian character of our people in the fullest sense of the word, and to strengthen the people and the youth in our diocese in the central truths of the Catholic faith.[110]

The cardinal reminded Hitler that episcopal zeal for the fatherland did not "stand in contradiction with the program of the National Socialist party," and he recalled Hitler's own words regarding this point. Preysing was embittered by these words and resigned his post as Fulda representative in matters of the press. He was even considering resigning from his post as bishop of Berlin. Pius recognized that disputes between bishops were at times unavoidable, but expressed great concern that the bishops remain united in their commitment to defend the Church.[111] The differences between the bishops were not reconciled, and they along with the pope supported Bertram's policies rather than risk the activist policy urged by Preysing.

The 1941 pastoral letter from the Bavarian bishops basically summarizes the approach of the episcopate to the National Socialist state. Appearing after the victories over Poland, France, and the Low Countries and before the Nazi attack on the Soviet Union reintroduced the "crusade against Bolshevism" aspect of the National Socialist program, this episcopal message and its appeal for unity and unstinting support of the war offer incontrovertible evidence that Bavarian Catholics would have received little encouragement from their bishops had they ever considered refusing to take part in Hitler's war. The letter reads in part:

> We Germans constitute one great community of life and destiny; we Christians constitute a community of belief in Christ and the love of Christ. And if

the commandment to love is always the greatest of all, this is especially true in times of danger and need. . . .

In the first years of the World War we saw with joy and pride the greatness that unity brings; but at the end of that war we had to learn how disunity can destroy all that greatness again. To be united is, therefore, the great commandment of this serious hour. To be united in love and in the service of the *Vaterland* is our wish, so that we may form one single community of sacrifice and effort for the protection of the *Heimat* . . . . To the free recognition of our religion guaranteed us in the Concordat belongs the freedom to remain loyal to the Faith and to defend it in every situation and circumstance, to attend Mass, to receive the sacraments, to educate and instruct our children and young people in the Catholic faith as is required of parents and clergy as a matter of duty and conscience. The freer and happier men are in the fulfilling of their duty to God, the more sacred to them will be the duties to the *Vaterland.*[112]

In an abstruse manner the pastoral informed the faithful that all was not well in the area of Church-state relationships as far as the enumerated rights were concerned. This patriotism-combined-with-protest theme is fairly consistent in the episcopal pastorals. Unfortunately, this very protest feature actually added emphasis to the patriotic moral content; the Catholic who heard this call to duty could easily conclude that, despite the antireligious aspects and policies of the Nazi government, the official leaders of the Church continued to stand united behind the national war effort. Some studies suggest that the stress on *Volk* or *Vaterland* in the public pronouncements of the bishops since the *Kulturkampf* as well as during the Third Reich and the patriotic birthday greetings to the führer would merely reinforce the political values held by most Germans. Such episcopal activities made it almost impossible to rally support against the regime, since most people part with their attitudes only with great reluctance. Generally, the intensity with which attitudes are held may be affected by an inundation of new information, but they are rarely altered completely. The Nazis were capable of inundating; the Church was not. The Christian religion emphasizes man's responsibility both to obey legitimate authority and, even more significantly, to treat his fellow human beings with respect and care. When asked to make a choice with respect to the war and eugenic aims of the Nazis, the average Christian usually would need pastoral guidance. Such leadership did not emerge from the episcopate as a united group.[113]

Bertram's *Eingabenpolitik* not only proved to be unworkable after 1936, but his refusal to consider any other course of action or to discuss openly his policy with the bishops has left him open to criticism. Unlike von Galen, Faulhaber, or Preysing, Bertram opposed mobilizing public opinion to any extent against the regime. His main weapon was the petition and the memo addressed to the bureaucratic apparatus of the State. Perhaps if voices had been raised against the crimes of the regime, the Nazis might have at least modified their attacks. But in general from hindsight it appears that Hitler easily reshaped tactics but not his strategic goals. The majority of the bishops favored Bertram's tactics, which did gain time for the Church and helped prevent the complete suppression of all Catholic activities—an accomplishment in itself. What ultimately saved the Church, however, was the beginning of war and Hitler's need for support. He told his intimates that he would delay dealing with the Church.

The nature of Bertram's policy, however, excluded any appeal for public support in order to force the Nazis to yield. Armed with this knowledge, the government officials were able to pursue fearlessly their goals by means of suppression, terror, and anti-Christian propaganda. Viewed from this perspective, Bertram's policy was ineffective and, after 1936, detrimental to the cause of the Church. Locked into a policy that held out the promise of security, Bertram and the majority of bishops were unwilling to risk everything including, possibly, their own lives, in pursuit of a more open condemnation of the regime and the party. Instead, the bishops sought to ward off the Nazi encroachments by protesting against violations of the Concordat and combining this type of opposition with declarations of loyalty to the state. The reasons for the hierarchy's half-hearted resistance to Hitler's regime are complex. But their anxiety to preserve the pastoral functions of the bishops and the clergy at all costs blinded them to suggestions of open resistance. For Bertram, as chairman of the Fulda Conference, the Concordat established official relations between the Hitler regime and the Church. As long as that treaty was in effect, Bertram felt obligated to recognize and loyally support the regime. Although its general attitude to the party and its policies had not changed during the entire period, many times the statements and actions of the Catholic clergy and laity certainly seemed to be less rigorous in opposition than they could have been. Through it all, the evidence supports the claim that the German hierarchy was opposed to the teachings of the National Socialists but maintained loyalty to the state as a legitimate political institution. Although the bishops may have been able to distinguish between patriotism and extreme nationalism, many in their congregations found such distinctions pointless. Likewise meaningless were the bishops' frequent attempts to separate conceptually the state from the party, since in reality the two were one in Nazism. Such a distinction conveniently allowed the bishops to remain loyal German Catholics and still consistently oppose the Nazi *Weltanschauung,* hoping that such a position would allow survival and highlight the Nazi value structure, which could either be destroyed or appropriately evolve. The party was to be separated from the basic needs of the country, the Church, and humanity. The distinction was not valid. Unfortunately, the religious community became enmeshed in its support for the sociopolitical order and lost its potential to be a source of dissent and disobedience.[114]

One point on which all the bishops seemed in agreement was in their lack of support for any revolution against the government. This concurrence is not surprising in view of the absence of a concept of legitimate revolution in most contemporary German theological and philosophical works. Frequently in Faulhaber's sermons and letters, for example, he inveighed against the evils of the time, vividly describing the persecution of the clergy or condemning the immoral laws of sterilization. He always concluded, however, with a protestation of loyalty to the state and, on several occasions, with a specific warning against revolutionary activity. Because of his association with Carl Goerdeler, Faulhaber was eventually interrogated by the Gestapo after the July 20, 1944 attempt on Hitler's life. His statement reflects his basic attitude:

> I am shocked to have been asked about a question that is in connection with men who have prepared and fulfilled the crime of July 20. I am shocked because as a bishop I must condemn before the whole world as crime the plan of a murder of the state's ruler. Before July 20 I would have thought impossible that such a plan could exist which would push our people into the most terrible chaos and would have made communism—in its most radical form—victorious.[115]

The circumstances surrounding the statement prohibit absolute acceptance without critical evaluation, but it does fit in with his earlier conceptions of the state and its authority. In 1960, Neuhäusler, Faulhaber's auxiliary bishop, also asserted that the cardinal could not have accepted political murder.

Catholic Patriots Supported the State at War

The bishops in general were convinced that the authoritarian state and its ruler were the embodiment of God's authority. They could not adjust to the Weimar Republic nor to the democratic and pluralistic principles of the twentieth century in general. They were faithful to an abstract ideal rather than to existential needs and demands. The inherent evil of the totalitarian state in its claim to the whole of a man's life was beyond their comprehension, and to the end they were caught up in a web of groundless distinctions between the party and the state. Defending the rights of the Church, they failed to defend the rights of the political community.

The German bishops became useful channels for Nazi control over their flocks, whether by general exhortations to loyal obedience to legitimate authority or by efforts to rally these followers to the support of *Volk, Vaterland,* and *Heimat* as a Christian duty. The formal and external controls of the Third Reich, a police state, as well as the secular myths of *Volk,* and so on, directed the average German toward acceptance of the dictates of the regime. A parallel set of social controls functioned within this institutional religious community as well. Very little could be done but conform. With respect to strictly political values, no selection process occurred, partially because the hierarchy seemed to view Hitler's guiding *Weltanschauung* as a cultural not a political issue. Catholic leaders distinguished between supporting, and later fighting, for the *Vaterland,* but not necessarily for the Third Reich. "The bishop is the real leader of his flock." In saying this about Faulhaber in 1936, Bishop Hauck helps explain the impact that the cardinal's (1939) statement that the faithful should serve *Vaterland* and *Heimat* would have. The value-impregnated beliefs men live and die for were apparently the same for both the Church and the state. Faithful performance of duty was made a moral obligation in both.[116] A few days after the start of the war the bishops issued a joint pastoral letter, asking Catholic soldiers to do their duty: "In this decisive hour we encourage and admonish our Catholic soldiers, in obedience to the führer, to do their duty and to be ready to sacrifice their whole person. We appeal to the faithful to join in ardent prayers that God's providence may lead this war to blessed success and peace for fatherland and people."[117] Supporting *Vaterland* and *Volk* was coupled with the attack on communism, common to both Hitler and the Catholic Church. Not surprisingly, little consensus could be reached on the more detailed ideology of either side both on the leadership and rank and file levels.[118]

The heart of the problem lay in the fact that both the state and the Church claimed ultimate jurisdiction over the individual's behavior. In Nazi ideology, the state held final and absolute rights, which the citizen had to respect regardless of how they might conflict with other personal or institutional values. The moral teachings of the Church, however, would resolve such conflicts in terms of the principle that it is better to serve God than man. In many respects, however, the two systems were not only highly compatible, but, to a significant degree, the religious value system specifically supported the secular system. Paul instructed the early Christians to be subject to the powers placed over them, and the gospel stresses that appropriate tribute be rendered Caesar. The Catholic Church—both in its theological formulations and in its acceptance of the natural law philosophy with its fundamental concern for the *bonum commune*—has historically usually baptized the secular myths and the subsidiary values derived from them. The bishops' stress on *Vaterland* and *Volk* verifies this general axiom. The religious value system specifically and intentionally supported the secular system, if only for its own survival. The Catholic Church, for example, was referred to as a *Volkskirche,* and the pastorals contained frequent references to *Vaterland, Volk,* and *Heimat.* There ultimately was no value-selection issue for Catholics. Once Nazi Germany was involved in actual warfare, however questionable the justice of her cause, the internal forces of patriotic and nationalistic sentiments could become fully operative in support of a regime destined to go beyond the normal political goals that traditionally had been supported in Germany.[119]

The Catholic, continually under pressure since the *Kulturkampf* and increasingly during the Hitler years to prove that he was as good a German as anyone else, remained sensitive to nationalist values. These internal pressures to conform by faithfully and loyally fulfilling whatever duties were placed upon him received public reinforcement and emphasis from religious superiors, to whom he was expected to turn for moral guidance. Such internal social controls clearly take on significance for the explanation of the German Catholic support for or acquiescence to Hitler's orders.[120] The Third Reich has offered several object lessons on the relationship between state power and individual rights within a specific society. More state authority means less individual capacity to survive, and a higher individual capacity to survive means less state authority. To presume obligations to the state is to assert not simply a theory of obedience, but rather that the state must insure the right to live without presuming the reasons for living or else the individual will lose his capacity for survival. The management of a society may extend to commands for obedience based on the need for mutual survival, but not beyond that point.[121] That the bishops failed to comprehend the optimum limitations on political power blunted any opposition that could have arisen between the Church and the state.

The Church has always respected the majesty of facts. Despite the wide reach of her jurisdiction, the Church as an indirect power has historically in modern times not accepted direct responsibility for political actions. The German bishops exercised the right to pass moral judgment on those measures of the Nazi state that impinged upon the Church's institutional vital interests and such cardinal points of doctrine as marriage legislation or euthanasia, but the bishops fell back on the indirect nature of their temporal jurisdiction whenever considerations of survival tactics required a more cautious course. The bishops adhered to the perennial political and philosophical norms of natural law. But in their case natural law plus prudence equalled flexibility.[122] Natural law is abstract and must be interpreted. Thus the gap between the abstract principles and the issue at hand is bridged by answers almost predetermined by the interests of the Church as an institution in the world trying to pursue religious goals. The bishops, then, could assault the Nazi *Weltanschauung,* but to preserve the spiritual efficacy of the Church they had to maintain peace with the state. Unfortunately, the bishops seemed unwilling to accept the fact that the state was the party and the dynamic force powering Nazism was Hitler. Normally the Church can influence individuals as the shaper of moral identity, the bearer of moral tradition, and the community of moral deliberation. Where moral identity is concerned, it is clear that the Church's actions (liturgy, preaching) function as socializing factors. Moral identity, however, would be difficult to create without the moral deliberation that occurs when abstract principles are applied to concrete cases.[123] Such an overt confrontation with the regime failed to materialize, leaving Catholics in a state of ambiguity due to the unclear signals sent by both the German episcopate and the pope. In essence it was the Nazi state—that is, Hitler himself—claiming absolute moral authority. The greater the claimed moral authority of Hitler became, the greater the demands on the citizens and ultimately the more far-reaching the process of the externalization of conscience and obedience to authority. The way was being paved for the Holocaust as a social policy.[124]

When it came down to specific issues that might seem to involve "bearing the cross," the bishops always stopped short of calling for the kind of concerted and open resistance that could have led to martyrdom on a massive scale. There are several reasons for their patriotism-protest combination. Perhaps the bishops may be faulted for a lack of vision and commitment, perhaps even for a failure of courage. In pragmatic terms, their decisions in favor of restraint were in all likelihood "dictated" by prudent circumspection. Indeed, they were probably quite right in their pessimistic assessment of their prospects of success for any determined stand they might have taken. Evidently the German hierarchy had concluded that they could not count on the loyalty of their "flock" in the event of a total Church-state confrontation. The controversy over the introduction of the *gottglaübig* designation as a religious category for personal registration is a case in point.[125] The structures of the Catholic Church aided and abetted the consolidation of the Nazi regime. There was a congruence between Catholic attitudes and those of the Nazi state, whose popularity was basically due to its endorsing the policies favored by the conservative elites, national revival, territorial expansion, abolition of democratic pluralism, and xenophobia.

Nationalist and racist ideologies helped mobilize social forces, but alone they could not sustain the regime. An organizational ideology that could mobilize social forces and sustain the political order was essential to the survival of the regime. In no way can any ideological analysis explain the sustenance, survival, or decay of the authoritarian system. Only when wedded to political organization did the Nazi ideology become an instrument of power. Ideology can offer cogent explanations for the beginnings of Nazism. The survival and sustenance of all modern totalitarian states, however, is explained by their innovative use of the monopolistic party and its auxiliary and parallel structures to manipulate mass societies. The Church can be seen as such a subsidiary structure. The bishops' actions emerged out of a context of real choice and reflected a selection of one among plural alternatives. But they chose to highlight patriotic themes to avoid a new *Kulturkampf.* This pattern of behavior was consistent with the general political theory of the Church as a whole as well as with the past experiences of German Catholics. The loyalty of the bishops, consistent with their past, should not be surprising. The conformity of the bishops as a group can warn of the danger that a stress on consistency can cause. Their patriotism as a group has helped reveal to us much about the contemporary issue of uncritical patriotism, although little about the bishops as individuals.[126] The bishops protested Hitler's incursions into their domain, but coupled their disagreements with patriotic exhortations. They were determined that no one could accuse them of disloyalty to the Reich. Their adherence to the normative German values helps illustrate the fact that the bishops were enmeshed in the patterns of behavior and values that had emerged and matured from the *Kulturkampf* to the Third Reich. Their behavior does not necessarily illuminate personal attitudes but does expose an institutional attitude. The bishops were protectors of and not prophets in the Church.

The directives inherent in cultural norms are based on the individual's generalized desire to conform to whatever it is that other people are observed to do, or what they say one should do, rather than what people may really want to do. While both external sanctions and conformity pressures certainly occur as the means of social control and are probably necessary, some studies suggest that these kinds of extrinsic motivators are rarely the primary types of control mechanisms in many societies, but they do seem to be most prevalent in such historical societies as post-1918 Germany, marked by social anomie and mental insecurity. Generally, the goals mandated within the cultural meaning system are also intrinsically rewarding. Through the process of socialization individuals come to find achieving culturally prescribed goals as well as following cultural directives to be motivationally satisfying and to find not achieving such goals or following such directives to be anxiety producing. Historically, the Church has usually sought to lend stabilizing support to varied societies and not to introduce dissonance into the lives of the faithful, compelling them to choose between God and mammon. In the case of Nazi Germany, the bishops supported the basic, historical values that Hitler represented. The concepts of *Volk* and *Vaterland* were part of the historical German learning environment for Hitler, the hierarchy, and the German people. Basically, culture consists of learned systems of meaning, communicated by language and other symbolic systems, and has representational, directive, and affective functions. Through these systems of meaning, groups of people adapt to their environment and structure their interpersonal activities.[127] To obstruct this adaptation could have threatened the institutional integrity of the Church.

In his seminal work on "groupthink," Irving Janis has maintained that the advantages of having policy decisions made by groups are often lost because of psychological pressures that arise when members work closely together, share the same values, and, above all, face a crisis situation in which everyone at the outset realizes that whatever the action that the group decides to take will be fraught with serious risks, but in which there is little hope for obtaining new information that will point toward a satisfactory solution. In these circumstances, the leader and his in-group are subjected to stresses that generate a strong need for affiliation. As conformity pressures increase, the striving for identification appears to foster a pattern of defensive avoidance of such unpleasant aspects as, for example, Hitler's policies, coupled with a characteristic lack of analytical vigilance, unwarranted optimism, sloganistic thinking, and a reliance on shared rationalizations that bolster the least objectionable alternative. The official position often becomes the one favored by the leader and other influential persons in the policymaking group on the basis of initial biases that remain uncorrected despite the availability of evidence indicating that it may well be inferior in achieving the results desired. The bishops, of course, could have employed a number of steps to reduce the threat of groupthink. For example, such individuals as Preysing could have been assigned the role of critical evaluator, a high priority could have been placed on airing doubts and uncertainties, and the Fulda agendas could have been arranged so that the bishops paid less attention to the initial preferences of Bertram and at least considered the competing alternatives. Moreover, if the group leader openly welcomes new ideas, groupthink effects can be countered. Free interchange within groups, however, is usually restricted because group members seek consensus in order to move toward group goals.[128]

In the case of the bishops, it is difficult to estimate the extent to which the external or the environmental force, that is, other people, could be responsible for the effects of the hierarchy's actions.[129] To a man the bishops were loyal to *Volk* and *Vaterland,* and so their values were congruent to the public Nazi pronouncements. Their behavior was also shaped, however, by the fact that the total loyalty to the Church of some

Catholic laity was questionable as well as by their concern to retain the ability of the Church to provide for the spiritual needs of the Catholic flock, by offering the Mass and maintaining the sacramental structure. Both internal and external pressures directed their activities. Jones and Davis suggest that if an environmental force is strong (patriotism)—and it was in Nazi Germany—and if it facilitates the same behavior as an internal disposition (patriotism), nothing can be concluded about the internal disposition of individual bishops. Although the actual disposition of individuals cannot be perceived, the "mentalities" of the group,[130] that is, the beliefs and ways of reasoning shared by the bishops of the era, can be discerned.

In general, the behavior of people is purposive and intentional, and that behavior is caused by a combination of internal (personal) and environmental-historical factors. Behavior can be seen to vary over actors, entities, and contexts. Generally, behavior that is consistent over context (consistency), in which many people engage (high consensus), and that is performed in the context of a particular entity (highly distinctive) is seen as caused by that entity.[131]

Along with other Catholics, the bishops had been historically patriotic, obedient to their rightful rulers, and supportive of *Volk* and *Vaterland*. Their behavior and attitudes had been consistent from the Second until the end of the Third Reich. The Catholic consensus supported such values. Patriotic values were manifested particularly at times of political crisis when the loyalty of Catholics might be questioned, for example, during the *Kulturkampf,* the Weimar era, and the *Hitlerzeit.* It would seem, then, that the bishops' behavior was forced not by either mere personal disposition or environment, but by both, since the interaction occurred when they attempted to respond to the totalitarian Third Reich, a system unique in the intensity of the political force that could be mobilized. From the inception of the Third Reich, Hitler moved to eliminate all organizational rivals to his führer state. Dissent could threaten his totalitarian order, and he was most effective in restricting criticism of the regime to the neighborhood and village arena, where a minimum of damage could be done. Only private jokes, saloon talk, gossip, and sermons proved useful when Germans wanted to critique the regime. He was successful in blunting such major institutions as the Church. The desire to preserve institutional integrity, the realization that their parishoners were Catholics *and* Germans, and the power of Hitler's state all conspired to sabotage the Church's mission as witness. Lack of public dissent weakened the ability of the Church to form consciences and to lead a concerted resistance against Hitler's crimes against humanity as these became institutionalized in the political order.

Notes

1. Martha Ziegler, "The Socioeconomic and Demographic Bases of Political Behavior in Nuremberg during the Weimar Republic, 1919-1933," Ph.D. diss., University of Virginia, 1976, esp. chap. 7.
2. Solomon Asch, *Social Psychology* (Englewood Cliffs, NJ: Prentice Hall, 1952).
3. For several works useful in understanding the interaction among these categories, see Philip Zimbardo and Ebbe B. Ebbesen, *Influencing Attitudes and Changing Behavior: A Basic Introduction to Relevant Methodology, Theory, and Applications* (Reading, MA: Addison and Wesley, 1969), pp. 1-23; C.I. Hovland et al., *Communication and Persuasion* (New Haven: Yale University Press, 1953).
4. Alfred Hero, *Opinion Leaders in American Communities* (Boston: World Peace Foundation, 1959); Kenneth J. Gergen, *Social Psychology* (New York: Harcourt Brace Jovanovich, 1981), pp. 321ff.
5. David Schneider et al., *Person Perception*, 3rd ed. (Reading, MA: Addison and Wesley, 1979), pp. 81ff. For an early seminal work on social exchange theory, see George Homans, *Social Behavior: Its Elementary Forms* (New York: Harcourt, Brace, and World, 1961).
6. Rokeach, "Long-Range Experimental Modification of Values, Attitudes, and Behavior," pp. 453-459; I. Janis and L. Mann, "A Conflict-Theory Approach to Attitude Change and Decision Making," in A. Greenwald et al. (eds.), *Psychological Foundations of Attitudes* (New York: Academic Press, 1968), pp. 327-360; T.M. Ostrom, "Between-Theory and Within-Theory Conflict in Explaining Context Effects on Impression Formation," *Journal of Experimental Social Psychology* 13 (1977):492-503; M. Fishbein and I. Ajzen, *Belief, Attitude, Intention, and Behavior: An Introduction to Theory and Research* (Reading, MA: Addison and Wesley, 1975).
7. Elizabeth Simpson, "Preference and Politics: Values in Political Psychology and Political Learning," in Renshon (ed.), *Handbook of Political Socialization: Theory and Research*, pp. 374-375; N. Rescher, "What is Value Change? A Framework for Research," in Kurt Baier and N. Rescher (eds.), *Values and the Future* (New York: Free Press, 1969).
8. Riede, "The Official Attitude of the Roman Catholic Hierarchy," p. 36; Fenn, p. 27.
9. Klaus Epstein, "A New Study of Fascism," in Henry Turner (ed.), *Reappraisals of Fascism* (New York: New Viewpoints, 1976), p. 16.
10. In his *Machtergreifung*, pp. 205ff., Bracher accuses the Church of permitting the Center party to collapse. Heinrich Brüning initially presented this view in his *Memorien, 1918-1934* (Stuttgart: Deutsche Verlagsanstalt, 1970), pp. 663-674. Volk has uncovered new evidence that seems to refute these charges in his *Reichskonkordat*, pp. 209-211.
11. Böckenförde, "German Catholicism," pp. 303-310; Buchheim, "Deutsche Katholizismus," has critiqued Böckenförde's interpretation by noting that the latter omitted portions of the Bishops' statements that qualify support. Such a critique, however, merely highlights the ambivalence of the German hierarchy during this era.
12. See Ian Kershaw, *Popular Opinion and Political Dissent in the Third Reich: Bavaria, 1933-1945* (Oxford: Oxford University Press, 1983).

13. Zahn, *German Catholics*, p. 75. In his article "German Catholicism," Böckenförde has concluded that it would have been best for German Catholics not to have followed the official episcopal advice and directives concerning their political responsibilities. His article offers a wealth of revealing quotations—some echoing the Nazi ideological concept of the *Volk* state—and has related these to traditional "theological-political" teachings, which bear examination in the view of later developments.

14. Bendersky, pp. 198-203.

15. Conrad Gröber, *Nationalkirche? Ein aufklärendes Wort zur Wahrung des konfessionellen Friedens* (Freiburg: Herder, 1934), pp. 63-66; Wilhelm Berning, *Katholische Kirche und Deutches Volkstum* (Munich: Georg D.W. Callwey Verlag, 1934), p. 9.

16. Anton Stonner, *Nationale Erziehung und Religionsunterricht* (Regensburg: Rustet, 1934), pp. 148, 153, 157. Stonner's book appeared with an *Imprimatur*. For a critique of Stonner's ideas, see Hugo Divald, "Sophistik des 'Brückenbanens': Kritische Betrachtungen zu Anton Stonners Buch . . .," *Der Christliche Ständestaat* 1 (1934): 13-16.

17. Uwe Lohalm, *Völkischer Radikalismus: Die Geschichte des Deutschvölkischen Schutz-und Trutz-Bundes, 1919-1933* (Hamburg: Leibniz Verlag, 1970).

18. Archepiscopal Ordinariat Breslau, *Diözesansynode des Erzbistums Breslau 1935* (Breslau, 1936), pp. 12-13.

19. For a superb study, utilizing Bertram's papers in the Archdiocesan Archives in Breslau (Wroclaw, Poland), on "petition-politics," see Rolfs, "The Role of Adolf Cardinal Bertram, Chairman of the Fulda Bishops' Conference, in the Church's Struggle in the Third Reich, 1933-1938."

20. Two works very nicely illustrate the full extent of the Nazi assault on the Catholic Church. Johannes Maria Lenz's *Christus in Dachau* (Vienna: Missionsdruckerei St. Gabriel, 1957) is a history of the experiences undergone by hundreds of priests sent to Dachau, written by one of those so imprisoned. Johannes Neuhäusler's *Kreuz und Hakenkreuz* is a heavily documented account of the methodical attack against the Catholic Church, written by a man who held a prominent post in the Munich chancery and after the war worked as an auxiliary bishop of that diocese. Neuhäusler's book has been criticized in an article that presents evidence that the texts of several documents have been altered by omissions without the customary indication of deletions and occasionally by changes in the wording. See Hans Müller, "Zur Behandlung des Kirchenkampfes in der Nachkriegsliteratur," *Politische Studien* 12 (1961), 474-481. Neuhäusler's reliability is thus weakened, but the description of the actions taken against the Church is not necessarily affected. These breaches of scholarly integrity appear to be attempts to suppress potentially embarrassing instances of compromise or conformity on the part of religious leaders. There is no suggestion that the Nazi assaults described in this literature have been fabricated or exaggerated.

21. Stasiewski, *Akten Deutscher Bischöfe*, doc. 77, p. 395. Unless otherwise noted, references to Stasiewski's *Akten* are in vol. I; Müller, *Kirche und NS*, pp. 210-213; Volk, *Episkopat*, p. 137; Kupper, *Staatliche Akten* p. 347.

22. Hans Buchheim, "Fördernde Mitgliedschaft bei der SS," *Gutachten des Instituts für Zeitgeschichte* (Munich: Institut für Zeitgeschichte, 1958), pp. 350-351; Gröber was a sponsoring member of the SS in 1933 and was expelled

from the organization in 1938, although he retained his party card. SS officials maintained that he had a liaison with a Jewess; Gröber claimed after the war that he was so hated by the Nazis that they planned to crucify him on the door of Freiburg Cathedral; see "Interrogation of Albert Hartl," C1-PIR/106, C1-11R/S3, C1-FIR/123, p. 20.

23. Berning, "Katholische Kirche," p. 41; for an excellent study of the *Reichs-ideologie*, see Klaus Breuning, *Die Vision des Reiches*.
24. Rolfs, p. 94.
25. *Germania*, no. 222, August 14, 1933.
26. Gill, pp. 96-97; Linz, p. 192.
27. Volk, *Kirchliche Akten*, p. 137.
28. Ibid., p. 241.
29. Rolfs, p. 103.
30. Volk, *Kirchliche Akten*, pp. 59-93, 148-150, 160, 166, 172; Stasiewski, *Akten*, p. 288; Nehäusler, 1:185ff.
31. Volk, *Kirchliche Akten*, pp. 174-177; Stasiewski, *Akten*, pp. 321-339.
32. Tinnemann, "Attitudes," 342.
33. *DGFP*, Series C, vol. 1 (1933-37), C 2, doc. 17, p. 24.
34. Gröber to Bertram and Faulhaber, October 27, 1933, in Stasiewski, *Akten*, pp. 420-422.
35. Bertram to the German bishops, October 30, 1933, in Ibid., pp. 423-424.
36. Faulhaber to the Bavarian bishops, October 31, 1933, in Ibid., pp. 426-430, 441-442.
37. November 3, 1933, in Ibid., p. 436.
38. Volk, *Episkopat*, pp. 150-152.
39. Bertram to the German bishops, November 5, 1933, in Stasiewski, *Akten*, p. 437.
40. Volk, *Episkopat*, pp. 152-153; Stasiewski, *Akten*, pp. 440-441.
41. Bracher, *Machtergreifung*, pp. 358-67. In Catholic Bavaria, the Nazis obtained well over 90 percent of the vote vs. 95 percent throughout the Reich; Conway, *Persecution*, p. 62.
42. Stasiewski, *Akten*, pp. 676-691. Episcopal concessions can be seen in "Draft of an agreement between Berning, Gröber and Bares, and the Reich representatives concerning the implementation of Article 31," in Stasiewski, *Akten*, pp. 731-732.
43. For Berning's report, June 27, 1934, see Stasiewski, *Akten*, pp. 731-732.
44. Bertram to the German bishops, see July 5, 1933, and Bertram to Pacelli, July 5, 1933, in Stasiewski, *Akten*, pp. 752-753.
45. Pacelli to Bertram, July 23, 1934, in Ibid., pp. 762-769.
46. Bracher, *Machtergreifung*, pp. 897ff.; Conway, *Persecution*, p. 94; Lewy, p. 171.
47. Rolfs, p. 133; Schulte's memorandum, Berlin, February 7,1934, in Stasiewski, *Akten*, pp. 704-705.
48. Pastoral letter of the German bishops, June 1934, in Stasiewski, *Akten*, pp. 704-715.
49. Rolfs, p. 137.
50. Müller, *Kirche und NS*, p. 328; Corsten in his *Kölner Aktenstücke* failed to cite this document, suggesting to Lewy, p. 379, that the Catholic author was trying to distort the role of the Church in the Third Reich.
51. Lewy, p. 199.
52. Rolfs, pp. 138-139; *DGFP*, C 3, doc. 470, p. 890.

53. Hermann Engfer, *Das Bistum Hildesheim, 1933-1945. Eine Dokumentation* (Hildesheim: August Lax, 1971).
54. See especially Broszat, *The Hitler State*; Carl J. Friedrich and Zbigniew Brzezinski, *Totalitarian Dictatorship and Autocracy* (New York: Praeger, 1965).
55. Walter Adolph, *Kardinal Preysing und Zwei Diktaturen*, p. 41; Mariaux, p. 75; Neuhäusler, *Hakenkreuz* 1:227; Gordon Zahn, "The German Catholic Press and Hitler's Wars," *Cross Currents* 10 (1960):373-374; Lewy, p. 150; Karl Aloys Altmeyer, "Der Episkopat und die katholische Presse im Dritten Reich," *Herder Korrespondenz* 14 (1959-60):374-381.
56. Karl Altmeyer, *Katholische Presse unter NS-Diktatur* (Berlin: Morus-Verlag, 1962), pp. 18-19.
57. Stasiewski, *Akten*, pp. 131-132, 247; Altmeyer, *Katholische Presse*, p. 20; Kupper, *Statliche Akten*, pp. 379-380.
58. For Faulhaber's Lenten pastoral (1920), see Lewy, p. 18.
59. Altmeyer, *Katholische Presse*, pp. 27-30; Rolfs, p. 158.
60. Altmeyer, pp. 35-36, 56, 85; Rolfs, pp. 160-165.
61. Altmeyer, pp. 75, 83-84.
62. Ibid., p. 84; Interview with Walter Adolph, December 10, 1971, in Rolfs, p. 166.
63. Stasiewski, *Akten*, pp. 704-715; Rolfs, pp. 168-169.
64. Lewy, p. 152; Corsten, *Kölner Aktenstücke*, pp. 29-32; Müller, *Kirche und NS*, pp. 292-293; *Studien zum Mythus des XX. Jahrhunderts! Amtliche Beilage zum Kirchlichen Amtsblatt für die Diözese Münster*, p. iii.
65. Altmeyer, *Katholische Presse*, pp. 109-111, 115-116.
66. Ibid., pp. 117-119; Rolfs, pp. 172-173; Corsten, *Kölner Aktenstücke*, pp. 108-109.
67. Rolfs, p. 173.
68. Corsten, *Kölner Aktenstücke*, p. 118.
69. Ibid.
70. See Ian Kershaw, *Der Hitler Mythos: Volksmeinung und Propaganda in Dritten Reich* (Stuttgart: Deutsche Verlagsanstalt, 1980).
71. Corsten, *Kölner Aktenstücke*, p. 123.
72. Rolfs, p. 174; Lewy, p. 203.
73. Altmeyer, *Katholische Presse*, pp. 122, 130-132; Neuhäusler, *Hakenkreuz* 1:207-208; Rolfs, pp. 175-176.
74. Altmeyer, *Katholische Presse*, pp. 127, 133-135.
75. Ibid., pp. 136-139; Rolfs, p. 177; Bischöfliches Generalvikariat Trier, *Kirche und Bolschewismus* (n.p., 1937).
76. Altmeyer, *Katholische Presse*, pp. 142-144, 150-151; Rolfs, pp. 178-179.
77. Volk, "Kardinal Faulhabers Stellung," p. 186.
78. Altmeyer, *Katholische Presse*, pp. 153-154; a partial list of diocesan weeklies and other publications suppressed by the government appears in Neuhäusler, *Hakenkreuz* 1:204; Lewy, p. 144; Rolfs, pp. 180-183.
79. Quotes in Tinnemann, "Attitudes," pp. 340ff.
80. Ibid., p. 341; Mariaux, p. 150.
81. Herbert F. Ziegler, "The SS Fuehrer Korps: An Analysis of Its Socio-Economic and Demographic Structure, 1925-1938," Ph.D. diss., Emory University, 1980, pp. 65-70; Klaus Scholder, "Die evangelische Kirche in der Sicht der Nationalsozialistischer Führung," *Vierteljahrshefte für Zeitgeschichte* 16 (1968):15-35.

82. Argyle, p. 117; Allen and Spilka, pp. 191-200; N.J. Pallone, "Explorations in Religious Authority and Social Perception," *Acta Psychologica* 22 (1964):324.
83. Rolfs, p. 188; Tinnemann, "Attitudes," p. 346.
84. Corsten, *Kölner Aktenstücke*, 156-161.
85. Ludwig Volk, "Die Enzyklika Mit Brennender Sorge," *Stimmen der Zeit* 183 (1969):179-181.
86. "Mit Brennender Sorge," in Mariaux, pp. 523-525, 532-534.
87. Neuhäusler, *Hackenkreuz*, 1:230-232; Volk, "Mit Brennender Sorge," p. 186.
88. See Hans Günther Hockerts, *Die Sittlichkeitsprozesse gegen Katholische Ordensangehörige und Priester 1936-1937* (Mainz: Matthias Grünewald Verlag, 1971).
89. Rolfs, p. 193; Helmreich, pp. 282-283.
90. See appendix in Ludwig Volk, *Akten Deutscher Briefe über die Lage der Kirche 1936-1939* (Mainz, 1981).
91. Adolph, *Hirtenamt*, pp. 102, 136-137; Mariaux, pp. 131, 143-144; Neuhäusler, *Hakenkreuz* 1:88-97; Rolfs, pp. 195-197.
92. Ulrich von Hehl (ed.), *Walter Adolph: Geheime Aufzeichnungen aus dem Nationalsozialistischen Kirchenkampf, 1935-1943* (Mainz: Matthias Grunewald Verlag, 1979). This study and collection of documents reveal Preysing's candid evaluations in his conversations with Adolph of his episcopal colleagues. The materials are important in assessing the overall policy of the Church toward the Nazi regime. The Vatican wanted to prevent a total break with the German government and in Nuncio Orsenigo, who was not liked by the German hierarchy, had a useful compromiser. This is an invaluable study for helping to understand the internal affairs of the Catholic Church in Germany under Hitler.
93. Adolph, *Hirtenamt*, pp. 136-137, 142-143.
94. Ibid., pp. 143-148.
95. Corsten, *Kölner Aktenstücke*, p. 231.
96. *Bayerische Katholische Kirchenzeitung*, vol. 14 (November 6, 1938), p. 316.
97. "Oberhirtlicher Erlass," October 5, 1938, *Amtsblatt Bamberg*, no. 61, October 6, 1938; *Münchener Katholische Kirchenzeitung*, no. 42, October 16, 1938, p. 669.
98. Pacelli to Bergen, April 30, 1937, *DGFP* D,1, doc. 649, pp. 944-965.
99. Encyclical letter *Summi Pontificatus* (October 20, 1939), *International Conciliation*, no. 335 (December 1939), p. 577; Order of Gestapo Munich, November 7, 1939, National Archives, T-175, roll 250, frame 2741860; *Münchener Katholische Kirchenzeitung*, no. 47, November 19, 1939, p. 584.
100. Zahn, in Littel and Locke, pp. 230-231.
101. Jim Castelli, "Unpublished Encyclical Attacked Anti-Semitism," *National Catholic Reporter* 9, no. 8 (December 15, 1972); *Summi Pontificatus,* October 1939; Gordon Zahn, "The Unpublished Encyclical—An Opportunity Missed," *National Catholic Reporter* 9, no. 8 (December 15, 1972), p. 9.
102. Adolph, *Hirtenamt*, pp. 161-162; Arthur C. Cochrane, *The Church's Confession Under Hitler* (Philadelphia: Westminster, 1962), p. 56.
103. Adolph, *Kardinal Preysing*, pp. 120-125.
104. Ibid., pp. 122-124.
105. Adolph, *Kardinal Preysing*, pp. 125-126.
106. Adolph, *Hirtenamt*, p. 149.
107. Mary Alice Gallin, "The Cardinal and the State," pp. 400-402.

108. Tinnemann, "Attitudes," p. 342.
109. Lewy, pp. 221-222; "Zum 20 April," by J.S., *Klerusblatt*, no. 15 (April 12, 1939), pp. 221-222.
110. Bertram to Hitler, April 10, 1940, in Rolfs, p. 211.
111. Rolfs, p. 211; Adolph, *Hirtenamt*, p. 164; Adolph, *Kardinal Preysing*, pp. 159-160, 169-170.
112. *Amtsblatt für die Erzdiözese München und Freising* (February 25, 1941), pp. 29-30.
113. Zahn, *German Catholics*, p. 62; E. Jackson Baur, "Opinion Changes in a Public Controversy," *Public Opinion Quarterly* 26 (1962):226; Melvin Small, "Some Suggestions from the Behavioral Sciences for Historians Interested in the Study of Attitudes," *Societas* 3 (1973):15; David C. Bock and Neil Warren, "Religious Belief as a Factor in Obedience to Destructive Commands," *Review of Religious Research* 13 (1972):186.
114. Zahn, in Littell and Locke, pp. 234-235.
115. Gallin, "Faulhaber," pp. 402-404.
116. Zahn, *German Catholics*, pp. 14, 18, 183, 193, 203-204; Robert M. MacIver, *The Web of Government* (New York: Macmillan, 1947), p. 4.
117. "Gemeinsames Wort der deutschen Bischöfe," *Martinus-Blatt*, no. 38 (September 17, 1939).
118. Sears, "Political Behavior," in Lindzey and Aronson, vol. 5, p. 410; Waldman, pp. 30-35.
119. Zahn, *German Catholics*, pp. 20-21, 24-27, 35-37.
120. Ibid., p. 37.
121. Horowitz, *Taking Lives*, pp. 83, 187.
122. August M. Knoll, *Katholische Kirche und Scholastisches Naturrecht: Zur Frage der Freiheit* (Vienna: Europa Verlag, 1962), pp. 24, 56-59; Ernst Böckenförde, "Der Deutsche Katholizismus im Jahre, 1933. Eine kritische Betrachtung," *Hochland* 53 (1961):239; *Summi Pontificatus*, p. 558; John C. Bennett, *Christians and the State* (New York: Scribner, 1958), p. 268.
123. Miller, pp. 32-44; Volk, *Akten deutscher Bischöfe*, vol. 4, (Mainz: Matthias Grünewald, 1981). The massive documentation in this volume edited by Volk shows that the failure to adopt a bold policy was the result not of weakness but of honest differences of opinion between conscientious pastors compelled to fight in the dark, with their backs to the wall, and with neither precedents nor prior experience to guide them.
124. John M. Steiner, "The SS Yesterday and Today: A Sociopsychological View," in Dimsdale, p. 423.
125. Zahn, in Littell and Locke, pp. 228-229; "Verkundigung Verordnet von Erzbischöflichen Ordinariat München und Freising mit Erlass," nr. 10900 (July 20, 1937). *Gottgläubig* as a midway designation between formal and specific religious identification and the "unchurched" classification was the subject of several chancery directives. Repeated references were made to this as a form of cowardice. But those references also testify to the effectiveness of the Nazi rule since they indicate that a sufficiently large number of Catholics did make use of this opportunity to stay in the good graces of the secular authority and still satisfy their conscience that they had not actually renounced their Christian faith.
126. Amos Perlmutter, *Modern Authoritarianism: A Comparative Institutional Analysis* (New Haven: Yale University Press, 1981), pp. 175, 185; E.E. Jones

and K.E. Davis, "A Theory of Correspondent Inferences: From Acts to Dispositions," in Berkowitz (ed.), *Advances in Experimental Social Psychology*, vol. 2, p. 328.

127. Robert G. D'Andrade, "Cultural Meaning Systems," in Robert McC. Adams et al., *Behavioral and Social Science Research: A National Resource*, pt. 2, (Washington, D.C.: National Academy Press, 1982), pp. 209, 232.

128. Irving Janis, "Preventing Groupthink in Policy-Planning Groups: Theory and Research Perspectives" (Paper delivered at the International Society of Political Psychology, Washington, D.C., 1979), pp. 8-9; M.L. Flowers, "A Laboratory Test of Some Implications of Janis' Group-Think Hypothesis," *Journal of Personality and Social Psychology* 35 (1977):888-896; L. Festinger, "Informal Social Communication," *Psychological Review* 57 (1950):271-282.

129. For an excellent analytical synthesis of attribution theory, see Schneider et al., *Person Perception*, pp. 41-50.

130. Ibid., p. 60; Charles M. Radding, "The Evolution of Medieval Mentalities: A Cognitive-Structural Approach," *American Historical Review* 83 (1978):395.

131. Schneider et al., *Person Perception*, pp. 42, 63; F. Heider, *The Psychology of Interpersonal Relations*; K. Davis and E. Jones, "Changes in Interpersonal Perception as a Means of Reducing Cognitive Dissonance," *Journal of Abnormal and Social Psychology* 61 (1960): 402-410; Kelley, "The Processes of Causal Attribution," 107-128.

6

The Theology of Adaptation and Critique

The fundamental principle organizing modern secular society in general is that each citizen is basically dependent upon the secular order for the establishment of a stable community. The resulting corollary is that the citizen must be ready to contribute whatever may be necessary for the preservation of that order and must act in a spirit of loyal dedication, usually motivated by patriotism. This rationale results in and simultaneously is maintained by complex patterns of value, accepted by members of the society. Every secular value system embraces its own set of principles that it designates as inviolable. The ideological concern for personalized relations based on a search for community meaning and a rejection of individualism was the goal of the Nazi secular society. In the Third Reich it led to an emphasis on the pseudoreligious and on the creation of a feeling of membership in the *Volk*.[1] Germans focused on the *Reich, Volk, Vaterland,* and, increasingly, on the *Rasse*. These basic values had been accepted by German Catholics as well, although *Rasse* tended to be relegated to the political-social-economic sphere where it was used to certify that the speaker or writer was a "true" German.[2]

To Catholic leaders only revelation was considered fixed and unchallengable, not susceptible to rational modification, at least in its essence. Similarly, they were also politically conservative. Some felt that adjustments in nonreligious areas, for example, might reduce pressure on the Church as it fulfilled its basic mission. Redemption, however, was a question of saving one's soul and not a moral commitment to the sociopolitical betterment of mankind.[3] Because of this basic orientation, Catholic leaders historically have been able to adapt to a wide variety of political regimes, but until the twentieth century none with a racist orientation.

By the 1920s *Rasse* had a certified biological foundation in the minds of many. Conceptually, *Rasse* was used to classify individuals biologically as well as socially according to "good" or "bad" racial qualities. There were, then, various degrees of racism, some resembling what Americans would refer to as ethnicity. *Vaterland* may be translated as "fatherland," but connoted as well to some Germans a measure of arbitrary authority exercised by legal rulers and of obedience on the part of the citizens. *Volk* designated a people organized along national lines and somehow organically fused together. Given Germany's pre-1871 disunity, some saw the *Volk* as the ultimate political reality. There were various cements for the *Volk*—race, religion, and culture. In this context, the Nazis could be classified as radical *völkisch,* stressing the racial element. Other Germans adhering to the *völkisch* ideal as the ultimate political reality, but rejecting the primacy of race, would be *völkisch* conservatives. Such concepts as *Volk* and *Vaterland,* which a person had to accept to behave appropriately as a member of society, are labeled culture, while the resulting values and attitudes are labeled personality.[4] In a review of studies focusing on the relationship between dogmatism and personality patterns, the dogmatic individual has been described as one characterized by dependency upon authority figures, by resistance to change, and by conformity to majority opinion. The dogmatic individual tends to be satisfied with what he has been taught to believe, inclined to accept statements or values despite inconsistencies, and in favor of tradition rather than change. In churches these intellectual, religious professionals devoted to understanding tradition and dogma and skilled in the reduction of dissonance are called theologians.[5] One mode of dealing with the dissonance, which arose when theological dogma confronted practical reality, was to stress the legitimacy of distinctions. Theologians were trained to do this as, for example, in the "just war" theory. In some respects, of course, inconsistency is in the mind of the beholder; theologians in Nazi Germany did not view their analysis as being inconsistent with Christian values or overtly as dissonance reducing. Theological commentators were merely delineating valid distinctions, although in the process they were dealing with the dissonance produced by the confrontation of the Nazi and Catholic *Weltanschauungen.* As they plied their skills, the theologians, unlike contemporary scholars, saw Nazism in fragmentation, not as a continuum. In hindsight, their experiences and errors in judgment can only serve to alert their successors to be vigilant in adhering to principles and hesitant in adapting to the sociopolitical order. Ideas and patterns of response do have consequences.

With both conservatives and Nazi radicals using the same terms, the ultimate effect was an inability to clarify the political values upon which the state was thought to rest. Ultimately, it became impossible to offer a coherent political analysis that could oppose Nazism. Conservative usage of such terms as *Volk* or *Reich* could imply that Nazism was a respectable movement, merely right of center. Nazi popular support suggested to many, indeed, that Hitler's government had legitimate popular support and that perhaps conservatives and radicals were "singing from the same hymnal." In time, some thought, the gap between them would close as *Reichskanzler* Hitler eliminated the more radical and uncontrollable members of his own movement. This latter development would occur as Hitler increasingly became convinced that the nonradical Germans supported his nationalistic aims. Indications of this capitulation on the part of the Catholic hierarchy were obvious by the spring of 1933, and the Concordat added the aura of respectability needed for compromise. Behind the public pronouncements of Church leaders, moreover, there was a substantial theological literature indicating that a broad basis of theological support existed for the bishops' political capitulation or that the theologians were beginning to conform to the official position or both.

Specific persons behave as they do because they want something from their interactions. They are influenced and guided by the exchanges they make, and they are shaped by their background of beliefs, values, and status investments. These "givens" help determine the concrete ways in which general psychodynamic propositions operate. Catholics held their values (*Volk, Vaterland*) due to a plethora of historical experiences in the German nation-state. What they did under the conditions of the Third Reich, a political form essentially distinct from past experience, is instructive. In the past, Catholics had achieved integration when they adhered to national values. Hence, allegiance to the new regime, they felt, would result in similar rewards. Adherence to national values in the post-*Kulturkampf* period had been a Catholic policy, and the remembrance of the suspicions of non-Catholics sensitized Church leaders to any activity that could be construed as disloyal. Having suffered discrimination in the past, Catholic leaders were determined to "fit" into the new Germany. The reward was great and so the high cost of adaptation was acceptable. Their selection and performance of activities was mainly governed by anticipated outcomes based on previous consequences that had been directly encountered or vicariously experienced. Their acquisition of proper behavior patterns occurred through their observation of others' activities. Their intensity of commitment in the past and then in 1933 was maintained and reinforced by beliefs about God's commands, the acceptance of historical political values, and the anxiety experienced over past seeming or real exclusions.[6] The initial response among Catholics was to adapt to the "New Germany."

German Theologians as Patriots

Among Catholic publicists there existed a corporatist-democratic tradition stressing some form of political participation, but virtually no strong support for a republican political system. Bavarian monarchists and other conservative Catholics, for example, generally opposed the "alien" republic during the Weimar era, an attitude that had widespread support among the bishops themselves. In 1926 Kurt Ziesche had commented that a common political battle involving true Christians should be waged against those liberals and Jews who favored the elimination of a viable national leadership in favor of control through the Jewish banks. Shortly thereafter, Friedrich Muckermann sounded the increasingly potent theme of the glories of the Reich, both past and future. One could not, he maintained, bury the historical idea of the Holy Roman Empire.[7] Attacking the liberal "Jewish" Republic, this *Reichstheologie* helped shape the intellectual patterns necessary for the initial adaptation to the Nazi *Weltanschauung* and reduced the possibility for Catholic resistance. Adherents to this *Reichstheologie* felt that the primary function of the state, however, was neither to wage war nor to control the lives of its citizens. The state was to create tranquility, security, and order.

By the end of March 1933, many in the Third Reich foresaw with enthusiasm the re-emergence of the Sacrum Imperium. The Enabling Act, for example, produced a decisive change in Carl Schmitt's attitude. He became more conciliatory toward Nazism. His previous attitude on constitutional revision, he felt, could be altered, since the constitution had now become irreversibly transformed. General-vikar Steinmann announced in August 1933 that what many had striven for had finally come to pass: Germany was one Reich with one leader. Naturally, Steinmann asserted that this leader should be followed. Confidently, Bishop Burger maintained that the goals of the new Reich government had for a long time been the goals of the Catholic Church. By 1935 Church representatives had assured the Nazi leaders that Catholics were *reichstreu* and *reichsverantwortlich.* Articles by Schmaus, Lortz, and Berning all provide examples of the general attempt to build bridges between the Church and National Socialism. In doing this the *Reichsidee* was a key element in the formula. Schmaus, for example, stressed the common front between Catholics and Nazis against liberalism and Bolshevism. Both *Weltanschauungen* also focused on a hierarchial ordering within society. For both Catholics and the Nazis the individualistic and Western democratic perception of man was unacceptable. Even Gundlach, for example, made the point that democracy was not a farce, but rather a legitimate political view, although he opposed, at least intellectually, the "atomistic" republic in which Weimar democracy was supposed to flourish.[8]

Gundlach, Rommen, Schilling, Brauer, and Schwer were all solidarists. Basically these solidarists opposed the liberal middle-class socioeconomic order and socialism. Along with the Nazis, they were committed to the fight against world-plutocracy and bolshevism, both of which were apparently supported by Jews. The social anti-Semitism of these Catholics was manifest in such comments as those made by Johannes Messner: "Germans should only marry Germans and avoid liaisons with other races. Hence, the immigration of Jews from the East should be subjected to careful supervision." Even so, Catholic theologians had hardly been completely consistent since 1918. Brauer, for example, in 1929 was a convinced republican. In 1930 he was committed to a universalistic solidarism and so attacked democracy. By 1931 he was demanding a strong state and saw the advent of Nazism as a blessing. Cooperation with the Nazis was necessary, he wrote in 1933. At the same time he perceived that the development of the German *Volk* demanded a basic cleansing in order to eliminate racial perversions.[9] In the case of Brauer, intellectual consistency was not a strong suit.

Almost universally by 1933, however, Catholic thinkers were seeking a rapprochement with the new Nazi state. Muckermann contended that there was a natural organic root to the *Volkstum,* and another organic principle directed the supernatural development of the Church. Frequently, both *Volk* and *Kirche* were enlisted to support one another. *Volkstum, Reich,* and *Rasse* intermingled at the base of the institutional state. The dominant signal being sent by the Catholic publicists was for reconciliation; they generally failed to explicate analytically the overt and covert meanings of these loaded "German values." Even liturgy journals typically avoided articles that offered scholarly analyses of the Jewish origins of early Christian liturgical developments. From the Christian perspective the real enemy seemed to be not the heathen or pagan, but rather the Jew. The *völkisch* Christians saw the hostile Church and loyal Christians as enemies on the side of the Jews. Clearly then, Church leaders had to emphasize their disdain although rarely outright hatred of the Jews. Their institutional survival seemed dependent on this. Anti-Semitism helped create the acceptance of Nazism among the Catholic populace. Based on hostility toward the Jews and connected to antiliberal and anti-Socialist resentment, a common ground existed between Catholics and Nazis. At least in the early phase, this congruence was of greater importance than the ideological and cultural differences. Eventually the latter elements, however, would play a central role in the official confrontation between leading Catholics and Nazis, as might be expected, when common ties were no longer able to be highlighted.[10]

The popular *Reichtheologie* orientation included a basic racist underpinning which by 1933 had become popularly familiar. Grosche (1934) saw the Reich as the secularized reflection of the kingdom of God. Rudolf Graber (1933-34) looked back through the mists of history and saw the Germanic race in its origins as a healthy, vibrant race. It entered a world that belonged to it then and presumably had now returned to reclaim its inheritance. Karl Adam, one of the foremost theologians of the twentieth century, claimed that it was the right and duty of the state to preserve the blood purity of the *Volk*. The expulsion of the Jewish mentality apparent in the press, literature, science, and art could be undertaken by the state as a necessary measure, although the Christian conscience was to insist that the legal ordinances be implemented in a spirit of justice and love. Apparently even at this early date having second thoughts, however, Adam did not conclude his essay in any of the subsequent issues of the *Theologische Quartalschrift*.[11]

In a paper serving Bavarian priests, an article (1935) on the revolution of 1918 exposed the role of the Jews in the *Dolchstoss* of the undefeated German army, thereby revivifying a seventeen-year-old accusation. "While the front made superhuman sacrifices and fought with admirable bravery against a world of enemies, the Jew Emil Barth equipped his *Untermenschen* (subhumans) with hand grenades and automatic pistols in order to attack the national defense from the rear . . ." These acts of treason, the article suggested, actually began in 1914, when the Jew Karl Liebknecht refused to vote for the war appropriations.[12] The anti-Semite theme persisted. The Jews had had a "demoralizing influence on religiosity and national character."[13] The Jews, as a spiritual community, had brought the German people "more damage than benefit."[14] The Jews had killed Jesus in their boundless hatred of Christianity and were still in the forefront of those seeking to destroy the Church.[15] These articles, written by priests, appeared in various journals and suggest the extensive network of prejudice entwined in support of the *Volk*. Some Catholic theologians attempted to promulgate a sophisticated *völkisch* anti-Semitism that could be acceptable to intellectuals with their "refined" sensibilities.

In *Theologie und Glaube* (1934), Algermissen perceived a synthesis emerging between *Vokstum* and *Christentum*. Just as the renewal of the *Volk* came from Christianity, so a vibrant Christianity was internally to develop within and grow from the living essence of the *Volk*. Part of this rebirth of the spirit in God had to be rooted in race and blood. In this view a baptized Jew remained a Jew according to race and blood, although for the moral worth of the individual the racial roots were insignificant compared to free-will acts. This modified racism still gave credence to the distinction contained in the insider-outsider array of values. Algermissen did, however, insist that Article 24 of the Nazi program was not totally valid since the *Volkstum* could not be the ultimate source of value, which was God. Essentially, the *Volk* and Christianity belonged together as nature and supernature. They were complementary. Algermissen contended that it was God's will that Christianity in Germany appeared in a form congenial and corresponding to the deepest values of the German *Volk*. Finally, Christianity had never destroyed anything worthwhile in the German soul, but rather had merely perfected everything beautiful and natural that lay at the origins of the race.[16]

Schmaus also attacked the Jews for believing that revelation was bound intrinsically to their nationality. He felt that the Jews should atone for this error.[17] These anti-Semitic views were reinforced by the hierarchy. On March 1, 1934, Cardinal Schulte said: "It is heathendom and apostasy from Christ and Christianity to see the essential element in religion only in the requirements of alleged blood and race. . . . It is heathendom and apostasy from Christ and Christianity . . . if people are no longer willing to be told that we are all sinful children of Adam in need of redemption through Christ and his sacred blood" (*Kirchlicher Anzeiger für die Erzdiöcese Köln,* March 1, 1934). Usually taken as an attack on Nazi ideology, such statements could actually be used to reinforce anti-Semitism by insisting that if one were not redeemed, then one could not be saved. By 1936 Cardinal Schulte was even more explicit when he allowed the following to be published in a catechism: "What was the greatest sin of the Jewish people? The greatest sin of the Jewish people was that it rejected the savior and his teaching."[18] The Jews as a people separate from Christians was a viewpoint that continued to be reinforced by the statements of the Catholic clergy.

Associated with the anti-Semitic theme were the general attacks on atomistic democracy by such theologians as Spann, Dempf, and Muckermann, all of whom felt that secular democracy was essentially alien to Christianity. An authoritarian state reflected true Christian values. Popular sovereignty could never be accepted since conceptually the true Reich reflected the same hierarchy that existed in the order of life.[19] Eschweiler summed up the 1933 Catholic consensus which seemed to be emerging and which reinforced the episcopal adaptation. The NSDAP and the state had become de facto unified. In his view, the Reich was once again to become the strong bulwark for the Christian West or civilization would sink into a *Volksgesellschaft,* characterized by a lack of faith, in which there would be no place for the chair of Peter. Article 24 so consistently attacked by Catholics was now given a new interpretation. Its stress on the moral feeling of the German people was meant to oppose the cleavages being created in human nature, i.e., individualism vs. the *Volk,* materialism vs. spiritualism. The grace of divine faith in Germans did not destroy their unique God-created natural dispositions. Grace was supportive of and presupposed nature. Referring to an earlier Bavarian episcopal letter, Eschweiler agreed with the bishops' conviction that the true renewal of the *Volk* could be derived solely from faith. Christianity should reinforce the natural life of the *Volk.* When he went so far as to approve the compulsory sterilization law enacted on July 14, 1933, Eschweiler was suspended and barred from teaching until he submitted to censure by Rome. His accommodation was too extensive. After his death (1936) an obituary in Alfred Rosenberg's gazette called him a "martyr to the Roman system."[20] The fact that all of these prominent men aligned themselves with the new regime could in all likelihood be viewed by "average" Catholics as proof that National Socialism, despite superficial faults, could not really be as evil as some had earlier suggested.[21] Practically all of these works, moreover, appeared with the approval of Church authorities and thus carried the stamp of orthodoxy.

The National Socialist state emphasized the term *Reich* to take advantage of the patriotic images that could be evoked. By supporting this thrust of Nazism, Catholics saw a distinct opportunity to escape completely the *Kulturkampf* ghettos to which they had been consigned for so long. The National Socialist state, it was hoped, would have to acknowledge these Catholics as supporters of Nazism. Catholics hoped from this position to eliminate the unacceptable aspects of the Nazi *Reichsgedanke*. This Catholic *Reichstheologie,* of course, was not universally supported. Keller, for example, felt that it was a web of theological errors. This *Reichsideologie* of 1929-34 was, he thought, an aberration, a dying echo of a theological tradition dating back to Constantine.[22] General support of the *Reichstheologie,* however, does reflect an unfortunate Catholic predilection, i.e., an overwhelming desire to adapt theological and philosophical attitudes to the contemporary socioeconomic and political reality instead of assuming the role of critic.

The thrust of theologians during the Weimar era and into the early Nazi Reich was to oppose the Republic rooted in liberalism and socialism as well as to repudiate democratic values shaped through nineteenth-century political experiences and not by Scholasticism. At the same time, at least until March 1933, most theologians were anti-Nazi, preferring their own authoritarian frame of reference. Indicating the lack of support that even the Catholic Center had in these circles are such remarks as those made by Muckermann who said that political Catholicism merely reflected the weakness found in the fragile political system of postwar Germany. In 1930 Cardinal Bertram had already proclaimed that there was a justified nationalism. Its sign is a love of the native tongue, love for the *Volkstum,* and praise to God for the inherited characteristics of this *Volk.*[23] This stress on *Volk* offered a bridge between the conservative Catholic and the Nazi *Weltanschauungen.*

Brauer stressed that the new leadership wanted to realize the potential of the *Volkstum* as fully as possible. The theologian used terms drawn from the traditional lexicon (*Blut, Boden,* and *Schicksal*) to bolster his arguments and suggested, for example, that the emergence of the *Volkstum* would require a *Saubererhaltung* (cleansing) from a racial perspective. Catholics could defend Hitler's view that he wanted the cultural and political leadership to be the expression of that elite racial segment which, thanks to its intrinsic talents, reflected the superior qualities inherent in the German people. With a favorable nod toward modern political issues, Brauer maintained that for a Catholic obviously the individual had intrinsic worth, but that this did not necessarily refer to the isolated individual. The individual only develops his true potential by living in the *Gemeinschaft*. All aspects of culture, therefore, should be directed to serve in the renewal of the *Volkstum*. Catholics, for their part, should be guided by those principles that unify their culture. Even scholarship should be placed in the service of reconstructing the true *Volk*.[24] Interestingly, Brauer and others viewed their tasks as reconstruction or renewal—the implication being that something was wrong with the old system that was now in need of repair. Here again they seem to be voicing the Nazi call-to-arms.

Accommodation, then, was reasonably complete in the hierarchy and among most theologians in 1933-34. Like many Germans, they seemed to feel that a Hitler in power could be molded into a rational statesman supporting their own traditional values. Indications of this attitude may be seen in the simultaneous critique of Rosenberg's *Mythus* and in support of Hitler as the legitimate political authority embodying the true values of the German people.[25] In a limited fashion Catholics attacked racist, but not politico-social anti-Semitism. Hitler engaged in the same political sleight of hand. He insisted that Rosenberg's book had no official status as the party's ideological bible and stressed common themes around which reconciliation might occur. In the end, Hitler won the contest since Catholic spokesmen praised Hitler and his ideas, while they attacked Rosenberg and his radical followers. Watching this political two-step, Catholics could not help but affirm their own confidence in the führer, since his nationalistic ideals had support in high clerical places.

While in hindsight this adaptation by Catholic thinkers may seem appalling, their analyses did contain the omnipresent qualification that God was the source of all legitimate power and values. Hence, obedience only to lawful authority was necessary. The issue they did not seem to address was what exactly constituted lawful authority. As its goal, the Church was to mediate to man his understanding of the absolute God and help apply divine law to the particular human situations that historically arose. Natural human developments were to be shaped by God's grace; by highlighting and supporting this grace, Catholics were told that they could actively insure that nature or man's world avoided perversion. Church leaders hoped that cooperation with Hitler would turn his movement into a force for good by reinforcing its positive contributions. In a decree of July 1933, Bishop Matthias Ehrenfried of Würzburg dutifully expressed this hope. He admonished the clergy of lower Franconia to observe a due subordination towards the lawful national government: "Under present conditions it is possible that subordinate officials might initiate wrongful and interfering measures, which might militate against our cooperation with the national movement and disturb our sympathetic attitude towards it. It is not, however, the duty of the individual priest to judge of such matters or to redress them."[26] The Church was prepared to support Hitler, even if not all his subordinates.

Attempts at adaptation and accommodation continued even as the Nazi regime revealed its true intentions and pursued its *Gleichschaltung* policies. In 1936 Emil Ritter and Kuno Brombacher issued a short work that reflected the thought patterns of those Catholics still at ease with the Nazis. They lay the blame for the then-current problems of the Church in Germany upon Bismarck and the liberals responsible for the *Kulturkampf* and the isolation of Catholics who had subsequently been forced to organize themselves socially and politically, thus forming a state within a state. They felt that one condition necessary for the revival of religious life had to be the clear separation in Germany of questions that touched upon faith and so belonged to the Church from other problems to which no specifically Catholic answer could be given. They were infuriated by what they termed the "spirit of confessionalism," which had made Catholics defensive and anti-Protestant. Because of historical circumstances, some maintained that German Catholics had a stronger spirit of kinship with Catholics of other countries than with their fellow countrymen. A consequence of this apparent lack of material identity was interpreted in some quarters as an essential opposition to the *Volk*. Both Ritter and Brombacher hoped to end the mistrust of non-Catholics. There must be, they felt, more stress upon the Church's spiritual character as the Bride and the Mystical Body of Christ, and less upon her outward and institutional forms. Similar to their contemporaries, both authors accepted the blessings of the Nazi regime without reserve. At the same time, however, after their initial flourish of support, these and other German Catholic writers as well as Pius XI himself ceased their praise of the new regime and began devoting their energy to the theological analyses through which they could oppose, although at times naively, at least the values of the Nazi *Weltanschauung* even if not the concrete results of Nazi activities.[27] By stressing that enmity existed between their party and the Church, the Nazis facilitated this transformation which eventually resulted in the realization of the dangers inherent in anti-Semitism.

Theological Challenges to the Totalitarian State

Hitler's conversion from indifference to religion to outright enmity was made certain by the resistance he encountered when he attempted the *Gleichschaltung* of the Church. The Concordat has been judged by some as a mistake, but it did offer the Church some leverage against the regime. Hitler, of course, felt that the Church should confine its attention strictly to spiritual matters; everything else was political, a position unacceptable to the Church. Having virtually no religious conscience himself, he could not see the connection of religion to political morality and could not accept the fact that clerical opposition was ultimately based on the realization that the basic Nazi *Weltanschauung* disagreed with Catholicism about the purpose of man on earth. Had he fully realized this basic contradiction, he might have been much more savage in his dealings with the Church right from the very beginning.[28] The Church's early desire for accommodation and Hitler's own needs for Catholic support domestically and for his foreign adventures resulted in a gradual and piecemeal, although increasingly intrusive, *Gleichschaltung.* The Church had ample indications of the characteristics of the enemy.

Signatures were initially affixed to the Concordat on July 20. The National Socialist government on July 25 published the compulsory sterilization law earlier enacted on July 14, 1933, but held up until the Concordat issue was resolved. Promulgation of the law was a good signal that the Concordat had not changed basic Nazi policies.[29] Dr. Schnabel, a professor at the University of Halle, wrote on July 4, 1935:

> In a certain sense National Socialism is a religion because it asks its followers not to become convinced of the truth of its doctrine, but to believe in it. Like any other religion, National Socialism possesses its own teaching on moral questions, and its own ethics, the classical expositions of which are, first, what the Führer wrote in his book *Mein Kampf* about Aryanism, and then the work of Alfred Rosenberg, *The Myth of the Twentieth Century.*[30]

In 1936 Victor Lutze continued to develop this theme. The totalitarian claims of the National Socialist philosophy, he felt, covered the life of every individual and would brook no opposition. The NSDAP, he asserted, had no time to reform religion or the Church and certainly did not want to introduce a new heathenism. Nazism had rolled back the tide of atheistic communism. Hence, the Church had no right to sabotage the work of the government. Lutze continued that he and his fellow Nazis were interested in everything that affected Germany in this world. Clearly, then, the Church had no right to protest the sterilization laws, because for the maintenance of the *Volk* the state, not the Church, bore responsibility. With respect to youth, a very sensitive issue to the German Catholics as well as to the pope, the NSDAP wanted full freedom to impregnate youth with the theory of the primacy of German blood and soil, the basis of racial survival.[31]

Significant attacks against the Church also appeared in Heinrich Himmler's paper *Das Schwarze Korps.* The following will suffice to provide the flavor of the SS position.

> That is the pestilential stench of a putrefying world; it stinks to heaven. We are referring to all those scandalous proceedings in those Church circles, both within and without the monasteries, in the midst of which not one crime is lacking from perjury to incest to sexual murder. . . . All this is the expression and consequence of a system that has elevated into a principle that which is against nature and of an organization that has withdrawn itself from public control. . . . We are actuated by no enmity to religion or Church in our demand for the State control of all Church organizations that work in public.[32]

Essentially reiterating Article 24, *Das Schwarze Korps* (1939) directed its readers to an aspect of Nazism that must have been particularly repulsive to Catholics. "A morality based on the demands of life is unable to set up an unchangeable moral code, because the eternal flux of life necessitates a progressive internal readjustment."[33] The Nazis and Soviets could at least agree on repudiating the transcendent in religion. In fact, as the Catholic thinkers analyzed Bolshevism they should have perceived that National Socialism was striving for the same goals. The point was probably muted because Hitler and his intimates kept mouthing religious phrases, although many Catholic thinkers had perceived from the beginning his lack of commitment to religious ideals.

Opposition to National Socialism was difficult to mount in light of the continuing Nazi suppression of the Catholic press. Those hostile to the NSDAP could not be inflammatory and had to be limited to the activities proper to priests, e.g., writing tracts that could undermine the arguments and ideals of the Nazi movement or adapt Nazi terms and symbols to Catholic activities. An internal report of the Gestapo (1937) about "political Catholicism," for example, warned that the Church was appropriating National Socialist symbols and terminology. Increasingly, one could hear such slogans as "Jesus is our *Führer,*" "Heil Bishop," etc. Thus, the Gestapo report charged, the Church hoped to conquer National Socialism as once she had overcome the German heathens. The difference between National Socialist and Catholic outpourings on the subjects of race, the leadership principle, nation, defense of the fatherland, etc., one writer complained, was minimal. Everywhere the Catholics seemed to be trying to outdo the Nazis in chauvinistic zeal.[34]

Although such complaints were justified, it would be wrong to conclude that any of the bishops or theologians completely identified themselves with the party's ideology. Many endorsements of specific points of the Nazi program and practice were hedged with reservations as the Nazis never ceased to complain. The bishops and theologians insisted repeatedly that race, although important, could not determine morality, and they opposed the idea of a master race. Though rejecting liberalism, Church leaders also alerted the faithful to the extravagant claims of the *Volksgemeinschaft* which, they contended, deprived the individual of his rights.[35] The Church insisted on not being entombed in the sacristy. The Church refused to be limited to worship and ritual, and stressed that its teaching encompassed all aspects of public and private life. The Church asserted the superiority of divine law over all man-made dogmas of nation and race, and coupled this with its claim to penetrate all areas of human existence. Such boldness infuriated the Nazis and made them see in the Church a most treacherous enemy. No matter what the tactics of the Church, declared a 1937 report, and regardless of whether the bishops used legal or illegal means, "between the National Socialist state and the Catholic Church there can be no peace. The totalitarian claims of the Church challenge those of the state."[36] Increasingly, Catholic adaptation was restricted to nationalistic goals held in common by the NSDAP and the Church, and was manifested in patriotic proclamations and in birthday greetings to the führer.

In 1933 Friedrich Fuchs wrote a response to Carl Schmitt's essay on the total state, which suggests that the Gestapo rightly sensed the serious threat being mounted by the Church. Fuchs viewed the Church as the visible representative of Christ, the *societas perfecta,* and insisted that only it had the power and responsibility to set the boundaries for the total state and by protecting religious freedom to safeguard the freedom of the spirit itself. The Church was "more totalitarian" than the Nazi regime. Operating from God-given principles, however, the Church could protect human freedom. Gustav Gundlach as well criticized the Nazi ideology by 1933. Naturally, he attacked the liberal conception of pluralism, which was purely formal and atomistic, since it denied an objectively grounded order and the unity of the human community. Natural law pluralism, however, emphasized hierarchical as well as organic *Ordnung* and stressed *Einheit* (unity). The most telling attack he made on Nazism early in 1933 was that it simply insisted on too much uniformity.[37]

His position was not supported with any enthusiasm by the general of Gundlach's Jesuit Order, Ledochowski. In 1933-34, Ledochowski and others felt that the Nazi system would not last and so they should focus their attention on their chief enemy, Bolshevism. Ultimately, they sensed the possibility for compromise with Nazism. Apparently, Ledochowski's opinion also was influential in the innermost circles of the Vatican and serves to illustrate the particularly weak position occupied by those who tried to defend the Church in Germany. Pius XI attacked Bolshevism in his encyclical *Divini Redemptoris* (1937), and then Nazism in his *Mit Brennender Sorge,* one of the most incisive and vigorous denunciations of racism during the 1930s. The Nazis were particularly stunned by this assault. Pius, however, saw this encyclical as only a first step. In 1934 he had already made known his position. A human norm, he felt, is unthinkable without its being anchored in God. The foundation for the norm cannot be some divinized race or the nation as an absolute.[38]

To expand on his 1937 assaults, Pius invited John LaFarge, S.J., a Jesuit well-known for his antiracist activities in the United States, to help draft an encyclical focusing on racism. LaFarge wrote from a pastoral viewpoint, Gundlach from a theoretical standpoint. The pope hoped to lay out systematically the social teaching of the Church on the state, nation, and race. Apparently the draft was submitted to Ledochowski who then delayed transference to the pope. In Gundlach's opinion, Ledochowski's fear of communism may well have stopped the appearance of the encyclical. Anyway, the delaying tactics probably were not questioned because of Pius' declining health. It is apparent from the sketch or draft of the encyclical that Pius hoped to offer a comprehensive analysis of the Catholic position against racism and its symbiotic connection to Nazism. Gundlach, LaFarge, and Pius saw that the Jewish question had to be addressed as a Christian problem before it could be handled from the racial dimension. At any rate, the encyclical was never published. Instead of a world-wide protest, Pius XII would decide for the silent helping deed.[39] Even in the 1930s, the question of a possible link between the age-old Christian teaching of contempt and the later catastrophes that threatened to overwhelm the Jews, so pejoratively portrayed, was not being ignored. The Holocaust was even in the 1930s on the way to becoming a Christian as well as Jewish problem. Pius XI seemed to see the insidious connection. While the German bishops and theologians might well have denounced anti-Semitism on the social level, although several did not, they simultaneously affirmed its theological underpinnings, thereby lending support to the tragedy about to ensue.

In Gröber's 1937 *Handbuch,* the prelate states:

> Every people bears itself the responsibility for its successful existence, and the intake of entirely foreign blood will always represent a risk for a nationality that has proven its historical worth. Hence, no people may be denied the right to maintain undisturbed their previous racial stock and to enact safeguards for this purpose. The Christian religion merely demands that the means used do not offend against the moral law and natural justice.[40]

Later, in 1939, Bishop Hilfrich of Limburg emphasized that "the Christian religion had not grown out of the racial nature of the Jews, but rather had advanced despite these God-killers."[41] In essence, both bishops and theologians confused and blurred the very issues it was in the interest of the religious community to define as sharply as possible. The patriotic rhetoric and statements intended to reinforce German *Volk* values in opposition to the more radical tenets of Nazism in fact probably reinforced the Nazis' own efforts to instill and exploit nationalistic pride.[42] Both the bishops and their theologians had identified values common to Nazism and German Catholicism which could facilitate an early adaptation. Outwardly the bishops, probably for political reasons, persisted in expressing nationalistic sentiments to avoid the ghettoization of the Church. Pius XI in 1937-38 appeared ready to go on an offensive that would become muted under his successor. Due to censorship, lack of newsprint, weak leadership from the German hierarchy, and a growing realization of the dangers inherent in the Nazi *Weltanschauung,* however, theologians in Germany after 1933-34 began to highlight those Catholic values that could be used in counterattacking Nazi totalitarian policies.

German Theologians Oppose Hitlerism

In the Catholic works that encouraged adaptation to National Socialism the intrinsic dangers of this hostile world view were not overlooked, but rather generally attributed to radical elements in the movement. Because of spy activities, Catholic clergy had to be cautious, even though the mismanagement and stupidity of the Gestapo were notorious. Spies were, however, endemic to the system. At the Nuremberg Trial one witness reckoned spies and informers inside various groups, societies, and churches at about 30,000.[43] Given the Christian tradition of obedience to political authority and the patriotic nationalism of most German Catholics, the tendency among theologians was to relate positively to what seemed good in the NSDAP. Of course, from a position of hindsight, it is difficult to judge with precision the subjective disposition of those who adapted to or adopted the principle tenets of what they felt might well be a basically healthy conservative national movement, although somewhat radical around the fringes. It is difficult to comprehend the naivete' of the *Kreuz und Adler* circle or of those engaged in *Reichstheologie* as these spiritual romantics searched for the roots of the Holy Roman Empire that had seemingly blossomed again in 1933. The antiregime political perception among the theologians could not be expressed openly, but became apparent, for example, in the sudden interest in developing materials on early Christian German saints.[44] To these men, there was another Germany.

By late 1933 the enthusiasm of some Catholic intellectuals for the regime had begun to wane, and the hierarchy began to respond more vigorously to the prominent errors supported by the party. Cardinal Faulhaber's sermons against the Nazis in 1933-34 offer a very good early example. In a series of three Advent sermons, the Munich cardinal sounded a critical note, but not a condemnation of anti-Semitism. He protested against the threatening relapse into the paganism of the ancient Germanic tribes, defended the Old Testament, and warned that "the individual must not be deprived of his own dignity . . . or treated as a slave without rights of his own."[45] A contemporary theologian, Friedrich Fuchs, perceived the meaning of the cardinal's comments. To Fuchs, the Old Testament was the basic theme of Faulhaber's sermons and not the Jewish question. In his defense against the Nazi ideologues, Fuchs stoutly maintained that the Old Testament contained revelation and so could not be separated from the Church. The Jewish issue was another question. Then Fuchs maintained that the cardinal's 1934 New Year's sermon emphasized the scripturally sound view that men are not saved because of German blood, but through Christ's blood. The unfortunate deduction that could be drawn was that only Christians were saved. But the Church was not speaking consistently. At Bremen, Bishop Berning declared before a mass meeting of Catholics that the führer had told him personally of his intention to build the German state upon Christian foundations, and the bishop exhorted his congregation to serve the new Germany with love. Although there were some criticisms, the Jesuit monthly *Stimmen der Zeit* adequately summed up the situation. The swastika had proven its creative potential: "the person of Hitler has become the symbol of the faith of the German nation in its existence and future." The speedy conclusion of the Concordat demonstrated that hostility need not prevail between the *Kreuz* and *Hakenkreuz*. "On the contrary: the symbol of nature only finds its fulfillment and consummation in the symbol of grace."[46]

Better than anything else, one episode epitomizes the situation in which the Church, despite all her protestations of goodwill, found herself at the end of the first year. Vicar General Mayer of Mainz, a vocal opponent of Nazism before 1933, now offered a burial for Peter Gemeinder, the Nazi *Gauleiter* of Hessen who had died in 1931, and, according to prevailing regulations, had been refused a Catholic funeral. The vicar general said that he had just received information that indicated that Gemeinder had indeed asked for a priest! Mayer now wanted to hold a belated funeral and blessing to which the local NSDAP would be invited. The Nazis rejected this offer of making amends. Gemeinder's widow replied that Reichsstaathalter Sprenger had ordered her to withhold her consent to the planned ceremony. This event and Faulhaber's sermon alerted most clerical leaders that the honeymoon, if it had ever existed, was finished. In 1934, Cardinal von Galen sponsored Professor Wilhelm Neuss-Bonn's *Studien zum Mythos des 20 Jh.* (1934), an attack against Rosenberg's work.[47]

The theological responses to Nazism developed along two lines. Almost without exception, major works contain virtually no attempt to accommodate Nazi axioms and, even though cut off from the literature of the universal Church in part before 1939 and almost totally after 1939, show a surprising creativity as well as stress on basic anti-Nazi values. A gradualist disenchantment with Nazism can be perceived in the journal offerings. Clearly the Nazis perceived opposition mounting in the theological area. Journals were halted; paper became scarce during the war; such theological faculties as those in Munich, Innsbruck, and Salzburg were closed.[48] Despite all the pressures some very perceptive works were published. A variety of apologetic works focusing on the papacy appeared. Because of Nazi falsehoods, such publications as those of Seppelt devoted to Church history had an eminent apologetic value, and the focus on the papacy reminded readers that the Church universal had persisted through other crises and had gained strength in persecution.[49] Noting the Nazi attempt to introduce "liturgical ceremonies" into their movement, several theologians also warned that the Church's sacraments and attendant ceremonies were grounded in the reality of grace and in Christ's continually living salvific mission.[50]

Likewise, there occurred a radical turn in the focus on apologetics. Rhetorically, Johann Beumer, S.J., asked, for example, whether the focus should be on apologetics or dogma in the Church. His answer was that theologians should concentrate both on apologetics and on the clarification of dogma, presumably so that Catholics could more adequately meet the assaults of a Nazi ideology supported by the wealth and power of the state. Even a study, purportedly only on dogma, seemed to confront some of the basic Nazi values. Michael Schmaus, for example, did not analyze dogma in an abstract fashion as derived from the ultimate unity that was God, but rather began with the salvific mission of the triune God historically stepping into man's world. His study is Christocentric, perhaps in contrast to the "führer-centric" Nazis, and focused on God's life among men.[51]

Naturally, given the Nazi transformation of societal values in part under the aegis of Social Darwinism, Catholic theologians felt compelled to reassert in a relevant manner the traditional precepts of morality. Fritz Tillmann fathered a school of moral theologians, simply an outbreak of religious life. Tillmann's Christocentric moral theology is not religious life. Tillmann's Christocentric moral theology is not merely a combination of the natural ethical norms and the demands resulting from the supernatural determination of man. Over and above this abstract approach, Tillmann analyzed Christ's injunction—"Follow me." A secular führer seemed to sensitize Tillmann to the need for a heavenly leader dynamically asserting His values. His moral theology was rooted in historical, scriptural events. Christians should model themselves on Christ's moral personality where three concentric patterns of duties could be discerned: love of God, love of neighbor, and love of self. Thus, not the avoidance of sin, but rather the positive virtues of love stand as the focal point of man's moral obligations.[52] These scholarly works were not read by nor written for the laity, of course, but rather for the use of the clergy in general and more so for professional theologians. Scholars very carefully responded to the principle thrusts of Nazism and carefully delineated Catholic teaching so that it responded to contemporary needs as well as reflected the perennial values residing in the historical Church founded by Christ. Although speculative, it was a comprehensive effort to maintain historical and dogmatic consistency as well as contemporary relevance. Likewise, theologians engaged in writing articles for journals, which viewed Nazism more critically after 1933-34. Initially, several of the theologians had tried to find "a common platform" for Nazism and Catholicism, a platform constructed from the planks of antiliberalism, antisocialism, and authoritarian thinking. This "spirit of 1933" was not maintained for long. Even this limited official acceptance of the Nazi order was deceiving since in the villages and small towns the Nazis remained to the end a minority and dependent on the toleration of the local populace.[53] Catholics in small towns maintained a more consistent opposition to the regime than did the bishops and theologians. Of course, the Catholic clerical leaders had to operate on "center stage" while trying to reconcile the irreconcilable.

Otto Schilling, Max Pribilla, and Erich Przywara offer very good examples of the struggle involved in dealing with Nazism. They published prolifically for a while, and so their almost daily intellectual turmoil can be observed. In 1933 Schilling published a standard analysis of social justice, which asserted that each person was to receive his just wages. The distribution of goods was to be guided by the calculated social necessity according to the needs of the common welfare, a position easily traced to Leo XIII.[54] Theologically, he opposed the Catholic view of the common good to that of the Nazis. In a compromising fashion, however, Pribilla accepted Hitler's promise in 1933 that the first step of the revolution had ended and that the positive reconstruction of Germany could now begin. Pribilla assured his readers that the revolution could only really be evaluated in a few years, thereby reflecting the almost universal caution of 1933. Few seemed to realize what National Socialism really was. Since he viewed Hitler's takeover as a positive development, he represented those who had only had disdain for the pluralistic, disorderly Weimar system. Nazism offered Germans, he felt, a chance to fight communism and an opportunity to escape the "ghetto" as well. In view of Hitler's apparent neutrality toward religion, even the bishops had retracted their earlier warning. Catholics themselves had a duty to infuse their spiritual contributions into the national life and could now work toward the inner reconciliation needed in the nation. They were urged to continue fighting for justice, particularly important in times of revolution. Pribilla, then, made a very interesting point, unfortunately not followed to its logical conclusion. The degree of political freedom in a state, he asserted, was directly related to the freedom allowed the minority; he was referring, however, to Catholics, not Jews. Catholics naturally were interested in the freedom of the Church, which was essentially the proclamation of the gospel through schools, the press, and sundry organizations. With respect to race issues, Pribilla thought that racial analyses were healthy as long as they were not restrictive or one-sided and could exist within the type of positive Christianity proclaimed by the Nazis. Finally, Pribilla insisted that the true "führer," who did not represent a specific interest, was needed and had, perhaps, arrived.[55] Similarly, another theologian, Przywara, maintained that "man-in-himself" existed nowhere; man only exists historically on earth and so must deal with temporal problems as they arise. Exhibiting a "normal anti-Semitism," he referred to Christ crucified by the unbelieving Jews. He and others seemed bent on affirming their "German orthodoxy." Simultaneously, however, the individual Christian, the state, and the nation were all obliged to pass through death into the one body, the Church, in order to be saved.[56]

Supporting the initial Nazi assumption of power, there continued into 1934 the attempt to reconcile scholarship to the new realities. Schilling now defended the right of the German people to "enlarged *Lebensraum*" and pleaded for the return of the colonies unjustly taken away from Germany after the World War. He argued that such a redress of national grievances would be in conformity with natural law. Support, however, was fading. By 1935 Pribilla had developed a guarded caution and skepticism in his commentaries on the Third Reich. In an article devoted to a critique of the *Deutsche Glaubensbewegung,* he reaffirmed the aximotic principle that *Christentum* and *Deutschtum* for centuries had formed a mutual bond with and had penetrated one another so that a symbiotic relationship clearly existed. Without faith in God, he continued, justice would lose its value. Lies and sheer power were not prerequisites for true spiritual victories. Still, opponents of the Church should not be confronted with hostility, but with love. If necessary, however, each Christian must stand up for his faith. He concluded this article by citing Pope Leo the Great, writing as Attila's hordes swept through Europe. Leo insisted that the true followers of Christ should adhere firmly to the quiet certainty of faith until the truth would shine on all men again and the darkness of unbelief vanished.[57] Pribilla's message was to endure patiently, just as previous Christians had stoically accepted seeming catastrophes.

The year 1935 seemed to be a key year in the transformation from a watchful acquiescence to a critique of the new regime. Negative analyses of the regime, however, were nearly always surrounded by patriotic camouflage. Usually considered critical of the regime, Preysing stated in 1935 that the battle to drive Christianity "from our Fatherland" was now being waged. In 1937 even the "Brown Bishop," Gröber, commented on the attacks against the Church "in our Fatherland." Catholics were struggling to emerge from the ghetto where they felt they had previously been relegated to the status of second-class citizens. At the same time they confronted the Nazi axiom that morality had no extrinsic basis, i.e., God was created by man. Rosenberg's statement that "National Socialism has always claimed the whole man and his entire personality" (*Frankfurter Zeitung* 1937) was particularly ominous and was more consistently opposed as the intention behind the *Gleichschaltung* became obvious. The patriotic camouflage probably confused Catholics who found it difficult in all the verbiage to discern the correct signal. In 1939 Rosenberg commented that true Nazis made no distinction between the state and its ideology, even for the benefit of those who were willing to accept the state but refused the ideology.[58] The ideologue saw compromise as impossible. All the patriotism in the world could not compensate for Catholic ideological intransigence. But both Catholics and Nazis were reluctant to wage full-scale war.

By 1938, Schilling was carefully analyzing the basic principle undergirding morality, which quite clearly opposed everything that the Nazis were promoting. He maintained that the ultimate goal was to become similar to God as He has revealed Himself in faith. The norm of this ethical life, of course, is love, not the hatred promoted by the NSDAP. He opposed the Reich of God to Satan's Reich and reiterated that the former was the eternal kingdom ruled by God. The basic norm shaping Catholic moral theology was love, not the *Reich Gottes* or even the imitation of Christ, since these latter flowed from the former.[59]

Concerned with Nazi eugenic policies, Pribilla urged that Catholic and not racist marriage manuals, for example, should be developed for the moral guidance of the faithful. In 1939 as the world approached war, Pribilla expanded his concern to the very survival of the Church and the moral decisions being made by Catholics. The Church itself, he asserted, had an unchangeable essence, and the crisis facing Christianity was only the most current in a long series. Christians had no right to be fatalists but should shape their era, since man is a social animal and so needs the help of society to develop properly. A good society was thought necessary to form a good man. Hence, a Christian education fully shapes a mature character grounded internally in faith. Indicative that the task of being a good Christian was becoming more difficult, Pribilla asserted that for many even the mere fulfillment of duty had become heroism. By citing the pressures that must have been felt by those trying to practice their faith,[60] Pribilla hoped to convince his readers that a considerable number of heroes existed. Resistance had become nonadherence to the regime.

By 1938 such scholars as Artweiler also were increasingly feeling the tension of being both Germans and Catholics. Some Germans waged war against God because He seemed too distant and so not able to understand their problems, others because the brotherhood of man was such a fragile concept in their minds. If brotherhood was unreal, he continued, fatherhood could not easily be accepted. Following the lead of Schmaus and Tillman, Artweiler insisted that exclusivistic or narrow apologetics were to be shunned. He felt men should focus on the spiritual life derived from faith in God and in the grace of Christ. The Church was the body of Christ, and the faithful were its members. Such a union should become visible. Love allowed men to exist in a stable relationship, not subject to the whims of the world. Focusing on the dangers of Nazi racism, Artweiler insisted that race was not absolute, but rather was limited by its very essence. All men belong to the human community since man is Man. Within this all-inclusive category, there were also such communities as the family and nation. The state was the organized form of the *Volk,* merely stressing connection by blood. Every community, however, was derived from God. Indeed, the Church was the community (*Gemeinschaft*) most closely approximating God's ideal.[61] Artweiler emphasized the Church as a union closely reflecting God's intended order, and certainly more worthy of adherence than Hitler's *Volk.*

In 1939 as the international tempo accelerated and pressures increased internally, Schilling as well tried to clarify some of the issues that Catholics were facing. To deemphasize the organic notion of the common good being promulgated by the Nazis, Schilling stressed that the basis of social justice was that the community has to give to the individual what was necessary. In essence, then, the individual was at the alpha and omega of the social order. Law was to have its basis in natural law, not in the will of the führer. Referring back to the Solidarist position, he reminded his readers that social justice and the organic principle could both belong to the traditional Christian pattern of thought, implying that only from this *Weltanschauung* was it possible to mediate values seemingly at odds with one another.[62]

As the threat and finally the reality of war emerged, Schilling tried to rework these theological opinions so that they would support what he perceived as acceptable wartime nationalism. Every German, he felt, surely viewed the Versailles Peace Treaty not as a document insuring peace, but rather as an instrument of force and injustice. If a superior opponent misused his power to deny to others their human dignity, then that rival was uniquely guilty of oppression. In his mind, then, the Germans were innocent victims of post-1918 European power politics. Abstractly, he admitted, all *Kulturvölken* should be united in a "League of Nations," since man's goal was the common good. In current circumstances, he felt, however, that the existence of such a league operating with justice seemed virtually unthinkable, since contemporary political realities did not reflect the axiom that the common good of peoples was the common goal. Clearly, if those fighting were seeking to destroy one another, then the presupposed community of justice was certainly not at hand.[63] During this "just" war, his work returned to a concern for private property, possibly reflecting the anti-Bolshevik theme so popular in Germany. To insure that private property could fulfill its social goal was the responsibility of the state. Only after careful consideration could the political leadership eliminate the right of private property or any other right. He reminded his readers that two extremes were to be avoided: individualism (liberalism) and collectivism (communism).[64] His flirtation with Nazism had been brief. Essentially he sharpened his basic theological speculation so that he could critically analyze the Nazi *Total Staat* and its place along the spectrum of political forms.

As the war intensified, paper supplies for theological journals and larger tracts "decreased," and those theologians still writing became even more compulsively abstract, as they tried to highlight traditional Catholic principles in opposition to National Socialism. Arnold, for example, stressed the increasingly relevant theme that the unity between Christ and all his members was a reality intrinsic to man's being and was even more intimate than that existing between husband and wife, but he failed to stress the commonality of mankind as did Pius XII in *Mystici Corporis* (1943), although even Pius took a Pauline view of the Church, emphasizing that members were those who had been baptized.[65] As did his pope, Arnold failed to proclaim publicly the role of the Jews in God's plan of salvation, even though on the abstract level the theologian certainly maintained that the majesty of God was reflected in the dignity of Man. Striking a patriotic theme, perhaps to insure publication, Arnold also highlighted the organic connection that should rightfully exist between the clergy and the *Volk*. The way to salvation led through the Church as a community (*Gemeinschaft*). To stress again the fact that Catholicism was fundamentally apolitical, however, Arnold pointed to the fact that Christianity was a religion of the spiritual, not the material man.[66]

As if to reemphasize these points, in 1943 Arnold analyzed Johann Möhler, Pelagius, and the general heritage of the Enlightenment, and concluded with an attack on anthropocentrism obviously intended to apply to Nazism or communism. The religious and existential relationship between God and man combined the natural freedom of man and the power of grace, a reality analyzed most carefully by St. Augustine in the early Church. Similar to Augustine, Arnold opposed man-made or natural religion.[67] As Brauer in 1935, for example, Arnold also opposed the false individualism rooted in the Renaissance and Thomas Hobbes. Brauer had already seen this stress on atomization as a forerunner to the mass politics of twentieth-century Europe. The rights and duties of the individual in society proved to be a good point of departure for Catholic thinkers, because the Nazis themselves had devoted a good deal of time and effort to the issue. Gundlach, for example, insisted that the NSDAP was basically sick in its collective view of race as the single, real source of value. Nazis eliminated a valid conception of the meaning of personality as well as the healthy interaction of free individuals.[68] In all of these commentaries, Catholic scholars meticulously avoided the real racial issue.

After 1934 the theologians as a whole ceased commenting on the so-called Jewish question from a biased standpoint. Apparently aware that Nazism was not "normal" racism, they even tended to stop their discussions of anti-Semitism itself, although not entirely. Moock noted that German leaders historically could be found with a variety of surnames, indicating that spiritual values, not blood, made a person German. Moock went even further in his insistence that the Church may well talk about a marriage blossoming in the *Volk,* but that the Church was not interested in racial breeding.[69] Respected members of the profession no longer commented on either *Volk* or *Blut* with the unabashed enthusiasm so apparent in the early years of the Third Reich. But, unfortunately, they did not chastise the Nazis for proclaiming their racist ideology and its subsequent implementation. Lack of comment could mean a realization that their publicized anti-Semitism was giving support to more than political racism. Perhaps they began perceiving that the Nazis were more than average conservative, authoritarian, and anti-Semitic politicians. There is no suggestion here, however, that anti-Semitism had died. Rather, it is clearly apparent in their works that the theologians stopped using the Jews as enemies in order more clearly to distinguish Catholic from Nazi ideals. Their continued use of such terms as *Volk* and *Vaterland,* however, allowed the insider-outsider matrix to persist. There is no condemnation, for example, as clear as the 1965 Vatican II statement in *Nostra Aetate* which stated that for the sake of her common patrimony with the Jews, the Church decried hatred, persecutions, and displays of anti-Semitism staged against

Jews at whatever time in history and by whomsoever. This document also affirmed that the spiritual bonds and historical links binding the Church to Judaism had to condemn, as opposed to the very spirit of Christianity, all forms of anti-Semitism.

In 1950, Max Pribilla wrote a fairly standard analysis of the reasons for the emergence of Nazism. The NSDAP derived its power more from its promises than from its theory, because it played on the weakness of German character accentuated by World War I and the disastrous post-1918 era. Pribilla failed to stress that Catholic leaders sought the fulfillment of at least the nationalistic promises and never questioned seriously the means to the end until the *Gleichschaltung* had nearly succeeded. By then, while they could and did question the means, the political and even racial ends could no longer effectively be challenged. As Pribilla suggests, the political inexperience of the German people was a factor in the Nazi success.[70] For their part, however, Catholic leaders had done nothing to educate Germans and make them politically more sophisticated. Since average individuals with conventionally oriented views of the state are hardly in positions to recognize offenses as such, intellectual leaders presumably have a responsibility to encourage a political consciousness sensitive to moral values.[71] Such theologians as Peter Lippert sensed this duty. His works of 1934 and 1935 are particularly pertinent. Man, he felt, must design his own history, since the essence of man was his personal relationship to God, not just in thought but in will. The truly religious man was a servant, giving instead of taking. His activities were to be encased in a spirit of love as he gave witness to God. Because man should be the bearer of God's love and His reflection, the truly religious man was to build *das Reich Gottes* and make it also into a home for humanity.[72] His emphasis on giving and not taking was stressed as a prominent theme in contrast to Hitler's seizure of power and the *Lebensraum* syndrome.

In "Der Gemeinschaftsmensch," Lippert saw the community as the highest form of human interaction. Communities of two or three or several hundred million as the Church overflowed with power and fullness. Each person receives much from each community in which he exists. He could agree with the Nazi slogan *Gemeinnutz geht vor Eigennutz* (Common need before the individual need), at least for specific socioeconomic dimensions of community life. Such an approach was not valid, however, where a specific spiritual good had the individual as its referent focus, i.e., all such created values of the spiritual person as truth and religion. The "common good" could not be decisive in a matter of conscience. Values proper to the person were to be defended against the *Gesellschaft,* since the well-being in a community was based on love, not hate. Ultimately the essence of the true community was to be the individual giving to those in need.[73] Lippert also analyzed the man of faith in a 1935 essay. National faith responded to the greatness and honor of the *Volk* or of the state. Religious faith was a humble acknowledgment of God and was manifested in love. The person living in real faith was greater than the individual without God and sought more than merely the development of the anthropocentric person.[74]

One more example illustrates the difficulties that the Catholic intelligentsia had in confronting Nazism and in formulating the relationship between *Volk* and *Kirche*. The Jesuit Ivo Zeiger had welcomed the Concordat and suggested that it marked a new beginning. But he wanted to make several clarifications. The Concordat, he reminded his readers, was not the result of a reversal of the Church's position as much as it was derived from the now moderate Nazi state seeking a reconciliation. Hence to Zeiger, the Church had not betrayed its ideals but was merely giving the Nazis another chance. Hitler's March 23 speech had convinced Church leaders of his good intentions, and the Church necessarily had to offer its hand in peaceful cooperation. Zeiger was cautiously optimistic for the future reconciliation of Church and state.[75] Under the *Gleichschaltung* pressure, however, he began to delineate a defensive position for the Church. In the very first paragraph of "Verrechtlichung der Kirche," he reminded his readers that there had been persistent attacks on faith and Christian morality. Part of the reason for the success of such assaults was the basic German characteristic of an obsessive sense of order. Germans, he felt, had a fixation on order and relentless loyalty to the law, which permeated both public and private life. In fact, if such order did not reign, Germans, he contended, felt disconcerted. Clearly, he saw this obsession as a weakness encouraging the lack of resistance in the Church—since law had its source in the frailty of human nature. Resulting from original sin, however, law as the sole social regulator should not govern the Church. The state embodies law per se. When the grace of Christ rules and law responds to the love of God, then freedom of the soul should not be regulated solely by law. The Church used canon law, but not merely defensively. The Church had always been an institution using law in order to regulate for the benefit of the community, since there had never been an era in which only love and the pneumatic charisma ruled. In conclusion, Zeiger emphasized that canon law was designed only to serve and regularize the inner life of the Church.[76] Apparently Zeiger hoped to refute accusations that the Church as a legal institution was a rival to the state. The law of the Church was designed for regulation to aid its members in conforming to its inner life based on the love and grace of Christ. He asserted, moreover, that the Church did not exist to support an amorphous religious spirit of experiential religion; the Church was a real institution. It objectively reflected Christ. Law served to help the members of the Church respond to the interior life of Christ's *Gemeinschaft.* Pointedly, he declared that even political law was not solely the will of the führer; the Church was not to be controlled by the state.

Zeiger's defense of the Church by 1938 had evolved into a defense of man himself. All discussion centering on the issue of morality and moral doctrine ultimately had to be referred back to anthropology, i.e., to man's image of himself. The moral law was peculiar to man. Hence, man only could become true Man when he totally obeyed moral precepts. His ideal was obedience to moral precepts, clearly a notion that radically differed from the National Socialist *Weltanschauung,* which had opted for a morality rooted in race. Although he did not discuss or even mention race, Zeiger emphatically insisted that revelation was God speaking to man and affirming that there was a personal deity superior to man. God speaks to mankind through creation, establishing a universe in which obedience to man's true nature as a creature of God is his natural law. Natural morality, then, was verified in revelation. In Christ, man became a new creature, and natural moral law was designed to help man reach the ideals originally created by God.[77] Later in 1938, Zeiger continued developing the dimension of morality. Catholic moral ideals were not based on speculative abstractions, but rather were rooted in the living Church. In this article, Zeiger reacted enthusiastically to Tillmann's work on the imitation of the historic Christ as the ultimate source of morality. It was in this way that the desire of contemporary man for a life formed according to a moral *Führergestalt* would be fulfilled.[78] This standard treatment of theological and moral issues suggests that at least some theologians had lost even their limited enthusiasm for an acceptance of the New Order. They seemed to be strengthening the traditional doctrinal fortifications as they prepared for the seige.

One other dimension of opposition emerged among those who felt that the Church should baptize Nazi terminology while opposing the essence of Nazi values. From hindsight such an attempt can be condemned as naive, but the Church has usually been praised for its ability to adapt to varied political situations. Walter Kampe, for example, asserted that the Church as an institution standing for specific values did not imply any superiority over secular communities, but the essence of the Church as the continuing life of the God-man, Christ, contained the ideal of humanity. Man's ever-changing organic culture was the living bond between man and God. Worried about Christ's life in a Jewish culture, Kampe quickly made the point that, because of Mary, Christ matured in his humanity in this particular *Blutgemeinschft* (racial community). But Christ was not really governed by the rule of Israel. Just as Christ conquered the death inflicted upon him by the Jews, so the resurrection of the flesh could also be seen as the salvation of peoples and races. Kampe suggested, then, that a Christian racial orientation could be constructed. He assured his readers that there is an absolute transcendence of grace over the limits of blood and that blood outside of a specifically saved race is incapable of constructive activity. Also, the saving-power of grace came through the blood of the God-man and will save mankind from the beguiling materialistic nationalism of the Jews. Kampe appears to be attempting to use arguments couched in such Nazi loaded terms as *Blut* and *Rasse* without really understanding their essential meaning, at least in Hitler's mind. Continuing this line of development, he viewed the *Volk* as a reflection of the ecclesiastical *Gemeinschaft*. The *Volk* was the arena in which the natural world and the Church would be mediated and through which the supernatural life would be transfused into members of the political community. Many, he felt, had also misunderstood the meaning of *führer*. The true *führer* could only represent the *Volk,* but never embody the *Volk* itself. One could also refer to the Church as a *Volk* and *Reich*; both concepts would only be valid because of their intimate union with Christ.[79] The terms in his mind seemed to be metaphorical, and so he could discuss the Church's mission in light of the contemporary and popular vocabulary. The hope perhaps was to suggest that the Church encapsulated values in many cases similar to those of the party. If such was the hope, it would fail. For the Nazi ideologues *Rasse, Blut,* etc., were real facts of life, not metaphors.

The theological dimension of Church life offers, then, a good reflection of various Catholic German patterns of thought as well as a growing realization that the Church's ideals were being compromised. Theologians during the Weimar era were nationalistic and did maintain a sociopolitical anti-Semitism. They praised Hitler as he apparently modified his own earlier radical position, and in 1933 they hoped for the best. By 1934 the coordination policy had begun in earnest. With few exceptions Catholic theologians turned to strengthen established ideals of morality and dogma, insisting that they were refining traditional maxims and axioms in light of the romantic nationalist patterns of thought then current, and they certainly felt that they were also simultaneously distancing themselves from the Nazi viewpoints gaining increased popularity after Hitler's accession to power. The hope was to remain German as well as Catholic; the Kulturkampf syndrome continued. While the theological and ideological themes could be analyzed abstractly with virtually no popular outbursts erupting among contemporaries and seemingly no immediate ramifications, the moral problems swirling around eugenic racism and euthanasia, as will be seen in chapter 7, were controversial in Weimar Germany, the Third Reich, and postwar reflections on Catholic responses, since these two issues were preludes to the Final Solution.

Catholic abstract moral treatises offer the scholar examples of ideological capitulation, heroism, and attempts to steer a course of compromise. But these reactions were confined to theological tracts and certainly went unread by the average Catholic layman and probably by the pastors serving their flocks as well. Still, since ideology sustains and helps institutionalize political structures,[80] Catholic theologians probably should have subjected the Nazi terminology expressing values to a more rigorous critique at an earlier date. Early adaptation and later opposition could only confuse those who looked to the Church for guidance and reflected the internal confusion characteristic within the German Catholic Church. Moral issues dealing with euthanasia provided incendiary focal points immediately relevant to contemporaries and significant to postwar scholars since the trail from eugenic racism to the Final Solution is now clear, although this was not quite so apparent in the Third Reich. Certainly it was not clear at the time that even sociopolitical anti-Semitism set the stage for the catastrophes of the Nazi genocidal program. The structure and ideology of the Church, however, abetted the consolidation of Nazi rule. There existed a congruence between Catholic attitudes and those of the Nazi regime, whose popularity was basically due to its endorsing the policies favored by the conservative elites—national revival, territorial expansion, the abolition of democratic pluralism, and ethnocentrism. The mobilization of heterogeneous elements of a society into the body politic can potentially create severe disorder if there is no overarching cultural system that integrates the diverse groups into a single ideological community. When Catholic theologians initially adapted to the Nazi value system and later failed sufficiently to highlight distinctions, they entwined the Church with the political regime. The development of conscience depends to an extent upon cultural and subcultural influences as well as upon age and mental level. Children are reared in accordance with and adults identify with the standards, values, and ideals of their particular society and in-group.[81] When Church leaders adapted to Nazism or responded to outrageous behavior in abstract tracts or with complex analyses, the faithful were deprived of leadership. Perhaps these leaders themselves undermined the development and maturation of moral reflection among their followers by reducing in themselves the conflict between such Christian virtues as charity, peace, and brotherhood and such Nazi values as Aryanism and *Lebensraum.*

Techniques for Coping in the Nazi Reich

Internal debate resulting in the subjective reconciliation or assimilation of competing values and interests does not always work.[82] There are, however, three useful ways in which an individual may attempt to cope with the stress that is aroused when diverse values are competing for satisfaction in a set of ideals that must be maintained: (1) conflict avoidance or reduction, (2) conflict resolution, and (3) conflict acceptance. A variety of specific psychological mechanisms have been identified which have in common that they enable the individual to banish or sharply reduce the motivational conflict experienced in making a decision, or, when exposed to pressures, in reexamining a decision already made. Three mechanisms[83] are:

1. Various tactics for *cognitive restructuring,* which help the individual to avoid or minimize the cognitive dissonance occasioned by information that is relevant to the decision being made, but which challenges some of the opposing principles; support of the *Volk,* while condemning such "radicals" as Rosenberg, would be one example.
2. The tactic of *devaluating* a value held by the self or significant others when that value loses out in competition; the bishops insisted, for example, that they were apolitical.
3. The tactic of reducing or abandoning one's identification with the significant others who suffer utilitarian loss as a result of the decision; given the extended anti-Semitic history, it was not difficult to deemphasize the Jewish roots of Christianity.

Conflict-reduction devices of this type may well have been functional for the clerical leaders as they maintained the loyalty of lay Catholics, but the consequences of coping with decisional stress in this way proved to be highly dysfunctional for the group in the long run as the consequences of such policies were discerned.

Motivational conflict may also be handled by conflict resolution that consists essentially in an effort by the leader to satisfy, to at least some extent, most of the competing considerations that are salient for his followers and himself in a problematic situation.[84] The individual tries to invent a single policy or option that will yield some satisfaction for most of the salient stakes and motivations involved. In some situations, a leader accepts and acts upon the fact that he cannot gain for himself all of the multiple stakes involved. Hence he selects some of the values as constituting the objectives he will strive for. The bishops and theologians accepted the continued existence of the institution itself as a paramount goal. By identifying with the clerical role and accepting themselves in this role, the bishops and theologians made difficult decisions, at least initially, with detachment and with a sensitivity to the pragmatic priorities of the Church. Ultimately, the desire to remain consistent made it increasingly difficult to diverge from their initial reconciliation. In public the bishops had to remain nationalistic, even though they could criticize radical Nazis. Theologians could, however, abandon their early accommodation, retreat behind theological abstractions, and nurture traditional Christian values. To reduce conflict both the bishops and theologians initially attempted to conform to the Nazi and Christian norms, which they felt could be reconciled. Conformity was aided by the strong group cohesion brought about, or accentuated by, the threatening, stressful environment of the *Gleichschaltung*.[85] Ultimately, at least abstractly, however, distinctions between the two normative systems had to be delineated.

Many common patterns of action are governed by internalized rules that are only focused upon in times of stress. Historically, Catholics had worked to become accepted as German citizens with all of the resulting rights and privileges. They persisted after 1933 in continuing their attempts to reconcile their political and religious roles. The distinctions made by the theologians and bishops enabled them to contain and reduce dissonance, and to function consistently as Catholics loyal to their legitimate government. Theological distinctions, of course, meant that many lay Catholics had to deal with the opposing Nazi and Catholic *Weltanschauungen* as best they could in their specific environments. If the laity doubted their actions or opinions, they should have been able to handle the induced dissonance by turning to their leaders. Such a course was not available. Early efforts at adaptation and later subtle theological distinctions or proclamations combining patriotism with protest could suggest to the average Catholic layman that the Church was supporting the basic policies of the regime and only differing over minor issues. The institutional homogeneity made it almost impossible to shape a laity able to resist on a broad-scale basis. Modeling and rule following contributed to the apparent public uniformity of Catholic patterns of behavior. Facing ambiguous conditions, people usually try to use the actions of others in shaping their own behavior. Lay German Catholics were offered few vigorous leaders whom they could model in resisting the regime, and they were usually enjoined to support at least Germany, if Nazism were unpalatable.[86]

The Nazi *Gleichschaltung* increased the pressure on Catholic leaders at the same time that they apparently began to realize that Hitler and his followers were not about to compromise even if the bishops and theologians stressed the importance of supporting the *Volk* and tactically identified with at least some of the Nazi maxims, although not with the full meaning of the principles. Such cognitive restructuring merely helped reduce dissonance for the average Catholic, who could now think that no essential conflict existed between the institutional Church and the NSDAP. Guided by their *Kulturkampf* experiences the bishops stressed German nationalism and carefully obscured their international connections. The long history of Christian anti-Semitism enabled Catholics to abandon very easily even normal links with the Jews as well as with the now discredited Weimar Republic. In essence, Church leaders chose those values with which Catholics could identify. As the leaders of the besieged Church, bishops and theologians accepted their roles and made compromises with their traditional value structure as they identified with acceptable elements of the regime. Their job was to preserve the institution and its sacramental life, and so compromises with the NSDAP leadership were necessary, even if not desirable.

Such tactical compromises as praising the Nazi stress on the *Volk* or withdrawal into theological treatises that would not be read by most Catholics eliminated by 1935 any real hope of widespread resistance because such opposition would mean the repudiation of past adaptive efforts and would result in swimming against the Catholic mainstream axiom which held that the Church could survive and prosper in virtually any political system. Since political systems were temporary and the Church eternal, full-scale attacks on the state were rare and not encouraged. Misunderstanding the full extent of the Nazi racial revolution, Church leaders compromised or retreated into abstractions. In doing so they were unprepared to oppose this totalitarian regime as it threatened the right to life of "racial undesirables." In ignoring their mission to offer and to publicize rigorous critiques of the Nazi *Weltanschauung* and political realities, they surrendered their ability to rally the faithful in support of religious values undergirding the right to life inherent in Man as God's creature.

Notes

1. Linz, p. 237; Merkl, *Political Violence Under the Swastika.*
2. Zahn, *German Catholics,* p. 21.
3. Michael Parenti, "Political Values and Religious Cultures: Jews, Catholics, and Protestants," *Journal for the Scientific Study of Religion* 6 (1967):268.
4. Zahn, *German Catholics,* p. 21; Lohalm, *Völkischer Radikalismus: Die Geschichte des Deutschvölkischen Schutz-und Trutzbundes, 1919-1933*; Adam, p. 228.
5. Cryns, p. 241; R.P. Vacchiano et al., "Personality Correlates of Dogmatism," *Journal of Consulting and Clinical Psychology* 32 (1968):83-85; R.P. Vacchiano et al., "The Open and Closed Mind: A Review of Dogmatism," *Psychological Bulletin* 72 (1969):261-273; Peter Berger, *The Sacred Canopy* (Garden City: Doubleday, 1966), pp. 53-80.
6. Richard Simpson, "Theories of Social Exchange," in John Thibaut et al., *Contemporary Topics in Social Psychology* (Morristown, N.J.: General Learning Press, 1976), pp. 82-83, 93-94; Homans, *Social Behavior: Its Elementary Forms,* p. 48; Albert Bandura, *Principles of Behavior Modification* (New York: Holt, Rinehart, and Winston, 1969), p. 132.
7. For a painstaking analysis of the *Reichsideologie,* see Klaus Breuning, *Die*

Vision des Reiches. Deutschen Katholizismus zwischen Demokratie und Dik-tatur (1929-1934); Muth, "Res Publica 1926," pp. 1ff.; Karl Muth, "Das Reich als Idee und Wirklichkeit-Einst und Jetzt," *Hochland* 30 (1932/33): 481ff.; Ziesche, pp. vii, 23, 56, 97f.; Friedrich Muckermann, "An den Pforten des Reiches," *Der Gral* 22 (1927/28): 208-209; Friedrich Muckermann, "Der Reichsgedanke als Kulturidee," *Schönere Zukunft* 63 (1927/28): 700ff.

8. Bendersky, p. 198; Breuning, pp. 179-180, 193; Wilhelm Reinermann, "Das Reich als deutsches Lebensgesetz und innenpolitische Zukunftsaufgabe," *Das Deutsche Volk* 1 (1933): 82; Schmaus, *Begegnungen*, p. 25; Greive, pp. 139-140; Gundlach discussed his views on democracy at a seminar of the Königswinter circle on May 12-13, 1932.

9. Greive, pp. 141-142; Johannes Messner, *Die soziale Frage der Gegenwart* (Innsbruck: Verlagsanstalt Tyrolia, 1934), p. 559; Brauer, *Der Katholik im neuen Reich*; Greive, pp. 144-145.

10. Muckermann, *Vom Rätsel der Zeit*, p. 102; A. Baumstark, "Wege Zum Judentum des neutestamentlichen Zeitalters," *Bonner Zeitschrift für Theologie und Seelsorge* 4 (1927): 24ff.; Lorenz Dürr, "Das Unsemitische und Übersemitische in der semitischen alttestamentlichen Religion," *Bonner Zeitschrift für Theologie und Seelsorge* 8 (1931): 1ff.; Greive, pp. 224-225.

11. Robert Grosche, "Die Grundlagen einer christlichen Politik der deutschen Katholiken," *Die Schildgenossen* 13 (1933/34): 48ff.; Rudolf Grober, "Deutsche Sendung. Zur Idee und Geschichte des Sacrum Imperium," *Werkblätter von Neudeutschland Älterenbund* 6 (1933/34): 169ff.; 232ff.; Adam, "Deutsches Volkstum und katholisches Christentum," pp. 40ff.; Lewy, p. 279.

12. "Vor 17 Jahren: Marxismus über Deutschland," *Klerusblatt* 16 (1935): 785-788.

13. F. Schülein, "Geschichte der Juden," *Lexikon für Theologie und Kirche*, 2nd rev. ed. (Freiburg: Herder, 1933), V: 687.

14. Lehmacher, p. 81.

15. Theodor Bogler, O.S.B., *Der Glaube von Gestern und Heute* (Cologne: Bachem, 1939), p. 150.

16. Konrad Algermissen, "Christentum und Germantum," *Theologie und Glaube* 26 (1934): 302-303, 312, 319, 321-322, 328.

17. Schmaus, *Begegnungen*, pp. 23, 33ff.

18. Corsten, pp. 136ff; Spael, p. 322.

19. Breuning, pp. 291, 298.

20. Eschweiler, "Die Kirche im neuen Reich," pp. 451, 453, 455-456; *Mitteilungen zur Weltanschaulichen Lage* II, 2 (1936): 1. Eschweiler had joined the NSDAP on May 1, 1933 and remained a member until his death; see Berlin Document Center, file Karl Eschweiler.

21. Lewy, p. 109.

22. Breuning, pp. 313-315, 350; Hermann Keller, OSB, "Zu uns komme dein Reich," *Benediktinische Monatschrift* 15 (1933): 357ff.

23. Muckermann, *Vom Rätsel*, pp. 119ff. For a pro-Nazi, Catholic analysis of the pre-1933 Nazi-Catholic situation, see Stark, *Nationalsozialismus und Katholische Kirche*; Nötges, p. 108.

24. Brauer, *Katholik im neuen Reich*, pp. 27, 32, 41, 57, 71.

25. Greive, p. 198.

26. Mariaux, p. 14.

27. Emil Ritter and Kuno Brombacher, *Sendschreiben Katholischen Deutschen,*

2nd ed. (Münster: Aschendorf, 1936); John Murray, "Problems of Church and Race," *Month* 168 (1936/37): 528-536.

28. Walker, *Hitler Youth and Catholic Youth*, p. 33.
29. Micklem, p. 95.
30. *Mitteldeutsche Nationalzeitung*, July 4, 1935.
31. See Walker on the Catholic youth issue and its importance to the Church. Victor Lutze, *Reden an die S.A.*, 4th ed. (Munich: Zentralverlag der NSDAP, 1936). For other pamphlets similar to those of Lutze, see Johannes Stark, *Zentrumsherrschaft und Jesuitenpolitik* (Munich: F. Eher, 1932) and G. Ohlemüller, *Politischer Katholizismus* (Berlin: Verlag des Evangelischen Bundes, 1936).
32. *Das Schwarze Korps*, April 15, 1937.
33. See Mariaux, p. 459.
34. Wilhelm Flosdorf, S.J., "Die deutschen Jesuiten unter dem Nationalsozialistischen Regime," *Jesuiten: Stimmen aus ihren Eigenen Reihen* 2 (1955): 106; Altmeyer, *Katholische Presse unter NS-Diktatur*, pp. 54-55, 59, 61-64.
35. Lewy, p. 166.
36. Müller, p. 393.
37. Friedrick Fuchs, "Der Totale Staat und seine Grenze," *Hochland* (1932-1933): 559; Schwarte, p. 48.
38. Friedrick Engel-Janosi, *Vom Chaos zur Katastrophe. Vatikanische-Gespräche, 1918 bis 1938* (Vienna: Herold, 1971), pp. 155-156; Schwarte, pp. 52, 73-74.
39. For an analysis of the drafting and then suppression of the text of the encyclical, see Schwarte, 77-119. For a favorable study of the efforts of Pius XII on behalf of the Jews, see Robert Graham, S.J., "Pius XII's Defense of Jews and Others: 1944-1945" (Milwaukee: Catholic League, 1982).
40. Conrad Gröber (ed.), "Rasse," in *Handbuch der religiösen Gegenwartsfragen* (Freiburg: Herder, 1937):536.
41. This material appeared in a pastoral letter for Lent in 1939; *Amtsblatt, Limburg*, no. 1, February 6, 1939, pp. 1-8.
42. Gordon Zahn, "Catholic Opposition to Hitler: The Perils of Ambiguity," *Journal of Church and State* 13 (1971):423.
43. Boberach, *Berichte des SD*, pp. xxx, xxxix, 23, 900, 902ff., 933; Reinhard Henkys, *Die NS Gewaltverbrechen* (Stuttgart: Kreuz Verlag, 1964); Zipfel, p. 296; Conway, *Persecution*, p. 402.
44. Wilhelm Moock, "Reich und Staat," *Hochland* (1933):97-111; Adolf Kolping, *Katholische Theologie: Gestern und Heute. Thematik und Entfaltung deutscher katholischer Theologie vom I. Vaticanum bis zur Gegenwart* (Bremen: Carl Schünemann Verlag, 1964), pp. 132-133.
45. Michael Cardinal Faulhaber, *Judaism, Christianity and Germany*, trans. George D. Smith (London: Burns, Oates, & Washbourne, 1934), pp. 55-56.
46. Friedrich Fuchs, "Ein Bischofswort über das Alte Testament," *Hochland* 31 (1933/34):471-472; Lewy, pp. 111-112.
47. Lewy, p. 112; Kolping, p. 113.
48. Kolping, pp. 133-134.
49. See, for example, Franz X. Seppelt, *Geschichte der Päpste von den Anfängen bis zur Gegenwart*, 2 vols. (Leipzig: Hegner, 1931-1941).
50. See, for example, G. Sohngen and A. Rademacher (eds.), *Symbol und Wirklichkeit im Kultmysterium* (Leipzig: Hegner, 1937).

51. See, for example, Michael Schmaus, *Katholische Dogmatik*, 3 vols. (Munich: Max Hueber Verlag, 1937-1941).
52. Fritz Tillmann, *Die katholische Sittenlehre. Die Idee der Nachfolge Christi* (Düsseldorf: L. Schwann, 1934). For an example of the influence Tillmann had, see Theodor Müncker, *Die psychologischen Grundlagen der katholischen Sittenlehre* (Düsseldorf: L. Schwann, 1934).
53. Amery, pp. 166-167.
54. Otto Schilling, "Die soziale Gerechtigkeit," *Theologische Quartalschrift* 114 (1933):271.
55. Max Pribilla, "Nationale Revolution," *Stimmen der Zeit* 125 (1933):156-158, 161-167.
56. Erich Przywara, "Nation, Staat, Kirche," *Stimmen der Zeit*, 125 (1933):371-376; see also Max Pribilla, "Nationalsozialistische Weltanschauung," *Stimmen der Zeit* 126 (1933):415-418; Max Pribilla, "Verfassungstreue," *Stimmen der Zeit* 125 (1933):57-61.
57. Otto Schilling, "Das moralische Recht des deutschen Volkes auf Kolonien," *Theologische Quartalschrift* 115 (1934):404; Max Pribilla, "Der Kampf der Kirche," *Stimmen der Zeit* 129 (1935):246-253.
58. Mariaux, p. 457.
59. Otto Schilling, "Das Prinzip der Moral," *Theologische Quartalschrift* 119 (1938):420, 423, 426.
60. Max Pribilla, "Ehe und Familie," *Stimen der Zeit* 134 (1938):53-56; Max Pribilla, "Christliche Haltung," *Stimmen der Zeit* 135 (1939):169-175.
61. Anton Artweiler, *Unser Glaube. Christliche Wirklichkeit in der Heutigen Welt* (Munich: Kösel-Pustet, 1938), pp. 8-10, 36, 152-153, 157-160.
62. Otto Schilling, "Von der sozialen Gerechtigkeit," *Theologische Quartalschrift* 120 (1939):198, 201.
63. Otto Schilling, "Quelle und Charakter des Völkerrechts," *Theologische Quartalschrift* 120 (1939):289-294.
64. Otto Schilling, "Eigentumslehre Leo XIII und Pius XI," *Theologische Quartalschrift* 121 (1940):206-207.
65. Kolping, p. 186; for a recent analysis of the Vatican diplomacy revealing this position, see John Morley, *Vatican Diplomacy and the Jews during the Holocaust, 1939-1943* (New York: Ktav, 1980) Morley's stance is not new, but he offers a good balanced account that leads to a more careful assessment of the controversial documents. In his work Morley contends that the Vatican could not have saved the Jews by a few words or actions. But more could have been done to use Vatican personnel and ecclesiastical prestige. Pius, however, was unwilling to confront realiy. In "Pius XII's Defense" (p. 34), Graham asserts the opposite. It should be noted (Graham, p. 5) that countless numbers of baptismal certificates were known by Church authorities to be forged and so were used to save Jews whenever possible.
66. Franz Arnold, "Das Prinzip des Gottmenschlichen und seine Bedeutung für die Seelsorge," *Theologische Quartalschrift* 123 (1942):149-168.
67. Franz Arnold, "Das Gottmenschliche Prinzip der Seelsorge in pastoralgeschichtlicher Entfaltung," *Theologische Quartalschrift* 124 (1943): 101-104, 111.
68. Theodor Brauer, "Die Stellung der Persönlichkeit in Gesellschaft und Staat. 'Individualismus'-Wahrheit und Irrtum," *Schönere Zukunft* 20 (1935):499-500; Schwarte, p. 391.

69. Wilhelm Moock, "Der Einzelne und die Gemeinschaft," *Hochland* 32 (1934-35): 193-203.
70. Max Pribilla, *Deutsche Schicksalsfragen. Rückblick und Ausblick* (Frankfurt: Josef Knecht-Carolusdruckerei, 1950), pp. 6, 19, 103.
71. Ekkehard Lippert, "Concerning the Relationship of Political Education and Moral Judgment," paper presented at the International Society of Political Psychology Meeting (May 24-26, 1979, Washington, D.C.).
72. Peter Lippert, "Der religiöse Mensch in der Gegenwart," *Stimmen der Zeit* 126 (1934):217, 221-224, 229.
73. Peter Lippert, "Der Gemeinschaftsmensch," *Stimmen der Zeit* 128 (1935): 361-370.
74. Peter Lippert, "Der gläubige Mensch," *Stimmen der Zeit* 129 (1935): 145-155.
75. Ivo Zeiger, "Das Reichskonkordat," *Stimmen der Zeit* 126 (1933): 2-4.
76. Ivo Zeiger, "Verrechtlichung der Kirche," *Stimmen der Zeit* 129 (1935): 38, 41-46.
77. Ivo Zeiger, "Werde, der du Bist," *Stimmen der Zeit* 133 (1938):298-307.
78. Ivo Zeiger, "Katholische Moraltheologie Heute," *Stimmen der Zeit* 134 (1938):149-150.
79. Walther Kampe, *Die Nation in der Heilsordnung. Eine Natürliche und Übernatürliche Theologie vom Volk* (Mainz: Matthias-Grünewald, 1936), pp. 2, 14, 77, 112-113, 157, 167, 171.
80. Perlmutter, p. 174.
81. Fenn, p. 23; S.N. Eisenstadt, "Social Change Differentiation and Evolution," *American Sociological Review* 29 (1964):375-386; Leonore Boehm, "The Development of Conscience: A Comparison of Upper-Middle Class Academically Gifted Children Attending Catholic and Jewish Parochial Schools," *Journal of Social Psychology* 59 (1963):101-102.
82. George in Coelho et al., pp. 183-186.
83. O.R. Holsti, "Cognitive Dynamics and Images of the Enemy: Dulles and Russia," in Finlay et al., pp. 25-96; M.B. Smith et al., *Opinions and Personality* (New York: Wiley, 1956), p. 251.
84. H.A. Simon, "A Behavioral Model of Rational Choice," *Quarterly Journal of Economics* 69 (1955):99-118.
85. George in Coelho, p. 193.
86. H. Garfinkel, *Studies in Ethnomethodology* (Englewood Cliffs, NJ: Prentice Hall, 1967); Festinger, "A Theory of Social Comparison Processes," pp. 117-140; C.L. Gruder, "Determinants of Social Comparison Choices," *Journal of Experimental Social Psychology* 7 (1971):473-489.

7

Racial Eugenics and the Final Solution

Like many Germans after 1918, Catholics were trapped in a cruel dilemma. To support the Nazi program in the Weimar era and then in the Third Reich could easily lead to a loss of moral credibility; to oppose Hitler's *Weltanschauung,* however, could result in the assault of Nazi propaganda, and after 1933 the power of state as well could be used against German Catholics. Both accommodation and circumscribed resistance highlight the story of the German Catholic approach to such sensitive and related issues as euthanasia and anti-Semitism. The response of Catholics was rooted in their historical politicization and intellectual experiences as well as situationally induced and illustrates the perennial issue of the relationship of church to state and morals to politics.[1]

In a Jewish-Christian culture, religion is expected, at least theoretically, to be at odds frequently with the surrounding world. But as Hans Küng has noted, the Church has constantly been tempted to make herself at home in the world, to see her temporal successes as the coming of God's kingdom, and to make herself secure from persecution.[2] The Church seems to have a dual goal. She is to preach and embody the word of God as well as preserve herself institutionally—potentially creating a conflict in such stressful historical environments as that of the Third Reich. To position Catholicism in the mainstream of the intellectual and political life of Germany, clerical leaders had historically made a number of lethal compromises, were frequently indifferent to vital issues, and often neglected to adhere to a course dictated by positive traditional values. They were Catholics who were German nationalists and intellectuals who tried to remain relevant within their milieu, supportive of circumscribed racial eugenics and an array of anti-Semitic orientations.

Analyzing the Catholic reactions to the eugenic-racist policies of the Nazis can help illuminate the nature of the relationship between twentieth-century political institutions and the traditional moral norms dominating society. Catholic responses to eugenic theories and Nazi racial policies, inconsistent with the ideal Christian values of brotherhood and love, can also offer a provocative insight into the dynamics undergirding Catholic religious values in the Third Reich and documented resultant behavior patterns. In general, the behavior of people is purposive and intentional. Specific behavior is caused by a combination of internal (personal) and environmental-historical factors. Behavior varies with respect to actors and their contexts. Research suggests that behavior that is consistent within specific contexts, in which many people engage, and that is performed in the presence of a particular entity is caused by that entity.[3] Anti-Semitism was not simply a manipulative device used by the Nazis. The occurrence of Catholic anti-Semitism or indifference toward Jews in the Third Reich should not be surprising in light of earlier Catholic historical interests focused on integration into the German nation and culture. The primary foundation for sustaining such negative values as eugenic-ethnic prejudice in society cannot be found solely in the pathological individual or in the dynamics of interpersonal relationships. Ultimately negative values are based on the salient historical conditions and the political-economic structures out of which intergroup relationships have been developed and sustained. Only in conjunction with specific societal and situational conditions did personal psychological factors become operationalized in response to the Nazi eugenic and racial policies.[4] Postunification Germans in the Empire and subsequently in the Weimar Republic matured in an eugenic and anti-Semitic environment and ultimately proved unable to mount a decisive opposition against the Nazi program.[5]

Sterilization and Euthanasia

Sounding a radical eugenics theme stressing sterilization and euthanasia in 1895, Adolf Jost asserted that the individual life had no value, but rather was subordinated to the community and to the development of the species.[6] Intellectually, Social Darwinism also reinforced eugenics but differentiated it from the vulgar racism acceptable in the beerhalls before 1933.[7] By 1930 the eugenics controversy in Germany had led, apparently, to a scientifically credible set of principles, which could be academically maintained. In the process science helped subvert faith by demoting the status of religious beliefs within the cognitive hierarchy. The result of the scientific debate on the eugenic issue was to separate in a most radical fashion the natural order from the moral. Euthanasia was not a discovery of Hitler's. Painless death for the incurably ill had already been recommended, for example, in 1920 by Karl Bindung and Alfred Hoche.[8] Essentially, the eugenic doctrines and practices, ultimately implemented in National Socialist Germany, postulated the existence of genetic differences between races and other categories of man that have much greater importance in determining the worth and performance of members of those groups than anything the individual man can do during his lifetime. Thus, according to this assumption *nature* outweighs *nurture*.[9] The issues emerging in the racial eugenics debate have persisted, of course, beyond the era of the Third Reich.[10]

In the National Socialist ideology and the minds of many Germans, the academic racial eugenics debate was contained in "vulgar" Social Darwinism, a viewpoint co-opted even by the socialists, and in the "normal" anti-Semitism so popular in Western Civilization.[11] Anti-Semitism became a popular theme for the volkists who turned into political issues such questions as those revolving around sex, ethics, and religion, which normally were answered only in the private arena. These traditionally private issues, turned into public debates, presented the Church with a forum that was unfamiliar. The party pursued abstract goals that seemingly could not have any concrete political effects: *Volk* unity, racial purity, *Lebensraum*. For their part, the National Socialists rejected as sterile the problems that politics can resolve, i.e., the development of institutional and legal frameworks within which a society can function. In essence, Nazi leaders politicized areas that have usually been reserved for decisions within the individual's conscience.

The eugenic policies of the Nazi regime should not have surprised anyone. Nazi written works, propaganda, and speeches were rife with references stressing the importance of achieving a pure and healthy race. At the annual party gathering at Nuremberg in 1929, for example, Hitler had held up ancient Sparta's policy of selective infanticide as a model. "If Germany every year would have one million children and eliminate 700,000-800,000 of the weakest, the end result would probably be an increase in (national) strength."[12] When he assumed power in Germany, Hitler's intentions were a matter of record. His presentation, although vulgar, did not provide a discordant note, since respectable eugenicists had reached similar conclusions, although expressing them in a more aesthetic fashion. Essentially, what emerged in scientific and academic journals on euthanasia and sterilization was transformed by Nazi politicos into racial purity, a moral-political issue.[13]

There had been a degree of hesitation on the part of Catholic moral theologians when the question of sterilization first emerged in the 1920s. Was it wrong to intervene surgically to prevent the proliferation of undesirable stock and so save the race from degeneration? Two moral theologians confronted one another from the late 1920s until the Nazi eugenic policies were implemented. The prominent advocate of the axiom that sterilization was forbidden by both Christian and moral law was Professor

Franz Hürth, of the Jesuit Theological Seminary at Valkenburg, later of the Pontifical Gregorian University. His antagonist on this issue was Professor Joseph Mayer of the philosophical-theological Paderborn Academy, who defended sterilization as probably licit and as certainly still a debatable academic issue. Ultimately, Hürth was to be sustained by the Holy See and the episcopate. In the 1930 encyclical *Casti Connubi (On Christian marriage)*, Pius XI declared that the body of man was inviolable, that the state had no authority to sterilize unless for medical reasons or as a punishment for crime, and that purely eugenic reasons would not suffice. *Casti Connubi* itself was promulgated to confront such views as that of Leo Just: "Without eugenics there can be no solution to the social question."[14] Unconvinced by this encyclical, Mayer went on to defend not only sterilization but also abortion. Eventually in a Nazi-sponsored memorandum, he justified euthanasia for the mentally ill.[15]

Eugenic sterilization had been keenly debated in Germany when in 1927 Mayer published his *Legal Sterilization of the Mentally Ill.* Opposing Hürth and the majority of moral theologians, Mayer suggested that the chief issue in the controversy was that the sterilized, according to canon law, at least if the primary goal of procreation in marriage were stressed, would not really have been capable of a proper marital relationship. Marriage, Mayer felt, however, should not focus so exclusively on procreation, but on sanctifying the souls of the partners. The only question that could logically be posed was whether sterilization intended a moral good. He concluded that neither private morality nor the moral world-order was endangered through the sterilization of the mentally ill. The healing of the community was viewed as more important than the physical integrity of the individual. Stressing that Thomas Aquinas accepted castration for sex offenders and that an extensive literature had developed emphasizing that the common good supersedes the individual benefit, Mayer asserted that the state does have the right to control the mentally and medically ill from "haphazard breeding." Since the goal of marriage, he insisted, is not just to beget children, sterilized individuals may certainly be allowed to marry and enjoy the other pleasures of connubial bliss. Mayer was very quick to point out that, conducted properly, legal sterilization measures would not lead to an undue interference of the state into the private lives of individuals.[16] In his scholarly treatise, Mayer asserted that it would be licit for the state to enforce sterilization for eugenic societal reasons. A person who is incapable of educating children, he maintained, had no right to beget them. The Jesuit Hürth almost immediately attacked the Mayer thesis, actually directed against his own earlier work.[17] Mayer had argued, for example, that in case of necessity an abortion could be procured. Hurth rejected this view and insisted: "Catholic moral theology sees in the life of a fully innocent person an inviolable good that is immune from a direct human attack by a private person or by the public authority."[18] Until 1933, the eugenics issue was consigned to encyclicals and theological journals.

On July 14, 1933, Hitler's regime formulated the "Law Preventing the Transmission of Hereditary Disease." This law for the prevention of progeny with hereditary disease, the basis for Hitler's racial purification program, was not unique, however, but was directly patterned on the model sterilization law proposed by the leaders of the American eugenics movement.[19] The publishing of this law (July 25) was particularly insulting, since it contradicted *Casti Connubi* and failed to take into account an earlier episcopal statement, voiced at the May 1933 Fulda Conference, opposing even voluntary sterilization. Also disturbing to Catholics was the fact that it was approved at the same cabinet session that had accepted the Concordat, which had been designed to resolve a plethora of Church-state concerns. This Reich statute, which provided for the compulsory sterilization of all persons afflicted with various hereditary diseases or disabilities, including alcoholism, was to take effect on January 1, 1934. Instead of opposing the law, the bishops at their August 1933 meeting decided to submit a memorandum to the Ministry of the Interior in order to explain the Catholic position. The government was to be asked to frame the implementing ordinances in such a way that Catholic physicians, judges, nurses, and other employees would not be subjected to conflicts of conscience. Catholics, especially parents and directors of asylums, were to be told later how to conduct themselves.[20] Bertram's protest said that as much as the Church regreted the conflict between Church and state legislation, she could not pass silently over this violation of the Catholic moral law. Respectable theologians carefully delineated the Catholic position. In an opinion prepared for Cardinal Bertram, Hürth distinguished between the goal and the content of the July 14, 1933 law on the prevention of hereditary disease. The goal was approved from a moral and theological standpoint, but the content of the law had to be repudiated because it was against natural and Christian moral law, clearly a confusing response for non-theologians. The challenge would be difficult to handle under the best of conditions, but was complicated in Nazi Germany where the press was already being carefully censored. Subsequently, Hürth commented that he wanted to publish an article on the new eugenics law, but as Robert Leiber, S.J., informed Pacelli, the cardinal secretary of state, it was impossible. Leiber commented that Mayer's 1933 article, published apparently supporting at least a Catholic position, could ultimately cause more damage in the long run than public support for the eugenic goals, if not means.[21]

By early November Bishops Konrad Gröber and Wilhelm Berning reported to their colleagues that the government was willing to exempt directors of Catholic institutions from the duty of applying for the sterilization of patients under their care. The Catholic directors would merely have to report the names of all their patients afflicted with diseases requiring sterilization. In the case of Catholic physicians employed in state institutions the situation was not as hopeful, the bishops thought, though the government was willing to consider the objections of the episcopate. The officials of the Ministry of the Interior, with whom the two bishops were negotiating, had granted the Church the right to inform the faithful of the Catholic position on sterilization. In January 1934 the faithful were told that according to Catholic doctrine it was forbidden to volunteer for sterilization or apply for another's. Such bishops as Galen and Faulhaber were somewhat more forceful than many of their colleagues in carrying out the injunction of their office.[22] There was, however, no public, frontal attack on the law as such.

Bertram felt that it was illicit cooperation in a sinful act for Catholic officials to file applications for sterilization. He felt, however, that priests did not need to deny the sacraments to officials who were not aware of the sinful character of such applications or who acted in good faith when they complied with the law to keep their positions and support their families. Bertram agreed with the opinion, formulated by moral theologians, on the illicitness of filing applications for sterilization, but expressed strong doubts on how to handle confessions. The Church could be accused of teaching something in theory but reconciling herself with the same sinful act in practice. The spread of such views "would lead to the loss of all respect for the moral law and for the authority of the Church." It would cause a scandal and thus in the bishop's opinion made it mandatory that the well-being of the official yield to the common good, that is, to "the preservation of morality among the people."[23]

Along with Mayer other Catholic intellectuals were not convinced by Bertram's insistence on conforming to the official view within the Church. Two Catholic theologians at the University of Braunsberg (East Prussia), Hans Barion and Karl Eschweiler, maintained that the sterilization law was not in conflict with Catholic doctrine. Even though the two professors had been suspended from their faculties by the Church, many lay Catholics, encouraged by their views, complied with the demands of the sterilization law—the path of least resistance. Eschweiler's and Barion's reaction was not isolated. Hürth had already privately written to Father Leiber, Pacelli's confidante, that a number of Catholic theologians were of the opinion that the state did not exist for man and that individuals were to be subordinated to the state. They offered, Hürth pointed out, Thomistic texts based on Aristotle's notion of the polity. Leiber added, however, that if Thomas were correctly interpreted such a position could not be sustained. Bertram himself had already admitted that very few Catholic officials were even bothered by the conflict of conscience that had arisen; and with this mood of theological uncertainty prevailing, several bishops decided to adopt a more conciliatory position. In particular, it proved impossible to obtain unanimity of opinion on how confessors were to treat Catholic officials who filed applications for sterilization. A pamphlet published at the Beuron monastery advised priests hearing confession not to pose troubling questions to persons known to be involved with the machinery of the sterilization law. The Cologne Bishops' Conference in March 1935 suggested that as long as no uniform stand could be reached no instructions should be issued so that confusion could be avoided.[24] Apparently, the Church had reconciled herself to the fact that most Catholic officials helped enforce the sterilization law, even though theologians generally opposed eugenics.

The theologian Otto Schilling, for example, had insisted that the Church wanted reason, not medical eugenics, applied to procreation but that within this context the focus should be on the valid welfare of the individual, of the community, and of the race. As an example of applied reason, for example, Pius XI in *Casti Connubi* had urged care in the choice of one's marital partner. The Church could not support artificial birth control or sterilization. Eugenicists, theologians reminded their readers, recommended noble motives for birth control, but, they stressed, in reality individual selfishness usually dominated. Schilling warned that by reducing the quantity of children one could also reduce the quality of the whole. With respect to the role of the state in eugenics, Schilling asserted that the state had the strict duty to protect the life of the innocent child, whose helplessness itself was a touching appeal to justice, the foundation of all political life. Naturally Schilling also condemned sterilization by reminding his readers that the sanctity of the family was to be respected by the state. A refined moral education, he felt, would be necessary for a national eugenics plan to operate within the parameters established by God. In essence, however, man had to use his reason while conforming to natural as well as God's law.[25]

In 1935 Karl Frank stated that in a *Volk* descended from a specific race or racial mixture there were valuable and less valuable offshoots. The current eugenics discussion, he maintained, was concerned with helping the hereditarily better elements attain victory over the inferior. Working with Mendel's laws, he felt that an intelligent approach would actually mean crossing races for a healthier stock. But he knew that from the Hitlerian national eugenics standpoint this mixing would be forbidden. Thus, in his view, a realistic eugenics policy was not being sought by the Reich. Selfishness, he insisted, should be opposed, and so religious ethics should be highlighted. Moreover, Frank stressed that the recent attacks on the family did not support the realization of eugenic goals, and that, as in nature, those elements of lesser value should never be obliterated. Eugenics, he felt, should reinforce that procreation that would strengthen the racial stock while still protecting the rights of the chronically ill. Frank pointed out that the goal of man was to seek fulfillment in eternal life. It was essential, he insisted, to leave to the creator how this goal could be achieved, even by the hereditarily mentally ill, since no one except God had control over all the possibilities inherent in procreation. Catholics, of course, could work to control marriages between the hereditarily ill as well as between the hereditarily ill and the healthy, but the efforts had to be guided by rational natural law. Also, constructive economic activities needed to be provided so that the unfortunates could assist in maintaining themselves.[26] In essence, then, Frank felt that eugenics could be practiced, but only within the confines of divine and natural law and only when motivated by proper charity. Apparently ignorant of Nazi goals, Frank naively maintained that euthanasia was not being seriously discussed in responsible governmental circles. Actually, however, as early as 1935 Hitler had decided on a euthanasia program to improve the quality of race, but he had hesitated to implement it for fear of the reaction of the Church. In the chaos of a wartime situation, he cleverly reasoned, opposition would not be mounted.[27]

Theologians were discussing the issues of racial differentiation as well. Frank, for example, insisted that all members of mankind from the beginning had been endowed with a rational essence, and that culture, of course, merely helped distinguish among human groups. Such a position developed more clearly and promoted vigorously would have obviated the entire concept of the *Untermensch* as well as the stress on racial eugenics either through sterilization or euthanasia. Who could tell when a particular quality could well be necessary for the next specialized formation in the onward development of mankind? Franz Walther felt that euthanasia was rooted in the historical collapse of religion in modern times and could never really improve God's creation. Walther found the deepest roots of the pro-euthanasia movement growing in soil characterized by the collapse of morality, conditioned through the experiences of the First World War as well as a materialistic world view, and powered by the surrender of a belief in God and immortality.[28] Theological opposition to Nazi racial eugenics was emerging.

Still, in 1934-36 approximately 168,000 persons were sterilized. The government was quite aggressive in implementing its law. Priests protesting against sterilization were penalized, frequently losing their right to give religious instruction in the public schools. In 1935 Wilhelm Frick, the minister of the interior, during a widely publicized speech, gave notice that the regime would not tolerate any further sabotage of the law. In several notes to the Reich government, Pacelli argued that the Holy See could not grant the state the power to determine the morality of legislation and so reserved the right of the Church to criticize ordinances in conflict with divine law. In fact, however, for all practical purposes, the episcopate was on a path of retreat. The Church's condemnation of sterilization was labeled sabotage of the national renewal and a malicious attack on the state and party. It was seen as an attack on the dynamic and legal foundation of the state.[29] The bishops were uncomfortable whenever their loyalty was attacked and continued their retreat, camouflaged by patriotic speeches focused on such other issues as the Saar plebiscite, which Hitler conveniently provided.

Aided by an intricate casuistry, the bishops had decided that Catholic physicians and social workers might report to the authorities those afflicted with ills that called for sterilization. This reporting was to be seen as "material cooperation," which was lawful, since such an act was morally indifferent and since the Catholic official in question might lose his job. To submit, on the other hand, an application for the sterilization of a person was "formal cooperation," which, being an essential part of an evil action, was sinful; but the Church did not attempt to enforce this position. When the question arose whether Catholic nurses might assist in sterilization operations, the Church replied negatively. But in 1940 even the Sacred Congregation of the Holy Office ruled that Catholic nurses in state-run hospitals could assist at such operations if a sufficiently important reason were present, such as the danger of replacement of Catholic nurses by staff hostile to the Church, who might prevent the administration of the sacraments. The bishops, then, opposed sterilization in theory, but accommodated themselves to the facts of life in the Third Reich, frequently accepting a lesser evil to avoid the greater. Also, they seemed to make decisions to accommodate lay Catholics who could have lost jobs and family stability had the moral ideals been strictly enforced. In general, then, they adjusted to the circumstances, applied moral precepts, and avoided burdening lay Catholics with ethical dilemmas. In 1936, the Munich courts decided that an objection to the sterilization law on religious grounds could not be upheld or considered. Further, the legal right of the priest, in distinction from his moral obligation, not to reveal the secrets of the confessional was very gravely qualified.[30] The obvious course, then, was to make sure that matters for the confessional were limited. Sterilization was, of course, only the first step in the racial eugenics program.

The transition to an offensive and aggressive foreign policy in 1937-38 went together with stepping up the domestic struggle against the Jews and the Church,[31] as well as against the largely conservative forces in the army, bureaucracy, and judiciary. Hitler's speech to the Reichstag on January 30, 1939, on the occasion of the sixth anniversary of his take-over of power, is worth recalling. Not since 1933 had Hitler attacked so fanatically in public the "spiritual weaklings," the decaying "social castes." He argued for the *völkisch* laws and predicted of the Jews that in the event of another world war "the result would not be . . . a victory for Jewry but the destruction of the Jewish race in Europe." For Hitler, war had a purpose more extensive than merely military victory. World War II was a "racial" action that had to be waged at home as a second stage of the National Socialist Revolution.[32]

There is an intrinsic connection between the sterilization law of 1933 and the euthanasia measures of 1939. The euthanasia policy did not originate in a vacuum but rather had a unique and traceable genesis. Its roots can be found in the medical, juridical, and moral-theological debates from the turn of the century until the 1930s. The infamous euthanasia order was a command to destroy the medically, socially, and, ultimately, the racially unwanted. There is a politico-ideological connection between this euthanasia action and the earlier laws on sound marriage, issued in 1933 and then reinforced in the 1935 Nuremberg laws. For these earlier laws special administrative and court authorities, however, were established with the legally prescribed process of submitting proposals and making decisions. But the cover organizations and secret authorizations concerned with the euthanasia action were deliberately constructed outside the law. Even the sterilization laws, however, had afforded a great deal of latitude of judgment for officials and so themselves had paved the way for the 1939 oral order from the führer.[33] Departmental cohesion had gradually dissolved; plenipotentiaries subordinate to the führer had emerged; all the conditions were by 1939 prepared for the euthanasia action, a crucial administrative step on the road to Auschwitz.

Hitler's euthanasia oral order was issued in late October 1939 after the successful Polish campaign. But it was predated to September 1, suggesting a connection with the war issues. Certainly it was connected to the race issue, but it also embraced, and now on a very basic level, the power of the state over the individual and highlighted the state, i.e., the führer, as the ultimate source of justice.[34] Such slogans as "Law is what serves the people" (*Recht ist, was dem Volk nutzt*) or "Common good before private good" (*Gemeinnutz vor Eigennutz*) now were brought to life as the basis for forthcoming arbitrary acts of the government. Euthanasia and its associated procedures embraced a massive assault on traditional morality (Christian and natural) and made the individual the instrument of the state or the race. Compounded with doctrines of racial supremacy, it was the prelude and preparation to the wholesale elimination of *Untermenschen* by any definition. Questionnaires and report forms, for example, provided blanks for information on patients who suffered from a variety of diseases or were criminally insane or were not German citizens or of German blood. Race and nationality were to be included.[35]

In the same month that Hitler issued his euthanasia order, Pius XII promulgated his first encyclical, *Summi Pontificatus,* which warned of the arbitrariness of political power that assimilated rights that belong to God alone. The state assumption of absolute autonomy asserted the encyclical, "puts itself in the place of the Almighty and elevates the state or group into the last end of life, the supreme criterion of the moral and juridical order, and therefore forbids every appeal to the principles of natural reason and of the Christian conscience." Against the background of the sterilization controversy and Pius XII's encyclical, the reaction of the German bishops to the 1939 Nazi euthanasia program was predictable: the opposition would be unconditional. Hitler seemed aware that a program to kill the mentally defective would meet strong resistance and so waited until the war began and patriotism made opposition more difficult.[36] Bishop Wurm, provincial bishop of the Lutheran Church in Württemberg, accurately prophesied: "There an be no stopping once one starts down this slope."[37] Hitler's order did not immediately touch Catholic institutions. The mentally ill patients had in previous years already been removed from Catholic institutions because of the Catholic opposition to the sterilization laws, and, in view of the intended operations, the institutes themselves had been confiscated.[38]

On August ll, 1940, Bertram as chairman of the Fulda Conference wrote to Hans-Heinrich Lammers, head of the Reich Chancellery, and reviewed the longstanding controversies in recent years in the field of eugenics. He stressed that assurances had been formally given that at least euthanasia was still illegal, even if sterilization was not. The point at issue, Bertram asserted, was the practice of government agencies to decree that the incurably insane, the so-called worthless lives, be either destroyed or used as experimental subjects in the search for new methods of curing other diseases. Particularly noteworthy in the Bertram letter are the uncompromising terms. He wrote of the "unqualified inadmissibility of acts of this kind," which were "most strictly forbidden" and "not only by the moral and religious teaching of the Catholic Church but by the religious and moral convictions of all Christians." The slightest exception, he maintained, would lead to grave consequences: "If this principle is once set aside, even with limited exceptions, on the ground of an occasional need, then, as experience teaches us, other exceptions will be made by individuals for their own purposes." The letter overflows with references to the sanctity of human life.[39] On November 6, 1940, Faulhaber wrote to the Minister of Justice Franz Gürtner. He reminded Gürtner that in 1934 the

German bishops had affirmed the irreconcilability of euthanasia with the Christian conscience. Panic, he continued, had seized the inmates of other welfare institutions, such as old people's homes and tubercular sanitaria. Concluding, he appealed: "But even during wartime one may not discard the everlasting foundations of the moral order, nor the fundamental rights of the individual." Because of the rigorous censorship the outcry was not as great rs it might have been. Often important public statements were not printed in the *Amtsblatt* of the diocese for fear of confiscation, but were sent secretly by courier to the local pastors, by whom they were often duplicated again. Some found their way to the foreign press in this form and were never officially printed.[40]

The pope's own immediate reaction to the euthanasia order was in the arena of doctrine. On December 6, 1940, *Osservatore Romano* published a decree of the congregation of the Holy Office in the traditional question-answer form:

> Whether it is licit, by the order of the public authority, to kill directly those who, although guilty of no crime worthy of death, nevertheless, because of psychic or physical defects can no longer be of use to the nation and are thought rather to be an impediment to it and to be an obstacle to its vigor and strength.

The answer was brief, but compelling.

> No, since this is contrary to both the natural and the divine positive law.

Pius gave his own explanation of this decree in a letter (December 15) to Bishop Konrad Preysing:

> About the shattering events which were the object of the courageous letter from Württemberg (Bishop Wurm's July 19 letter), the Holy Office has in the meantime issued a public condemnation on the general principle. We have had our highest tribunal speak as briefly and trenchantly as was possible. We would not think we had done our duty, if we had kept silent about such deeds. It is now for the German bishops to judge what the circumstances of time and place permit to be done.[41]

Such German bishops as Preysing presented the decree in public sermons (March 9, 1941). Clemens August Galen published it in the *Amtsblatt* of the Münster diocese.[42] The Nazis quite clearly were concerned with its publication. On April 7, 1941, the police and intelligence services were alerted in Düsseldorf, Münster, Aachen, Bielefeld, Dortmund, Osnabrück, and Cologne. The Nazi police official, Walter Bierkamp (later head of an *Einsatzgrupp,* an execution squad in the Ukraine), enclosed the translation of the Latin text and forecast trouble: "Since we may expect that discussions and rumors about this problem will increase notably from now on, the respective agencies responsible should follow the situation most attentively and report without delay to the Reich Main Central Office any eventual information, and also in writing to me."[43]

Confidential protests by the bishops resulted in little satisfaction from the Reich authorities. In February 1941, a new murder clinic was set up at Hadamar near Frankfurt. It was equipped with gas chambers for the extermination of those who were to be its victims and crematories for the disposal of their bodies. On June 24-26, 1941, the bishops met at Fulda. Ignoring the campaign against the Soviet Union, they dwelt on the mortal peril facing the German Church. "The very existence of the Church and of Christianity," they said, "is at stake in Germany." They cited among other threats to religion and society the suppression of those "lives unworthy to live." Bertram was to present their grievances to the government in writing.[44]

Following these varied papal and episcopal responses to the new eugenics crisis, Bishop Galen of Münster created an international uproar by his three famous sermons of July 13 and 20 and August 3. The third dealt with the suppression of "lives unworthy to live." These unfortunates die, he emphasized, "not because they are guilty of anything but because in the opinion of some doctor, in the view of some committee, they are 'unworthy to live' because in their eyes they belong to the unproductive citizens." Galen focused on the fundamental issue of the entire Nazi era, i.e., genocide as public policy:

> If once it is admitted that people have the right to kill unproductive persons—it concerns at the moment poor, defenseless lunatics—then the murder of all unproductive persons, that is, of incurables, of cripples, of folk maimed by war or work, indeed of us all, when we grow old and feeble and unproductive [will be possible]. . . . None of us will be sure of his life.

Pius praised Galen for his stand in 1941, and, on February 24, 1943, in a letter to Galen, he wrote: "Perhaps never in modern church history have these three—human dignity, the family, and the Church—been so fatefully linked as today. It is always for us a consolation when we learn of an open and courageous word from a German bishop or the German bishops."[45]

Galen's service is that he produced a great deal of publicity, reinforced a mobilized public opinion, and helped prevent the recurrence of euthanasia, at least in Germany. Reich officials also noted that the Church was still a major "uncoordinated" force. Galen's protest provided the Church with a renewed public credibility and offered it the possibility of retaining a consistency in its moral theology. Unfortunately, Church officials did not extend and continue their critique once the Nazis moved their racial purification machinery east. The Nazis were clearly upset over Galen's sermons especially that of August 3, which had an immense effect on the Germans domestically as well as on the soldiers in the field. It is indicative of their rage that a Gaustableiter, Arnold F. (Essen), accused Galen of being a paid English agent. But in all of the furor at home and abroad concerning Galen's sermons, it should be recalled that he attacked the National Socialist state and ideology, not his German fatherland.[46] The bishops seemed able to attack Nazi policies, but not the political organization that made such actions possible. They remained loyal to Germany, even if not to the particular policies of the Reich.

Other protests now followed those of Galen. Anton Hilfrich, bishop of Limburg, on August 13 sent a letter to the Ministry of Justice condemning the extermination of so-called lives unworthy of being lived at Hadamar. He called for an end to further violations of the fifth commandment. Albert Stohr, the bishop of Mainz, asked in a sermon: "Who gives a man the right to say that a life is unworthy of being lived?. . . . It is wrong to kill directly the life of the innocent." Bishop Franz Bornewasser on September 14 stated that the killing of these so-called unproductive and unworthy but harmless persons "cried to heaven for vengeance." On the feast of Christ the King, Bishop Stohr preached against euthanasia: "Not merely the individual man is not permitted to lay violent hands on his neighbor, but also the community *Gemeinschaft* is forbidden to do evil. At no time is it permitted to extinguish a human life." It is particularly noteworthy that Stohr stressed that the community or state could not do that which was forbidden to the individual person by natural or divine law. On November 2 Bishop Preysing warned in a sermon: "Woe to us if the eternal moral law can be changed or set aside for purely expediency reasons. When the right to life of the innocent, the sanctity of life, is denied, then there is no stop in this descending road."[47]

On December 10, 1941, a most bitter message was sent to the Nazi authorities. Ultimately, the main points were made public. The bishops had catalogued the Hitlerian promises callously dishonored. One complaint stated:

> With deep horror Christian Germans have learned that, by order of the state authorities, numerous insane persons, entrusted to asylums and institutions, were destroyed as so-called unproductive citizens. At present a large-scale campaign is being made for the killing of incurables through a film *Ich klage an* recommended by the authorities and designed to calm the conscience through appeals to pity. We German bishops shall not cease to protest against

the killing of innocent persons. Nobody's life is safe unless the command-ment "Thou shalt not kill" is observed.[48]

To an extent, although they expressed it in a very abstract fashion, the German bishops were not exclusively concerned about the lives of defense-less Germans. In the Fulda pastoral of September 12, 1943, they urged the defense of all those in danger: "Killing is wrong in itself, even when al-legedly exercised in the interest of the common good against the innocent and defenseless weak and infirm of mind, on the incurable, those mortally wounded, those with hereditary diseases, infants unable to live, innocent hostages and disarmed war or penal prisoners, or on men of another race and origin."[49] Belatedly, the bishops had observed that eugenic reasons justifying racial purification seemed to be connected inexorably to mass murder. Until it was too late, however, they failed to perceive that the soil had been prepared for this growth by the earlier nationalistic anti-Semitism and stress on the *Volk,* rarely criticized by Church leaders.

On August 24, 1941, Hitler's order had reduced the proportions of the euthanasia program in Germany and transferred its functions east. The bishops' protests, in particular those of Galen but more significantly the reactions of the German people themselves, had caused Hitler to reduce the dimensions of the program in Germany. The Nuremberg trials have made clear how Hitler and his doctors prepared themselves for the mass slaughter of the Jews by first killing nearly a hundred thousand of their fellow citizens in Germany.[50] Postwar testimony, a memo from Mayer on the Catholic position related to euthanasia, the role of Heinrich Wienken, the bishops' liaison representative to the government, and the delay of the Catholic response are issues that have clouded the historical response of the Church to the regime.

The defense strategy in the 1967 euthanasia trials was to show that the killing of the insane and the hopelessly ill was thought to be respectable and had also been practiced in other countries. An opinion by Professor Joseph Mayer was introduced through the testimony of Albert Hartl, a former SS officer and Gestapo official, who insisted that he had commissioned from Mayer a memorandum on the subject in 1939, although 1940 was probably the real year. Mayer had responded with a theological opinion of over 100 pages in favor of euthanasia. Hartl allegedly circulated the document to those engaged in the euthanasia program. A Catholic moral theologian was thus brought in to ease the political consciences of the Nazis at the very inception of the euthanasia program. Hartl, the chief of the Catholic sec-tion of the SD (secret intelligence), declared that on Hitler's order he had asked Mayer for an opinion on the euthanasia problem from the Catholic viewpoint. The theologian, said Hartl, anticipated no fundamental objection from the Church. In Hartl's words, "Only then did Hitler decide to begin the 'mercy killing' program."[51]

There is no need to doubt whether Mayer could have given such an opinion. His earlier views on sterilization and abortion had already predisposed him for such a conclusion and were indeed the reason why he was approached by the Nazis. Still, if Hartl had really wished to provide his Nazi superiors reliable information on the views and potential reactions of the bishops, he obviously misled these leaders. Mayer's opinion was completely out of harmony with Catholic doctrine. It also seems unlikely that Hitler would have personally wished to sound out legitimate Catholic opinion about "Action T-4." Likewise, he would scarcely have needed the assurances of the *Pfaffen* before proceeding on his course. The text of the alleged Mayer *Gutachten* has never been found under Mayer's name.[52] Professor Mayer himself ultimately left the Paderborn Academy after 1945 and ceased writing on moral issues. The reasons for his departure are obscure but perhaps relate to his links as a spy to Hartl. Mayer apparently supplied not only learned dissertations to the Nazis, but also other information as well. He thus appears to have been a Nazi informer all during the war.[53]

Based on past ecclesiastical adaptation, some Nazis apparently also thought that the Church would not be so unequivocally opposed to euthanasia if specific concessions could be made. Hans Hefelmann was the executive assistant to Victor Brack, a member of the führer's personal chancellery. On April 7, 1964, Hefelmann affirmed during his trial that the Catholic bishops were willing to moderate their stand if opportunities to perform pastoral functions were made available. At least according to Hefelmann, Catholic bishops had been wiling to tolerate a limited euthanasia restricted to certain categories of persons. Hefelmann alleged that he was himself present at two interviews between Bishop Heinrich Wienken (the Fulda bishops' liaison with the government) and the minister of the interior, Wilhelm Frick. He said that the arrest of Bishops Galen and Hilfrich was averted because Wienken, with authorization from the bishops, had agreed to accept specific government regulations, i.e., that only completely insane persons would be eliminated. Little credence need be attached to the Hefelmann testimony. To the bishops, the lives of the mentally ill were sacrosanct and inviolable. Hence, in their view no "limited euthanasia" could be permitted. No other evidence substantiates Hefelmann's testimony, and he contradicted it himself several weeks earlier. In the middle of March he had claimed that the arrest of Galen and Hilfrich, demanded by Heydrich and Himmler, had been avoided by Victor Brack's intervention with Hitler—that is, not by any "concessions" on the Catholic side. He also testified that Hitler had personally made the decision to suspend the program in order not to give the churches any further occasion for public protest. There is no indication that the Church representatives were willing to compromise.[54]

The testimony of Hefelmann, Hartl, and Wienken during the euthanasia trials of the 1960s has offered additional insights, however, into the Church's relatively slow response to Hitler's back-dated order.[55] The suggestion of a "deal" being made by Wienken, Bertram's liaison in Berlin, does not seem likely. Wienken was an unobtrusive, diligent church bureaucrat with an enormous capacity for optimism in his role as liaison officer between the German Catholic hierarchy and the Nazi state. Determined not to provoke any quarrels and believing in the compatibility of loyalty to Christ's Church and Hitler's Germany, both Bertram and Wienken were cut from the same cloth. Wienken weathered the storms of political controversy, but at no little cost to his personal image of integrity. The most controversial issue over which he is alleged to have capitulated was that of the Nazi euthanasia program. Indeed, Wienken's optimism that problems could be negotiated opened the way for ambiguous interpretations even though he did not compromise on the episcopal position that euthanasia violated the Fifth Commandment.[56]

As the Fulda representative, Wienken had to deal with the National Socialist government at a particularly important time. The *Blitzkrieg* had been an almost unprecedented victory. The campaigns in the west had astounded the world. In this victorious Germany, Wienken was certainly susceptible to Nazi blandishments. By November 1940 Wienken had several times discussed the euthanasia theme. But the development of the Church's case was interrupted in early autumn by the insistence of the propaganda ministry representatives that all churches respond more carefully to the political needs of wartime Germany. To insure pastoral care under wartime conditions, Wienken recommended to the episcopate great care in the handling of the wartime doctrinal decisions of the Church and the renunciation of anything injurious or harmful to the political welfare of wartime Germany.[57] Wienken's discussions of euthanasia and its problems cannot be comprehended without understanding his personality. He wanted to remain in contact with the opponents of the Church, while hoping that, without capitulation, he could still avoid conflict. Counterbalancing what appears to be an overzealous desire to compromise, Wienken during these same weeks petitioned against the beginning Jewish deportations and for the alleviation of the sufferings being endured by the priests in Dachau. To the aggressive Bishop Preysing, Wienken on November 5, 1940, confided what probably was his own motivation. Wienken maintained that there were in the Nazi party two camps—one was anti-Church and anti-Christian and one hoped to use the Church to support the regime. He hoped to strengthen the compromise party but was unsure where the führer stood. The role of Wienken is unclear because his sole accuser, Hefelmann, took a variety of positions and was not privy to all of the discussions.[58]

Whether Mayer performed his role of informer and spy willingly or unwillingly, under blackmail fear or through personal conviction, he was certainly not the foremost representative of German Catholic clerical thought or action.[59] The murder ethic of the Nazis was possible only in their concept of the absolute power of the state, an institution they saw as unanswerable to any moral claims except the imperatives of race. Once on this slope there could be no internal corrective or brake. In his 1927 book Mayer promoted sterilization, but did not maintain that it would be licit to kill the mentally ill. The bishops did not initially launch a full-scale assault against sterilization except in theory; they compromised on a pastoral level. Human rights were being hierarchically scaled by Catholic leaders in a Nazi Germany where no human rights were sacrosanct. Wienken hoped that a patriotic Church could reshape radical Nazi policies. On April 28, 1972, Professor Georg Siegmund of Fulda during a broadcast over Vatican Radio cited a proverb that epitomizes what occurred in the Church during these years: "If you give the devil your finger, he will take your hand."[60] Success in the nearly total elimination of the domestic euthanasia program in Germany is in part a credit to the Catholic Church, which otherwise was tarnished by its noteworthy failure to oppose the Holocaust publicly. The reproduction of the experiences of the T-4 organization (bureaucracy in charge of euthanasia) and the continuation of the purification of the German *Volk* from supposedly less worthy strains into the purification of Europe from inferior races form a unified policy.[61] Euthanasia in Germany was protested; the Final Solution from the initial restrictions to the death camps in the east received little public comment during this entire period.

The majority of people who had been outraged over the euthanasia issue, because it touched their friends and relatives, failed to react when their Jewish neighbors were deported and killed. The disaster befalling the Jews, the culmination of years of anti-Semitic propaganda, did not result in similar humane feelings.[62] That German public opinion and the Church were a force to be reckoned with in principle and could have played a positive role in averting the Jewish disaster as well—that is a lesson to be derived from the fate of Hitler's euthanasia efforts. But, lest the power of the Church and public opinion be overestimated, it must be recalled that sterilization and euthanasia were merely component of the intricate, but secretive, Nazi racial eugenic policy. By 1941 the Final Solution along with *Lebensraum* as the twin goals of the regime were being implemented, although ultimately the latter would be hampered to insure the success of the former. Hitler could afford surrender on the relatively minor euthanasia program to achieve his major ideological goal. Success in war and the Final Solution would allow him to focus later on the Church, and his intentions there were clear.

Nazi eugenic policies led from sterilization to the death camps in a logical progression. First, those who were thought likely to pass on hereditary defects were deprived of their procreative powers. Their children and those members of "inferior races" could be legally aborted. Then defective Germans were put to death. But since membership in an "inferior" race was considered in itself to be a hereditary, transmissable defect, the euthanasia program was simply broadened to become the mass extermination of entire populations. A number of individuals who had worked in the euthanasia *Aktion,* for example, eventually cooperated in the Final Solution.[63] The Final Solution could be implemented because of the anti-Semitism prevalent in virtually every class and section in Germany, not always, of course, in equal intensity.

Anti-Semitism and the Institutional Church

Instead of emphasizing a spontaneous eruption of popular anti-Semitism in the socio-psychological crisis brewing in Weimar Germany, some recent interpretations have stressed the conscious manipulative exploitation of anti-Semitism, which the Nazis used as a tool of integration and mass mobilization. In some interpretations anti-Semitism served the interests of finance capital; in others it seemed a cementing element that diverted attention from the failures of Nazi socioeconomic policies and held together the antagonistic forces of the Nazi movement.[64] But as Kershaw has recently noted, public opinion did not support radicalized anti-Semitism. In essence popular opinion was indifferent and guided by latent and historically rooted anti-Semitism. Such opinion, however, did supply a climate within which Nazi ideology and programs could advance unchallenged.[65]

The Catholic anti-Semitic experience during the *Kulturkampf* may be seen as a phenomenon that at least reinforced an existent anti-Semitism and simultaneously aided Catholics in their struggle for integration into a potentially hostile authoritarian Reich. Parliamentary liberalism, viewed by many as a Jewish political ideology, was not accepted in the 1870s, nor would it be approved thereafter enthusiastically by many Catholics. Even if most Catholics were not racially anti-Semitic, therefore, they could hardly be jaundiced against the Nazis in light of their own post-1871 experiences. Anti-Semitism served the Catholic Center party as a functional mechanism for political mobilization to the right. After 1880 it could be directed against liberal Jews, Social Democrats, or against any problem that seemed insoluble or rooted in an "anti-German" conspiracy.[66]

After 1918 a variety of clerical Catholic leaders assaulted the Jews with theological and political diatribes. The Jesuit Gustav Gundlach argued for a mild political anti-Semitism and contended that fighting the Jews' "exaggerated and harmful influence" was permitted as long as it used moral means. Vicar General Mayer of Mainz, anti-Nazi in other respects, maintained that *Mein Kampf* had outlined the bad influence of the Jews in the press, theater, and literature. Father Senn called even elements of German Catholicism *verjudet* and labeled the Hitler movement radical, but really the last good opportunity to throw off the Jewish yoke.[67]

During the Weimar years, the German bishops preached against the Nazi glorification of race and blood but generally had almost nothing specific to say about the widespread anti-Semitic propaganda. On August 27, 1922, Faulhaber characterized the November Revolution as perjury and high treason, an unfortunate condemnation since in the minds of many this political system was part of the liberal-Jewish conspiracy. In 1923, Cardinal Faulhaber, for example, declared that every human life was precious, including that of a Jew—a backhanded compliment. Faulhaber also noted in 1924 that even if Hitler's subordinates did not realize that the German nation required the support of Christianity, the führer did. Other Catholics, most notably those in the *Katholikenbund,* urged combat against the enemies of Germany and the Church—Marxists, Freemasons, and Jews.[68] Clearly, then, many Catholics could see in Nazism at least some programs they could support. Still, for the most part the "Jewish Question" was important only to a minority of Germans. The general population was never actively instrumental in driving Jews from Germany or in their annihilation. Hitler and his radical followers pursued the Final Solution.[69] After 1933 moderate anti-Semitism appears to have been a success, because the population accepted legal and "moderate" measures against the Jews in Germany. Extreme anti-Semitism was apparently a failure in terms of public opinion after 1933. But the simple fact that Hitler could find enough collaborators to exterminate most German and European Jews seems to indicate that public opinion, at least in this area, had become irrelevant during the war,[70] since sensitivity toward Jewish rights had been undermined in the past. Although the ambivalent attitude of the papacy and of the Catholic hierarchy to the Jewish Question has been subjected to a thorough analysis, the stance adopted by the theologians and parochial clergy has not been completely delineated.[71] In all likelihood, of course, it was the parish clergy who were most able to exert a direct influence upon their flock.

Almost universally by 1933, Catholic thinkers were seeking a rapprochement with the new Nazi state, although such Catholics as Waldemar Gurian and Provost Lichtenberg of Berlin vigorously attacked anti-Semitism and asserted that the political actions in the 1930s constituted the prelude to the physical destruction of the Jews.[72] Typically, however, the dominant mood was moderation. Friedrich Muckermann, for example, contended that there was a natural organic root to the *Volkstum* and that another organic principle directed the supernatural development of the Church. Frequently, both *Volk* and *Kirche* were enlisted to support one another. *Volkstum, Reich,* and *Rasse* intermingled at the base of the institutional Nazi state. The dominant signal being sent by the Catholic publicists was for reconciliation; they generally failed to explicate analytically the overt and covert meanings of these loaded "German values." Even liturgy journals typically avoided articles that offered scholarly analyses of the Jewish origins of early Christian liturgical developments. In the Christian perspective the real enemy was not the heathen or pagan, but rather the Jew. Since the *völkisch* Christians saw the hostile Church and loyal Christians as enemies on the side of the Jews, Church leaders had to emphasize their disdain or even outright hatred of the Jews. Their institutional survival seemed dependent on this. Anti-Semitism had a role in the relationship between the Catholic populace and the Nazis. Based on a common political hostility to the Jews, connected to antiliberal and anti-socialist resentment, a solidarity existed between Catholics and Nazis. This congruence had a greater impact on the Catholic laity than the ideological and theological ruminations of their leaders. Catholic theological principles played a central role mainly in the official reactions of leading Catholics to the Nazis, although common ties as well had been highlighted in the early reconciliation phase.[73]

Although the research conclusions are not unequivocal about the exact cause, there is sufficient evidence to indicate that self-concern lessens willingness to help others. Like their episcopal predecessors, the German bishops had as their basic interest the maintenance of the Church in Germany and the elimination of any second-class status that might accrue to it. As bishops they had certainly identified with the institution. The Church's concern was theirs as well. Hence, to help purported enemies of the Nazi ideology would isolate the Church as an enemy of the regime. Given the institutional stakes, lack of concern was not surprising. When a sympathetic audience was watching, the bishops responded to euthanasia. The Church's leaders could act vigorously. When an anti-Semitically imbued congregation went to Church, they heard little. A correlation seems to exist between the individual's willingness to help and the audience's expectations and attitude.[74]

Shortly after the Concordat (1933), which seemed to regularize relations between Nazi Germany and the Vatican, Catholic leaders continued their traditional support of "normal" anti-Semitism to maintain the allegiance of the Catholic laity and to allow them to deal with what they hoped would develop into the moderate wing of Nazism. Both before and after Hitler assumed the chancellorship, the German bishops continued declaring their unwavering support of the important national values of ethnicity and culture and limited dissent to an insistence that this goal could not be achieved by resorting to immoral means.

Lesser Church leaders took their cue from the hierarchy. A canon in Regensburg advised Catholic teachers to point out to pupils that the sacred books of the Old Testament were not only beyond the Jewish mentality, but in direct conflict with it. "The greatest miracle of the Bible is that the true religion could hold its own and maintain itself against the voice of Semitic blood."[75] Anti-Semitism was not merely voiced by Church leaders for political reasons, but historically had been an accepted position through the ranks.

Anti-Semitism was pervasive and some of its main tenets were accepted as credible axioms. The Jews had a "demoralizing influence on religiosity and national character." The Jews had displayed a mortal hatred for Jesus, while the Aryan Pontius Pilate would gladly have let him go free. The Jews had been "the first and most cruel persecutors of the young Church."[76] These are some relevant examples of Catholic writing during the years 1933-39, all published in journals edited by priests or in books bearing the Church's *imprimatur*. A climate of opinion was being formed. Along the same lines, a principle function of theology has historically been to foster dissonance reduction where significant items of information can be perceived as inconsistent with established beliefs, values, and collectively sanctioned behavior. Theologians are the professionals responsible for dissonance reduction. The defamation of the Jews can be seen as at least partly motivated by the desire to handle potentially disconfirming items of information (the Jews as outsiders, Christians as a loving community, the stress on the Jews as the chosen people) by discrediting the source of Judaism, which was viewed by the Jews as a religion of history and not myth and so could be perceived by gentiles as threatening the values of Christianity.[77]

Given this general orientation, the Church retreated in the face of Nazi anti-Semitic legislation even where these ordinances touched upon such vital domains of ecclesiastical jurisdiction as the sacrament of matrimony. In 1934, for example, the Church had made clear to the regime that the enactment of a law forbidding "racially mixed" marriages (*Mischehe*) would create a very difficult situation. If two baptized persons of racially mixed stock insisted on being married by a priest, the latter would have to comply, even were the state to prohibit such a union.[78] The Nuremberg Laws of 1935 did prohibit racially mixed marriages. What could the Church do? In some instances priests circumvented the law by using a provision of the Concordat of 1933, which in cases of "great moral emergency" permitted a Church marriage without a preceding civil ceremony. By and large, however, the Church conformed to the law, agreeing to what had earlier been termed an unwarranted infringement on her spiritual jurisdiction. While Waldemar Gurian denounced the Nuremberg laws as violations of natural law and of the moral teachings of the Church and declared that they were only a stage on the way toward the complete physical destruction of the Jews, an article in the January 1936 *Klerusblatt* justified the new anti-Jewish statutes as indispensable safeguards for the qualitative makeup of the German people.[79]

Frequently, the bishops tried to protect non-Aryan Catholics, for whom the Church felt a special responsibility. In 1936 the Ministry of Ecclesiastical Affairs requested statistics about the number of Jews converted to the Church in the years 1900-35. Cardinal Bertram agreed to comply to this request.[80] But when the ministry later sought permission to consult the diocesan files on conversions and mixed marriages, the Church withheld consent "on grounds of pastoral secrecy." Similarly, in 1938, Bertram refused to open the diocesan archives to researchers working for a new state institute for the study of the Jewish question. As an institution, however, the Church extended neither aid nor sympathy to other than non-Aryan Catholics. Even during the *Kristallnacht* of November 1938, the bishops remained silent in the face of burning temples and the first roundup of the Jews.[81]

With the war in the Soviet Union, the possibilities for emigration finally became unrealistic. The Reich faced the unwelcome prospect of absorbing millions more unwanted and unexpellable Jews. All moral restraint could be abandoned in the Soviet Union, where the war with Jewish Bolshevism could be waged. On July 31, 1941, Heydrich was charged "with making all necessary preparation ... for bringing about a complete solution of the Jewish question in the German sphere of influence in Europe."[82] On September 1, 1941, all Jews and post-1935 converts were compelled to wear the yellow star. Only non-Aryans married to an Aryan partner were exempt from this order. Bertram's response was that the segregation of Catholic non-Aryans would violate Christian principles and so should be avoided as long as possible. Perhaps, he suggested, priests should advise Jewish Catholics to attend an early Mass whenever possible. If Aryan Catholics caused difficulties, he continued, special services might have to be offered.[83]

Mass deportations of German Jews toward the east began on October 15,

1941. Berning requested some amelioration for the Catholic non-Aryans. He was told that Christian non-Aryans would be evacuated only in exceptional cases. At least for the time being non-Aryans of mixed marriages would not be effected by these measures. If deported, Christian non-Aryans would participate in Polish liturgies. These promises made by the Gestapo to Berning were not honored. Wienken was asked to take up the matter of the lack of preferential treatment and by early November replied to the Bishop of Limburg that negotiations about the deportation of Catholic non-Aryans had been started at the highest levels.[84] The bishops were preoccupied solely with the pastoral care administered to Catholic non-Aryans.

In 1941 and 1942, the bishops were kept well-informed about the destruction of the Jews.[85] The response seemed to be an increased concentration on the *Mischlinge* (half-Jews, quarter-Jews) and non-Aryans married to Aryan Christians. The regime had determined that mixed marriages were to be dissolved and the Jewish partner deported to the east. On November 11, 1942, Bertram protested the planned compulsory divorce legislation. His intervention on behalf of the bishops, he insisted, was not due "to lack of love for the German nationality, lack of feeling of national dignity, and also not to underestimation of the harmful Jewish influences upon German culture and national interests." The bishops did want to stress that humane treatment also should be extended to those of other races. Respect for the religious rights of Catholic Christians was an indispensable condition for the peaceful cooperation of church and state, never more necessary than in the present condition. The bishops hoped, the letter ended, that the government would withdraw the planned divorce ordinance. In fact, the bishps did not have as much an effect in stopping compulsory divorce as 6,000 Aryan wives demonstrating in Berlin and howling for their non-Aryan husbands did.[86] An outraged conscience apparently could still achieve victory, even against Hitler's terror apparatus.

Ordinances continued to be applied to the *Mischlinge.* Bertram by 1944 could assert that these measures aimed "clearly at segregation at the end of which threatens extermination." He pointed out that any change in the meaning of the term Jew after the 1935 Nuremberg laws would seriously undermine confidence in the law. Ordinances segregating *Mischlinge* would seriously threaten the unity of the inner front, a danger to be avoided at all cost.[87] In his Christmas 1943 sermon and in March 1944, Archbishop Frings reiterated the words of his fellow bishops by emphasizing that it was wrong to kill innocents just because they belonged to another race.[88]

Ever since 1945, such pronouncements have been cited as proof that the bishops did publicly protest the extermination of the Jews. Possibly some

Catholics did think of the Jews when their spiritual leaders castigated the murder of those not of Aryan blood. But the word Jew did not cross the bishops' lips. The Nazi administrators of the Regensburg area, for example, reported in October 1943 that the joint pastoral letter castigating the killing of innocents had not had any lasting effect: "The population pays scant attention to such involved pronouncements burdened with stipulations."[89] The bishops and others did not mince words in the euthanasia controversy and had an effect. Their insipid protests focused on the Final Solution achieved no result. Close to half the population of the Greater German Reich (43.1 percent in 1939) was Catholic, and even in the SS, despite all the pressures to leave the Church, almost a fourth (22.7 percent on December 31, 1938),[90] belonged to the Catholic faith. The bishops had potential support, at least statistically, but Catholics were not mobilized against Hitler's racist policies. The machinery of extermination continued to function smoothly.

In sharp contrast to what happened in the countries of western Europe,[91] in Germany only a handful of Jews were hidden by the clergy or otherwise helped by them in these distressful circumstances. Generally only a few helped the persecuted; the large majority failed.[92] The deportations were not opposed. The reports of the *Regierungspräsidenten* (provincial administrators), generally candid, noted that the deportations had caused no adverse public reactions. From Ansbach in Bavaria comes one of the shortest: "Except for some suicides and attempted suicides, no trouble whatsoever was encountered."[93] The German Church was in the center of the maelstrom of the Third Reich and could have been more courageous, perhaps, had the vicar of Christ, Pius XII, exhibited more forthright leadership.

Ever since Hochhuth's play, *The Deputy*, the debate has swirled around the character and role of Pius XII.[94] Although Pius may not have made explicit references publicly to the horrors of the Final Solution for diplomatic or other reasons, there can be no doubt about his genuine humanitarian concern during the war. The fact that Pius wrote several German bishops asking them to speak for human rights irrespective of race or nationality would seem pertinent to any discussion of his policies. That some bishops in 1942-43 publicly opposed the killing of persons merely because of race was in part a consequence of papal influence. On June 2, 1943, in speaking to a group of cardinals, Pius expressed his sorrow for people suffering solely because of nationality or race, some even to the extent of "forceful methods of extermination."[95] Unfortunately, the Jews were never cited by name.[96] Reserve and prudence were the criteria of papal actions. Such a cautious approach could not coexist with humanitarian concern. To avoid offending Germany and to maintain a prudent reserve, the Vatican acted in ways that ignored the depth of suffering so widespread among Christians and Jews. Prudence rather than human-itarian concern betrayed the ideals of Christianity. Given this lack of lead-ership from Rome, the pressures from the regime and the traditional anti-Semitism in Germany itself, it is not surprising, albeit unfortunate, that the bishops were constrained from exercising a leadership role.

Since the Vatican documents, many now edited and published,[97] attest to the deep concern of the pope for all the oppressed, to his horror at the atrocities being committed, to his dilemma about the value of a public statement, and to his belief that he could do little to aid the persecuted, they do not support the charges of Hochhuth and others that Pius XII's silence was criminal. But since the Pope knew of the German determina-tion to annihilate the European Jews, it is difficult to avoid the conclusion that he had an obligation to speak candidly and decisively to the bishops in 1941, 1942, and 1943, and publicly to European Catholics in 1944, when substantial harm to Catholics was unlikely. Hochhuth's *Stellvertreter* as well as the real Pius XII faced a moral quandry that proved impossible for the prudent diplomat to resolve, but then a leader can only be as coura-geous as his followers.[98] Theologians themselves argued abstractly from a pro-*Volk* position, simultaneously putting forward the moderate anti-Sem-itic arguments that had become common currency among the Catholic hierarchy and theologians. Theirs was a latent, not blatantly radical anti-Semitism. Both the bishops and the theologians were intellectual anti-Semites. But what were the opinions of local priests and their con-gregations? In his popular sermons in the *Frauenkirche* in December 1936, the Jesuit Hermann Muckermann concluded that Christ's teaching was not Jewish in origin but, rather, opposed Jewry. He expressly maintained "the facts of heredity and race" and insisted that, at least in principle, the Church could support the eugenic and racial policies of the regime. He had already in the spring of 1936 in Bamberg described a "healthy racial stock" as "a lofty magnificent gift of heaven" and regarded it as a Christian duty to strengthen and multiply the home race (*Heimrasse*). Though not opposed to God's plan as such, he stated that combining the home race with alien races should be rejected.[99] Muckermann was concerned with theoretical racial and eugenic problems, not prepared to see the crucial issues at hand.

A few clergymen spoke out publicly on the "racial problem" from the Nazi perspective. A Catholic Redemptorist from Cham in 1939 praised the Nazi state, mentioned the Jewish Question, and portrayed Jews as the murderers of Christ. A Catholic priest from the Bamberg district in March 1939 offered such a pro-Nazi sermon that about thirty people left the Church in protest. He called out as they went: "Let them go, they're nothing but Jew-servers."[100] But Nazi racial views as such were rare among the parish clergy. Although not preaching racial hatred, however, some priests did reveal a racist attitude and a basic acknowledgement that there existed a racial problem. Frequently, Catholic clergy opposed the racial policy of the regime and occasionally even sided openly with the persecuted Jews. Allegedly, a speaker in Bamberg declared in a sermon: "For God there are no *völkisch* matters and no national laws. . . . For him there are no racial differences."[101] A Catholic priest in Neustadt an der Saale in October 1934 condemned human hatred and a lack of charity with respect to anti-Jewish actions and repudiated anti-Jewish songs in the *Hitlerjugend* since these produced hatred towards the Jews and implanted prejudice in young people.[102] One Catholic priest in the district of Neustadt an der Aisch in Middle Franconia was presented a summons in the summer of 1940 for allegedly saying in his sermon that "the Jews should not be cast out since they too are human beings."[103] Following the "Crystal Night" of 1938 a priest in Neumarkt in der Oberpfalz compared those who smashed Jewish windows with the purest Bolsheviks.[104] Disorder, not necessarily anti-Semitism, was to be condemned.

In Bavaria the attitudes of the clergy toward the Jews suggest division on the "race question." Some clergy approved the exclusion of Jews from German society. Most rejected the Nazi dogma of hate toward a particular part of mankind. Still, latent anti-Semitic feelings were expressed. A number of government reports show, for example, that local clergy did not condemn the discrimination itself, but rather the deplorable excesses of the Jewish persecution. In the final analysis, the evidence illustrates that the overwhelming majority of priests and pastors, modeling their superiors, made no public comments and silently watched the persecutions.[105]

A variety of reasons can be offered to explain the surprising lack of response. Clearly the vulnerable position of the priests in the Third Reich, the power of the police state, and the generally pervasive atmosphere of fear and repression explain a great deal. Defense of the Church itself had a high priority, but the Jewish Question, in the opinion of Church leaders a political matter, was scrupulously avoided after 1933. Moreover, the Jewish Question did not seem to be regarded by the clergy as a central theme to be addressed. The parish priest could generally count on the popular support of his flock in response to Nazi interference in local Church affairs as well as on full support from his superiors. In the Jewish Question, however, the clergy encountered primarily indifference or at the most abstract and latent anti-Semitism.[106] In Munich, for example, the police interpreted the considerable success of the annual sales at Jewish department stores as a sign that many women still "had not understood, nor want[ed] to understand, the lines laid down by the Führer for solving the Jewish Question."[107] Such complaints were common throughout Germany in these years before the war.[108] Intimidation, however, also helped reinforce the anti-Semitic ideology. Merchants saw a chance to ruin rivals by reporting their Jewish background to communities normally deaf to a racial consciousness.[109] Businessmen greedy for money, intellectuals mired in anti-Semitic traditions, all combined to negate any effort to oppose Nazi racism vigorously. For the peasants, economic self-interest, revealed in comments to the effect that Jewish animal traders offered better deals, helps explain the unwillingness of rural Catholics to accept Nazi racial dogma. In the Jewish Question the clergy tended to follow and reflect rather than mold popular opinion. Priests certainly rejected Nazi inhumanities, but living in a historical as well as socioeconomical climate hostile to the Jews, they mirrored the anti-Semitism and indifference of their fellow Germans. Blatant, idological hatred of the Jews was absent in both the clergy and the laity. Certainly Christian precepts of humanity were present as well as the widespread opposition to the Nazi party for its assault on the Church, which resulted for some in a rejection of some Nazi values. In the final analysis latent anti-Semitism could coexist with traditional Catholic religious precepts.

The hierarchy, theologians, and parish priests did little to construct antiracist attitudes. The ambivalent attitude of the Church toward race, however, allowed the retention of anti-Semitic views by the faithful. In essence, Jews were not to be hated, but they did not necessarily have to be loved.[110] Nazi paganism was rooted in racial inequality, which should have been seen as diametrically opposed to God's commandments and the expressed values of the Catholic Church. Defending themselves against Nazism, Catholics should have rejected racism. In the real world of the Third Reich, however, the Church saw the ideological contest mainly as a struggle for the faithful in a religious sense exclusively and as a defense of Church institutions. The real racial issue as a question of human values was touched upon only tangentially. Voices of protest were not significant in the "Church struggle," nor did they find support from the hierarchy. The Jewish Question was basically a matter of indifference to the clergy as well as to most Catholic parishoners.[111] As Kershaw has recently noted in his study of Bavaria, popular opinion was largely neutral to the fate of the Jews but infused with a populistic anti-Jewish feeling, consistently reinforced by Nazi propaganda.[112] Such a condition provided the environment within which Nazi legal and then murderous assaults on the Jews could take place unchallenged, especially as the war began to take its physical and psychological toll on Germans. With respect to the Church, Nazi racial policies based on universal hatred were ignored, and Catholics seemed indifferent toward the larger human issues.

Public opinion followed by the forceful reaction of the Catholic Church were the key factors in Hitler's decision to abandon the euthanasia program. The episcopal public protests helped form and consolidate public opinion and contributed to the general feeling of outrage that eventually led the führer to suspend the domestic euthanasia program. Here is an example of the strength, power, and influence of public opinion in Hitler's totalitarian state, occurring at a time when Hitler stood at the zenith of his military success. Had German public opinion responded similarly against such other crimes as the Final Solution, the results might well have been similar. Euthanasia and the Final Solution were concrete manifestations of Nazi ideology and became gradually institutionalized after 1933.[113] Euthanasia in Germany was protested; the Final Solution in the East received little vehement or meaningful opposition.

The majority of people who had been outraged over the euthanasia issue, because it touched their friends and relatives, failed to react sufficiently when their Jewish neighbors were exposed to discrimination, ghettoization, deportation, and execution. The disaster befalling the Jews, the culmination of years of anti-Semitic propaganda, did not stimulate similar humane feelings.[114] That German public opinion and the Church were a force to be reckoned with in principle and could have played a more positive role in averting the Jewish disaster as well is a lesson to be derived from the failure of Hitler's euthanasia efforts. But the power of the Church and public opinion should not be overestimated, since sterilization and euthanasia were merely components of the Nazis' intricate eugenic policy, almost unbelievable in magnitude until the war was well underway. Rumors of extermination camps were probably circulated among many Germans, for most of whom the Jewish Question was hardly a topic of concern.[115] By 1941 the Final Solution along with *Lebensraum* as the twin goals of the regime were being implemented. Success in war and the Final Solution would free Hitler to wreak vengeance on the Church, one of the few institutions not yet fully "coordinated." Nazi eugenic policies led from sterilization to the death camps in a consistent ideological progression, although the bureaucratic procedures differed.[116] In the final analysis, the dynamic hatred of the masses proved unnecessary. Latent anti-Semitism, reinforced by and combined with compromises over the sterilization issue and concern only over fellow Germans in the euthanasia controversy, as well as apathy toward such issues before and during the war, allowed the criminal and dynamic Nazi hatred to result in the Holocaust.

Latent Anti-Semitism and the Final Solution

There are two basic philosophical positions that are equally important in the examination of the social and ethico-religious issues of the Third

Reich. These philosophies—utilitarianism and formalism—represent extreme polarities in terms of viewpoints regarding the rights and worth of individuals in society. A utilitarian philosophy holds that an individual has only those rights granted to him by the larger society. Formalism as a system of values, however, maintains that the individual has basic rights that can be neither abrogated nor curtailed by society. The individual's rights are superordinate to those of society. Neither of these two extremes is workable in pure form in a complex society. Somewhere between the two extremes is the optimum position never achieved in Hitler's Germany.[117] Rarely has formalism been achieved in the twentieth century. Such an analysis as that of Horowitz,[118] however, would argue that the goal of society is to achieve the maximum individual liberty. The struggle to achieve this goal would probably result in the discovery of the so-called optimum position and safeguard the person from the state with its overwhelming power. In this context, Pius XII, for example, insisted on the rights of all individuals to be protected from the advancing pretensions of state power. Some argue as well that bureaucracy had originally been developed to protect individual rights, but as seen in Nazi Germany it can just as easily be maintained that it was the key to destroying that same liberty by creating an insider-outsider condition. In the milieu of the Third Reich, deviance was not merely an instance of behavior defined as a breach of the social order but was also applied to a category of persons, viewed as somehow less than fully human, less than normal, not up to normal human capabilities or dispositions. According to Nazi eugenic policies, the dominant social group was to define deviance by making the rules whose infraction constituted deviance, and by applying those rules to a particular people, thereby labeling them as outsiders. From this point of view, deviance was viewed not as a quality of a person's action, but rather as a consequence of the application by others of rules and sanctions to the "offender" group. The deviant became the one to whom the label could be successfully applied; deviant behavior can be seen, then, as the behavior that people so label and was found useful in reinforcing centralized control in the modern state.[119]

Eugenics and anti-Semitism, culminating in genocide as public policy, appears directly connected to the maintenance of the nation-state, but the Holocaust was a specifically German phenomenon. The Nazis defined the Jews as nonhuman, identified "misfits" who should be expunged from the Aryan race, and proceeded in their highly industrialized state to liquidate nearly entire groups. The features relevant to the German case were an intense focus on the political and social significance of eugenics, an extended history of anti-Semitism, and an extremely stressful situation during the Weimar years, resulting in overt political aggression coupled with a documented virulent prejudice and, finally, the metamorphosis of a state founded on legally defined rights and duties into a state based on Hitler's will.[120]

Initially, Catholics opposed the NSDAP as a radical and vulgar party, but not necessarily hold the same view toward the full Nazi political and ideological stance. As both Guenter Lewy and Gordon Zahn have asserted, Catholics were subject to such normal social controls as obedience to the state and were susceptible to such values as *Volk* and *Vaterland*.[121] A Catholic could feel that he or she was ultimately supporting Germany, and only temporarily Hitler, thereby allowing adherence to the law while objecting to specific applications of it. In the process, faced with extraordinary evil, the Church erred by compromising its moral essence when it focused on "reasons of state."[122] Over the years, then, political, sociological, theological, and historical reasons have been offered for the behavior of Catholics in the Third Reich.

Equally significant, however, is the psychological undergirding of those Catholic value and behavior patterns, which had historically developed. Since the *Kulturkampf* in Germany, Catholics had consistently struggled to prove that they were not second-class citizens, but were good, loyal, and obedient Germans. Catholics saw themselves as loyal Germans, and so bishops as well as some theologians felt they had to permit moral compromises on the sterilization issue, limited discussion with the government on euthanasia, and only felt strong enough to condemn the latter as their flock protested and felt threatened. Likewise, anti-Semitism since 1871 had served as a vehicle bearing Catholic patriotic values. Naturally the anti-Semitism of theologians and bishops was not identical with that of the radical Nazis. Many could assume, however, that Catholics were just in a different position on the anti-Semitic spectrum, just as all Nazis were not Himmlers. Anti-Semitism helped support patriotic credentials. By the time Church leaders realized that Nazi racism was not a gentle cleansing of the body politic, they were at war and could not attack the Nazi hierarchy without appearing unpatriotic to their flock and reversing previous stances.

Leon Festinger's cognitive dissonance theory assumes that people cannot tolerate cognitive inconsistency and will work to eliminate it or reduce it whenever it exists. Cognitive systems tend toward a state of harmony, balance, and consistency. How could Catholics valuing love, peace, and brotherhood be anti-Semitic and accept portions of the eugenic program? Zimbardo suggests that these opposite sides of human nature can be explained by deindividuation, a complex process in which a series of social conditions leads to changes in perception of self and of other people. The individual does not monitor his or her own behavior and becomes less concerned about evaluation by others. Consequently, there is a weakening of the controls on behavior based upon guilt, shame, fear, and commitment. Thus, behavior that is normally restrained and inhibited is "released" in violation of the established norms of appropriateness. Such behaviors in some contexts may be characterized as selfish, greedy, or hostile. But people may be more willing to engage in antisocial acts if they do not feel personally responsible for the consequences. This sense of diffused responsibility can result from sharing it with others, turning it over to some higher authority, or being unable to see the relationship between an action and its consequences. The presence of a group not only promotes anonymity and diffused responsibility but can provide the necessary models by triggering behavior in a given direction or toward a given object. In general, people will try to become anonymous in a threatening environment and will not individuate themselves.[123]

Also operating in the Nazi environment was the process of dehumanization, the psychological erasure of human qualities. In this context people are treated as objects rather than as complete human beings. Dehumanization may be: (1) imposed socially, (2) imposed in self-defense, (3) imposed deliberately for self-gratification, (4) rationalized as the necessary means toward a noble end, or (5) effected by a combination of the above. One technique that seemed useful in Nazi Germany was relabeling. Employment of pejorative labels used to describe people is one way of making them appear more objectlike and less human. Jews were, for example, "Christ-killers" and therefore unworthy of normal love just as the devil was not worthy of love.[124] Cognitive dissonance and dehumanization theories suggest that, reinforced by secular political figures, Catholics as loyal Germans may well have seen little reason to stress their "good" Christian attitudes and behavior until it was too late, and even then they did so mildly. Their statements directed toward Nazi atrocities were general and gave solace to the enemy. During the war, the bishops usually responded to atrocity reports that the duty of humane treatment also existed toward the members of other races.[125]

The cover organizations and secret authorizations concerned with the euthanasia action were deliberately constructed as instruments outside the law and actually functioned through bypassing the state authorities set up by the Nazi government itself. Even the legally regulated process of sterilization and termination of pregnancy afforded a great deal of latitude of judgment for official doctors and the courts concerned with healthy stock. Because of grave consequences the government had removed these "laws" a long way from moral principles and the protection of law. Thus, Nazi legislation itself had helped pave the way for lawlessness. The collapse of administrative and departmental cohesion, the use of plenipotentiaries and offices directly subordinate to Hitler, and the earlier general devaluation of the legislative processes through the führer authorizations all con-stituted the essential preconditions of the euthanasia action. The fact that the policy had to be abandoned in 1941 because of complaints from the public, the judiciary, such ministers as Gürtner and Lammers, who insisted to Hitler on a legal ruling, and the bishops can be seen as proof of the fact that constitutional developments in the *Führerstaat* had not yet evolved to such an extent that friction could be prevented. Even in 1941 Hitler's authority clashed with the bureaucracy, generated conflict, and opposed the remaining legal restraints of the old Reich. To resolve the conundrum, of course, the eugenic policies were implemented in the more remote east-ern conquests administered by Himmler.[126]

From hindsight it seems that extraordinary evil can be prevented only by a careful analysis of ordinary, seemingly minor, moral compromises as well as by a constant questioning of the validity of attitudinal consistency in a historically changing milieu. Nazi eugenic policies suggest that racial puri-fication and the Holocaust itself may well be partially rooted in the psycho-logical human need for cognitive stability. To counter this need required a courage and imagination that Church leaders did not have, unless pushed forward by their flock. In essence, Catholic leaders sacrificed a complete commitment to their moral value system by consistently adhering to Ger-man patriotic norms, reasons of state, and their historical experiences, thereby sacrificing the meaning of their legitimate Christian roots. The lack of reaction was made easier as the eugenic policies were transferred from Germany to the east. The Christian system of ethics emphasizes charity and brotherly love. But a variety of activating conditions may be present that will move people not to help others. People may decide that the need for active help is low, particularly if full knowledge of the extent and direc-tion of Nazi policies, for example, had not been realized. Little response may be elicited if the person in need does not seem to deserve help. After 1939 the concerns of most Germans were so focused on the war that Nazi eugenic policies may not have seemed of crucial importance unless, as in the case of euthanasia, they hit home. Moreover, frequently the high cost of helping leads to inactivity. Cost can be measured in terms of time, effort, risk of safety, sacrifice of one's goals, or the possibility of appearing foolish.[127]

Psychological research indicates that only under specific conditions do people feel responsible for helping others. When many other people are present, however, the feeling of responsibility gets diffused. A person alone also feels less responsible to act. To offer assistance in an emergency a number of steps must be followed. First, one must notice that something is happening. Second, one has to interpret the event. Third, if one perceives the activity and interprets it as an emergency, then one must assume responsibility for providing help. Fourth, the individual must then decide what to do. Finally, the observer must actually carry out the action decided on.[128] Germans found opposition to Nazi eugenics difficult, since the regime propagated values and norms that depersonalized and dehumanized Jews, who became increasingly isolated in German society after 1933, as well as other groups and made their suffering not only a matter of indifference or acceptable, but even something desirable from a variety of motives. Economically some Germans, for example, profited from the elimination of their Jewish competitors. This approach to the "Jewish outsider" became a dominant motive for the responses of some. Not only do such motives result in mistreatment, but, over time, the student of the Nazi phenomenon can perceive a progressive decrease in the likelihood of empathetic feelings toward the Jews in this type of environment.[129] Naturally antagonism toward Jews per se did not automatically lead to the Final Solution, but when other factors were present, for example, war, a long-standing anti-Semitic tradition, and eugenics as a respected science, tragedy became more likely.

A complex dynamic was present as the Final Solution unfolded. People generally find the suffering of innocent people—those who have done nothing to bring about their own suffering—unacceptable. But observers can reason that if innocent people can suffer, they themselves can suffer without cause. To defend themselves from this possibility they have to engage in a defensive psychological act; if they cannot attribute the cause of others' suffering to their actions, they must then attribute it to their character. Thus, the innocent victims will be negatively evaluated, devalued, so that the observers' belief in a just world can be maintained. If people bring about suffering by their own actions or character, an appropriate fit exists and belief in a just world can be maintained. In this case, devaluation of the person may seem to be necessary. If members of a group suffer without having acted badly or stupidly, then it might be that such individuals are undesirable as persons; they are being treated equitably.[130] The diffusion of responsibility, seen in the Nazi and Church bureaucracy, can also lead to less adherence to valued social conduct. It seems to contribute to a condition of deindividuation that can serve to diminish a sense of personal responsibility for the welfare of other human beings. If other people can suffer innocently, therefore, the observer can suffer innocently, and so the victims must be devalued to make their suffering more deserved. A victim's membership in groups that are subject to prejudice may also make devaluation easier. In fact, seeing others suffer could certainly make the observer suffer, but could also lead to dislike of the victim.[131]

Theoretically, official Catholic doctrine on racial hygiene and the sanctity of the person diametrically opposed the National Socialist

Weltanschauung. But by compromises as Catholics reacted to sterilization, by delaying their wholesale condemnation of euthanasia, by adhering to historical anti-Semitism, and by defending Jewish converts to the faith and not Jews as persons, Catholics did participate in softening up the consciences of the nation for radical racial policies. Catholics may have originally adhered to and consistently supported German anti-Semitism to the degree they did because, at least psychologically, there is a tendency for those least accepted by the group to be the most conformist. Generally, however, Catholics did not identify with racial anti-Semitism, but rather with the religious and socioeconomic perspectives that supported racism. After 1933, Carl Schmitt, a leading Catholic jurist, for example, began inserting anti-Semitic remarks into his publications. But although he mentioned such terms as race and blood, he never succumbed to a belief in the biological racism of National Socialist ideology.[132] Limited decisions and daily actions, however, do add up. The "Catholic conscience" did not develop in some ideal or rarified atmosphere. Whereas Kohlberg, for example, may well locate the problem of obedience in the stages of individual moral development, one can hear in Milgram the much more familiar march of politics. Milgram's work on the obedience of individuals to a designated authority rightly focuses on how the surrounding social structure distributes such opportunities that support or inhibit moral reasoning and the subsequent moral advance of society itself. Justice, then, seems less a reflection of the developmental psychology of the individual than the social psychology of the group.[133]

Human behavior, according to Staats, gains its complexity through building up more and more constellations of behavior patterns. When the individual's array of constellations has reached a certain complexity, composed of repertoires that have been permanently learned and thereby providing continuity, such contellations of behaviors are usually labeled as aspects of personality. Germans had matured in an anti-Semitic and nationalistic milieu, one resulting not surprisingly in behavior patterns that were racist and hyperpatriotic. As a result, Nazi aggressive eugenic policies were accepted or were only opposed when the policies touched specific individuals residing in communities supportive of their members' rights. Under such conditions, euthanasia could be opposed; anti-Semitism was either ignored or accepted. Aggressive anti-Semitic behaviors had been reinforced by language and by adherence to such terms as *Volk* and *Gemeinschaft*. Aggression is not a single behavioral action but is rooted in such a complex repertoire. It has been found, for example, that individuals can be conditioned to either positive or negative attitudes toward ethnic or national names, depending on the direction of language conditioning. Since individuals learn negative attitudes, a person identified with a "negative" group will elicit negative attitudes that can result in aggressive behavior. The acceptance of negative attitudes virtually invited either passive or active aggressive action. The conditions in a society, supporting a system of preferences, help determine the behavior of the members of that society as they make social and political decisions. With their specific nationalistic interests, Germans had historically developed specific ethnocentric preferences, which had been rewarded through the unification and the development of Germany into a dominant power. Within such a context Germans made political decisions. In the Third Reich, Hitler wielded governmental power and could force decisions from Berlin but was ultimately only successful in his racial policies only because Germans were unwilling to view Nazi racism as the beginning of the destruction of the rights of all persons within the state. The resources of the Catholic Church, which could have been used to influence others, were restricted by the adherence of the clergy to nationalistic values and by their inability to perceive that "normal" anti-Semitism was the first step toward the Final Solution.

Notes

1. Blackbourn, "Roman Catholics, the Centre Party, and Anti-Semitism in Imperial Germany," in Kennedy and Nicholls (eds.), pp. 106-129; Uriel Tal, *Christians and Jews in Germany*; Werner Mosse (ed.), *Entscheidungsjahr 1932*.
2. Glock and Stark, *Christian Beliefs and Anti-Semitism*, p. ix; Hans Küng, *The Council: Reform and Reunion*, trans. Cecily Hastings (New York: Sheed and Ward, 1961), pp. 21-22.
3. Schneider et al., *Person Perception*, pp. 42, 63; F. Heider, *The Psychology of Interpersonal Relations*; K. Davis and E. Jones, "Changes in Interpersonal Perception as a Means of Reducing Cognitive Dissonance," pp. 402-410; Kelley, "The Process of Causal Attribution," pp. 107-128.
4. Ehrlich, *The Social Psychology of Prejudice*, pp. 160ff.
5. Pulzer, *The Rise of Political Anti-Semitism*; Kelley, *The Descent of Darwin*.
6. Adolf Jost, *Das Recht auf den Tod* (Göttingen: Dieterich 'sche Verlagsbuchhandlung, 1895).
7. Loren Graham, "Science and Values: The Eugenics Movement in Germany and Russia in the 1920s," *American Historical Review* 82 (1977):1134. For an outstanding survey of pre-1933 German works and the National Socialist literature on virtually every aspect of racial eugenics, see Klaus Dörner, "Nationalsozialismus und Lebensvernichtung," *Vierteljahrshefte für Zeitgeschichte* 15 (1967):121-152. For a recent analysis of euthanasia in the Third Reich, see Ernst Klee, '*Euthanasie' im NS-Staat. Die 'Vernichtung Lebensunwerten Lebens'* (Frankfurt: S. Fischer, 1983). Klee has presented how the mass murder of the mentally ill was interwoven into the tawdry history of the Third Reich.
8. Karl Bindung und Alfred Hoche, *Die Freigabe der Vernichtung lebensunwerten Lebens, Ihr Mass und Ihre Form* (Leipzig: E. Strache, 1920). See also E.

Meltzer, *Das Problem der Freigabe der Vernichtung lebensunwerten Lebens* (Weimar: Marhold, 1925), Ernest Gellner, *Legitimation of Belief* (London: Cambridge University Press, 1974), chap. 8.

9. For a well-documented, although somewhat biased, perhaps because of its East German orientation, presentation of the sterilization issues before and after 1933, see Kurt Nowak, *Euthanasie und Sterilisierung im Dritten Reich Die Konfrontation der Evangelischen und Katholischen Kirche mit dem "Gesetz zur Verhütung erbkranken Nachwuchses" und der "Euthanasie"—Aktion* (Göttingen: Vandenhoeck & Ruprecht, 1978). Nowak has carefully analyzed the contributions made to the ongoing debate by jurists, medical doctors, and theologians. His development of the pre-1933 Catholic position, however, is decidedly one-sided, since he never cites the works of Franz Hürth (see below) and his debate with Joseph Mayer.

10. For the most recent official Catholic position on euthanasia, see *Declaration on Euthanasia*, issued by the *Sacred Congregation for the Doctrine of the Faith*, pub. no. 704, United States Catholic Conference.

11. Paula E. Hyman, "The History of European Jewry: Recent Trends in the Literature," *Journal of Modern History* 54 (1982):303-319. The literature on anti-Semitism in Germany is massive. Some coherent scholarly accounts of the intricacies involved in creating such an attitudinal dimension may be found in Pulzer, *Political Anti-Semitism*, and Katz, *From Prejudice to Destruction*. Anti-Semitism, of course, was hardly peculiar to Germany. See Martin Blumenson (ed.), *The Patton Papers: 1940-1945* (Boston: Houghton Mifflin, 1974), p. 751; on September 17, 1945, Patton made the following comment on displaced persons in his Bavarian zone of command: "[Earl G.] Harrison [State Department] and his ilk believe that the Displaced Person is a human being, which he is not, and this applies particularly to the Jews who are lower than animals."

12. *Völkischer Beobachter*, no. 131, August 7, 1929. The evolution and institutionalization of the Nazi eugenics policy can be seen in Larry V. Thompson, "*Lebensborn* and the Eugenics Policy of the *Reichsführer-SS*," *Central European History* 4 (1971):54-77.

13. Horowitz also convincingly argues that to raise the issue of "personality," the key to this entire issue, is to present the case for the restoration of individualism on a new basis Irving Louis Horowitz, *Taking Lives: Genocide and State Power* (New Brunswick, NJ: Transaction Books, 1980).

14. Albert Niedermeyer, *Handbuch der speziallen Pastoralmedizin*, vol. 4 (Vienna: Verlag Herder, 1949-52), p.222; K. Just, *Eugenik und Weltanschauung* (Berlin: Deicert, 1932).

15. Robert Graham, "The 'Right to Kill' in the Third Reich. Prelude to Genocide," *The Catholic Historical Review* 62 (1976):56-76. In volumes 4 and 6 Niedermeyer has presented a thorough review of the literature covering the debates and opinions on sterilization, abortion, and euthanasia in Weimar and Nazi Germany. Before *Casti Connubi*, for example, the well-known Catholic priest-eugenicist at the Kaiser Wilhelm Institute, Professor Hermann Muckermann, supported sterilization legislation (Herman Muckermann, *Rassenforschung und Volk der Zukunft. Ein Beitrag zur Einführung in die Frage vom biologischen Werden der Menschheit* (Berlin: A Metzner, 1932).

16. Joseph Mayer, *Gesetzliche Unfruchtbarmachung Geisteskranker* (Freiburg: Herder, 1927), pp. 113, 121, 124-25, 128, 352, 373-86, 422, 434 Mayer was already attacking Hürth's position (see p. 352 in Mayer, *Gesetzliche*).

17. After Mayer's 1927 work, the parameters of the debate may be seen in the following: Franz Hürth, "Die 'aequalitas institutiae in ihrer Beziehung zur 'aequivalentia obiectorum' bei strengen Rechtsverbindlichkeiten," *Scholastik* 3(1928):481-505; Joseph Mayer, "Sexualprobleme zur Strafrechtsreform," *Theologie und Glaube* 21 (1929):137-162; Franz Hürth, "Zur Frage des Tötungsrechtes aus Notstand," *Scholastik* 4(1929):534-560. The 1927 Mayer book was later cited in a bibliography of the "most important writings on the subject," in an analysis of the 1933 sterilization legislation, published by four Nazi doctors, Franz Rüdin et al. (eds.), *Zur Verhütung erbkranken Nach-wuchses-Gesetz und Erläuterung* (Munich: F. Eher, 1934).

18. As late as 1933 Mayer was still pleading for support of sterilization legislation. See Joseph Mayer, "Zum Gesetz gegen erbkranken Nachwuchs," *Germania*, no. 221, August 13, 1933; and the warning of Leiber to Pacelli, cited in Volk, *Das Reichskonkordat*, p. 248.

19. Martin Broszat, *The Hitler State*, p. 284ff.; Allan Chase, *The Legacy of Malthus* (New York: Knopf, 1977), p. 349; *Reichsgesetzblatt* 1 (1933): 529-531.

20. For a variety of quotes that consistently oppose euthanasia from Faulhaber in 1934 to Bertram in 1943, see Friedrich Stöffler, "Die 'Euthanasie' und die Haltung der Bischöfe im Hessischen Raum 1940-1945," *Archiv für Mittelrheinische Kirchengeschichte*, 13 (1961):321-323; see also Herman Berg (ed.), *Albert Stohr, Gottes Ordnung in der Welt* (Mainz: Matthias Grünewald, 1960), pp. 25-28, 59; *Protokoll der Verhandlungen der Plenar-Konferenz der deutschen Bischöfe vom 29 bis 31 August 1933*, p. 12.

21. Bertram in Lewy, p. 259. See Niedermayer, vol. 4, p. 280 for Hürth's *Gutachten* submitted to Bertram; Mayer's opinions at this point can also be found in Joseph Mayer, "Zum Gesetz gegen erbkranken Nachwuchs," *Germania*, no. 221, August 13, 1933; Joseph Mayer, "Vorschläge für ein eugenisches Aufbauprogram," *Schönere Zukunft* May 21, 1933:814-815; May 28, 1933:837-839; Leiber in Volk, *Das Reichskonkordat*, p. 248.

22. Lewy, pp. 259-260; Corsten, pp. 17-18.

23. Bertram to the German bishops, in Lewy, p. 261.

24. *Münchener Katholische Kirchenzeitung*, no. 49, December 2, 1934, p. 714; *Ecclesiastica* 14 (1934):345-46. Both Barion and Eschweiler had joined the Nazi party in May 1933 and have files in the Berlin Document Center; Leiber to Pacelli in Volk, *Reichskonkordat*, August 17, 1933, p. 247; *Sterilisierung und Seelsorge* (Beuron, 1935), in Lewy, pp. 261-262.

25. Otto Schilling, "Richtiges und Falsches bei der sog. Eugenik," *Schönere Zukunft* 7 (1932):570-572, 597-598.

26. Karl Frank, "Zur Eugenik," *Stimmen der Zeit* 128 (1935):316-324.

27. Alexander Mitscherlich and Fred Mielke, *Doctors of Infamy* (New York: Henry Schuman, 1949), p. 91.

28. Karl Franke, "Rassenkunde und Rassengeschichte der Menschheit," *Stimmen der Zeit* p. 127 (1934):110; Franz Walther, *Die Euthanasie und die Heiligkeit des Lebens. Die Lebensvernichtung im Dienste der Medizin und Eugenik nach christlichen und materialistischer Ethik* (Munich: Kaiser, 1935), p. 22; Nowak, p. 128.

29. Lewy, p. 262; Norman St. John-Stenas, *Life, Death and the Law* (Bloomington, IN: Indiana University Press, 1961), p. 174; Niedermeyer, vol. 4, p.265.

30. *Protokoll der Verhandlungen der Plenar-Konferenz der deutschen Bischöfe in*

Fulda am 5, 6 und 7 Juni 1934, p. 6. Expert opinion of Professor Wehr, Trier, December 4, 1935, DA Trier, 59/23, Lewy, p. 262. For an extensive treatment of the distinctions between material and formal cooperation as well as the other moral precepts that could be applied by pastors in handling the sterilization issue, see Niedermeyer, vol. 4, pp.288ff.

31. Schleunes, *The Twisted Road to Auschwitz: Nazi Policy Toward the Jews, 1933-1939* (Urbana: University of Illinois Press, 1970).

32. Max Domarus, *Hitler. Reden und Proklamationen, 1932-45*, vol. 2 (Munich: Süddeutscher Verlag, 1965), pp. 2, 1058.

33. Nowak, pp. 64ff, 87ff. For a discussion of the euthanasia categories used by the Nazis, see Helmut Ehrhardt, *Euthanasie und Vernichtung "lebensunwerten" Lebens* (Stuttgart: Ferdinanrd Enke Verlag, 1965), p. 43. Ehrhardt also offers a succinct analysis of the medical, historical, and psychological roots of euthanasia as well as a careful analytical treatment of Nazi policy.

34. A trenchant exposition of the plight of lawyers has been provided by Lothar Gruchmann's "Euthanasie und Justiz im Dritten Reich," *Vierteljahrshefte für Zeitgeschichte* 20 (1972):235-279. The article exposes the operations of both Gürtner and Lammers as they tried to handle legally Hitler's oral order, which in reality had the force of law. The legal problems were certainly exposed when Nazi lawyers wanted to respond to Galen and his sermons. How does a government ministry, for example, prosecute a person for breaking an unpublished law? By keeping his order secret, Hitler made it difficult to restrict opponents of the regime. But to publicize the order would mobilize public opinion against the government.

35. Graham, "Right to Kill," p. 57; Werner Catel, *Grenzsituationen des Lebens. Beitrag zum Problem einer begrenzten Euthanasie* (Nürnberg: Glock und Lutz, 1962). There is probably no way in which to achieve limited euthanasia, (see Mitcherlich, *Medicine*, p. 98). The opposition of the Catholic Church is recounted in Nowak, pp. 158-177. The focus of the program was on eliminating those who were diseased as well as ultimately those who were socially unfit. Even under the pressure mobilized by the state, however, a majority of the German doctors during this period repudiated the entire concept of the elimination of the *lebensunwerten Leben* (see Georg Zillig, "Über Euthanasie," *Hochland* 42 :351).

36. *Acta Apostolica Sedis* 31 (1939):466, par. 48. United States vs. Karl Brandt et al., Nuremburg Trials, transcript, vol. 7a, p. 2413, in Graham, "Right to Kill," p. 60.

37. *Nazi Conspiracy and Aggression* (Washington, DC, 1947), suppl. A, pp. 1218-1225.

38. Stöffler, p. 317.

39. Neuhäusler, vol.2, pp. 357-359.

40. Ibid., pp. 359-363.

41. *Actes et documentesdu* 2:102-103.

42. Ibid., pp. 208-209.

43. National Archives, Washington, DC, T 175/409/293 z 690-92.

44. The letter (July 16, 1941) was considered too weak by many of the bishops and too strong by the minister for church affairs, Hans Kerrl, who on August 4, 1941, rejected it. See *Actes et Documentes* 2:224. See also Ludwig Volk, "Die Fuldaer Bischofskonferenz von der Enzyklika Mit Brennender Sorge bis zum Ende der NS-Herrschaft," *Stimmen der Zeit* 178 (1966):241-267.

45. Heinrich Portmann (ed.), *Bischof Graf von Galen Spricht: Ein Apostolischer Kampf und Sein Widerhall* (Freiburg: Herder, 1946), pp. 66-76; *Actes et Documentes* 2:230, 308.
46. Gitta Sereny, *Into that Darkness: From Mercy Killing to Mass Murder* (New York: McGraw-Hill, 1974), p. 295. Sereny offers the purported opinions of the now dead Burkhart Schneider, S.J., one of the editors of the materials of Pius XII. If made, Schneider's comment is unfounded, at least with respect to content. Martin Höllen, "Katholische Kirche und NS-'Euthanasie,' Eine vergleichende Analyse neuer Quellen," *Zeitschrift für Kirchengeschichte* 91 (1980):81. Nowak, pp. 163, 169.
47. *Nazi Conspiracy and Aggression* 3:449-451; Stöffler, pp. 325, 342ff.; Neuhäusler, *Kreuz*, vol. 2, pp.371-373; *Actes et Documentes*, 2:253.
48. Konrad Hofmann, *Zeugnis und Kampfe des deutschen Episkopats. Gemeinsame Hirtenbriefe und Denkschreiben* (Freiburg: Herder, 1946), p. 72. The letter was repeated in a variety of sermons during early 1942 (See Corsten, pp. 260-77, and Neuhäusler, *Kreuz*, vol. 2, p. 373).
49. Neuhäusler, *Kreuz*, vol. 3, pp.373ff.
50. Graham, "Right to Kill," pp. 72-73.
51. *Süddeutsche Zeitung*, February 15, 1967. In an interrogation (National Archives, Rg 238, 106, C1-11R/S3, C1-FIR/123) Hartl states that the memo was commissioned in 1940, but he allegedly had a poor memory for dates; see pp. 25, 42 in the interrogation testimony.
52. An Erich Warmund did issue a memo, *Euthanasie im Lichte der katholischen Moral und Praxis* (Vienna, 1940). The work appears to be the "lost" memo of Josef Mayer, issued, not surprisingly, under a pseudonym. The textual content matches the brief summary of the *Gutachten*, given in 1949 by Albert Hartl (*National Archives*, RG 238, Records of the National Archives, Collection of World War II War Crimes, Cl-PlR/106, Cl-llR/S3, Cl-FIR/123). No records of Erich Warmund can be located at the Berlin Document Center, where they most likely would be stored, as indicated in a letter (February 14, 1984) from the director of the center to this author; Robert Graham, S.J., has written this author that the Warmund memo "must be" the Mayer memo. Graham contends that Hartl merely typed the name Warmund onto the second, revised version of the Mayer memo, but the interrogation indicates that the Mayer memo was really written in 1940, not 1939. The Warmund memo may be the original, and the memo would have been needed by the government more in 1940 than in 1939. The Warmund memo may be found in the National Archives 1021, roll 11.
53. Hartl estimated that he had about 200 informers, both Catholic and Protestant, in ecclesiastical circles. (See Reinhard Henkys, *Die Nationalsozialisten Gewaltbrecher* [Stuttgart: Krenz-Verlag, 1964] p. 178).
54. Graham, "Right to Kill," pp. 73-74. See *New York Times*, March 19, 1964, for the early reports on the trial.
55. The most recent study of the role of Albert Hartl in the SS and in his dealings with the Catholic Church is being done by Georg Denzler. See Georg Denzler, "SS-Spitzel mit Soutane," *Die Zeit*, no. 36, September 3, 1982, pp. 9-10.
56. Martin Höllen, *Heinrich Wienken, der 'unpolitische' Kirchenpolitiker. Eine Biographie aus drei Epochen des deutschen Katholizismus* (Mainz: Matthias Grünewald, 1981), pp. 86-100. Höllen is convinced that one can only speculate whether an earlier or more decisive protest by the Catholic hierarchy could have been effective.

57. Heinrich Missalla, *Für Volk und Vaterland. Die Kirchliche Kriegshilfe im Zweiten Weltkrieg* (Königstein: Athenäum, 1978), pp. 115ff.
58. Ulrich Hehl (ed.), *Walter Adolph*, pp. 276ff. Höllen, "Katholische Kirche," p. 73.
59. Robert Graham, "Spie Naziste attorno al Vaticano durante la Seconda Guerna Mondiale," *La Civilta Cattolica* 121, (1970):21-31; Hartl's indiscreet revelation on Mayer was made to Sereny, pp. 64-76.
60. Siegmund's comment in Graham, "Right to Kill," p. 76.
61. Dörner, p. 152.
62. Leon Poliakov, *Harvest of Hate* (Westport, CT: Greenwood Press, 1971), p. 283. The Final Solution program was reasonably well known in Germany (see Lawrence Stokes, "The German People and the Destruction of the European Jews," *Central European History* 6 [1973]:167-191). Intimidation and passive security militated against any resistance to this outrage.
63. Höllen, *Wienken*, p. 90.
64. Kershaw, pp. 224-225; K. Patzold, *Fascismus, Rassenwahn, Judenverfolgung* (Berlin: Niemeyer, 1975), pp. 28-32; M. Broszat, "Soziale Motivation und Führer: Bindung des Nationalsozialismus," *Vierteljahrshefte für Zeitgeschichte* 18 (1970):400ff.
65. Kershaw, p. 277.
66. Zangerl, pp. 220-221, 239-240; David Blackbourn, "Class and Politics in Wilhelmine Germany: The Center Party and the Social Democrats in Württemberg," *Central European History* 9 (1976):220-249; Ernst Heinen, "Antisemitische Strömungen im politischen Katholizismus während des Kulturkampfes," in Heinen and Schoeps, pp. 259-299.
67. Gustav Gundlach, S.J., "Antisemitismus," in *Lexikon für Theologie und Kirche*, vol. 1, p.504; Lewy, pp. 80, 271.
68. Faulhaber, *Deutsches Ehrgefühl*, pp. 13, 19; *Münchener Katholische Kirchenzeitung*, no. 31, July 31, 1932, p. 332; *Der Rütlischwur* 114, no. 1 (1924):4.
69. Uwe Adam, *Judenpolitik im Dritten Reich* (Düsseldorf: Droste Verlag, 1972); Jäckel, *Hitler's Weltanschauung: A Blueprint for Power*.
70. Gordon, *German Opposition to Anti-Semitic Measures*, Ph.D. diss., pp. 410-411.
71. Lewy, chap. 10; Conway, *The Nazi Persecution of the Churches*; B. van Schewick, "Katholische Kirche und nationalsozialistische Rassenpolitik," in Klaus Gotto and Konrad Repgen (eds.), *Kirche, Katholiken, und Nationalsozialismus* (Mainz: Matthias-Grünewald, 1980), pp. 83-100; Dietrich, "Historical Judgments and Eternal Verities," pp. 31-35.
72. *Deutsche Briefe*, no. 52, September 27, 1935, pp. 6-7; Alfons Erb, *Bernhard Lichtenberg: Dompropst von St. Hedwig zu Berlin* (Berlin: Morus, 1949), p. 43.
73. Muckermann, *Vom Rätsel der Zeit*, p. 102; Baumstark, pp. 24ff.; Dürr, pp. 1ff.
74. David Aderman and Leonard Berkowitz, "Self-Concern and the Unwillingness to Be Helpful," *Social Psychology Quarterly* 46 (1983):301; F. Gibbons and R. Wicklund, "Self-Focused Attention and Helping Behavior," *Journal of Personality and Social Psychology* 43 (1982):462-74.
75. J. Scherm, "Der alttestamentliche Bibelunterricht: Planungen und Wegweisungen," *Klerusblatt* 20 (1939):225.
76. F. Schühlein, "Geschichte der Juden," *Lexikon für Theologie und Kirche* 5:687; "Verdienst die katholische Kirche den Namen 'Judenkirche'?" *Klerusblatt* 18 (1937):542.

77. On the role of theologians, see Berger, *The Sacred Canopy*, pp. 53-80; Richard Rubenstein, "The Unmastered Trauma: Interpreting the Holocaust," *Humanities in Society* 2 (1969):425.

78. Lewy, p. 280.

79. Alfred Richter, "Parteiprogramm der NSDAP und Reichskonkordat: Zum dritten Jahrestag der Unterzeichnung des Reichskonkordats (July 20, 1933)," *Deutschlands Erneuerung* 20 (1936):468; *Deutsche Briefe*, no. 52, September 27, 1935, pp. 6-7; Regierungsrat Münsterer, "Die Regelung des Rassenproblems durch die Nürnberger Gesetze," *Klerusblatt* 17 (1936):47.

80. Bertram's letter to the German bishops (October 14, 1936) in Lewy, p. 282.

81. Vicar General Buchweiser to Kerrl (November 18, 1937) in Lewy, p. 63; Poliakov, *Harvest of Hate*, p. 17; Hugh Martin et al., *Christian Counter-Attack* (New York: C. Scribner's Sons, 1944), p. 24; Lewy, p. 282.

82. Raul Hilberg, *The Destruction of the European Jews* (Chicago: Quadrangle Books, 1961), p. 262. Hitler made the decision for the implementation of the Final Solution. See Martin Broszat, "Hitler und die Genesis der 'Endlösung': Aus Anlass der Thesen von David Irving," *Vierteljahrshefte für Zeitgeschichte* 25 (1977):739-75; for an explication of the Broszat position, see Christopher Browning, "Zur Genesis der 'Endlösung': Eine Antwort an Martin Broszat," *Vierteljahrshefte für Zeitgeschichte* 29 (1981):97-109.

83. Lewy, p. 286.

84. Ibid. pp. 286-287.

85. Thomas Dehler, "Sie Zuckten mit der Achsel," in Fritz J. Raddatz (ed.), *Summa Inuria oder Durfte der Papst Schweigen?* (Reinbek bei Hamburg: Rowohlt, 1963), p. 231; Lewy, p. 288.

86. Bertram to Thierack (November 11, 1942) in Lewy, pp. 288-289; Ruth Andreas Friedrick, *Berlin Underground, 1938-1945* (New York: Knopf, 1947), p. 92; Philip Friedman, *Their Brother's Keepers* (New York: Crown Publishers, 1957), p. 93.

87. Bertram to Thierack (January 29, 1944) in Lewy, p. 291.

88. Corsten, p. 269.

89. In Lewy, p. 292.

90. National Archives, Washington, T-580, roll 42, file 245.

91. See the Gröber's pastoral letter (March 27, 1941) in Lewy, pp. 294-295. For an analysis, weak in some respects, of the varied responses to genocide, see Helen Fein, *Accounting for Genocide: National Responses and Jewish Victimization During the Holocaust* (New York: The Free Press, 1979) and Michael Marrus and Robert Paxton, *Vichy France and the Jews* (New York: Schocken Books, 1983). Marrus and Paxton, *Vichy France and the Jews* are excellent studies of the implementation of genocide in Nazi occupied states.

92. Kurt Grossmann, *Die unbesungenen Helden* (Berlin: Arani Verlags, 1957), p. 153; "Thesen christlicher Lehrvekündigung in Hinblick auf umlaufende Irrtümer über das Gottesvolk des Alten Bundes," *Freiburger Rundbrief* 2, (1949-50):nos. 8-9, p. 9.

93. In Lewy, p. 295.

94. Dietrich, "Historical Judgments and Eternal Verities," pp. 31-35.

95. Pierre Blet et al., *Lettres de Pie XII aux Eveques Allemands, 1939-1944*.

96. John F. Morley, *Vatican Diplomacy and the Jews during the Holocaust, 1939-1943*, Ph.D. diss., New York University, 1979, p. 468.

97. Pierre Blet et al., *Actes et Documentes du Saint Siege relatifs a la Seconde*

Guerre Mondiale, 9 vols., (Vatican City: Libreria Editrice Vaticana, 1965-1975).

98. Leonidas Hill, "The Vatican Embassy of Ernst von Weizsaecker, 1943-1945," *The Journal of Modern History* 39 (1967):138-59; Wall, pp. 437-456.

99. H. Witetschek (ed.), *Die kirchliche Lage in Bayern nach den Regierungspräsidentenberichten, 1933-1943*, vol. 1, *Regierungsbezirk Oberbayern* (Mainz: Matthias Grünewald, 1966), pp. 175ff; H. Witetschek (ed.), *Die kirchliche Lage in Bayern nach den Regierungspräsidenten 1933-1943*, vol. 2, *Regierungsbezirk Ober-und Mittelfranken* (Mainz: Matthias Grünewald, 1967), p. 80.

100. Witetschek, *Kirchliche Lage*, vol. 2, p.317; ibid., vol. 1, pp.175ff.

101. Ibid, vol. 2, p. 218.

102. Kershaw, *Popular Opinion*, p. 252.

103. Witetschek, *Kirchliche Lage*, vol. 2, p. 353.

104. W. Ziegler (ed.), *Die kirchliche Lage in Bayern nach den Regierungspräsidentenberichten, 1933-1945*, vol. 4. *Regierungsbezirk Niederbayern und der Oberpfalz* (Mainz: Matthias Grünewald, 1973), p. 224.

105. Kershaw, *Popular Opinion*, pp. 253-255.

106. Schleunes, pp. 88-89; P. Hanke *Zur Geschichte der Juden in München zwischen 1933 und 1945* (Munich: Stadtarchiv, 1967), pp. 83-86; Kershaw, *Popular Opinion*, pp. 245-246, 254.

107. Kershaw, *Popular Opinion*, p. 245.

108. Ian Kershaw, "The Persecution of the Jews and German Popular Opinion in the Third Reich," *Leo Baeck Institute Yearbook* 26(1981), hereafter cited as Kershaw, "Persecution."

109. B.Z. Ophir and F. Wiesemann, *Die jüdischen Gemeinden in Bayern, 1918-1945. Geschichte und Zerstörung* (Munich: Knapp, 1979), p. 472; Kershaw, *Popular Opinion*, p. 246.

110. Van Schewick, pp. 90-91, in Kershaw, *Popular Opinion*, 256.

111. Kershaw, *Popular Opinion*, p. 257; H. Witetschek (ed.) *Die Kirchliche Lage in Bayern nach den Regierungspräsidentenberichten, 1933-1943*, vol. 3, *Regierungsbezirk Schwaben* (Mainz: Matthias Grünewald, 1971), p. 28.

112. Kershaw, *Popular Opinion*, p. 277. Because the study focused on Bavaria, its conclusions are certainly tentative with respect to the rest of Germany but are certainly suggestive and probably accurately reflect the multiplicity of Catholic and non-Catholic responses during this period; cf. Heinz Boberach, *Berichte des SD und der Gestapo über Kirchen und Kirchenvolk in Deutschland, 1934-1944* (Mainz: Matthias Grunewald, 1971).

113. Dörner, p. 152.

114. Poliakov, *Harvest of Hate*, p. 283. The Final Solution program was reasonably well-known in Germany (see Stokes, "People and the Destruction of the European Jews," pp. 167-191). Intimidation and passive security seemed to militate against any resistance to this outrage.

115. Stokes, 184-185; M.G. Steinert, *Hitler's Krieg und die Deutschen* (Düsseldorf: Econ-Verlad, 1970), pp. 258-259.

116. Broszat, *Hitler State*, pp. 322-323.

117. A.J.A. Tymchuk, "A Perspective on Ethics in Mental Retardation," *Mental Retardation* 14 (1976):45. The social and ethical issues surrounding sterilization and euthanasia in contemporary America are surveyed in Philip C. Chinn et al., *Mental Retardation: A Life Cycle Approach* (St. Louis: Mosby, 1979), pp. 438-474.

118. Horowitz, *Taking Lives.*
119. Hewitt, p. 204; Howard Becker, *Outsiders: Studies in the Sociology of Deviance* (New York: Free Press of Glencoe, 1963), p. 9.
120. Dietrich, "Holocaust," 445-462.
121. Lewy, op. cit.; Gordon Zahn, *German Catholics and Hitler's Wars: A Study in Social Control,* (New York: E.P. Dutton, 1969).
122. Lewy, pp. 341ff.; Zahn, *German Catholics,* chaps. 2, 3, 11, 12; Joseph L. Featherstone, "Did the Church Fail?" *Commonweal* 79 (February 28, 1964):650.
123. Leon Festinger, *A Theory of Cognitive Dissonance*; P.G. Zimbardo, "The Human Choice: Individuation, Reason, and Order versus Deindividuation, Impulse, and Chaos," in W.J. Arnold and D. Levine (eds.), *Nebraska Symposium on Motivation 1969* (Lincoln: University of Nebraska Press, 1969); Leon Berkowitz, *A Survey of Social Psychology,* pp. 72-73, 149.
124. A. Bandura et al., "Disinhibition of Aggression", pp. 253-269; A. Koriat et al., "The Self-Control of Emotional Reactions to a Stressful Film,"*Journal of Personality* 40 (1972):601-619.
125. Bertram to Thierack, November 11, 1942, Archives of the Ministry of Justice, Bonn, R 22 Gr. S/XXII-2; T.W. Brehm and A.R. Cohen, *Explorations in Cognitive Dissonance* (New York: Wiley, 1962); Philip G. Zimbardo, *Psychology and Life,* 10th ed. (Glenview, IL: Scott, Foresman, 1979), pp. 651-653; Hilberg, *Destruction,* pp. 1-17.
126. Broszat, *Hitler State,* pp. 322-323.
127. Glenn Wilson and Christopher Bagley, "Religion, Racialism and Conservatism," in Glenn Wilson (ed.), *The Psychology of Conservatism* (New York: Academic Press, 1973), p. 117; Ervin Staub, *Positive Social Behavior and Morality,* vol. 1, p.58; I.M. Piliavin et al., "Costs, Diffusion, and Stigmatized Victim," *Journal of Personality and Social Psychology* 13 (1975):429-438; S.H. Schwartz, "Normative Influences on Altriusm," in L. Berkowitz (ed.), *Advances in Experimenal Social Psychology,* vol. 10, (New York: Academic Press, 1965-1977).
128. Staub, vol. 1, pp.74-76; B. Latane and J.M. Darley, "Group Inhibition of Bystander Intervention," *Journal of Personality and Social Psychology* 6 (1968):215-221; B. Latane and J.M. Darley, *The Unresponsive Bystander: Why Doesn't He Help?* (New York: Appleton, Century, Crofts, 1970).
129. Staub, vol. 1, p. 429.
130. Lerner, "Observer's Evaluation of a Victim," pp. 127-135; M.J. Lerner and G. Matthews, "Reactions to Suffering of Others under Direct Conditions of Indirect Responsibility," *Journal of Personality and Social Psychology* 5 (1967):319-325.
131. Staub, vol. 1, pp.155, 159, 161-162; E. Walster, "Assignment of Responsibility for an Accident," *Journal of Personality and Social Psychology* 3 (1966):73-79.
132. Simpson, p. 86; Bendersky, p. 208.
133. Laurence Kohlberg, "Stage and Sequence: The Cognitive-Developmental Approach to Socialization," in David A. Goslin (ed.), *Handbook of Socialization Theory and Research* (Chicago: University of Chicago Press, 1969); Stanley Milgram, "The Sociology of Justice: Kohlberg and Milgram," *Political Theory* 10 (1982):427-428.
134. Staats, *Social Behaviorism,* pp. 155, 164, 168, 221, 506-507; A.W. Staats and C. K. Staats, "Attitudes Established by Classical Conditioning," *Journal of Abnormal and Social Psychology* 57 (1958):37-40.

8

Catholic Resistance: Still Waters Run Deep

Given the pressures of living in a totalitarian political system, German Catholics utilized several familiar strategies for avoiding or coping with stress caused, at least in part, by cognitive complexity as they tried to reconcile their traditional value structure with the Nazi *Weltanschauung*. Avoiding heroism they adopted a satisfying rather than an optimizing strategy. Some chose an approach labeled "incrementalism" or "muddling through." The hierarchy in particular seemed to base their response on "consensus politics." They couched their critique within a framework of what their flock wanted and would support, and did not attempt to master the cognitive complexity of the Catholic-Nazi problem by analysis, especially since such a rigorous approach could have led to open warfare between the Church and the Reich. Most of the bishops had a keen sense of history and did not want a repetition of the *Kulturkampf.* The bishops, moreover, generally felt that the Church was a long-lived institution, while states rose and fell. The crucial goal was to maintain the Church intact until the state could be transformed. Church leaders could also, of course, narrow their focus to strictly religious matters and avoid comment on political issues unless such remarks could be viewed as patriotic and so reinforce their nationalistic credentials. In this way the bishops could be good Catholics and good Germans simultaneously. Lay Catholics had to employ an "operational code" in their daily interactions with Nazi party representatives. These Catholics did not develop sophisticated and complex political or religious theories, but they did have a workable set of beliefs about the nature of politics and history as well as about correct political strategy and tactics. They could well support the nationalistic policies of Hitler as he realized their patriotic hopes, but they could also defend the historical insularity of their villages and neighborhood communities as well as the integrity of their traditional faith. From their perspective in many cases the Nazis, not their Jewish neighbors, were the outsiders. Their tactics were not heroic demonstrations, but usually were

259

jokes, small acts of kindness, and gossipy complaints. None of these acts really merited any organized state assault on their behavior, but did indicate to the authorities that an unmobilized resistance persisted in Germany.[1]

Resistance to the regime was lively throughout the 1930s and clearly feared by the Nazis.[2] The joint pastoral letter of the Bavarian bishops, for example, protesting the unpopular dismissal of all nuns teaching in the public schools and scheduled to be read on June 21, 1936, had been forbidden by the Bavarian political police. The letter was read, but the government did not arrest the priest offenders. Afterward, a number of provincial administrators reported that in the event of arrests the population would not have accepted these measures without resistance, and that disturbances would probably have resulted. "The priest," the administrator noted, "is still a person enjoying the greatest respect and that is true especially in rural districts. Even the currency and immorality trials have been unable to change this fact to any substantial degree. When the priest yet appears as a martyr for his convictions, he is defended even by people who normally have little to do with the Church." Other instances of popular resistance can also be cited, for example, surrounding the government's attempts to remove crosses from public buildings between 1936 and 1941.[3] Certainly the names of Rupert Mayer, S.J., Alfred Delp, S.J., and Augustinus Rosch, S.J. stand out heroically as well. Ultimately, of course, victory in war would enable the regime, Hitler thought, to crush that "reptile," the Church.[4] Resistance to the regime developed slowly because totalitarianism as a comprehensive challenge is difficult to discern in a modern society where the essence is on the diffusion of conflicts. The fragmentation characteristic of Germany made it difficult to see "evil" until it was too late, but unorganized resistance to the *Gleichschaltung* was present from 1933 until the end.

No political authority could expect to remain in power if it had to maintain constant supervision and continuous reinforcement through terror to gain compliance with its commands. After 1933, the "führer myth" had as its purpose the total identification of the people and their leader as they united in the fight for Germany's future. In the view of many, the Nazis had created a united nation out of the shambles of Weimar democracy. Opposition existed, but before the disasters in Russia there is no doubt that Hitler, if not all of his policies, was popular. The failures and bitterness engendered in the Reich were only tolerable because most people could identify with the führer. This weakened in the later war years and resulted in a significant escalation of terror.[5] Hence the lack of acquiescence among Catholics is significant. Catholic resistance surfaced through newspaper or journal articles, sermons, pastoral letters, and *Amtsblätter* as long as these functioned. Official documents used to reflect institutional resistance, however, do not provide a complete picture. Nazi records themselves document resistance and suggest that all was not serene within the supposedly monolithic Reich. In the *Kirchenkampf*, past critics and defenders have customarily relied almost exclusively upon official ecclesiastical source materials. The failure to consult the full range of the National Socialist documents dealing with religious affairs has resulted in a large body of works characterized by a constricted perception of Catholic resistance. Even though Conway, Zipfel, and Lewy[6] have effectively utilized many of the available National Socialist sources, they cite only occasionally the reports of the *Sicherheitsdienst* (SD), the internal intelligence agency of the SS. From the fall of 1939 to mid-1944 the SD submitted regular reports to the Nazi leadership at least twice a week. The SD reports, for example, show that the desire for peace was strong from the beginning of the war and not just from the defeat of Stalingrad onward.[7] These reports also contain detailed descriptions of public reactions and attitudes toward conditions of life in wartime Germany and furnish evidence that could incriminate the enemies of the regime. Although it never worked in practice, theoretically the SD was to handle all general and fundamental questions relating to ideological matters, and the Gestapo was to deal with all the individual cases in which the executive state police measures came into question.[8] Besides providing surprisingly comprehensive factual accounts of parish activity during the often neglected war years, the reports bring into sharp relief the bitter ideological and institutional conflict between the Church and the regime. Much of the information, of course, which seems useful, was vague hearsay. Its presentation was often biased by Himmler's pathological theories of conspiracy, of the secret power of the Church, and of its desire to overthrow the state.[9] As can be seen, some of the material, for example, was incredibly misleading: "The ecumenical movement is unthinkable without the background of a liberal-democratic world. It bears a Marxist, pacifist, and Jewish stamp. The influence of the ecumenical movement on German church life is very great."[10] With their fixed ideas as well as power, the bureaucratic SD chiefs naturally desired and subsequently received information from extensive sources calculated to confirm their stereotypic ideas. Albert Hartl, an ex-Catholic priest and from 1937 an *Obersturmbannführer*, for example, led the subdepartment on the churches and claimed that among his informers were 200 clergymen of all denominations.[11] His postwar testimony cannot be accepted without extraneous corroboration, and there is nothing to suggest that as a Nazi bureaucrat he was any more reliable. Even though biased, the reports do, however, indicate that the Nazis recognized that they had yet to achieve full control in their society.

Passionate commitment to National Socialism prompted SD agents to search relentlessly for forces, attitudes, and enemies that might weaken the regime, even after Himmler and Bormann had ceased to place confidence in the *Sicherheitsdienst* reports, which they felt were undermining morale. On June 18, 1938, a meeting in Berlin of Gestapo representatives from all the Reich ordered the collection of proofs of illegal activity by the Church, a watch upon the Catholic clergy and gentry, the Catholic festivals, the theological faculties of Tübingen, Freiburg, and Heidelberg, and an investigation into the attitude of 'denominationally committed' professors to party and state.[12] In a letter to the religion specialists in the fall of 1941, Heydrich pointed out that the expanded war in the east had forced the regime to postpone a major attack against the Church. Consequently, the agents were to concentrate on collecting such religious materials as sermons, pastoral letters, records of meetings, and special pamphlets, that could be produced later as evidence of treasonable activities. At a meeting of religion specialists in September 1941, one of Heydrich's assistants declared: "Each one of you must . . . work with your whole heart and a true fanaticism. . . . The immediate aim: the Church must not regain one inch of ground it has lost. The ultimate aim: destruction of the confessional churches."[13] Knowledge of the reportorial competence of the SD agents is not available, and so the reports must be used with caution, although the Himmler-Bormann reaction suggests that they may have been trying to bury valid reports.

Most of the available SD reports emanated from Bielefeld, Frankfurt, Koblenz, Dortmund, and Aachen. In June 1942 the Bielefeld agents issued a fifty-page summary of the basic religious situation, based upon observations from all parts of Germany. It contained in summary form the substance of nearly all the shorter biweekly reports. The suggestion is that the Bielefeld reports were typical of the national situation. The SD's basic appraisal of the Church problem, which upset the regime from 1933 until the end, may be seen in the following:

> From numerous reports at the time of the outbreak of war, it appeared that a large part of the population had become somewhat indifferent toward the churches. The political propaganda about the Church, its history, its institutions, and its dogma, together with ideological indoctrination, had caused an increasing number of people to become disenchanted with the Church. . . . The influence of Protestants had diminished more than that of Catholics, although only a relatively small number had made a complete break with either Church. Now, however, both confessions, but especially Roman Catholicism, have broadened and deepened their influence.[14]

The secrecy that enveloped *Amt III*'s public opinion gathering, necessary in view of the police work it also performed and in any case inevitable in the closed society of Nazi Germany, removed all effective checks on the correctness of the information assembled concerning popular morale. The SD's *V-Leute* (agents) passed along to their responsible *Aussenstelle* the gist of conversations overheard or provoked at work, on streetcars, in bars and restaurants, and among relatives, friends, and acquaintances. All each *Aussenstelle* could do was accumulate as much "raw material" on a particular topic as possible; on the basis of this, multiplied several hundred times over, the superiors made their judgments on the opinions and morale of the German people. Even with high-quality informants, the anonymity of the reporting system lessened the certitude of accuracy. Still, these are revealing documents reflecting the domestic political situation in the Third Reich and offer the perceptions of SD agents who reported on such minor matters as the lack of enthusiasm encountered by the bishop of Mainz when he visited Nieder-Oelm in June 1939. The local group leader reported the number of men (thirty-six) and women (fifty) who had assembled in front of the church to greet him, as well as the number of families (five) whose houses had been decorated for the occasion. His report noted with satisfaction that the majority of those present were elderly people, that "the reception had never been so miserable," and that the bishop had "certainly been disappointed by it."[15] Such a report, of course, must be used with care since it neglects to tell the reader how many people, for example, could have potentially been present. The report does indicate the level of observation as well as the keen interest that the regime had in the reactions of German Catholics to their Church and Reich. Thus, the reports contain a wealth of material, but interpretations must be cautiously derived.

Resistance Among the Bishops as Loyal German Citizens

The hierarchy usually couched their expressions of protest in patriotic public sermons or letters. Along with their endorsement of Hitler's foreign policy, the German bishops failed to raise questions whether a war waged for the führer's expansionist aims would be just or unjust. Hitler explicitly stated his goals and was persuasive. The patriotic bishops agreed with many of his goals, but always not with his means. To convey meaningfully their nuances to the faithful was much more difficult than Hitler's presentation of the regime's aims. His popular statements encouraged agreement; the bishops' verbal and written messages provided little activist leadership on the national level, but served merely to reinforce the martial commands of the Reich's leaders and to illustrate the Church's loyalty to the *Vaterland*. They taught the faithful to be prepared to serve the fatherland. Gröber noted that Catholic theologians had "never left it to the judgment of the individual Catholic, with all his shortsightedness and emotionalism, in the event of war to decide its permissability or lack thereof. Instead, this final decision has always been in the province of the lawful authority."[16] The joint pastoral letter of the Cologne and Paderborn Church provinces of March 1942, which reaffirmed the natural rights of life, liberty, and property, and decried the arbitrary detention and killing of innocents, ended with the following typical admonishment to the faithful:

> That which we bishops had to tell you today with grievously moved soul may not however serve anyone as an excuse to neglect his national duties. On the contrary! With the full authority of our holy office we urge you again today! In this time of war fulfill your patriotic duties most conscientiously! Don't let anyone surpass you in willingness to make sacrifices and readiness to do your share! Be faithful to our people.[17]

Although not viewed by the bishops as resistance, this type of support was perceived by some in the regime as being dangerous. In December 1939 Rosenberg had written Göring that the Church was out to regain her lost positions by delivering martial sermons, and in May 1941 Bormann warned all *Gauleiters* not to be misled by the clever tactics of the Church, which was propagandistically exploiting the fact that many clerics at the front had received medals for bravery and was bragging about the number of priests killed in action, all in order to improve her bargaining position at the day of reckoning after the war. In talks between officials of the propaganda ministry and the Party Chancellery held in December 1941, it was argued that German propaganda abroad should ignore the declarations of the bishops in support of the German war effort in order not to strengthen their position at home. A Gestapo bulletin of June 1942 decried the fact that many party members were still attending divine services and attributed this state of affairs to the growth of religious sentiment caused by the tribulations of war. The Church, the report continued, systematically used National Socialist concepts and expanded her influence by pointing to the large number of priests in the armed forces as proof that being a Catholic not only did not detract from heroism, but actually made it possible.[18] The Church was loyal to the *Vaterland*, distrusted the party, and was reinforcing the Catholic presence among the German people, an intolerable situation in the eyes of some Nazis.

Such Nazi leaders would certainly find the letter (1940) of Faulhaber to Gürtner obnoxious:

> We understand when extraordinary measures are taken in wartime to assure the security of the nation and sustain the *Volk*. And we instruct the *Volk* that it must be prepared to assume the burden of wartime sacrifices, even that of

blood, in the Christian spirit of sacrifice and to honor the women they encounter on the streets of the city who wear the veil of sorrow signifying that
they have offered the sacrifice of a precious life for the *Vaterland*.[19]

Galen's message of 1944 evoked the same theme:

> In this hour I must direct a word of greeting and acknowledgement to our
> soldiers. I wish to express our gratitude to them for the loyal protection they
> have furnished the *Vaterland* and its borders at the price of unspeakable
> strains and sheer superhuman effort. In particular for the defense against the
> assaults of godless Bolshevism! And a word of deep-felt remembrance for
> those who, in the performance of their duty, have offered their lives and the
> last drop of blood for their brothers. May these all-sacrificing efforts succeed
> in wining for us an honorable and victorious peace![20]

Perhaps the Church leaders had found another way to undermine
Nazism. They would adopt the basic values of the "cause" as German
patriotic norms and thus a' la Bismarck steal the planks of the enemy's
program. After the war the Church hoped to be still in a position too strong
to be assaulted.

It is partly a misunderstanding of the existing conditions of wartime
Germany to blame the Church either for acting cautiously or for calling for
obedience to the führer and performance of duty at home and at the front,
since understandably most ecclesiastics were staunchly nationalistic and
patriotic. Orseniga exposed the dissonance present in the German Church
in a report of April 13, 1940:

> As long as the conflict only involved domestic policies, it was easy for anyone
> to distinguish between Anti-National Socialist and subversive behavior; as
> was its duty, the clergy was against National Socialism but was not subversive.
> Now that it concerns foreign policy, this distinction is significantly more
> difficult; only a few understand that one can be against Hitler without being
> against the state, i.e., without being a traitor.[21]

Hitler's decision to postpone anti-Church measures for the duration of
the war and his call for a *Burgfrieden* also can help explain the Church's
discretion or modified loyalty. Having noted the negative reaction to his
anticlericalism, he urged all party bureaus to avoid further friction between
Church and state, a "wish" that factions within the party struggling for
control over ecclesiastical policies did not fully heed, despite repeated re-
minders. This neutrality, of course, did not extend to surveillance, since
reports on Church activities were intensified. A *Burgfrieden* was particularly attractive because most Catholic Germans remained faithful to
the Church and hostile to anti-clericalism despite Rosenberg's efforts. Both

Catholics and Nazis could now call for loyalty to führer, *Volk,* and *Vaterland* and both could continue to owe allegiance to the Church and Germany, at least during the war.[22]

In defending Pastor Johannes Kraus, the rector of the Eichstätt Cathedral parish, Bishop Michael Rachl offered a typically institutional defense. Kraus had been ordered to leave his post after some purportedly antiregime sermons. Kraus had said: "I am an old front-line officer and have given my heart's blood for the *Vaterland.* . . . I have proven my love for the *Vaterland*; I prove it everyday as one of Christ's officers when, in keeping with the words of the dying Field Marshall von Hindenburg, I see to it that Christ is preached in Germany." Rachl's defense was standard: "And once again an officer of the *Vaterland* has become in addition an officer of the Catholic Church, an officer of Jesus Christ, and an officer of God—then that loyalty which is inscribed on his banner is a loyalty toward state and *Vaterland* as well. No one loves his *Vaterland* more truly than the Catholic priest." The pattern is the same as that found in much of the formal, public Catholic opposition to the regime, combining strong explicit protest and equally powerful affirmations of patriotism and national loyalty. By using these tactics Rachl and his colleagues may well have reinforced, albeit inadvertently, however, the hold the Nazis had upon the ordinary German citizen who also happened to be a member of the Catholic Church. Hidden behind the lack of ostensible Catholic resistance is the suspicion that the religious leaders never really thought the outcome of organized resistance could be other than defeat. From the very beginning they seemed to operate on the prudential (and probably correct) assumption that if they were to issue a call to spiritual arms against the state, their troops might not have rallied to the cause.[23] The bishops and their Nazi opponents waged the *Kirchenkampf* without engaging in a direct confrontation. They fought a battle for position. The German bishops retained a patriotic stance during the Third Reich even while criticizing such specific policies as euthanasia by appealing, for example, to the Concordat.[24] To undermine the legitimacy of Catholicism while not attacking the Church head-on, the Nazis had conducted a sustained, although unsuccessful, attack against recalcitrant priests in general and the Jesuits in particular. Jews and Jesuits were popularly depicted as the two sides of the same coin.[25] Despite the "petition politics" of the Church and the number of priests imprisoned, this limited resistance of the Church has, not surprisingly, been overshadowed by its aptitude for adaptation. Even in response to the persecution of the Jews, official Catholic reactions have been correctly judged as mild, vague, and belated,[26] especially in view of the Nazi hatred of the Church. While the hierarchy responded diplomatically, other Catholics resolutely faced the Nazi anti-Semitism in the 1930s and in its muted post-1939 form.

The Clergy and Racial Persecution

Heydrich's despisal of the Catholic Church, which to only a slightly lesser degree permeated the entire SS, render the SD reports on religious subjects somewhat questionable sources on the response of the Church toward Nazism. But they are certainly valuable as evidence of the Nazi elites' own views on religion. Once identified, however, the prejudices of the SD and its chief do not seriously impair the "Meldungen aus dem Reich" or the *Berichte* (1939-44) as trustworthy "barometers" of German public opinion. In Heydrich's view the Catholic Church was Nazism's most dangerous ideological enemy. He had an almost pathological hatred of the Church. In *Das Schwarze Korps* (May-June 1935), he attacked the "politically minded" Catholic clergy who were "continuing their old, embittered struggle for the secular domination of Germany" on the pretense that an irreligious National Socialism threatened Christian virtues and German culture. Wilhelm Patin, an ex-priest and cousin of Himmler, was in charge of reporting on "political Catholicism." The SD from 1933 onward participated in the harassment of the Bavarian clergy and other measures directed against the Church.[27] Martin Bormann offered the most articulate statement of the party's monopolistic claim not only to the outer but also the inner man. In his well-known letter of June 6, 1941, to the Gauleiter of Münster and sent three days later to all Gauleiters, he defined the "relationship of National Socialism to Christianity." In his opinion they were mutually exclusive; Christianity was based on human uncertainty, National Socialism on "scientific foundations." For centuries the Church had ruled the people, now "for the first time in German history the *Führer* had taken over public leadership. . . . All influences that could impair, or even damage, the *Führer's* and the Party's rule must be eliminated. More and more the *Volk* must be wrested away from the Churches and their agents, the pastors."[28] To reduce pressure on the institution, Church leaders as a group unfortunately did not respond negatively to the heightened anti-Semitism and the Final Solution.

The anti-Jewish propaganda was disseminated through nearly every possible channel to Germans. A 1935 leaflet stated that the "Jew destroys your Church, rapes your wife, and corrupts your race."[29] Hermann Reinecke's *Der Jude als Weltparasit* (1944), although distributed only through official channels, summarized the propaganda campaign that had been waged since the late nineteenth century. The pamphlet highlighted Jewish "crimes" by asserting that the Jews had consolidated power in disparate arenas and that they had polluted for all eternity the blood of many German families. Likewise, Jewry was seen as the coagulation of antisocial, criminal, sick, perverted, and the expelled elements of all the possible races of the ancient world. Jewry was an artificial race produced by inbreeding. The fact that such publications were economically viable is evidence that many average Germans eventually swallowed the regime's propaganda against the Jews.[30] Probably because of prior experiences consisting of ghettoization, pogroms, and general discrimination, the popular reaction to the introduction of the "yellow star" was slight. Anti-Semitism was greeted by apathy and indifference during the war. Such latent anti-Semitism ultimately allowed the Nazis to implement the Final Solution.[31]

This populist attitude toward the Jews helps explain why the Germans as a whole never took a strong position with respect to the Final Solution. Simultaneously, they were too bourgeois to accept the eugenic policies of the regime.[32] It seems undeniable that much, although not all, of the terror and destruction inflicted upon the Jews of Europe by the Nazis was generally known among the German people. Not only were the infamous *Einsatzgruppen* activities known, but they were explicitly discussed. In 1939 a priest in Passau referred to such actions while addressing a group of secondary students. The massacres inflicted on the *Volksdeutschen* by the Poles, he declared, "were not at all so serious when one considered the sort of atrocities our soldiers committed in Poland."[33] The SD reports indicate that the general public was informed through rumors about the murder of the Jews in Poland and other occupied territories, although the extent of knowledge concerning the extermination camps is unclear.[34] Knowledge of the German persecution of the Jews seems apparent and an array of unorganized protests can be discerned.

Bishop Johannes Sproll's sermons, carefully watched and noted by the police, had been giving the party concern for several months, and, in the autumn before the campaign against him, material was collected with a view to his prosecution. Sproll spoke against the errors of blood and race applied to religion and said so in the pulpit.[35] Only a few church leaders, however, spoke out vehemently against prewar anti-Semite measures and their subsequent implementation leading to the Final Solution. No amount of research can basically alter the Church leaders' moral responsibility for these events. Their aquiescence to anti-Semitism has been covered in a variety of texts and the specific extent of their culpability has been established.[36] Church leaders were reluctant to speak out against racial persecution in a consistent fashion after 1933 not only because of their long history of religious anti-Semitism, but also because of such objective factors as the battle with the Nazi regime for institutional autonomy and the difficulty of publicly opposing the racial policies of the regime without encountering harsh countermeasures.[37]

Some Catholic leaders attempted to ameliorate the effects of racial persecution. Dean Lichtenberg of St. Hedwig's Cathedral in Berlin, for example, condemned the *Kristallnacht* pogrom, praying for Jews and prisoners in concentration camps. In 1941, he said: "If it is said that Germans, by supporting Jews, commit treason, I enjoin you not to be misled by such unchristian sentiments, but to act in obedience to Christ's commandment, and to love your neighbor as yourself."[38] His criticisms of anti-Jewish actions during the war were considered dangerous to public order and resulted in two years' imprisonment. In 1943 he died en route to Dachau. At that time he said: "Nothing would be better than for an old clergyman like me to stand by baptized Jewish Christians as I die."[39]

In general, however, the hierarchy was cautious. As early as 1930 Cardinal Bertram had attacked Nazi racial theories.[40] In 1933, prior to the April boycott of Jewish businesses, he requested assistance for Jews from Gröber. In September 1933 he complained to Pacelli regarding the Concordat between the Catholic Church and the Nazi state, because it endangered the rights of Jewish Catholics. In 1941 he issued instructions for Church leaders to treat Jewish converts as they did other Christians, but perhaps to invite them to attend earlier services to prevent incidents. More significantly, he protested against the death of Jews in concentration camps in letters to Himmler and to the Ministry of the Interior.[41] His "petition politics" was pursued with some courageous moral thrusts. But in the bulk of these statements only the persecution of Jewish Christians was condemned. Although not as vocal as some in defending Jews, Bishop Preysing did help baptized Jews and set up an agency that assisted them after 1941. Earlier he had submitted documents that helped shape *Mit Brennender Sorge*. In 1942 he contributed to a *Hirtenbrief* of the Catholic opposition which condemned Nazi violations of God's laws, although he did not mention Jews by name. But by 1943 he said: "Primitive rights, such as the right to live, to be free, to have possessions, to marry whom one chooses, etc., cannot and must not be denied even to those who are not of our blood."[42] Hardly a blanket condemnation of genocide, the statement exceeded the cautious position taken by many of his colleagues.

Although major Catholic leaders did not speak out vehemently against persecution during World War II, there are certainly indications that they disapproved of it. In 1940 the reports mention that Christ was frequently designated as the highest führer. In August 1940 an SD report on German public opinion indicated that anti-Semitic propaganda was not well-received in Catholic circles. There was also Catholic opposition to the introduction of the yellow star and the attempt to exclude Jews from religious services in 1941. The Church opposed compulsory divorce of Catholics and Jews, but, hedging his position, Bertram insisted that pastoral letters to this effect should not be interpreted as "underrepresentation of the harmful Jewish influences upon German cultural and national interests." His opposition to race theory was primarily theological, and he avoided confrontations with the Nazis over the "Jewish Question" when this was expedient for the Church. The Church, however, circulated *Hirtenbriefe* which criticized racial ideology, referred to Jesus as king of the Jews, and called for the blood brotherhood of all men. One of these letters written by the bishops in the Church district around Cologne cast suspicion on the legality of the Third Reich's treatment of foreign races and claimed that the regime rested solely on power rather than on legality. The archbishop of Cologne also hid Jews. This Catholic prelate spoke out very strongly in favor of equality for all races and attacked their persecution. His sermon was well attended for the time of day and his collection box was unusually full of money. In 1942 the *Sicherheitsdienst* also complained that Catholic leaders were still willing to marry Catholics and baptized Jews.[43]

Other clerics objected to the Nazi attack on the Jews. Father Leffers of Paderborn, for example, spent a year and a half in prison because he criticized Rosenberg's *Myth of the Twentieth Century.* Others received varying sentences for similar offenses. Bishop Berning of Osnabrück helped baptized Jews emigrate, and the general secretary of the St. Raphael Association, which aided Jews who were emigrating, was imprisoned for a number of months by the Gestapo. The Archbishop of Paderborn and Bishop Berning looked upon the bitter suffering of the Jews in April 1933 with a deep sense of regret, and both were later castigated by the Nazis for sympathizing with Jews.[44] Cardinal von Galen criticized Rosenberg's book in 1934, yet did not openly attack the Nazis for racial persecution. Not until 1943 did he attribute German war losses to God's punishment for the atrocities committed against the Jews. Still, the Gestapo obviously realized that he opposed their policies and kept a close watch on him during the war, probably because of his nationally known opposition to euthanasia.[45] Cardinal Faulhaber defended the Old Testament, but could not bring himself to speak out for Jews during Hitler's Third Reich. Such reticence did not hurt the Nazi cause. In contrast, the Jesuit Alfred Delp, belonging to the Kreisau circle, excoriated the Church for failing to accept any moral responsibility for racial persecution.[46] Even though Catholic leaders did not offer more than a pittance of support for or aid to Jews unless they were also baptized Catholics, they consistently opposed the racial ideology of the Nazi regime, especially as articulated by Rosenberg. Here was an institutional issue. Rosenberg's glorification of race rather than religion undermined the foundations and dogmas of the Church itself. The persecution of nonconverted Jews never appeared to arouse much serious interest among Catholic leaders. But when the Nazi party attempted to infringe upon the Church's ministrations to its Jewish converts, they were opposed and were able to preserve the right of these individuals to participate in religious services well into the war. Also, they tried to save Jews married to Catholics.[47]

There was considerable anti-Semitism in the Church, but it was based upon religious rather than racial axioms. Even during the Weimar Republic some Catholic publications had condemned Rosenberg's theories, and during the Third Reich there were numerous examples of Catholic attacks on Rosenberg's ideas.[48] Insofar as these attacks were based on moral as well as institutional considerations, they offer one of the most favorable examples of courage on the part of Catholic leaders at all levels of the hierarchy. Nazi reports portray the opposition that the regime was trying to crush.

It has long been recognized that cognitive limits on information and knowledge needed for rational decision making can be a source of acute stress.[49] To relieve the stress of cognitive dissonance and consequently direct Catholics away from the Church and toward the regime, the Nazis were most sensitive to information and opinions that conflicted with their own. Lewy argues that very few Catholics opposed racial persecution and that this was one reason for the reluctance of Catholic leaders to speak out against it. Were that the case, there would be few references to persecution in other sources. Yet quite a few examples of opposition among less prominent Catholic leaders and the Catholic population can be found in the currently available sources.[50] In April 1933, at the very inception of the Reich, a priest published an article in the *Rheinmainische Volkszeitung* condemning violent illegal attacks on Jews. In the same year another priest was brought to trial for slander against the state because he said that he did not understand the measures against the Jews, that they were also men, and that he would say so in his next sermon. He also said that good Germans should not disturb Jewish property and that there was no special type of Christianity for the separate races. Another priest wrote a flyer in which he said, "What is going on in the Church struggle? . . . Salvation comes not from the Aryans, but as Christ said, from the Jews." In 1935 the police seized the Catholic weekly *Ketteler Wacht* because it contained an article entitled "Christianity and Judaism," which was contradictory to Nazi racial ideology. A Catholic priest from Duisburg gave a lecture in 1935 condemning the anti-Semitic scientist, Muckermann. The meeting was stormed by the *Hitlerjugend,* and the audience sang the *Judenlied* in protest. Also, in 1935 Gerhard Kehnscherper had written that religion under the Nazis had been secularized into race-hygiene. In the Nazi system the care of blood was becoming the prime duty of men.[51]

A 1935 report of the *Regierungspräsident* in the Aachen Government District indicated that strong anti-Semitic propaganda would not be well received there, since a large part of the population disapproved of it especially as it appeared in *Der Stürmer.* It was suggested that very serious differences with the Catholic Church would result if such propaganda continued.[52] Another report reads as follows:

> The treatment of the Jewish Question in my district has in any case elicited the greatest indignation, since in their values the Catholic population appraise the Jews first as men and only secondarily judge the matter from a racial-political standpoint.[53]

Still another report quoted and commented upon an ironic sermon as typical of the sense of injustice with which racial persecution was perceived by Catholics:

> Why do many people venerate the Virgin Mary, perhaps because she is not of Aryan descent? When men are dead and buried, it is irrelevant to which race they belonged, and when they come before the divine judges, they will also not be asked: 'Are you of Aryan descent or do you belong to another race?' [Comment: Pastor Coenen's statement produced general laughter among the congregation.][54]

Attacks on Jewish property were also condemned in this largely Catholic district. Catholic publications tried to undermine Nazi racial ideology by continuing traditional references to marriages between Protestants and Catholics as *Mischehe* to mock the Nazi use of the term for marriages between non-Jews and Jews.[55] The press was forbidden to discuss *Mischehe* except in a racial sense to foil the Catholics. The continuance of "racial" intermarriage, of course, suggests that Nazi ideas were irrelevant to many Catholics since it was their *own* norms that mattered to them.

In 1936 a priest from Lauterbach made the following statement while instructing Catholic children: "*Das Schwarze Korps* and *Der Stürmer* are hateful newspapers; whoever reads them commits a sin." A member of the Catholic Young Men's Association also sought support for a "free Jerusalem" in March of 1938; the confidential agent who reported this commented that all good Nazis would agree he belonged in a concentration camp. In 1937 a *Deutschland-Bericht* reported that priests were being attacked for their *judenfreundliche* attitudes and their hostility to Rosenberg during instructional sessions. Another *Deutschland-Bericht* reported in 1937:

> In the Catholic question far-reaching decisions were awaited; instead of this the Führer denied that Jews possessed any intelligence whatsoever, which statement has but strengthened the opinion of the people that he is becoming really megalomaniacal.[56]

A Catholic chaplain was brought to trial in 1937 because he attacked

Nazi ideology regarding "race, blood, and soil" as the worst form of materialism. He also said that leaders in Bolshevik Russia had given an order to publish an anti-Semitic book of Ludendorff's that represented the doctrines of National Socialism quite well, thus indicating how really inferior the Nazis were. In the same year a report on public opinion stated that Jewish shops prospered in Catholic areas because of the Church's opposition to persecution as well as because Jews could offer better prices.[57]

Several sources also indicate that Catholics disapproved of the pogrom of November 1938. A priest in Düsseldorf, for example, took in a Jew during the *Kristallnacht*. The Jew had been stabbed, a tendon in his right hand was severed, and he would have bled to death. The Church remained critical of *Kristallnacht* long after the population had generally accepted it as a bygone occurrence. Nevertheless, the churches were expected even by the Nazis to sponsor a more orchestrated propaganda campaign against the regime because of this pogrom; they did not do so. Individual Catholics who aided Jews at that time were more courageous than their leaders, who lost a golden opportunity to destroy the moral credibility of the Nazi regime. *Kristallnacht* was probably the unique occasion during which the Church could have taken a stance, because a large part of the public appears to have opposed the pogrom. Yet the Church remained silent just as it basically did during the Roehm purge.[58]

During World War II there were varied cases of aid to Jews by Catholics in positions of only modest authority. One *Pfarrer*, for example, paid the medical bills of a Jewish cancer patient in 1941 and was subsequently sentenced to two and a half months in prison plus a 2,000 RM fine. Another attempted to help a Jewess cross the border, resulting in criminal proceedings that were begun against him. One arrested priest in 1942 had said: "I am a minister and in this capacity cannot adopt hostility toward any man, including Poles, Russians, or Jews." In Berlin a priest was arrested in 1943 because he gave 350 RM to a Jew from the *Caritashilfe* and associated with them in public. A cleric was arraigned before the *Volksgerichthof* in 1943 because in a store he had said that the allied air forces' "terror" attacks against Cologne were revenge for the legal and illegal persecution of Jews. He also referred to a picture of Hitler with the following comment: "This guy is to blame for everything."[59] In Villingen another clergyman spoke very admiringly of Jews. The report on his activity was as follows:

The Roman Catholic Church recognizes nothing of the war against the world—enemies, Judaism and Bolshevism. Certainly she stands at the front and prays with her 'believers' for peace, but never for a German victory, and many party members pray with her.[60]

In 1944 a chaplain was sent to Dachau because he secured lodging for a "submarine" (Jew in hiding) even though he knew what was involved. A Catholic nun in a hospital was condemned to death in 1945 at the age of 27 because she helped Jews in Germany. A number of nuns were helpful to Jews during the war. Catholic hospitals regularly took in Jews for real and invented reasons to protect them. Two Catholic women, Else Heidkamp and Gertrud Luckner, aided Jews through the St. Raphael Society and the *Caritasfund.* In one instance they placed a Jewish child in a Catholic home illegally, and subsequently it was also discovered that Gertrud Luckner had aided many Jews to cross the border into Switzerland. She spent the rest of the war in a concentration camp, while Else Heidkamp was sent to prison, where it is known that she remained until at least August 1943.[61]

These are only a few examples of reported opposition among the hierarchy, lower clergy, and Catholics in general. Still, if these examples are at all representative, it would appear that Lewy's assumption that the Catholic population approved of racial persecution should be reexamined. In any case, most acts on behalf of Jews seem to have been performed by lesser clergymen and the laity; the institution, at least openly, failed to imitate their heroism. But it is doubtful that these individual Catholics would have acted so heroically had their behavior not been sanctioned by the norms of the Church and perhaps even by the hierarchy acting in a private rather than public fashion. An apparent, although not overwhelming, opposition to the regime's anti-Jewish policy existed within the Church.

The Resistance of the Parish Clergy

With respect to its own institutional integrity, the Church's opposition was more intense, perhaps because the Nazis were intervening in the traditional relationships between Germans and their religious mentors. One directive of 1938 from the *SD-Oberabschnitt Südwest* described the key points at which informers should be placed: among diocesan officials, in religious orders, bishops' residences, lay organizations, youth groups, theological faculties, cultural institutions, and the ecumenical movement. Open opposition in the Church, therefore, was difficult to mobilize because of SD informers. Not only violations of existing laws or such agreements as the 1933 Concordat were to be reported; the informants were also to forestall "all plans and measures which the Churches are legally allowed to pursue within their own areas of competence but which if they were carried out in public would not be tolerated from the standpoint of the Party's ideological principals." Sermons, in particular, were to be regularly overheard and noted. Finally, the financial and economic resources of the churches were to be uncovered for propaganda exploitation and possible administrative and legal countermeasures.[62] Resistance, then, could be mobilized around those "rights" still existent in the Concordat as well as on the regime's obvious desire not to alienate the Church during wartime. Clerical leaders could also focus their critiques on Rosenberg's *Mythos*, which had not been officially made part of the Nazi ideological canon. Rosenberg, for example, had insisted that Germans had to choose between Christ and the German *Volk*. The bishops declared:

> We German Catholics reject such a choice with burning indignation. We love our German people and serve them, if need be, to death. At the same time we also live and die for Jesus Christ and want to remain united with him, now and for all eternity. . . . If we take pains to preserve Christianity among our people, we thereby also stand for the individual right and dignity of every German . . .[63]

Local clergymen could resist on a level that the regime found difficult to control without highlighting its inability to contain the Church. To reduce anxiety, both the regime and the Church promoted community integrity, which was helpful for those who would find coping difficult.[64] Hence, the role of the local pastor in maintaining a well integrated *Gemeinschaft* responded to a very important coping need prevalent among members of his local parish, who may well have felt uncomfortable when faced with "outside" political forces (Nazi bureaucrats) and then war. Catholic clergymen, for example, increased their efforts to administer the sacraments secretly to those who wished to retain the designation *Gottglaübige* for political reasons. Because of the Church's flexibility, the number of withdrawals had dropped sharply since the beginning of the war. Although it did not supply precise statistics, the SD reported that among the many who had rejoined the Church were party members from whom "one would expect more conviction in ideological matters." The SD reported that Catholics were quite negative even in the early *Gleichschaltung* phase. They referred to Christ as the highest führer, to which Goebbels responded that the word had never been applied to Christ before it was coined by the party.[65]

Catholic priests continuously made the point that religion went beyond the church doors and was to pervade the whole of a person's life. Most priests did not launch attacks on the leaders of the regime with the exception of Rosenberg. Generally, priestly denunciations focused on Nazi racism and neoheathen observances. Priests would use their religious instruction classes to ask such questions as: "Are you Christian or heathen? Is Hitler God, or is Jesus Christ?" Also, priests removed swastikas from their churches. Resistance to local Nazis is apparent, probably because local priests resented the intrusion of Nazi outside forces into their village or parish. There does not seem to be a great deal of opposition to Hitler's nationalistic goals or to his anti-Bolshevism.[66]

The establishment of special classes in religious instruction also demonstrated the Church's flexibility and resourcefulness. By 1941 the regime had reduced the number of class hours in school devoted to religious instruction, and had cancelled such education in all schools after the eighth year. In response, clergymen set up special religion classes on church premises, enrolled students over age 14 for evening classes twice a month, included worship services, dancing, singing, and even cowboy films. Apparently, teachers and students discussed such topics as "Counteracting National Socialist Ideology through the Formulation of a Catholic *Weltanschauung,* Christianizing the Germans, and Jesus Christ and the Jews." Younger children attended regular religion classes in the secular schools. In areas where significant numbers of clerical teaching personnel had been replaced by National Socialist laymen, clergymen established special religion classes. In 1943 an SD agent pointed out that the Church's educational program was far more successful than that of the *Hitlerjugend.* He wrote:

> The Church's educational activities have greatly extended its influence over family life. The Church has consistently demonstrated a deep personal concern for and involvement in the needs of parents and children. In the effort to provide religious education for children the Church has been particularly successful in securing the cooperation of the German woman.[67]

Although a sizable number of women opposed the Nazi *Weltanschauung,* female antagonism was by no means universal. The new paganism argued that racial purity and selective breeding were the necessary instruments of progress in the human as in the animal world, thus insisting that social policy be oriented accordingly. In general, Catholic women were disturbed by the purely biological role that National Socialism assigned them. Catholic women opposed the Nazi view that the role of women was grounded in racial procreation, making women merely "fair game" for Aryan males devoted to the eugenic goals of the *Weltanschauung. Casti Connubi* may well have urged women to remain in the home, but they did not agree that the encyclical supported Nazi eugenic goals. In such organizations as *Katholischer Frauen und Mutterverein,* Catholic women visibly opposed Nazi racism as a view irreconcilable with their credal tenets. Only a couple of million women, however, joined Catholic organizations where they could register their disapproval of their government's racist policies.[68] In all likelihood Catholic women chose not to support such organizations as *Caritas* to avoid public conflict with Nazis. The mediocre support of Catholic women's organizations by Germans reflects a familiar desire to remain anonymous and free of conflict. While many women remained apolitical, those in Catholic organizations did perceive and confront the issue of racism so highly touted by the regime. In the Third Reich, schools, media, and rallies all stressed that Christian charity should be terminated in the interest of the racial purity of the *Volk*.[69]

When Nazi welfare personnel, who worked in sterilization and euthanasia programs, came to Catholic institutions to take away the mentally handicapped and the infirm elderly, it was not the staff in *Caritas* headquarters who acted, but local volunteers. Berlin women hid the feeble-minded protectively to shield them from referral to one of those houses where imminent death was certain. Members of the Elizabeth Society cared for non-Aryan Catholics as much as for other needy persons. Some Catholic women felt that their Church acted in pusillanimous fashion except, of course, when it came to euthanasia. Members of the Berlin Elizabeth Society, however, maintained that an open dispute was not the way the *Caritas* organization was to defend its God-given duties. If individual women wished to counteract the evil of their government, they generally had to act alone and on their own initiative. Some met the challenge and some did not.[70] It is inadequate simply to posit anti-Semitism as a reason for the Church's uneven handling of the racist question, because the issue contradicted Catholic doctrine and Christian principles so completely that it posed a threat to the Church itself. Quite apart from their posture on the Nazi treatment of Jews, the hierarchy recognized the ultimate threat which neopagan racism posed for the institutionalized Christian tradition, but provided weak leadership. Psychologists suggest two ways in which individuals deal with anti-Semitism. The more a person allows another to suffer, the more one will derogate or dehumanize the hapless victim. An act that injures another is not viewed as inequitable if the victim deserves to be harmed. Thus, an obvious way in which a person who has practiced anti-Semitism can persuade himself that his act was equitable is by devaluating the victim's actions. Latent anti-Semitism or apathy perhaps encouraged Catholics to offer only minimal and individual responses to Nazi eugenic policies. Behavior, however, that departs from the consensual norms is also significant. Joining avowedly Catholic organizations in Nazi Germany was a significant act of protest against and resistance to anti-Semitism.[71] Such resistance may not have been heroic, but it worried the regime, whose representatives were concerned about all manifestations of religion and the conflict in allegiance, which might be shaped.

Gauleiter Wagner's order of April 23, 1941, to remove all crucifixes from classrooms and end school prayers, for example, provoked public indignation. Everywhere demonstrations, litigations, and riots resulted—even

Mutterkreuze were returned. Women barged into schools, threatening to keep their children at home. There was talk of a work strike and even threats to bring their complaints to the führer. When in early September Wagner rescinded his order under the pressure of events, protests continued because the cancellation had occurred secretly and it took time for the lifting of these restrictions to spread. In their eagerness to neutralize their opponents, party bureaus also made numerous tactical errors that often produced the opposite of the desired effect. Such a blunder was the decision to observe traditional religious celebrations, processions, pilgrimages, etc., on Sundays or holidays instead of weekdays. Refusal to comply could result in prohibition of the event. In one Silesian locality, women reportedly retaliated by boycotting Mother's Day celebrations put on by the Women's League.[72]

In sending religious literature to members of the armed forces, the Church was also particularly resourceful. In 1939, Hans Kerrl, minister of Church affairs, prohibited clergymen from sending to the Front any kind of religious publication apart from Bibles and hymnals. Nor could they compile address lists of parishioners in the armed forces. Clergymen found, however, that they could send material without violating Kerrl's law. Surprisingly, the regime allowed civilian clergymen to send all religious literature to frontline chaplains in postage-free packages weighing less than ten kilograms. The chaplains, of course, could then distribute such literature freely to the men. Also, since the prohibition did not apply to laymen, the clergy urged families to send pamphlets and journals. They also organized groups of members who sent literature in envelopes bearing an unknown return address. The SD agent caustically observed that "clergymen feel themselves to be especially ingenious by practicing these subterfuges."[73]

Besides being flexible and resourceful, the SD found clergymen conducting themselves with uncharacteristic boldness. The regime had restricted religious activities in hospitals. Violations, however, were frequent, especially in Catholic hospitals. Priests often made calls without the request of the patient. Nuns urged patients to request priests to call, sang religious songs in the wards, and baptized infants. An SD agent in the Bielefeld area observed that Catholics seemed to know that the shorthanded Gestapo was unable to enforce hospital restrictions. By 1943 priests conformed to the government's restrictions in public hospitals, but defied the regime in Catholic ones. Occasionally defiance in military hospitals, where restrictions were similar, went beyond urging patients to request the visit of a clergyman or singing religious songs in the wards. An SD agent reported that a nun in a military hospital made an insult about Hitler in the presence of an SS man and told a soldier about the euthanasia program that had been cancelled in 1941 after vigorous protests by clergymen. The soldier reportedly replied: "If German people are being treated like that, I am going to throw away my rifle." The nun was summarily dismissed by the chief doctor.[74]

Catholic clergy also violated restrictions designed to regulate foreign laborers. The SD reported numerous and flagrant violations. Roman Catholic clergy, for example, conducted services in Polish and in German churches near the labor camps. The Gestapo in the Saarbrücken area arrested a German priest who actually arranged transportation for Polish workers, especially women, so that they might worship in his parish. Such joint German-Polish activities as Corpus Christi processions and social evenings for young people in convents were common. Polish workers did not always wear the prescribed "P," but even when they did, German Catholics, including servicemen on leave, apparently were delighted to worship with their fellow-Catholics. On July 3, 1942, Father Josef Bär, for example, was imprisoned because he allowed Poles and Russians to participate in services, despite a previous warning. In the view of the SD agent, Catholics consorting with Poles displayed a complete disregard for racial doctrine:

> They show no understanding of the insidious and vengeful character of the Poles. . . . The struggle against the Poles in the villages is in vain so long as Germans and Poles sit together in Church. . . . The necessary evil of Poles working on German soil is compounded by the Church, which does not seem to grasp the enormity of Polish crimes against Germans.[75]

The SD charged the Church with defying the regime and undermining its programs in the area of youth work. According to a report submitted to one *Gauleiter,* the Catholics had succeeded by 1943 in reviving two illegal youth organizations, the Marian Congregation and *Neu-Deutschland.* Through intensive indoctrination of an ever-increasing number of altar boys, priests in Aachen had formed "an *ersatz* youth organization." From the regime's point of view a more ominous development in some Catholic parishes was the formation of a *Stosstrup,* a group of ten to fifteen young "activists" whose purpose was to "counteract militantly the effects of the regime's youth program by infiltrating the Hitler youth and undermining it subversively from within." Referred to once, this is the only recorded instance of an overtly subversive activity planned by the Church. But each year the Gestapo observed the Catholic Youth Festival carefully and was dismayed, particularly at the fact that the festival consistently attracted large numbers of parents and children. In the words of one agent: "The young people seem to prefer this service to the often boring ceremonies of the Hitler Youth."[76]

By late 1942 many of the clergy and laity had also become alarmed at the child-evacuation program. According to rumors allegedly fostered by the Church, the regime not only failed to provide for the children's religious needs, but also fed and housed them inadequately. The SD charged the Church with opposing the program from the beginning and cited protests from Bishop Galen and the Fulda Bishops' Conference. In a pamphlet allegedly dropped from an airplane, Gröber described the program as "a plan of the SS to de-Christianize German children." By 1943 such protests had prompted Berhard Rust, minister of education, to issue an official guarantee that children in the program would receive religious instruction. To what extent Rust's decree was actually implemented is not known, but the SD interpreted the minister's directive as "a major setback for National Socialism in its ideological confrontation with the Church."[77] An agent described the efforts of officials to implement the child evacuation program in Trier (1944):

> The parents, deeply concerned about religious instruction for the children, sarcastically asked such Jesuitical questions as: 'Is there a law requiring us to enroll our children?' The women jeered and hooted at the *Kreisleiter.* One was reminded of the *Kampfzeit!* It was disconcerting to learn how un-enlightened the people are in Trier and how little the Party has impressed them. Obviously, hostile powers are at work here to sabotage all that the Party does. . . . Only 50 percent of the eligible children registered for the program.[78]

The extent to which clergymens' protests turned laymen against the program cannot be measured, but by making religious education of the children a major issue, the Church helped arouse suspicion about the entire child-evacuation program. The SD reports are replete with lengthy excerpts from pastoral letters, sermons, and the Fulda Bishops' Conferences as well as statements, rumors, and jokes attributed to specific clergymen or to "confessional circles." To the SD these protests were designed "to undermine the people's confidence in the NSDAP leadership." The vast majority of clergymen were hardly revolutionary. Basically, the clergy usually endorsed Hitler's military ventures, at least initially, and merely charged the regime with undermining the people's morale through specific policies. Naturally protests resulted when the moral teachings of Christianity were impinged upon. These moral protests suggested to the SD that the Church was a subversive threat to the regime.[79]

The Church made relatively little effort to avert the extermination of the Jews or even to speak out against this atrocity. But the clergy did appear sensitive to the regime's brutality as in the euthanasia controversy. Also, especially after Stalingrad, the clergy often asserted that the horrors of war were God's punishment for Germany's treatment of Russians, Poles, and

Jews. According to a *Gauleitung* report of 1943, priests in Lübeck told their parishioners: "The regime has no right to protest the murders at Katyn in view of the SS methods of butchering Jews in the East. God will punish our people for what the SS is doing." Another theme of "confessional propaganda" was that National Socialism with its nihilism, brutality, and persecution of the Church was no better than Bolshevism and, like communism, was doomed to destruction. The SD charged clergymen with convincing large numbers of fighting men that the struggle against Bolshevism was in vain so long as the party used Bolshevist tactics on the churches at home.[80]

The SD found that clergymen often publicly read letters of fighting men who had had religious experiences under fire or whose Christian faith had favorably impressed unbelievers. The following passage illustrates this point:

> All of us at the front need courage and faith in this struggle between Christian Europe and godless Russia. We pray that there will soon be peace and that Christian love for all men will replace hatred for the Jews. . . . We soldiers at the front have again learned that we cannot get along without faith or religion. We urge you at home to train our children in the faith of our fathers, so that the German people will remain strong, pious, and true.[81]

Other examples can also be cited. A son, for example, who had rejected the Church and had for some time ceased praying requested his mother to send a rosary: "Experiences at the front have opened my eyes and taught me the power of prayer." A popular, although somewhat melodramatic, letter described the experience of a German soldier devoutly praying his rosary. Because he was praying, he did not see an approaching Russian soldier. Upon seeing the rosary, however, the Russian immediately laid down his rifle and embraced the German.[82]

From the regime's point of view the most dangerous letter of this kind was that allegedly written by Germany's leading air ace, Colonel Werner Mölders, killed in a plane crash in November 1941. In a letter written to a Roman Catholic clergyman, the devoutly Catholic fighter pilot pointed out that his example of Christian courage, when facing death, had converted, or at least impressed, many of his anti-Christian colleagues. The letter, of course, was immediately printed, circulated, and read from hundreds of Roman Catholic and Protestant pulpits in Germany. It was also accompanied by a rumor that the SS had killed Mölders because his prowess and courage in the air derived from a faith hostile to National Socialism. Although the Gestapo secured public denials of the letter's authenticity from Mölder's mother and even from the clergyman to whom it was written, millions of Germans believed the letter to be genuine. "The Church is capitalizing on the letter," wrote an SD agent, "even though its falsity has been well-established. Confessional circles believe that the incident demonstrates the real attitude of the führer and National Socialism toward Christianity." Even if the Gestapo had known that a British intelligence agent had written the letter and dropped it from a Royal Air Force plane, the people probably would have remained unconvinced. The British intelligence agent, Sefton Delmer, had learned from a captured Luftwaffe officer that Mölders, shortly before his death, had written a letter to a Roman Catholic clergyman, who had read it to a youth group. The actual letter was not critical of the regime, but merely reflected the pilot's deep religious conviction. Very cleverly, Delmer worded the forgery so that it contained no direct reference to National Socialism or its leaders, but only a description of the powerful impact of Mölder's Christian witness upon skeptics and scoffers. The letter was credible.[83] Because Germans knew that the regime falsified the news, they were susceptible to rumors. The Church took advantage of such rumors both to discredit the regime as well as to defend the faith.

In what was clearly an example of moral outrage, Roman Catholic clergymen spoke out against SS eugenic practices. Already in 1940, Faulhaber had attacked "Himmler's appeal to the SS to do its biological duty." Two years later clergymen had become more explicit. They denounced the practice of encouraging and even paying girls in the Reich Labor Service to engage in sexual relations with members of the Waffen SS. An SD agent vigorously denied the claim and attacked Roman Catholic clergymen, who, "in their allegations that girls in the Labor Service are required to father a child by an SS man, will stop at nothing to defame the regime." Clerical attacks did not compel the SS to revise its eugenic policy, but they may have deterred some women from voluntarily offering themselves to SS men. In any case, Himmler could hardly have been pleased with the final results. The SS *Lebensborn,* established in 1936 to care for the offspring of selective mating, had recorded only 11,000 births by 1945, an inauspicious beginning for the "Thousand-Year Reich."[84]

While the SD did not supply statistics on the incidence of clerical protest, the reports indicate that it was frequent, widespread, and persistent. Although anti-Christian measures were applied more harshly in such areas as Württemberg, Bavaria, and the Rhineland, the reports also reveal that protests were not centered in these areas. For almost five years agents from all over Germany consistently reported the same phenomena, with the incidence of clerical protests increasing after late 1941. After Stalingrad the reports became gloomy. A Catholic priest, for example, was arrested in Düsseldorf for saying that it would not be so bad if the Bolsheviks came. Another said that the bombing of Cologne was the punishment for Hitler's destruction of the Jewish stores before the war.[85] Internment in concentration camps or execution would have silenced many clergymen, but the regime was reluctant to take such drastic measures. With the exception of Bishop Sproll of Rottenburg,[86] bishops were generally inviolate as can be seen by the regime's failure to take action against Galen after his attack on euthanasia in 1941. Goebbels, Bormann, and other leaders wanted to hang Galen for what they considered a treasonous act, but agreed that capital punishment for the bishop might turn Westphalians and Roman Catholics in general into active opponents of the regime. The number of priests arrested was relatively small. Approximately 1.5 percent of the Catholic clergy was interned during the war. Leaders of the regime also ruled out an intensive propaganda campaign against the Church during the war. "Because the war has required the regime to exercise the utmost restraint in public discussion of internal affairs and ideological questions," wrote an SD agent, "confessional propaganda has become increasingly blatant and effective." Priests, then, took advantage of the regime's restraint, even though their protests were not part of a systematic campaign designed to undermine the people's confidence in the Nazi leadership.[87]

The SD divided clerical protests into two categories. The first consisted of overt criticism or negative reaction to specific events, policies, programs, and leaders. In a second category were numerous sermons and pastoral letters enjoining the faithful to do their Christian duty by obeying God's laws, practicing brotherly love for all men, and providing religious training for children and youth. The second category was almost as dangerous as the first, for the SD believed that the New Order could never become a reality as long as millions of Germans were Catholics. Consequently, the propagation of the Christian law and gospel, even if couched in non-political terms, was an obstacle to the establishment of a truly totalitarian society. Despite the limitations of restraint imposed by the exigencies of war, bureaucratic incompetence, and personnel shortages, the National Socialists were unwilling to concede that the totalitarian ideology was incapable of displacing Christianity. Responding to this conviction, party leaders initiated in 1940 a program designed to make National Socialist celebrations more spiritually and psychologically fulfilling than those of the Church.[88]

Catholics also surpassed Nazis in social work as well. Gau Baden complained about "insidious agitation" by "blacks" (Catholics) in episcopal letters and described the Lroba Sisters as especially dangerous because of their "harmful work within the family." Similar reports by the Nazi Woman's League in other areas clearly reveal a basic professional jealousy at the root of this conflict with the Church. Members of the Reich Chancellery were also envious of "noticeably higher Church collections," far surpassing Winter Relief results. Church youth work was viewed with particular alarm, and a circular from the Reich Youth Directorate of March 19, 1941, repeated demands that any situation tending to aggravate the "confrontation of ideologies" was to be avoided.[89]

Opposition to Nazism and Catholic Values

Zahn, Müller, and Lewy have asserted that the Catholic Church failed to exert the kind of moral and political leadership that might have mitigated the horrors of National Socialism.[90] In an introduction to Müller's work, Sontheimer states: "By failing to protest the gross injustices of the regime as vigorously as those measures which affected its institutional structure, the Church violated its own moral teachings."[91] Sontheimer has also contended that Catholic endorsement of such specific aspects of National Socialism as authoritarian government, intense nationalism, and fervent opposition to liberalism and communism "prevented the formation of a general political principle which could have prompted Catholics to defend freedom and equal rights resolutely." This dualism of patriotism and opposition robbed the churches and resistance movements of their ability to act decisively.[92] The SD reports on religious affairs, however, supply an intriguing dimension to the study of the *Kirchenkampf* during the war. They suggest that the Church acted more in accordance with Christian principles than some of its critics are willing to concede. The Church did not lead an organized resistance movement, but clergymen boldly criticized National Socialism and meaningfully and lovingly ministered to millions active in this tragic war. The SD reports indicate that the Church maintained its institutional and doctrinal integrity. The Church did not win the *Kirchenkampf,* but survived and maintained its institutional opposition to Nazi totalitarianism. Conversely, however, the SD reports, by documenting the Church's spiritual power in defying the regime and undermining its programs, provide the basis for an indictment. If more vigorously applied, the Church's considerable influence might well have significantly mitigated the horrors of National Socialism. The SD reports are useful, therefore, to both the defenders and critics of the Church. The reports also contribute to a deeper understanding of the Church's varied responses to National Socialism as it tried to survive in the lives of its people, particularly in villages.

In Catholic villages the pastor traditionally selected mayors and teachers as well as determined important political matters, thus making him a prime target of the NSDAP. At least in the village studied by Rinderle, Kirchheim, the party never achieved its goal of winning the loyalty of the villagers away from their Church and home town. Nazi officials faced a tightly knit society which they could not effectively penetrate from without and which the local group leader could not control from within. These leaders could not substitute Nazi celebrations and holidays for traditional religious festivities nor turn the schools into indoctrination centers. The villagers were not anti-Nazi per se, but rather wanted to preserve their traditional way of life in the face of threats from such forces as that of the central government and modernization in general. Nazi attempts to utilize social or political power outside the range of its legitimacy tended to increase resistance to its influence.[93] Village and town politicians maintained their influence despite the *Gleichschaltung,* and the local Catholic priests continued to play their roles in village life.

The concern of the SD with the Catholic Church is not difficult to understand, since the latter formed one of the remaining counterweights to state totalitarianism in Germany, opposing the state with its own claims on the individual. In Catholic communities, pressures toward uniformity in values seem greatest when traditional or religious values were directly threatened, since such norms were necessary for the maintenance of the social integrity of the local Catholic community. Two principles help explain the response of Catholics to the regime: (1) a person will resist real or cognitive changes in situations that are central to his self-concept or to his self-esteem, and (2) persons will resist changing an environment that offers a source of stability.[94]

Elements of opposition existed from the inception of the regime in Catholic circles even though compromises were made with the "legitimate authority." Had the resistance been mobilized more effectively and had the pronouncements of the bishops been more clearly antiregime, then the moral prestige of the Church would have been enhanced. But would Catholics have supported their leaders in attacking the legitimate regime and after 1939 a government fighting a war? Sustained overt resistance probably could not have been incited or sustained, given the regime's power, German nationalistic values, and the tendency toward concern with personal problems especially as the war commenced. Apparently, however, what is perceived by Lewy, Zahn, Conway, and others as capitulation or, at the very least, lack of resistance, was viewed by Nazi leaders as posing a very serious threat. In trying to maintain the Church as a viable institution and continuing their pressure on the regime, perhaps the bishops chose a course between Scylla and Charibdis—not very heroic but practical. Popular resistance indeed seems to have focused on the objections to governmental interference in local situations, not initially on hostility to the goals of the regime, at least until these became too costly for the sacrifices being made.[95] The SD reports indicate that institutional "silence" is not always assent and that patriotic sermons, for example, may simply have been the vehicle used to gain a hearing. Not every German was a fanatical, heel-clicking, hand-raising Nazi. Even numerous party members became disenchanted enough with Hitler to oppose the NSDAP and so open themselves to the vigorous trials before the *Parteigericht*.[96] Religion is inherently a conservative force, since its function is to consecrate the status quo. If the task of religion, and so of theology, is to bestow ultimate meaning, and if meaning is the order that a true religious society projects upon the universe, then religion cannot but be seen as the consecration of the structures of society. At least on the local level, Catholics viewed Nazism as disturbing the traditional societal configurations, and these included parish life. Hence, Nazism was to be viewed by local Catholic leaders as a danger to the traditional society in which religion played a key role.[97]

Humans are reward-seeking and punishment-avoiding creatures. Catholics could support their bishops' and Hitler's nationalistic patriotism and simultaneously oppose local Nazi incursions. Some local resistance was probably mere stubbornness to outside resistance. Exchange theories help in explaining the paradox of resistance and adaptation, anti-Semitism and help for individual Jews, patriotism and opposition to Nazi incursions on the local level. An individual can independently learn to respond to each of two stimuli sets. A person can be, therefore, a good German, not necessarily a Nazi, and a good Catholic, especially if a community network support system is present. Confronted with a compound value configuration, a novel integrated response composed of the two systems seemed to occur. Patriotism and protest, articulated by the clergy, seemed to fall on ready ears in the Third Reich. In their role as teachers, Catholic clergy reinforced patriotism to the nation and loyalty to the Church. They emphasized the faults of the individual Nazis who were failing to administer properly and so were undermining the *Vaterland*, village-town society, and the Catholic Church. In this way traditional patriotism could be nurtured, while the specific government then in power could be attacked.[98]

Generalized values tend to be weak constraints on political beliefs, but this is not true of needs. Some Catholics, for example, apparently saw the need for condemning the treatment of the Jews to affirm their own humanity, religious values, or village autonomy. Some could be indifferent and achieve a similar result. Some cheered *völkisch* statements, but resented Nazi attempts to create a homogeneous *Volk* by annihilating particularistic communities. To an important degree the organization of modern social life seems to demand that humans be treated as statistics. By considering their immediate neighbors, Jew and Aryan, as persons, some Catholics played an outstanding role in nurturing moral responsibility. Erroneously, Baum has insisted that there were virtually no debates on the values held in the Third Reich. A mere perusal of the SD reports should indicate that the debate on values persisted even in Nazi Germany. It may not have been a debate publicized through the media, but resistance through sermons, actions, comments in bars, etc., constituted perhaps a more significant critique of the Nazi *Weltanschauung* than any that could have occurred in learned journals. Marrus and Paxton, for example, have contended that German policy as well as the ability of the Nazis to apply their power, were decisive in determining how far the destructive process went by 1945.[99] Perhaps such a thesis was operant in Germany as well as occupied Europe. Because of resistance to the regime and even coordinated adaptation, a monolithic Third Reich was never allowed to emerge and wreak even more carnage than it had by 1945.

What damages religion and undermines belief in God, some scholars feel, is not the denial of the transcendent as much as its separation as a distinct category from the rest of life. The Catholic clergy very carefully constructed a framework in which Catholics could be loyal to the *Volk* and so remain rooted in the traditional German value system. Support even for the Nazis could be tendered insofar as they remained in this community of traditional political values, thus making protest and patriotism simultaneously possible. Bishops adapted for an institutional *raison d'etre*; many Catholics resisted local incursions of Nazis for personal or community reasons. Thus, religion remained a part of everyday life where it counts—in the actions of persons, not just in official missives. For Kant the essence of sin is making exceptions. This "sin" is difficult to avoid for a Christian living in a world in which the prophetic spirit and the spirit of order are at work, sometimes in cooperation but more frequently in conflict. From the experience of German Catholics in the Third Reich it has become increasingly clear that religious thinkers making distinctions should never put a stamp of approval upon any given system of society. Resistance could be mounted in support of the Church as either a national or local institution. But religious opposition to racism did not enjoy broad support, since the clergy generally and unfortunately mirrored the indifference of their congregations. In most Catholics the party had failed to inculcate an *active* hatred of the Jews, although the Nazis had succeeded in convincing most Germans that there was a "Jewish Question" that had to be answered. Kershaw's general assessment is that the road to Auschwitz was built by hate, but paved with indifference.[100] SD reports and other documents indicate that the apathy was not universal, but that paths of resistance had to be chosen cautiously if the individual hoped to criticize the regime and maintain his local religious community intact.

Notes

1. Simon, "A Behavioral Model of Rational Choice,' pp. 99-118; C.E. Lindblom, "The Science of 'Muddling Through,'" *Public Administration Review* 29

(1959):79-88; D. Bobrow, "The Chinese Communist Conflict System," *Orbis* 9 (1966):931; A. Schlesinger, "The Roosevelt Era: Stimson and Hull," *Nation*, June 5, 1948; George in Coelho, pp. 187-188.

2. See Beate Ruhm von Oppen, *Religion and Resistance to Nazism*, Center of International Studies, Princeton University, 1971, for a succinct analysis of Catholic resistance. For a carefully crafted analysis of resistance focusing on the "Jewish question," see Sarah Gordon, *Hitler, Germans, and the "Jewish Question"* (Princeton: Princeton University Press, 1984). Several collections of governmental materials highlighting Catholic resistance may be found in: Helmut Prantl (ed.), *Die Kirchliche Lage in Bayern nach den Regierungspräsidentenberichten, 1933-1943: Regierungsbezirk Pfalz, 1933-1940* (Mainz: Matthias Grünewald, 1978); Ziegler, *Die Kirchliche Lage in Bayern*; Witetschek, *Die Kirchliche Lage in Bayern*; Klaus Wittstadt (ed.), *Die Kirchliche Lage in Bayern nach den Regierungspräsidentenberichten, 1933-1943: Regierungsbezirk Unterfranken, 1933-1944* (Mainz: Matthias Grünewald, 1981). An older but still useful work on resistance may be found in Mary Alice Gallin, *German Resistance to Hitler: Ethical and Religious Factors* (Washington, D.C.: Catholic University Press, 1961). For an incisive analysis of the structure and functions of the SD, see Wall, pp. 438-440. The reports were so candid that by 1943 such leading Nazis as Himmler and Bormann had concluded that the materials were unsuitable because their explicit coverage of Germany's deteriorating condition actually fostered a defeatist mentality. Bormann even withheld these reports from Hitler. After 1943, the reports remained objective, but less explicitly critical of events, personalities, and policies.

3. Neuhäusler, 2:104-109; Lewy, pp. 314-315. For a recent study of the Oldenburg Crucifix struggle, see Jeremy Noakes, "The Oldenburg Crucifix Struggle of November 1936: A Case Study of Opposition in the Third Reich," in Peter Stachura (ed.), *The Shaping of the Nazi State* (London: Croom and Helm, 1978):210-233.

4. "Reptile," *Monologe*, August 11, 1942, p. 337, in MacGregor Knox, "Conquest, Foreign and Domestic in Fascist Italy and Nazi Germany," *Journal of Modern History* 56(1984):56.

5. Damico, p. 424; Ian Kershaw, "The Führer Image and Political Integration: The Popular Conception of Hitler in Bavaria during the Third Reich," in Gerhard Hirschfeld and Lothar Kettenacker (eds.), *Der "Führerstaat": Mythos und Realität. Studien zur Struktur und Politik des Dritten Reiches* (Stuttgart: Klett-Cotta, 1981), pp. 155, 159, 161.

6. See Conway, *Persecution*; Lewy, *Catholic Church*; Friedrich Zipfel, *Kirchenkampf in Deutschland, 1933-1945*.

7. Heinz Boberach (ed.), *Meldungen aus dem Reich. Auswahl aus den geheimen Lageberichten des Sicherheitsdienstes der SS, 1939-1944* (Neuwied: Luchterhand, 1965), x; Aryeh L. Uunger, "The Public Opinion Reports of the Nazi Party," *Public Opinion Quarterly* 29 (1965-66):565-582.

8. See Lawrence Stokes, "The *Sicherheitsdienst* (SD) of the Reichsführer SS and German Public Opinion, September 1939-June 1941," Ph.D. diss., Johns Hopkins, Baltimore, 1972.

9. Josef Ackermann, *Heinrich Himmler als Ideologe* (Göttingen: Musterschmidt, 1970), pp. 48-49.

10. Boberach, *Berichte*, p. 291 (February 15, 1938).

11. Ibid., p. xxxix. Boberach's work reinforces the accepted interpretation that the Gestapo was crude, stupid, wasted time, and was mismanaged. His work includes a list of pro-Nazi Catholic books (201), examples of anti-Nazi literature (205-207, 217), and a number of antiregime sermons that appear in no other collection.

12. Boberach, *Berichte*, pp. xxx, 902ff.

13. National Archives, T-175, roll 409, frames 2932603-05; Wall, p. 440.

14. National Archives, T-175, roll 271, frames 2766976-77. Lewy and Conway describe the Church's earlier loss as a result of the prior compromises with National Socialism; see Lewy, p. 223 and Conway, *Persecution*, p. 231.

15. Stokes, "The *Sicherheitsdienst*," pp. 242, 253; National Archives, T-81, 119/139, 907-8.

16. Zahn, *German Catholics* has offered a thorough examination of the German Catholic response to the war; Cohen, p. 7; Lewy, p. 225.

17. Corsten, *Kölner Aktenstücke*, p. 261.

18. National Archives, T-81, roll 676, frame 5485216; T-81, roll 673, RPL 172; T-175, roll 271, frames 2766979-7001.

19. Neuhäusler, 2: 361, 363.

20. *Kirchliches Amtsblatt für die Diözese Münster*, vol. 78 (September 1, 1944), p. 111.

21. Marlis Steinert, *Hitler's War and the Germans: Public Mood and Attitude during the Second World War* (Athens, Ohio: Ohio University Press, 1977), p. 52.

22. Zipfel, p. 226; Bundesarchiv, NS Misch/474, Vol. 112, 809; Conway, *Persecution*, 232.

23. Zahn, "Catholic Opposition to Hitler," 415-416, 418, 420-422.

24. See Faulhaber's letter to Gürtner, the minister of justice, in which the cardinal protested against the liquidation of the sick and feebleminded, expressly appealing to his obligations arising out of Article 16 of the Concordat, in Donohue, pp. 61ff.

25. See Boberach, *Berichte*, pp. 242ff., for a special SD report on the Jesuits; Lapomarda, p. 242; Flosdorf, pp. 1-2; Hockerts, *Die Sittlichkeitsprozesse*.

26. Alan Davies, *Anti-Semitism and the Christian Mind* (New York: Herder & Herder, 1969), pp. 23-67.

27. Stokes, "The *Sicherheitsdienst*," pp. 54, 59, 239-240.

28. Zipfel, p. 511; Steinert, p. 91.

29. John Mendelsohn, *The Holocaust*, vol. 4, *Propaganda and Aryanization, 1938-1944* (New York: Garland Publishing, Inc., 1982), p. 116.

30. Ibid., pp. 10, 28; Erich Ebermayer, " . . . *Und morgen die ganze Welt." Erinnerungen aus Deutschlands dunkle Zeit* (Bayreuth: Hestia, 1966), p. 420.

31. Rainer C. Baum, *The Holocaust and the German Elite: Genocide and National Suicide in Germany, 1871-1945* (Totowa: Rowman and Littlefield, 1981), p. 55. For an interesting perspective on the complexity of anti-Semitism as found in the Polish experience, see Michael Checinski, *Poland: Communism, Nationalism, Anti-Semitism* (New York: Kary-Cohl, 1982); Kershaw, "The Persecution," p. 289.

32. See Thompson, pp. 54-77. The eugenics policies were not enthusiastically greeted by the vast majority of Germans who could not or would not adjust their personal relationships and moral values so that these could be congruent with Nazi racial aims.

33. Stokes, "The German People," p. 190; National Archives, T-175/258, 2750848, 2750978/9.
34. Boberach, *Meldungen*, pp. x, 63, 383, 386; Stokes, p. 185.
35. For an analysis of the explusion of Sproll from his diocese, see Paul Kopf and Max Müller, *Die Vertreibung von Bischof Johannes Baptiste Sproll von Rottenburg, 1938-45* (Mainz: Matthias Grünewald, 1971).
36. Lewy, pp. 268-309; Bracher, *German Dictatorship*, p. 389; Hans Peter Bleuel and Ernst Klinnert, *Deutsche Studenten auf dem Weg ins Dritte Reich: Ideologien, Programme, Aktionen 1918-1935* (Gütersloh: Sigbert Mohn Verlag, 1967), p. 150; Jochen Klepper, *Unter dem Schatten deinen Flügel; aus den Tagebüchern der Jahre 1932-1942* (Stuttgart: Deutsche Verlags Anstalt, 1966), pp. 47, 682, 730; Hans Joachim Fliedner, *Die Judenverfolgung in Mannheim 1933-1945* (Stuttgart: Deutsche Verlags Anstalt, 1971), p. 228.
37. Allen, "Objective and Subjective Inhibitents in the German Resistance to Hilter," in Littell and Locke, pp. 121-123.
38. Heinz Leuner, *When Compassion was a Crime: Germany's Silent Heroes, 1933-1945* (London: Wolff, 1966), p. 138.
39. Ger von Roon, *German Resistance to Hitler: Count von Moltke and the Kreisau Circle* (London: Van Nostrand Reinhold, 1971), p. 238. See also Steinert, *Hitler's War*, p. 245; Günther Weisenborn (ed.), *Der lautlose Aufstand. Bericht über den Widerstandsbewegung der deutschen Volkes, 1933-1945* (Hamburg: Rowohlt Verlag, 1962), pp. 52-53; Leon Poliakov, *Das Dritte Reich und die Juden: Dokumente und Aufsätze* (Berlin: Arani, 1955), pp. 432, 434.
40. Freya Moltke and Annelore Leber, *Für und Wider; Entscheidungen in Deutschland 1918-1945* (Berlin: Mosaik Verlag, 1962), p. 70.
41. Stasiewski, *Akten*, pp. 375, 402; Boberach, *Berichte*, pp. 195-197; Steinert, *Hitler's War*, p. 259.
42. Moltke and Leber, pp. 76-79; Leuner, pp. 105, 137, 140.
43. Boberach, *Berichte*, pp. xxxiii, 481; NA T-175, R 259, F 2752165-12.8.40 (*Meldungen aus dem Reich*); Steinert, *Hitler's War*, pp. 239, 248; Conway, *Persecution*, p. 266; NA T-175, R 260, F 2753097-99-23.1.41; Boberach, *Berichte*, pp. 643, 768; Portmann, pp. 95-98; Historisches Archiv der Stadt Köln, *Ausstellung: Widerstand und Verfolgung in Köln* (Cologne: Archiv, 1974), p. 209.
44. Miles Ecclesiae, *Hitler Gegen Christus. Eine katholische Klarstellung und Abwehr* (Paris: Societe d' Editions Europeennes, 1936), pp. 168, 181, 190; Müller, *Katholische Kirche*, p. 95; Moltke and Leber, p. 77.
45. Boberach, *Berichte*, p. 7.
46. Alfred Delp. *Zur Ende Entschlossen. Vorträge und Aufsätze* (Frankfurt: Josef Knecht, 1949); Frank Tennenbaum, *Race and Reich: The Story of an Epoch* (New York: Wiley, 1956), pp. 76, 439; Leuner, pp. 103-104; Heinrich Portmann, *Der Bischof von Münster. Dokumente um den Bischof von Münster* (Münster: Aschendorff, 1947), p. 103; Boberach, *Berichte*, p. 21; Stasiewski, *Akten*, p. 38.
47. Lewy, pp. 289-291.
48. Pridham, *Hitler's Rise to Power*; Gordon, "German Opposition to Nazi Anti-Semitic Measures", pp. 366-367.
49. George, in Coelho, p. 186; R.C. Snyder et al., *Foreign Policy Decision-Making* (New York: Free Press of Glencoe, 1962).

50. Historisches Archiv der Stadt Köln, pp. 207-208, 225-236; Moltke and Leber, pp. 72, 75; Müller, *Katholische Kirche*, p. 106; Stasiewski *Akten*, pp. 88, 688, 703; Bernhard Vollmer, *Volksopposition im Polizeistaat* (Stuttgart: Deutsche Verlagsanstalt, 1957), pp. 17, 21-22, 142, 276-277, 284-285.

51. Boberach, *Berichte*, pp. 77, 208. *Hauptstaatsarchiv Düsseldorf*, G 21/5, 30655d-4, 5, 33, G/90 rep. 27, no. 45-6 JS 722/35 (1935).

52. Vollmer, p. 259-260.

53. Ibid., p. 277.

54. Ibid., pp. 290-291.

55. Gordon, "German Opposition," p. 369.

56. Ibid., p. 370.

57. *Hauptstaatsarchiv Düsseldorf.* G/90 rep. 27, no. 50-5.9.37 (18 Js1811/37); National Archives, T-81, R 225, F 5006310.

58. Stasiewski, *Akten*, pp. 300-301; Steinert, p. 74; Gordon, "German Opposition," p. 371.

59. Boberach, *Berichte*, pp. 651-684, 709, 783, 891.

60. Portmann, p. 74.

61. Boberach, *Berichte*, p. 888; Leuner, p. 64; Else R. Behrend-Rosenfeld, *Ich Stand Nicht Allein. Erlebnisse einer Jüdin in Deutschland, 1933-1944* (Frankfurt: Euro Verlag, 1963), pp. 126, 160; Weisenborn, p. 47; Hauptstaatsarchiv Düsseldorf, file 296.

62. Stokes, "Sicherheitsdienst," pp. 128-129; Sereny, 64077; NA, C1-PIR/106, C1-11R/S3, C1-FIR/123/Interrogation of Albert Hartl.

63. *Bundesarchiv* Koblenz, R58/162.

64. Irving Janis, "Vigilance and Decision Making in Personal Crises" in Coelho, p. 170; G.V. Coelho et al., "The Use of the Student TAT to Assess Coping Behavior in Hospitalized, Normal and Exceptionally Competent College Freshmen," *Perceptual and Motor Skills* 14 (1962):355-365; R.S. Lazarus, *Psychological Stress and the Coping Process.*

65. National Archives, T-175, roll 265, frames 2759350-54, frames 2759341-44; Boberach, *Berichte*, pp. 118-121.

66. Lawrence Walker, *Hitler Youth*, pp. 75-89.

67. Ernst Helmreich, *Religious Education in German Schools* (Cambridge: Harvard University Press, 1959); Berlin Document Center, T-581, roll 50; National Archives, T-175, roll 258, frames 260-261; T-175, roll 265, frames 2759153-154; T-175, roll 265, frame 2759242.

68. Gerhard Weinberg, "The World Through Hitler's Eyes," *Midway* (1970):56; Michael Phayer, "Challenges Met and Opportunities Missed: Catholic Women in Nazi Germany," paper presented at the American Historical Association, San Francisco, December 30, 1983. For a comprehensive treatment of women and religion in Nazi Germany, see the forthcoming book by Michael Phayer, *Martha and Mary: Protestant and Catholic Women in Twentieth Century Germany.*

69. Nowak, pp. 69-70; Berthold Hinz, *Art in the Third Reich* (New York: Pantheon, 1979); David Hull, *Film in the Third Reich* (Berkeley: University of California Press, 1969).

70. Phayer, *Martha and Mary*, chap. 6.

71. Walster, pp. 9-10; Schneider, pp. 62-63.

72. Steinert, *Hitler's Wars*, p. 92.

73. Wall, pp. 443-444; National Archives, T-175, roll 260, frames 2752779-81; Zipfel, pp. 228-229.

74. National Archives, T-175, roll 272, frame 2768538; roll 408, frame 2932105; roll 270, frames 2766308, 2766368; roll 272, frame 2768450; roll 264, frame 2758875.
75. Boberach, *Berichte*, p. 688; National Archives, T-175, roll 264, frames 2757696-700; roll 270, frame 2766212.
76. Berlin Document Center/Hoover, T581, roll 50; National Archives, T-175, roll 265, frame 2759286; roll 272, frame 2769118; Heinrich Roth (ed.), *Katholische Jugend in der NS-Zeit unter besonderer Berücksichtigung des Katholischen Jungmannerverbandes. Daten und Dokumente* (Düsseldorf: Hans Altenberg, 1959).
77. National Archives, T-175, roll 266, frames 2760739-745.
78. National Archives, T-175, roll 272, frames 2769062-64.
79. National Archives, T-175, roll 270, frame 2766403; Lewy, p. 31; National Archives, T-81, roll 185, frames 0334431-437.
80. National Archives, T-175, roll 270, frame 2766923; T-175, roll 262, frames 2755-168-170; T-175, roll 271, frame 2767008; Wall, p. 449.
81. National Archives, T-175, roll 271, frame 2766984.
82. National Archives, T-175, roll 271, frame 2766999.
83. Helmut Witetschek, "Der gefälschte und der echte Mölders Brief," *Vierteljahrshefte für Zeitgeschichte* 16 (1968):61-65; National Archives, T-175, roll 262, frame 2756532.
84. National Archives, T-175, roll 262, frame 2756538; T-175, roll 258, frame 604; T-175, roll 270, frame 2766400; Conway, *Persecution*, p. 273.
85. Boberach, *Berichte*, p. xxxii.
86. See Kopf and Müller (eds.), *Die Vertreibung von Bischof Johannes Baptista Sproll von Rottenburg, 1938-1945*.
87. Wall, p. 451.
88. National Archives, T-175, roll 264, frame 2757698; T-175, roll 258, frames 275-6453-455. For accounts of the pseudo-religious activities within the party, see Hans-Jochen Gamm, *Der Braune Kult* (Hamburg: Rütter and Leoning, 1962); Hans Müller, "Der Pseudo-Religiöse Charakter der Nationalsozialistischen Weltanschauung," *Geschichte im Wissenschaft und Unterricht* 6 (1961):337-352. For a succinct analysis of the Catholic reaction to the Nazi *Lebensfeiern*, see Wall, pp. 453-455.
89. Steinert, *Hitler's Wars*, p. 91.
90. Zahn, *German Catholics*; Müller, *Katholische Kirche*; Lewy, *Catholic Church*. All three focus on the hierarchy and are based primarily on the documents emanating from the episcopal administrative sections of German dioceses.
91. Müller, *Katholische Kirche*, xxii.
92. Ibid., p. xxiv; Steinert, *Hitler's Wars*, p. 125.
93. Rinderle, pp. 135, 221-223, 236-237; Pallone, p. 324.
94. Fenn, p. 221; J. Stacy Adams, "Inequity in Social Exchange," in Berkowitz (ed.), *Advances in Experimental Social Psychology*, pp. 295-296.
95. See Steinert, *Hitler's Wars*, pp. 14-15, 50. The *Meldungen* document the increasingly critical responses of Germans to the regime. Even at the beginning of the war the mood of the German people in general was merely one of "reluctant loyalty."
96. Donald McKale, *The Nazi Party Courts: Hitler's Management of Conflict in His Movement, 1921-1945* (Lawrence, KS: University Press of Kansas, 1974), p. 135.

97. Berger, *The Social Reality of Religion*, p. 41.

98. Walster, p. 5; A.W. Staats, *Complex Human Behavior* (New York: Holt, Rinehart & Winston, 1963); G.J. Whitehurst, "Production of Novel and Grammatical Utterances by Young Children," *Journal of Experimental Child Psychology* 13 (1972):502-515; A. Bandura, "Influence of Models' Reinforcement Contingencies on the Acquisition of Imitative Responses," *Journal of Personality and Social Psychology* 1 (1965):584-95; D.C. Butler and N. Miller, "'Power to Reinforce' as a Determinant of Communication," *Psychological Reports* 16 (1965):705-709.

99. Robert E. Lane, "Patterns of Political Belief," in Knutson (ed.), *Handbook of Political Psychology*, p. 111; Baum, pp. 321ff; Michael Marrus and Robert Paxton, "The Nazis and the Jews in Occupied Western Europe, 1940-1944," *Journal of Modern History* 54 (1982):714.

100. Gellner, p. 160; Jeffrey Burton Russell, *A History of Medieval Christianity: Prophecy and Order* (New York: Crowell, 1968), p. 1; Kershaw, *Popular Opinion*, pp. 275-277.

9

Conclusion

Hitler's rise to power confronted German Catholics with three moral dilemmas as they sought to regulate their behavior after 1933. How were they to fulfill their duties as citizens in the totalitarian Third Reich? Was Hitler's war legitimate and, if so, how were Catholics to fulfill their patriotic obligations and simultaneously secure their faith in the increasingly oppressive Reich? How were Catholics to respond to the vitriolic racism of Nazi Germany and to the implementation of Hitler's eugenic policies? Each of the three issues was a moral quandary of the first order and could easily have resulted in extensive debate among Catholics as they continued their efforts to leave the ghetto of the *Kulturkampf* era and join the nation. Branded *Reichsfeinde* by Bismarck, Catholics were anxious thereafter to prove that they were not a dissident minority but rather were German to the core. They longed for acceptability and respectability. Hence they were willing to insure their rights and institutional position within the state through the Concordat of 1933—Hitler's first foreign policy triumph and German Catholicism's seemingly last opportunity to safeguard the Church-state relations so laboriously constructed since 1871. Even so, after 1933, just as before, the battle of ideologies continued. In the Third Reich, however, the conflict had to be joined in earnest.

Nazi ideology combined the doctrines of race and space, both of which had significant implications for the daily conduct of domestic and foreign affairs. Publicly explicit about both before 1933, Hitler did not highlight these doctrines in a radical fashion quite so openly after 1933, perhaps giving the illusion to Catholic leaders that now in power he was becoming moderate. This helps explain the persistence among the hierarchy that there were stable and radical elements within the party. The goal of the bishops was to use "good" Nazis to tame Hitler on behalf of the patriotic Catholic Church. Insistently they repeated to everyone available that the Church could become an element of support in the new Germany. What helped suggest to them the possibility of political flexibility was Hitler's own mode of governing, which appeared to the bishops to sanction policy debates within the regime. In the Nazi state, however, the plurality of organizations merely introduced into totalitarianism an element of heterogeneity resulting in feudal rather than bureaucratic forms.[1] Not unlike others, the bishops felt they could maneuver within this "bureaucracy" to achieve their goals. Hitler, however, had instituted this chaotic struggle for bureaucratic power to insure that all final decisions were submitted, after a period of internecine squabbling, to himself as führer. The bishops perceived normalcy and opportunity where none existed.

No centers of power capable of challenging the authority of the führer were allowed to surface, since the struggle for power between the subleaders and organizations was one of the characteristics of the system encouraged by Hitler as he followed a system of *divide et impera*. The struggle took place within the party and its affiliate organizations as they devised alliances with pretotalitarian structures or the emerging social interests of Germany's complex industrial society. Frequently, Hitler even contracted segments of his authority to individual agents on the basis of intensely personal relationships rather than to bureaucratic officials or legally established institutions.[2] This necessitated, for example, the bishops to file protests against the violations of the Concordat either with impotent Reich officials or with those who were causing the abuse of law in the first place. Given Hitler's system of government, or lack thereof, the bishops as representatives of such a rationalized, bureaucratic institution as the Church found it difficult to deal with the Nazis. "Petition politics" was doomed to failure from the beginning.

Although Hitler was not making all the decisions in the literal sense, the men chosen or tolerated by him acted in the system as they thought he expected. Thus, there existed a very intimate relationship between Hitler's *Weltanschauung* and the bloody events that proceeded from them.[3] He challenged the Church's moral and political traditions, its assumptions about man's nature, and its understanding of the role of God in man's destiny. Because of the nature of the NSDAP, the Church was unable to succeed in effectively restraining the regime. Historically, the Catholic Church traditionally has tried to accommodate to the de facto political power in exchange for the freedom to pursue its religious goals. To be sure, the road was rocky even in authoritarian states, but would have proved ultimately to have been impassable in the totalitarian regime envisioned, but never achieved, by Hitler. Catholic Church leaders joined others in failing to understand the malevolent nature of Hitler's totalitarian rule in its pure form which, even if not capable of being actualized, carried with it enough power to curtail the freedom and dignity of the individual as the regime attempted to sever the relationship between the Church and Catholic Germans.

Politically the Church failed to control Hitler and his minions. Its more traditional mission, however, was religious in nature. Christian faith and its structured theology historically has had as its concern the communication of belief with both "integrity and intelligibility." Integrity reflects a concern to transmit the faith in a manner true to the distinctive parameters of the community's understanding. Intelligibility signals the need to present the faith in a manner accessible to its hearers, making sense of their experience. There is necessitated, then, a continuing inquiry into the relation between the sovereign God and human experience. The theologian's task is to construct a reinterpretation of what is presently known about the human condition in light of the interpreted experiences that make up the Church's accumulated tradition as it seeks to unfold the meaning of revelation. Theology, therefore, should attend to the integrity of the community's classical perceptions of God, to the plurality of perspectives on human life and the world, and to ordinary notions of sound judgment.[4] The clerical leaders proved unable to perceive the nature of the regime and the ultimate threat it posed to religious norms in the world.

Leading figures in the Church were hard pressed to communicate crucial religious principles and their applications through the normal avenues of pastoral care. Such associations as Catholic youth groups were curtailed. Journals and newspapers were initially heavily censored and then finally stopped. Even the gazettes used to maintain communication links between bishops and their clergy were restricted. To maintain its ability to critique the regime, Church leaders resorted to couching their attacks on hostile acts within a patriotic framework, not too difficult in light of the Church's previous patterns of behavior.[5] Patriotically extolling *Vaterland* and *Volk* or sending birthday greetings to their "beloved" führer, they could criticize specific acts of Nazi officials. While to the bishops this may well have appeared to be a clever tactic, it most likely served only to confuse the laity. Every government has stupid and corrupt officials who should be attacked, but that does not necessarily mean that loyal citizens should attack the system. The bishops operated on this normal premise of political behavior. Supportive of national goals throughout the Second Reich and very intensively during the Weimar years, Catholic bishops praised Hitler's foreign policy in the pre-war years as a reflection of valid German goals. Equally, although noting the cruelties of war, they urged their fellow Germans to fight for the *Vaterland* after 1939. Most helpfully, Hitler made this an anti-Bolshevik crusade after 1941, insuring solid public support, at least initially.

Religion and law have traditionally been the two sustaining pillars for the values of Western civilization. Both now became nearly impotent when confronted with the arbitrary authority of Hitler's state as its officials isolated and/or exterminated any group hostile to the regime, totally ignoring the normal considerations of justice. Why did Germans and in particular the Catholic Church allow him to proceed virtually unhindered? The bishops failed to make normative decisions. Procedures followed by the bishops either individually or as a group were designed to buttress and secure the institutional Church. In his study of "groupthink," Janis[6] has offered a variety of ways to achieve a viable decision, including the active search for new information, the evaluation of a wide range of policy alternatives, consideration of information and advice that does not support actions initially preferred, and the reexamination of the positive and negative consequences of all known alternatives, even those originally regarded as unacceptable. The bishops certainly had a wide range of information sources, but generally preferred politically astute consensus in order to present a unified front. Such a public position is not surprising except that even behind the scenes there does not appear the active and coordinated planning by Church officials devoted to the implementation of basic religious values in light of the serious ramifications of the regime's intentions. They were content with meetings and exchanges of letters, dedicated to the creation of a uniform stance. The bishops apparently were concerned with short-term survival, hoping that in the long-run either Hitler would fail or be grateful. For reasons of institutional survival their approach is comprehensible, even though not particularly praiseworthy. Their goal was maintenance of the institution to insure the administration of the sacraments and to support the spiritual viability of their flock so that the Church could fulfill its spiritual mission. Even more troublesome is the nagging suspicion that most of the flock would have been reluctant to follow their shepherds into open resistance unless local parochial interests could somehow have been given universal meaning.

Had Hitler been a "normal" dictator, the policies of the Church would certainly be questionable. But the postwar controversy that has swirled around the response of the Catholic Church is rooted in the genocidal policy pursued by Hitler and his followers. From hindsight one can readily understand that the gradual nature of the process, the legal legitimation, and the bureaucratic organization can be offered as factors that facilitated Catholic indifference. The research devoted to this genocidal holocaust alone has been of monumental proportions. Complex functional behavior, however, is learned. In fact, man is distinguished by his extraordinary ability to learn. Able to discriminate, humans can learn different responses to similar stimuli. They can be normal anti-Semites and not necessarily killers.[7] The result has been a vast array of interpretations, which has still resulted in merely reinforcing the troublesome thought that lack of resistance was not surprising, that genocide may well not be foreign to man in his twentieth-century society, and that many features of contemporary life may well encourage an easy resort to the "Final Solution."[8]

Still, to say as some suggest that the Third Reich appears as neither admirable nor repulsive but incomprehensible also will not suffice. Answers continue to be sought by those wishing to understand human behavior and by those who hope to comprehend why even religious institutions responded as they did. Religion is supposed to contribute to the integration of the whole society and the functioning of other social institutions by providing a unifying value system. Religion is supposed to sustain social stability and provide an adaptation mechanism for the whole social system.[9] When such adaptation is impossible because the political leaders of a country have chosen a perverse system of values, the religious leaders, if they are to remain true to their calling, should confront the alien system. When Nazi eugenic policies touched the faithful, they were attacked in sermons, articles, and official letters, but anti-Semitism was rarely condemned nor were the atrocities actively resisted.

Since 1945 scholars and interested commentators have been obsessed with understanding how men could actively or passively participate in this event which once again has highlighted what St. Augustine saw as a basic evil in the composition of man himself. Such atrocities cannot be fully explained by the pathology of the perpetrators. But to say that the atrocities of the Holocaust defy both cognitive and emotional assimilation because they are off the scale of established human knowledge[10] is rationally unsatisfying, since even theological mysteries can be partially penetrated to help satisfy human inquisitiveness. Racial anti-Semitism was Hitler's central guiding principle, and so its role as an ideology affecting such groups as German Catholics must be studied to understand the behavior patterns that emerged. At the same time, it must be recalled that terror, murder, and racism are not a German monopoly, and so the Nazi experience can be viewed as a phenomenon capable of being replicated in any twentieth century politicization process.

German racial anti-Semitism, not to be confused with everyday anti-Jewish prejudice, was an ideology rooted in the nineteenth century and elevated to public policy by the Nazis. Its emergence presupposed centuries of preparatory anti-Semitism which had developed, at least until recently, into an integral component of Western civilization. For Hitler and others the "Final Solutions" varied according to political expediency, but gradually, as temporary options were closed, evolved into extermination as the absolute priority of the regime. Auschwitz, not 1933, was the real "German

Revolution"—the overthrow of one set of historically and religiously evolved norms, values, and social formations. Historical anti-Semitism, the nature of the institutional stimuli in the Third Reich, the historical labels applied to the Jews and indicative of the emotional states of non-Jewish Germans, reveal that the feelings and behavior patterns of Catholics in Hitler's Germany were the natural and disastrous result of an extensive historical development.[11] On this issue the Church could have made a stand since the Nazis clearly were proceeding beyond "normal" political authoritarianism and anti-Semitism.

Nazi eugenic policies called for the dehumanization of specific human persons and linked the creation of a better society with their destruction. In the eyes of a Himmler the Holocaust became a painful duty at the service of historical tasks for which future generations would be grateful. To implement the dehumanization policies, the regime sought to decrease each Aryan person's sense of individuality so that the humanity of others could be eliminated. Rallies and a stress on the common good could be utilized for this purpose. Continued focus on the Jews as bad humans, a view favored by those who could not accept the Jews as subhumans, justified maltreatment although not necessarily extermination. One question was asked, but never answered, as the socio-psychological dynamics of anti-Semitism wreaked havoc with supposedly accepted social norms. When and where was the line to be drawn? Stereotyping increased the emotional distance from those "outsiders" being persecuted. Obeying orders served to diminish the sense of personal responsibility for the consequences of one's actions. When would the situation be grave enough to evoke disobedience? Involvement with procedural problems served to compartmentalize human needs, and individuals typically found it difficult to oppose dominant group attitudes.[12] In this complex of forces leading to dehumanization, the Church could have interposed itself more vigorously to support those individuals who were making or wanted to take a stand against the regime. In the euthanasia controversy, opposition from the Church helped modify some of Hitler's plans. But this opposition only succeeded because German Catholics realized that those close to themselves were being killed. Historically affected by anti-Semitism, the Church could not convincingly argue that Catholics love Jews as brothers, at least until after their conversion. To make Catholics less susceptible to the currents of popular attitudes, Catholic leaders needed to correct the corrupted images of Judaism present from the early fathers and to develop theological patterns based on understanding the intrinsic connection in the Jewish-Christian revelation experience. Such a change of direction would take time, energy, and certainly great courage in the Third Reich.

The Catholic Church did virtually nothing to erase the stereotypes of

Jews, which had developed over the centuries. Support of Jewish converts was commendable, but not sufficient for an institution that was staking its own existence on illuminating the relationship between God and all his creatures. The official Church followed a business-as-usual approach. It would, however, have been difficult after 1939 and after the existence of the death camps became known suddenly to change its attitude toward the Jews. To be fair, Catholic anti-Semitism was a religious, not racial, bias. Until it was too late Catholic leaders did not realize that centuries of stereotyping had prepared the way for the Holocaust and that the traditional Catholic response to the Jews made it difficult to distinguish Hitler's public policies from those of his predecessors. Religious prejudice provided labels and terminology as well as reinforced the insider-outsider dichotomy, which proved so lethal. In a broader sense the causes of anti-Semitism are not found only in the psychology of a person or in mere interrelationships. Prejudice is developed within the historical conditions and political-economic-religious structures out of which intergroup relations develop and are sustained. Situational conditions activate stereotypes. Obviously, a sustained campaign to destroy the stereotype would reduce the material available for actualization. Generally not racists themselves, Catholics were latently anti-Semitic. It was their indifference that helped make possible the murders. The Nazis themselves, of course, interpreted Catholic objections to Nazi neopaganism as opposition to racism. All Christians, Catholics included, however, must bear a responsibility for creating the environment that allowed the Nazis to proceed unhindered well into the war. It was the Church's challenge to enlarge the population of intrinsically religious people, but the struggle was not joined vigorously. There is evidence of a strong correspondence between the absence of prejudice and committed faith. Hence, the role of religion is ambivalent; it makes and unmakes prejudice, depending on how committed or conventional the members of the flock are.[13] In this instance the Catholic Church sustained secular patterns of prejudice.

Hitler's racist anti-Semitism was the motor of the Third Reich. Ideas do have consequences. In 1921, Hitler claimed that race was the driving force of world history. Later in *Mein Kampf* he described it as "the key not only to world history, but to all human culture." History was the chronicle of race struggle. Hence, in Hitler's opinion, National Socialism was more than a political system; it was a science, appealing to twentieth-century minds obsessed with the need to be integrated into a rational, secular paradigm.[14] But other Germans did not see in racism *the* guiding principle of their lives. Yet they ultimately succumbed to the implementation of Nazi eugenic policies. Racist determinism, of course, conflicts with evidence from many philosophical, psychological, and sociological perspectives that indicate that personalities may be altered by the course of events and by participating in such communities as a church.[15] Hitler's science was based on ideological principles. Public declarations by Catholic officials, however, failed to challenge effectively the Nazi viewpoint.

Despite the alleged secularistic dilution of religious devotion,[16] the beliefs held regarding man's nature, his redemption, and commitments to this and the next world compose a crucial component of that ideational environment that helps define responses toward political conditions. Even practical speculation depends in part on a religious foundation, and the Jewish-Christian theological tradition does provide highly useful resources for practical moral thinking.[17] The Church, therefore, had ideological weapons at its disposal for even the political struggle. Unfortunately, the arsenal was never fully utilized. The Church was not solely the victim of Nazi persecution for it sought to combine incompatible loyalties to God and to the legal Nazi government. The visceral nationalism so prevalent among German Catholics combined with ruthless Nazi tactics of intimidation and resulted in the institutional capitulation of the Church. At any moment in time, various elements in the individual's sociopolitical environment have *relative* intensity. It is the relative value of the reinforcers in the individual's system of preferences that determine behavior. Faced with war, hardship on the homefront, and the need for patriotic support of the *Vaterland,* concern or compassion for Jews no longer in their midst would be difficult for Catholic leaders to mobilize.[18]

To be both German and Catholic opened a potential conflict between two value systems. Each configuration of specific rights and duties as well as general norms was partially a culturally based entity, rooted in constitutive rules learned and passed onto succeeding generations. Each value pattern was designed to guide the individual's behavior in an organized and coordinated fashion. Thus, for very consistent reasons, Catholics could adapt to or resist the regime or do both on different levels, depending on the question and their intrinsic commitment to the nation or to their religion over a specific issue.

Human behavior gains its complexity through the construction of increasingly intricate constellations of behaviors. The behavior constellation eventually reaches a complexity characterized by repertoires that have been permanently learned and so provide continuity. Latent and even blatant anti-Semitism was part of the nationalistic and Catholic *Weltanschauung* in Germany. Such a world view helped Catholics determine complex social actions and could allow the individual Catholic to be anti-Semitic, nationalistic, and a churchgoer. Such a development was especially likely since the representatives of the institutional Church did not ask the questions that could have provoked dissonance. Social learning theory also suggests that the behavior of some Germans toward Hitler's regime was acquired through imitating the behavior and attitudes of successful Nazis. Other Germans may well have adhered to Catholic value and behavior patterns because of the particular reinforcements available to them. For example, neighborhoods, villages, or circles of friends and acquaintances could exert powerful influences. Thus, a person could be loyal to his local Catholic pastor and simultaneously support Hitler's war effort and the solution of the "Jewish problem," especially as the numbers of Jews diminished and the issue became abstract. Each person asks: Can a specific model person or group offer needed rewards? The answer varies according to the observer's personality and the environment.[19] Seemingly contradictory value and behavior patterns can be compatible and need not produce dissonance.

Prosocial religious behavior, of course, could have been induced by a number of determinants. A less ambiguous response from the Church could have helped form a more solid front. Focusing and highlighting responsibility for helping others could have guided Catholics. The sight of someone suffering should serve as an emotion-eliciting stimulus as well as a negative reinforcing stimulus and a directive stimulus that should elicit such avoidance behavior as that aimed at stopping the condition causing a person to suffer. This did not happen in Germany because of the anti-Semitism and the removal of the Jew through a slow process of restriction, isolation, and then deportation. Naturally the wartime conditions were also conducive to this general indifference. The gradual escalation of the racist policy and war made it easy to avoid helping. To a considerable extent emotional responses were extinguished through conditioning. Relying solely on initiative and individual decision-making serves to limit prosocial behavior. The Church's institutional response, therefore, was important for her members. If the type of action necessary for help is acceptable, desirable, and appropriate, the individual can act. In essence, given a political crisis, leadership was needed to clarify and support the norms necessary for activity.[20] The Church failed to provide that leadership.

Unlike psychoanalytical theories, non-Freudian principles can help explain the relationship between Hitler and the German people by the same principles that govern other forms of social and group behavior. Such principles can help link the events of the Third Reich with the behavior of individuals in groups. Not surprisingly, Catholics behaved like other Germans. Exchange theories postulate that individuals must undergo psychological costs to get psychological rewards. The goal is to minimize the costs. Some Catholics chose to be active Nazis and so compromised their religious values. Some persisted in their faith and were consigned to concentration camps. Other Catholics, the majority, felt that Catholicism and Nazism were compatible, at least with respect to nationalistic values. The same principle (i.e., reward-seeking and punishment-avoiding) applies to individuals and to such macro-structures as the Church, which behaved *as if* it were an individual seeking rewards while avoiding punishment. Some psychologists warn of the overestimation of either personal or dispositional factors[21] since, ultimately, both personal and situational factors lead to actions. Thus, psychological principles can help sensitize one to the role of history in a culture and in individual life because human action is based on reinforcers, and some of these are products of the past. Of course, there could be an infinity of historical reinforcers. For the psychologist, it may not be necessary for theory to take total historical conditionality into account. The limited task is merely to show the role of contemporary reinforcement in shaping the social structure.[22] The historian can separate significant from accidental causes and include the former as the principal reinforcers for specific activities. To use historical data as reinforcing causes requires a sensitivity to the array of past facts and present psychological theories. The features relevant to the German genocidal public policy were: (1) an extended history of anti-Semitism; (2) an extremely stressful situation during the Weimar years, resulting in increased aggression coupled with a documented virulent prejudice; and (3) the metamorphosis of a state founded upon legally defined rights and duties into a state based on Hitler's will. Psychological and bureaucratic dynamics served as the foundation for this transition, since people essentially learn through diverse experiences which activities of sociopolitical life are morally relevant. Without positive models, prosocial learning is nearly impossible. Germans had a variety of reasons for following Hitler. Some shared his racist vision; some saw a moral significance in the Nazi movement and hoped to achieve a higher form of culture through struggle; some ignored the ideology and concentrated on personal success; and some merely wanted to continue their traditional patterns of livelihood. Individuals, however, did make discriminating judgments in opposing the regime if the issue were important enough. Unfortunately, the fate of the Jews was not viewed as a matter of importance by many. This failure of courage is the real measure of the German and Catholic disaster. The Church failed to provide a model for normative moral decision-making as Hitler implemented his totalitarian and eugenic policies.

People are different. All humans have in common, however, the means of ego defense, self-concept formation, active nervous systems, and motives. The development, learning, and growth of people takes place in terms of a limited number of such principles as conditioning, modeling, identification, and learning through the resolution of cognitive discrepancies. Knowledge of such principles helps reveal the salient patterns of cultural assumptions, particular social tensions, racial myths, ideal self-images, and political expectations. Psychological theories act as an adrenalin, a substance that heightens consciousness without destroying it. Knowledge of psychological principles and the historical data can help explain social behavior, sensitize the scholar to specific patterns of facts, help organize the experiences of groups of people, integrate isolated entities, and decompose erroneous understanding.[23]

Although one might expect a religious institution to defend its norms, preach brotherhood, and resist the Nazis, the historical experience of Catholics in the Third Reich refutes this assumption, and the current salient psychological principles help explain why Catholics behaved as others (both German and non-German) when confronted by the complexities of Hitler's plans and political manipulations. The reaction of German Catholics, members of a well organized Church, does offer an example of the power of a modern state and the inhibiting pressures that characterize twentieth-century society. German Catholics were neither better nor worse than anyone else faced with the brutal force of Hitler's racial revolution. Their reaction and that of others, however, does suggest that mechanisms must be constructed to avoid such brutality in the future. Essentially the permanent modification of behavior to avoid future totalitarian states requires organizing social structures that will retard such developments.[24] Several lines of development seem possible. One direction would be to encourage the broad participation of people in collective social endeavors. Public pressure also can be mobilized to arouse officials to control institutions that threaten established norms. Individualized initiatives and responses can be mobilized to alleviate everyday problems. Success here should help participants gain courage to tackle larger issues. Efforts can be made to induce the government to serve the public more equitably at the expense of vested interests. Social demands can be converted into formal legal codes backed by sanctions and so reduce the likelihood of civil strife. In the light of Nazi experiences, society must be organized to eliminate the potentials that allow the genocidal state to take shape. Aggression is not an inevitable aspect of man, but a product of aggression-promoting conditions operating within a society. Hence man has the power to reduce the level of sociopolitical dissonance by reforming the structure of his environment. Here churches can take a leading role as established communities mediating the goals of the state and those of individuals.

Since its foundation, Christianity has stood for human dignity. Its early appeal was its refusal to distinguish between slave and freeman, male and female, Jew and gentile. Through the centuries this heritage has emerged in a variety of reform movements ranging from the Puritans' search for freedom to the social encyclicals of Leo XIII, and to the proclamations of John Paul II on the dignity and freedom of the individual. But the Church has persecuted as well—Jews since patristic times and Moslems in the Middle Ages, to name but two examples. As an institution it has aimed to persist in order to administer the sacraments, frequently placing more stress on survival than on the meaning behind the sacraments. The experience of Catholics in the Third Reich can impress on all observers the importance of psychologically discerning patterns of values and behavior in specific historical situations in order to avoid the easy or low-level compromise, made on the assumption that discord must be avoided for the good of the community. Christians as a whole have also come to realize that religious anti-Semitism helped pave the way for the Holocaust and that strident nationalism gave birth to widespread support for the *Führerstaat.* This is not to say that anti-Semitism of itself automatically led to the Final Solution, only that it predisposed many not to act as they focused on Hitler's successes and then the very survival of Germany itself.

The use of mass violence to create a society that conforms with radical ideological principles tempts all modern governments. Alerted by their experiences in the Third Reich with its exaggerated claims of nationalism and racism, the Catholic and other Christian churches should have learned to be prepared to proclaim publicly their consciences against any misuse of power, no matter how small and insignificant it may initially appear. Acceptance of authority and the desire to be true Germans crippled Catholic resistance, at least institutionally. The Holocaust now has forced all men to create barriers to such a repetition. The Church has historically and consistently been tempted to adapt to the world, to view its success as the imminence of God's kingdom, and to free itself from persecution.[25] During the *Hitlerzeit,* Catholic leaders and many in their flocks sacrificed a complete commitment to their normative moral value system by consistently adhering to German patriotic ideals as well as by invoking anti-Semitic terminology and stereotypes to emphasize their adherence to the German *Volk.* They sacrificed the meaning of their legitimate moral roots. Their response to the challenge lacked courage, but is comprehensible given the unprecedented and unique experience they were facing. Others responded in a similarly pragmatic and nonheroic manner. Hindsight is always better than foresight. Having confronted the possibilities of the modern state powered by a demonic ideology, German Catholics as one among many groups have illustrated the pitfalls of submission to political authority for pragmatic purposes and have exposed the danger of prejudice that denigrates human dignity in any form.

Nazi Germany offers the unusual case of an advanced technological society virtually eliminating a targeted group as part of an attempt to redefine the normative values governing society. The psychological, social, and political factors that made the Holocaust possible can offer a reflective model for a continuing and critical analysis of the state and can create a compelling interest in the preservation of the rights of man in society. The patterns of behavior woven by Catholics in response to Hitler's regime and the moral values embedded in their activities can offer to post-1945 commentators a perspective useful in measuring current responses to the incursions of state power into human societies at all levels. German Catholics wrestling with the questions posed in the Third Reich can help us focus more precisely on such issues as those of state power, collectivism, bureaucracy, human rights, and individualism, which have yet to be fully faced. The German Catholic experience has also illuminated very clearly the need for the articulation of moral values in political environments and has made the compelling case that morals and politics cannot be compartmentalized. Totalitarian Germany and its Holocaust, then, have served to sensitize subsequent generations to the need for refining moral values in order to evaluate political actions and to choose those that insure that man remains a social being striving for ultimate ideals. From 1933 to 1945, German Catholic bishops, theologians, and laity, through both pragmatic and heroic decisions, touched both with failure and success, helped intensify the perennial debate on the role of morals in politics and the rights of social man in the political state. Even more than in previous centuries the issues in this debate must be resolved no longer simply for intellectual satisfaction. The issue has now become the survival of human dignity and, perhaps, even man himself.

Notes

1. Linz, p. 237; Robert Koehl, *RKFDV: German Resettlement and Population Policy 1939-1945* (Cambridge: Harvard University Press, 1957); Robert Koehl, *The Black Corps: The Structure and Power Struggles of the Nazi SS* (Madison: University of Wisconsin Press, 1983).
2. Orlow, pp. 7-12; Linz, 207. For a recent study of the structure of Hitler's state, see Hirschfeld and Kettenacker (eds.), *Der Führerstaat: Mythos und Realität*; even with all of the literature on the Third Reich, a new comprehensive treatment integrating the roles of groups and individuals is needed.
3. Dawidowicz, *Holocaust*, p. 31.
4. Douglas F. Ottati, "Christian Theology and Other Disciplines," *Journal of Religion* 64 (1984):173, 178, 187.
5. See, for example, Stewart A. Stehlin, *Weimar and the Vatican, 1919-1933: German-Vatican Diplomatic Relations in the Interwar Years* (Princeton: Princeton University Press, 1983).
6. Janis, "Preventing Groupthink," p. 2.

7. Several recent studies offer a survey of directions that can be taken to understand the roots, implementation, outcome, and analysis of the Holocaust. See Heiko Obermann, *The Roots of Anti-Semitism in the Age of the Renaissance and Reformation* (Philadelphia: Fortress, 1984); Franz Mussner, *Tractate on the Jews: The Significance of Judaism for the Christian Faith* (Philadelphia: Fortress, 1984); J. Marcus, *Social and Political History of the Jews in Poland, 1919-1939* (Berlin: Murton, 1983); Philip Friedman, *Roads to Extinction: Essays on the Holocaust* (Philadelphia: Fortress, 1980); Staats, *Social Behaviorism*, pp. 18, 25; N. Guttman and H.I. Kalish, "Experiments in Discrimination," *Scientific American* 198 (1958):77-82.

8. Horowitz, *Taking Lives*; Kuper, p. 137.

9. Hamerow, p. 72; Argyle, p. 203.

10. George M. Kren, "Psychohistorical Interpretations of National Socialism," *German Studies Review* 1(1978):166; George Kren and Leon Rappaport, *The Holocaust and the Crisis of Human Behavior* (New York: Holmes & Meier, 1980) p. 125.

11. Moishe Postone, "Anti-Semitism and National Socialism: Notes on the German Reaction to 'Holocaust,'" *New German Critique* (1980):114; Staats, *Social Behaviorism*, pp. 82-83.

12. Viola Bernard et al., "Dehumanization: A Composite Psychological Defense in Relation to Modern War," in Schwebel, pp. 64-77.

13. Ehrlich, pp. 160-161.

14. Jeffrey Herf, "Reactionary Modernism: Some Ideological Origins of the Primacy of Politics in the Third Reich," *Theory and Society* 10 (1981):824; Adolf Hitler, *Sämtliche Aufzeichnungen, 1905-1924*, Eberhard Jäckel and Axel Kuhn, eds. (Stuttgart: Deutsche Verlagsanstalt, 1980), p. 89; Knox, 1-57. For an analysis of Hitler's determinative role in the Final Solution, see Gerald Fleming, *Hitler und die Endlösung. "Es ist der Führers Wünsch"* (Munich: Limes Verlag, 1982).

15. Ottati, p. 176; Edward O. Wilson, *Sociobiology: The Abridged Edition* (Cambridge: Harvard University Press, 1975), p. 286.

16. Parenti, p. 269; Gill, pp. 85-86; Peter Berger, *The Social Reality of Religion*.

17. Don Browning, "Psychology as Religioethical Thinking," *Journal of Religion* 64 (1984):141.

18. For a recent study of the problems faced by Church organizations in the Reich, see Heinz-Albert Raem, *Katholischer Gesellenverein und deutsche Kolpingsfamilie in der Ära des Nationalsozialismus* (Mainz: Matthias Grünewald, 1982); Staats, *Social Behaviorism*, pp. 114-115.

19. Adams et al., pp. 224, 228; A. Bandura and R.H. Walters, *Social Psychology and Personality Development* (New York: Holt, Rinehart, and Winston, 1963), p. 106; Staats, *Social Behaviorism*, pp. 155-158.

20. Staub, 2: 8-10; Staats, *Social Behaviorism*, p. 193. For a rigorously constructed study of behavior modification, see Albert Bandura, *Principles of Behavior Modification*.

21. Edward E. Jones, "The Rocky Road from Acts to Dispositions," *American Psychologist* 34 (1979):107-117; L. Ross, "The Intuitive Psychologist and His Shortcomings: Distortions in the Attribution Process," in L. Berkowitz (ed.), *Advances in Experimental Social Psychology*, vol. 10, p. 84. The interconnections existing among Hitler, the German people, and Nazi ideology are intricate; for a comprehensive study focusing on the subtleties of these interconnections, see Weinstein, pp. 117-163.

22. George Homans, *The Nature of Social Science* (New York: Harcourt, Brace, and World, 1967); Peter Knapp, "Can Social Theory Escape from History? Views of History in Social Science," *History and Theory* 23 (1984):34-52.

23. Brugger, pp. 25-26; Robert L. Hanbein and John H. Kunkel (eds.), *Behavioral Theory in Sociology: Essays in Honor of George C. Homans* (New Brunswick, NJ: Transaction Books, 1977).

24. Bandura, *Aggression*, pp. 319-323.

25. Küng, pp. 21-22.

Bibliography

Archival Materials

Abel Collection from the Hoover Institution.
Archives of the Ministry of Justice, Bonn.
Berlin Document Center.
Bundesarchiv, Koblenz.
Diözesan Archiv, Aachen.
Diözesan Archiv, Trier.
Hauptstaatsarchiv, Düsseldorf.
Historisches Archiv der Stadt, Cologne.
Nachlass Faulhaber.
National Archives.

Newspapers and Diocesan Gazettes

Allgemeine Zeitung des Judentums.
Amtsblatt (Specific dioceses are identified in the footnotes).
Archepiscopal Ordinariat Breslau.
Bayerische Katholische Kirchenzeitung.
Bischöfliches Generalvikariat, Trier.
Die Christliche Frau.
Deutsche Briefe.
Ecclesiastica.
Frauenland.
Frau und Mutter.
Germania.
Klerusblatt.
Martinus Blatt.
Mitteilungen zur Weltanschaulichen.
Mitteldeutsche Nationalzeitung.
Monologe.
Münchener Katholische Kirchenzeitung.
Nationalzeitung.
New York Times.
Osservatore Romano.
Der Rütlischwur.

Das Schwarze Korps.
Süddeutsche Zeitung.
*Verkündigung Verordnet von ErzbischRöflichenOrdinariat München und
    Freising mit Erlass.*
Völkischer Beobachter.
Waldse'er Wochenblatt.

Published Primary Sources

Albrecht, Dieter. *Der Notenwechsel zwischen dem Heiligen Stuhl und der
    Deutschen Reichsregierung. Von der Ratifizierung des Reichskonkor-
    dats bis zur Enzyklika "Mit Brennender Sorge."* Mainz: Matthias-
    Grünewald-Verlag, 1965.
Baynes, Norman (ed.). *The Speeches of Adolf Hitler, April '22-August '39.*
    London: Oxford University Press, 1942.
Bischöflichen Ordinariat, Berlin (ed.). *Dokumente aus dem Kampf der
    katholischen Kirche im Bistum Berlin gegen den Na-
    tionalsozialismus.* Berlin: Morus-Verlag, 1946.
Blet, Pierre, et al. (eds.). *Actes et Documentes du Saint Siege relatifs a la
    Seconde Guerre Mondiale,* 9 vols. Vatican City: Libreria Editricl Vat-
    icana, 1965-75.
Blet, Pierre, et al. *Lettres de Pie XII aux eveques allemands, 1939-1944.* 9
    vols. Vatican City: Libreria Editrice Vaticana, 1965-75.
Blumenson, Martin (ed.). *The Patton Papers: 1940-1945.* Boston:
    Houghton Mifflin, 1974.
Boberach, Heinz. *Berichte des SD und der Gestapo über Kirchen und
    Kirchenvolk in Deutschland, 1934-1944.* Mainz: Matthias-
    Grünewald-Verlag, 1971.
Boberach, Heinz (ed.). *Meldungen aus dem Reich. Auswahl aus dem
    geheimen Lageberichten des Sicherheitsdienstes der SS, 1939-1944.*
    Neuwied: Luchterfand, 1965.
Buchberger, Michael. *Lexikon für Theologie und Kirche.* 9 vols. Freiburg:
    Herder, 1930.
Catholic Church. *Acta Apostolica Sedis: Commentarium Officiale.* Vatican
    City: Libreria Editrice Vaticana, 1909.
Corsten, Wilhelm (ed.). *Kölner Aktenstücke. Zur Lage der katholischen
    Kirche in Deutschland, 1933-1945.* Cologne: J.P. Bachem, 1949.
Domarus, Max. *Hitler, Reden und Proklamationen, 1932-45.* Munich:
    Süddeutschen Verlag, 1965.
Engfer, Hermann. *Das Bistum Hildesheim, 1933-1945. Eine Dokumenta-
    tion.* Hildesheim: Verlagsbuchhandlung August Lax, 1971.
Germany. *Auswärtiges Amt, Documents on German Foreign Policy,
    1918-1945.*Series C, 1.
Hehl, Ulrich von. *Katholische Kirche und Nationalsozialismus im
    Erzbistum Köln, 1933-1945.* Mainz: Matthias-Grünewald-Verlag,
    1977.

Hitler, Adolf. *Mein Kampf.* Munich, Eher, 1935.

Hitler, Adolf. *Mein Kampf.* Trans. Ralph Manheim. Boston: Houghton Mifflin, 1943, 1970.

Hofer, Walter (ed.). *Der Nationalsozialismus: Dokumente, 1933-1945.* Frankfurt: Fischer-Bücherei, 1957.

Hofmann, Konrad (ed.). *Zeugnis und Kampf des deutschen Episkopats. Gemeinsame Hirtenbriefe und Denkschriften.* Freiburg: Herder, 1946.

Hürten, Heinz. *Deutsche Briefe, 1934-1938: Ein Blatt der katholischen Emigration, 1, 1934-1935, 2,1936-1938.* Mainz: Matthias-Grünewald-Verlag, 1969.

International Military Tribunal. *Trial of the Major War Criminals.* Nuremberg: Germany, 1947.

Jäckel, Eberhard, and Axel Kuhn (eds.). *Adolf Hitler: Sämtliche Aufzeichnungen, 1905-1924.* Stuttgart: Deutsche Verlags Anstalt, 1980.

Kirchliches Handbuch. Amtliches statistisches Jahrbuch der katholischenKirche Deutschlands. Freiburg: Herder, 1914 + .

Kopf, Paul, and Max Miller (eds.). *Die Vertreibung von Bischof Joannes Baptista Sproll von Rottenburg, 1938-1945. Dokumente zur Geschichte des kirchlichen Widerstands.* Mainz: Matthias-Grünewald-Verlag, 1971.

Kupper, Alfons. *Staatliche Akten über die Reichskonkordatsverhandlungen, 1933.* Mainz: Matthias-Grünewald-Verlag, 1969.

Lutze, Viktor. *Reden an die S.A. Der politische Katholizismus.* 4th ed. Munich: Zentralverlag der NSDAP, 1936.

Mendelsohn, John (ed.). *The Holocaust: Selected Documents in Eighteen Volumes.* New York: Garland Publishing, 1982.

Müller, Hans. *Katholische Kirche und Nationalsozialismus. Dokumente, 1930-1935.* Munich: Nymphenburger Verlagshandlung, 1963.

Neuhäusler, Johann. *Kreuz und Hakenkreuz: Der Kampf des Nationalsozialismus gegen die katholische Kirche und der kirchliche Widerstand.* 2 pts. Munich: Katholische Kirche Bayerns, 1946.

Prantl, Helmut (ed.). *Die Kirchliche Lage in Bayern nach den Regierungspräsidentenberichten 1933-1943. Regierungsbezirk Pfalz, 1933-1940,* Mainz: Matthias-Grünewald-Verlag, 1978.

Sacred Congregation for the Doctrine of the Faith. *Declaration on Euthanasia,* no. 704, n.d.

St. John-Stenas, Norman. *Life, Death and the Law.* Bloomington, IN: Indiana University Press, 1961.

Schneider, Burkhart (ed.). *Die Briefe Pius XII. An die Deutschen Bischöfe, 1939-1944.* Mainz: Matthias-Grünewald-Verlag, 1966.

Stasiewski, Bernhard. *Akten Deutscher Bischöfe über die Lage der Kirche 1933-1945. 1, 1933-1934.* Mainz: Matthias-Grünewald-Verlag, 1968.

Stasiewski, Bernhard. *Akten Deutscher Bischöfe über die Lage der Kirche,*

1933-1945. Vol. 2, *1934-1935.* Mainz: Matthias-Grünewald-Verlag, 1976.

Strachey, James, et al. *The Standard Edition of the Complete Psychological Works of Sigmund Freud.* 24 vols. London: International Psychoanalytical Press, 1953-1975.

United States Government. *Nazi Conspiracy and Aggression.* Washington, DC: U.S. Government Printing Office, 1947.

Verhandlungen des Reichstags, Berlin, 1936.

Volk, Ludwig. *Akten Deutscher Bischöfe über die Lage der Kirche, 1936-1939.* Mainz: Matthias-Grünewald-Verlag, 1981.

Volk, Ludwig. *Akten Kardinal Michael von Faulhabers, 1917-1945* 1, 1917-1934. Mainz: Matthias-Grünewald-Verlag, 1975.

Volk, Ludwig. *Der Bayerische Episkopat und der Nationalsozialismus, 1930-1934.* Mainz: Matthias-Grünewald-Verlag, 1965.

Volk, Ludwig. *Der Bayerische Episkopat und der Nationalsozialismus, 1930-1934.* 2nd ed. Mainz: Matthias-Grünewald-Verlag, 1966.

Volk, Ludwig (ed.). *Kirchliche Akten über die Reichskonkordatsverhandlungen, 1933.* Mainz: Matthias-Grünewald-Verlag, 1969.

Volk, Ludwig. *Das Reichskonkordat vom 20. Juli 1933. Von den Ansätzen in der Weimarer Republik bis zur Ratifizierung am 10. September 1933.* Mainz: Matthias-Grünewald-Verlag, 1972.

Witetschek, Helmut (ed.). *Die Kirchliche Lage in Bayern nach den Regierungsprasidentenberichten, 1933-1943, Regierungsbezirk Ober- und Mittelfranken.* Mainz: Matthias-Grünewald-Verlag, 1967.

Witetschek, Helmut (ed.). *Die Kirchliche Lage in Bayern nach den Regierungspräsidenterberichten, 1933-1943. Regierungsbezirk Oberbayern.* Mainz: Matthias-Grünewald-Verlag, 1966.

Witetschek, Helmut (ed.). *Die Kirchliche Lage in Bayern nach der Regierungspräsidentenberichten, 1933-1943. Regierungsbezirke: Oberbayern, Ober-und Mittelfranken, Schwaben, 1943-1945.* Mainz: Matthias-Grünwald-Verlag, 1981.

Witetschek, Helmut (ed.). *Die Kirchliche Lage in Bayern, nach den Regierungspräsidentenberichten, 1933-1943. Regierungsbezirk Schwaben.* Mainz: Matthias-Grünewald-Verlag, 1971.

Wittstadt, Klaus (ed.). *Die Kirchliche Lage in Bayern nach den Regierungsprasidentenberichten, 1933-1943. Regierungsbezirk Unterfranken, 1933-1944.* Mainz: Matthias-Grünewald-Verlag, 1981.

Zieger, Walter (ed.). *Die Kirchliche Lage in Bayern nach den Regierungspräsidentenberichten, 1933-1943. Regierungsbezirk Niderbayern und Oberpfalz, 1933-1945.* Mainz: Matthias-Grünewald-Verlag, 1973.

Zipfel, Friedrich. *Kirchenkampf in Deutschland, 1933-1945: Religionsverfolgung und Selbstbehauptung der Kirchen in der nationalsozialistischen Zeit.* Berlin: DeGruyter, 1965.

Books

Abel, Theodore. *The Nazi Movement: Why Hitler Came to Power*. New York: Atherton Press, 1965.

Abraham, David. *The Collapse of the Weimar Republic: Political Economy and Crisis*. Princeton: Princeton University Press, 1981.

Ackermann, Josef. *Heinrich Himmler als Ideologe*. Göttingen: Musterschmidt, 1970.

Ackermann, Konrad. *Der Widerstand der Monatschrift Hochland gegen den Nationalsozialismus*. Munich: Oldenbourg, 1965.

Adam, Uwe. *Judenpolitik im Dritten Reich*. Düsseldorf: Droste Verlag, 1972.

Adams, Robert McC., et al. *Behavioral and Social Science Research: A National Resource*. Pt 2. Washington, D.C.: National Academy Press, 1982.

Adolph, Walter. *Hirtenamt und Hitler-Diktatur*. 2nd ed. Berlin: Morus-Verlag, 1965.

Adolph, Walter. *Im Schatten des Galgens. Zum Gedächtnis der Blutzeugen in der nationalsozialistischen Kirchenverfolgung*. Berlin: Morus-Verlag, 1953.

Adolph, Walter. *Kardinal Preysing und zwei Diktaturen. Sein Widerstand gegen die totalitäre Macht*. Berlin: Morus-Verlag, 1971.

Adolph, Walter. *Verfälschte Geschichte. Antwort an Rolf Hochhuth*. Berlin: Morus-Verlag, 1963.

Adorno, Theodor W., et al. *The Authoritarian Personality*. New York: Harper, 1950.

Albrecht, Dieter (ed.). *Katholische Kirche im Dritten Reich. Eine Aufsatzsammlung*. Mainz: Matthias-Grünewald-Verlag, 1976.

Algermissen, Konrad. *Die Gottlosenbewegung der Gegenwart und Ihre Überwindung*. 2nd ed. Hannover: Verlag Joseph Giesel, 1933.

Allen, William Sheridan. *The Nazi Seizure of Power: The Experience of a Single German Town, 1930-1935*. Chicago: University of Chicago Press, 1965.

Altmeyer, Karl Aloys. *Katholische Press unter NS-Diktatur. Die katholischen Zeitungen und Zeitschriften Deutschlands in den Jahren 1933 bis 1945*. Berlin: Morus-Verlag, 1962.

Amery, Carl. *Capitulation: The Lesson of German Catholicism*. Trans. Edward Quinn. New York: Herder & Herder, 1967.

Anderson, Margaret Lavinia. *Windthorst: A Political Biography*. Oxford: Clarendon Press, 1981.

Andics, Hellmut. *Der ewige Jude. Ursachen und Geschichte des Anti-Semitismus*. Vienna: Molden, 1965.

Anschütz, Gerhard. *Die Verfassung des deutschen Reichs vom 11. August 1919. Ein Kommentar für Wissenschaft und Praxis*. 3rd ed. Berlin: G. Stilke, 1930.

Apostle, Richard A., and Charles Y. Glock, et al. *The Anatomy of Racial Attitudes*. Berkeley: University of California Press, 1983.

Arendt, Hannah. *The Origins of Totalitarianism*. New York: Harcourt, Brace & World, 1966.

Argyle, Michael, and Benjamin Beit-Hallahmi. *The Social Psychology of Religion*. London: Routledge and Kegan Paul, 1975.

Arnold, W.J., and D. Levine (eds.). *Nebraska Symposium on Motivation, 1969*. Lincoln: University of Nebraska Press, 1969.

Artweiler, Anton. *Unser Glaube. Christliche Wirklichkeit in der Heutigen Welt*. Munich: Kösel-Pustet, 1938.

Asch, Solomon. *Social Psychology*. Englewood Cliffs, NJ: Prentice Hall, 1952.

Bachem, Karl. *Vorgeschichte, Geschichte, und Politik der Deutschen Zentrums Partei*. 9 vols. Cologne: J. P. Bachem, 1927-1932.

Baier, Helmut. *Die Deutschem Christen Bayerns im Rahmen des bayerischen Kirchenkampfes*. Nürnberg: Selbstverlag des Vereins für bayerische Kirchengeschichte, 1968.

Baier, Helmut. *Kirchenkampf in Nürnberg, 1933-1945*. Nürnberg: Korn u. Berg, 1973.

Baier, Kurt, and N. Rescher (eds.). *Values and the Future*. New York: Free Press, 1969.

Baird, Jay W. *The Mythical World of Nazi War Propaganda, 1939-1945*. Minneapolis: University of Minnesota Press, 1974.

Balfour, Michael. *The Kaiser and His Times*. Boston: Norton, 1964.

Bandura, Albert. *Principles of Behavior Modification*. New York: Holt, Rinehart and Winston, 1969.

Bandura, Albert. *Aggression: A Social Learning Analysis*. Englewood Cliffs, NJ: Prentice-Hall, 1973.

Bandura, A., and R. H. Walters. *Social Psychology and Personality Development*. New York: Holt, Rinehart and Winston, 1963.

Bauer, Clemens. *Deutscher Katholizismus: Entwicklungslinen und Profile*. Frankfurt am Main: Josef Knecht, 1964.

Baum, Rainer C. *The Holocaust and the German Elite: Genocide and National Suicide in Germany, 1871-1945*. Totawa: Rowman and Littlefield, 1981.

Baumgärtner, Raimund. *Weltanschauungskampf im Dritten Reich. Die Auseinandersetzung der Kirchen mit Alfred Rosenberg*. Mainz: Matthias-Grünewald-Verlag, 1977.

Becker, Howard. *Outsiders: Studies in the Sociology of Deviance*. London: Free Press of Glencoe, 1963.

Beer, Alfred. *Erzbischof Dr. Conrad Gröber. Ein Lebensbild*. Konstanz: Verlagsanstalt Merk & Co. KG, 1958.

Behrend-Rosenfeld, Else R. *Ich Stand nicht Allein. Erlebnisse einer Jüden in Deutschland, 1933-1944*. Frankfurt: Euro Verlag, 1963.

Bellah, Robert M. *Beyond Belief*. New York: Free Press, 1970.

Bellig, Michael. *Fascists: A Social Psychological View of the National Front*, London, Academic Press, 1978.

Bendersky, Joseph W. *Carl Schmitt: Theorist for the Reich.* Princeton: Princeton University Press, 1983.

Bennett, John C. *Christians and the State.* New York: Charles Scribner's Sons, 1958.

Berg, Hermann (ed.). *Albert Stohr, Gottes Ordnung in der Welt.* Mainz: Matthias-Grünewald-Verlag, 1960.

Berger, Peter. *The Sacred Canopy.* Garden City: Doubleday, 1966.

Berger, Peter. *The Social Reality of Religion.* London: Faber, 1969.

Berger, Peter, and Thomas Luckmann. *The Social Construction of Reality.* Garden City, NY: Doubleday, 1967.

Berkowitz, Leonard. *Aggression: A Social Psychological Analysis.* New York: McGraw-Hill, 1962.

Berkowitz, Leonard (ed.). *Advances in Experimental Social Psychology.* 10 vols. New York: Academic Press, 1965-1977.

Berkowitz, Leonard. *A Survey of Social Psychology.* Hinsdale, IL: Dryden Press, 1975.

Berning, Wilhelm. *Katholische Kirche und deutsches Volkstum.* Munich: Georg D.W. Callweg Verlag, 1934.

Bertram, Adolf. *Die Stellung der katholischen Kirche zu Radikalismus und Nationalismus: Ein offenes Wort in erster Stunde am Jahresschlusse, 1930.* Breslau: G.P. Aderholz, 1930.

Bielfeldt, Johann. *Der Kirchenkampf in Schleswig-Holstein, 1933-1945.* Göttingen: Vandenhoeck & Ruprecht, 1964.

Bierstedt, Robert. *The Social Order: An Introduction to Sociology.* New York: McGraw-Hill, 1975.

Binder, Gerhart. *Irrtum und Widerstand. Die deutschen Katholiken in der Auseinandersetzung mit dem Nationalsozialismus. Mit einführung von Felix Messerschmid.* Munich: Verlag Pfeiffer, 1968.

Bindung, Karl, and Alfred Hoche. *Die Freigabe der Vernichtung lebensunwerten Lebens, Ihr Mass und Ihre Form.* Leipzig: E. Strache, 1920.

Binion, Rudolph. *Frau Lou: Nietzsche's Wayward Disciple.* Princeton: Princeton University Press, 1968.

Binion, Rudolf. *Hitler Among the Germans.* New York: Elsevier, 1976.

Blackbourn, David. *Class, Religion, and Local Politics in Wilhelmine Germany: The Centre Party in Württemberg Before 1914.* New Haven: Yale University Press, 1980.

Blackbourn, David, and Geoff Eley. *Myther deutscher Geschichtschreibung! Die gescheiterte bürgerliche Revolution.* Frankfurt: Ullstein, 1980.

Blau, Peter. *The Dynamics of Bureaucracy.* Chicago, Univèrsity of Chicago Press, 1955.

Blau, Peter. *Exchange and Power in Social Life.* New York, J. Wiley, 1964.

Bleuel, Hans Peter, and Ernst Klinnert. *Deutsche Studenten auf dem Weg*

ins Dritte Reich: Ideologien-Programme-Aktionen, 1918-1935.
Gütersloh: Sigbert Mohn Verlag, 1967.

Bogler, Theodor. *Der Glaube von Gestern und Heute.* Cologne: Bachem, 1939.

Boyer, John W. *Political Radicalism in Late Imperial Vienna: Origins of the Christian Social Movement, 1848-1897.* Chicago: University of Chicago Press, 1981.

Bracher, Karl Dietrich. *Die Auflösung der Weimarer Republik. Eine Studie zum Problem des Machtverfalls in der Demokratie.* 3rd ed. Villigen: Ring Verlag, 1960.

Bracher, Karl Dietrich, et al. (eds.). *Die nationalsozialistische Machtergreifung. Studien zur Errichtung des totalitären Herrschaftssystems in Deutschland, 1933-34.* 2nd ed. Cologne: Westdeutscher Verlag, 1962.

Brandenburg, Hans-Christian. *HJ-Die Geschichte der HJ.* Cologne: Verlag Wissenschaft und Politik, 1968.

Brauer, Theodor. *Der Katholik im neuer Reich: Seine Aufgabe und sein Anteil.* Munich: Kösel and Pustet, 1933.

Brehm, T.W., and A.R. Cohen. *Explorations in Cognitive Dissonance.* New York: Wiley, 1962.

Breuning, Klaus. *Die Weg in die Diktatur 1918 bis 1933. Zehn Beiträge.* Munich: Nymphenburger Verlagshandlung, 1962.

Breuning, Klaus. *Die Vision des Reiches. Deutscher Katholizismus zwischen Demokratie und Diktatur (1939-1934).* Munich: Max Hueber Verlag, 1969.

Brodie, Fawn. *Thomas Jefferson: An Intimate History.* New York: Norton, 1974.

Broszat, Martin. *The Hitler State: The Foundation and Development of the Internal Structure of the Third Reich.* Trans. John W. Hiden. London: Longman, 1981.

Browning, Christopher R. *The Final Solution and the German Foreign Office. A Study of Referat DIII of Abteilung Deutschland, 1940-1943.* New York: Holmes & Meier, 1978.

Brüning, Heinrich. *Memoiren, 1918-1934.* Stuttgart: Deutsche Verlagsanstalt, 1970.

Brugger, Robert, ed. *Our Selves/Our Past; Psychological Approaches to American History.* Baltimore: Johns Hopkins University Press, 1981.

Buchheim, Hans. *Das Dritte Reich: Grundlagen und politische Entwicklung.* Munich: Kösel-Verlag, 1958.

Buchheim, Hans. "Fördernde Mitgliedschaft bei der SS." In *Gutachten des Instituts für Zeitgeschichte.* Munich: Selbstverlag, 1958.

Cardauns, Hermann. *Adolf Gröber.* Munich-Gladbach: H. Ludwig, 1921.

Cartwright, Darwin, and F. Zander (eds.). *Group Dynamics: Research and Theory.* 2nd ed. New York: Harper & Row, 1960.

Catel, Werner. *Grenzsituationen des Lebens. Beitrag zum Problem einer begrenzten Euthanasie.* Nurnberg: Block und Lutz, 1962.

Cecil, Robert. *The Myth of the Master Race: Alfred Rosenberg and Nazi Ideology*. New York: Dodd, Mead & Co., 1972.

Chamberlain, Houston Stewart. *Worte Christi*. Munich: Oldenbourg, 1903.

Charles-Roux, Francois. *Huit ans au Vatican, 1932-1940*. Paris: Flammarion, 1947.

Chase, Allan. *The Legacy of Malthus*. New York: Knopf, 1977.

Checinski, Michael. *Poland: Communism, Nationalism, Anti-Semitism*. New York: Karz-Cohl, 1982.

Chinn, Philip, et al. *Mental Retardation: A Life Cycle Approach*. St. Louis: Mosby, 1979.

Cochrane, Arthur C. *The Church's Confession under Hitler*. Philadelphia: The Westminster Press, 1962.

Coelho, George V. *Coping and Adaptation*. New York: Basic Books, 1974.

Cohen, Arthur A. *The Tremendum: A Theological Interpretation of the Holocaust*. New York: Crossroads Publishing Co., 1981.

Cohen, Arthur D. *Attitude Change and Social Influence*. New York: Basic Books, 1964.

Cohen, Jeremy. *The Friars and the Jew: The Evolution of Medieval Anti-Judaism*. Ithaca: Cornell University Press, 1983.

Cohn, Norman. *Warrant for Genocide*. New York: Harper, 1967.

Congar, Yves, M.-J. *The Catholic Church and the Race Question*. Paris: Unesco, 1953.

Conway, John S. *The Nazi Persecution of the Churches, 1933-45*. New York: Basic Books, 1968.

Conze, Werner. *Die Zeit Wilhelms II und die Weimarer Republik*. Tübingen: Wunderlich, 1964.

Dahrendorf, Rolf. *Society and Democracy in Germany*. Garden City: NY: Doubleday, 1967.

Davies, Alan T. *Anti-Semitism and the Christian Mind: The Crisis of Conscience After Auschwitz*. New York: Herder and Herder, 1969.

Dawidowicz, Lucy *The Holocaust and the Historians*. Cambridge: Harvard University Press, 1981.

Dawidowicz, Lucy. *The War Against the Jews, 1933-1945*. New York: Holt, Rinehart and Winston, 1975.

Delp, Alfred. *Zur Erde Entschlossen. Vorträge und Aufsätze*. Frankfurt am Main: Verlag Josef Knecht, 1949.

Deuerlein, Ernst. *Das Reichskonkordat*. Düsseldorf: Patmos, 1956.

Deuerlein, Ernst. *Der Deutsche Katholizismus, 1933*. Osnabrück: Verlag A. Fromm, 1963.

Dicks, Henry V. *Licensed Mass Murder: A Socio-Psychological Study of Some SS Killers*. New York: Basic Books, 1972.

Diehn, Otto. *Bibliographie zur Geschichte des Kirchenkampfes, 1933-1945*. Göttingen: Vandenhoeck and Ruprecht, 1958.

Dimsdale, Joel E. (ed.). *Survivors, Victims, and Perpetrators: Essays on the Nazi Holocaust*. Washington: Hemisphere Publishing Corp., 1980.

Doetsch, Wilhelm Josef. *Württembergs Katholiken untern Hakenkreuz, 1930-1935.* Stuttgart: W. Kohlhammer Verlag, 1969.

Donohoe, James. *Hitler's Conservative Opponents in Bavaria, 1930-1945: A Study of Catholic, Monarchist, and Separatist Anti-Nazi Activities.* Leiden: E.J. Brill, 1961.

Duberman, Martin (ed.). *The Anti-Slavery Vanguard: New Essays on the Abolitionists.* Princeton: Princeton University Press, 1965.

Eberle, Joseph. *Zum Kampf um Hitler. Ein Reform program für Staats-, Wirtschafts-und Kulturpolitik zur Überwindung des Radikalismus.* Vienna: Verlag "Schonere Zukunft," 1931.

Ebermayer, Erich. " . . . *Und Morgan die ganze Welt." Erinnerungen aus Deutschlands dunkle Zeit.* Bayreuth: Schmidt Verlag, 1966.

Ebers, G.J. (ed.). *Katholische Staatslehre und Volksdeutsche Politik.* Freiburg: Herder, 1929.

Ecclesiae, Miles. *Hitler Gegen Christus. Eine katholische Klarstellung und Abwehr.* Paris: Societe d' Editions Europeennes, 1936.

Eckert, Willehad. *Judenhass-Schuld der Christen.* Essen: H. Driewer, 1964.

Ehrhardt, Helmut. *Euthanasie und Vernichtung "Lebensunwerten" Lebens.* Stuttgart: Ferdinand Enke Verlag, 1965.

Ehrlich, Howard J. *The Social Psychology of Prejudice: A Systematic Theoretical Review and Propositional Inventory of the American Social Psychological Study of Prejudice.* New York: Wiley, 1973.

Eisenstadt, S.N. *Traditions, Change, and Modernity.* New York: Wiley, 1973.

Engel-Janosi, Friedrich. *Vom Chaos zur Katastrophe. Vatikanische Gespräche, 1918 bis 1938.* Vienna: Herold, 1971.

Epstein, Klaus. *Matthias Erzberger and the Dilemma of German Democracy.* Princeton: Princeton University Press, 1959.

Erb, Alfons. *Bernhard Lichtenberg: Dompropst von St. Hedwig zu Berlin.* Berlin: Morus-Verlag, 1949.

Erikson, Erik. *Childhood and Society.* New York: Norton, 1950.

Erikson, Erik. *Young Man Luther.* New York: Norton, 1958.

Erler, Ludwig. *Historisch-kritische Übersicht nationalökonomischen und sozialpolitischen Literatur.* Mainz: Matthias-Grünewald-Verlag, 1879-1885.

Erzberger, Matthias. *Christliche oder sozialdemokratische Gewerkschaften.* Stuttgart: Deutscheuerlagsanstalt, 1898.

Evans, Ellen. *The Center Party, 1870-1933: A Study in Political Catholicism.* Carbondale, Il: University of Southern Illinois Press, 1981.

Evans, Richard J., and W.R. Lee (eds.). *The German Family: Essays on the Social History of the Family in Nineteenth and Twentieth Century Germany.* London: Croom Helm, 1981.

Faulhaber, Michael Kardinal. *Deutsches Ehrgefühl und katholisches Gewissen.* Munich: Pfeiffer Verlags, 1925.

Faulhaber, Michael Kardinal. *Judaism, Christianity and Germany.* Trans. George D. Smith. London: Burns, Oates and Washbourne, 1934.

Fein, Helen. *Accounting for Genocide: National Responses and Jewish Victimization During the Holocaust.* New York: Free Press, 1979.

Fellmeth, Adolf. *Das kirchliche Finanzwesen in Deutschland.* Karlsruhe: I.B.G. Braun, 1910.

Festinger, Leon. *A Theory of Cognitive Dissonance.* Stanford: Stanford University Press, 1957.

Field, Geoffrey G. *Evangelist of Race: The Germanic Vision of Houston Stewart Chamberlain.* New York: Columbia University Press, 1981.

Finlay, David J., et al. (eds.). *Enemies in Politics.* Chicago: University of Chicago Press, 1967.

Fishbein, M., and I. Ajzen. *Belief, Attitude, Intention, and Behavior: An Introduction to Theory and Research.* Reading, MA: Addison-Wesley, 1975.

Fisher, Desmond. *Pope Pius XII and the Jews: An Answer to Hochhuth's Play, Der Stellvertreter (The Deputy).* Glen Rock, NJ: Paulist Press, 1963.

Fleischner, Eva (ed.). *Auschwitz: Beginning of a New Era.* New York: Ktav Pub. Co., 1977.

Fleming, Gerald. *Hitler and the Final Solution.* Berkeley: University of California Press, 1982.

Fliedner, Hans Joachim. *Die Judenverfolgung in Mannheim, 1933-1945.* Stuttgart: Deutsche Verlags Anstalt, 1971.

Forgie, George. *Patricide in a House Divided: A Psychological Interpretation of Lincoln and His Age.* New York: Random House, 1979.

Freidlander, Henry, and Sybil Milton (eds.). *The Holocaust: Ideology, Bureaucracy, and Genocide. The San Jose Papers.* Millwood, NY: Kraus International Publications, 1980.

Freytag, Gustav. *Soll und Haben.* Berlin: Wegmeiser, 1855.

Friedländer, Saul. *L'Antisemitisme Nazi: Histoire d'une psychose collective.* Paris: Editions du Seuil, 1971.

Friedman, Philip. *Their Brothers, Keepers.* New York: Crown Publishers, 1957.

Friedman, Philip, *Roads to Extinction: Essays on the Holocaust.* Philadelphia: Fortress Press, 1980.

Friedman, Saul. *The Oberammergau Passion Play: A Lance Against Civilization.* Carbondale: Southern Illinois University Press, 1984.

Friedrich, Carl J., and Zbigniew Brzezinski. *Totalitarian Dictatorship and Autocracy.* New York: Praeger, 1963.

Friedrich, Ruth Andreas. *Berlin Underground, 1938-1945.* New York: Knopf, 1947.

Gager, John. *The Origins of Anti-Semitism: Attitudes Toward Judaism in Pagan and Christian Antiquity.* New York: Oxford University Press, 1983.

Galen, Clemens von. *Die Pest des Laizismus.* Münster: Aschendorff, 1932.

Gallin, Mary Alice. *German Resistance to Hitler: Ethical and Religious*

Factors. Washington, DC: The Catholic University of America Press, 1961.

Gamm, Hans-Jochen. *Der braunne Kult. Das Dritte Reich und seine Ersatzreligion: Ein Beitrag zur politischen Bildung.* Hamburg: Rütter und Loening Verlag, 1962.

Garfinkel, H. *Studies in Ethnomethodology.* Englewood Cliffs, NJ: Prentice Hall, 1967.

Garr, Ted Robert. *Why Men Rebel.* Princeton: Princeton University Press, 1970.

Gebhardt, Bruno (ed.). *Handbuch der deutschen Geschichte.* Stuttgart: Union Deutsche Verlagsgesselschaft, 1963.

Geerbig, Dr. *Die Parität an den öffentlichen höheren Schulen der Rheinprovinz im Schuljahr, 1928.* Birkenfeld: Volk u. Wissen, 1928.

Geis, Robert Raphael and Hans-Joachim Kraus. *Versuche des Verstehens, Dokumente jüdisch-christlicher Begegnung aus den Jahren, 1918-1933.* Münich: Chr. Kaiser Verlag, 1966.

Gellner, Ernest. *Legitimation of Belief.* London: Cambridge University Press, 1974.

Gergen, Kenneth J. *Social Psychology.* New York: Harcourt Brace Jovanovich, 1981.

Gerhart, Walter. *Um des Reiches Zukunft. Nationale Wiedergeburt oder politische Reaktion?* Freiburg: Herder & Co., 1932.

Gibbard, Graham, et al. *Analysis of Groups.* San Francisco, Jossey-Bass Publishers, 1974.

Gilbert, Felix. "Bismarckian Society's Image of the Jew." New York: Leo Baeck Institute, 1978.

Gill, Robin. *The Social Context of Theology: A Methodological Enquiry.* London: Mowbrays, 1975.

Glaser, Hermann. *Spiesser-Ideologie, von der Zerstörung des deutschen Geistes im 19. und 20. Jahrhundert.* Freiburg: Rombach, 1964.

Glock, Charles Y., and Rodney Stark. *Christian Beliefs and Anti-Semitism.* New York: Harper & Row, 1966.

Glum, Friedrich. *Der Nationalsozialismus, Werden und Vergehen.* Munich: Beck, 1962.

Golde, Günter. *Catholics and Protestants: Agricultural Modernization in Two German Villages.* New York: Academic Press, 1975.

Gordon, Harold J. *Hitler and the Beerhall Putsch.* Princeton: Princeton University Press, 1972.

Goslin, David A. (ed.). *Handbook of Socialization Theory and Research.* Chicago, University of Chicago Press, 1969.

Gotto, Klaus, and Konrad Repger (eds.). *Kirche, Katholiken und Nationalsozialismus.* Mainz: Matthias-Grünewald-Verlag, 1980.

Gottron, B. *Erlebtes und Erlauschtes aus dem Mainzer Metzgergewerbe im 19. Jahrhundert.* Mainz: Matthias-Grünewald-Verlag, 1928.

Graham, Robert, S.J. *Pius XII's Defense of Jews and Others: 1944-1945.* Milwaukee: A Catholic League Publication, 1982.

Greenstein, Fred I., and Nelson W. Polsby. *Macropolitical Theory Vol. 3 of Handbook of Political Science*. Reading, MA: Addison Wesley, 1975.

Greenwald, Anthony et al. (eds.). *Psychological Foundations of Attitudes*. New York: Academic Press, 1968.

Grieve, Hermann. *Theologie und Ideologie: Katholizismus und Judentum in Deutschland und Österreich, 1918-1935*. Heidelberg: Lambert Schneider Verlag, 1969.

Grill, Johnpeter Horst. *The Nazi Movement in Baden, 1920-1945*. Chapel Hill: University of North Carolina Press, 1983.

Gröber, Conrad (ed.). *Handbuch der religiösen Gegenwartsfragen*. Freiburg: Herder, 1937.

Gröber, Conrad. *Kirche, Vaterland, und Vaterlandsliebe. Zeitgemässe Erwägungen und Erwiderungen*. Freiburg: Herder, 1935.

Gröber, Konrad. *Nationalkirche? Ein aufklärendes Wort zur Wahrung des konfessionellen Friedens*. Freiburg: Herder, 1934.

Groner, Franz (ed.). *Kirchliches Handbuch: Amtliches statistisches Jahrbuch der katholischen Kirche Deutschlands*. Cologne: Bachem, 1957.

Grossmann, Kurt. *Die unbesungenen Helden*. Berlin, Arani Verlags, 1957.

Gundlach, Gustav, S.J. *Zur Soziologie der katholischen Ideenwelt und des Jesuitenordens*. Freiburg: Herder, 1982.

Gurland, Arkadij (ed.). *Faktoren der Machtbildung*. Berlin: Duncker and Humblot, 1952.

Gutteridge, Richard. *The German Evangelical Church and the Jews, 1879-1950*. New York: Barnes and Noble, 1976.

Hackey, Thomas E. (ed). *Anglo-Vatican Relations, 1914-1939: Annual Reports of the British Ministers to the Holy See*. Boston: Beacon Press, 1972.

Hadrossek, Paul. *Die Bedeutung des Systemgedankens für die Moraltheologie in Deutschland seit der Thomas-Renaissance*. Munich: Karl Zink Verlag, 1950.

Häuser, Philipp. *Jud und Christ oder Wem gehört die Weltherrschaft?* Regensburg: G.J. Manz, 1923.

Häuser, Philipp. *Pazifismus und Christentum*. Augsburg: Aschendorff, 1925.

Häuser, Philipp. *Wir deutsche Katholiken und die moderne revolutionäre Bewegung*. Regensburg: J.G. Manz, 1921.

Haffner, Sebastian. *The Meaning of Hitler*. New York: Appleton-Century-Crofts, 1979.

Hahn, Helmut. *Der Einfluss der Konfessionen auf die Bevölkerungs-und Sozialgeographie des Hunsrück*. Bonn: Selbstverlag des Geographischen Instituts der Universität, 1950.

Hambrecht, Rainer. *Der Aufstieg der NSDAP in Mittel und Oberfranken (1925-1933)*. Nürnberg: Stadtarchiv, Korn u. Berg (Vertrieb), 1976.

Hamilton, Richard F. *Who Voted for Hitler?* Princeton: Princeton University Press, 1982.

Hanbein, Robert L., and John H. Kunkel (eds.). *Behavioral Theory in Sociology: Essays in Honor of George C. Homans*. New Brunswick, NJ: Transaction Books, 1977.

Hanke, P. *Zur Geschichte der Juden in München zwischen 1933 und 1945*. Munich: Stadtarchiv, 1967.

Hartmann, Edward v. *Das Judenthum in Gegenwart und Zukunft*. 2nd ed. Leipzig: W. Friedrich, 1885.

Hartup, W.W., and N.L. Smothergill (eds.). *The Young Child: Review of Research*. Washington, DC: National Association for the Education of Young Children, 1967.

Heberle, Rudolf. *From Democracy to Nazism: A Regional Case Study on Political Parties in Germany*. Baton Rouge: Louisiana State University Press, 1945.

Hecker, A. *Vor Judas Weltherrschaft?* Achern: I.B., Unitas Gmbh, 1921.

Hehl, Ulrich von (ed.). *Walter Adolph: Geheime Aufzeichnungen aus dem Nationalsozialistischen Kirchenkampf, 1935-1943*. Mainz: Matthias-Grünewald-Verlag, 1979.

Heiber, H. *Walter Frank und sein Reichsinstitut für die Geschichte des neuen Deutschland*. Stuttgart: Deutsche Verlags-Anstalt, 1966.

Heider, F. *The Psychology of Interpersonal Relations*. New York: International Universities Press, 1958.

Heinen, Ernst, and Hans Julius Schoeps (eds.). *Geschichte in der Gegenwart. Festschrift für Kurt Klupen*. Paderborn, Ferdinand Schöningh, 1972.

Heller, Celia. *On the Edge of Destruction*. New York: Macmillan, 1970.

Helmreich, Ernst. *The German Churches Under Hitler: Background, Struggle, and Epilogue*. Detroit: Wayne State University Press, 1979.

Henkys, Reinhard. *Die Nationalsozialistischen Gewaltverbrechen. Geschichte und Gericht*. Stuttgart: Kreuz-Verlag, 1964.

Hero, Alfred. *Opinion Leaders in American Communities*. Boston: World Peace Foundation, 1959.

Hersen, Michel, et al. (eds.). *Progress in Behavior Modification*. Vol. 16. New York: Academic, 1978.

Hewitt, John P. *Self and Society: A Symbolic Interactionist Social Psychology*. Boston: Allyn and Bacon, 1976.

Heydt, Fritz von der. *Die Parität bei der Anstellung der Beamten*. Berlin: Säemann-Verlag, 1931.

Hilberg, Raul. *The Destruction of the European Jews*. Chicago: Quadrangle Books, 1961.

Hillgruber, Andreas. *Hitlers Strategie: Politik und Kriegsführung, 1940-41*. Frankfurt: Bernard and Graege Verlag für Wehrwesen, 1965.

Hinz, Berthold. *Art in the Third Reich*. New York: Pantheon Books, 1979.

Hirschfeld, Gerhard, and Lothar Kettenacker (eds.). *Der "Führerstaat": Mythos und Realität: Studien zur Struktur und Politik des Dritten Reiches*. Stuttgart: Klett-Cotta, 1981.

Hochhuth, Rolf. *The Deputy.* New York: Grove Press, 1964.

Hockerts, Hans Günter. *Die Sittlichkeitsprozesse gegen Katholische Ordensangehörige und Priester, 1936/1937: Eine Studie zur nationalsozialistischen Herrschaftstechnik und zum Kirchenkampf.* Mainz: Matthias-Grünewald-Verlag, 1971.

Hollander, E.P. *Leadership Dynamics: A Practical Guide to Effective Relationships.* New York: Free Press, 1978.

Höllen, Martin. *Heinrich Wienken, der 'unpolitische' Kirchenpolitiker. Eine Biographie aus drei Epochen des deutschen Katholizismus.* Mainz: Matthias-Grünewald-Verlag, 1981.

Homans, George. *The Nature of Social Science.* New York: Harcourt, Brace & World, 1967.

Homans, G.C. *Social Behavior: Its Elementary Forms.* New York: Harcourt, Brace & World, 1961.

Homeland, C.I., et al. *Communication and Persuasion.* New Haven: Yale University Press, 1953.

Hommes, Jakob. *Lebens-und Bildungsphilosophie als völkische und katholische Aufgabe.* Freiburg: Herder, 1934.

Hommes, Ulrich (ed.). *Gesellschaft ohne Christentum? Zum Beitrag der Christen für die Erhaltung der Freiheit.* Düsseldorf: Patmos-Verlag, 1974.

Hoose, Amine. *Katholische Presse und die Judenfrage: Inhaltsanalyse katholischer Periodika am Ende des 19. Jahrhunderts.* Berlin: Brückenverlag, 1875.

Horowitz, Irving Louis. *Genocide: State Power and Mass Murder.* New Brunswick, NJ: Transaction Books, 1976.

Horowitz, Irving Louis. *Taking Lives: Genocide and State Power.* New Brunswick, NJ: Transaction Books, 1980.

Hudal, Alois. *Rom, Christentum, und Deutsches Volk.* Innsbruck: Tyrolia Verlag, 1935.

Hudal, Alois. *Die Grundlagen des Nationalsozialismus Eine ideengeschichtliche Untersuchung.* Leipzig: Johannes Günther Verlag, 1937.

Hull, David. *Film in the Third Reich.* Berkeley: University of California Press, 1969.

Hunt, James. "Between the Ghetto and the Nation: Catholics in the Weimar Republic." In *Towards the Holocaust: The Social and Economic Collapse of the Weimar Republic,* ed. Michael Dobrowski and Isidor Wallimann. Westport, CT: Greenwood Press, 1983.

Hüsgen, Manfred. *Die Bistumsblätter in Niedersachsen während der nationalsozialistischen Zeit. Ein Beitrag zur Geschichte der katholischen Publizistik im Dritten Reich.* Hildesheim: August Lax Verlagsbuchhandlung, 1975.

Huss, Hermann, and Andreas, Schröder (ed.). *Antisemitismus: Zur Pathologie der Bürgerlichen Gesellschaft.* Frankfurt: Europäische Verlagsanstalt, 1966.

Iggers, George G., and Harold T. Parker (eds.). *International Handbook of Historical Studies: Contemporary Research and Theory*, Westport, CT: Greenwood Press, 1979.

Jäckel, Eberhard, *Hitler's Weltanschauung: A Blueprint for Power*. Trans. Herbert Arnold. Middletown, CT: Wesleyan University Press, 1972.

Janis, Irving. *Victims of Groupthink: A Psychological Study of Foreign-Policy Decisions and Fiascoes*. Boston: Houghton Mifflin Co. 1972.

Johnson, P.E. *The Psychology of Religion*. New York: Abingdon Press, 1959.

Jones, E.E., and R. E. Nisbett. *The Actor and the Observer: Divergent Perceptions of the Courses of Behavior*. New York: Appleton-Century-Crofts, 1967.

Jost, Adolf. *Das Recht auf den Tod*, Göttingen: Dieterich 'sche Verlagsbuchhandlung, 1895.

Just, K. *Eugenik und Weltanschauung*. Berlin: Deichert, 1932.

Kampe, Walther. *Die Nation in der Heilsordnung. Eine Natürliche und Übernatürliche Theologie vom Volk*. Mainz: Matthias-Grünewald-Verlag, 1936.

Kater, Michael. *The Nazi Party: A Social Profile of Members and Leaders, 1919-1945*. Cambridge: Harvard University Press, 1983.

Katz, Jacob. *From Prejudice to Destruction: Anti-Semitism, 1700-1933*. Cambridge: Harvard University Press, 1980.

Kaupel, H. *Die antisemitische Bekampfung des Alten Testaments, vom Standpunkt katholischer Bibelbetrachtung beleuchtet*. Münster: Aschendorff, 1933.

Kelley, Alfred. *The Descent of Darwin: The Popularization of Darwinism in Germany, 1860-1917*. Chapel Hill, NC: University of North Carolina Press, 1981.

Kennedy, Paul, and Anthony Nicholl (eds.). *Nationalist and Racialist Movements in Britain and Germany Before 1914*. London: Macmillan, 1981.

Kershaw, Ian. *Der Hitler Mythos: Volksmeinung und Propaganda in Dritten Reich*. Stuttgart: Deutsche Verlagsanstalt, 1980.

Kershaw, Ian. "The Persecution of the Jews and German Popular Opinion in the Third Reich." In *Leon Baeck Institute Yearbook* 26 (1981).

Kershaw, Ian. *Popular Opinion and Political Dissent in the Third Reich: Bavaria, 1933-1945*. Oxford: Oxford University Press, 1983.

Ketteler, Wilhelm. *Freiheit, Autorität und Kirche. Erörterungen über die grossen Probleme der Gegenwart*. Mainz: Matthias-Grünewald-Verlag, 1862.

Kidd, Robert, and Michael Sales (eds.). *Advances in Applied Social Psychology*. Hillsdale, NJ: Lawrence Erlbaum, 1980.

Kidder, Louise H., and V. Mary Stewart. *The Psychology of Intergroup Relations: Conflict and Consciousness*. New York: McGraw Hill, 1975.

Kirchlicher Anzeiger für die Erzdiözese Köln. *Grundfragen der Lebens-auffassung und Lebensgestaltung Fünfter Teil der 'Studien zum Mythos des XX. Jahrhunderts'.* Cologne: J.P. Bachem, 1935.

Klee, Ernst. *'Euthanasie' im NS-Staat. Die 'Vernichtung Lebensunwerten Lebens'.* Frankfurt: S. Fischer, 1983.

Klein, Charlotte. *Anti-Judaism in Christian Theology.* Trans. Edward Quinn. Philadelphia: Fortress Press, 1978.

Kleineidam, Erich. *Die Katholisch-Theologische Fakultät der Universität Breslau, 1811-1945.* Cologne: Wienand-Verlag, 1961.

Klepper, Jochen. *Unter dem Schatten deinen Flügel; aus den Tagebüchern der Jahre, 1932-1942.* Stuttgart: Deutsche Verlags-Anstalt, 1956.

Klonne, Arno. *Hitlerjugend. Die Jugend und die Organisation im Dritten Reich.* Hanover: O. Goedel, 1955.

Knoll, August M. *Katholische Kirche und Scholastisches Naturrecht: Zur Frage der Freiheit.* Vienna: Europa Verlag, 1962.

Knutson, Jeanne N. (ed.). *Handbook of Political Psychology.* San Francisco: Jossey-Bass, 1973.

Koch, H.W. *The Hitler Youth: Origins and Development, 1922-1945.* London: MacDonald and Jones, 1975.

Koehl, Robert. *The Black Corps: The Structure and Power Struggles of the Nazi SS.* Madison: University of Wisconsin Press, 1983.

Koehl, Robert L. *RKFDV: German Resettlement and Population Policy, 1939-1945. A History of the Reich Commission for the Strengthening of Germandom.* Cambridge: Harvard University Press, 1957.

Köfler, J.A. *Katholische Kirche und Judenthum.* Munich: F. Enke, 1928.

Kolping, Adolf. *Katholische Theologie: Gestern und Heute. Thematik und Entfaltung deutscher katholischer Theologie vom I. Vaticanum bis zur Gegenwart.* Bremen: Carl Schümann Verlag, 1964.

Kornhauser, William. *The Politics of Mass Society.* London: Routledge and Kegan Paul, 1960.

Kren, George M., and Leon Rappoport. *The Holocaust and the Crisis of Human Behavior.* New York: Holmes and Meier, 1980.

Küng, Hans. *The Council: Reform and Reunion.* Trans. Cecily Hastings. New York: Sheed and Ward, 1961.

Kuper, Leon. *Genocide: Its Political Use in the Twentieth Century.* New Haven: Yale University Press, 1981.

Küppers, Heinrich. *Der Katholische Lehrerverband in der Übergangszeit von der Weimarer Republik zur Hitler-Diktatur. Zugleich ein Beitrag zur Geschichte des Volksschullehrerstandes.* Mainz: Matthias-Grünewald-Verlag, 1975.

Lambert, W.E., and O. Klineberg. *Children's Views of Foreign Peoples.* New York: Appleton-Century-Crofts, 1967.

Lapide, Pinchas E. *Three Popes and the Jews.* New York: Hawthorn Books, 1967.

Latane, B., and J.M. Darley. *The Unresponsive Bystander: Why Doesn't He Help?* New York, Appleton Century Crofts, 1970.

Lazarus, R. *Psychological Stress and the Coping Process.* New York: McGraw-Hill, 1966.

Lehr, Stefan. *Antisemitismus religiöse Motive in sozialen Vorurteil aus der Frühgeschichte des antisemitismus in Deutschland, 1870-1914.* Munich: Oldenbourg, 1974.

Leuner, Heinz. *When Compassion Was a Crime: Germany's Silent Heroes, 1933-1945.* London: Wolff, 1966.

Levin, Nora. *The Holocaust: The Destruction of European Jewry, 1933-1945.* New York: Thomas Y. Crowell Co., 1968.

Levy, Richard. *The Downfall of the Anti-Semitic Liberal Parties in Imperial Germany.* New Haven: Yale University Press, 1975.

Lewy, Guenther. *The Catholic Church and Nazi Germany.* New York: McGraw Hill, 1964.

Lewy, Johann M. *Christus in Dachau.* Vienna: Missionsdruckereai St. Gabriel, 1957.

Lifton, Robert J. (ed.). *Explorations in Psychohistory.* New York: Simon & Schuster, 1974.

Lindzey, Gardner, and Elliot Aronson. *The Handbook of Social Psychology.* 4 vols. 2nd ed. Reading, MA: Addison-Wesley, 1969.

Linz, Juan, and Alfred Stepan (eds.). *The Breakdown of Democratic Regimes.* Baltimore: Johns Hopkins University Press, 1978.

Lipset, Seymour Martin. *The First New Nation.* New York: Basic Books, 1963.

Lipset, Seymour Martin. *Political Man: The Social Bases of Politics.* Baltimore, MD: The Johns Hopkins University Press, 1981.

Littell, Franklin H., and Hubert G. Locke (eds.). *The German Church Struggle and the Holocaust.* Detroit: Wayne State University Press, 1974.

Lohalm, Uwe. *Völkischer Radikalismus: Die Geschichte des Deutschvölkischen Schutz-und Trutz-Bundes, 1919-1933.* Hamburg, Leibniz Verlag, 1970.

Lortz, Joseph. *Katholischer Zugang zum Nationalsozialismus kirchengeschichtlich gesehen.* Münster: Aschendorff, 1933.

Lortz, Joseph. *Katholischer Zugang zum Nationalsozialismus.* 2nd ed. Münster: Verlag der Aschendorsfschen Verlagsbuchhandlung, 1934.

Lutz, Heinrich. *Demokratie im Zwielicht. Der Weg der deutschen Katholiken aus dem Kaiserreich in die Republik, 1914-1925.* München: Kösel-Verlag, 1963.

Macaulay, J., and L. Berkowitz (eds.). *Altruism and Helping Behavior. Social Psychological Studies of Some Antecedents and Consequences.* New York: Academic Press, 1970.

Maccarrone, Michele. *Il Nazionalsocialismo e la Santa Sede.* Rome: Editrice Studium, 1947.

MacDonald, Dwight. *Memoirs of a Revolutionist: Essays in Political Criticism.* New York: Farrar, Straus and Cudahy, 1957.

MacIver, Robert M. *The Web of Government*. New York: Macmillan, 1947.

Mann, Golo. *Der Antisemitismus*. Munich: Ner-Tamidverlag, 1960.

Marcus, J. *Social and Political History of the Jews in Poland, 1919-1939*. Berlin: Mouton, 1983.

Mariaux, Walter, S.J. *The Persecution of the Catholic Church in the Third Reich. Facts and Documents*. Trans. from German. London: Burns Oates, 1940.

Marrus, Michael, and Robert Paxton. *Vichy France and the Jews*. New York: Schocken Books, 1983.

Martin, David (ed.). *Sociology and Theology: Alliance and Conflict*. New York: St. Martin's Press, 1980.

Martin, Hugh, et al. *Christian Counter-Attack; Europe's Churches Against Nazism*. New York: Charles Scribner's Sons, 1944.

Mason, John B. *Hitler's First Foes: A Study in Religion and Politics*. Minneapolis: Burgess Publishing Co., 1936.

Massing, Paul. *Rehearsal for Destruction: A Study of Political Anti-Semitism in Imperial Germany*. New York: Harper, 1949.

Masur, Gerhard. *Imperial Berlin*. New York: Basic Books, 1970.

Matheson, Peter (ed.). *The Third Reich and the Christian Churches*. Grand Rapids, MI: William B. Eerdmans, 1981.

Matthias, Erich, and Rudolf Morsey (eds.). *Das Ende der Parteien: 1933*. Düsseldorf, Droste, 1960.

Mayer, Joseph. *Gesetzliche Unfruchtbarmachung Geisteskranker*. Freiburg: Herder, 1927.

McClelland, David, and Robert Steele (eds.). *Human Motivation: A Book of Readings*. Morristown, NJ: General Learning Press, 1973.

McKale, Donald M.. *The Nazi Party Courts: Hitler's Management of Conflict in His Movement, 1921-1945*. Lawrence, KS: University Press of Kansas, 1974.

Meissner, Otto. *Staatssekretär unter Ebert-Hindenburg-Hitler*. Hamburg: Hoffmann und Campe, 1950.

Merkl, Peter. *Political Violence under the Swastika: 581 Early Nazis*. Princeton: Princeton University Press, 1975.

Meltzer, Ewald. *Das Problem der Freigabe der Vernichtung lebensunwerten Lebens*. Weimar: Marhold, 1925.

Messner, Johannes. *Die soziale Frage der Gegenwart*. Innsbruck: Verlagsanstalt Tyrolia, 1934.

Morsey, Rudolf, and Erich Matthias (eds.). *Das Ende der Parteien: 1933*. Düsseldorf: Patmos, 1960.

Micklem, Nathaniel. *National Socialism and the Roman Catholic Church. Being an Account of the Conflict Between the National Socialist Government of Germany and the Roman Catholic Church, 1933-1938*. London: Oxford University Press, 1939.

Milgram, Stanley. *Obedience to Authority: An Experimental View*. New York: Harper & Row, 1969.

Missalla, Heinrich. *Für Volk und Vaterland. Die Kirchliche Kriegshilfe im Zweiten Weltkrieg.* Königstein: Athenäum, 1978.

Mitchell, Otis C. *Hitler Over Germany: The Establishment of Nazi Dictatorship (1918-1934).* Philadelphia: Institute for the Study of Human Issues, 1983.

Mitscherlich, Alexander. *Doctors of Infamy: The Story of the Nazi Medical Crimes.* Trans. Heinz Norden. New York: Henry Schuman, 1949.

Möckl, Karl. *Die Prinzregentenzeit. Gesellschaft und Politik während der Ära des Prinzregenten Luitpold in Bayern.* Munich: Oldenbourg, 1972.

Moltke, Freya, and Annelore Leber. *Für und Wider; Entscheidungen in Deutschland 1918-1945.* Frankfurt: Mosaik Verlag, 1961.

Mommsen, Hans. *Beamtentum im Dritten Reich.* Stuttgart: Deutsche Verlags-Anstalt, 1966.

Moody, Joseph N. (ed.). *Church and Society: Catholic Social and Political Thought and Movements, 1789-1950.* New York: Arts, 1953.

Morley, John F. *Vatican Diplomacy and the Jews during the Holocaust, 1939-1943.* New York: Ktav Publishing House, Inc., 1980.

Morsey, Rudolf. *Die deutsche Zentrumspartei.* Düsseldorf: Droste, 1966.

Morsey, Rudolf (ed.). *Zeitgeschichte in Lebensbildern. Aus dem deutschen Katholizismus des 20. Jahrhunderts.* Mainz: Matthias-Grünewald-Verlag, 1973.

Mosse, George. *The Crisis of German Ideology: Intellectual Origins of the Third Reich.* New York: Grosset & Dunlap, 1964.

Mosse, George C. *Toward the Final Solution: A History of European Racism.* New York: Howard Fertig, 1978.

Mosse, Werner (ed.). *Deutsches Judentum in Krieg und Revolution, 1916-1923. Ein Sammelband.* Tübingen: Mohr, 1971.

Mosse, Werner (ed.). *Entscheidungsjahr 1932. Zur Judenfrage in der Endphase der Weimarer Republik.* Tübingen: Mohr, 1965.

Mosse, Werner E. (ed.). *Juden im Wilhelminischen Deutschland, 1890-1914.* Tübingen: Mohr, 1976.

Muckermann, Friedrich, S.J. *Der Deutsche Weg. Aus der Widerstandsbewegung der deutschen Katholiken von 1930-1945.* Zurich: NSN-Verlag, 1946.

Muckermann, Friedrich. *Vom Rätsel der Zeit.* Munich: Kösel and Pustet, 1933.

Muckermann, Hermann. *Rassenforschung und Volk der Zukunft. Ein Beitrag zur Einführung in die Frage vom biologischen Werden der Menschheit.* Berlin: A. Metzner, 1932.

Müncker, Theodor. *Die psychologischen Grundlagen der katholischen Sittenlehre.* Düsseldorf: Druck u. Verlag L. Schwann, 1934.

Mussner, Franz. *Tractate on the Jews: The Significance of Judaism for the Christian Faith.* Philadelphia: Fortress, 1984.

Natterer, Alois. *Der bayerische Klerus in der Zeit dreier Revolutionen:*

1918-1933-1945. 25 Jahre Klerusverband, 1920-1945. 3rd ed. Munich: Verlag der Kath. Kirche Bayerns, 1946.

Nebraska Symposium on Motivation. Lincoln, NE: University of Nebraska Press, 1967.

Neher, Anton. *Die wirtschaftliche und soziale Lage der Katholiken im westlichen Deutschland.* Rottweil: Druck und Verlagtes Emmanuel, 1927.

Nellessen-Schumacher, Traute. *Sozialprofil der deutschen Katholiken: Eine konfessionsstatistischen Analyse.* Mainz: Matthias-Grünewald-Verlag, 1978.

Nellessen-Schumacher, Traute. *Sozialstruktur und Ausbildung der deutschen Katholiken.* Weinheim: Beltz, 1969.

Neuhäusler, Johann. *Saat des Bösen, Kirchenkampf im Dritten Reich.* Munich: Manz Verlag, 1964.

Niedermeyer, Albert. *Handbuch der speziellen Pastoralmedizin.* 6 vols. Vienna: Verlag Herder, 1949-1952.

Noakes, Jeremy. *The Nazi Party in Lower Saxony, 1921-1933.* London: Oxford University Press, 1971.

Nötges, Jakob, S.J. *Nationalsozialismus und Katholizismus.* Cologne: J.P. Bachem, 1931.

Norden, G. van. *Kirche in der Krise.* Düsseldorf: Verlag Presseverband der Evangelischen Kirche im Rheinland, 1963.

Nowak, Kurt. *"Euthanasie" und Sterilisierung im "Dritten Reich." Die Konfrontation der Evangelischen und Katholischen Kirche mit dem "Gesetz zur Verhütung erbkranken Nachwuchses" und der "Euthanasie"-Aktion.* Göttingen: Vandenhoeck and Ruprecht, 1978.

Obermann, Heiko. *The Roots of Anti-Semitism in the Age of the Renaissance and Reformation.* Philadelphia: Fortress, 1984.

Ogiermann, Otto. *Bis zum letzten Atemzug. Den Prozess gegen Bernhard Lichtenberg, Dompropst an St. Hedwig in Berlin.* Leipzig: St. Benno-Verlag, GMBH, 1968.

Ohlemüller, Gerhard. *Politischer Katholizismus.* Berlin: Verlag des Evangelischen Bundes, 1936.

Ophir, B.Z., and F. Wiesemann. *Die jüdischen Gemeinden in Bayern, 1918-1945. Geschichte und Zerstörung.* Munich: Knapp, 1979.

Orlow, Dietrich. *The History of the Nazi Party: 1919-1933.* Pittsburgh: University of Pittsburgh Press, 1969.

Papen, Franz von. *Der Wahrheit eine Gasse.* Munich: P. List, 1952.

Patzhold, K. *Fascismus, Rassenwahn, Judenverfolgung.* Berlin: Niemeyer, 1975.

Perlmutter, Amos. *Modern Authoritarianism: A Comparative Institutional Analysis.* New Haven: Yale University Press, 1981.

Peterson, Edward N. *The Limits of Hitler's Power.* Princeton, Princeton University Press, 1969.

Pflanze, Otto. *Bismarck and the Development of Germany: The Period of Unification, 1815-1871.* Princeton: Princeton University Press, 1963.

Phayer, Michael. *Martha and Mary: Protestant and Catholic Women in Twentieth Century Germany*. Forthcoming.

Pieper, Josef. *Das Arbeitsrecht des neuen Reiches und die Enzyklika Quadragesimo anno*. Münster: Verlag der Aschendorffschen Verlagsbuchhandlung, 1934.

Plum, Günter. *Gesellschaftstruktur und politisches Bewusstsein in einer katholischen Region, 1928-1933. Untersuchung im Beispiel des Regierungsbezirks Aachen*. Stuttgart: Deutsche-Verlags-Anstalt, 1972.

Poliakov, Leon. *The Aryan Myth: A History of Racist and Nationalist Ideas in Europe*. New York: Basic Books, 1974.

Polaikov, Leon. *Das Dritte Reich und die Juden: Dokumente und Aufsätze*. Berlin: Arani, 1955.

Poliakov, Leon. *Harvest of Hate. The Nazi Program for the Destruction of the Jews of Europe*. Westport, CT: Greenwood Press, 1971.

Portmann, Heinrich (ed.). *Bischof Graf von Galen Spricht! Ein apostolischer Kampf und Sein Widerhall*. Freiburg: Herder, 1946.

Portmann, Heinrich. *Der Bischof von Münster: Das Echo eines Kampfes für Gottesrecht und Menschenrecht*. Münster: Verlag Aschendorff, 1947.

Portmann, Heinrich. *Kardinal von Galen: Ein Gottesmann seiner Zeit, Mit einem Anhang: Drei Weltberühmten Predigten*. Münster: Verlag Aschendorff, 1948.

Pribella, Max. *Deutsche Schicksalsfragen. Rückblick und Ausblick*. Frankfurt: Josef Knecht-Carolusdruckerei, 1950.

Pridham, Geoffrey. *Hitler's Rise to Power: The Nazi Movement in Bavaria, 1923-1933*. New York, Harper & Row, 1973.

Pross, Harry (ed.). *Die Zerstörung der deutschen Politik*. Frankfurt: Fischer Bücherei, 1959.

Przywara, Erich. *Analogia Entis, Metaphysik*. Munich: J. Kösel and F. Pustet, 1932.

Przywara, Erich. *Logos, Abendland, Reich, Commercium*. Düsseldorf: Patmos-Verlag, 1964.

Pulzer, P.G.J. *The Rise of Political Anti-Semitism in Germany and Austria*. New York: Wiley, 1964.

Raddatz, Fritz (ed.). *Summa Inuria oder Dürfte der Papst Schweigen*. Reinbek bei Hamburg: Rowohlt, 1963.

Raem, Heinz-Albert. *Katholischer Gesellenverein und deutsche Kolpingsfamilie in der Ära des Nationalsozialismus*. Mainz: Matthias Grünewald-Verlag, 1982.

Raem, Heinz-Albert. *Pius XI und der Nationalsozialismus. Die Enzyklika "Mit Brennender Sorge" vom März 1937*. Paderborn: Ferdinand Schöningh, 1979.

Rahner, Karl, et al. (eds.). *Sacramentum Mundi: An Encyclopedia of Theology*. London: Burns and Oates, 1970.

Ratzinger, Georg. *Die Volkswirtschaft in ihren sittlichen Grundlagen. Eth-*

isch-soziale Studien über Cultur und Civilisation. Freiburg: Herder, 1881.

Rebbert, Joseph. *Blicke in's Talmudische Judenthum. Nach den Forschungen von Dr. Konrad Martin, Bischof von Paderborn, dem christlichen Volke enthüllt.* Paderborn. Bonifacius Druckerei, 1876.

Die Religion in Geschichte der Gegenwart. Handwörterbuch für Theologie und Religionswissenschaft. 5 vols. 3rd ed. Tübingen: Mohr, 1957-1962.

Rengstorf, Karl Heinrich, and Siegfried von Kortzfleisch (eds.). *Kirche und Synagoge. Handbuch zur Geschichte von Christen und Juden,* 2 vols. Stuttgart: Ernst Klett Verlag, 1968.

Renshon, Stanley Allen (ed.). *Handbook of Political Socialization: Theory and Research.* New York: Free Press, 1977.

Rhodes, James M. *The Hitler Movement: A Modern Millenarian Revolution.* Stanford: Hoover Institution Press, 1980.

Rich, Norman. *Hitler's War Aims: Ideology, The Nazi State, and the Course of Expansion.* 2 vols. New York: Norton, 1973.

Riegel, Klaus. *Psychology of Development and History.* New York: Plenum, 1976.

Ritter, Emil, and Kuno Brombacher. *Sendschreiben Katholischen Deutschen.* 2nd ed. Münster: Aschendorff, 1936.

Rohling, August. *Der Talmudjude. Zur Beherzigung für Juden und Christen aller Stände.* 4th ed. Münster: Adolph Russell's Verlag, 1873.

Rokeach, Milton. *The Open and Closed Mind.* New York: Basic Books, 1960.

Roon, Ger von. *German Resistance to Hitler. Count von Moltke and the Kreisau Circle.* London: Van Nostrand Reinhold, 1971.

Rosenberg, Alfred. *Der Mythus des 20. Jahrhunderts.* Munich: Hoheneichenverlag, 1934.

Ross, Ronald. *The Beleagured Tower: The Dilemma of Political Catholicism in Wilhelmine Germany.* Notre Dame: University of Notre Dame Press, 1976.

Rost, Hans. *Christus, nicht Hitler.* Augsburg: Haas and Grabherr, 1932.

Rost, Hans. *Erinnerungen aus dem Leben eines beinahe glücklichen Menschen.* Westheim: Antiquariat, II, 1962.

Rost, Hans. *Gedanken und Wahrheiten zür Judenfrage.* Trier: Paulinus, 1907.

Rost, Hans. *Katholische Familienkultur.* Augsburg: Haas und Grabherr, 1926.

Rost, Hans. *Die Parität und die deutschen Katholiken.* Cologne: J.P. Bachem, 1914.

Rost, Hans. *Die wirtschaftliche und kulturelle Lage der deutschen Katholiken.* Cologne: J.P. Bachem, 1911.

Roth, Armin. *Nationalsozialismus und katholische Kirche. Mein Schriftwechsel mit der Gauleitung Rheinland und der Reichsparteileitung der N.S.D.A.P. sowie mit der Kanzlei Adolf Hitlers.* Munich: Ludendorffs Volkswarte-Verlag, 1931.

Roth, Heinrich. *Katholische Jugend in der NS-Zeit unter besonderer Berücksichtigung des Katholischen Jungmännerverbandes. Daten und Dokumente.* Düsseldorf: Verlag Hans Altenberg, 1959.

Roth, Josef. *Katholizismus und Judenfrage.* Munich: Eher, 1923.

Rubenstein, Richard L. *The Cunning of History: The Holocaust and the American Future.* New York: Harper & Row, 1978.

Rüdin, Franz et al. (eds.). *Zur Verhütung erbkranken Nachwuchses-Gesetz und Erläutereung.* Munich: Eher, 1934.

Ruether, Rosemary Radford. *Faith and Fratricide: The Theological Roots of Anti-Semitism.* New York: Seabury Press, 1974.

Ruhm von Oppen, Beate. *Religion and Resistance to Nazism.* Princeton: Center for International Studies, Princeton University, March 1971.

Russell, Jeffrey Burton. *A History of Medieval Christianity: Prophecy and Order.* New York: Wiley, 1968.

Sackett, Robert Eben. *Popular Entertainment, Class, and Politics in Munich, 1900-1923.* Cambridge, MA: Harvard University Press, 1982.

Sampson, Edward. *Social Psychology and Contemporary Society.* New York: Wiley, 1971.

Sarason, S.B. *Psychology Misdirected.* New York: Collier Macmillan Publishing, 1981.

Scharnagl, Anton. *Die völkische Weltanschauung und wir Katholiken.* Munich: Graphische Kunstanstalt, 1932.

Scheible, Hartmut. *Joseph Roth: Mit einem Essay über Gustave Flaubert.* Stuttgart: Kohlhammer, 1971.

Schleunes, Karl. *The Twisted Road to Auschwitz: Nazi Policy Toward the Jews, 1933-1939.* Urbana, IL: University of Illinois Press, 1970.

Schlund, Erhard. *Katholizismus und Vaterland.* Munich: F.A. Pfeiffer, 1923.

Schmaus, Michael. *Begegnungen zwischen katholischem Christentum und nationalsozialistischer Weltanschauung.* 2nd ed. Münster: Verlag der Aschendorffschen Verlagsbuchhandlung, 1934.

Schmaus, Michael. *Katholische Dogmatik.* 3 vols., Munich: Max Heuber Verlag, 1937-41.

Schmaus, Michael. *Katholische Dogmatik.* 5 vols. 5th ed. Munich: Max Heuber Verlag, 1954-1958.

Schmidt, W. *Die Stellung der Religion zu Rasse und Volk.* Augsburg: Haas und Grabherr, 1932.

Schnabel, Franz. *Deutsche Geschichte im neunzehnten Jahrhundert.* 4 vols. Freiburg: Herder, 1951.

Schneider, David, et al. *Person Perception.* 3rd ed. Reading, MA: Addison-Wesley, 1959.

Scholder, Klaus. *Die Kirchen und das Dritte Reich: Vorgeschichte und Zeit der Illusionen, 1918-1934.* Frankfurt am Main: Ullstein, 1977.

Schorsch, Ismar. *Jewish Reactions to German Anti-Semitism, 1870-1914.* New York: Columbia University Press, 1972.

Schreiber, G. *Auslandsdeutschtum und Katholizismus.* Münster: Aschendorff, 1927.

Schubert, Günter. *Anfänge Nationalsozialistischer Aussenpolitik.* Cologne: Verlag Wissenschaft und Politik, 1963.

Schwarte, Johannes. *Gustav Gundlach, S.J. (1892-1963). Massgeblicher Repräsentant der katholischen Soziallehre während der Pontifikate Pius XI und Pius XII,* Munich: Verlag Ferdinand Schöningh, 1975.

Schwebel, Milton (ed.). *Behavioral Science and Human Survival.* Palo Alto: Science and Behavior Books, 1965.

Senn, Wilhelm Maria. *Katholizismus und Nationalsozialismus. Eine Rede an den deutschen Katholizismus.* Münster: Abwehr-Verlag, 1931.

Seppelt, Franz X. *Geschichte der Päpste von den Anfängen bis zur Gegenwart.* 2 vols. Leipzig: Hegner, 1931-1941.

Sereny, Gitta. *Into that Darkness: From Mercy Killing to Mass Murder.* New York: McGraw-Hill, 1974.

Sheehan, James J. *German Liberalism in the Nineteenth Century.* Chicago: University of Chicago Press, 1978.

Sherif, Muzafer. *Social Psychology.* New York: Harper, 1969.

Showalter, Dennis E. *"Little Man, What Now?" Der Stürmer in the Weimar Republic.* Hamden, CT: Archon Books, 1982.

Sills, David (ed.). *International Encyclopedia of the Social Sciences.* 7 vols. New York: Macmillan, 1968.

Slobin, D.I. (ed.). *The Ontogenesis of Grammar.* New York: Academic Press, 1971.

Smith, Bradley F. *Adolf Hitler: His Family, Childhood, and Youth.* Stanford: Stanford University Press, 1967.

Smith, M.B., et al. *Opinions and Personality.* New York: Wiley, 1956.

Snyder, R.C., et al. *Foreign Policy Decision-Making.* New York: Knopf, 1962.

Sohngen, G., and A. Rademacher (eds.). *Symbol und Wirklichkeit im Kultmysterium.* Leipzig: Meyer, 1937.

Sontheimer, Kurt. *Antidemokratisches Denken in der Weimarer Republik. Die politischen Ideen des deutschen Nationalismus zwischen 1918 und 1933.* Munich: Nymphenburger Verlagshandlung, 1962.

Spael, Wilhelm. *Das katholische Deutschland im 20. Jahrhundert. Seine Pionier-und Krisenzeiten 1890-1945.* Würzburg: Echter Verlag, 1967.

Späth, Alfons. *Johannes Baptista Sproll der Bekennerbischof.* 2nd Ed. Stuttgart: Schwabenverlag, 1963.

Speckner, K. *Die Wächter der Kirche.* Munich: J. Kösel and F. Pustet, 1934.

Staats, A.W. *Child Learning, Intelligence, and Personality.* Kalamazoo, MI: Behaviordelia, 1977.

Staats, A.W. *Complex Human Behavior.* New York: Holt, Rinehart and Winston, 1963.

Staats, A.W. (ed.). *Human Learning.* New York: Holt, Rinehart and Winston, 1964.

Staats, A.W. *Learning, Language, and Cognition.* New York: Holt, Rinehart and Winston, 1968.

Staats, A.W. *Social Behaviorism.* Homewood, IL: Dorsey Press, 1975.

Staatslexikon der Görres Gesellschaft. 5th ed. Freiburg: Herder, 1929.

Stachura, Peter (ed.). *The Shaping of the Nazi State.* London: Croom and Helm, 1978.

Stark, Johannes. *Nationalsozialismus und Katholische Kirche.* Munich: Eher, 1931.

Stark, Johannes. *Zentrumsherrschaft und Jesuitenpolitik.* Munich: Eher, 1932.

Staub, Ervin. *Positive Social Behavior and Morality.* 1, *Social and Personal Influences.* 2, *Socialization and Development.* New York: Academic Press, 1978-79.

Stehle, Hansjakob. *Eastern Politics of the Vatican, 1917-1979.* Trans. Sandra Smith. Athens, OH: Ohio University Press, 1981.

Stehlin, Stewart A. *Weimar and the Vatican, 1919-1933. German-Vatican Diplomatic Relations in the Interwar Years.* Princeton: Princeton University Press, 1983.

Steiner, John M. *Power Politics and Social Change in National Socialist Germany: A Process of Escalation into Mass Destruction.* The Hague: Mouton Publishers, 1976.

Steinert, M.G. *Hitler's Krieg und die Deutschen.* Düsseldorf: Econ-Verlag, 1970.

Steinert, Marlis G. *Hitler's War and the Germans: Public Mood and Attitude During the Second World War,* Trans. ed. Thomas E.J. DeWitt. Athens, OH: Ohio University Press, 1977.

Stern, Fritz. *The Failure of Illiberalism: Essays on the Political Culture of Modern Germany.* New York: Knopf, 1972.

Stern, Fritz. *Gold and Iron: Bismarck, Bleichröder, and the Building of the German Empire.* New York: Knopf, 1977.

Stern, Fritz. *The Politics of Cultural Despair.* Berkeley: University of California Press, 1961.

Stonner, Anton. *Nationale Erziehung und Religionsunterricht.* Regensburg: Pustet, 1934.

Stromberg, Roland. *Redemption by War: The Intellectuals and 1914.* Lawrence, KS: University of Kansas Press, 1982.

Stürmer, Michael. *Regierung und Reichstag im Bismarcksstaat, 1871-1880: Cäsarismus oder Parlimentarismus.* Düsseldorf: Droste, 1974.

Tal, Uriel. *Christians and Jews in Germany: Religion, Politics, and Ideology in the Second Reich, 1870-1914.* Ithaca: Cornell University Press, 1975.

Tal, Uriel. *Religious and Anti-Religious Roots of Modern Anti-Semitism.* New York: Leo Baeck Institute, 1971.

Tennenbaum, Frank. *Race and Reich: The Story of an Epoch.* New York: Wiley, 1956.

Thibaut, John, et al. *Contemporary Topics in Social Psychology.* Morristown, NJ: General Learning Press, 1976.

Thibaut, J.W., and H.H. Kelley. *The Social Psychology of Groups.* New York: Wiley, 1959.

Thiele, Friedrich, et al. *Das Kirchensteuerrecht.* Herne, Westfalen: Neue Wirtschaftsbriefe, 1947.

Tillmann, Fritz. *Die katholische Sittenlehre. Die Idee der Nachfolge Christi.* Dusseldorf: Druck u. Verlag L. Schwann, 1934.

Tillmann, Fritz, *Die katholische Sittenlehre. Die Verwirklichung der Nachfolge Christi. Die Pflichten gegen Gott,* Pts. 1 and 2. Düsseldorf: Druck u. Verlag L. Schwann, 1935-1936.

Tilten, Timothy. *Nazism, Neo-Nazism and the Peasantry.* Bloomington: Indiana University Press, 1975.

Toury, Jacob. *Die politischen Orientierungungen den Juden in Deutschland.* Tübingen: Möhr, 1966.

Turner, Henry. *German Big Business and the Rise of Hitler.* New York: Oxford University Press, 1985.

Turner, Henry (ed.). *Reappraisals of Fascism.* New York: New Viewpoints, 1976.

Vaillancourt, Jean-Guy. *Papal Power: A Study of Vatican Control over Lay Catholic Elites.* Berkeley: University of California Press, 1980.

Vollmer, Bernhard. *Volksopposition im Polizeistaat.* Stuttgart: Deutsche Verlagsanstalt, 1957.

Vorländer, Hewart. *Kirchenkampf in Elberfeld, 1933-1945. Ein kritischer Beitrag zur Erforschung des Kirchenkampfes in Deutschland.* Göttingen: Vandenhoeck and Ruprecht, 1968.

Waite, Robert G.L. *The Psychopathic God: Adolf Hitler.* New York: Basic Books, 1977.

Walker, Lawrence D. *Hitler Youth and Catholic Youth, 1933-1936: A Study in Totalitarian Conquest.* Washington, DC: Catholic University of America Press, 1970.

Walterbach, C. *Katholiken und Revolution: Eine Verteidigung gegenüber den Angriffen auf die Führer der deutschen Katholiken.* Berlin: E. Schmidt, 1922.

Walther, Franz. *Die Euthanasie und die Heiligkeit des Lebens. Die Lebensvernichtung im Dienste der Medizin und Eugenik nach christlichen und materialistischer Ethik.* Munich: Kaiser, 1935.

Warloski, Ronald. *Neudeutschland: German Catholic Students, 1919-1939.* The Hague: Martinus Nijhoff, 1970.

Weber, Christoph. *Aufklärung und Orthodoxie am Mittelrhein, 1820-1850.* Paderborn: Schöningh, 1973.

Webster, Richard A. *The Cross and the Fasces.* Stanford: Stanford University Press, 1960.

Wehler, Hans-Ulrich. *Das deutsche Kaiserreich, 1871-1918*. Göttingen: Vandenhoeck und Ruprecht, 1973.

Weinberg, Gerhard, *The Foreign Policy of Hitler's Germany: Starting World War II, 1937-1939*. Chicago: University of Chicago Press, 1980.

Weinstein, Fred. *The Dynamics of Nazism: Leadership, Ideology, and the Holocaust*. New York: Academic Press, 1980.

Weisenborn, Günther (ed.). *Der Lautlose Aufstand: Bericht die Widerstandsbewegung des deutschen Volkes, 1933-1945*. Hamburg: Rowohlt Verlag, 1953.

Wild, Alfons. *Nationalsozialismus und Religion: Kann ein Katholik Nationalsozialist sein*. Augsburg: Haas und Grabherr, 1930.

Wilson, Edward O. *Sociobiology: The Abridged Edition*. Cambridge: Harvard University Press, 1975.

Wilson, Glenn D. (ed.). *The Psychology of Conservatism*. New York: Academic Press, 1973.

Winkler, August. *Mittelstand, Demokratie und Nationalsozialismus*. Cologne: Kiepenheuer and Witsch, 1972.

Zahn, Gordon C. *German Catholics and Hitler's Wars: A Study in Social Control*. New York: E.P. Dutton, 1969.

Zang, Gert (ed.). *Provinzialisierung einer Region. Regionale Unterentwicklung und liberale Politik in der Stadt und im Kreis Konstanz im 19. Jahrhundert. Untersuchungen zur Entstehung der bürgerlichen Gesellschaft im der Provinz*. Frankfurt: Syndikat, 1978.

Zeische, K. *Das Königtum Christi in Europa*. Regensburg: G.J. Manz, 1926.

Zimbardo, Philip. *Psychology and Life*. 10th ed. Glenview, IL: Scott, Foresman, 1979.

Zimbardo, Philip, and Ebbe B. Effesen. *Influencing Attitudes and Changing Behavior: A Basic Introduction to Relevant Methodology, Theory and Applications*. Reading, MA: Addison-Wesley, 1969.

Articles

Aberbach, Joel D. and Jack L. Walker. "Political Trust and Racial Ideology" *American Political Science Review*. 64 (1970):1199-1219.

Adam, Karl. "Deutsches Volkstum und katholisches Christentum." *Theologische Quartalschrift* 114 (1933):40-63.

Aderman, David and Leonard Berkowitz. "Self-Concern and the Unwillingness to be Helpful." *Social Psychology Quarterly* 46 (1983):293-301.

Algermissen, Konrad. "Christentum und Germanentum." *Theologie und Glaube* 26 (1934:)302-330.

Allen, Russell O., and Bernard Spilka. "Committed and Consensual Religion: A Specification of Religion-Prejudice Relationships." *Journal for the Scientific Study of Religion* 6 (1967):191-206.

Allport, G.W., and J.M. Ross. "Personal Religious Orientation and Prejudice." *Journal of Personality and Social Psychology* 5 (1967):432-443.

Allport, Gordon. "The Religious Context of Prejudice." *Journal for the Scientific Study of Religion* 5 (1966):447-457.

Altmeyer, Karl A. "Der Episkopat und die katholische Presse im Dritten Reich." *Herder Korrespondenz* 14 (1959-60):274-81.

Anderson, Terry. "Becoming Sane with Psychohistory." *Historian* 41 (1978):1-20.

Anon. "Thesen christlicher Lehrverkündigung in Hinblick auf umlaufende Irrtümer über das Gottesvolk des Alten Bundes." *Freiburger Rundbrief* 2(1949-50):9.

Arnold, Franz. "Das gott menschliche Prinzip der Seelsorge in pastoralgeschichtlicher Entfaltung." *Theologische Quartalschrift* 124 (1943):99-133.

Arnold, Franz. "Das Prinzip des Gottmenschlichen und seine Bedeutung für die Seelsorge." *Theologische Quartalschrift* 123 (1942):145-176.

Asher, Harvey. "Non-Psychoanalytic Approaches to National Socialism." *Psychohistory Review* 7 (1979):13-21.

Bagley, Christopher. "Relation of Religion and Racial Prejudice in Europe," *Journal for the Scientific Study of Religion* 9 (1970):219-225.

Bandura, A.,et al. "Disinhibition of Aggression through Diffusion of Responsibility and Dehumanization of Victims." *Journal of Research in Personality* 9 (1975):253-269.

Bandura, Albert. "Influence of Models' Reinforcement Contingencies on the Acquisition of Imitative Responses." *Journal of Personality and Social Psychology* 1 (1965):584-95.

Baumstark, A. "Wege zum Judentum des neutestamentlichen Zeitalters." *Bonner Zeitschrift für Theologie und Seelsorge* 4 (1927):19-37.

Baur, E. Jackson. "Opinion Changes in a Public Controversy." *Public Opinion Quarterly* 26 (1962):212-226.

Bendix, Reinhard. "Social Stratifications and Political Power." *American Political Science Review* 46 (1952):357-375.

Bernhart, Joseph. "Um das Alte Testament." *Hochland* 1(1934-1935):99-118.

Benan, W., "On Getting in Bed With a Lion." *American Psychologist* 35(1980):780-790.

Binion, Rudolph. "Review: Fred Weinstein, The Dynamics of Nazism: Leadership, Ideology, and the Holocaust." *Journal of Modern History* 54(1982):409-411.

Blackbourn, David G. "Class and Politics in Wilhelmine Germany: The Center Party and the Social Democrats in Württemberg." *Central European History* 9(1976):220-249.

Blasius, Dirk. "Psychohistorie und Sozialgeschichte." *Archiv für Sozialgeschichte* 17(1977):383-403.

Bock, David C., and Neil Clark Warren. "Religious Belief as a Factor in

Obedience to Destructive Commands." *Review of Religious Research* 13(1972):185-191.

Böckenförde, Ernst-Wolfgang. "Der Deutsche Katholizismus im Jahre 1933. Eine kritische Betrachtung." *Hochland* 53(1961):215-239.

Böckenförde, Ernst Wolfgang. "Der deutsche Katholizismus im Jahre 1933. Stellungnahme zu einer Diskussion." *Hochland* 54(1962):217-245.

Böckenförde, Ernst-Wolfgang. "German Catholicism in 1933." *Cross Currents* 11(1961):283-304.

Boehm, Leonore. "The Development of Conscience: A Comparison of Upper-Middle Class Academically Gifted Children Attending Catholic and Jewish Parochial Schools." *Journal of Social Psychology* 59(1963):101-110.

Bornkamm, Heinrich. "Die Staatsidee in Kulturkampf." *Historische Zeitschrift* 170(1950):1-50.

Brauer, Theodor. "Die Stellung der Persönlichkeit in Gesellschaft und Staat:'Individualismus'-Wahrheit und Irrtum." *Schönere Zukunft* 20(1935):499-500.

Broszat, Martin. "Hitler und die Genesis der 'Endlösung'" Aus Anlass den Thesen von David Irving." *Vierteljahrshefte für Zeitgeschichte* 25 (1977):739-75.

Broszat, Martin. "Soziale Motivation und Führer-Bindung des Nationalsozialismus." *Vierteljahrshelte für Zeitgeschichte* 18 (1970):392-409.

Browning, Christopher. "Zur Genesis der 'Endlösung': Eine Antwort an Martin Broszat." *Vierteljahrshefte für Zeitgeschichte* 29 (1981):97-109.

Browning, Don. "Psychology as Religioethical Thinking," *Journal of Religion* 64 (1984):139-157.

Buchberger, Michael. "Wir Katholiken in den Kämpfen und Gefahren der Zeit." *Schönere Zukunft* 7 (July 17, 1932):975-977.

Buchheim, Hans. "Der deutsche Katholizismus im Jahre 1933: Eine Auseinandersetzung mit Ernst-Wolfgang Böckenförde." *Hochland* (1960/61):497-515.

Budner, S. "Intolerance of Ambiguity as a Personality Variable." *Journal of Personality* 30 (1962):29-50.

Butler, D.C., and N. Miller. "'Power to Reinforce' as a Determinant of Communication." *Psychological Reports* 16 (1965):705-709.

Castelli, Jim. "Unpublished Encyclical Attacked Anti-Semitism." *National Catholic Reporter* 9 (December 15, 1972).

Chadwick, Owen. "The Present Stage of the 'Kirchenkampf' Enquiry." *Journal of Ecclesiastical History* 24 (1973)33-50.

Christie, R., and R.K. Merton. "Procedures for the Sociological Study of the Value Climate of Medical Schools." *Journal of Medical Education* 18 (1958):125-153.

Coelho, G.V., et al. "The Use of the Student TAT to Assess Coping Behavior in Hospitalized, Normal and Exceptionally Competent College Freshmen." *Perceptual and Motor Skills* 14 (1962):355-365.

Conzemius, V. "Eglises chretiennes et totalitarisme national-socialiste." *Revue d' Histoire Ecclesiastique* 63 (1968):868-948.

Conzemius, Victor. "German Catholics and the Nazi Regime in 1933." *Irish Ecclesiastical Record* 103 (1967):326-335.

Cryns, Arthur. "Dogmatism of Catholic Clergy and Ex-Clergy: A Study of Ministerial Role Perseverance and Open-Mindedness." *Journal for the Scientific Study of Religion* 9 (1970):239-243.

Damico, Alfonso. "The Sociology of Justice: Kohlberg and Milgram." *Political Theory* 10 (1982):409-433.

Davis, K., and E. Jones. "Changes in Interpersonal Perception as a Means of Reducing Cognitive Dissonance." *Journal of Abnormal and Social Psychology* 61 (1960):402-410.

Denzler, Georg. "SS-Spitzel mit Soutane." *Die Zeit* (Sept. 3, 1982,):9-10.

Deuerlein, Ernst. "Hitler's Eintritt in die Politik und die Reichswehr." *Vierteljahrshefte für Zeitgeschichte* 7 (1959):177-227.

Deuerlein, Ernst. "Zur Vergegenwärtigung der Lage des deutschen Katholizismus 1933. Dritten Teil: Die Gewinnung der Konkordatslinie." *Stimmen der Zeit* 168 (1961):1-23;90-116;196-223.

Dicks, H.V. "Personality Traits and National Socialist Ideology: A War-Time Study of German Prisoners of War." *Human Relations* 3 (1950):111-154.

Dietrich, Donald J. "Historical Judgments and Eternal Verities." *Society* 20 (1983):31-35.

Dietrich, Donald J. "The Holocaust as Public Policy: The Third Reich." *Human Relations* 34 (1981):445-462.

Dietrich, Donald J. "Psychohistory: Clio on the Couch-or Off?" *Historical Methods* 15 (1982):83-90.

Divald, Hugo. "'Sophistik des Brückenbonens': Kritische Betrachtungen zu Anton Stonners Buch ... " *Der Christliche Ständestaat* 1 (1934):13-16.

Dörner, Klaus. "Nationalsozialismus und Lebensvernichtung." *Vierteljahrshefte für Zeitgeschichte* 15 (1967):121-152.

Dürr, Lorenz. "Das Unsemitische und Übersemitische in der semitischen alttestamentlichen Religion." *Bonner Zeitschrift für Theologie und Seelsorge* 8 (1931):1-13.

Eisenstadt, S.N. "Social Change Differentiation and Evolution." *American Sociological Review* 29 (1964):375-386.

Emmerich, Alex. "Katholizismus ohne Politik." *Zeit und Volk* 1 (1933):1-19.

Engelbert, Kurt. "Adolf Kardinal Bertram-Fürstbischof von Breslau 1914 bis 1945." *Archiv für Schlesische Kirchengeschichte* 7 (1949):7-37.

Epstein, Ralph. "Aggression Toward Outgroups as a Function of Authoritarianism and Imitation of Aggressive Models." *Journal of Personality and Social Psychology* 3 (1966):574-579.

Eschweiler, Karl. "Die Kirche im neuen Reich." *Deutsches Volkstum* 15 (1933):451-458.

Esh, Shaul. "Words and Their Meanings. Twenty-five examples of Nazi Idiom." *Yad Vashem Studies* (1963):133-167.

Featherstone, Joseph L. "Did the Church Fail?" *Commonweal* 79 (February 28, 1964):649-654.

Fenn, Richard K. "Toward a New Sociology of Religion." *Journal for the Scientific Study of Religion* 11 (1972):16-32.

Festinger, Leon. "Informal Social Communication." *Psychological Review* 57 (1950):271-282.

Festinger, Leon. "A Theory of Social Comparison Processes." *Human Relations* 7 (1954):117-140.

Fitzer, Joseph. "J.S. Drey and the Search for a Catholic Philosophy of Religion." *Journal of Religion* 63 (1983):231-246.

Flosdorf, Wilhelm, S.J. "Die deutschen Jesuiten unter dem Nationalsozialistischen Regime." *Jesuiten. Stimmen aus ihren Eigenen Reihen* 2 (1955):104-119.

Flowers, M.L., "A Laboratory Test of Some Implications of Janis' Group-Think Hypothesis." *Journal of Personality and Social Psychology* 35 (1977):888-896.

Frank, Karl. "Rassenkunde und Rassengeschichte der Menschheit." *Stimmen der Zeit* 127 (1934) 102-110.

Frank, Karl. "Zur Eugenik." *Stimmen der Zeit* 128 (1935):316-324.

Fuchs, Friedrich. "Ein Bischofswort über das Alte Testament." *Hochland* 31 (1933/34):469-483.

Fuchs, Friedrich. "Der totale Staat und seine Grenze." *Hochland* 1 (1932-33):558-560.

Gall, L. "Die Problematik des badischen Kulturkampfes." *Zeitschrift für die Geschichte Oberrheins* 113 (1965):151-196.

Gallin, Mary Alice. "The Cardinal and the State: Faulhaber and the Third Reich." *Journal of Church and State* 12 (1970):385-404.

Gergen, Kenneth. "Social Psychology as History." *Journal of Personality and Social Psychology* 26 (1973):309-320.

Gibb, C.A. "An Interactional View of the Emergence of Leadership." *Australian Journal of Psychology* 10 (1958):101-110.

Gibbons, F., and R. Wicklund. "Self-Focused Attention and Helping Behavior." *Journal of Personality and Social Psychology* 43 (1982):462-474.

Gilmore, William. "Critical Bibliography." *Psychohistory Review* 5 (1976):4-33, 6 (1977):88-96, 6 (1977-78):106-111, 6 (1978):60-65, 7 (1978):40-47.

Graham, Loren R. "Science and Values: The Eugenics Movement in Germany and Russia in the 1920s." *American Historical Review* 82 (1977):1133-1164.

Graham, Robert A. "The 'Right to Kill' in the Third Reich. Prelude to Genocide." *Catholic Historical Review* 62 (1976):56-76.

Graham, Robert. "Spie Naziste attorno al Vaticano durante la Seconda Guerra Mondiale." *La Civilta Cattolica* 121 (1970):21-31.

Grill, Johnpeter Horst. "The Nazi Party's Rural Propaganda before 1928." *Central European History* 15 (1982):149-185.

Grober, Rudolf. "Deutsche Sendung. Zur Idee und Geschichte des Sacrum Imperium." *Werkblätter von Neudeutschland Älterenbund* 6 (1933/34):169-176.

Grosche, Robert. "Die Grundlagen einer christlichen Politik der deutschen Katholiken." *Die Schildgenossen* 13 (1933/34):48-57.

Gruchmann, Lothar, "Euthanasie und Justiz im Dritten Reich." *Vierteljahrshefte für Zeitgeschichte* 20 (1972):235-279.

Gruder, C.L. "Determinants of Social Comparison Choices." *Journal of Experimental Social Psychology* 7 (1971):473-489.

Gundlach, Gustav, S.J. "Fragen um die berufsständische Ordnung," *Stimmen der Zeit* 125(1933):217-226.

Guttman, N. and H.I. Kalish. "Experiments in Discrimination." *Scientific American* 198 (1958):77-82.

Haecker, Theodor. "Zur europäischer Judenfrage." *Hochland* 24 (1926/27):607-627.

Hamerow, Theodore S. "Review Essay: Guilt, Redemption, and Writing German History." *American Historical Review* 88 (1983):53-72.

Harrigan, William. "Hochhuth as Historian." *Continuum* (1964):166-182.

Harrigan, William. "Nazi Germany and the Holy See, 1933-1936: The Historical Background of *Mit Brennender Sorge*." *Catholic Historical Review* 47 (1961):164-198.

Harrigan, William. "Pius XII's Efforts to Effect a Detente in German-Vatican Relations, 1939-1940." *Catholic Historical Review* 49 (1963):173-191.

Hatfield, W. "*Kulturkampf*: The Relationship of Church and State and the Failure of German Political Reform." *Journal of Church and State* 23 (1981):465-484.

Herf, Jeffrey. "Reactionary Modernism: Some Ideological Origins of the Primacy of Politics in the Third Reich." *Theory and Society* 10 (1981):805-832.

Hill, Leonides E. III. "The Vatican Embassy of Ernst von Weizsäcker, 1943-1945." *Journal of Modern History* 39 (1967):138-159.

Hochhuth, Rolf, et al. "The Papcy and the Holocuast: A Symposium." *Society* 20 (1983):4-35.

Holborn, Hajo. "Der deutsche Idealismus in sozialgeschichtlicher Bedeutung." *Historische Zeitschrift* 174 (1952):359-384.

Höllen, Martin. "Katholische Kirche und NS-'Euthanasie.' Eine vergleichende Analyse neuer Quellen." *Zeitschrift für Kirchengeschichte* 91 (1980):53-82.

Hommes, Jakob. "Katholisches Staats-und Kulturdenken u.d. Nationalsozialismus." *Deutsches Volk* (1933):279-296.

Horn, Daniel. "The Struggle for Catholic Youth in Hitler's Germany: An Assessment." *Catholic Historical Review* 65 (1979):561-582.

Horowitz, Irving Louis, and M. Liebowitz. "Social Deviance and Political Marginality: Toward a Redefinition of the Relation Between Sociology and Politics." *Social Problems* 15 (1968):280-296.

Hürth, Franz. "Die *aequalitas justitiae* in ihren Beziehung zur *aequivalentia objectorum* bei strenger Rechtsverbindlichkeiten." *Theologie und Glaube* 3 (1928):481-505.

Hürth, Franz, S.J. "Zur Frage des Tötungsrechte aus Notstand." *Scholastik* 4(1929):534-560.

Hughes, John Jay. "The Popes 'Pact with Hitler': Betrayal or Self-Defense." *Journal of Church and State* 17 (1975):63-80.

Hughes, John Jay. "The Reich Concordat 1933: Capitulation or Compromise?" *Australian Journal of Politics and History* 20 (1974):164-175.

Hunt, James. "Review: Margaret Lavinia Anderson, *Windthorst: A Political Biography.*" *Review of Politics* 44 (1982):465.

Huston, James. "The Allied Blockade of Germany, 1918-1919." *Journal of Central European Affairs* 10 (1950).

Hyman, Paula. "The History of European Jewry: Recent Trends in the Literature." *Journal of Modern History* 54 (1982):303-319.

Jarausch, Konrad, "Illiberalism and Beyond: German History in Search of a Paradigm." *Journal of Modern History* 55 (1938):268-284.

Jones, Larry Eugene. "'The Dying Middle': Weimar Germany and the Fragmentation of Bourgeois Politics." *Central European History* 5 (1972):23-54.

Juan, Isabel, and Harold B. Haley. "High and Low Levels of Dogmatism in Relation to Personality, Intellectual, and Environmental Characteristics of Medical Students." *Psychological Reports* 26 (1970)535-544.

Katz, Elihu. "The Two-Step Flow of Communication: An Up-to-Date Report on an Hypothesis." *Public Opinion Quarterly* 21 (1957):61-78.

Keller, Hermann, OSB. "Zu uns komme dein Reich." *Benediktinische Monatschrift* 15 (1933):356-365.

Kelley, K., and D. Bryne. "Attraction and Altruism: With a Little Help from My Friends." *Journal of Research in Personality* 10 (1976):59-68.

Kelley, H.H. "The Process of Causal Attribution." *American Psychologist* 28 (1973):107-128.

Kelman, Herbert. "Attitudes are Alive and Well and Gainfully Employed in the Sphere of Action." *American Psychologist* 29 (1974):310-324.

Keniston, Kenneth. "Student Activism, Moral Development, and Morality." *American Journal of Orthopsychiatry* 40 (1970):577-592.

Kent, George O. "Pope Pius XII and Germany: Some Aspects of German-

Vatican Relations, 1933-1943." *American Historical Review* 70 (1964):59-78.

Knapp, Peter. "Can Social Theory Escape from History? Views of History in Social Science." *History and Theory* 23 (1984):34-52.

Knox, MacGregor. "Conquest, Foreign and Domestic in Fascist Italy and Nazi Germany." *Journal of Modern History* 56 (1984):1-57.

Kohlberg, Lawrence. "The Development of Children's Orientations Toward a Moral Order, 1: Sequence in the Development of Moral Thought." *Vita Humana* 6 (1963):11-33.

Koonz, Claudia. "Nazi Women before 1933: Rebels Against Emancipation." *Social Science Quarterly* 56 (1976):553-563.

Koriat, A., et al. "The Self-Control of Emotional Reactions to a Stressful Film." *Journal of Personality* 40 (1972):601-619.

Kren, George M. "Psychohistorical Interpretations of National Socialism." *German Studies Review* 1(1978):150-172.

Krieger, Leonard. "Nazism: Highway or Byway." *Central European History* 11 (1978):3-22.

Kupper, A. "Zur Geschichte des Reichskonkordats." *Stimmen der Zeit* 163 (1958-59):362-375.

Lane, Barbara Miller. "Nazi Ideology: Some Unfinished Business." *Central European History* 7 (1974):3-30.

Langer, William L. "The Next Assignment." *American Historical Review* 63 (1958):283-304.

Lapomarda, Vincent A., S.J. "The Jesuits and the Holocaust." *Journal of Church and State* 23 (1981):241-258.

Latane, B., and J.M. Darley. "Group Inhibition of Bystander Intervention." *Journal of Personality and Social Psychology* 6 (1968):215-221.

Lehmacher, Gustav. "Rassenwerte." *Stimmen der Zeit* 126 (1934):73-82.

Leiber, Robert. "Pius XII + ." *Stimmen der Zeit* 163 (1958):81-101.

Leiber, Robert, S.J. "Reichskonkordat und Ende der Zentrumspartei." *Stimmen der Zeit* 167 (1960-61):213-223.

Lerner, M.J. "Observer's Evaluation of a Victim: Justice, Guilt, and Veridical Perception." *Journal of Personality and Social Psychology* 20 (1971):127-135.

Lerner, M.J., and G. Matthews. "Reactions to Suffering of Others under Direct Conditions of Indirect Responsibility." *Journal of Personality and Social Psychology* 5 (1967):319-325.

Levinson, D.J. "Authoritarian Personality and Foreign Policy." *Journal of Conflict Resolution* 1(1957):37-47.

Lindblom, C.E. "The Science of 'Muddling Through'" *Public Administration Review* 29 (1959):79-88.

Lippert, Peter. "Der Gemeinschaftsmensch." *Stimmen der Zeit* 128 (1935):361-370.

Lippert, Peter. "Der gläubige Mensch." *Stimmen der Zeit* 129 (1935):145-155.

Lippert, Peter. "Die religiöse Mensch in der Gegenwart." *Stimmen der Zeit* 126 (1934):217-229.

Littell, Franklin H. "*Kirchenkampf* and Holocaust: The German Church Struggle and Nazi Anti-Semitism in Retrospect." *Journal of Church and State* 13 (1971):209-226.

Loewenberg, Peter. "The Psychohistorical Origins of the Nazi Youth Cohort." *American Historical Review* 76 (1971):1457-1502.

Loomis, C.P. and J.A. Beegle. "The Spread of German Nazism in Rural Areas." *American Sociological Review* 11 (1946):724-34.

McCormick, Richard. "Notes on Moral Theology: 1980." *Theological Studies* 42 (1981):74-121.

Madden, Paul. "Some Social Chracteristics of Early Nazi Party Members, 1919-1923." *Central European History* 15 (1982):34-56.

Marrus, Michael, and Robert Paxton. "The Nazis and the Jews in Occupied Western Europe, 1940-1944." *Journal of Modern History* 54 (1982):687-714.

Martin, Konrad. "Blicke ins talmudische Judenthum." *Theologische Vierteljahresschrift* (1848).

Mayer, Joseph. "Sexualprobleme zur Strafrechtsreform." *Theologie und Glaube* 21 (1929):137-162.

Mayer, Joseph. "Vorschläge für ein eugenisches Aufbauprogram." *Schönere Zukunft* (May 21, 1933):814-815, (May 28, 1933):837-839.

Maynes, May Jo. "Theory and Method in Recent German Historical Studies." *Journal of Interdisciplinary History* 10 (1979):311-317.

Michelat, Guy, and Michael Simon. "Religion, Class, and Politics." *Comparative Politics* 10 (1977):159-186.

Mikat, Paul. "Zur Kundgebung der Fuldaer Bischofskonferenz über die nationalsozialistische Bewegung vom 28. Marz 1933." *Jahrbuch für Christliche Sozialwissenschaften* 3 (1962):209-235.

Miller, Jeremy. "Ethics within an Ecclesial Context." *Angelicum* 57 (1980):32-44.

Moock, Wilhelm. "Der Einzelne und die Gemeinschaft." *Hochland* (1934-35):193-203.

Moock, Wilhelm. "Reich und Staat." *Hochland* 2 (1933):97-111.

Mork, Gordon. "Bismarck and the Capitulation of German Liberalism." *Journal of Modern History* 43 (1971):59-75.

Mörsdorf, Klaus. "Zur Eheprozessordnung für die Diözesangerichte vom. 15.8.1936." *Theologische Quartalschrift* (1939):206-219.

Morsey, Rudolf. "Hitlers Verhandlungen mit der Zentrumsführung am 31. Januar 1933." *Vierteljahrshefte für Zeitgeschichte* 9 (1961):182-194.

Muckermann, Friedrich. "An den Pforten des Reiches." *Der Gral* 22 (1927/28):205-214.

Muckermann, Friedrich, S.J. "Die Positive Überwindung des Nationalsozialismus." *Gral* 26 (1932):269-277.

Muckermann, Friedrich. "Der Reichsgedanke als Kulturidee." *Schönere Zukunft* 63 (1927/28):700-702.

Muckermann, Friedrich. "Wir Katholiken und der Nationalsozialismus." *Schönere Zukunft* 7 (1932):927-928.

Müller, Hans. "Zur Behandlung des Kirchenkampfes in der Nachkriegs-literatur." *Politische Studien* 12 (1961):474-481.

Müller, Hans. "Der pseudoreligiöse Charakter der nationalsozialistischen Weltanschauung." *Geschichte in Wissenschaft und Unterricht* 6 (1961):337-352.

Müller, Max. "Neudeutsche Jugend und neuer Staat." *Leuchtturm* 27 (1933-34):131-143.

Murray, John. "Problems of Church and Race." *Month* 168 (1936/37):528-536.

Muth, Karl. "Das Reich als Idee und Wirklichkeit-Einst und Jetzt." *Hochland* 30 (1932/33):481-492.

Muth, Karl. "Res Publica 1926. Gedanken zur politischen Krise der Gegenwart." *Hochland* 24 (1926/27):1-28.

Nunnally, Jim C., and Howard Bobren. "Attitude Change with False Information." *Public Opinion Quarterly* 23 (1959):260-266.

Ostrom, T.M. "Between-Theory and Within-Theory Conflict in Explaining Context Effects on Impression Formation." *Journal of Experimental Social Psychology* 13 (1977):492-503.

Ottati, Douglas. "Christian Theology and Other Disciplines." *Journal of Religion* 64 (1984):173-187.

Pallone, Nathaniel. "Explorations in Religious Authority and Social Perception I." *Acta Psychologia* 22 (1964):321-337.

Parenti, Michael. "Political Values and Religious Cultures: Jews, Catholics, and Protestants." *Journal for the Scientific Study of Religion* 6 (1947):259-269.

Peitzmeier, J. "Vom Sinn der Rasse." *Theologie und Glaube* 26 (1934):405-426.

Pflanze, Otto. "Bismarcks Herrschaftstechnik als Problem der gegenwartigen Historiographie." *Historische Zeitschrift* 234 (1982):562-599.

Phelps, Reginald. "Hitler als Parteiredner im Jahr 1920." *Vierteljahrshefte für Zeitgeschichte* 11 (1963):274-330.

Piliavin, I.M. et al. "Costs, Diffusion, and Stigmatized Victim." *Journal of Personality and Social Psychology* 13 (1975):429-438.

Pois, Robert A. "Ideology, Totalitarianism, and National Socialism: The Historian's Dilemma." *Societas: A Review of Social History* 8 (1978):177-192.

Postone, Moishe. "Antisemitism and National Socialism: Notes on the German Reaction to 'Holocaust.'" *New German Critique* 4 (1980):97-115.

Pribilla, Max. "Christliche Haltung." *Stimmen der Zeit* 135 (1939):169-179.

Pribilla, Max. "Ehe und Familie." *Stimmen der Zeit* 134 (1938):53-56.

Pribilla, Max. "Der Kampf der Kirche." *Stimmen der Zeit* 129 (1935):242-253.

Pribilla, Max. "Nationale Revolution." *Stimmen der Zeit* 125 (1933):156-168.

Pribilla, Max. "Nationalsozialistische Weltanschauung." *Stimmen der Zeit* 126 (1933):415-418.

Pribilla, Max, S.J. "Verfassungstreue." *Stimmen der Zeit* 125 (1933):57-61.

Przywara, Erich, S.J. "Judentum und Christentum: Zwischen Orient und Okzident." *Stimmen der Zeit* 110 (1925/26):81-99.

Przywara, Erich. "Nation, Staat, Kirche." *Stimmen der Zeit* 125 (1933):370-379.

Pulke, Engelbert. "Geschichte der politischen Parteien in Kreis Recklinghausen bis zum Ende des Kulturkampfes 1848-1859." *Vestische Zeitschrift* 41 (1934):3-163.

Radding, Charles M. "The Evolution of Medieval Mentalities: A Cognitive-Structural Approach." *American Historical Review* 83 (1978):577-597.

Rausch, H.L. "Interaction Sequences." *Journal of Personality and Social Psychology* 2 (1965):487-499.

Redfield, R. "The Primitive World View." *Proceedings of the American Philosophical Society* 96 (1952):30-36.

Reinermann, Wilhelm. "Das Reich als deutsches Lebensgesetz und innenpolitische Zukunftsaufgabe." *Das Deutsche Volk* 1 (1933):81-93.

Repgen, Konrad. "Das Ende des Zentrumspartei und die Entstehung des Reichskonkordats." *Militarseelsorge* 12 (1970):83-122.

Repgen, Konrad. "Zur Vatikanischen Strategie beim Reichskonkordat." *Vierteljahrsheft für Zeitgeschichte* 38 (1983): 506-535.

Richter, Alfred. "Parteiprogram der NSDAP und Reichskonkordat: Zum dritten Jahrestag der Unterzeichnung des Reichskonkordats (20 July 1933)." *Deutschlands Erneuerung* 20 (1936)):466-479.

Rim, Y. "Values and Attitudes." *Personality: An International Journal* 1 (1970):243-250.

Rokeach, M. "Long-Range Experimental Modification of Values, Attitudes, and Behavior." *American Psychologist* 26 (1971):453-459.

Rost, Hans. "Der Zerfall des deutschen Judentums." *Hochland* 11 (1913-1914):545-558.

Rubenstein, Richard. "The Unmastered Trauma: Interpreting the Holocaust." *Humanities in Society* 2 (1979):421-429.

Ruhm von Oppen, Beate. "Catholics and Nazis in 1933. Anatomy of Nonconformism." *Wiener Library Bulletin* 16 (1962):8.

Sampson, Edward. "Cognitive Psychology as Ideology." *American Psychologist* 36 (1981):725-737.

Sarason, S.B. "The Nature of Problem Solving in Social Action." *American Psychologist* 33 (1978):370-380.

Sauer, Wolfgang. "National Socialism: Totalitarianism or Fascism?" *American Historical Review* 73 (1967):404-424.

Schankol, Richard V. "Studentenrecht und Judenfrage." *Schönere Zukunft* 27 (December 1931):303-304.

Scherm, J. "Der alttestamentliche Bibelunterricht: Planungen und Weg-weisungen." *Klerusblatt* 20 (1939):219-229.

Schilling, Otto. "Die Eigentumslehre Leos XIII und Pius XI." *Theologische Quartalschrift* (1940):205-210.

Schilling, Otto. "Das moralische Recht des deutschen Volkes auf Kolo-nien." *Theologische Quartalschrift* (1934):397-404.

Schilling, Otto. "Das Prinzip der Moral." *Theologische Quartalschirft.* (1938):419-426.

Schilling, Otto. "Quelle und Charakter des Völkerrechts." *Theologische Quartalschrift* (1939):289-295.

Schilling, Otto. "Richtiges und Falsches bei der sog. Eugenik." *Schönere Zukuuft* 7 (1932):570-572, 597-598.

Schilling, Otto. "Die sozial Gerechtigkeit." *Theologische Quartalschrift* (1933):269-277.

Schilling, Otto. "Von der sozialen Gerechtigkeit." *Theologische Quar-talschrift* (1939):197-205.

Schlesinger, Arthur. "The Roosevelt Era: Stimson and Hull." *Nation* 5 (June 1948).

Schlund, Erhard. "Religion, Christentum, Kirche und Na-tionalsozialismus." *Gelbe Heft* 8 (1931):114-145.

Scholder, Klaus. "Die evangelische Kirche in der Sicht der Na-tionalsozialistischer Führung." *Vierteljahrshefte für Zeitgeschichte* 16 (1968):15-35.

Simon, H.A. "A Behavioral Model of Rational Choice." *Quarterly Journal of Economics* 69 (1955):99-118.

Sinofsky, Faye, et al. "A Bibliography of Psychohistory." *History of Child-hood Quarterly* 2 (1975):517-562.

Small, Melvin. "Some Suggestions from the Behavioral Sciences for Histo-rians Interested in the Study of Attitudes." *Societas* 3 (1973):1-19.

Sorge, Bartolemeo. "Civilta Cattolica." *The Jesuits* (1975-76):147-55.

Spahn, M. "Das deutsche Zentrum und die Wahlen." *Das Neue Reich* (May 9, 1920):510-515.

Sperber, Jonathan. "Roman Catholic Religious Identity in Rhineland-Westphalia, 1800-70: Quantitative Examples and some Political Im-plications." *Social History* 7 (1982):305-318.

Sperber, Jonathan. "The Transformation of Catholic Associations in the Northern Rhineland and Westphalia, 1830-1870." *Journal of Social History* 14 (1981):253-263.

Spitzer, Allen B. "The Historical Problem of Generations." *American His-torical Review* 78 (1973):1353-85.

Staats, A.W., and C.K. Staats. "Attitudes Established by Classical Con-ditioning." *Journal of Abnormal and Social Psychology* 57 (1958):37-40.

Stasiewski, Bernhard. "Die Kirchenpolitik der Nationalsozialisten im War-thegau, 1939-1945." *Vierteljahrshefte für Zeitgeschichte* 7 (1959):46-74.

Stehle, Hansjakob. "Motive des Reichskonkordats." *Aussenpolitik* 7 (1956):556-573.

Stempel, Guido H. "Selectivity in Readership of Political News." *Public Opinion Quarterly* 25 (1961):400-404.

Stöffler, Friedrich. "Die 'Euthanasie' und die Haltung der Bischöfe im Hessischen Raum 1940-1945." *Archiv für Mittelrheinische Kirchengeschichte* 13 (1961):301-325.

Stokes, Lawrence D. "The German People and the Destruction of the European Jews." *Central European History* 6 (1973):167-191.

Thompson, Larry V. "*Lebensborn* and the Eugenics Policy of the *Reichsführer-SS*." *Central European History* 4 (1971):54-77.

Tinnemann, Ethel Mary SNJM. "Attitudes of the German Catholic Hierarchy toward the Nazi Regime: A Study in German Psycho-Political Culture." *Western Political Quarterly.* 22 (1969):333-349.

Tinnemann, Ethel Mary. "The Silence of Pius XII." *Journal of Church and State* 21 (1979):265-285.

Trevor-Roper, H.R. "Hitlers Kriegsziele." *Vierteljahrshefte für Zeitgeschichte* 8 (1960):117-130.

Tymchuk, A.J.A. "A Perspective on Ethics in Mental Retardation." *Mental Retardation* 14 (1976):41-47.

Uunger, Aryeh. "The Public Opinion Reports of the Nazi Party." *Public Opinion Quarterly* 29 (1965-1966):565-582.

Vacchiano, R.P., et al. "The Open and Closed Mind: A Review of Dogmatism." *Psychological Bulletin* 72 (1969):261-273.

Vacchiano, R.P., et al. "Personality Correlates of Dogmatism." *Journal of Consulting and Clinical Psychology* 32 (1968):81-89.

Volk, Ludwig. "Die Enzyklika *Mit Brennender Sorge*." *Stimmen der Zeit* 183 (1969):174-187.

Volk, Ludwig. "Die Fuldaer Bischofskonferenz von der Enzyklika *Mit Brennender Sorge* bis zum Ende der NS-Herrschaft." *Stimmen der Zeit* 178 (1966):241-267.

Volk, Ludwig, S.J. "Kardinal Faulhabers Stellung zur Weimarer Republik und zum NS-Staat." *Stimmen der Zeit* 177 (1966):173-195.

Walker, Lawrence. "The Nazi 'Youth Cohort': The Missing Variable." *Psychohistory Review* 9 (1980):71-73.

Walker, Lawrence. "'Young Priests' as Opponents: Factors Associated with Clerical Opposition to the Nazis in Bavaria, 1933." *Catholic Historical Review* 65 (1979):402-413.

Wall, Donald D. "The Reports of the *Sicherheitsdienst* on the Church and Religious Affairs in Germany, 1939-1944." *Church History* 40 (1971):437-456.

Walster, E. "Assignment of Responsibility for an Accident." *Journal of Personality and Social Psychology* 3 (1966):73-79.

Weatherly, D. "Anti-Semitism and the Expression of Fantasy Aggression." *Journal of Abnormal and Social Psychology* 62 (1961):454-457.

Weima, J. "Authoritarianism, Religious Conservatism and Sociocentric Attitudes in Roman Catholic Groups." *Human Relations* 18 (1965):231-239.

Weinberg, Gerhard L. "The World Through Hitler's Eyes." *Midway* (1970):53-75.

Wernick, Uri. "Cognitive Dissonance Theory, Religious Reality and Extreme Interactionism." *Psychohistory Review* 7 (1979):207-232.

Whitehurst, G.J. "Production of Novel and Grammatical Utterances by Young Children." *Journal of Experimental Child Psychology* 13 (1972):502-515.

Wiedemann, A. "Stimme aus der katholischen Jugend." *Deutsches Volkstum* 15 (1933):565-577.

Williams, R.M. "Religion, Value Orientation, and Inter-group Conflict." *Journal of Social Issues* 12 (1956):12-20.

Witetschek, Helmut. "Die Bayerischen Regierungspräsidentenberichte 1933-1943 als Geschichtsquelle." *Historisches Jahrbuch* 87 (1967):355-372.

Witetschek, Helmut. "Der Gefälschte und der echte Mölders-Brief." *Vierteljahrshefte für Zeitgeschichte* 16 (1968):60-65.

Zahn, Gordon C. "Catholic Opposition to Hitler: The Perils of Ambiguity." *Journal of Church and State* 13 (1971):413-425.

Zahn, Gordon C. "The German Catholic Press and Hitler's Wars." *Cross Currents* 10 (1960):337-351.

Zahn, Gordon. "The Unpublished Encyclical: An Opportunity Missed." *National Catholic Reporter* 9 (December 15, 1972).

Zangerl, Carl H.E. "Courting the Catholic Vote: The Center Party in Baden, 1903-13." *Central European History* 10 (1977):220-240.

Zeender, John. "German Catholics and the Concept of an Interconfessional Party, 1900-1922." *Journal of Central European Affairs* 23 (1964):424-439.

Zeiger, Ivo. "Katholische Moraltheologie Heute." *Stimmen der Zeit* 134 (1938):143-153.

Zeiger, Ivo. "Das Reichskonkordat." *Stimmen der Zeit* 126 (1933):1-8.

Zieger, Ivo. "Verrechtlichung der Kirche." *Stimmen der Zeit* 129 (1935):38-46.

Zeiger, Ivo. "Werde, der Du Bist." *Stimmen der Zeit* 133 (1938):298-307.

Zillig, Georg. "Über 'Euthanasie.'" *Hochland* 42 (1949-50):337-352.

Zmarzlik, Hans-Günter. "Der Antisemitismus im Zweiten Reich." *Geschichte in Wissenschaft und Unterricht* 14 (1963):273-286.

Unpublished Material

Gordon, Sarah Ann. "German Opposition to Anti-Semitic Measures Between 1933 and 1945, with Particular Reference to the Rhine-Ruhr Area." Ph.D. diss., SUNY—Buffalo, 1979.

Ihorst, A. "Zur Situation der katholischen Kirche und Ihren Caritative Tätigheit in der ersten Jahren des Dritten Reiches." Diplomarbeit, University of Freiburg, 1971.

Janis, Irving. "Preventing Groupthink in Policy-Planning Groups: Theory and Research Perspectives." Paper delivered at the International Society of Political Psychology, June 1979, Washington, D.C.

Kitterman, David Harold. "National Diary of German Civilian Life During 1940: The SD Reports." Ph.D. diss., University of Washington, 1972.

Lippert, Ekkehard. "Concerning the Relationship of Political Education and Moral Judgment." Paper delivered at the International Society of Political Psychology, June 1979, Washington, D.C.

Morley, John F. "Vatican Diplomacy and the Jews during the Holocaust, 1939-1943." Ph.D. diss., New York University, 1979.

Pease, Louis Edwin. "After the Holocaust: West Germany and Material Reparation to the Jews—From the Allied Occupation to the Luxemburg Agreements." Ph.D. diss., Florida State University, 1976.

Phayer, Michael. "Challenges Met and Opportunities Missed: Catholic Women in Nazi Germany." Paper presented at the American Historical Association, San Francisco, December 30, 1983.

Riede, David. "The Official Attitude of the Roman Catholic Hierarchy in Germany Toward National Socialism, 1933-1945." Ph.D. diss., State University of Iowa, 1957.

Rinderle, Walter J. "Struggle for Tradition: One German Village in a Radical Era, 1929-1936." Ph.D. diss., Notre Dame, Department of History, January 1977.

Rolfs, Richard William. "The Role of Adolf Cardinal Bertram, Chairman of the Fulda Bishops' Conference, in the Church's Struggle in the Third Reich: 1933-1938." Ph.D. diss., University of California-Santa Barbara, 1976.

Schmidt-Clausing. "Judengegnerische Strömungen in deutschen Katholizismus des 19. Jahrhunderts, eine religionspolitische Untersuchung." Unpub. diss., University of Jena, 1942.

Schnitzer, Paul. "Die katholische Kirche und der Nationalsozialismus bis 1933." Unpublished Staatsexaminarbeit, Frankfurt University, 1960.

Stokes, Lawrence. "The *Sicherheitsdienst* (SD) of the *Reichsführer* SS and German Public Opinion, September 1, 1939-June 1941." Ph.D. diss., Johns Hopkins, 1972.

Waldman, Loren K. "Models of Mass Movements: The Case of the Nazis." Ph.D. diss., University of Chicago, 1973.

Ziegler, Herbert F. "The SS Fuehrer Korps: An Analysis of Its Socioeconomic and Demographic Structure, 1925-1938." Ph.D. diss., University of Virginia, 1980.

Ziegler, Martha Moore. "The Socio-Economic and Demographic Bases of Political Behavior in Nuremberg during the Weimar Republic, 1919-1933." Ph.D. diss., University of Virginia, May 1976.

Index